MASSACRE IN MALAYA

MASSACRE IN MALAYA EXPOSING BRITAIN'S MY LAI

CHRISTOPHER HALE

'The truth is that there is no pure race and that to make politics depend upon ethnographic analysis is to surrender it to a chimera.'

Ernst Renan, 'What is a Nation?' (1882)

'A nation is like a fish. If we are merdeka [independent] we can enjoy the whole fish head, body and tail. At the moment, we are only getting its head and bones.'

Sutan Jenain, Indonesian nationalist

'This is how one pictures the angel of history. His face is turned toward the past. Where we perceive a chain of events, he sees one single catastrophe that keeps piling ruin upon ruin and hurls it in front of his feet. The angel would like to stay, awaken the dead, and make whole what has been smashed. But a storm is blowing from Paradise; it has got caught in his wings with such violence that the angel can no longer close them. The storm irresistibly propels him into the future to which his back is turned, while the pile of debris before him grows skyward. This storm is what we call progress.'

Walter Benjamin, 'Ninth Thesis on the Philosophy of History'

'I am hampered by ignorance of conditions of the past.'

Sir Harold MacMichael, King's Special Representative to Malaya, 1945

First published 2013

The History Press
The Mill, Brimscombe Port
Stroud, Gloucestershire, GL5 2QG
www.thehistorypress.co.uk

© Christopher Hale, 2013

The right of Christopher Hale to be identified as the Author
of this work has been asserted in accordance with the
Copyright, Designs and Patents Act 1988.

British Library Cataloguing in Publication Data.
A catalogue record for this book is available from the British Library.

ISBN 978 0 7524 8701 4

Typesetting and origination by The History Press
Printed in Great Britain

CONTENTS

A BRIEF NOTE ON TERMS

The 'Batang Kali Massacre' of December 1948 took place not in the predominantly Malay town of that name but on on the Sungai Remok Estate, which is about 5 miles (8.29km) distant. Before 1957, Malaya was part of the British Empire but was never a unitary colony. 'British Malaya', the term used in this book, was a composite colonial territory that encompassed the 'Straits Settlements' of Singapore, Penang and Malacca and a number of Malay sultanates in both the peninsula and northern Borneo. These were subdivided into federated and unfederated states. These Malay states were nominally ruled by sultans (or rulers) but governed as protectorates by the British through the appointment of 'Residents'. The British imposed semi-centralised federal rule across Malaya after 1945 though Singapore remained administratively separate. In 1957, the British granted independence, or *merdeka*, to the Federation of Malaya. The British retained control of Singapore and Crown Colonies in northern Borneo – Sabah and Sarawak. Kalimantan, the southern region of Borneo, was part of Indonesia. In 1963, Malaya was enlarged to include Singapore, for a short period, and the Borneo states of Sabah and Sarawak as the Federation of Malaysia. Singapore left or was ousted from the federation (depending on your point of view) in 1965. It is now an independent city republic. I have used 'Malayan' to refer to all the non-European peoples (Malays, Indians and Chinese) of both colonial and independent Malaya who became 'Malaysians' after 1963. It has been necessary, for reasons that will become clear to the reader, to refer to 'the Chinese', 'the Indians' and 'the Malays'. It would be wearisome to insert inverted commas for these catch-all terms throughout the text of this book – but they are implied. 'Race' was a pseudo-scientific idea imported to Asia by the European colonial powers and imposed through census operations and other administrative devices across a diverse ethnic landscape. Modern biology has shown that, in scientific terms, these old ideas of immutable racial differences can no longer be regarded as useful. There is some controversy about terminology used to refer to the indigenous people of the Malayan Peninsula. 'Aboriginal' is a common term in anthropological publications and was used by the British during the colonial period but 'Orang Asli' (meaning original people) is now preferred. Some regard the term 'aboriginal' as confusing and derogatory. In the past, Malays referred to 'Sakai', which definitely is pejorative since it means 'slave'. Throughout the book I have used the most accessible or familiar spellings of Chinese and Malay family and place names consistent with documentary sources. The history of currency in colonial Malaya is complex, as explained at http://moneymuseum.bnm.gov.my. In the text that follows 'dollars' generally refers to Straits or Malayan dollars unless otherwise stated.

PREFACE

'GROSSLY UNREASONABLE FORCE'

'Once we started firing, we seemed to go mad […] I remember the water turned red with their blood.'

William Cootes, Scots Guards

LONDON, MAY 2012

For two days in May 2012 the restless spirits of twenty-four men shot dead more than half a century ago by British soldiers near a tiny Malayan village called Batang Kali haunted court number three inside the Royal Courts of Justice in London. On a bright spring morning, British and Malaysian lawyers gathered with their frail and elderly clients in front of the cathedral-like main entrance. They held up banners demanding justice. They had waited a very long time. It was not difficult to be reminded of the case of *Jarndyce v. Jarndyce* dragging its way through the Court of Chancery in Charles Dickens' *Bleak House*, which began serialisation in 1852, bang in the middle of the imperial century:

> hard by Temple Bar, in Lincoln's Inn Hall, at the very heart of the fog, sits the Lord High Chancellor […] Never can there come fog too thick, never can there come mud and mire too deep, to assort with the groping and floundering condition which this High Court of Chancery, most pestilent of hoary sinners, holds this day in the sight of heaven and earth.

The claimants in the Batang Kali massacre case are only too familiar with the thick fog of cover-up.

The Royal Courts of Justice heralded a new era in British justice, or so it was hoped, when they were commissioned and designed in the 1870s. The old Court of Chancery that Dickens had so savagely pilloried had been demolished. This was an era of boundless national confidence: the high tide of empire. Factories churned out the tools that changed the world: steamships, railways and Gatling guns. At the time the new courts were under construction, work undertaken by German strike breakers in the late 1870s, a good number of the curious Englishmen and women who paused briefly in the Strand to watch the slow upward progress of its spires, vaults and transepts, constructed from millions of blocks of Portland stone, saw their race as new Romans. They, like their toga-clad forebears, held sway over a global empire through force of character and an innate genius for leadership. For the many devout readers of Edward Gibbon's history of the Roman Empire, arrogance was shaded by uncertainty, even fear. Might Britain's imperial majesty suffer the same precipitous decline and fall that Gibbon's had unfolded in such matchless English prose? The first volume of his great history was published in 1776 when Britain's thirteen American colonies were under attack from a motley guerrilla army commanded by George Washington. No wonder, after this traumatic loss, Gibbon saw the future written in the ruined monuments of the Roman Forum. But having lost an empire in the West, Britain rebuilt another in the East. India, the 'jewel in the crown' and the crescent of imperial territories that stretched from Rangoon to Sydney, seemed more than ample recompense for the traumatic loss of the American colonies.

By the end of the next century, that once-resurgent empire had, as Rudyard Kipling prophesied, suffered the same fate as every other world empire: 'Far-called our navies melt away–/On dune and headland sinks the fire–/Lo, all our pomp of yesterday/Is one with Nineveh and Tyre!' In the wreckage of empire, the successors of Edward Gibbon would examine afresh how and why the British had held sway over a quarter of the earth's surface. The modern history of empire has become a polarised enterprise. In their classic *1066 and All That*, published in 1930 and comprising '103 Good Things, 5 Bad Kings and 2 Genuine Dates', W.C. Sellar and R.J. Yeatman had concluded that the Roman invasion of Britain was a 'good thing' because Britons were 'only natives at the time'. The American Revolution, however, was a 'bad thing'. How should the British Empire be judged – was it a 'good thing' or a 'bad thing'? Did high-minded British imperialists act as the standard-bearers of civilisation to 'make the modern world', as many conservative historians still affirm? Or was the empire a global business racket founded on profiteering, violence and tyranny?

The imperial imagination certainly brought forth monsters. Many colonial administrators with long experience of serving overseas returned to Britain with the racist and xenophobic views that were commonly held about native peoples in the colonies. They were appalled to discover that their homeland had become, in their absence, a more liberal, open and democratic society. (Or so they imagined.) Such men felt betrayed and many, such as the fascist A.K. Chesterton, embraced conspiratorial theories that blamed national moral decay on the Jews or the Irish, the Germans or the Bolsheviks. The notorious traitor 'Lord Haw-Haw', whose real name was William Joyce, had developed his political vision in the loyalist community in Northern Ireland. He saw the partitioning of Ireland as the first step towards the disintegration of the Empire. Joyce was an imperialist traitor. The British fascist movements of the 1930s feared above all the end of empire.

The long afterglow of imperialism finally guttered in Hong Kong in 1997, but the British, as a people, often appear to be unreconciled to decline. In 1981, the British government belatedly rallied to the cause of the Falkland islanders, the long-forgotten inhabitants of a relic micro colony in the southern Atlantic. Britain, with grudging American support, stumbled into a war with Argentina, a faraway nation conveniently ruled by a tinpot dictator who was easy to demonise. The British wallowed in an orgy of 'Hope and Glory' patriotism that E.P Thompson called 'imperial atavism, drenched in nostalgia'. The 'Falkland Factor' and a blizzard of tabloid posturing prolonged the reign of Margaret Thatcher and revived a kind of warmed-up nostalgia for all our pomp of yesterday. All British political leaders have subsequently longed for their own 'Falklands moment'. Gibbon warned that 'to hold in obedience remote countries and foreign nations, in opposition to their inclination and interest' was 'adverse to nature'. At the time he was writing his long history, this caution went unheeded. Gibbon's prescience now seems all too evident. In the spring of 2012, British dominion in a 'remote country' and its methods of rule would be held to account inside the Royal Courts of Justice.

The Batang Kali incident has been called 'Britain's My Lai'. In March 1968 American troops of 'Charlie Company' of the 20th Infantry Regiment attacked the village of Son My, in Quang Ngai province in South Vietnam, which comprised a number of hamlets: My Lai 1, 2, 3, and 4. It was believed that the 48th Battalion of the communist National Liberation Front, the NLF, known as the Viet Cong or 'Victor Charlie' by the Americans, had taken shelter in Son My. The Americans referred to the village as 'Pinkville'. It was supposedly a guerrilla stronghold. Two months earlier on 30 January, the NLF had launched the 'Tet offensive', striking for the first time at cities in South Vietnam including the capital Saigon. Although the Viet Cong attack was repelled, the Tet offensive changed the course of the war in Vietnam. According to Michael Walzer's classic *Just and Unjust Wars* (1977), on the evening before the attack Captain Ernest Medina briefed 'Charlie Company': 'They're all V.C. [Viet Cong guerrillas], now go and get them …'. One of the soldiers asked: 'Who is my enemy?' Medina replied: 'Anybody that was running from us, hiding from us, or appeared to be the enemy. If a man was running, shoot him, sometimes even if a woman with a rifle was running, shoot her.' During the course of the attack the Americans killed at least 300 villagers, mainly women, children and elderly men. Many women were raped; bodies were mutilated. At the time General William Westmoreland congratulated 'Charlie Company' for a job well done. The truth emerged slowly. On the evening of the attack, a helicopter pilot called Hugh Thompson, who had rescued a number of children from Son My, protested to his superior officers about the indiscriminate killing of women and children he had witnessed. Soon afterwards, an investigation carried out by a 31-year-old major called Colin Powell into the My Lai attack exonerated 'Charlie Company' of any wrongdoing. In the meantime, another American officer, Ronald Ridenhour, had talked to members of 'Charlie Company' and become convinced that something 'dark and bloody' had taken place in Son My. He wrote to thirty members of Congress urging them to investigate the 'Pinkville incident'. His campaign led to the secret military prosecution of platoon leader Lt William Calley and twenty-five other officers who had taken part in the attack. It was not until November 1969 that journalist Seymour Hersh broke the story in thirty American newspapers, including *The New York Times*. His report had a traumatising impact on a public that was already weary of the war and the way it was being fought. At his trial in 1970, Calley claimed:

> I was ordered to go in there and destroy the enemy. That was my job that day. That was the mission I was given. I did not sit down and think in terms of men, women and children. They were all classified as the same, and that's the classification that we dealt with over there, just as the enemy. I felt then and I still do that I acted as I was directed, and I carried out the order that I was given and I do not feel wrong in doing so.

In other words, Calley was 'just following orders' – and many believe that he was. In Vietnam the murder of unarmed civilians was normal procedure.

The 'Malayan Emergency' – the British war against communist insurgents in Malaya – had ended nearly ten years before 'Charlie Company' rampaged through the Vietnamese village of Son My. The revelations of the Calley trial had unintended consequences in Britain. The veteran BBC journalist William Hardcastle quizzed the notoriously bibulous politician George Brown, who had been foreign secretary and deputy leader of the Labour Party, on *World at One*. Brown's response was oddly equivocal: '… William, could you put your hand on your heart, and say in all the time Britain has been playing a similar role […] whether we could have turned up a Pinkville [My Lai] on the way […] I hope not but I just don't know.' Pressed by Hardcastle, Brown went further: 'People when they are fighting, when they are frightened do terrible things […] I suspect there are an awful lot of spectres in our cupboard too.' Brown seemed to have no doubt that British soldiers might have been capable of killing unarmed civilians as Calley and 'Charlie Company' had in Vietnam. Since 1945, British soldiers had fought many 'small wars' across the territories of the waning empire. But even at the end of the liberal 1960s, Brown's remarks sounded like an outrageous slur on 'our boys', especially those who had fought to defend Malaya from communism. Robert Edwards, the truculent editor of the Sunday newspaper *The People*, decided to challenge the former foreign secretary in an editorial headlined 'Where's the evidence, George?' What troubled Edwards was the implication that 'since all war is horror, since we bombed Dresden and the Americans Hiroshima, what's the difference?' Brown seemed to be saying that the war hero who lived next door might have shot women and children in cold blood. Edwards insisted: 'Withdraw this slur, Mr Brown!' It was Sunday 30 November 1969.

On that freezing morning in Stretford, Greater Manchester, where a 40-year-old former Scots Guardsman called William Cootes lived with his new girlfriend, the couple were starting breakfast when their copy of *The People* was pushed noisily through the letterbox. The 'Voice of the People' editorial was on page two. As Cootes absorbed Edwards' ringing words, he struggled with the chilling realisation that he could answer the headline question, 'Where's the evidence, George?' Cootes had done his national service in Malaya. He had served with the Scots Guards. He had been a member of the patrol that had marched into Batang Kali twenty-one years earlier. Cootes knew what had happened. Two days later, on Tuesday 2 December, Cootes walked into the Manchester offices of *The People* and asked to talk to a journalist. He had a story to tell. The first journalist to hear the story of Britain's My Lai was William Dorran, the northern news editor. By the following weekend, Cootes was in London at the newspaper's head office near Covent Garden talking to Bob Edwards, described in his obituary as 'a champagne socialist with Savile Row suits, hand-rolled cigars and a castle in Oxfordshire', who had once been the editor of the Labour Party weekly magazine *Tribune* but had defected to the *Daily Express* for ten times the salary. Edwards was, however, a hard-nosed journalist in the classic mould. He had published the memoirs of Christine Keeler and led investigations of corruption and protection rackets in London's Soho. He was shocked by the story the former national serviceman had to tell.

Cootes had joined the Scots Guards and been sent to Malaya at the beginning of the 'Emergency'. At the beginning of December 1948, the Guards were based about 40 miles north of the colonial capital of Kuala Lumpur in Kuala Kubu Bharu. On the morning of 11 December, Cootes joined a platoon that had been ordered to a small settlement of Chinese rubber tappers on the Sungai Remok Estate close to the village of Batang Kali. According to Cootes, a guards officer called George Ramsay had given explicit orders to 'wipe out anybody they found there'. He described the way platoon leaders had dealt with a young villager who was 'grinning in an insolent way':

> [Sergeant] Douglas dropped to one knee, aimed his rifle and shot the youth in the back [...] I could see the youth on the path on his back and his stomach was ripped open by the shot. I was amazed to see him suddenly raise his head from the ground and I shouted to Sergeant Hughes, nearby, that the boy was still alive. He walked over with his Sten gun and put a bullet through his head where he lay ...

The following day, Cootes alleged, the Scots Guards divided the male villagers into groups, led them to the bank of the nearby river and shot them all in cold blood. One man had managed to escape but this was not known until some time later. When the patrol returned to the camp at Kuala Kubu Bharu, Ramsay and

other officers called the men together. Another former Scots Guards private told
a BBC reporter years later:

> *Remedios*: We were told by the sergeant after the incident that if anyone said
>   anything we could get fourteen or fifteen years in prison. We were more or
>   less threatened by the sergeant.
> *BBC*: So you got together and conspired to fabricate a story?
> *Remedios*: Yes, more or less.
> *BBC*: All the platoon?
> *BBC*: More or less, yes.

Edwards was under no illusion that the story Cootes had told him was incendiary.
George Brown had been right to suspect that Britain's military establishment
had 'closeted spectres' lurking in its historical cupboard. How many more might
now spill out? The Scots Guards was an elite division, with a proud history. The
British establishment would no doubt defend its record fiercely. Edwards could
not publish without corroboration. But he was prepared to commit resources to
proper investigation. Bill Dorran persuaded other former Scots Guards who had
been present in Batang Kali that day in December 1948 to come forward. Most
corroborated Cootes' version of events. The villagers had not been running away:
British troops had perpetrated a massacre in cold blood.

The investigation took two months to complete. It was an impressively
thorough job. On 1 February 1970, Edwards was confident enough to run the
story: 'Horror in a Nameless Village' was headlined on the front page. Edwards
contributed an editorial statement:

> A newspaper has a simple duty to its readers which is best summed up by the
> biblical phrase, 'Ye shall know the truth'. The truth in this case illustrates the
> corrupting and fearful effect of war on otherwise decent men, and what can
> happen when the highest standards of discipline are allowed to fall. That is the
> lesson, and it can never be taught too often.

Edwards pointed out that this was not 'another Pinkville'. The British soldiers
had *spared* women and children. But what had happened in that Malayan village
was, he insisted, 'appalling enough'.

When Hersh had published his celebrated account of the My Lai massacre in
The New York Times, American soldiers were still fighting and dying in Vietnam
and a clamorous anti-war movement ensured that the story would not be
ignored. The exposure of the My Lai massacre contributed to ending the war.
In 1970, when *The People* published the Batang Kali story, Malaysia had been an
independent nation for more than a decade. The last British troops had left years
before. Britain was racked by economic calamity and dissent. Edwards recalled

ruefully that 'The country was shocked, I felt, but wanted the matter quietly dropped, and that is what happened.' What Edwards meant of course was that circulation figures had dropped after he had published the story. Few, it seemed, wanted to hear about a 'British My Lai'. On the threshold of the 1970s, public opinion was still in the grip of a long drawn-out victory party that had begun on VJ Day in 1945. We had won the war. We were a good people defended by morally righteous men and women in uniform who didn't shoot people in cold blood. It was not difficult for the government to launch a cover-up that has lasted to this day.

To begin with, Minister of Defence Denis Healey ordered Scotland Yard to set up a task force to investigate the allegations, and Cootes and the other Scots Guards were reinterviewed under oath. But in June, 1970, the Conservative Party led by Edward Heath won a surprise general election victory. The new attorney general, Sir Peter Rawlinson, quietly cancelled the new investigation for 'lack of evidence'. In the four decades that have passed since William Cootes walked into the offices of *The People*, successive British governments have resisted calls for a public enquiry to discover what happened at Batang Kali. Official statements have reiterated that the villagers were 'shot trying to escape' and that no evidence has been produced to justify an enquiry. By the end of 2011, this long, 'very British cover-up' seemed to be close to collapse – thanks to a long campaign fought by British and Malaysian lawyers and the journalists Ian Ward and Norma Miraflor. Lawyer Quek Ngee Meng recalls:

> Back in 2004 my father, the late Quek Cheng Taik, used to visit the hot springs in Ulu Yam near Batang Kali to treat an illness. He used to go from Serdang to that area and eventually bought a house in Ulu Yam. He listened to the stories of villagers. It is still a talked-about topic there more than sixty years on. Those killed were from Ulu Yam. If you go there you won't miss the cemetery. Every Qing Ming (a day to pay respect to one's ancestors) they go back. They still feel it. It is still a stigma. The official account says they were suspected of being bandits. When we followed the case, we found a lot of cover-ups.

At the beginning of May 2012 Quek Ngee Meng and his legal team flew from Kuala Lumpur to London where lawyers John Halford and Danny Friedman had been masterminding the campaign. The most important members of Quek's party were the 'claimants': the surviving relatives of the men killed at Batang Kali. Their principal demand was for a public enquiry. In dry legalese:

> The Claimants challenge decisions of the Defendants (or 'the Secretaries of State') of 29 November 2010 and 4 November 2011 (a) not to pay 'reparations' or financial compensation in respect of killings at Batang Kali, Selangor, Malaya on 11–12 December 1948 ('the killings') and (b) not to establish a public

inquiry under the Inquiries Act 2005 ('the 2005 Act') or any other inquiry or investigation into the killings.

The purpose of the trial, in other words, was to contest decisions made by the British government, the defendants, not to hold an enquiry into the Batang Kali killings. The trial in May was *not* an enquiry – though, as it would turn out, the two-day proceedings yielded a great deal of new information about British counter-insurgency operations in Malaya. The claimants were asking the High Court to overturn the government's refusal to investigate. At previous hearings the Secretaries of State for Defence and Foreign and Commonwealth Affairs insisted that they were unwilling to do anything to make public the truth of what happened. No apology has ever been offered. This means that the government continues to maintain that the killings at Batang Kali were 'necessary and justified'.[1] What was at issue was whether the defendants had acted lawfully when they refused the claimants' application for a public enquiry. The claimants' lawyers argued that 'This case is about truth and reconciliation. It concerns a continuing injustice of deeply troubling proportions.' This became very clear at a press conference when the four elderly Malaysians spoke of their experiences.

Loh Ah Choy recalled: 'It was about 5 in the evening when the soldiers came to our Kongsi [hut]. Women and children were herded to one place. At 7, my uncle walked to the vegetable garden, followed by a soldier. I heard three shots. My uncle didn't come back, but the soldier came back …'. Madam Lim had just turned 11 at the end of 1948. She remembered the way the British soldiers treated her mother: 'They pulled her by the arm and we clung on to the other arm, and when she was led away, we heard shots and thought that they had shot her. But she was spared.' Madam Lim's father was not so fortunate. He was shot: 'We were asked to get on to a lorry and then we heard several shots fired and then saw flames.' A week later, the women and their children returned to Batang Kali to fetch the bodies for burial: 'The stench was really bad. There were worms coming out of the eyes and mouths …'. Even in death, there was no dignity for the men who were killed that day in December at Batang Kali.

The first report of the killings in *The Straits Times* sounded a shrill note of triumph: 'Police, Bandits kill 28 [sic] bandits in day […] Biggest Success for Forces since Emergency Started'. It would not take long for the official story to unravel. The Chinese Consul in Kuala Lumpur complained to the colonial government. The dead villagers had not been communists, he asserted. The journalists at *The Straits Times* who had been so gung-ho when news of the Scots Guards' action was first released now demanded a public enquiry. The colonial government was forced on the defensive. Now, they insisted, the dead men had been 'shot while trying to escape'. The killings, in short, were justified. Since 1948, successive British governments have stubbornly pedalled the same story. The massacre that took place at Batang Kali is not of course the only 'closeted spectre' of British imperial history. In May 2013, the British government began negotiating payments to thousands of Kenyans who were detained and tortured during the 'Mau Mau' insurgency in Kenya. Long-concealed documents released by the National Archives in 2012 revealed incriminating new evidence. Eric Griffiths-Jones, the attorney general in colonial Kenya, had once described the treatment of detainees as 'distressingly reminiscent of conditions in Nazi Germany and Communist Russia' but nevertheless sanctioned beatings of suspects as long as it was done in secret: 'If we are going to sin, we must sin quietly.' One of the victims was Hussein Onyango Obama, Barack Obama's grandfather. British soldiers rammed pins into his fingernails and squeezed his testicles between metal rods. Other prisoners were 'roasted alive'.[2] Historian Caroline Elkins revealed that, in 1957, the colonial government in Kenya decided to subject the detainees who still refused to co-operate and comply with orders to a torture technique known as 'the dilution technique'. This was a grotesque euphemism. Dilution meant the systematic use of brute force to overpower alleged 'Mau Mau' adherents, using fists, clubs, truncheons and whips. This treatment would continue until the detainees co-operated with orders, confessed and repented. Martyn Day, the lawyer who acted on behalf of the Kenyan claimants, has written that the British government hid for years 'behind technical legal defences to avoid any legal responsibility. This was always morally repugnant …'.

We will come back to what *The People* newspaper called 'Horror in a Nameless Village' in due course. For historians of the British Empire and its long decline and fall, the 'Batang Kali trial' has already shed new light on the longest overseas war fought by British troops in the twentieth century – the 'Malayan Emergency'. The counter-insurgency tactics developed by British forces in Malaya have long been regarded as exemplary. The communists were defeated; Malaya became happily independent. This book will seek to demonstrate that this comforting historical narrative is a myth, and a dangerous one. For the 'lessons' of the Malayan counter-insurgency campaign influenced American strategy in Vietnam and even today are invoked to rationalise military tactics in Iraq and Afghanistan. Viewed through the lens of that tragedy, the entire history of British rule in Malaya, both direct and indirect, is thrown into sharp relief as a long and troubling chronicle of slaughter and deception. We seem to cherish a rosy view of the long ago and far away world of 'British Malaya'. In *Eastern Journey*, published in 1939, J.H. MacCallum Scott eulogised on the eve of the Second World War: 'Malaya is as happy a land as one could ever hope to find – a Tory Eden in which each man is contented with his station, and does not wish for change.' This nostalgic folk memory is infused with a congratulatory sense that we 'got Malaya right': we had learnt hard lessons from the bloody catastrophe of Indian partition and the ignominious flight from Palestine and so made decent exit from Malaya. Look, too, at *modern* Malaysia, with its booming economy, multiracial society, stable government and teeming shopping malls. Malaysians surely owe a tremendous debt to the old empire builders whose roll call of honour is still evoked by place names like Port Swettenham, the Cameron Highlands and Jalan Gurney. We surely bequeathed to Southeast Asia a decent prosperous nation. This is the fundamental reason why the British government has resisted an enquiry into the slaughter at Batang Kali. What happened by the banks of the Sungai Remok contradicts a treasured national mythology. The secret history of British Malaya and the making of modern Malaysia was, from the very beginning, founded on chicanery and violence, on skulduggery and conquest. That true history is the one that must now be told .

PART ONE

THE FOUR C'S

OF COLONIALISM

1

THE BATTLEFIELD

The Least Known Part of the Globe

'Public opinion,' lamented Isabella Bird in 1879 'never reaches these equatorial jungles; we are grossly ignorant of their inhabitants and of their rights [...] unless some fresh disturbance and another "little war" should concentrate our attention for a moment on these distant states, we are likely to remain so, to their great detriment [...] I felt humiliated by my ignorance.'

For much of the nineteenth century Malaya lay in the shadow of British India. A position in the Malayan Civil Service, the MCS, was for second-raters: the elite served the Raj. It was not until Britain lost Malaya and Singapore to the Japanese in 1942 that its value was fully appreciated. When the Japanese surrendered in 1945, the near-bankrupted new Labour government in London would do everything in its power to hold onto 'these equatorial jungles' and their wealth. The Malayan Peninsula divides the Bay of Bengal from the South China Sea and resembles a misshapen limb bent towards the vast Indonesian Archipelago and the Philippine Islands. Once called 'Further India' or the 'Far Eastern Tropics', this arc of islands and peninsulas was demeaned as an extension of India or a tropical appendage of the Far East. With the exception of Thailand, Europeans who came here encountered not a single polity that resembled a nation state. Burma, Cambodia, Laos, Vietnam, Malaysia, Indonesia, Brunei are all creations of imperialism – French, British, Dutch and American. It was the Japanese armies that rampaged through the Malayan Peninsula and into the Philippines and Indonesia in 1942 that definitively stamped out a grander regional identity, a fact of conquest recognised by British military commanders when they established 'South East Asia Command', or SEAC, to oust these impertinent Asian imperialists. For Alfred Russell Wallace (with Charles Darwin, co-discoverer of evolution by natural selection) Southeast Asia was the 'Malay Archipelago'. This plucky naturalist spent little time in the peninsula: it was the archipelago that fascinated him most. He began his engrossing account:

To the ordinary Englishman this is perhaps the least known part of the globe. Our possessions in it are few and scanty; scarcely any of our travellers go to explore it; and in many collections of maps it is almost ignored, being divided between Asia and the Pacific Islands [...] Situated upon the Equator, and bathed by the tepid water of the great tropical oceans, this region enjoys a climate more uniformly hot and moist than almost any other part of the globe, and teems with natural productions which are elsewhere unknown. The richest of fruits and the most precious of spices are indigenous here ...

Wallace published *The Malay Archipelago* in 1869. Three decades later, this hot, wet and teeming world was transformed utterly by Portuguese, Dutch, French and English colonisers. Territorial borders that were once contested between European powers now demarcate the political boundaries of the brand new nations like Malaysia and Indonesia, which emerged in the aftermath of the Second World War. From the point of view of Asian nationalists, the colonial powers violently dismembered a unified ethnic and cultural domain. There is no territorial logic that can rationalise severing modern Malaysia from the rest of the Indonesian Archipelago. When Portuguese admiral Afonso de Albuquerque sailed into Malacca harbour with guns blazing on 2 May 1511, he inaugurated the destruction of a distinct 'Malay World' encompassing much of modern Southeast Asia, whose legendary splendour rivalled that of Mogul India. Nations depend on such assertions of antiquity and unity. According to Gandhi, 'India was one undivided land [...] made by nature.' Nehru spoke of an 'impress of oneness' going back 6,000 years. 'Mother India' is a myth. In pre-modern times, the Indian subcontinent was never a single political or cultural entity. It was in fact a mutable hotchpotch of petty and middle-sized kingdoms that had little in common. Arguably, 'India' was a European invention: there is no equivalent term in any indigenous language. Likewise, 'Indonesia', which yokes together the Greek 'Indus' and 'nèsos', meaning islands, was first used by English ethnologists and popularised by German anthropologist Adolf Bastian. Nations, in short, demand a prestigious genealogy. Today, the legend of a once glorious 'Malay World' inhabited by a unitary indigenous people nourishes chauvinist racial politics that enshrines Muslim Malays as indigenous 'Bumiputera' or 'Princes/sons of the Soil'. The idea is profoundly atavistic. It is a truism to say that we are all the children of migrants. Modern genetics has sketched a global cartography of human interconnectedness, the consequence of a history of incessant wandering, settlement and emigration.

This axiom is especially pertinent to Southeast Asia where successive waves of migrants have churned back and forth to forge unique regional cultures. These are the 'Lands of the Monsoon' straddling the equator, much warmer than China and wetter than the greater part of the Indian subcontinent. For millennia, Southeast Asia has been a maritime crossroads. Its rugged and intricate topography is deeply incised by oceanic waters, and copious rainfall has generated an intricate network of interlaced waterways. The first classical geographers, such as Ptolemy, recorded jewel-like clusters of ports in the region they called the *Chersonesus Aurea*, the

Golden Chersonese. Though on its northern borders Southeast Asia was cut off from the continental interior and its ancient centres of human dispersal by the icy ramparts of the Tibetan plateau, the entire region to the south has been exposed to seaborne settlement and incursion of peoples and cultures as well as ceaseless internal migration from island to island. These convergences and dispersals have over tens of thousands of years created a human topography of remarkable diversity that in many ways evokes the civilisations of the ancient Aegean, which Plato compared to 'ants and frogs around a pond'. Thousands of years before Europeans came here, Southeast Asia was globally interconnected. Archaeologists have excavated the bones of Stone Age humans in Perak whose ancestors evolved in Africa. Modern humans, with their big, inquisitive brains, were wanderers and explorers who seem to have loped across the ancient land bridge connecting Asia with the far reaches of the archipelago before the end of the last Ice Age. These long-vanished people may well be the distant forebears of the Malayan aboriginals, called in Malay 'Orang Asli', the 'original people'. The Malays, too, were intruders once. They probably migrated southward from the Asian interior and then spread across the entire archipelago. Later, the great pump of the monsoon brought Greeks, Arabs, Persians and Indians from the west and Chinese from the east. Here, for 1,000 years, was one of the great centres of Hindu culture centuries before the coming of Islam. This astonishing human and cultural liquescence renders meaningless the idea of a single race of indigenes. Before the first Europeans sailed tentatively into the Straits of Malacca, fleets from India and China sailed to Southeast Asia with one monsoon and returned home with another. For millennia, the great migrational pump of the monsoon churned and shuffled the gene pool.

In the vast water world of Southeast Asia, the Malayan Peninsula is in some ways anomalous. Unlike the islands of Indonesia and the Philippines, this slender rocky limb is attached to the Eurasian landmass and forms its south-eastern extremity. Modern Malaysia, of course, shares the peninsula with Burma and Thailand. Many borderland regions become battlegrounds and this one is no exception. Thai rulers once claimed sovereignty over the northern Malay states of Perlis, Kedah, Kelantan, and Terengganu; it was here that Japanese armies landed in December 1941 and it was to the Thai border that Malayan communist guerrillas retreated in the mid-1950s. Many retired communist freedom fighters still live in 'Peace Villages' close to the Malaysian border in Thailand. For some years radical Muslim insurgents linked to 'Jemaah Islamijah' have been engaged in a campaign of bombings and assassinations in the southern Thai state of Patani. The colonial administrator, Sir Hugh Clifford, in his book *In Court and Kampong*, left us a wonderful account of the pristine peninsula rain forests as they were in the late nineteenth century:

> These forests are among the wonderful things of the Earth. They are immense in extent, and the trees which form them grow so close together that they

tread on one another's toes. All are lashed, and bound, and relashed, into one huge magnificent tangled net, by the thickest underwood, and the most marvellous parasitic growths that nature has ever devised. No human being can force his way through this maze of trees, and shrubs, and thorns, and plants, and creepers; and even the great beasts which dwell in the jungle find their strength unequal to the task, and have to follow game paths, beaten out by the passage of innumerable animals, through the thickest and deepest parts of the forest. The branches cross and recross, and are bound together by countless parasitic creepers, forming a green canopy overhead, through which the fierce sunlight only forces a partial passage, the struggling rays flecking the trees on which they fall with little splashes of light and colour. The air 'hangs heavy as remembered sin', and the gloom of a great cathedral is on every side. Everything is damp, and moist, and oppressive.

Mountain, river and jungle. These are the physical protagonists that have channelled and sculpted the incessant flow of migrations and settlements, the drama of encounters, skirmishes and wars. It is a topography that can be both a barrier and a refuge. Some seven or eight major mountain ranges ripple down the peninsula separated by deep furrows. The most impressive is the prosaically named Main Range, which extends uninterrupted from the Thai border to Negeri Sembilan before tapering into the flat lands of Johor. The granite cores of the Main Range are encrusted with a patina of sedimentary limestone that has been eroded to a distinctive topography of towering bluffs and spires riddled with caves and fissures. This rocky landscape is itself sheathed up to a level of about 2,000ft by immense evergreen rainforests that once covered four-fifths of the peninsula. This ancient jungle is now being steadily eroded by desolate plantations of oil palms.

To east and west, the long green spine of the central ranges descends to rolling foothills and coastal plains. The west coast facing across the narrow Straits of Malacca towards the great island of Sumatra is edged along its entire length by tangled mangrove swamps and shimmering expanses of mud. These mud flats can deceive the unwary. When British troops landed on Morib Beach near Port Swettenham in September 1945, what in aerial photographs appeared to be solid ground turned out to be a deceptive crust concealing layers of silt that ensnared tanks and trucks. On the other side of the Main Range, the east coast possesses an entirely different character. The north-east monsoon that batters its shores between November and February checks the spread of mangroves. Long sandy beaches stretch for mile upon mile broken by shingle spits and rocky headlands. The east coast is notoriously treacherous, as thousands of Japanese soldiers discovered when they struggled through pounding waves towards the beaches at Kota Bahru in December 1941. On the west side of the peninsula, the Straits of Malacca are sheltered by the island of Sumatra and the Malayan highlands and are for much of the year as placid as an inland sea. For merchants and travellers propelled across the Bay of Bengal by the monsoon, the straits are the maritime gateway to Southeast Asia. Sir Hugh Clifford called the straits the 'front door' of the peninsula – the east, across the Main Range, was 'the other side of silence'.

The peninsula can boast no grand relics of ancient civilisations like the pyramidal Buddhist temple of Borobudur on Java or the ruins of Angkor Wat in Cambodia. Excavations at Sungai Batu in the Bujang Valley in Kedah have uncovered evidence that the Chola (or Chozhan) kingdom in southern India established some kind of settlement here on the banks of the Muda River to mine and export local deposits of iron ore. Malaysian archaeologists have claimed the Bujang Valley as early evidence of Malay civilisation. Although Chinese records from the first century seem to refer to a kingdom called 'Lang-ya-xiu' or 'Langkasuka', excavations have so far uncovered not a shred of evidence of an indigenous culture. Malays were thoroughly Indianised before their conversion to Islam. 'Singapura' is believed to derive from a Sanskrit term meaning 'Lion City'. In the north-east, the Malay states of Kelantan, Terengganu and northern Pahang may have developed similarly derivative ties with the Mon-Khmer lands to the north. The simple fact is that the peninsula was hard to settle. Granite, the bedrock of the peninsula, does not yield fertile soils – and from whatever direction the peninsula was approached early settlers found their way to the interior blocked by jungle. Settlement was localised in a few relatively favoured lowland areas and in clusters scattered along the coastal edges of the peninsula, where rivers met the sea. It was not that the Malays and the other peoples passing through the peninsula were in some way deficient. The ancient civilisations of Burma, Thailand and Cambodia all flourished in great fertile river basins. Well-fed rice growers built the great monuments of central Java. The main factor shaping the history of the Malayan Peninsula is a severely limited capacity to grow food crops, which over time has handicapped the development of political power. Malaya has been described as a 'causeway and breakwater of massive proportions', but as English political geographer Halford Mackinder always insisted, even a sea power has to be 'nourished by land-fertility somewhere'. Even Malacca, the great west coast emporium of the spice trade, which dominated all the small river-basin sultanates of the peninsula as far north as Kedah and Patani, was held back by the limited food production capacity of its hinterland. According to a Chinese observer, the soil of Malacca was barren and saline; rice had to be imported from Java. For much of its history, the peninsula was a backwater.

As the classical geographers suspected, the 'Golden Chersonese' were endowed with riches. But the most valuable were secretive – and inedible. Iron, as we have already noted, was mined in the Bujang Valley in Kedah and exported to southern India more than 1,000 years ago. It was only much later in the nineteenth century that Malaya's mineral resources became unique assets – tin above all was the making of Malaya. In wet tropical climates, granite weathers swiftly. As the core rock crumbles, quartz, feldspars and other silicate minerals break down to form clays which are carried away by streams. The toughest crystals coalesce as gravels. Concentrated inside these alluvial gravels is a heavy mineral called cassiterite that accumulates in what geologists call lenses that are distributed along a horizon in the gravel. This, in brief, is the creation story of tin. So it was that the lodes, veins and scattered crystals released from the granitic cores of the peninsula ranges were washed into the foothills of western Malaya to form a band of alluvial fans impregnated with this dull silvery ore. Tin in this form is not difficult to extract – and Malays had extracted small amounts for centuries. It was Chinese immigrants who first saw the immense potential of Malaya's alluvial tin deposits. The tin rush that began in the Larut field in 1848 would transform Malaya from a backwater into an economic powerhouse controlled by people feared as outsiders. The Malayan wars had begun.

The Sudden Rampage, 8 December 1941

Early morning, 4 December 1941: Samah harbour on the Japanese occupied island of Hainan in the Gulf of Tongkin. As a sheet white moon set in the western sky, the sun burst above the horizon making the still ocean surface shimmer gold and silver. This picture-postcard vista delighted Colonel Masanobo Tsuji as he stood on the bridge of the amphibious assault ship *Ryujo Maru*, 'The Dragon and the Castle'. Designed as an aircraft carrier, this odd flat-topped vessel was the temporary headquarters of the Japanese 25th Army, commanded by Lt General Tomoyuki Yamashita. Colonel Tsuji owed nothing to privilege and everything to intelligence and grit. He loved kendo fencing – but spurned most other time-wasting sports, as well as alcohol and women. He had vowed to abstain from any sexual activity until after Singapore had fallen. Tsuji was notoriously short-tempered and regarded as a killjoy by many of his fellow officers. But that morning the lurid splendour of the rising sun perfectly matched his exultant mood.

If the diminutive colonel was a prig, he was one with clout. He was the strategic mastermind behind a plan of conquest that would, in less than two months, bring more than a century of colonial rule in Malaya to an inglorious end. As the moon dipped out of sight, and the hot-red sun rose ever higher above the horizon, the *Ryujo Maru* and an armada of Japanese troopships, led by the flagship *Chokai* and flanked by two lines of destroyers and minesweepers, began steaming south-west towards the coast of Thailand. The die, as Tsuji reflected, had been cast. As the lush tropical coast of Hainan Island receded slowly astern, he conjured up the faces of his mother, his wife and children waiting at home in Japan. The fate of the nation hinged on the success of his plan.

Crammed inside the *Ryujo Maru* and the other transport ships were 83,000 soldiers, squatting or sprawling just a few inches apart. Most of the men were horribly seasick. Tsuji was one of the few onboard who seemed immune. This was the Japanese 25th Army – their mission: the invasion of British Malaya and the capture of Singapore. Tsuji had begun detailed planning at the Taiwan Army Research Centre at the beginning of 1941 for the conquest of Southeast Asia. The Chinese had ceded Taiwan (called Formosa by the Portuguese) to the Japanese in 1895 and the island had become a fortress with a large garrison. Japanese soldiers had very little experience of fighting in the tropics. At the research centre, Tsuji and just ten staff officers struggled to gather every scrap of information they could lay their hands on about tropical warfare. They staged exercises on the sandy beaches of the southern Japanese island of Kyushu to simulate the rigours of disembarkation. Tsuji and his team investigated ways to cope with heat, mosquitoes and snakes; they advocated hygiene and recommended swallowing the raw livers of tropical snakes for stamina. As the Japanese armada turned into the Gulf of Thailand, the emperor's soldiers in their cramped and uncomfortable quarters below deck longed desperately for the voyage to be over. They were confident of victory. A lucky few had the stomach to wolf down meagre rations of rice, miso and pickled radish. Some pored over Colonel Tsuji's pamphlet *Read this Alone and the War can be Won*. This was both a practical guidebook and propagandist exhortation:

> … at stake in the present war, without a doubt, is the future prosperity or decline of the [Japanese] Empire […] Regard yourself as an avenger come face to face at last with his father's murderer. Here before you is the [Westerner] whose death will lighten your heart …

Although Tsuji stressed that the task of the Imperial Army was to build a new 'Asia for Asians', they should not 'expect too much of the natives'. Malays, many Japanese believed, were backward peasants. The Chinese, on the other hand, Tsuji warned, were mere 'extortionists' – not fit to join the 'Asian Brotherhood'.

The Japanese convoy closing in on the Malayan Peninsula was one part of an audacious master plan intended to oust the European powers that had for centuries abused and exploited the peoples and treasure of Asia. This imperial crusade was a desperate gamble. Japanese armies were still at war with Chiang Kai-Shek's nationalist forces in China; in Europe, the German onslaught against Stalin's Red Army was foundering in the ice and snow of the Russian winter.

Although Japanese and American diplomats continued to wrangle in Washington, General Hideki Tojo and his planners were convinced that speed, deceit and surprise would win the day. The strategic blueprint hatched in Tokyo was to smash British forces in Hong Kong, Singapore, Malaya and Borneo; oust the Americans from the Philippines; seize flanking positions in southern Burma and the Bismarck Archipelago; and set up a kind of perimeter line of defence in the Andaman and Nicobar Islands. Once this immense region had been secured, the victors could feast on the oil riches of Borneo and Sumatra. That was the plan and it very nearly succeeded.

The supreme commander of the Japanese 'Southern Expeditionary Army' who would lead the assault on Southeast Asia was Count Hisaichi Terauchi. The capture of Malaya, Singapore, southern Sumatra and British Borneo fell to Lt General Tomoyuki Yamashita. He defied every colonial stereotype of a Japanese warrior. In stark contrast to the frugal and ascetic Colonel Tsuji, the tall bulky Yamashita was once described as an 'Oriental Falstaff'. His father was a rural doctor on the smallest Japanese island of Shikoku, celebrated for its arduous eighty-eight-temple pilgrimage route and magnificent cedar trees. His mother descended from a samurai clan whose fortress was still a local monument. For much of his career, Yamashita, who was married to a willowy general's daughter, had been a punctilious, hard-working bureaucrat, who had done well enough to serve as military attaché in Germany and Austria. In Vienna, he had acquired girth, a passion for literature, and a mistress called 'Kitty'. By the time he returned to Japan, Yamashita had an enviable reputation as a diplomat but very little experience of combat.

By the mid-1930s, Japan had become, as historian Rikki Kersten has shown, an ultranationalist quasi-fascist society, imbued with an aggressive imperialist foreign policy, and a national creed of spiritual superiority towards the West and racial superiority to other Asians.[3] The dominance of the 'Emperor System' led to an all pervasive psychological coercion. The Japanese state was authoritarian; its society was rigidly conformist. In February 1936, a group of radical young army officers, known as the 'National Principle' faction, staged a *coup d'état* under the slogan 'Revere the Emperor, expel the evils'. The plan was to 'execute the disloyal and unrighteous'. The uprising was crushed and its ringleaders committed suicide or were executed. The main consequence of the coup was to deepen the power of the Imperial Army. A few of the rebels had talked of Yamashita as a role model or mentor and, though he was not directly involved, he was disgraced by association and banished to Korea. But Yamashita had many supporters in the War Office. After serving out his time in Seoul, he was recalled and appointed to lead a mission to Germany. Japan had been a German ally since 1936 and in 1940 joined the Three Power Pact with Italy and Germany. In the spring of 1941, Yamashita was personally briefed by Adolf Hitler on 'Operation Barbarossa' – the invasion of the Soviet Union. Although Hitler reminded Yamashita of a 'bank clerk', he was convinced that Britain could not win the war. This was the message he conveyed to Minister of War and Prime Minister Hideki Tojo. There was no better time to strike the Asian bastions of the British imperialists. Yamashita flew to Saigon in French Indochina to prepare the invasion based on Colonel Tsuji's blueprint. He promised the emperor that he would secure Singapore by the New Year.

Yamashita's confidence was well founded. A year earlier, on 11 November 1940, the Blue Funnel Line steamer the *Automedon* had been intercepted north-west of Sumatra by the German surface raider *Atlantis*. The *Automedon* stood little chance of escaping this ruthless maritime predator that rapidly overtook the wallowing steamer, guns blazing. Six crew died instantly; all lifeboats were destroyed; the *Automedon* began listing. There followed a classic moment of historical serendipity. When one of the English passengers, a Mrs Ferguson, insisted that the German captain, Bernhard Rogge, retrieve her baggage, which contained a prized tea-set, he despatched First Lt Ulrich Mohr to search the rapidly sinking ship. Once onboard, Mohr could not resist scavenging the wrecked chart room of the *Automedon* and, as he recalled:

> Our prize was just a long narrow envelope enclosed in a green bag equipped with brass eyelets to let water in to facilitate its sinking. The bag was marked 'Highly Confidential [...] To be destroyed' and contained the latest appreciation of the Military strength of the Empire in the Far East [...] What the devil were the British about, sending such material by a slow old tub like *Automedon*, I puzzled? Surely a warship would have been a worthier repository? We could not understand it ...

That puzzle remains unsolved. Captain Rogge, who spoke good English, immediately understood the significance of this serendipitous discovery and, through the German naval attaché in Tokyo, sent the captured documents to his counterpart in Berlin who forwarded them on to the Japanese. By mid-December, the implications of the British report had begun to sink in. As Tsuji put it: 'Such a significant weakening of the British Empire could not have been identified from outward appearances.'

Also onboard Yamashita's invasion fleet was Iwaichi Fujiwara. He too had fought in China, with the 21st Army, but at the end of the 1930s he returned to Tokyo to join the 8th Section concerned with intelligence and propaganda. Fujiwara passionately believed that the embryonic nationalist movements in Southeast Asia fitted with Japanese imperial ambition. His Fujiwara Kikan (Agency) had begun to develop a relationship with the Indian nationalist Subhas Chandra Bose, who had fled to Berlin, and had its eye on a tiny group of Malay nationalists, the Kesatuan Melayu Muda (KMM) led by Ibrahim Yaacob. A year earlier, Fujiwara had taken part in the tsunami of nationalist celebrations commemorating the 2,600th anniversary of the Japanese Empire. He had met many of the foreigners who had come to Tokyo to take part in the celebrations, along with members of the 'Hitler Youth'. Indian, Vietnamese and Burmese nationalists, among them Aung San, eagerly embraced Japan as leader of their anti-colonial liberation struggles. Fujiwara ensured his visitors that once the hated British, Dutch and American imperialists had been sent packing, they would be welcomed as members of a 'Greater East Asian Co-Prosperity Sphere'. 'Banzai!' they all shouted. A year later, soldiers of the 25th Army onboard their convoy ships that pitched and rolled across the Gulf of Thailand, took to heart Colonel Tsuji's vitriolic words : 'These white people may expect, from the moment they issue from their mothers' wombs, to be allotted a score or so of natives as their personal slaves. Is this really God's will?'

For two days, the Japanese invasion fleet ploughed through heavy seas across the Gulf of Tonkin towards the Malayan coast. For the soldiers packed below decks, conditions were unimaginably foul. But for General Yamashita and his headquarters staff, the thick roiling storm clouds were a blessing. From the air, the Japanese armada was well-nigh invisible. British pilots would surely not risk flying into a typhoon.

Yamashita could not know that in Singapore and Kuala Lumpur British commanders were overwhelmed by a typhoon of doubt, confusion and geriatric dithering. It had long been understood that should the Japanese ever choose to invade Malaya, the back door to Singapore, they would almost certainly establish a bridgehead on the Kra Isthmus, where the peninsula narrows close to the border with Thailand. In the northern Malay state of Kelantan the long sandy beaches of Kota Bahru offered a near perfect site for landing troops; to the north on the other side of the border, there was an excellent harbour at Singora (Songkhla) as well as an airfield at Patani. The British devised a 'forward defence' plan codenamed 'Operation Matador' to defend the vulnerable 'neck' of the peninsula by launching a pre-emptive strike across the border. And there, in a nutshell, was the problem. The Kingdom of Thailand, as Siam was now called, was the only independent nation in Southeast Asia.[4] Sir Josiah Crosby, the influential British minister in Bangkok, was terrified that an incursion like the one envisaged by the 'Matador' planners would have ruinous consequences: the Thais, he informed the Foreign Office in London, were fully convinced of the power of the Japanese to 'do them harm', but 'have no faith at all in our power to protect them'. (As it turned out, the Japanese would not secure Thai agreement for 'free passage' until 21 December.)[5] With some irony, the British also feared provoking the wrath of the Americans. The United States remained a neutral power, and President Roosevelt's contempt for British imperialism was well known. This delicate international conundrum was compounded by a confused and confusing chain of command. 'Matador' became synonymous with indecision and inaction. These dilemmas tormented the 63-year-old Commander-in-Chief of the British Far East Command, Air Chief Marshal Sir Robert Brooke-Popham, disrespectfully known as 'old pop off' by his subordinates. As rumours and portents of catastrophe swirled around him, Brooke-Popham vacillated. Then, on 1 December, Roosevelt finally gave the nod to 'Matador' and a few days later London signalled Brooke-Popham that the plan was green lit *if* Japan invaded Thailand or was seen to be approaching with hostile intent. The decision to go to war was his, and his alone, it seemed. In any event, Brooke-Popham never squeezed the 'Matador' trigger.

At a point roughly midway across the Gulf of Thailand, to the south of Phu Quoc island, the Japanese armada split: three transports (supported by four destroyers and the cruiser *Sendai*) headed south towards Kota Bahru in Malaya, while the main

Japanese force steamed on towards the Thai coast. There the fleet would divide again to disembark the bulk of the Japanese Army at Singora and Patani. Not long after this parting of ways, the storm abated. Yamashita and Colonel Tsuji observed the sky clearing with dread. Tsuji had flown reconnaissance missions the length and breadth of Malaya and had spotted numerous British airfields gashed out of the jungle. What the Japanese commanders feared most was aerial attack. As it happened, Tsuji had grossly overestimated the fire power of the RAF in Malaya.

From rain-saturated runways at Pengkalan Chepa, 5 miles east of Kota Bahru, three antiquated Lockheed Hudsons lumbered into the sky, banking sharply to follow a course along the Malayan coast. An hour or so after take-off, the Australian pilots spotted the Japanese armada – they reported perhaps seventy vessels, with warships in attendance. As this shattering news sped down the wire to Singapore and then London and Washington, the weather over the Gulf deteriorated again. Yamashita's fleet sailed on out of sight as British hesitancy took on an epic dimension. Where were the Japanese? What did they intend? Was this war? Then came much more ominous news. A twin engine Catalina flying boat, with a range of 4,000 miles, had been despatched from Singapore to reconnoitre the region south of Phu Quoc island. Now radio contact had been lost. Flying Officer Edwin Beddell had not sent a distress message. Despite the Catalina's famous resilience, the most likely explanation was the worst: the aircraft had been shot down. In his memoir Tsuji revealed that Japanese Ki 27s had bathed the ill-fated Catalina in ferocious fire. It exploded at 400m. Beddell and his seven-man crew had become the first casualties of the Pacific War.

Just after midnight on 8 December, the southern Japanese invasion fleet anchored 3 kilometres off the Kota Bahru beaches. Onboard the three transports was a 6,000-strong brigade of the 18th Chrysanthemum Division, led by Major General Hiroshi Takumi. His task was to secure the airfield at Pengkalan Chepa and divert British attention from the main Japanese landings at Singora and Patani on the Thai coast. It is a myth that the British did not defend Malaya – and that the mainly Indian troops ran away at the first sight of the Japanese. From Takumi's point of view the first wave of landings on the Kota Bahru beaches were touch and go. As the *Sendais'* 8in guns pounded shore defences, he and his officers struggled to get as many of their men into the landing craft fast enough. It was a nasty business timing the jump from the rolling transport ships to the bobbing landing craft. Clouds veiled the moon, it was pitch dark and the sea was already running high. Takumi's men had been issued with life jackets, but burdened as they all were with rifles and packs, those who fell short of the landing craft and ended up in the water rarely came back up. As the heaving boats filled up, British Hudsons suddenly roared low across the waves hurling 250-pounders at the now vulnerable Japanese invasion fleet. They scored direct hits on the *Awagisan Maru* – where Takumi and his staff officers huddled in the dark. Fire erupted from the superstructure and thick oily smoke billowed across the sea. When Takumi's men finally reached the beaches they faced withering fire from behind a labyrinth of entangled barbed wire, punctuated by a rain of bullets sprayed from pill boxes. Japanese soldiers were forced to dig their way under the wire with spoons.

To be sure, the Japanese received a bloody nose at Kota Bahru – but the attack was in any case diversionary. Fifty miles north north-east of Kota Bahru, on the other side of the Thai border, Yamashita's armada was anchored in Singora's fine harbour, and thousands of soldiers poured from the transports and into their landing craft. Since 'Matador' had been stillborn, the Japanese landed unopposed. At both Singora and further south at Patani, hundreds of gleaming Japanese aircraft, including the formidable new Zeros, lined up on airfields that had been secretly constructed months before. As Yamashita mustered his forces to march south towards the Malay border, Takumi's troops had begun pushing into the dense network of canals and waterways that lay between the coast and Kota Bahru town – but Australian and Indian forces continued to fight back hard. The Pacific War was just six hours old. In less than a day the Japanese had utterly transformed the scale and scope of the war. In whirlwind succession the emperor's army, navy and air force attacked the British colonies of Hong Kong and Malaya, followed, only an hour and a half later, by the attack on the US Navy's Pacific Fleet in Pearl Harbor. In Singapore, General Arthur Percival was perversely optimistic. The first reports from Kota Bahru suggested that the 'little men' had been 'seen off'. But by the end of that momentous first day the mood had changed. The Japanese had dealt a mortal blow to the empire.

The back door to Singapore now swung precariously on its hinges. Soon it would be kicked wide open. The Malayan campaign would be the prelude to the shaming of Malaya's colonial masters by a determined Asian army that had been dismissed by General Sir Archibald Wavell as 'highly trained gangsters'. The narrative of how the Japanese '*kiramoni sakusen*' (the 'driving charge') swept down through the Malayan Peninsula to capture, in just fifty-five days, Britain's iconic and supposedly impregnable bastion of Singapore – the symbol of imperial power and prestige in the Far East – has been told many times. Historians continue to fret over who was to blame for this humiliating rout, and whether the loss of Singapore was the inevitable consequence of a wrong-headed strategic concept that sought to defend a two-hemisphere empire with a one-hemisphere navy. The penalties of defeat are not in doubt. They went deeper than military defeat. The Japanese shamed the colonial European masters of Asia and galvanised anti-colonial nationalist movements that had emerged in Burma, the Philippines, Indonesia and, more tentatively, in Malaya. Because Japan was still at war with nationalist China, the occupiers of Southeast Asia whetted the struggle between the long-divided ethnic communities of British Malaya. They forced Chinese nationalists and communists to take up arms against the occupiers, and recruited Malays to keep the peace. In the turbulent course of an occupation that would last for three years and eight months, the Japanese primed a long and bloody conflict.

2

THE MAKING OF BRITISH MALAYA

Murder in the Bath

Early on the morning of 2 November 1875 James Wheeler Woodford Birch, the first British 'Resident' of the Malayan state of Perak, chose the wrong time and the wrong place to take a bath. For more than a year, Birch, an abrupt cantankerous man, had been struggling to impose his authority on the young state ruler, Sultan Abdullah. Birch was under tremendous pressure. Recently widowed and with four young children to support, he was heavily in debt. Although he was building a house in Bandar Bahru fit for a British Resident, he was unaware that Governor Sir William Jervois was pondering whether he should have him replaced. Birch and the sultan had clashed repeatedly. 'We are unfortunate in the Sultan,' he wrote to colleagues in Singapore: 'He riles me awfully. He is so childish.' Birch deplored Abdullah's use of opium, and his refusal to release his slaves. For his part the sultan resisted Birch's efforts to bring 'good government' to his state, or sort out claims by rival rulers. By the beginning of November, during the Muslim festival of Hari Raya Puasa, rumours had reached Birch that trouble was brewing. At midnight on 1 November, Birch, accompanied by a small company of sepoys, a Lieutenant T.F. Abbott and his interpreter, Mat Arshad, moored his boat the *Naga* at Pasir Salak on the Perak River. Early the next day, while it was still cool, Birch moved the *Naga* to the other side of the river and tied up alongside a riverside bathhouse owned by a Chinese goldsmith. The bath was a modest affair: a wooden frame sheathed in braided palm leaves. While Lt Abbott set off to do some hunting, Birch sent Arshad to post proclamations declaring in no uncertain terms that he was determined to 'administer the Government of Perak in the name of the Sultan'. It was now very hot and Birch, after posting a sepoy to stand guard, disappeared inside the little riverside bathhouse. As he set to work nearby, clutching an armful of proclamations, Mat Arshad was attacked by a large party of at least fifty Malays, many armed with spears. As the interpreter fled, the Malays surrounded the hut. Birch splashed happily inside. As the men with spears closed in, the sepoy panicked and hurled himself into the river. The Malays thrust their spears through the thin palm leaf walls of the bathhouse. Birch, taken by surprise, naked and vulnerable, died instantly. His blood gushed into the sluggish waters of the Perak as his assassins hacked another sepoy to death. The other sepoys managed to reach the boats and make their escape as Birch's bloodied corpse floated past. Wounded, Mat Arshad was dragged onboard one of the fleeing boats, but died soon afterwards. A few days later, Birch's mutilated corpse was recovered and sent to Bandar Bahru where, on the spot he had planned to build his official residence, he was buried with full military honours. When his son Ernest Birch visited Pasir Salak ten years later, he met many people who said they had known his father. An elderly man returned the murdered Resident's gold watch and gun to his astonished son.

The Four C's

The murder of James Birch, the first British Resident in Perak, was a pivotal moment in the slow emergence of what came to be known as 'British Malaya'. It was a long drawn-out and tortuous process that defied conventional ideas about the nature of empire building and imperial rule. Likewise, the departure of the British from Malaya and other overseas possessions in the 1950s and 1960s was equally protracted and has been just as mythologised. The rise and fall of the British Empire remains in many ways enigmatic. Just what was the nature of British rule? How and why did it end? Historians have never ceased to wonder about the nature of the beast and to pick over its carcass. It is useful to have in mind Peter Borschberg's 'Four C's' model of colonialism: curiosity, collaboration, commerce and conflict. All four will be much in evidence in the narrative of this book. Borschberg might have added a fifth C – civilising. But this would mean falling for the Victorian fantasy that the purpose of empire was to bring enlightenment to benighted natives: the 'white man's burden'. Commerce, not compassion, drove the imperial project. Lord Palmerston, who served as foreign secretary and then prime minister and was one of the architects of empire, told Parliament in 1839 that 'The great object of the Government in every quarter of the world was to extend the commerce of the country.' The empire was a world system of feverish commercial activity whose principal article of faith was global free trade. The big players were not politicians but merchant houses based in the big port cities of London, Liverpool and Glasgow. India was the jewel in the crown of the British Empire for good reason. By 1850 the Raj generated a revenue of about £30 million a year. India was also 'an English barrack in the Oriental seas' that supplied the manpower demands of the rest of the empire – at low cost. In 1914, 1.3 million Indians mustered to fight for king and country. The empire was a commercial republic headquartered in the City of London that, octopus-like, extended its tentacles of influence and power into every region of the world, from treaty ports in China, to Malaya, through Burma, India, the Persian Gulf, the Mediterranean, West Africa and Zanzibar, then across the Atlantic to the Caribbean, the River Plate republics in South America and North America.

The management of the British 'world system' depended on apparently clashing strategies of coercion and collaboration. The Indian Army was the biggest employer in the Raj, and India remained a garrison state until independence. Indian historian B.B. Misra admits that 'Indian troops conquered the country for Britain.' The Indian Army was regularly deployed to quash revolt in far-flung regions of the empire. By the 1880s, the British had built up a powerful police apparatus in India – the vanguard of repression. But naked coercion, the shades of the prison houses so familiar to anti-colonial nationalists, was not sufficient on its own. The empire relied on collaboration – and collaborators. So, too, would the Japanese after 1941 when they ousted the British from Malaya and Indonesia. In the case of British India, two-fifths of the Raj territory and more than one-fifth of its population was nominally ruled by native princes guided and advised by British 'Residents'. In the Malay states the sultans took on much the same role with varying degrees of reluctance and were rewarded with a salary and pension. These rulers owed the maintenance of their power and prestige to the empire. Princes and rulers of various kinds were the most prominent and ostentatious beneficiaries of the colonial regime. Merchants, manufacturers, lawyers and administrators – in the words of historian Lord Macaulay 'a class of persons, Indian in blood and colour, but English in taste, in opinions, in morals and in intellect' – shared the burden of rule. The empire was a modernising force, for good or ill. This 'class of persons' was also the human seedbed of nationalist movements that would bring down the empire.

The modern obsession with the British Empire and its decline has obscured and demeaned the political movements and individuals who challenged British hegemony. The former imperial power still clings to a mildewed narrative of empire. British historians dominate the telling of imperial history. Ronald Hyam in his *Britain's Declining Empire: the Road to Decolonisation 1918–1968* (2006) turns to that most traditional of British sporting pastimes to sum up contesting theories of imperial decline: 'Either the British were bowled out (by nationalists and freedom fighters), or they were run out (by imperial overstretch and economic constraints) or they retired hurt (because of a collapse of morale and "failure of will"), or they were booed off the field (by international criticism …).' The insinuation of Hyam's witty précis is that decolonisation was all about the British losing the match. The opposing team – the nationalists and freedom fighters – lurk on the margins of history. In former colonies this conveniently narrow focus is echoed in a struggle for historic ownership of the nationalist movement. In Malaysia, for example, the ruling government elite insists that the communist guerrillas who fought the colonial power after the Second World War were not nationalist 'freedom fighters' but terrorists. This is propaganda not history. The decline and fall of the British Empire is simultaneously the story of the emergence of Asian and African nationalisms. Every empire in history has hatched the nationalist ideas that will plot the destruction of its rulers.

Benedict Anderson has described the history of Southeast Asia as mottled: the blotchy consequence of intrusions, interferences and involvements. Southeast Asia can be imagined as a palimpsest: 'a membrane or roll cleansed of its manuscript by reiterated successions'. Beneath the map of empire, we can dimly perceive the lineaments of an older world. By the 1920s, nearly all of Southeast Asia – which is bounded by India, China, the South Pacific and Australia – had been claimed in some form by one or other of the imperial powers of Great Britain, France, the Netherlands and the United States. European *arrivistes* profoundly reordered the networks and nodes of Asian trading powers. Look forward from the end of the First World War to the present day and Western colonial rule has been obliterated, replaced by the modern ASEAN nation states. Decolonisation can, it would seem, be reinterpreted as a creative process of nation building rather than embarrassing degeneration – but on whose terms? Was nationalism a European import or did it assume a distinct Asian form?

In 1913, the Inter-Parliamentary Union met in The Hague to celebrate the opening of the Peace Palace and to debate the frightening escalation of the arms race between European nation states. That same year the Dutch government subsidised celebrations to mark the liberation of the Netherlands from French imperial rule 100 years earlier. On the other side of the world, in the Dutch East Indies, the liberation of the fatherland was remembered just as exuberantly. A tidal wave of nationalist revels spread from the colonial epicentre of Batavia. Governor General A.W.F. Idenberg insisted that every community contribute to the festivities – whether they were Dutch, Eurasian, Chinese or 'native'. On 13 July *De Expres* published a now famous polemic written, in Dutch, by a young man called Soewardi Soerjaningrat (also known as Ki Hajar Dewantoro). The title 'Als ik eens Nederlander was' means 'What if I were for once a Dutchman?' Soewardi wrote:

> At the moment we [he is speaking as if he were Dutch] are very happy because we are celebrating our own independence in their native country [...] Does it not occur to us that these poor slaves are also longing for such a moment as this? [...] If I were a Dutchman, I would not organize an independence celebration in a country where the independence of the people has been stolen.

Soewardi's insight was precocious for its time and place. Nationalism developed unevenly, and in fits and starts, across Southeast Asia, beginning in the Philippines with the armed uprising against Spanish rule in 1896, which was swiftly quashed by the United States. The emergence of the idea of 'Indonesia' to enfold the very diverse peoples and territories of the Dutch East Indies was a kind of miracle, driven by the fragmentation of a colonial empire that encompassed an archipelago comprising more than 17,000 islands. In Peninsula Malaya, by contrast, nationalism flickered into life at the end of the 1930s, immediately before the Japanese invasion. On the peninsula, the breaking of what Anderson calls 'the last wave' of nationalism was shaped by envy and fear of other Asian 'races' as much by a desire to expunge colonial outsiders.

During the last century, the maritime peoples of Southeast Asia were battered by successive waves of violent upheaval that profoundly altered the political cartography and varieties of political consciousness of this vast and intricate region. The new nations emerged not from deep time but from colonial happenstance, conflict and war which, for example, incised an imaginary political boundary along the narrow Straits of Malacca culturally severing East Sumatra from the Malayan Peninsula, even though the peoples of both regions understood each other's speech, shared the same ethnicity and prayed to the same God. Today, Indonesia, which is territorially nearly identical to the former Dutch East Indies, yokes together the Sumatran Acehnese with, for example, the Ambonese, who live on the faraway Maluku islands and share neither religion, ethnicity nor mother tongue with their fellow Indonesian citizens. The making of nations and the breaking of older bonds is always accompanied by violence. The price of nationhood is paid in blood. It was the warriors of the emperor's imperial armies who, by so deeply shaming the Dutch and English masters of the Malayan Archipelago, unleashed the pent-up energies of modern Asian nationalism. When American and British armies defeated the Japanese in 1945 they inaugurated another violent chapter in Southeast Asian history as Asian nationalists fought to eject their former, now decrepit, colonial masters, who had staged a comeback in the atomic shockwave of Hiroshima and Nagasaki. Inevitably these new wars were fought not only against Europeans but with other Asians too as different factions and groups sought to stamp their mark on the new states. In Malaya, and its successor state of Malaysia, a poisonous combination of pre-colonial semi-feudal social relations and European imported ideas about racial difference and hierarchy deformed the struggle for independence – and continues to shape the modern state. The tangled roots of these never-ending conflicts reach back across turbulent centuries of near continuous political and cultural transformation.

Before

The history of the 'Malay World' in the centuries before the momentous fall of Malacca to the Portuguese in 1511 is predominantly a convoluted narrative of maritime statelets, technically called thalassocracies. Although it may offend Malay nationalists to say so, the history of the modern nations of Southeast Asia has only the most tenuous ties to the pre-colonial 'Malay World'. We can still get glimpses of this older world in parts of modern Malaysia. As historian Farish Noor writes:

[The Malay state of] Sabah has always been, and remains, an extraordinarily cosmopolitan space where cultures and peoples overlap and share common lives and interests [...] In Sabah it is not uncommon to come across indigenous families where the siblings happen to be Muslim and Christian, all living under the same roof and celebrating Muslim and Christian festivals together. Sabah society also seems more de-centred compared to other communities in the region: The Kadazandusuns do not have a concept of Kingship, and instead govern themselves along the lines of communal leaders (Orang Kaya Kaya) and their symbolic grand leader called the 'Huguan Siou'. So tolerant and open is Sabah society that inter-ethnic marriages are common, with Kadazandusuns and Muruts marrying Malays, Chinese, Arabs as well as Suluks, Bugis, Bajaos, Bruneians. It has been like this for hundreds of years.

The long-vanished, poorly documented Malay-speaking trading kingdoms of the past have significance today as *myths* – and, for a nervous political elite, as models of deferential semi-feudal social relations. Nor will the most fervent nationalists happily embrace the fact that for many centuries a succession of Chinese emperors regarded the '100 Kingdoms' of the 'Nanyang', or 'Southern Ocean', as tributary or vassal states. From the eighth century, the growth of trade in the archipelago was driven by the tremendous gravitational field of the vast Chinese markets. Most of the truly historical information we possess about the Malay Peninsula comes from Chinese sources that record the business of traders. It was a Chinese merchant who described the Straits of Malacca as a 'gullet through which the foreigners' sea and land traffic must pass in either direction'. The contrariwise annual rhythm of the monsoon forced the great trading armadas from India and China to spend months waiting in sheltered spots along the straits where they bartered for local commodities like spices and aromatic woods. Over time these bustling little ports grew in size and power. Chinese documents begin referring to trade centres like 'Kan-t'-Li' on the south-east coast of Sumatra, and 'Melayu' on the Jambi River north of Pelambang. T'ang dynasty records provide more information about these embryonic kingdoms, all of which enjoyed close ties to China, showing how they slowly developed traditions of local government, legal systems and treasuries. Trade with China brought wealth and power. One local ruler, it was reported, possessed a fleet of 300 vessels and 'sits on a three tiered couch facing north and dressed in rose coloured cloth [...] more than a hundred soldiers mount guard.' Historian Anthony Reid points out that the consequence of these very early trading interactions was intense 'hybridisation' of genes, language, dress, food and material culture. The fundamental factor, he points out, was that female emigration from China was prohibited until the late nineteenth century, whereas male Chinese settled in large numbers in ports all over Southeast Asia, where they took wives from the local population. The most prosperous Chinese married into the indigenous aristocracies. As early as the 1290s a Chinese commentator called Zhou Daguan noted that 'since rice is easily had, women easily persuaded, houses easily run, furniture easily come by, and trade easily carried on, a great many Chinese sailors desert to take up permanent residence'. This predated the great migrations from India and China set in motion by Europeans in the nineteenth and early twentieth centuries. As Reid argues, this demolishes the colonial distinction between 'Malays' and 'Chinese': we need to think instead in terms of polyglot diasporas of seafaring, trading peoples with a substantial Chinese admixture that may have had little in common with indigenous rural peoples of the hinterlands.

The Myths of Malacca

According to nineteenth-century historian Thomas Babbington Macauley 'the history of our country [Britain] during the last hundred and sixty years is eminently the history of physical, of moral, and of intellectual improvement.' This was a terse definition of what became known as the 'Whig' school of history. Macauley was its greatest practitioner. For him and his followers, British history offered a landscape of unfolding perfection. Its end result was continuous enlightenment that gave Britain 'the place of umpire among European powers'. The task of the British historian was to demonstrate 'how her opulence and her martial glory grew together; how, by wise and resolute good faith, was gradually established a public credit fruitful of marvels which to the statesmen of any former age would have seemed incredible'. Whig history is no longer fashionable. Roger Scruton, the political philosopher, does not pull his punches: Whig history 'is an extremely biased view of the past: eager to hand out moral judgements, and distorted by teleology, anachronism and present-mindedness'. But for most modern nations, especially new ones, a thick dollop of 'Whiggism' is always desirable. In museums dedicated to telling the story of the nation state, a magnificent past leads us down a single unbroken road towards the glorious present. The 'Muzium Kebudayaan' (Museum of Culture) in Malacca is a perfect example. Built at a cost of 2.5 million ringgits, the museum was opened by Malaysian Prime Minister Dato' Seri Dr Mahathir Mohamad in 1986. It is crammed with more than 1,000 objects that represent the history of the Malay Sultanate of Malacca. A few of the galleries nod to the different communities that have settled in Malacca, but its main purpose is to enshrine Malay culture and history inside a modern reproduction of the palace of the sultans of Malacca. The 'Muzium Kebudayaan' is one of the most revered landmarks in a Malaysian city that is itself a living museum or '*bandaraya bersejarah*'. Its streets and monuments, even its tacky craft shops, embody national history – or, to be precise, *a* national history. For the Malay nationalists who confronted resurgent British imperialism at the end of the Second World War, Malacca was 'the soul of independence'. It was here that the first Malay Nationalist Conference was held in 1945; here that the first prime minister of independent Malaya, Tunku Abdul Rahman, announced that the British had, at last, agreed to hand over power on

31 August 1957. Malay nationalists commemorate Malacca as the quintessential symbol of a golden age and the continuity of the *bangsa*, the Malay community. This identity has many different levels but Malays are, above all, the Muslim subjects of a ruler. This royal community is called, in Malay, the *Kerajaan*. Inside the 'Muzium Kebudayaan', which reproduces the form of a sultan's palace, we encounter the legendary figure of Hang Tuah, the iconic loyal courtier. These are useful myths for an authoritarian state.

Few national monuments give space to the fractures and dissents of actual history. The museum city of Malacca is a case in point. We have already seen that *mobility*, not stasis, is the essence of Southeast Asian history. Over time, both rulers and their subjects, the *rakyat*, were in continuous flux, shifting their courts from one region to another to establish new settlements and mini states. There is a telling story of a man from Patani in southern Thailand, who, in the early part of the last century, left his home for the Malay state of Terengganu. Here he established a small settlement which prospered. Later, his son refused to acknowledge the authority of the Sultan of Terengganu and 'gave himself airs as if he were the Sultan'. He built a splendid pavilion and had himself carried around in a litter. British visitors sometimes called the Sultanate of Brunei on the island of Borneo 'the Venice of the East' but there were many sultan's palaces that were little more than squalid shacks in the jungle. The *institution* of the raja was the fixed point in a fluid world. It linked sultanates large and small in a sacred network of Muslim monarchs who were the 'Shadow of Allah on Earth'. The Muslim raja, it seems, expressed purpose or meaning in a community. The full title of the famous 'Malay Annals' the *Sejarah Melayu* is *Penurunan Segala Raja-Raja*: 'Origin and Descent of the Malay Rajas'. The 'Annals' is not a 'people's history'. It may have begun as a simple list of kings. The text affirms the moral sovereignty of the raja. In another famous 'Annal', the *Hikayat Hang Tuah*, we learn of a wealthy but ill-starred Indian merchant who has the misfortune to live in a land without a raja. So he 'expends his property' (i.e. sells land) to buy in a ruler because 'the property of this world can have no use' in a ruler-less world. Subjects, we are being told, need rulers as much as rulers need subjects. Better to be the poorer subject of a raja than a wealthy landowner without one.

Malacca was no exception to this pattern of incessant social flux around the symbolic figure of the raja. The 'Malay Annals', which may have originated as a simple list of kings, opens the story of Malacca in the island kingdom of 'Temasek', now modern Singapore. We are told that Sri Tri Buana, a descendant of Alexander the Great, the ruler of Palembang on the island of Sumatra, set off to find a site for a new city. He landed on an island of gleaming white sands that one of his companions said was called 'Temasek'. When Sri Tri Buana explored his new-found land, we are informed, he encountered a terrifying animal 'with a red body and black head' that, for some reason, the king's advisor identified as a lion. So Temasek became Singapura, the Lion City. As well as semi-mythic histories, the 'Annals' offer political morality tales. The scribes tell us that though Singapura prospered, the last sultan offended a court minister, who treacherously invited the ruler of Majapahit, a much more powerful kingdom in Java, to attack Singapura. 'Blood flowed like a river,' say the 'Annals'. The sultan fled north to found a new kingdom. A prime location was found in the shade of a malaka tree. The city of Malacca rose in prominence at the hub of a grand empire. It was the ideal Malay state.

The 'Annals' is a propagandist work and is legendary rather than historical: 'From below the wind to above the wind Melaka became famous as a very great city, the Raja [ruler] of which was sprung from the line of Sultan Iskandar Zul-karnain ...'. The anonymous Malay scribes were clear about their purpose: their task was 'to set forth the genealogy of the Malay Rajas [...] and the ceremonial of their courts for the information of the [ruler's] descendants [...] that they may be conversant with the history and derive profit therefrom ...'. The 'Annals' were written as lessons in power. From the perspective of the seventeenth century, when the 'Annals' were written, Malacca is fashioned as a kind of ideal kingdom in which everyone knows their place. The most celebrated tales in the 'Malay Annals' concern the semi-legendary character of Hang Tuah, who was instructed by the sultan to kill his childhood friend Hang Jebat. Hang Tuah is reputed to have sworn, '*Takkan Melayu Hilang di Dunia!*' – 'Malays will never vanish from the face of the Earth.' Hang Tuah has enjoyed a remarkable afterlife as an icon of Muslim fealty and was portrayed as such in a famous film by the great Malay actor Tan Sri P. Ramlee. Malaysian historian Khoo Kay Kim ruffled a great many feathers when he pointed out that there was not a shred of evidence that Hang Tuah was a real person. 'Legend is a lie that has attained the dignity of age', as H.L. Mencken liked to say. Malays, one might say, have 'printed the legend'.

The founding ruler of Malacca was, it seems, a Hindu prince. To be sure, the 'Malay Annals' grudgingly imply this to be the case. But what the Malay scribes could not admit was how much the rise of Malacca as a trading emporium owed to the new Ming dynasty in China, which emerged in 1368. Even harder to acknowledge, and unrecognised by the Malay scribes, was the part played by Chinese Muslims in the conquest of the archipelago by Islam. The first Ming emperor, Hong-wu, revolutionised mercantile relations with the Nanyang region by suppressing private trade and promoting instead trade that accompanied tribute: the acknowledgement by local rulers of Chinese suzerainty. Many Chinese traders already well established in Java and Sumatra and used to independence resented the new policy and tried to thwart the emperor's plan. At the beginning of the next century, Ming interaction intensified. The new emperor, Zhu Di (who adopted the reign title of Yong Le), embarked on a course of aggressive territorial expansion into Yunnan and the region of modern Vietnam. He established a new 'Maritime Board' and sent formidably armed armadas to the 'Western Ocean': i.e. maritime Southeast Asia to the west of the island of Borneo and extending as far as the Indian Ocean. His intention was to display the might of the Ming throughout the known world and hoard treasures for his court. The most celebrated of the emperor's naval commanders was a court eunuch called Zheng He or San-bao (the 'Three Treasures').

The other remarkable fact about Zheng He is that he was a Muslim originally called Ma He who was captured when Ming armies raided his home village in Yunnan. He was castrated to serve as a palace official and became a close confidante of the emperor. The emperor's 'Chief Envoy' Zheng He commanded a colossal fleet that was clearly intended to inspire 'shock and awe'. According to maritime historian Geoff Wade:

> A typical [naval] mission comprised, in the senior ranks, almost 100 envoys of various grades, 93 military captains, 104 lieutenants, 103 sub-lieutenants as well as associated medical and astrological staff members. In one case cited, 26,800 out of 27,400 on board were the rank and file, the irregular troops, the crack troops, as well as the sailors and clerks. It is likely that all of the missions carried something in excess of 20,000 military men. In a Ming era document of 1427, there is reference to '10,000 crack troops who had formerly been sent to the Western Ocean' also suggesting that a relatively large ratio of the members of these fleets were military men.[6]

These were not 'voyages of friendship' as some Chinese historians claim. This was the Ming version of gunboat diplomacy. Like the British Royal Navy three centuries later, the Ming fleets set up staging posts or depots called 'guan-chang' strategically positioned in an arc across the Western Ocean.

The Chinese built a garrison-cum-treasury at Malacca. This means we now have a *third* source of information about the foundation of Malacca. The Chinese records appear to confirm some of the details in the Portuguese 'Chronicles' and contradict others. It seems that Parameśvara, a prince of Palembang, fled after the state was attacked by rival power Majapahit. At the beginning of the fifteenth century, he somehow made his way to Malacca where he found a good port, situated at the narrowest part of the straits and accessible all year round. With the assistance of local Malay privateers known as 'orang laut' or 'sea people', Parameśvara 'persuaded' passing ships to call in and Malacca soon had a stranglehold on the great volumes of trade passing between China and Malaku in the east to East Africa and as far as the Mediterranean in the west. Just as Parameśvara was beginning to build up this new port empire, the mighty armada of Admiral Zheng sailed into Malacca harbour, bristling with arms and crammed to the gunwales with soldiers. We can imagine that Parameśvara had not forgotten why he had been forced to flee his home state of Palembang. He feared his bellicose neighbours, Majapahit and the proto-Thai kingdom of Ayudhya to the north. Emperor Yong Le offered protection in return for tribute and Parameśvara was not ashamed to accept.

From as early as 1405 the Malacca ruler despatched frequent missions to the Ming court. For the new king, submission to the Chinese shored up status and protection so that, by the mid-fifteenth century, Malacca grew to become one of the greatest trading emporiums in the world. With the backing of the Chinese emperor, Parameśvara and his successors, Megat Iskandar Syah and Sultan Muzaffar Syah, built Malacca into a regional hegemon – enriched by the burgeoning flow of trade through the 'gullet' of the straits. Wade confirms that:

> the chronological collocation between [the rise of Malacca] and the Ming voyages was no coincidence. It is obvious that the military support provided by the Ming forces allowed Malacca to disregard the threats posed to new polities at this time by both Majapahit in Java and Ayudhya in what is today Thailand.

Malacca connected the intricate trading networks of the archipelago to a semi-globalised system that embraced India, Persia, Arabia, East Africa and the Mediterranean, as well as China and Japan. Malacca sucked in and disgorged an astonishing cornucopia of raw material and commodities that were gloatingly catalogued by the Portuguese chronicler Tomé Pires: 'gold, pepper, silk, wood resins (like benzoin), sulphur, iron, cotton, rattan, rice, nutmeg, clove, mace, honey, wax, tamarind […] and slaves'. Pires' lists occupy many pages of his report. But it was the Ming emperor and the formidable fleets of Admiral Zheng He that had made all this possible. It was no wonder that the first Europeans to sail into the gullet of the straits became so covetous of the wealth of Malacca.

The Things of Mohammed

The rise to power of the quintessential Malay state depended on the power and protection of the Ming emperor. By becoming a vassal, Parameśvara, the first ruler of Malacca, founded an empire. We must now turn our attention to another ingredient of the myth of Malacca.

The rise of Malacca brought not only wealth and trade to Southeast Asia, but a new faith – Islam. The turn to Islam was a momentous caesura in the cultural and political history of the region. Islam comprehensively defined Malay identity for the first time: a definition that remains fundamental today. Once again we discover some intriguing paradoxes and a link to Imperial China. Parameśvara, the probable founder of Malacca, was a Hindu-Buddhist prince. A Portuguese chronicler tells us that he or a successor came to 'like the "Mullahs" [probably meaning Sufi teachers] who accompanied Muslim merchants to his port and sought to convince the ruler "to turn Moor"'. After his conversion, the Malacca ruler, as a good Muslim, set out to 'instruct' the kings of other states 'in the things of Mohammed, because he knew all about them …'.[7] But this turn to Islam was a lot more complicated than the chronicler implies. The first Indianised states of the archipelago, such as

Śrīvijaya and Majapahit, were rigidly hierarchical, ruled by semi-divine kings who acknowledged a multitude of different gods. The faith of the Prophet asserted the equality of all men before one God. Mohammed himself was, it is believed, hostile to secular rulers: 'whenever a man accedes to authority he drifts away from God.' When an Arab chief acclaimed the Prophet a prince, he insisted 'the prince is God, not I'. So it would take many centuries for the Asian rulers to embrace such an egalitarian faith. From the seventh century at the latest, the time of the third caliph, Muslim traders and emissaries from Arabia voyaged through the islands of maritime Southeast Asia – and yet Islam had almost no impact on the Hindu and Buddhist courts or their subjects. Most of these daring Muslim itinerants were on their way to the Chinese court, following the sea routes of the archipelago. We should keep in mind that in this period Europe was relatively undeveloped: European states were neither especially dynamic nor advanced. Islam and Imperial China were the two great vibrant poles of the pre-modern world and there was a strong mutual attraction. By the end of the ninth century there were several thousand Muslim merchants resident in Canton alone. This great reservoir of traders and scholars would come to have a transforming impact.

There is no single, reliable account of the eventual triumph of Islam. The historical evidence is meagre and fragmentary. What is certain is that it was only when Muslim scholars changed their minds about *kingship* that the Islamic revolution gathered real momentum. For reasons too complex to go into here, Shiite Muslims in Persia had begun to re-evaluate the ethical value of kingship. According to *The Iranians: Persia, Islam and the Soul of a Nation* (1996) by Sandra Mackey:

> In Safavid Iran, absolute monarchy in its secular form ruled as the dominant feature of the state built on Islam. Consequently, the king and the Shia clerics became dual poles in which political power based on the traditions of Persian kingship weighed against the legitimacy of the clerics derived from the theology of Shia Islam. At the same time, the king and the clerics reflected more than the question of authority. They stood as symbols of a whole culture in which Persia and Islam continually meet and mesh, repel and divide.

This new conception of the 'Shah' or 'Khalifah' made a lot of sense to the rulers of the old Malay states. According to the refashioned faith, a sultan could assume the power of the 'Shadow of God upon Earth'. Islam could, in other words, be used to buttress secular power since 'He who obeys the Sultan obeys God.' There was another novel strand in Islamic thought that tied in with the elevated role of the ruler. All over Asia, Sufi mystics had followed in the wake of Muslim traders and merchants. According to Sufism, the 'Perfect Man' was a kind of saint who had achieved oneness with God: an idea borrowed perhaps from the figure of the *Bodhisattva* in Buddhism. Sufi mystics were tolerant of older kinds of religious faith – not just Hinduism and Buddhism but the animist practices that infused the everyday lives of the peoples of the archipelago. In the Muslim Malay courts, Islam absorbed the old royal titles and arcane rituals rather than supplanting them. Sultans, as we have seen, could be referred to as rajas, an Indian term and, in Malay, as Yang Di-Pertuan Agong: 'he who is made lord'. These ethical innovations and subtle accommodations made Islam a great deal more attractive to the archipelago rulers and their courts. This was no longer a faith of rigorous egalitarianism, though that strain would persist. Slowly but surely Hindu and Buddhist kingdoms become sultanates. Inscriptions begin to refer to a sultan as the 'Shadow of God', or as 'one who governed on earth in place of God'. Some rulers aspired to become the Sufis' 'Perfect Man' and dabbled in esoteric knowledge. Many claimed to possess supernatural powers.

As well as power Islam was associated with wealth. In the past, historians argued that foreign Muslim traders intermarried locally and formed Islamic communities. As these grew, their egalitarian ethos drew Hindus, oppressed by the caste system, to the new faith. It has become evident, however, that in practice there was nothing egalitarian about Islam. The first Muslims who came to the archipelago were merchants, daring and rich enough to seek out far-flung markets in China and the fabled 'Spice Islands' of Maluku in East Indonesia. It may have been the sudden and spectacular enrichment of the kingdom of Samudra Pasai, a Muslim statelet and port on the northern coast of Sumatra, that first tipped the scales in favour of Islam. The king, whose Sanskrit name was Mara Siluh, converted to Islam in 1267 and ruled as Sultan Malik as-Salih. His decision was probably influenced by close contact with the vibrant community of wealthy Sunni Muslim merchants and Sufi scholars already based in the kingdom: a case of wanting what *they* had. According to the Pasai chronicle, the *Hikayat Raja-raja Pasai*, when the Sultan accepted Islam he manifested magical powers. To be sure his little kingdom boomed as Muslim Arab merchants rushed to exploit the wealth of its once-neglected hinterland. From the mountains of Bukit Barisan came camphor and gold dust; by the early sixteenth century Pasai was producing 8,000 to 10,000 *bahar* (about 1,500 metric tons) of pepper annually; cloves, nutmegs, precious gaharu wood and other perfumes and sandalwood could be bought in its markets in exchange for stoneware artefacts from Burma and Thailand and silk from China. God was good.

Islam meant wealth, and wealth meant power. The Malay rulers, one after the other, began to proclaim their Islamic credentials. The pivotal moment came when Parameśvara, the ruler of the mighty Malaccan Empire, embraced the brash new faith. Parameśvara had married a Pasai princess and he may simply have envied the good fortune enjoyed by his Muslim father-in-law. The 'Malay Annals' describe his conversion in fascinating detail. The Prophet appears to the king in a dream and teaches him the Confession of Faith, gives him a new name, Mohammed, and tells him to expect the arrival of a teacher whom he must obey. When the king wakes, he finds that he has been miraculously circumcised and repeats the confession to his courtiers in Arabic. No one understands him. The king has gone mad. But then a boat sails into Malacca harbour as the Prophet had promised and the teacher Sayyid Abdul Aziz steps ashore and begins to pray. His ritual gestures astonish the people and the courtiers. The king takes the new title of Sultan Muhammad Syah and commands the people to embrace Islam. This is, of course, a legendary account. But the story makes clear that conversion was an elite affair. A Malay king had the power to command his people. Sultan Muhammad Syah would not regret his decision. It is the duty of every Muslim to spread the faith of the Prophet – if necessary by force.

The aura of Islam added to the protection granted to the sultan by the Chinese emperor to make Malacca a regional power. It is not coincidental that the Chinese 'Special Envoy' to the Nanyang, Admiral Zheng, was himself a Muslim, though apparently with Taoist sympathies, and that many other Muslim scholars and merchants travelled on his ships. His Muslim chronicler, Ma Huan, provides us with a fascinating snapshot of Javanese society in the period of Ming expansion. He describes three types of people encountered in the trading cities of the archipelago: Muslim traders from the west who dressed and ate properly (i.e. according to Muslim dietary doctrine); Chinese from Guangdong and Fujian who were also Muslim and observant; and local people who consumed improper foods, lived with dogs and practised pagan rituals. This intense contact with China inevitably led to an injection of Chinese personnel and technologies – one of which was the sailing junk which became ubiquitous throughout the 'Nanyang' maritime world. By the time Muslim scribes began work on the 'Malay Annals', Islam had become a critical and defining ingredient of the Malay identity. The 'things of the Prophet' were not, however, indigenous. Even before the shadow of the Europeans fell across the archipelago at the beginning of the sixteenth century, religious and institutional forces originating in Arabia, China and India had been regional protagonists for centuries.

The Muslim Malay Court and the People

History would be unimaginable without borders and frontiers. Lines drawn across maps shape the dynamics of how nation states interact: wars, negotiations, treaties and the affiliation of peoples. Borders define national struggles. We are free or not within a frontier. Borders can be punitive – as any German citizen who grew up before 1945 can testify. Lines on maps become concrete gateways and iron fences. Borders can incarcerate or unshackle; they sculpt the great migrations of the modern era. For the rulers of Malay sultanates before the arrival of Europeans, the idea of a state border was tenuous. As late as the 1870s the Sultan of Terengganu admitted to an English visitor that he was uncertain where the border of his state ran. Territoriality mattered less than the allegiance and activities of people. In 1827 an Englishman called Charles Gray had little sense of crossing state borders when he travelled to the capital of Pahang. Instead, when he reached the village of Kampong Brah he discovered that its people were 'under the control of the Rajah of Pahang'. Territorial markings mattered less than control of people and the right to take tax and tribute. A locally made map of Perak showed just a tangle of rivers and no other details. Since people lived on rivers, this was a kind of human geography which had no need for any other kind of topographical detail. The Malay word '*negeri*' can be roughly translated as 'state' but not in any unitary sense. A ruler could possess one or more negeri and the contents of each was 'the people' not state institutions of any kind. This conception of the Malay polity defined what Anthony Milner calls '*Kerajaan*', ideology founded on the ties between ruler and *rakyat*. These were naturally unequal. The sultan, the 'Shadow of God', and his princes and courtiers were set apart from the people by their manner of dress and the obligatory use of a special court language. Ceremonial splendour signified power and patronage. European visitors to Brunei were astonished by the silk wall hangings of the sultan's audience hall. Sultans were obliged to build fine palaces and beautiful mosques. The imperative of show extended to copies of the Koran. Conversion was, as we have seen, a top-down process. Court texts refer to Islamic Sharia law as 'laid down by the ruler' or 'in the hands of the ruler'. A corollary was the creation of exquisite court copies of the Koran decorated in royal yellow and gold.

Splendour set the raja apart. When John Anderson visited Siak in the 1820s he entered the sultan's audience hall 'fitted up with elegant canopies of gold and silk'. The body of the king was also richly decorated. 'Nothing can surpass', Anderson reported, 'the elegance and richness of the fabrics worn by the king and the royal family'. The Siak ruler was 'in fact like one beautiful sheet of embossed gold'. Clothes really did make the man. When the sultan offered promotion, he offered, along with rank, appropriate 'robes of honour'.

The Muslim rulers of Malacca insistently proclaimed the rewards of unflinching loyalty, or *Daulat*. The antithesis of *Daulat* was the odious crime of treason – *Derhaku*, which necessitated the severest of punishments. *Daulat*, though, was not a one-way street. The ruler had responsibility to the *rakyat*. He had to be addressed properly, but was also praised and honoured for speaking appropriately, with refinement and grace, *to* his subjects. The 'Malay Annals' spelt out some of these mutual obligations:

> If any ruler puts a single one of his subjects to shame, that shall be a sign that his kingdom will be destroyed by Almighty God. Similarly, it has been granted by Almighty God to Malay subjects that they shall never be disloyal or treacherous to their rulers, *even if their rulers behave evilly or inflict injustice upon them.*

Mutuality, it seems, favoured the raja.

All this splendour came with a price. Historian Paul Kratoska has written that 'in the indigenous Malay economy human labour was the form of capital that underlay economic relations'. A great sultan was therefore one to whom many people owed allegiance and paid taxes as '*kerah*', or labour service. Labour could be mortgaged in a system of debt slavery in order to borrow money. One of the rulers of Malacca tried to impress the Chinese emperor by sending him a ship full of sago. He informed the emperor that he had instructed each of his subjects to roll a single grain – the cargo was thus a tally of the human capital he owned. The Malay rulers were hungry for people and lamented their loss for the *rakyat* was highly mobile. In 1816, historian Khoo Kay Kim tells us that the Sultan of Perak lamented the loss of 80 per cent of his people who had fled to another ruler. In the 1880s, some 2,000 people, 'all hungry', migrated from the eastern states of Patani, Kelantan, Patalung and Songkhla, to Kedah where they offered their rice-growing skills to a delighted sultan. Mobility meant that labour mattered more than land. People had proprietary rights, not absolute ownership. According to a legal text from Johor, anyone who reclaimed unused or 'unappropriated' land 'shall not be molested in his possession'. There would seem to be little difference between this concept of land ownership and that exercised by pejoratively labelled 'Chinese squatters' who were demonised after the Second World War.

Before we turn to the European conquest of the archipelago, we should examine precisely what the term 'Malay' meant over time. The Emergency war of the 1950s erupted on the periphery of a struggle between opposed conceptions of national identity. Ethnic Malays asserted foundation rights and denied them to other Malayans of Chinese and Indian origin. And yet the historical record shows that the idea of a Malay identity and of a 'Malay World' postdates the advent of colonialism. To be sure, the Malay language, at least in its written *Jawi* form, was remarkably uniform across the archipelago. In the eighteenth century a British official called William Marsden commented on the 'striking consistency in the style of writing, not only of books in prose and verse, but also of epistolary correspondence'. The Malay language was the lingua franca of maritime Southeast Asia. It was a prestige language that flowed across ethnic boundaries. So, too, did Islam. Nor, it would seem, did the sultans and the ruling ideology of *Kerajaan* trouble much with ethnic identities. Just as one could convert to Islam, the people-hungry states of the archipelago frequently embraced newcomers including many Chinese who were taught to speak Malay, and adopt Islam and its customs and styles of dress. All over the peninsula, aboriginal peoples were absorbed as 'Malays'. We have documented examples from Patani and Kedah. In the Sultanate of Brunei many Muslim *rakyat* were converts from local Dyak groups, many of whom acquired *Kerajaan* titles. Assimilation was in a sense a kind of 'recruitment'. Some converts to Islam and the *Kerajaan* referred to 'becoming Malay' – but in Borneo use of the term 'Malay' was introduced by the British Brooke administration while Iban peoples referred to 'Laut' and Orang Asli to 'Gop'. This linguistic slipperiness suggests that a Malay identity was an innovation that emerged after the traumatic conquest of Malacca. In the seventh century,

'Malayu' referred to the Jambi region of Sumatra where there is a 'Malayu' river. Intriguingly, the Javanese referred to the people of Sumatra as 'Malayu' – and called the inhabitants of the peninsula 'Pahang'. 'Malay' remained securely attached to the regions of East Sumatra for a long time. The step change came along with the Portuguese. The chronicler Tomé Pires uses 'Malay' to refer to peoples of East Sumatra and Malacca. He *excludes* the peoples of the other peninsula states like Kedah, Pahang and Brunei. The bond between Malacca and Malay reappears in the word list compiled by the Magellan expedition which renders the 'ways of Malacca' as coterminous with the 'ways of Malayu'. This reinforces the link with Sumatra, of course, since the founder of Malacca was a Hindu prince of Palembang. The definition was later extended to Johor for reasons that will become clear shortly. So 'Malay' was used in a remarkably fluid and 'fuzzy' way. It was mercurial. It was only when Europeans led by Sir Stamford Raffles and his collaborator John Leyden imported the notion of *race* that a Malay identity became truly fixed. It is important to note that as late as 1930 a British census taker lamented that 'most Oriental peoples have no conception of race'.

Incursions and Conquests

The conquest of Malacca by the Portuguese in 1511 and the settlement of Singapore two centuries later by an agent of the British East India Company possess iconic significance in the history of Southeast Asia. Both of these indubitably momentous encounters between the Malay-speaking world and Europeans have acquired a thick patina of legend. They have become fables of colonial conquest and yet neither the destruction of Malacca nor the founding of Singapore was a true turning point. The attack on Malacca epitomises, to be sure, Borschberg's '4 Cs of colonialism': curiosity, conquest, commerce and collaboration. The Portuguese king, Dom Joâo II, proclaimed a mercantile crusade to seize control of the incalculably valuable spice trade and break the monopoly of the Muslim Arab trading empires. His most fanatical crusader was Afonso de Albuquerque. In 1510, Afonso had seized Goa in India – and it was just a matter of time before he turned his attention eastwards to Malacca. In 1509 a Portuguese squadron was repelled by Sultan Mahmud Syah. This impertinence was the 'Great' Afonso's opportunity. On 2 May 1519 a more formidable force of eighteen ships manned by Portuguese and South Indian Malabaris left India. Two months later Sultan Mahmud was dismayed to hear blasts of trumpet and cannon as the Great Afonso sailed into Malacca harbour and began a terrifying bombardment of the city. The sultan mustered at least 20,000 soldiers including Javanese, Persian and Turkish mercenaries, armed with bows, arrows and light artillery pieces, to defend his empire against just 1,200 Portuguese soldiers. But the sultan's troops were no match for heavy cannon. Modern artillery fire alone cannot explain why Malacca succumbed to the Portuguese. Afonso owed his victory as much to the Chinese merchants who had provided the flat-bottomed junks (which the Portuguese used to land) and to the sultan's Javanese mercenaries who defected, as to his cannon. After a bombardment that lasted forty days, and a great deal of bloodshed, the Portuguese wantonly incinerated the sultan's palace and destroyed the royal mosque.

There was another factor that helped the Portuguese. According to the 'Malay Annals' the Malaccan court was riven by internal rivalries. Some time before the Portuguese ships sailed into Malacca harbour, Sultan Mahmud had ordered the execution of a palace noble, the '*Bendahara*'. This was unwise, for his queen was the noble's daughter. For reasons that remain obscure the sultan then abdicated in favour of his son, Sultan Ahmad Syah. As Portuguese forces overwhelmed the Malaccans, the two rulers fled to Bintan in the Johor-Riau-Lingga Archipelago. Here the former Sultan had his son murdered – and took back the throne. From his new base in Bintan the Sultan launched a succession of attacks on the Portuguese assisted by 'Orang Laut' sea traders. By 1526 the Portuguese had had enough of Sultan Ahmad and smashed his fragile new state – forcing the sultan to flee again, this time to the east coast of Sumatra. Here, in his ancestral home, the Sultan died. The dynastic story seemed to have come full circle. But another son who was now Sultan Alauddin Syah returned to the peninsula sometime in the 1530s where he established a royal residence at Pekan Tua on the Johor River. The Malay state of Johor is thus regarded as the successor state to Malacca and its rulers have often followed their own political and cultural path.

By seizing Malacca, the Portuguese broke open the sea routes to the fabulous riches of the 'Spice Islands'. The trade was no longer an Arab and Asian monopoly. The engine of colonial conquest is mercantile ambition. The fall of Malacca can also be understood as a clash of civilisations. When the Portuguese soldiers attacked the famous Malacca bridge they bellowed 'St James!' After the conquest, Afonso de Albuquerque built a fort on the site of the sultan's palace using stones from the royal mosque. This was not merely opportunist. Christendom had crushed its most formidable rival, Islam. The Portuguese exhibited crusading zeal – and yet, as Mark Frost points out, they were also *curious*. Like the Spanish conquistadores, the Portuguese compiled voluminous commentaries about the peoples, wealth and history of their new possession. For their part the Malays called the Portuguese '*Bengali Putih*', 'white Bengalis'. This was perfectly logical since the Portuguese fleet had sailed from Goa on the other side of the Bay of Bengal. Like the medieval Crusades, the conquest of Malacca resonates as a flagrant act of cultural and ethical vandalism. In the ruins of Malacca the old Malay state perished; the spirit of independence, or *merdeka*, would rise from its ruins.

We see again that the idea of Malacca nourishes myths. A more credible narrative emphasises the irruption of competitive new rivals in the maritime world of the archipelago. European traders joined the regional melee that had scrapped and skirmished here for many centuries. The Portuguese followed in the long wake of Indians, Chinese and Arabs and after subduing Malacca fought the Achenese, the Javanese and then the heirs of Malacca on the peninsula. It was the entry of a rival European power, represented by the 'United Netherlands Chartered East India Company', the Vereenigde Oostindische Compagnie (VOC), that began to fundamentally reconfigure this regional struggle for power. Conflict between European colonial powers would utterly and irrevocably reshape the archipelago and Peninsula Malaya and give birth to modern nation states. The VOC 'Supreme Government' was intricately linked to the Dutch state, and its charter granted its directors, many of whom also held government posts, quasi-sovereign powers. The VOC was a floating state within a state, bristling with advanced weaponry, and endowed with the power to make treaties or wage war. Its command centre in Southeast Asia was the city of Batavia (now Jakarta), founded in 1619 on the island of Java. From here, the VOC's 'Council of the Indies' schemed to dislodge the Portuguese from their Malacca stronghold. To achieve this the VOC magnates thought and acted much like local Malay rulers: they looked for allies. They sought out collaborators. They knew that Sultan Iskander Muda of Aceh had already tried to dislodge the Portuguese from Malacca but his forces had been soundly defeated. The Dutch strenuously courted the sultan but he showed little interest. As negotiations foundered the sultan died. The Sultan of Johor, much battered by Acehnese aggression, was more amenable. In August 1641, a VOC army, backed by the sultan's troops, laid siege to Malacca. The Portuguese capitulated in January 1641. A few years later the Dutch governor general, Antonio van Diemen, wrote to the company directors in The Hague emphasising that 'the Johor people have contributed substantially to the conquest of Malacca ...'. This allegiance, as the Dutch now found out to their cost, was expedient. As Portuguese power declined the Dutch faced a challenge from within the archipelago. The Sultan of Johor, fearing the growing power of the VOC, forged an alliance with Bugis refugees from the island of Sulawesi to push out the Dutch. The Bugis mercenaries were renowned warriors who eventually turned the tables on the Johor ruler and came to dominate his court – forcing a later sultan to go back to the Dutch for assistance. Soon a Bugis army was at the gates of Malacca, now a Dutch trading enclave. The hundred years war that ensued between the Dutch and the Bugis and other regional powers dominated the eighteenth century – and was only ended when the Dutch government despatched a mighty fleet to deliver a knockout punch in 1784. Colonial conquest was in no sense ever a walkover. It took the Dutch a long time to get the measure of the ferocious Bugis.

After 1511, a European power stood on the threshold of Southeast Asia and would soon be followed by jealous rivals, but the old Malay polities had not vanished overnight. Our view of what unfolded in the archipelago and on the peninsula after 1511 is clouded by European historical narratives that, for their own purposes, imposed a story of decay and decline. These accounts of the Malay states refer insistently to their pettiness, incessant squabbling and habit of piracy.

An English report described the Malay states as 'mouldering in self decay and mutual destruction'. But Malacca was not the last successful Malay state. Travellers in the region were astonished by the splendours of Brunei, for example, with its harbour crammed with 'a hundred prows'. On the peninsula, Patani was judged to be 'strong and may hardly be conquered', and the deep water port at Songkhla (Singora) attracted merchants and migrants from Thailand, Cambodia, Japan and beyond. Malacca's successor state, Johor, was equally impressive. The throng of ships in Riau, the first capital, was said to be 'so great that the river was scarcely navigable'; the Sultan of Johor was said to hold audiences in front of thousands.

The power and prestige of the different Malay rulers waxed and waned. The Sultans of Johor claimed descent from Malacca but as a consequence of an intricate succession of royal marriages. So too did Perak: 'I am the oldest of all the kings in these parts,' a Sultan of Perak told the British a century later. The most powerful Malay kingdom after Johor was on the other side of the straits in Aceh. Like the Malacca kings, the Sultan of Aceh claimed descent from Alexander the Great, now refashioned as a Muslim Prophet. Situated at the mouth of the straits, Aceh reaped tremendous wealth from the increasingly globalised trade that flowed back and forth between Europe, India and China. Aceh was the Asian Mecca of Muslim scholarship. The sultan commissioned Malay-Jawi editions of Islamic texts that reinforced the tie between divine obedience and loyalty to the ruler: *Daulat*. The old idea of *Derhaku*, or treachery, inferred disobedience to God. These Muslim scholars deepened the bond between faith and ethnic identity. To be a Malay was to be a Muslim.

Relations between Aceh and the other Malay kingdoms were rarely harmonious. At the beginning of the seventeenth century, the Sultan of Perak permitted Dutch merchants to make inroads into the tin trade. Sultan Iskander Muda of Aceh disapproved – and launched attacks on Perak, Pahang, Kedah and Johor. The Acehnese captured some 22,000 slaves. But Aceh's heyday did not last long. When the sultan sent his armies to Portuguese Malacca, they were rebuffed. All the Malay states were squeezed between the increasingly powerful proto-Thai Ayudhya state to the north, the Javanese to the south, and the *arriviste* European powers. The northern Malay states like Patani, Terengganu and Kedah were all forced to pay tribute to Ayudhya – the *bunga mas dan Perak*, the gold and silver flowers: gifts, cloth, weapons and slaves. The Malay rulers valued the protection and stability that came with Thai suzerainty. But it was resented by the ordinary people, the *rakyat*, whose taxes paid for tribute.

It was another, the Manchu emperor of the Qing dynasty, who incited a new upheaval in the Malay world, and intensified the competition between the European powers for regional dominance. In 1727, the emperor repealed prohibitions against junk traffic between South China and the 'Nanyang' ports. Malay rulers and nobles profited from royal monopolies on highly valued products like rattan and even birds' nests (used in making soup). European interest in the China trade expanded – mainly due to the demand for tea. Because Chinese merchants disdained most European products, British traders began to use Southeast Asia to exchange textiles and opium from India for tin and spices, commodities that were highly valued in China. The problem for newcomers like the British was that the Dutch had already woven a network of monopolies in Perak, and on the other side of the straits in Palembang. This provoked a commodities rush to find alternative sources of metals and spices. This commodity rush led to profound dislocations of the Malay world.

Traditionally the Malay rulers had not troubled to define the territorial frontiers of their states. Since the sultans could take a cut of profits from mines and plantations, the precise location of tin deposits or gold seams was suddenly a matter of importance. So when tin, for example, was found in a remote border region along the Kerian River, whose ownership was claimed by both Perak and Kedah, a bitter dispute erupted between the state rulers about ownership. The position of a line on a map could impact positively or negatively on the tax revenues of the royal court. This rapidly developing economy unsettled the old feudal bonds between the sultan and the datos, or local chiefs. According to Malay custom a dato acted on behalf of the ruler, but if a productive new mine or plantation was built on the dato's land, he might become very rich – and a troublesome rival for power. Wealth challenged tradition.

The human landscape of the Malay Archipelago has always been molten. This is a region of ceaseless migration, not permanence. In the late eighteenth century the changing economies of the Malay world lured the first great waves of pioneers from southern China. They joined the already rooted 'Baba' communities that had been flourishing in the peninsula and archipelago for a very long time. But now instead of becoming traders and shopkeepers, like their forebears, many Chinese turned to agriculture and mining, focusing on such valued commodities as pepper, gambier and, of course, tin. Dutch and English reports give us a good sense of this metamorphosis of the ethnic landscape, noting Chinese pepper growers in Brunei, and Chinese tin miners in Selangor and Perak. And it did not take the Chinese miners long to introduce innovative technologies. The Chinese would soon become masters of tin.

As well as these enterprising newcomers, by the mid-eighteenth century English private 'country traders' had begun to make inroads into the Malay kingdoms. The British government had very little interest in the region of the world on the other side of the Indian Ocean. The country traders, for their part, did not export to London but focused on profiting from the movement of commodities through the labyrinthine waterways of the East. But as the East India Company tightened its grip on the Indian textile trade, British merchants began importing cheaper raw materials manufactured in the cotton mills of Lancashire and strangling the livelihoods of local producers. At the same time, the company seized control of poppy-growing regions. These brutal economic upheavals would revolutionise the old 'country trade'. Together, cloth and opium would become the commodities that the British exploited to dominate the China trade – which, of course, had to be conveyed through the gullet of the Straits of Malacca. Those ports that had resisted Dutch control became busier and wealthier. A huge leap had been taken towards globalisation, which would have shattering consequences for the peoples of Southeast Asia.

The Muslim Malay world was and still is bounded to the north by a Buddhist state. At the end of the eighteenth century, an aggressive new Thai ruler emerged – an army general called Chakri, who reigned as Rama I. To fund a war with the rival kingdom of Burma, Chakri demanded increased tribute from the northern Malay states. Not only that, but Chakri insisted that the rulers come to his court and personally pay obeisance – *tawai bangkom*. In the northern Malay courts there was outrage; the legendary hero Hang Tuah, who had refused to kowtow to Ayudhya, was invoked. Resistance severely provoked the new Thai king: the Malay kingdom of Patani was razed, its women and children trampled to death by elephants (it was said). Patani was forcibly fused with the southern Thai province of Singora. By now the British country traders, awash with profits from the textile and opium trade, had developed close relations with the Malay courts. Sir Francis Light, who spoke fluent Malay as well as other Asian languages, had to all intents and purposes become the unofficial advisor to Sultan Abdullah of Kedah. Hoping desperately that the British might protect him from the Thai ruler, the sultan offered to lease the island of Penang to the East India Company.

Light deftly handled the negotiations – and, on behalf of King George III, formally took possession of Penang in 1786 and renamed the new East India Company 'Residency', Prince of Wales Island. The other beleaguered northern states now hoped to persuade the British to pull various other irons out of their own fires. The Sultan of Perak wanted Light to get rid of the Bugis; the Bugis powers in Riau hoped to win over a new ally to fight the Dutch. But the Company refused to get involved and Light had to disappoint his many suitors. Sultan Abdullah petulantly demanded that the British leave Penang. When Light dug his heels in, the Kedah nobles proclaimed an ecumenical Jihad: 'All Muslims, that is Bugis, Acehnese, men of Minangkabau, Malays and Chulias [Indians]: God will assist us and our Lord Muhammad the Guardian of the Muslims and last of all the prophets …'. It was one of the first Malay rebellions against British rule. It was also the least effective. Company troops easily quashed the rebels and peace was restored. As a 'free port', Penang became, for a short period, a vibrant East India Company outpost.

It was at this pivotal juncture that tremendous political upheavals in continental Europe and across the Atlantic in the American colonies reconfigured the colonial game on the other side of the world in Southeast Asia. The peoples of the Malay Archipelago had been drawn inexorably into a globalising world economy. A constantly shifting pattern of allegiances and rivalries, fragile friendships and bitter hostilities, had built a rickety hierarchy of winners and losers in a game increasingly dominated by outsiders. The British already knew the pain of imperial defeat. In the 1770s, an American guerrilla army had, with French backing, gouged a deep rent in the ramshackle edifice of scattered colonies that aspired to become the New Rome. When news of the humiliating British surrender at Yorktown reached London, Lord North sobbed that 'Oh God, it is all over!' Like the Japanese conquest of Singapore nearly two centuries later that so deeply upset Prime Minister Winston Churchill, the loss of the thirteen colonies of North America was interpreted as a harbinger of national doom. In 1737, Sir George Macartney had coined the celebrated refrain that the sun would never set on the British Empire. Now, lamented Lord Shelbourne, the empire had 'tumbled to disgrace and ruin' from 'a pitch of glory and splendour perfectly astonishing and dazzling'. Anxiety about empire was a dominant theme of the age. It was a time of passionate moral crusade directed at the Atlantic slave trade and fierce domestic repression. Soon after the American debacle, the prodigious energies that were released by the French Revolution and the rise to power of Napoleon Bonaparte, who became emperor in 1804, spawned swarms of disquiet throughout Europe and across the Channel. The French revolutionaries, who seemed bent on liquidating the entire French aristocratic class, were the communist bogey men of their time. The poet William Cowper spluttered: 'Oh how I detest them [...] Apes of Sparta!' In the bleak aftermath of two calamitous revolutions, the government of the bibulous Prime Minister William Pitt the Younger – though faced with a parlous economy – sanctioned a fresh burst of colonial expansion in Asia. Since Britain could not hope to master the unnerving flow of events on the other side of the Channel and, aggrieved by the loss of the thirteen colonies, the government sanctioned a fresh eruption of imperial ambition in another hemisphere. The French, above all, must not be permitted to dominate Asia. Lord Cornwallis, who had shamed the nation by capitulating to George Washington at Yorktown, now became Governor General of India. In 1792, he won a historic victory against the Indian ruler Tipu Sultan (who sat on a throne shaped and striped like a tiger) at the Battle of Seringapatam (Shrirangapattana). This new empire would be won by the sword. Instead of settlement there would be conquest by force of arms. Lord Castlereagh, the Secretary of State for War and the Colonies, admitted that the British must change from traders to sovereigns in India. Midwife to the rough birthing of the British Raj was rampant fear of those Spartan apes in Paris. It was not entirely groundless: the French had backed the American revolutionaries. If Jacobinism spread to Asia the consequences would be chilling indeed: 'Adieu to power, influence and respectability …'. fretted a British captain in Bombay. The main actor in this new bout of imperialism was the East India Company. This commercial behemoth, which had been chartered by Queen Elizabeth I on New Year's Eve 1600, was traditionally reluctant to step outside its role as a mercantile business operation devoted to enriching its members and the nation. Now it was permitted to establish trading outposts known as 'factories' – not colonies.

Conquest was expensive; so too was administration. Profit was all. Headquartered at India House in Leadenhall Street in London, 'John Company' was a bloated and increasingly sclerotic institution burdened by a byzantine bureaucracy. In the age of sail, communication between India House and the various factories were sluggish. Members and employees of the Company devoted a great deal of their time to writing reports and so-called narratives, but it could take up to a year to get a response. The main consequence of this snail-speed intranet was that the Company governors developed a managerial culture of localised decision-making. Initiative was with the periphery not the centre. This accounts for the rise to power of Company conquistadores, epitomised by Clive of India, whose sepoy army defeated the mighty Indian ally of the French Suraj-ud-daulah, the Nawab of Bengal. As well as conquest, many 'John Company' men on the spot were rapacious bullies who shed few tears when their greed killed one-third of the population of Bengal through famine. Such men would be the vanguard of empire building.

The struggle between the European powers, Britain, France and the Netherlands, would shatter the old Malay polities and inflict a completely new territorial grid on the palimpsest of Southeast Asia. At the beginning of 1795, Napoleon invaded and occupied the Netherlands. The 'Stadtholder', or chief executive, of the Dutch Republic, William IV Prince of Orange, fled to England – where he took up residence at the 'Dutch House' in Kew. The British government feared that the French would now seize control of the Dutch possessions in the Indies: the domino theory of its time. They persuaded William to transfer the VOC colonies in Java and the Malayan Peninsula to Britain for 'safekeeping'. The stadholder's decision was unwelcome and confusing news to the governors of Dutch enclaves in southern India and the Malay Archipelago. Some, such as the Governor of Malacca, complied; others resisted.

With the fall of Napoleon, the Dutch Republic was liberated and normal competitive relations between the British and the Dutch resumed. British advance in India led by the avaricious agents of the East India Company had by the end of the Napoleonic wars confirmed Britain as a global power. Dominion depended – or was understood to depend – on both the Raj and the British Royal Navy. Britannia was determined to rule the waves – which inspired a wave of conquests and annexations that created a string of fortified bases stretching from Gibraltar to Malta and Corfu in the Mediterranean, to the Cape of Good Hope (annexed from the Dutch in 1806) and then on and in an ever widening arc across the Indian Ocean towards the great gullet of the Straits of Malacca. The British seized Mauritius from the French and grabbed Ceylon, the 'grand imperium of Oriental commerce', from the Dutch. So it was that in 1819 the British stood on the threshold of Southeast Asia, face to face with the Dutch.

The British East India Company was the vanguard force of the new imperialism and backed by the might of the Royal Navy. Company magnates in India House and in Calcutta spoke the language of commerce and worshipped at the altar of free trade. The bottom line was profit not wasteful territorial conquest. The architect of Britain's Far Eastern empire was an ambitious and talented young man who, loathed by his colleagues and frequently admonished by Company moguls for a succession of money-losing misdemeanours, rose to become 'Sir Stamford Raffles of the eastern isles', the 'Father of Singapore'. Born onboard his drunken father's ship in the Caribbean, young Thomas grew up in shabby Walworth. His family was impecunious and his education unimpressive. Raffles joined the East India Company as a junior clerk aged just 14 in the secretary's office. But young Raffles was pushy, ambitious and a classic autodidact, eager to learn about the byzantine ways of John Company, and the exotic new worlds in the East where Company men could make their mark and their fortune. In 1805, when he turned 26, Raffles was despatched to the new Company 'residency' on Prince of Wales Island, Penang, the first British possession in the Malay Peninsula. On the long voyage out, Raffles devoted his time to learning Malay. It was a shrewd decision: Raffles' obvious talents made his rise to power irresistible. Then, in 1808, Emperor Napoleon Bonaparte, the terrifying bogeyman who stalked through the nightmares of Englishmen, sent a new administrator, Marshall Herman Willem Daendels, to Batavia in Java. Thoroughly rattled, the British despatched a fleet bearing an army of 10,000 troops to annex Java and appointed Raffles as lieutenant governor. The British campaign was brutal and destructive. Raffles was just 30 and had immense ambitions. Some of his plans were enlightened. He wanted to reform the Dutch-imposed system of land tenure and abolish the local slave trade. But he committed the cardinal sin of losing a great deal of money for the East India Company as well as wasting his time on reform – and he was recalled in disgrace. The Company had few regrets in handing Java back to the Dutch.

For the East India Company directors in London, and Raffles' many envious rivals, the disconcerting rise of 'Sir Knight' (as some disparagingly called the honours-conscious Raffles) was inconvenient. So they sent him back east to the health-sapping backwater of Bencoolen in eastern Sumatra. The place would kill four of his children. It was in benighted Bencoolen that Raffles' vision of an eastern empire, which would contest the monopolistic Dutch, flowered like one of the giant endoparasitic *Rafflesia* plants that he and his surgeon Doctor Joseph Arnold discovered in Sumatra. The problem, as Raffles pointed out to the new Governor General of Bengal, Frances Rawdon-Hastings, Marquess of Hastings and Earl of Moira, was the Dutch stranglehold on the southern end of the straits: the British, he lamented, 'have now not an inch of ground to stand upon between the Cape of Good Hope and China …'. The solution was to secure a port that would release the Dutch grip. As he put it: 'one free port in the seas must eventually destroy the spell of Dutch monopoly.' Like his masters in Leadenhall Street, Raffles was an ardent believer in the gods of free trade. The Southeast Asian shrine of free trade would be the port city of Singapore.

Raffles, it need hardly be pointed out, neither discovered Singapore nor was he the founder of a settlement on the island, which is so perfectly situated at the southern tip of the Malay Peninsula. It commanded the straits, as he told Lord Hastings, and was at the confluence of the monsoon winds. The history of Singapura, the Lion City, was older than Malacca's. It was, to be sure, decayed and neglected when Raffles sailed into its great natural harbour. Wa Hakin, who was 15 when the English ships dropped anchor, recalled eighty years later the day that Raffles and Major William Farquhar set foot on the sandy rat-infested beach on 19 January 1819: 'there were two white men and a Sepoy [...] they went straight to the Temenggong [prime minister]'s house [...] who gave them rambutans and all kinds of fruit. The Sepoy carried a musket.'[7]

The foundation of Singapore was indeed a pivotal moment in British imperial history. The port city would become one of the great synapses of imperial trade and power and would be one of the last imperial bases abandoned by the British as the sun finally set on the empire in the 1960s. The city expanded with breathtaking speed. Singapore would become the Babylon of the East. It owed its diversity and astonishing growth to Raffles' vision of a free port: a truly globalised emporium that surpassed the old Malay empires like Malacca and Śrīvijaya where, as one observer, George Windsor Earl, observed with awe, 'Ships from all parts of the world are constantly arriving [...] and the flags of Great Britain, Holland, France and the America may often be seen intermingled with the streamers of the Chinese junks, and the fanciful colours of the native *parahus*'. When Alfred Russell Wallace spent time in Singapore between 1854 and 1862, he observed:

> The government, the garrison, and the chief merchants are English; but the great mass of the population is Chinese, including some of the wealthiest merchants, the agriculturists of the interior, and most of the mechanics and labourers. The native Malays are usually fishermen and boatmen, and they form the main body of the police. The Portuguese of Malacca supply a large number of the clerks and smaller merchants. The Klings of Western India are a numerous body of Mahometans, and, with many Arabs, are petty merchants and shopkeepers [...] Besides these, there are numbers of Javanese sailors and domestic servants, as well as traders from Celebes, Bali, and many other islands of the Archipelago.

The point we should draw out is the manner in which the British exploited, coerced, manipulated and in the end cheated the local rulers. A great deal of tortuous plotting by all sides had preceded the famous landing by Raffles and Major Farquhar and their meeting with the Temenggong, the hereditary prime minister of the Johor-Riau-Lingga Sultanate. Raffles had exploited a petty dynastic squabble, as European colonisers would on many future occasions.

Raffles' trap was sprung with due pomp and circumstance. He had a cunning sense of theatre. To set the stage, he ordered Chinese plantation workers to erect a little colony of tents and a mast. The most imposing was the scarlet-coloured 'Treaty Tent' where the business of appropriation would shortly be conducted. From the tent a carpet of the same vibrant hue led down to the riverbank. At about one o'clock, a cannon boomed – and the local ruler, the portly Sultan Hussain, resplendent in bright yellow royal apparel, stepped from his boat and proceeded slowly down the red carpet to the 'Treaty Tent' flanked by an escort of Company soldiers. As soon as the various parties were seated inside, the nine article 'Treaty of Friendship between Sir Thomas Stamford Raffles and Sultan Hussain and Temenggong Abdul Rahman' was read aloud – in English. Under its terms, Sultan Hussain would enjoy an annual salary of 5,000 Spanish dollars. The Temenggong was rewarded for his role in Raffles' dealing with a salary of 3,000 Spanish dollars. Both the new sultan and the Temenggong promised to 'aid and assist [the English] against all enemies'. The Union flag was hauled to the top of the mast. Raffles had his free port and the sultan his throne. The Malays, it was observed, 'sat down promiscuously with the British' who happily slurped 'royal bumpers' of alcohol with gleeful abandon, their faces becoming as red as Raffles' 'Treaty Tent'.

Neither Raffles nor the new sultan imagined that their dealings had fixed the pattern of British rule in Malaya. It would be a full half-century before other Malay rulers bowed the knee to devious British empire builders – but the ruse by which the Malay rulers would become the instruments of a foreign colonial power was hatched that day in Raffles' blood-red 'Treaty Tent'. For that service the Malay rulers would be rewarded with pensions – and contempt. The British captain of the survey ship *Investigator* observed the ceremony with undisguised scorn. The sultan's dress, he remarked, was inelegantly put on, and displayed 'a disgusting breast and stomach'. As Raffles read out the 'Treaty of Friendship', 'the vulgarity of the Sultan's expression, the want of expression and perspiration running down his face, raised in the feelings of the English spectators a horrible and disgusting loathing ...'. Sir Stamford, he suspected, 'inwardly accorded'. The humiliation of the Malay rulers had begun.

Skulduggery

As Singapore ascended to its zenith as a city port, Southeast Asia became entangled in a globalised imperial economy that would shatter the ancient bonds between Malays and all other peoples of the region – above all the Chinese and Indians. An immediate consequence of the rise of British Singapore was the commercial ruin of Malacca. Raffles' teacher and translator, Munshi Abdullah, compared Malacca to a 'woman bereaved of her husband'. 'How ephemeral are the things of this world!' he lamented. As Singapore prospered, agents of the East India Company settled their differences with the Dutch and reached out to another Asian power in the region, Siam, to secure an ally against the Burmese Empire, which contested

British control of north-east India. There was deep-rooted enmity between the Thais and the Burmese. The first Anglo-Burmese war began in 1824. It was the beginning of a protracted and, for the East India Company, expensive conflict. For the Burmese the wars were a catastrophe. The alliance was humiliating too for the Malays. Before becoming the Resident in Singapore, East India Company agent Dr Crawfurd led a trade mission to the court of King Rama II. A few years later, in 1826, the king's successor, Rama III, and another company agent, Henry Burney, signed a 'Treaty of Amity and Commerce', thus recognising Siam as a nominal ally of Britain. The treaty had immediate consequences in the Malay Peninsula because Burney agreed to recognise Siamese claims over the northern Malay states of Perlis, Kedah, Kelantan and Terengganu.

The high watermark of this great territorial carve-up came in 1824. The 'Anglo-Dutch Treaty' (or 'Treaty of London'), concluded after four years of negotiations between the British and the government of the Netherlands, was yet another reinscription of the Southeast Asian territorial palimpsest. The treaty recognised British sovereignty over Singapore and severed the Malay Peninsula from Sumatra and the archipelago – the Dutch East Indies. Dutch Malacca and Dutch posts in India were formally turned over to the British, who in turn surrendered Raffles' insalubrious old fiefdom of Bencoolen. Unofficially, the 'Treaty of London' tacitly recognised that the British had superseded the Dutch as the most powerful naval and commercial force in Southeast Asia. It defined British and Dutch spheres of interest – and was a rough draft of the future territories of modern Malaysia and Indonesia. It would, however, take more than half a century for the British and the Dutch to completely subjugate their respective spheres of interest. In August of the same year (1824) Crawfurd formally stripped Sultan Hussein and the Temenggong of all residual power. He had cleverly exploited the innate weaknesses of the Malay royal courts. Since the sultan and his minister had signed the treaty with Raffles five years earlier their retinues of followers and hangers-on had grown to match their apparent new status. Royal courts were expensive to maintain and Crawfurd had only to make a good enough cash offer to achieve what he wanted politically – that is, full British possession of Singapore. So in return for renouncing 'full judicial and legal control throughout Singapore' the sultan and the Temenggong received grants of 30,000 and 15,000 Spanish dollars respectively as well as regular monthly allowances. Their downfall was complete. As Munshi Abdullah realised, 'a new world was being created'.

3

THE RACIAL STATE

The grandees of the British East India Company, headquartered on the far side of the Bay of Bengal, had scant interest in the interior of the Malayan Peninsula. The maxim of the Company was trade, not territory. The Straits Settlements of Penang, Malacca and Singapore functioned as outward looking maritime power bases that guaranteed and protected the lucrative flow of commodities to and from India and the great Chinese emporiums. But by the end of 1875, when J. W. W. Birch took that fatal bath in the Perak River, a new 'forward policy' was beginning to supplant the traditional 'hands off' ad hoc style of colonial rule. There was no imperialist master plan. What drove this slow, evolutionary transformation of the Malay world was not a grand strategy but the spectacular success of Singapore and its newly empowered Anglo-Chinese commercial oligarchs. A complex synergy between global and regional commercial energies would soon transmute the old Malayan kingdoms into 'British Malaya'.

Tin Wars

In 1867, the shock of the Indian Mutiny had led to the humiliating demise of the much decayed East India Company. 'The Company' was, it turned out, not too big to fail. Benjamin Disraeli's 'India Act' of 1868 ushered in a new era of imperial government. The India Act created two executive posts: the Secretary of State for India, who answered to Parliament, and the viceroy, who presided over a quasi-cabinet in Calcutta, which included the compliant Indian princes. Beneath the viceroy was the old Company pyramid of hierarchical offices, provincial governors, magistrates, commissioners, tax collectors and clerks, who were now all servants of the British Crown. The 'India Act' added a kind of ideological patina to the old patterns of conquest and avaricious colonial rule. High-minded imperialism added another C to the 'Four C's of Colonialism': civilising. The *Edinburgh Review* proclaimed that the 'glorious destiny of England was to govern, to civilise, to educate and to improve the innumerable tribes and races whom Providence had placed beneath her Sceptre.' As the British embarked on this great mission, the other European powers rattled imperial sabres. A new power wanted in. German

Chancellor Otto von Bismarck had exploited a succession of wars to engineer German unity. Exultant German nationalists demanded their own foreign colonies to play imperial catch-up with the French, the Dutch and the British. The industrial age reshaped colonial conquest as imperial aggrandisement. The steamship had slashed journey times between London and Singapore, and the completion of the Suez Canal in 1868, by French engineers, had further narrowed the gap between Europe and Asia. In this swiftly globalising world, the new British Colonial Office kept a beady eye trained on the unnerving activities of European rivals. The French were busy empire building in North Africa and Southeast Asia. Could Burma be next? Rumours of suspicious German activities in Siam focused British minds on the northern Malay states that had for centuries paid tribute to the Thai kings. Could these become weak links in the imperial chain? Was it sufficient to control the coastal Straits Settlements and not reach out into the Malay interior? Many began to fear that the peninsula might offer a wide open back door to the great imperial synapse of Singapore. Something needed to be done and Sir Stamford Raffles' perfidious treaty with Sultan Hussein seemed to offer a ready model.

The British frequently described the Malay states as 'decayed'. This was symptomatic of a racialised contempt. But there is no doubt that Malay kingdoms had been weakened since the glory days of Malacca. In 1837, Abdullah bin Abdul Kadir who was known simply as 'Munshi Abdullah' embarked on a journey through the peninsula and wrote a remarkable report called the *Hikayat Abdullah* ('The Account of Abdullah'): a Malay language version of William Cobbett's *Rural Rides*. Abdullah had been employed by Raffles as translator and teacher, but he had no illusions about the rapacious nature of British colonialism. His sharp eye spared no one: Sultan Hussein, the nominal ruler of Singapore, he wrote, grew 'plumper and plumper as time went on ...'. He had never seen a fatter man. In his book, *The Malay World*, the world Abdullah reported on was barely a community. Malays were mainly preoccupied by their differences, not by what they had in common. They were not citizens in any sense but the subjects of rulers. This severely limited their mental world. According to Abdullah, 'ignorant', 'uneducated' Malay rulers occupied shabby dilapidated palaces: in Terengganu, for example, he describes the sultan's palace as 'in the Chinese style' with crumbling walls made of 'dirt, spittle, betel juice and moss'. The ruler's subjects naturally occupied even meaner dwellings that 'emitted foul odours'. Abdullah deplored the miserable condition of Malay peasants and blamed it squarely on 'the tyranny and injustice of the government of the rajas [...] to live close to a raja is like making friends with a poisonous snake.' The courts were preoccupied with custom, ritual and the frequent awarding of titles and not at all with the well-being of their subjects. Abdullah did not pull his punches:

I have mentioned the injustices of the rajas because it is always the custom of the Malay ruler to despise his subjects, as though he thought of them as animals. Whenever a common man meets his ruler he is obliged to squat on the ground in the mud and filth […] The laws and subjects which he imposes on his subjects depend solely on his own private whim …

The Malay rulers, however, faced a fundamental problem. The sultan was in many respects merely a master of ceremonies, a curator of ritual. Real power was vested in district chiefs, or datos, and village headmen, the *penghulas*. In Perak, the chiefs were non-royal, but their families had usually held power for many generations. In Selangor, with its Bugis-dominated sultanate, the territorial chiefs were rajas, or princes. Each dato was obligated to pay obeisance to the sultan but could, if he possessed the means to do so, exercise near despotic power in his own fiefdom. The sultan's political control over his realm was thus ritualised rather than real.

In Perak, the richer and more important datos controlled territory from armed riverside stockades. They administered local justice and had the right to demand free *corvée* labour (*kerah*) from the peasantry (the *rakyat*). Malay peasants worked the fields, mines, plantations and, whenever necessary, defended the district. The power and wealth of a dato depended on extracting revenue from the resources of the district he ruled. Traditionally in a riverine state like Perak, taxes on river traffic yielded lucrative rewards. The datos used these revenues to maintain their families and an entourage of servants, agents and bodyguards as emblems of prestige. A good number of the datos' retinues were slaves. All slaves were of course non-Malays since Sharia law permits only the enslavement of non-Muslims. The sultan, at the apex of this socially rigid hierarchy, was obligated to build and maintain alliances with the datos and their headmen. But if a chief 'struck it rich' he might be tempted to defy the sultan. Not only that, but the system of Malay inheritance often produced numerous rival claimants to the throne. The Malay states thus presented a paradox – they were socially rigid, but inherently unstable. It was this intrinsic fragility of the sultan/chief relationship that allowed an English adventurer James Brooke, who had been brought up in India and, like Raffles, had nourished a fascination with Malay culture, to establish a dynasty of 'White Rajas' in Sarawak on the island of Borneo. A Malay state might remain intact so long as the sultan successfully played off and kept in balance the power of his many competitive chiefs. The ruler might have been a symbol, but symbols can be potent – and in this feudal world the *rakyat* would never dare question the sultan's authority, which derived from God. In the mid-nineteenth century in some Malay states this delicate balance would be smashed asunder. This violent upheaval began in Perak – and it was all to do with tin.

Tin had already made the Sultan of Perak wealthy. It was mined by both Malays and Chinese workers from the great alluvial deposits of ore washed out of the Main Range along the Larut River. The tin deposits were not, of course, evenly distributed. As well as the rich Larut valley deposits, tin ore had been discovered on the Linggi near Malacca and the Klang in Selangor. The distribution of these tin deposits would shape the power struggles to come. Tin had been mined in the Malay Peninsula for many centuries. For much of this time the industry was lucrative but small in scale. What drove the rise of tin mining was the invention of the tin can in the early nineteenth century to preserve food, and the widespread use of can openers during the American Civil War in the 1860s. The extraction of tin would dominate the economies of Southeast Asia. By mid-century, tin plate manufacturing had expanded in Britain and in 1853 the government repealed duties on tin imports and demand grew very rapidly.

Since the founding of Singapore, Chinese involvement in both plantation agriculture and mining had also been expanding, sucking in huge numbers of new immigrant workers fleeing poverty and violent unrest in South China. Most of these *sinkheh*, or 'new men', as older Baba, or 'Straits' Chinese, contemptuously called them, came to Singapore and Malaya under the exploitative credit ticket system, which bound them to Chinese employers for long periods of time. 'Chinese', it should be noted, encompassed speakers of many different languages: Teochew and Cantonese, Hokkien, Hakka, and Hainanese. This was a diverse community that did not yet think of itself as 'Chinese'. By 1845, fully half the population of Singapore spoke one of these languages or their dialects. Many came to the promised land of Singapore hoping to emulate Hoo Ah Kay, or 'Whampoa' (his birthplace), who was just 15 when he arrived in Singapore to work for his father. It did not take long for this clever and indomitable young man to accumulate a spectacular fortune and learn to speak excellent English. For the majority of Chinese *sinkheh*, a 'new life' in the Straits Settlements or Malaya meant decades of back-breaking badly paid work. In some Chinese immigrant communities the death toll from disease and labour exhaustion could be above 50 per cent. It was these labouring Chinese legions that would build the modern economies of the Malay states.

By mid-century the global tin boom had depleted the older Malay-owned mines that had used the same extraction techniques for centuries. As a consequence, demand rose for new innovative technologies to dig deeper, and this led to a demand for new sources of capital investment. Since Malay rulers and chiefs habitually frittered away reserve capital on ostentatious ceremonial displays, they were forced to turn to the wealthy Baba Malay oligarchs such as Chee Yam Chuan and See Boon Tiong in Malacca and Penang. In the early part of the century these Baba Malay merchants outnumbered the British and European financiers involved in the tin mining industry. ('Engaged in the native trade' was the formula used at the time.) The Baba were local born. Their ancestors, who were mainly Hokkiens from the south-eastern province of Fukien, had first come to Malacca in the fourteenth century. Many developed close ties to the Malay royal families. Chee Yam Chuan, for example, was one of the major creditors of Sultan Muhammad of Perak, whose debts in 1847 amounted to an eye-watering $169,000. But even with Baba backing, by the 1840s the Malay chiefs faced fierce competition from a fast-rising new breed of Chinese entrepreneurs, who had made their piles in Singapore and were often allied with British or European merchant houses. These 'new men' had a tremendous advantage. While the Malay world revolved around the sultan's court, Chinese entrepreneurs had brought with them a uniquely Chinese way of doing business that had first emerged among Hakka communities in Yunan and had been refined over many centuries. This was the 'Kongsi' system. 'Kongsi' literally means 'meeting hall' and it will be recalled that the Chinese villagers shot dead by members of the Scots Guards in Batang Kali in December 1948 lived in 'Kongsi huts'. The entrepreneurial 'Kongsi' was, in essence, an association of risk takers, who shared both profit and loss. The entire system was a lucrative investment and profit-making machine: the typical Kongsi was both a brotherhood of shareholders and a proto-corporation. It also offered a way out of poverty. A European observer remarked that he 'always looked upon a Sinkheh [newcomer] as a Towkay Labur [financier], Towkay Bantu [advancer], or a Capitan China in embryo and respected him accordingly.' This was astute. The humble Chinese indentured labourer was the future.

In the Malay state of Perak it was Kongsi capital and Chinese waged labour that revolutionised tin mining by funding innovation. Chinese miners were soon digging deeper and wider, opening up highly profitable new seams and deposits. In the southern state of Johor, the rulers and datos had developed bonds with Chinese entrepreneurs through land grants. But this was unusual. In most other states, the Malay chiefs, who tended to value retinues more highly than revenues, could not compete with the flood of new Chinese capital. As the power of the chiefs eroded, the Kongsis began to take direct control of tin mining operations. In a very short period of time the Kongsis tightened their grip on the tin mines and plantations, to the dismay of many anxious Malays.

Tin mining reconfigured social and ethnic relations and transformed the physical landscape of Malaya. Tin made fortunes and built new cities. In the vicinity of the tin mines, jerry-built rough-and-ready settlements sprang up to accommodate Chinese mine workers and cater to their needs. These primitive little towns were controlled by 'headmen', who lived in separate, often quite grand houses with their new families: many 'sinkheh' married local Orang Asli women. Ipoh, the 'city of millionaires', was a creation of the tin mining industry. In 1850, few people lived in the Larut river valley. Its development was the tin revolution in microcosm. The story begins with a Malay trader called Che Long Jaafar, a tax collector for the sultan within the Larut area. The first big tin deposits were discovered near his house and he was not slow to recognise their potential. At the time only three Chinese lived in the Larut area but when news spread that tin had been struck thousands flocked to the valley to seek their fortunes. This was when Che Long Jaafar made his first mistake. Since he could extract a substantial tax or royalty on the metal, he was happy to sit back and let the Chinese get on with the job. They did – with prodigious energy. Between 1863 and 1879 the human landscape of the Larut valley was utterly transformed. More than 30,000 Chinese workers toiled in the mines, far outnumbering the 2,000 to 3,000 Malays who lived nearby. Further south in Selangor, close to tin mines at Ampang and Pudu, now part of greater Kuala Lumpur, a few score Chinese traders set up a cluster of shop houses or stores selling general provisions on the muddy confluence, or 'kuala lumpur', where the sluggish, brown waters of the Klang and Gombok rivers met and joined, before flowing down to discharge into the straits at Klang. In June 1869, the Selengor Raja Mahdie, who was struggling to hold on to power, appointed a dynamic Hakka Chinese from the Guangdong province of southern China called Yap Ah Loy to serve as the headman, or 'Kapitan Cina', for this brash, fast-expanding new settlement. Ah Loy had arrived in Malacca in 1854 and, legend has it, lost his ticket home. He was a smart boy and a ferocious fighter who, when he left Malacca, worked as a mining coolie and cook. He had come to Kuala Lumpur after serving as the 'Kapitan Cina' in Sungai Ujong and within two years owned tin mines, a 'druggist store' and had helped found the city's first temple. His arrival coincided with the rapid growth of the new town and intensifying competition over commercial and mining rights between Malays and Chinese alike – that culminated in the Selangor wars. When Raja Mahdie formally invested Yap Ah Loy the new 'Kapitan' wore the Malay dress of a raja and was carried through town in a sedan chair, flanked by his head fighting men in military uniform, like a Chinese official. As his power grew, Yap Ah Loy invested in plantations and brickyards, as well as prostitution houses, gambling booths, and opium farms. He would turn a wild tin-mining village into a mighty city. Yap Ah Loy was also a leading member of a mysterious organisation called the Hai San.

The Hai San was a secret society, or 'Hui'. Though Chinese secret societies were both exploited and feared by the colonial powers, they were, in many respects, comparable to English 'friendly societies' or the Freemasons. Both the Hui and the Kongsi, as David Ownby points out, stem from a common tradition of Chinese ritual brotherhood dedicated to social justice and equality. According to historian Heng Pek Koon, the secret societies probably originated at least 2,000 years ago among bands of dispossessed peasants who had been driven from their homes and villages by war, flood, famine, or the whim of tyrants. These vulnerable, displaced peoples sought out charismatic leaders to organise and resist authority. The members of this early kind of Hui were bonded together by arcane rituals of initiation and secret oaths of loyalty that represented a kind of theatrical fusion of shamanism, Taoism, Buddhism and Confucianism. During the Qing dynasty, which ruled China from the seventeenth century until the revolution of 1911, the old secret societies matured into highly effective quasi-political organisations for mobilising support against government and authority. They also offered a means of bypassing the rigid Chinese hierarchies topped by scholars and administrators and acted as 'leadership academies'. In south-east China the most influential were the Triad Brotherhood of societies that had offshoots like the

Heaven and Earth League and the Hung Brotherhood. The Triads had a powerful grip on urban and rural communities as well as the emerging proletariat of the Asian ports. All secret societies were dominated by a patriarchal leadership sect and were rigidly hierarchical, though the best and brightest could ascend through the ranks. The occult society rituals and oaths that both frightened and fascinated outsiders encouraged absolute loyalty. From early in the nineteenth century, the secret societies dominated the social and political life of the new *sinkheh* Chinese communities in Singapore and the other Straits Settlements, and had developed closely woven ties with the Kongsis. For British colonial administrators these clandestine and uncontrollable networks were a threat.

As the Straits Settlements prospered, both the Hui and Kongsi businesses thrived. In Singapore, the big three secret societies were the 'Ghee Hin', the 'Ho Seng' and the 'Hai San'. Members had to swear elaborate oaths and take part in arcane rituals. Some were exclusively Chinese; but Malays, Portuguese and Indians (including the mixed Jawi Peranakan) could join the smaller societies. As the Hui became increasingly influential and their members more numerous, the British colonial administrators in the Straits Settlements and the Malay elites, who were struggling to control the internecine conflicts of the new tin mining areas in Selangor and Perak, became more perturbed by these clandestine webs of intrigue and influence. Since Hui activity was by definition secretive, it was easy to imagine any number of fantastical imaginings of plots and conspiracies. These were not always imaginary. In 1846 the Ghee Hin had allegedly incited riots in Singapore; local papers began reporting so-called 'Hoey [sic] disturbances'; and in 1867, in Penang and Province Wellesley, a small war erupted between rival Hui militias, some armed with artillery. It was not just a 'Chinese problem', for the warring secret societies were allied with rival Malay and Indian gangs. (Any sign of communal allegiance troubled the British.) In July, skirmishing between the 'Malay White Flag Society', the 'Ghee Hin' and 'Toh Peh Kong' societies exploded in ten days of rioting – forcing the British governor, Major General Harry Ord, to order a public enquiry. The commissioners delivered their report a year later: they concluded that 'the late riots had their origin in a trifling quarrel between two rival Muhammadan Societies during the late Mohurrum Festival [New Year] and that they were fostered by two other rival societies of Chinese [...] [these are] extremely dangerous to the peace and welfare of the community.' It was not the Muhammadan but the Chinese who bore the brunt of subsequent legislation, the 'Dangerous Societies Suppression Ordinance', passed in 1869. The ordinance was a blunt weapon. It had almost no impact on the activities of the secret societies in Penang or anywhere else. In 1872, there were riots in Singapore and another Commission of Enquiry was set up, whose members included the then Colonial Secretary, James Birch.

In the Malay interior, far from the cities of the straits, the Kongsi and the secret societies dominated the tin mining communities in Perak and Selangor. The flow

of revenue was spectacular. So too were the taxes flowing into the coffers of
Malay nobles. But where there is profit, there is envy. Where there is envy, there is
conflict. The Chinese Kongsi and their Hui followers fought bitterly one against
the other to maximise their rights and revenues. Tensions between the Chinese
secret societies coincided with a fresh bout of dynastic infighting between some
of the Malay rulers. It was traditional for embattled rivals to promiscuously seek
out allies with greater firepower. In the past the Malay rulers had turned to
Bugis mercenaries – as well as European powers, the Dutch or the British – but
whoever or whatever the client, they naturally took full advantage of their weak
Malay patrons. This was how Raffles and Farquhar had acquired Singapore. Now
another set of power brokers were added to the mix. Malay royal contenders
turned increasingly to local Chinese power brokers to support their claims. In
Selangor, for example, the famous 'Kapitan Cina', Yap Ah Loy, who was a member
of the Hai San society, backed one royal claimant while the 'Kang Yeng Chew'
society allied with his rival. In Perak, the tin boom amplified these overlapping,
interwoven conflicts between rival Malay princes and their Chinese allies. As the
Chinese and their Malay allies squabbled, profits began to tumble. In Singapore
and the other Straits Settlements, hard-nosed British businessmen and their
Chinese partners became greatly alarmed. A Singapore notable called William
Henry Macleod Read of A.L. Jonston & Co., Freemason, former policeman,
founder of the Singapore Turf Club and leading member of the Legislative
Council of the Straits Settlements, lobbied for what he and others had begun
calling the 'forward policy': in other words, the Colonial Office must intervene in
the Malay States, or, they warned, Perak would be– as future Governor and High
Commissioner of the Malay States Sir Frank Swettenham put it – reduced to a
'disorderly, penniless state'. Read knew a great deal about Malay dynastic disputes
and the Perak wars through his business associate, the fabulously wealthy Tan Kim
Cheng. Both feared that anarchy would erode profits.

The Humbling

As in Singapore, British rule in the Malayan Peninsula would be founded on
an act of outrageous skulduggery. As the Malay rulers and their Chinese allies
brawled, and as revenues from the Larut mines plummeted, the Colonial Office
in London anxiously read financial reports, fretted about losses and did nothing.
There were many in the British establishment who shared Disraeli's view that
colonies were a 'millstone round our necks'. But as the Perak tin wars showed no
sign of abating, the Secretary of State for the Colonies, John Woodhouse, the 1st
Earl of Kimberley, sent a request that the new Governor of the Straits Settlements,
Sir Andrew Clarke, should find out more about the baffling conflicts in the Malay
States – and send a report. Kimberley had in fact been stirred into action by
reports of worrying German activity in Siam that conceivably threatened the

northern Malay states, which were vassals of the Thai king. Like many other 'men on the spot' in the British Empire, Clarke was, like Sir Stamford Raffles before him, used to thinking, and in many cases acting, independently of his faraway masters in the Colonial Office. Once he had received Kimberley's rather vague instructions, Clarke turned to the shrewd W.H. Read to get a grip on what was happening in Perak and find a solution that would restore business confidence in the tin industry.

Read explained that for some time Perak had been plagued by increasingly acrimonious wrangles between rival royal heirs and their backers. In 1871, Sultan Ali Al-Mukkammal died. His natural successor should have been the heir apparent (or Raja Muda) Abdullah. But Abdullah was the bad boy of Perak. He was, or so it was rumoured, promiscuous, addicted to opium, fond of gambling and cock fighting, and, unsurprisingly, virtually bankrupt. For a later generation of Malay nationalists and even communists like Abdullah C.D., Abdullah would become a symbol of resistance. But he was not, historian Khoo Kay Kim implies, especially bright. He was something of a peacock with a fondness for personal display.

When Abdullah churlishly refused to attend Sultan Ali's funeral, the Perak chiefs retaliated by electing the *Bendahara*, a court minister, called Raja Ismail. Ismail's most powerful backer was the chief of the Larut river valley, Ngah Ibrahim, who had made a fortune by taxing the tin mines in his fiefdom and had close ties to the Hai San society. He may even have been a member. Ibrahim *also* had designs on the throne. Not to be outdone, Abdullah turned to the bitter rivals of the Hai San, the Ghee Hin, to support *his* claim. Perak was now ruled in effect by two sultans – and both were backed by competing Chinese secret societies. W.H. Read's business partner, Tan Kim Cheng, was a member of the 'Ghee Hin' and supported Abdullah. In short, a tangled web of allegiances had been woven. Read had no hesitation urging Clarke to cut the Malay Gordian knot. Intervention was the only answer; the 'forward policy' must prevail. Years later, Read confessed that he had had in mind to intervene much earlier: 'There is no doubt that the Malay Peninsula would have been opened up in 1865 [...] as it had been a favourite scheme of mine ...'.

Read took the first step. He prompted, or rather persuaded, Abdullah to write to Clarke proposing that in return for the British endorsing him as sultan, he, Abdullah, would permit the appointment of 'a man of sufficient abilities to show us a good system of government'. Here in a nutshell we have the device that would become the main instrument of British rule in Malaya: the Residential System. It was neither original nor unique. Colonial powers invariably invited indigenous princes or rulers to govern as proxies. It is worth noting here that the Dutch got rid, by and large, of the Javanese rulers.

With Abdullah's agreement, Clarke now called a conference to settle matters in Perak. The various warring parties met at the beginning of 1874 aboard the British steamer *Pluto* that was moored just off Pangkor Island. Clarke's ostensible purpose was to end hostilities and find a solution to the dispute between the Malay royal claimants. That was his overt agenda. The less transparent purpose of the Pangkor Conference was to impose indirect rule in Perak. Chinese expert William Pickering, who could speak Cantonese, Hakka, Hokkien, Foochew, Teochew and Mandarin fluently, and would be appointed the 'Chinese Protector' of the Straits Settlements a few years later, had already warmed up the Chinese delegates, and all twenty-six of them quickly agreed to a truce. They were all weary of fighting, and to convince any waverers Clarke threatened to levy a fine of $50,000 if they failed to come to terms. The negotiations with the Malays proved much stickier. Abdullah's two rivals, Sultan Ismail and Raja Yusuf, failed to appear at the conference. (Frank Swettenham, the 'Malay expert' in Clarke's entourage, was unaware at the time of the Pangkor meetings of Yusuf's claims and possibly that he existed.) Since Abdullah appeared to be willing to kowtow, Clarke formally recognised him as the legitimate ruler of Perak. Ismail was consoled with a pension of $1,000 a month. The big loser was the *Mantri* Ngar Ibrahim, who had been forced to attend the conference at gunpoint and refused a chair to sit on. He was stripped of power in the tin rich Larut valley and made to pay compensation for the cost of the wars. The agreement was drawn up on 19 January and signed the next day. Surrounded by British soldiers, some of the Malay delegates were frightened out of their wits.

In the longer term it was Sultan Abdullah and his successor rulers who paid the highest price. The nub of their deceit was in a single word. According to the terms of the Pangkor Treaty, both Ibrahim and Sultan Abdullah were obliged to accept the appointment of a British Resident:

VI. Sixth. – That the Sultan receive and provide a suitable residence for a British Officer to be called Resident, who shall be accredited to his Court, and whose advice must be asked and acted upon on all questions other than those touching Malay Religion and Custom.

This was the English language version. It was translated into Malay by Swettenham. To describe the role of the Resident, he used the word *muafakat*, which means or strongly implies consultation between equal parties. The all-important phrase '*whose advice must be asked and acted upon*' in the English version was thus obfuscated. Swettenham's use of *muafakat* deliberately misled the Malay negotiators who would have assumed that the proposed Resident would take part as an equal or advisory partner in the traditional court, *mesyuarat bicara*, or 'meetings for discussions'. These usually took place over several days and participants were obligated to reach consensus decisions. Since the sultan had no remit to impose a resolution, it was unimaginable that a foreign official could abrogate the decision-making powers of a Malay court. Arguably, too, the qualifying phrase '*in all questions other than those touching Malay Religion and Custom*' was meaningless in a Muslim culture that did not comprehend, let alone accept, any separation of powers. Secular and religious realms were not pigeonholed. Every aspect of life touched on 'Malay religion and custom'. The sultan was 'the Shadow of God'. By limiting that power under the rubric of 'advice that must be acted upon', the British walked roughshod over some fundamental Muslim ethics.

Clarke later admitted that he had indeed hustled the Malay rulers to come to an agreement. If he had not, he claimed, nothing would have been achieved. The truth was that the Pangkor Conference was negotiation by diktat. The British imposed a solution by recognising Sultan Abdullah because they believed he would do their bidding. The former Lieutenant Governor of Penang, Colonel Archibald Anson, had no doubt that 'these chiefs did not fully realise what they were asked to agree to; or if they did had no intention of acting up to it'. What the British meant by advice was *control* and between the twin poles of advice and control the history of British Malaya would now be enacted.

The 'Residential System' that had been duplicitously imposed on the Sultan of Perak would take time to bed down. It had to be refined, slowly and painfully, and would always reflect a tricky balance struck between the capacity of the Malay ruler to resist and the personal and diplomatic skills of the British Resident to get his way. Mr J.W.W. Birch seems not to have possessed the appropriate facility, though he had a great deal of experience. Soon after the signing of the treaty, he pressured Clarke to appoint him as temporary Resident on the Perak River. Clarke was not, it seems, completely convinced that Birch was the right man to take on a tough and, as yet, ill-defined job. It was said of Birch that he had spoken to the Sultan of Selangor 'peremptorily': he was known to have excoriated Malays for dilatoriness and 'shilly-shallying'. Birch was not convinced that 'Easterners' were capable of 'good government'. He saw his new task as enforcing 'good government'. That was not negotiable. Two years later his mutilated corpse would be floating down the Perak River.

The Pangkor Treaty's notorious Article 6 was not the only bone of contention between the Malay rulers, the datos, and the British. According to Article 10 of the treaty, the British Resident would 'regulate the collection and control of state revenue'. This clause antagonised the datos, who were used to taxing revenues in their riverine fiefdoms. Now they would get fixed salaries from a central state treasury – a salary which might, they suspected, be withheld if they did not toe the line. Even worse, the British insisted that 'no slavery could be permitted to exist in any state under British protection'. For the Malay rulers and their chiefs this constituted intolerable interference. They depended on forms of slavery: in the 1870s some 6 per cent of the total Malay population could be classified as slaves of one sort or another. Islam permitted the enslavement of non-Muslims, which was anathema to the high-minded British. It was, in one respect, humbug. For at least two centuries British merchants and the British government had made handsome profits from a global slave trade that linked together, in a chain of misery and profit, the African trading ports, West Indian and American plantations and port cities such as Bristol, Manchester and Liverpool. The great and the good of the British establishment had vested interests in this barbaric trade, the continued practice of which was morally justified by the alleged inferiority or non-human status of their human cargoes. The slaving community in London vociferously resisted the campaign to abolish the slave trade, Wordsworth's 'pilgrimage sublime' that was led by abolitionists William Wilberforce, Thomas Clarkson, Olaudah Equiano and other courageous individuals. But in 1833 that battle had at last been won, the chains had been broken and slavery was outlawed across Britain's fast-expanding empire. It would be wrong to condemn the British campaign to extinguish the slave trade as mere hypocrisy. But the institution of slavery in the Malay States was very different from the Atlantic trade. The majority of the sultan's subjects, or *rakyat*, were free peasants. But, as the British discovered, there were also significant numbers of *orang berhutang*, or 'debt bondsmen', who had contracted loans with their chiefs and to repay their debt took on a period of indentured labour. In theory, the debt bondsman (or woman) could purchase his or her freedom from the chief, but in practice the majority were unable to do so and remained trapped in service. Since these debt bondsmen were in fact Muslims they cannot be described as slaves; nevertheless, they were *enslaved*. As well as the Malay *orang berhutang*, the chiefs and sultans owned numerous non-Malay and thus non-Muslim slaves, or *hamda abdi*. A number of them were aboriginal Orang Asli. Others had been bought by pious Malays returning from the Haj (the pilgrimage to Mecca). Slaves had been traded throughout the Malay Peninsula and the Indonesian Archipelago for many centuries. Clarke understood that the matter would have to be handled delicately. Under pressure to prove both his own suitability for the job and the efficacy of the Residential System itself, Birch concluded that he could not afford to be subtle.

Sultan Abdullah owed his position to the British, but once he felt secure he refused to play the game. Birch harboured an intense and personalised dislike of Abdullah: he referred to him as a 'young fool … We are unfortunate in the Sultan,' he concluded. Two years after the signing of the treaty, Birch had made little progress in bringing Abdullah to heel. For his part he had antagonised the sultan by giving refuge to runaway slaves. His job was on the line. Clarke's concerns about Birch were shared by his successor, the new Straits Governor, Sir William Jervois, who concluded that 'there is not the "holy calm" reigning in the [Malay] peninsula which the Pangkor Treaty is supposed to have inaugurated …'. He summoned Birch to a meeting in Penang in late June. Birch blamed Sultan Abdullah: he was not fit to rule and should be deposed. He persuaded Jervois that direct annexation, since it was now difficult to switch to one of the other claimants, was the only realistic option. Jervois was also dismayed to find out that Perak owed the Straits Settlements $18,000. How was this to be recovered if Perak descended into anarchy? Jervois spent two weeks touring Perak and trying to help Birch force Abdullah into line. At a meeting with Abdullah and Perak chiefs he threatened to impose direct rule.

Trouble was brewing. At another meeting, this time with Birch alone, Abdullah, surrounded by a cohort of followers, demanded $5,000 – and the return of the runaway slaves Birch was sheltering. In response, Birch delivered another pious lecture to the sultan. Birch did not just have to deal with Abdullah. The Malay chiefs fiercely opposed the terms of the treaty, and the 'Menteri' Ngah Ibrahim, who had so badly lost out at Pangkor, warned Abdullah: 'I think bye and bye that Mr Birch will bring many more Europeans to take charge of the country [...] It is improper for your majesty to follow the Resident for his rank is only that of a Datuk.'

On 20 July 1875, a Bugis slave trader called Maharaja Lela Pendak Lam called the sultan's supporters to a meeting at Durian Sebatang and an agreement was concluded that the troublesome Birch must be removed. Birch had some idea what was happening and the danger it posed but, with Frank Swettenham's assistance, pressed on with plans for direct rule. Jervois' idea was to govern in the sultan's name through British officers and a Malay Council. Under pressure, Sultan Abdullah temporised and signed two official proclamations of his intent to comply. In October, Birch was warned that plans were afoot to do him harm. He said: 'I will take good care [...] if one Mr Birch is killed, ten Mr Birches will take his place.' On 1 November, Birch arrived on the 'Naga' at Pasir Selak on the Perak River, which happened to be the home village of Maharaja Lela. The following morning a Dato Sagor arrived and asked to speak with Birch – but Birch was too busy posting copies of the sultan's proclamations in the village. When he had finished the job, Birch walked down to the river's edge and the little bathhouse. Dato Sagor tore down the proclamations, and a group of armed Malays employed by Maharaja Lela rushed the bathhouse and speared Birch to death.

In the aftermath of the assassination of the British Resident, sporadic attacks against the British or their allies flickered across the three tin states. Turkish flags were spotted – that implied that a general uprising might be in progress. Jervois anxiously called for assistance, and troops were despatched from India and Hong Kong. The British pursued Birch's assassins and both the sultan and his old rival and co-conspirator Ismail fled into hiding. The suspected assassins, including Maharaja Lela, were rounded up and hanged. It did not take the British long to find the sultan, and Abdullah was exiled to the Seychelles – along with Raja Ismail and several rebellious datos. They would never return. For Swettenham, writing long after the event, this ruthless campaign accomplished in a few months what years of 'advice' would have failed to achieve. With Abdullah banished, the British rewarded Raja Yusuf (whose existence had come as such a surprise to Swettenham in 1874) by appointing him regent.

The creation of British Malaya was not in any sense a gentlemanly business of sending out a few 'Residents' to the Malay states and expecting the sultans to do what they were told. The Residential System was frequently resisted – and, if necessary, imposed by force of arms. Nevertheless, resistance to indirect rule was sporadic. As the British tightened their grip on the Malaya Peninsula, the Dutch were busy vanquishing the old Malay kingdom of Aceh in northern Sumatra. The 'Aceh Wars' were protracted and bloody. The last rebels were still fighting and dying as late as 1912. For many Acehenese today, the war has *never* ended – as successive Indonesian governments have repeatedly discovered to their cost. The Dutch colonial armies mapped out in blood the territorial borders of what, after the agonies of a world war, would become a modern Asian nation. Three points should be noted about Dutch strategy in the East Indies. The first is that relatively small numbers of European combatants, roughly equivalent to a single European military division, subdued and then pacified a vast new colonial estate step by step. The British deployed troops in Peninsula Malaya but on nothing like the same scale as the Dutch in the archipelago. Second, for the 37 million newly acquired colonial subjects of the Netherlands government, the idea of an 'Indonesian' identity was just a murmur and not yet a shout. The peoples of Java, for example, took little interest in what was happening to 'foreigners' in far away Sumatra. The final point is a direct consequence of the second. All colonial powers depend on collaborators. The Dutch took the practice of divide and rule to an extreme. At least 30,000 Javanese, Ambonese, Sundanese, Madurese, Bugis and Malay mercenary recruits joined in the violent conquest of the indigenous island realms of the vast and unruly archipelago of the Dutch East Indies. The Dutch exploitation of indigenous peoples as proxy colonial combatants would have lasting and ultimately calamitous consequences.

For those in the Colonial Office in London who had opposed the 'forward movement', the troubles in Perak proved their point. Direct intervention merely led to expensive wars. Jervois was accused of reckless sabre-rattling. In the aftermath of the 'Perak War' he resorted to more devious tactics – exploiting the ambitions of the ruler of Johor, Abu Bakar, to unite the fractious 'Negeri Sembilan' (meaning 'Nine Lands') states of Sungai Ujong, Jelebu, Johol and Rembau – with the sultan acting as a kind of proxy Resident. Then in the 1880s another bout of great power anxiety erupted in the Colonial Office in London. The French had got their perfidious hands on Indochina (Laos, Cochin China, Vietnam and Cambodia), and the worryingly busy Germans had already grabbed a few islands in the Pacific. After three wars, Burma was at last under control but in Siam the new Thai king, Chulalongkorn, was energetically importing European 'specialists' to help modernise his kingdom. Not all were British. Fears about the potential vulnerability of the northern Malay states bubbled up once again. The nightmare scenario for the British was a Germanised Siam pushing decisively into Kedah, Kelantan and Terengganu. The Malay state of Patani had long been broken up and absorbed by the Thai rulers. More than a decade after Clarke had cobbled together the Resident system at Pangkor the status of the Malay states remained vulnerable. The forward movement was again resurgent.

Lord Curzon, who became Viceroy of India at the turn of the century, put it like this: 'India is like a fortress [...] with mountains for her walls [...] beyond these walls extends a glacis of varying breadth and dimension.' That 'glacis' was formed by Malaya and Singapore. He went on: 'We do not want to occupy it, but we cannot afford to see it occupied by our foes. We are quite content to let it remain in the hands of our allies and friends, but if rivals and unfriendly influences creep up on it [...] we are compelled to intervene.' From Singapore a new governor, Frederick Weld, saw his mission as pushing British power and control right up to the border with Siam. He was persuasively backed by Swettenham – who believed himself the new Raffles, bringing civilisation and good government to Malays who would, he believed, benefit as much as the British.

After the signing of the Pangkor Treaty in 1874 it took nearly half a century for the British to erect that curious and ramshackle edifice of Crown Colonies and protectorates that came to be known as 'British Malaya'. By the end of the First World War, British Malaya comprised the old Straits Settlements and a federation of Malay states governed from Kuala Lumpur. Ever closer federation had been punctuated by rebellions and petty wars. Over time the British stripped more powers from the sultans. Federation left open the status of the troublesome but resource rich northern states. The final push to complete incorporation was yet again inspired by 'Germanophobia': the British, fearful that mysterious German engineers had been reported infiltrating into Kelantan, clinched a deal with the Thai government in 1909. All the northern states, with the exception of Patani, now became an integral part of British Malaya as the 'Unfederated Malay States'. Only Sultan Zainal Abidin of Terengganu held out. In 1914, the Turkish government allied itself with Germany and declared a global Jihad against France and Great Britain. Convinced that the infidel British would lose the war with the kaiser and the caliph, the devout sultan refused to comply with British demands. It was only in 1918, with the defeat of Germany and the collapse of the Ottoman Empire, that the new sultan, Mohammed Shah II, capitulated and accepted a Resident – who then forced him to abdicate. The Terengganu court in any event was bankrupt.

For its most privileged British residents this Malaya appeared to be a 'magical world'. After independence, memories of this equatorial paradise tugged at retired hearts and minds in the Home Counties. 'It was enough for me to fall for everything,' recalled Sjovald Cunyngham-Browne, 'for the mountains and plains and the streams and the empty coasts of sand so golden in the dusk; for the charm of the inhabitants, the elegance of their gestures, and, when young, the ineffable grace of their physique ...'. In reality, British Malaya was a tropical dystopia of simmering discontent, where tens of thousands of Chinese and Indian coolies toiled under a pitiless equatorial sun in plantations or sweated in tin mines to feed the coffers of empire.

The Plantation Realm

Tin began it all – but it was the viscous product of the Pará tree *Hevea brasiliensis* that would remake Southeast Asia into a vast plantation economy that made the different colonies of the region the fiscal engine houses of European wealth and power. The engine of colonial power was race.

Race has become, in the majority of modern human cultures, a dirty word. It carries multiple stigma of irrational prejudice, persecution, enslavement and, since the Second World War, the worst genocide in human history. It need hardly be pointed out that bigotry has not become extinct, but the idea of racial difference is no longer a driving force of state governance as it was in Nazi Germany. Not so in modern Malaysia. Malaysians today remain obsessed with different races and racial difference. And that's not surprising: race is integral to the Malaysian constitution. The reason why this modern nation state continues to ratify an obsolete and vicious idea is all to do with its colonial history.

The idea that humans are divided into distinct immutable types with distinct characteristics can be traced back at least as far as the biblical story of the sons of Noah – Shem, Ham and Japheth – who gave rise to the three races of man: the 'Semitic' (or Asiatic) peoples, the 'Hamitic' Africans and the 'Japhetic' types of Central Asia and Northern Europe. This classificatory system was also judgemental. Ham had witnessed the nakedness of his drunken father, Noah, and was cursed for telling his brothers. Later traditions in Judaism, Islam and Christianity associated Ham's transgression with the possession of black skin: he was 'cursed with blackness'. In the seventeenth century the story of the supposedly unfortunate Ham was used by Christian merchants to exonerate their treatment of black Africans. Likewise, Christian persecutors of Jews had invoked the alleged betrayal of Christ by Jewish religious authorities to vindicate pogroms and banishments. Such myths may seem arcane, but Holy Writ continued to infect emerging new ideas about the races of man that began to flourish in the early modern period to make sense of the remarkable diversity of peoples encountered by European explorers in Asia and Africa. The old classifications of biblical lore were suddenly in need of drastic revision. In the age of the encyclopaedists, it would be science that offered new solutions and classifications. Race and colonialism were closely interwoven from the start.

In the nineteenth century these new ideas of racial difference refashioned biblical myths under the aegis of science. The herculean efforts of eighteenth-century naturalists Carolus Linnaeus, Johann Friedrich Blumenbach and the Comte de Buffon, reduced all flora and fauna, including humans, to members of distinct species and subspecies. Blumenbach was the first to display a graduated range of human skull types. By the mid-nineteenth century a crude appropriation of Darwin's theory of 'evolution by means of natural selection' led 'Social Darwinists' to propose not only the existence of different races, but that these races had separately evolved to form qualitatively different, hierarchically arranged subspecies. They placed white-skinned Europeans at the apex of a human pyramid of races with black-skinned Africans at the bottom. As Europeans took on the white man's burden of empire building this new racial ideology, which was sanctified by Science with a capital S, turned out to be a persuasive way of condoning severely restricted democracy at home and colonial authoritarianism abroad. Europeans were now morally obligated to govern lesser races regarded as incapable of self-organisation. This was the order of things.

In India and Southeast Asia, British rule was underpinned by rigid classifications – stereotypes, in other words – that captured and solidified the multitude of different Asian ethnicities, as if on the silvered plate of a Victorian daguerreotype. Ethnicity was reconfigured as race – and race justified imperial rule for, like the 'Sons of Ham' in Africa, Asians were incapable of proper government. This meant they had to *be* governed.

The edifice of all colonial administrations rested on the foundation of stereotypes. The naturalist Alfred Russell Wallace concluded that 'The intellect of the Malay race seems rather deficient. They are incapable of anything beyond the simplest combinations of ideas and have little taste or energy for the acquirement of knowledge.' Frank Swettenham, in his book *British Malaya* described the Malays as a 'shy and reserved race' who were 'inherently lazy', with 'no stomach for really hard and continuous work …'. The typical Malay was 'hospitable, generous, extravagant, a gambler, a coxcomb …'. He was 'Nature's Gentleman', blessed with singular dignity and good manners but fickle, indolent and, to borrow a phrase from Kipling's poem 'Recessional', 'a lesser breed without the Law'.

Swettenham knew very well that Malays were capable of resisting colonial rule – but by the time he wrote *British Malaya* he seems to have forgotten all about the Malay assassins who despatched J.W.W. Birch: 'you will not wish for a better servant, no more pleasant and cheery companion' he rhapsodised. Malays were placid, compliant and servile. These stereotypes would become the immoveable mental furniture of colonial minds. In his classic study *The Myth of the Lazy Native* (1977), Syed Hussein Alatas showed that before the colonial period Malays had been active in farming, industry, trade, commerce, war and government: it was after the arrival of the Portuguese that the Malay merchant class declined. 'Natives' did not avoid permanent routine work but disdained the 'exploitative type in other people's mines and plantations. Refusing to work for wages was, Alatas argued, a rational choice. There were 'Lazy Malays' – but they belonged to the upper class, above all the native rulers and chiefs paid off by the colonial rulers. The purpose of the 'image of the indolent, dull, backward and treacherous native' was to reinforce dependency: 'requiring assistance to climb the ladder of progress'.

The French anthropologist Claude Levi-Strauss argued that myths were essentially binary systems energised by opposites. In the colonial mind the lazy Malays were the antithesis of the industrious Chinese. British attitudes to the Chinese were ambivalent – and volatile. Remember that 'the Chinese' *did not exist*.

They had to be constructed from the many different language and dialect groups who came to Southeast Asia over many centuries. To be sure, many Chinese do have a passion for educating their children and for wealth creation. Migrant people work hard. Chinese communities are rarely stagnant. They are dynamic and volatile. Most Europeans who lived and worked in the Straits learnt to have a grudging respect for the Chinese they met or partnered in business. Singapore magnate Tan Kim Cheng cultivated mutually beneficial bonds with the Straits government and W.H. Read, the architect of the 'forward movement'. Another British businessman declared that the Chinese 'are, as a race, capable of civilisation of the highest kind. They have great mercantile capability: we are pleased to see them flocking to [Malaya and Singapore] as they do in thousands.' At the same time there was resentment: 'Whenever money is to be acquired [...] there will be found the greedy Chinese.' Colonial paternalism did not work with the Chinese, though not for want of trying. Swettenham admitted that 'The Chinese have, under direction, made the protected [Malay] states what they are. They are the bees who suck the honey from every profitable undertaking ...'. But: 'It is almost hopeless to expect to make friends with a Chinaman ...'. Resentment shaded into *anxiety*. In the nineteenth century the British both feared and exploited the Chinese secret societies; later they would grossly exaggerate the threat posed by the Chinese-dominated Malayan Communist Party (MCP).

The Malay peninsula and the archipelago had been tied to the Indian subcontinent for at least two millennia. It was Hindu peoples from southern India who created the entrepôt civilisation of the Bujang Valley. At the end of the eighteenth century, with the rise of the British East India Company, Indian migration eastward across the Bay of Bengal to the Malay Peninsula began to increase. In 1824 there were just 756 people of Indian origin resident in Singapore; by 1860 that number had risen to 13,000. The majority of the Indian settlers were Muslim men from southern India. Many of the new arrivals married Muslim Malay women. Malays began referring to their children as *Jawi Peranakan* – *Jawi* is the Arabic word for the Malay Archipelago, *Peranakan* is Malay meaning 'born of'. (Other variations include *Jawi Pekan* and *Peranakan Kling*.) The new *Jawi Peranakan* community became wealthy and invested its money in culture and education. In 1888, Munshi Muhammad Said bin Dada Muhyiddin founded the first Malay language newspaper, the *Jawi Peranakkan*. This remarkably vibrant community was just one aspect of the Indian revolution. Many Indians found work as government clerks in the Straits' administration. Sikhs were recruited as policemen. Those who belonged to the 'Chettiar' sub-caste conventionally turned to money lending. Before the Indian Mutiny, the East India Company recruited its native clerks mainly among the Singhalese – and this had a direct impact on migration to the Malay Peninsula. English-speaking Jaffna Tamils, who had a good idea of British administrative laws and customs, streamed across the Indian Ocean to do the same kind of jobs in the Straits. Many of the European planters in Malaya had also worked in Ceylon and felt at ease with Tamil workers, whom they considered easier to manage than Chinese plantation workers. For some time emigration from southern India was very strictly regulated – but in the last decades of the nineteenth century demand for cheap labour increased so quickly that most restrictions were abolished. The Indian community that rapidly took shape at the beginning of the twentieth century was just as heterogeneous as the Chinese one. The *Jawi Peranakan* formed a wealthy, culturally unique elite, with strong ties to both the Malay community and the British colonial government. The majority of later migrants came to Malaya as plantation workers through the *kangani* system. While Ceylonese Jaffna Tamils dominated the estates as supervisors, and regarded themselves as a managerial class, their labourers originated from all over the subcontinent, belonged to a multitude of castes, and spoke mutually incomprehensible languages. The Indian working community was fragmented, impoverished, and cut off from other workers.

These great movements of peoples from southern China and from India to Southeast Asia have overshadowed the way the Malay community was itself continuously reconfigured by migration. For the colonial government this presented problems of definition. In the 'Malay Reservations Act' of 1913, the colonial government defined, for the first time, a Malay as 'any person belonging to any Malayan race', who 'habitually spoke Malay' or 'any other Malayan Language' and 'professes the Muslim religion'. But this definition was a kind of categorical fudge, reflecting more than a century of confusing discussion and debate, that began when Raffles insisted: 'I cannot but consider the Melayu nation as one people, speaking one language, though spread over so wide a space …'. This was all very well, but later colonial administrators became increasingly baffled by the complexities of ethnic identity in the 'Malay World'. Just who was a 'Malay'? Did the term apply to *all* the native peoples of the region? The answer seemed to be yes, for as the British tightened their grip on the 'Malay States' it made sense to insist that 'Malay' identity applied to 'any Malayan race', i.e. not Chinese or Indian that inhabited the peninsula, as well as northern Borneo. Something rather different was taking place in the Dutch-ruled islands of the archipelago. The colonial recasting of Malay racial identity shaped the way 'Malays' regarded themselves. This was already apparent in the writings of Munshi Abdullah, who in the *Hikayat Abdullah* uses the Malay word *bangsa* in the sense of race: for example the 'bangsa Inggeris' (the English race), the 'bangsa Arab' – and the 'bangsa Malay'. When he scolds the Malay rulers, Abdullah implies that *the* Malays suffer under their tyrannous rule. His definition of 'Malayness' modifies the older *Kerajaan* idea of the Malay world as a community of monarchies bound together by a top-down transmission of courtly values. What is especially interesting is that Abdullah understands the Malay *bangsa* as inclusive and capable of absorbing outsiders: he himself, he points out, is a 'Tamilian of Southern Hindustan'.

By 1913 such ethnic boundaries had become less forgiving. That crucial phrase 'any Malayan race' sanctioned almost continuous enlargement of the Malay *bangsa*, even though this diluted any notion that all 'Malays' were indigenous to the peninsula. In the northern Malay states, for example, Thai-speaking Muslims and Malay-speaking Thais, formerly called 'Sam-Sam', were counted as 'Malay'. Throughout the twentieth century, Malay-speaking peoples from Sumatra and Java, with distinctive cultural identities, have flowed back and forth across the Straits. These Minangkabau, Rawa, Mandailang, Acehnese, Batak and Javanese peoples began thinking and referring to themselves as Malays within a single generation. Unlike the Chinese and Indian migrants, these new arrivals in the peninsula spoke the same language and worshipped the same God. It suited the colonial government to simplify the human landscape for its own purposes.

The Power of Numbers

The British colonial government used a banal administrative tool to mould Asian ethnic complexity into a settled domain of different races. This was the census. The census both defined and reinforced racial differences. The bureaucratic apparatus of census taking mirrored the territorial or quantitative expansion of British Malaya but at the same time crystallised ethnic categories in terms of racially defined, impermeable boundaries. The encounter between the census enumerator and the colonial subject was highly charged: it was the moment when the individual entered the record-taking process as a racial type. In 1871, the first modern census took in only the Straits Settlements of Singapore, Penang and Malacca – in other words, port cities and their hinterlands. As the British 'forward movement' reached into the interior of the peninsula the census enumerators followed in the wake of the newly appointed Residents: in 1891, state censuses were taken in Selengor, Perak, Sungai Ujong (later part of Negeri Sembilan) and Pahang. In 1901, the colonial government conducted the first unified census of the Federated Malay States – and ten years later carried out the same exercise for both Federated and Unfederated Malay States. In 1921, the colonial government launched a new census encompassing the Straits Settlements, the Federated Malay States and the Unfederated Malay States – *all* 'British Malaya'.

In Malaya and other colonial territories the impact of census taking was profound. The administrators of the earliest colonial censuses appear to have been 'feeling their way' – bewildered by the astonishing variety of possible 'nationalities'. The history of census taking shows a pattern of strategic simplification that replaces an ethnic grid with a racial one. In 1871, the census enumerators worked from a simple tabular set of classifications. At the top it listed 'Western' peoples: Europeans and Americans, Armenians and Jews. Next came 'Eurasians', meaning people of mixed inheritance, and then followed a list of no less than twenty-three populations from A for Abyssinians to S for Singhalese.

By 1881 the census had been broadened to include Chinese dialect groups or 'tribes'. From 1891 major headings signal a sustained effort by the colonial authorities to harmonise and control the ethnic complexities of their expanding colonial property: we now have 'Europeans', 'Eurasians', 'Chinese', 'Malays and other Natives of the Archipelago', 'Tamils and other Natives of India', and then 'Other Nationalities'. 'Race' was alluded to in an appendix. Then between 1901 and 1911, 'Races' completely replaces 'Nationalities': 'Malays and Allied Races'. In the next decades the census takers tinkered with details but retained this broad racial straitjacketing.

In British Malaya, the publication of census data and associated reports, which grew longer and more prolix over time, was the responsibility of the Department of Statistics. Each report carried the name of a senior colonial administrator. What they had to say is often revealing. In 1931, for example, Charles Vlieland offered his reflections on the meaning of 'race'. He admitted that 'it is in fact impossible to define the sense in which the term "Race" is used for census purposes …'. He goes on: 'it is, in reality, a judicious blend, for practical ends, of the ideas of geographic and ethnographic origin, political allegiance, and racial and social affinities and sympathies …'. Vlieland admits that 'most Oriental peoples have themselves no clear conception of race …'. and points out: 'The Malay, for instance, habitually regards adherence to Islam in much the same light as a European regards a racial distinction …'. He points out that: 'a Chinese convert to Islam who describes himself as 'Melayu' is to all intents and purposes a member of the Malay community'. So he proposes that the idea has to be *made accessible* to 'the Oriental': when the census enumerator asks 'What is your race?' he is asking 'What is that man?' The implication of Vlieland's remarkably candid rumination is that the census is a kind of education in racial thinking so that: 'Race is used in the sense that it is understood by *the man in the street* …'.

The Department of Statistics was staffed by an elite governing class that regarded Asians as employees or servants, rarely as friends and colleagues. Over time, as the British crystallised the territorial identity of Malaya, the census data reflected less and less the ethnic complexity of Southeast Asia, and more a kind of European racial fantasy concocted as an instrument of political control. When 'Race' replaced the more neutral 'Nationality' after 1891, it signalled acceptance of the hierarchy of qualitatively distinct races and the innate superiority of Europeans who were morally responsible for leading lesser races up the ladder of civilisation. The racial categories – Malay, Chinese, Indian and others – set in stone by the Department of Statistics, was a shorthand for supposedly innate racial attributes. The Chinese were cunning and avaricious; Malays lazy and shiftless; Indians amenable workers ('the mild Hindoo'), and so on. As the British colonial nobility co-opted the Malay rulers, they saw their own qualities reflected in the sultans and their courts. The majority of colonial administrators had been educated at English public schools and in many cases at Oxford or Cambridge

(Charles Vlieland – Exeter School and Balliol College, Oxford). 'British Malaya' was jointly the creation of an increasingly compliant and well-rewarded Malay elite and the British.

The Rubber Men

Census taking was not a scholastic exercise. It was a means of quantifying and controlling the working peoples of colonial Malaya. If the Indian Raj was the jewel in the imperial Crown, Malaya was the backyard factory of empire; its throbbing engines fuelled and greased by the people Karl Marx called the 'disposable reserve army' of Asian labourers. In the mid- to late nineteenth century the Chinese tin miners, who flooded to the west coast Malay states such as Perak and Selangor, enriched the empire. Just as the revenues extracted by Dutch colonists in the East Indies fuelled an economic miracle in the Netherlands, so too did the wealth of Malaya and other colonies feed the coffers of the most powerful imperial nation in the world. Since the discovery of the big tin fields in Perak at Larut and Kinta, the impact of the Chinese as workers and entrepreneurs on the mining industry had been spectacular. By the end of the century, at least 80,000 Chinese coolies worked in mines owned by European and Chinese entrepreneurs. Capital meant innovations like steam pumps and enormous new dredgers, and innovation led to bigger profits. In the first decade of the twentieth century, another raw material eclipsed tin – and would come to symbolise the world of colonial Malaya for nearly sixty years. This was, of course, the viscous product of the Pará rubber tree, *Hevea brasiliensis*.

The coming of rubber to Asia is encrusted with myth. The traditional hero of the story was a maverick planter called Henry Wickham, who smuggled 70,000 hevea seeds from their native habitat in the Amazon rainforest of Brazil and brought them to the eminent botanist Joseph Hooker, the Director of the Royal Botanic Gardens at Kew. Wickham became celebrated as the self-proclaimed 'father of rubber', who had literally seeded the great plantations of Asia and ruined the Brazilian wild rubber trade. If the rubber business had a parent it was not Henry Wickham, but the British government and the India Office in London, which had begun looking for ways of exploiting wild rubber long before he had thought of collecting those famous seeds on the banks of the Tapajós River. It is true that the Pará rubber tree is native to the Amazon rainforest. Three thousand years ago the Olmec and Maya extracted primitive rubber from the trees to make balls. In 1839 the discovery of 'vulcanisation', by Thomas Hancock and Thomas Goodyear, revolutionised the potential of hevea. The process, in brief, cross bonds the long polymer chains of natural rubber thus making processed rubber less sticky and more elastic. Hancock used rubberised leather to manufacture waterproof mackintoshes. Demand for wild rubber exploded – and there was a rubber boom in Amazonia. The British government took note. How could Brazil's monopoly be broken?

In 1859 a former British naval officer called Clements Markham led an expedition to Peru to procure seeds of the cinchona plant. The bark is a source of quinine, which was the first effective treatment (though not a cure) for malaria. Markham successfully established cinchona plantations in India and Ceylon. The mass production of quinine vastly improved the lives and survival rates of the British servants of empire. Rewarded with a knighthood, Sir Clements began looking around for other potentially lucrative botanical treasures and soon focused his attention on the Pará tree and its sticky sap. Markham acquired a handful of hevea seeds from the British Consul in Pará – the port-of-entry to the rubber lands of the Amazon basin. He despatched them to Hooker who did some experiments but failed to make the hevea seeds germinate. It was at this point that the frustrated Hooker contacted Wickham, who was eking out a precarious livelihood in Santarem in Brazil. Most of his family had perished in this disease-infested Amazonian backwater. Wickham then collected the famous 70,000 hevea seeds which he despatched to Liverpool, where a Customs Office Bill of Entry notes the arrival of 'The Amazonas' and a cargo of '171 cases of rubber'. When they arrived at Kew, Hooker's staff immediately planted the hevea seeds in carefully prepared seedbeds. Evidently it was an urgent matter. The archives of the Royal Botanic Garden show that the decision to transplant hevea was taken at the highest levels of the India Office. Botany would have to serve the interests of empire. A few weeks later a relieved Hooker reported that 2,397 had germinated: less than 10 per cent. Some 2,000 seedlings were then sent to Ceylon and Singapore. The seeds' story is not quite as simple as it might seem. Hooker had not taken any chances. He had also sent botanist Robert Cross to Brazil in case Wickham's mission failed, and Cross had also returned to Kew with hevea seeds – so there is some uncertainty about the paternity of the seedlings that ended up in Singapore. Cross may be a better candidate as 'father of the rubber plantation industry'. In any event, H.J. Murton, Director of the Singapore Botanic Garden, planted his twenty-two seedlings – and every one of them survived. In Perak, the British Resident Hugh Low planted hevea seeds in the garden of his residency in Kuala Kangsar – also with great success. So rather than being Henry Wickham's story, the key figure was Sir Clements Markham who was himself acting on behalf of the Secretary of State for India. The coming of wild rubber to Southeast Asia was managed, not fortuitous.[9]

Rubber was not an overnight success story. In Singapore, the irector of the Royal Botanic Gardens, Henry Ridley, who was obsessed with the potential of wild rubber, was dubbed 'Rubber Ridley' and less politely 'Mad Ridley'. A rubber tree takes six years to reach 'profitable maturity' and wild rubber simply did not look like a good enough investment. Then in the last decade of the nineteenth century, blight ravaged the coffee and tea plantations of Sumatra and Malaya. At the same time, sugar planters were hit by intense competition from the European beet industry. It was a Chinese businessman and philanthropist who showed the way forward. In 1895, Tan Chay Yan 'interplanted' hevea seedlings with tapioca on his forty-three-acre estate at Bukit Lintang near Malacca. In the meantime, John Lloyd Dunlop, the Scottish inventor, had patented the pneumatic rubber tyre, commercially produced by the Dunlop Company from 1898. In the same year 'Mad Ridley' reported receiving requests for 1 million seeds on a single day. The bicycle and then the automobile pushed demand for rubber to astronomical levels. By 1908 rubber was being planted and tapped in every Malayan state. The triumph of rubber can be illustrated by the fortunes of the Ramsden family, who controlled numerous plantation businesses at the turn of the century. The family owned the 'Penang Sugar Estates', which began planting rubber rather half-heartedly in 1900 but were reluctant to give up sugar. The correspondence of a company executive called E.L. Hamilton shows that he worried about labour shortages, a possibly fickle market – and the vulnerability of the hevea trees to white ants and root disease. As it turned out, a plague of rats attacked not the rubber trees but the sugar beet: they had sharp teeth and a sweet tooth. Five years later, Sir John Ramsden had switched entirely to rubber planting. Penang Sugar changed its name to Penang Rubber.

As with coffee, the global rubber market was chronically unstable. But by 1915 rubber had overtaken tin as Malaya's most valuable export – and was worth 40 per cent of the colony's total export value. Rubber accounted for four-fifths by volume of all agricultural output. The first rubber estates were small-scale affairs run by owner operators, but as the production boomed bigger conglomerates began to dominate the market. On the eve of the First World War, the Asian plantations had overtaken the Amazonian growers for the first time. The Brazilian industry would never recover.

These were the halcyon days of rubber: the 'Golden Age' of the planters. But the big new Malayan plantations with their great armies of cheap regimented labour and scientific methods had an inherent weakness. They produced so much rubber that buyers could stockpile for their needs – and so the growers faced a buyer's market. From peak prices of six to eight shillings per pound from the boom years around 1910, three years later rubber was selling at between one and sixpence to two shillings. Rubber prices would never stabilise again. Demand climbed during the war but plummeted again in 1918. The rubber industry was for ever afterwards plagued not by blight or infestation but rollercoaster price fluctuations. The typical rubber planter, like Sir John Ramsden, was a committed advocate of free trade. But the industry's lobby group in London, the Rubber Growers' Association, demanded help. The result was the Stevenson Plan proposed by Sir John Stevenson, who had made his pile from Johnnie Walker whisky. His proposal was that rubber producers should be allocated strict quotas to prevent overproduction pushing down prices. The Stevenson Plan, which the American rubber tyre king Harvey S. Firestone accused of price fixing, was disastrous. It inflicted misery on small-scale producers – and in colonial records we hear for the first time of the Chinese 'squatters', who had begun planting land with rubber trees illegally in Johor. The Governor of the Straits Settlement, Sir Cecil Clementi, recommended 'punitive action'. For producers who buckled down, the plan was so complex that few understood its most intricate workings. The plan, it became all too evident, did not serve British interests. For the Dutch planters in Sumatra, it was a bonanza. According to the American firm Lee Tire & Rubber, production of rubber in the Dutch East Indies increased by 300 per cent between 1922 and 1927. Most of the 'Dutch' rubber was produced by native smallholders. As a Goodyear executive commented: 'it was the little brown man who in the end broke the British monopoly.' The plan was scrapped in 1928. It would not be mourned.

The end of the Stevenson era coincided with the Great Crash of 1929 and a global depression. Across the vast plantation world of Southeast Asia tens of thousands of workers were laid off. There was widespread misery and distress – and the emergence of a vociferous new labour movement. By the end of the 1930s the worst of the Depression was over and rubber prices and production had begun to rise again. By the time Rupert Emerson began research in Malaya, the total area of land 'alienated' for agriculture was 6 million acres – 5 million of which was planted for the great 'money-crop' – rubber. On the eve of the Second World War the Malayan rubber industry was larger than before the Great Crash. Though smallholders were making significant inroads, 75 per cent of the total acreage was still in European hands. The rubber estates were massive industrial enterprises with enormous workforces and infrastructure. In the mid-1930s the British Dunlop estate in Johor was treating 7,000lbs of rubber every day in its on-site factory, which was equipped with state-of-the-art processing machinery. Plantations like this one had their own light railways and electricity-generating equipment, as well as workshops, hospitals and – in some cases – schools for the tappers' children.

For the British or French or Dutch planter the rubber estate was a world within a world. 'He hadn't much to talk about but rubber and games, tennis, you know, and golf and shooting …'., Somerset Maugham wrote of a planter called Bronson, 'he had the mind of a boy of eighteen. You know how many fellows when they come out east seem to stop growing.' Many of the young Europeans employed on the rubber estates of Southeast Asia worked as assistant planters or 'creepers'. They were the backbone of estate operations, because a colour bar prevented coolies rising above the level of clerk. The 'creepers' were an odd bunch. James Mill said that the main purpose of empire was to 'provide outdoor relief for the British upper classes'. Many were misfits or black sheep exiled by their families. Others were restless fellows who had fled enervating office jobs in the City. In Malaya, at least one-third of the assistant planters were Scottish. The Ramsden company archive is chockfull of reports of assistants sacked because they were alcoholic, prone to violence, mentally ill, or just bone idle time-wasters. A surprising number ended up destitute on the streets of Singapore, waiting or begging for a passage home, sometimes in vain. For others colonial service offered a step up. They enjoyed powers that were not easy to attain in the normal run of things at home. These 'Tuan Besars' and 'Tuan Kechils' – the 'great gentlemen' and 'junior masters' – who strutted about their domains in stained khakis, tropical whites and solar topees, periodically lunging at coiled snakes with a stick, were the petty lords of all they surveyed. A good number were unashamed racists who fervently believed in the civilising ethos of empire and the natural inferiority of native lesser breeds. The best and the brightest admittedly turned into decent linguists – learning the rudiments or more of Tamil, Malay, Javanese and the Chinese dialects often with the assistance of Asian 'wives' known as 'sleeping dictionaries'. Work was hard and most of the Tuans had to endure recurrent bouts of debilitating malaria. After a day on the estate, checking and rechecking the work of the tappers, they fled to their bungalows to sip whisky *stengahs*, and bitter English beer. Who can blame them? The Dutch, too, were 'tremendous soaks', who could, as one memoir admitted, 'put away an incredible amount of beer at an incredible pace'. An Australian journalist reported from Papua that an appropriate coat of arms for the territory would be 'a white man rampant, with a boy couchant, bearing a bottle of beer proper'. 'Beer, Boy!' was the most distinctive cry of the species. Many of the French planters in Indochina were veterans of the Foreign Legion – and some were distinctly unsavoury types. The British recruited their planters from the 'great' public schools such as Eton and Rugby, or 'lesser' public schools and elite state grammar schools (many of the Scots had been educated at Fettes School near Edinburgh). Life in the tropics was rarely comfortable. It was often lonely. The working day began in the cool before dawn – and no one, Tuan or coolie, stopped work until the setting of the hot and merciless sun. A Scot called Ian Matheson recalled that on his estate in Sumatra he had to live in a leaking bungalow with no running water or electricity, and a 'thunder box which needs no description'. Leopold Ainsworth, who was sent to an estate near Penang, could not forget the 'miserable dreary light' of the single oil lamp in his quarters, and a malodorous mildew-ridden mattress and rotting 'Dutch Widow' pillow. With the onset of the monsoon, a 'solid, streaming, crashing wall of water' broke through the roof. He had first come to the estate after a long journey by cart. He arrived late and his new employer, a cantankerous old Scot, had whipped the cart driver with cruel abandon and retired, exhausted, to bed. Supper was a 'disgusting meal' of tinned soup with ants floating on its greasy surface. Coffee was strained through an old sock. Ainsworth was woken the next morning, bowels churning, by a barrage of hammering on his door and a cry of 'Get up you lazy bastard!' Strong drink was a refuge. Not a few sodden, prematurely aged, and pickled Tuans lost their wits and ended up in the Singapore Lunatic Asylum before being shipped back home [...] if they were lucky. The planter elite was a predominantly male enclave. The rubber companies actively discouraged marriage. 'Creepers' were forbidden to tie the knot until the fourth year of their contracts. Lonely, and far from hearth and home, it was unusual for a young planter not to seek relief and solace in Malay 'kip shops', or in the arms of Asian concubines known as 'Keeps' (short for 'housekeeper') in Malaya. Some planters treated their Asian mistresses with respect, fathered families and sent their children to school. A tiny minority of European planters married their 'Keeps', but the hypocritical Victorian values of the colonial elite that informed the poisonous gossip of the club and tea party spurned the mixed-race Eurasian children of these unions. Most 'Keeps' were sent packing with their light-skinned children when a respectable 'Memsahib' finally turned up to share the planter's world.

The privations suffered by the European planters in the tropics should be set against the harrowing privations endured by the coolie labourers who toiled in their thousands on their estates. 'Coolie' is a demeaning term but it is unavoidable. ('Do not use this word' insists Longman's Dictionary.) The great diaspora of indentured Asians that unfolded at the same time as millions of Europeans fled the distress and unemployment brought by industrialisation in Britain and Europe to the Americas and Australia was in fact a rescue package for colonial sugar plantations in the West Indies. In August 1834, the British abolished slavery in most of their empire by Act of Parliament.[10] This humanitarian gesture coincided with the rapid emergence of a globalised economy that had an insatiable appetite for cheap labour. As one British Royal Commissioner put it: 'Every consideration of humanity [...] must concur with a due regard for the interests of property ...'. In other words, slaves would need to be replaced. In the rapidly expanding colonial world, the coolie filled the labour gap. Many *were* slaves. Famine in India and war in southern China made 'Cooliedom' alluring for millions of Asians. As indentured labourers, coolies endured incessant corporal punishment, wage arrears and the notorious 'double cut system' that cut two days' wages for every day missed. This great movement of Asian peoples began in 1829, reached a peak mid-century – and only came to an end in 1929 when the system was finally ended.

Only a tiny minority of coolies who came to French Indochina, British Malaya and the Dutch East Indies were native to Southeast Asia, which was turning into great emporium of labour.[11] The majority originated from densely populated and troubled regions of China, India and Java. In ports all over Asia, rickety ships disgorged armies of men who were herded into a 'coolie ghat', where officials logged names (as they heard them), place of origin and date of arrival in a register. Each person was photographed, then housed in sweltering sheds before being individually selected by plantation owners. The 'ghat' was not much different from a slave market. In Indochina the French barred the import of Chinese coolies and relied on the so-called 'rice deficit' regions of Tonkin and northern Annam to procure labourers. Coolies enriched European plantation owners and transformed the human landscape of Southeast Asia. By 1911, Malays made up a mere 7 per cent of the workforce on the rubber plantations in Malaya – rising to just under 13 per cent by 1940. The hunger for coolie labour was insatiable but since the prices of rubber and tin fluctuated, often wildly, plantation labour had to be dispensable. The colonial economy thus acted like a vast bellows sucking in labour forces in times of plenty and spewing them out when prices dropped.

By 1912 some 550,000 Tamils had been brought from India to Ceylon, where they worked in the plantations alongside 150,000 Singhalese labourers. By the late 1920s more than half a million migrant workers toiled in Ceylon. By 1941, on the eve of the Japanese invasion, 350,000 coolies worked in the rubber plantations in Malaya: over 220,000 from India and 86,000 from China. British Malaya, the world's largest producer of rubber, sucked in these enormous human reserves and acted as a distribution centre, funnelling the great coolie streams to the Dutch East Indies. The flood of Chinese workers, which was known as the 'pig business', began to slow when reports trickled back about the treatment of workers on the plantations. A new generation of Chinese nationalists resented what they regarded as a new kind of slave trade. The coolie supply business was managed by rapacious Asian middle men, known as 'Crimps', who sold Chinese labourers, or 'Kongsi men', to plantation owners at $10 a head. Like the European slavers, these labour contractors held new recruits in 'pig stations' in the ports of southern China until sufficient numbers had been recruited to make up a cargo for shipment south. This was, strictly speaking, a system of indentured labour, for the Kongsi men owed money to the 'Crimps' for transportation costs and sundry expenses. These debts could take years to pay off. The moral distance between slavery and a system of indentured labour was a narrow one. According to British planter Leopold Ainsworth the Kongsis had joined a labour force that was 'to all intents and purposes comprised of slaves'. The colonial authorities made some efforts to reform these practices but with only limited success. It was a maxim of British rule that no one race should predominate in Malaya, and from quite early on colonial administrators fretted about the status of the 'native' Malays. The cornerstone of colonial power is a compliant 'native elite'. It would be disastrous if that elite withered away. The coolie diaspora that sustained the colonial economies of Southeast Asia would lead to a fundamental demographic revolution that had, the British rightly feared, unpredictable consequences. They were creating a new working class, a plantation proletariat that from early on showed signs of radicalisation. This was why the British came to prefer the supposedly more tractable Indian coolies from the Madras region, the Tamil districts and the Coromandel Coast to the better organised, often defiant and frequently rebellious Chinese. The Chinese Revolution that overturned the Ching dynasty in 1911 reverberated across the world of the overseas Chinese. The Governor of the Straits Settlements, Sir Fredereick Weld, hoped that the 'peccable and easily governed' Indians would be a counterpoise to the Chinese.

The British struggled to regularise this human traffic – which one official condemned as 'a regularly organised system of kidnapping'. Efforts to reform the system of recruitment were rarely effectual. Tran Tu Binh (1907–67), the

Vietnamese communist and labour organiser, wrote a visceral memoir of the coolie life. Recruiting advertisements for the French plantations overflowed, he said, with 'sugar and honey'. Once the French steamers docked at Saigon the cowed and bewildered new recruits entered a frightening world of threats and violence. As they emerged from the foetid holds to stumble down narrow gangplanks, Tran says that French and Vietnamese guards swarmed like flies, flailing about them with clubs and bellowing insults: 'exactly like a concentration camp'. After miserable days in a holding depot the recruits would be trucked to plantations in Cochin China or crammed into rickety river steamers and sent upriver to Cambodia. They were sucked into a kind of total institution – the plantations were mini states with their own rules and regulations and governed by tyrannical European managers. The coolie found himself in a foreign country, surrounded by wild animals and malicious insects, where the drab and dusty hevea lines stretched endlessly to the distant horizon. It was a world of dirt, poor hygiene, foul food, disease and epidemic. Malaria and dengue fever were endemic as were tropical ulcers, anaemia and beriberi – and the plantations were periodically ravaged by water-transmitted diseases such as dysentery and cholera. Harder to quantify was the psychological toll of depression and other mental illnesses that blighted the coolie's world. In 1919, a Dutch writer wrote about conditions in the rubber district of Asahan in Sumatra:

> At the point of destination [for the labourers], there was no accommodation whatsoever. Mud and dirt were their mattress. Many were starving because they had sold their rice rations to some sly Malay [...] There were no permanent houses [...] Mortality was high, reaching as much as 30% because of the appallingly poor washing facilities.

Many coolies suffered injuries from falling trees, or were bitten by poisonous snakes and insects. Their feet were frequently lacerated by sharp slivers of bamboo that lay strewn on paths and tracks. These agonising wounds usually turned septic. Festering bamboo injuries must have been a common sight, for the Dutch came to call all their plantation workers 'stinkers'. Conditions were not much better on the 'Coolie Lines' in Malaya. In 1890, as the rubber boom was just taking off, Dr S. Patrao, the acting civil surgeon in Negapatam in India, complained about the 'deplorable' death rate on rubber plantations in Malaya. He blamed the 'unhealthy conditions of most of the estates, and the climatic influence, overwork'. A British manager complained about 'weaklings from India [...] who build up our hospital bill', but the Ramsden company archives show that the Indian doctor was not exaggerating. Conditions on the British estates could be just as lethal as those on the notorious Dutch plantations: in some cases the mortality rate was higher than 30 per cent. It was only under persistent pressure from the British 'India Immigration Committee' that the Ramsden company managers agreed to do anything to reduce such heinous rates by, for example, supplying fresh water. The plantation gulag was a realm of violence. Leopold Ainsworth witnessed numerous cruel punishments – and came to enjoy administering retribution himself as 'a new and rather amusing form of sport'. On one occasion he witnessed a manager 'quivering with rage' while confronting a group of coolies who had refused to continue working because their pay day had been postponed. With the estate 'Creepers' covering the 'mutineers' with Schneider rifles, he 'beat the stuffing out of them'. Workers were often referred to as 'boys' – as in 'Beer, boy!' A good number of the estate managers and their assistants had been educated in a society that relished the corporal punishment of children. In their eyes, mutinous coolies were a lower form of the recalcitrant younger boys they had flogged in their youth. The colonial administration did not turn a blind eye to the arbitrary violence of the Malayan estates. Europeans who assaulted workers could be fined, sacked and arrested. But they had to step a long way over the line. On a Malayan estate in 1910, a 'creeper' called R.C. Gray beat two Javanese women to within an inch of their lives, and the police were forced to step in. His boss, General Manager Mr William Duncan, refused to sack Gray because he 'got on so well with the natives' – so he was fined and quietly packed off to another estate.

Like the slaves of the American plantations, the coolies resisted through the cultural weapons of religion and song. One folksong lamented the life of the bonded labourer with these eloquent words:

> I hoe all day and cannot sleep at night
> Today my whole body aches, Damnation to you arkatis. [recruiters]
> I have toiled day and night
> from the moment I entered your house.
> The skin of my body has dried
> And happiness has become but a dream …[12]

It is hardly surprising that the Malays and other ethnic groups like the Bataks in Sumatra, the Khmers in French Indochina and the Papuans in Australian New Guinea chose to resist the labour economies of the colonial plantations. To become a wage labourer meant submitting to the rigid and merciless rhythms of the working day that were enforced by plantation managers. This perfectly rational choice angered the European managerial class. A Danish writer, quoted by John Tully, complained that: 'Mentally, the Papuans and Melanesians range with European children of about twelve years of age […] The white man's device for reckoning time is beyond their comprehension.' The plantation revolution overturned the natural time of seasons and the rhythms of dawn and dusk, wet and dry seasons, the monsoon, planting seasons and traditional rites and festivals. Wage labour was despised as unnatural, unpleasant and unnecessary.

The plantations would be one of the main battlefields of the Malayan Emergency. The seeds of revolution had been sowed like the mythical dragon's teeth by the cruelties of the coolie diaspora.

Indirect Rule

In 1932, a young American academic called Rupert Emerson arrived in Malaya. A graduate of Harvard and the author of a well-received book on modern Germany, Emerson had been awarded a travel and study grant by the 'Bureau of International Research'. He travelled all over Malaya and Indonesia – and ventured into Siam and French Indochina. Emerson returned to Harvard full of outrage and with a voluminous collection of research materials. His now classic study *Malaysia: a Study in Direct and Indirect Rule* was published in 1937. An idealistic young American, a typical Boston Brahmin, Emerson despised the moral righteousness of the British colonial class and their exploitation of indigenous peoples. On the very first pages, he denounced British imperialists 'setting out on new and bloody conquests'. It is not surprising to discover that Emerson's book was detested by old Malaya hands like Sir Frank Swettenham, who attacked Emerson for 'seeking to ride a title against all Imperialism'. By the time Emerson published his analysis of the iniquities of empire, there were many fervent young people in the colonial domains of British Malaya, Dutch Indonesia and French Indochina who would 'ride a title against Imperialism'.

As Emerson realised, the British ruled 'indirectly' through the Malay aristocracy, which had been radically reconfigured to serve colonial interests. Under British tutelage, the Malay courts had become ornamental institutions that not only served colonial commercial ends but satisfied English pseudo-medieval nostalgia. Nineteenth-century Britain was a grossly unequal society: its ruling class was drawn exclusively from a closed world of some fifteen public schools and, for the crème de la crème, two elite universities. The colonial governing class was not only elitist – it was staunchly anti-democratic. Those men and women who took up the 'white man's burden' in the burgeoning British Empire brought with them attitudes to social hierarchy and class that had been bred in the bone. Tradition served imperial purposes. In 1927, Governor Sir Hugh Clifford vowed to preserve the 'Muhammadan Monarchies' since his government had received no mandate from the 'Rajas, Chiefs or the people' to 'vary the system of Government which has existed in these territories from time immemorial'. In the theatre of imperial power, all had their allotted role. Europeans would govern; the sultans would perform their traditional ceremonies and hand out awards and titles; the Malay peasants would till their fields and fish their rivers; the Chinese and Indians would labour in mines and plantations. The British tin mine entrepreneur Charles Warnford-Lock explained with brutal concision:

From a labour point of view, there are practically three races, the Malays the Chinese and Tamils. By nature, the Malay is an idler, the Chinaman is a thief, and the Indian is a drunkard. Yet each, in his special class of work, is both cheap and efficient when properly supervised.

The imperial machine was lubricated by racial caricature. While the sultans profited from their allotted role in the colonial regime, the traditional Malay administrative classes suffered a decline. The British enhanced the ornamental status of the sultans but threatened the old elites with extinction. To survive, these elites would have to change. For Sultan Idris ibni Raja Iskandar of Perak, who came to the throne in 1887, the solution was education – *English* education. The sultan had spent time in London trying to retrieve the Perak royal regalia, which had been seized during the Perak wars, and had come to believe that it was the English public schools that had made Britain a great power. Back in Perak the sultan established a 'Raja Class' – a school for princes – at his riverside palace in Kuala Kangsar. This eventually became the 'Clifford School' in 1927. In Selangor, the heir apparent, or Raja Mudah, followed Sultan Idris's lead and established his own 'Raja School', as the British Resident William Maxwell put it, to 'educate the sons of Rajas and chiefs, whose *hereditary influence we desire to be used to the advantage of the State* …'. (my italics). These Malay schools mimicked the British public schools to instil the values proclaimed in the words of Sir Henry Newbolt's excruciating ditty:

> This is the word that year by year,
> While in her place the school is set,
> Every one of her sons must hear,
> And none that hears it dare forget.
> This they all with a joyful mind
> Bear through life like a torch in flame,
> And falling fling to the host behind–
> 'Play up! play up! and play the game!'

As in British India, only a tiny elite benefitted from these new schools.

PART TWO

THE JAPANESE

CRUCIBLE

1

A NATION IS LIKE A FISH

'Forgetting, I would even go so far as to say historical error, is a crucial factor in the creation of a nation [...] Historical enquiry brings to light deeds of violence which took place at the origin of all political formations, even of those whose consequences have been altogether beneficial. Unity is always effected by means of brutality ...'.

Ernest Renan

The Malayan Emergency that erupted in June 1948 lasted 'officially' for twelve years. Victory was declared in 1960 but the communist insurrection sputtered on for another three decades. In the same period, the Malaysian armed forces fought a war with Indonesia and race riots erupted in Kuala Lumpur. The war, it might be said, took a long time to end. Recent events in the Malaysian state of Sabah, which was invaded by Filipino insurgents from the Sulu islands, have shown that the violent energies of the region have not yet been exhausted. The aftershocks of colonial rule still reverberate. In many historical accounts the Malayan Emergency war is represented as exemplary. This approach tends to shrink real history to parable – a kind of 'Just So' story for the lecture halls at the Royal Military Academy, Sandhurst or West Point. The history of the Malayan Emergency defies closure. It was a war of skirmishes fought by a resurgent colonial power that sought to dominate the destiny and soul of a nation. Arguably, the war began when Sir Stamford Raffles first set foot on Singapore island – and has yet to end.

Forgetting and Remembering

In the turbulent aftermath of the Second World War, anti-colonial nationalist movements began to contest the European empires that sprawled across Africa, the Indian subcontinent and Southeast Asia. The winds of change gusted across mapped territories that had been marked out not by Asian or African nationalists but by the cartographers of empire. The anti-colonial nationalist leaders were forced to accept the intricate web of arbitrary colonial borders that would define and contain the struggles for independence. Entirely new Asian and African nation states would break up the old European empires. The same shattering metamorphosis from decayed empire to a patchwork of autonomous nations is a recurrent narrative of modern history that began with the destruction of the Holy Roman Empire by Napoleon in 1806. Nineteenth-century European history can be viewed as a long drawn-out tournament between empires and nations. The first global war of the twentieth century, that ended in 1918, shattered four great empires and precipitated a volatile patchwork of new, and often fragile, successor states. The main purpose of the Paris Peace Conference in 1919 was to divvy out the spoils of the old European empires between the victorious 'Great Powers', and settle the vociferous claims of various nationalist claimants.

The famous 'Fourteen Points', which had been set out by American President Woodrow Wilson before the Paris Peace Conference in a speech made in January 1918, highlighted the ethical imperative of national self-determination and sovereignty. Wilson spoke of 'nations we wish to see safeguarded and assured' that would 'be accorded the freest opportunity to autonomous development'. He promised 'a free, open-minded, and absolutely impartial adjustment of all colonial claims ...'. What this meant in practice was that Britain and France gobbled up the colonies of defeated Germany and took control of huge areas of the defunct Ottoman Empire in the Middle East as mandates. The 'mandate system' obligated the British, in Palestine for example, to govern 'until such time as they [the people of the mandated territory] are able to stand alone ...'. Wilson's idealistic talk of self-determination had drawn many hopeful Asian nationalists to Paris including Ho Chi Minh – but every one of them went away empty-handed. The message was clear: they would have to fight for independence. They would also have to define just what it was they hoped to achieve. The post-war settlement in Europe resurrected the Polish nation which had been dismembered nearly two centuries earlier. But Poland had once been a nation state: it had a language, a culture and, as the Fourteen Points put it 'indisputably Polish populations'. Beyond the borders of Siam, there was not a single recognisable nation in Southeast Asia. The Asian nationalists would now need to forge the very idea of a nation before it could be liberated – and sovereign.

The French philosopher and historian Ernest Renan mischievously remarked that members of a national community must 'forget their history'. Or rather, as Benedict Anderson argues in his classic study *Imagined Communities* (1983), members of nations must *both* remember and forget. Every schoolboy and girl remembers – or remembered – William the Conqueror as a founding father of the English nation. The same schoolchild must simultaneously forget that this Norman king was 'the Conqueror *of* the English', and certainly did not speak the language of the peoples he subdued: 'English' did not exist in 1066. Nationalism insists on remembering and forgetting in the same moment. The founders of nations are compelled to contrive 'national' traditions. Conservative historians insist that schoolchildren cram into their heads a sacralised list of English kings and queens stretching back to the Dark Ages, but overlook the very recent invention of the British constitutional monarchy and the fact that its dynastic line was 'Made in Germany'. The national touchstone of modern Malaysian nationalism is the 'living museum' of Malacca, the 'soul of independence' and the hub of a lost Malay empire. What is remembered in Malacca and what is forgotten?

For nationalists in the British, French and Dutch colonial realms of Southeast Asia, the nation state had to be *invented* before it could be fought for and become independent. It was not, however, a simple matter of importing a European political commodity. Many streams flowed into the broad rivers of Asian nationalisms. Their head waters rose from the ancient universities of the Netherlands and France – and from the Masjid al-Haram in Mecca and Al-Azhar University in Cairo. It would be the rise of 'Meiji' Japan, a formidable Asian power modelled on militaristic Prussia, that would turn these burbling brooks into a fearsome torrent that would wash through China, India, Vietnam and into the islands of the Indonesian Archipelago.

The Idea of a Nation

Before the end of the nineteenth century there was no Indonesia and no 'Indonesians'. The term was manufactured. In 1850 a proto-version 'Indu-nesians' was coined by an English traveller and ethnographer called George Samuel Windsor Earl who was casting around for a way to refer to 'the brown races of the Indian Archipelago'. Earl was dissatisfied with his coinage and abandoned it in favour of 'Malayunesians' but it was taken up and adapted as a purely geographic term by his colleague, John Logan, who was the first to refer to a rather broadly defined Indian archipelago as 'Indonesia'. Then in the early 1880s, the renowned German anthropologist Adolf Bastian gave the term academic respectability when he published his imposing five-volume study *Indonesien oder die Inseln des Malayischen Archipel*. Bastian's distinguished imprimatur inspired G.A. Wilken, an ethnologist at the University of Leiden, to refer to both the geographical 'Indonesian archipelago' and more broadly to 'Indonesian' peoples roughly sharing ethnic characteristics, cognate languages and cultural traits. These rather abstract 'Indonesians' had yet to step onto the historical stage. They did not exist outside the rarefied world of the university lecture hall or the pages of an academic tome. It would be the violent aggregation of Dutch colonial power 'to the furthest nooks and crannies of the archipelago' after the 1870s that would create an indigenous national identity.

For a long time, Dutch power had been centralised in Java. From 1898 and the introduction of the 'Short Contract' the native states recognised Dutch sovereignty – and pledged obedience to the colonial government. Mercenary colonial armies brought to heel any state that resisted. The horizontal or territorial integration of the Dutch East Indies was reinforced by enhanced transport infrastructures, like roads, railways and a network of shipping routes, and centralised taxation, legal and postal services. Rapid Dutch-directed economic growth stimulated spasms of internal migration from the outer islands to Java and beyond to the plantations of Sumatra. This brought the many different ethnic groups into closer contact and encouraged the usage of a single tongue, Malay, as a lingua franca. By 1907 the National Geographic's Eliza Ruhamah Scidmore, reporting on a visit to Java, could confidently refer to 'all Indonesians as they are, under the rule of the one governor-general of Netherlands India, representing the little Queen at The Hague'. Dutch imperialism thus provided the conditions for a self-conscious sense of national identity – they did not create it. Unlike the British in Malaya, who actively promoted the civil use of their own tongue, the Dutch did not encourage the learning and use of Dutch by inferior 'natives'. Nevertheless, the first nationally conscious Indonesians were the handful of students who travelled to the Netherlands to pursue higher studies and unlock 'the treasure house of western civilisation'. Most were ambitious young Javanese aristocrats known as 'priyayi', who had been supported by the liberal-minded 'Indies Association' ('Indische Vereeniging') and became a vanguard of a nationalist Indonesian consciousness. The other source of a new national identity was the experience of the Haj, the pilgrimage to Mecca. The Dutch scholar and 'Advisor on Native Affairs' Christiaan Snouck Hurgronje was fascinated by the transformative impact of these often hazardous voyages into the unknown. He wrote that: 'On the sea voyage, and still more in Mekka [...] pilgrims come together from the most remote parts of the archipelago: their exchange of ideas acquires a deeper significance because their country-folk, settled in Mekka, give them a lead ...'. For some of these pilgrims, and for students from Java and Sumatra who studied at the Al-Azhar University in Cairo, it was possible to imagine a unified Islamic movement to resist the 'kafir' (non-Muslim or infidel) colonial state.

There is, however, a profound tension between the ethics of Islam and the ideological rigours of nationalism. Islam is a world community, or 'Ummah' – the Islamic nation or 'ummat al-Islamiyah' – that lived under the symbolic authority of a *Kaliph*. Islam is ecumenical rather than nationalist and territorial. It is portable rather than local. Islam was carried into Asia by merchants, bankers and travelling Sufi scholars, who presented their faith to converts as a universalising world view. The paradox of Islam was that the average Malay peasant may have imagined him or herself as part of a global 'Ummah', but at the same time did not think beyond the local mosque and the sultan who had endowed it. Theirs was not a faith of state builders. Instead, Islam inspired radical Asian nationalists who professed themselves Muslims because it was traditionally hostile to 'the West' and to Western colonialism. Pankaj Mishra offers a number of pithy examples in his book *From the Ruins of Empire* (2012). The Ottoman historian Asim, writing in 1801, was horrified by the French Revolution: 'its ultimate basis is an evil doctrine consisting of the abandonment of religion and the equality of rich and poor'. Parliamentary deliberations reminded him of 'the rumblings and crepitations of a queasy stomach'. Westerners urinated in public and their women did not veil themselves; they had 'intercourse with women who please them' and buried their dead in a barbaric manner. Abd al-Rahman al-Jabarti was horrified when Napoleon claimed that 'all people are equal in the eyes of God': 'this is a lie, and ignorance and stupidity!' Al-Jabarti was impressed, however, to discover when he visited the new 'Institut d'Égypte' that French scholars had 'translated the glorious Koran'.

Japanese Thunderclaps

Many Muslim scholars exposed to the iniquities of the West came to grudgingly admire the workings of modern European nations and chafe at their own sclerotic rulers and institutions. The West, in other words, offered a challenge. Europe had to be confronted not just despised. But the challenge of the West would be taken up not by a Muslim nation – but by modern Japan. And it was the new Japan that rose from the Meiji restoration at the end of the nineteenth century that became a Mecca for Asian nationalists. The Japanese oligarchs who drove the Meiji restoration and reimagined the idea of a Japanese nation clearly understood that isolation and petulant xenophobia, which had long been practised by the reactionary Shogunate, could not solve the dilemma posed by superior Western powers. For this new generation Japan appeared abject and weak. So they set about, with astonishing brilliance, inventing a modern nation state that bristled with armed might. They took as their model the modern German state, which had been wrought from the ruins of the Holy Roman Empire by the reactionary Otto von Bismarck. Modern Germany was a Frankenstein creature stitched together in 1871 by military conquest. The Meiji elite took on the identity of 'Asian Hohenzollerns' and adapted the German-Prussian model of nation building. They brought the emperor out of seclusion and renovated the role as the symbolic apex of a patriotic cult. Buddhism was demoted and Shintoism proclaimed a state religion. It was as if the Meiji oligarchs were following, step by step, a secret manual of nation building. The cult of the emperor and the arcane rituals of Shinto fused and guided a reinvented people. Japanese intellectuals and students travelled to the West as willing apprentices of advanced civilisation and, likewise, European experts were embraced in every realm from schoolroom to barracks. Christian missions were tolerated. The Japanese upper and middle classes adopted Western styles of dress. Civilisation, in short, was not a white man's monopoly. The Meiji oligarchs launched a programme of modernisation from above, lavishly, by ruthless taxation. As in Germany, industrial modernisation and remarkably rapid growth buttressed nationhood and was focused on armaments manufacture. By the beginning of the twentieth century, Japan had been remade as a formidable military and naval power. That an upstart Asian nation was on the threshold of becoming a world power was proclaimed to an astonished world in May 1905 when a Japanese fleet commanded by the famously taciturn Admiral Tōgō Heihachirō, who had studied in Britain and would be fêted as the 'Nelson of the East', shattered the Russian Baltic fleet in the Tsushima Strait. Lord Curzon, the Viceroy of India, described this epochal victory as a 'thunderclap reverberating through the whispering galleries of the East'. Asian nationalists exalted. Mohandas Gandhi heard the news in Pretoria, South Africa. The Japanese victory would put forth such broad roots, he prophesied, that their fruits could not yet be visualised. When the Chinese nationalist Sun Yat-Sen stepped off a boat in Egypt he was congratulated by Arab port workers who thought he was Japanese. A young Jawaharlal Nehru began to imagine the end of the 'thraldom of Europe'.

Japan's rise to power as a militarised Asian nation state would inspire the leaders of Asian anti-colonial movements but would also have profoundly contradictory consequences. Since the new rulers of Japan modelled their new nation on the most bellicose Western states epitomised by Imperial Germany, it was natural to perceive great nations as mighty conquerors. The case for an aggressively imperialist Japan was made most forcibly in the infamous *Nihon Kaizō Hōan Taikō* ('Outline for the Reconstruction of Japan'), written a few years after the First World War by the ultranationalist scholar and socialist political philosopher Ikki Kita. Ikki grumbled that Japan was still a 'proletarian' among nations and dwarfed by the 'millionaire' British Empire. Since it was reasonable for the working class 'to overthrow unjust authority by bloodshed', it was, by the same token, a matter of just cause for Japan to 'rectify unjust international frontiers'. Ikki had come to the same conclusion as German nationalists who had argued that for Germany to compete with Britain it was essential to acquire an empire. He called for expansion into Korea and Manchuria and war with 'landlord nations' like Britain. Japanese armies would eventually strike at the British Empire. But it was China that first paid the terrible price of Japanese imperial ambition.

Japan first invaded China in 1894 and seized the Liaotung Peninsula. The famous scholar and admirer of all things Japanese, Lafcadio Hearn, admitted that 'the real birthday of the New Japan began with the invasion of China'. This relish for conquest led Japan to conclude an alliance with the imperialist British in 1902. Japan's martial spirit did nothing to deter the many Asian and Muslim intellectuals who were lured to Tokyo. The city became the Mecca of Asian nationalism. Many were convinced that Japan would be the saviour of an Asia disfigured by Europeans. How is it, asked the Vietnamese Phan Boi Chau, 'that these blue-eyed, yellow bearded people [the French], who are not our fathers or elder brothers, can squat on our heads, defecate on us?' The tragedy of Asian history is that the Japanese Imperial Army would do much the same to the peoples of the Philippines, Singapore, Malaya, the Dutch East Indies and Burma.

'Mi Patria Idolatrada'

In the aftermath of the First World War, the great dynastic European empires collapsed. Austro-Hungary, Germany, and Tsarist Russia fractured into scores of nation states. Some of these 'new' nations, like resurrected Poland, had deep historical footings; others, such as the Baltic states Lithuania, Latvia and Estonia, had shallow and tenuous foundations. This seismic dismemberment followed the military defeat of Imperial Germany and the allied 'Central Powers'. They would be humiliated at the Paris Peace Conference in Versailles. The Allied Powers would be fattened by victory. The French and the British carved up the relic territories of the obsolete Ottoman Empire and tightened their grip on Asia and Africa. The reputation of the empire had been badly tarnished by the conduct of the Boer War and its treasuries depleted by the 'war to end all wars'. The sun had reached its zenith and had begun to dip towards a faraway horizon. The iron claws of empire may have been corroded, but they were not blunted. The passionate eloquence of Indian nationalist leader Mohandas Gandhi was brutally countered by the rifles of General Reginald Dyer at the Jallianwala Bagh Gardens in Amritsar.

By the time General Dyer's bullets ripped into Indian bodies in Amritsar, the imperial map of Southeast Asia was complete. The British in Burma and Malaya, the Dutch in the vast archipelago of islands that some were already referring to as 'Indonesia', the French in Indochina and the Americans in the former Spanish East Indies, the Philippines, were busy refining the political and cultural map of the region, gouging hard-edged territorial borders across the palimpsest of a vanishing and once more fluid world. The indigenous peoples of this 'mottled' territory interacted with their European rulers in very different ways: fighting, resisting, accommodating and adapting. Only the Thai rulers of Siam had resisted the imperial deluge. Nationalist movements would emerge in fits and starts.

The most precocious anti-colonial nationalist movement emerged at the very end of the nineteenth century, not in British Malaya nor the Dutch East Indies, but in the Spanish Philippines. We tend to forget that in the late nineteenth century, Europe was bookended by two empires that were in chronic disrepair. In the east the Ottoman caliph presided over a decaying patchwork of territories, the final disintegration of which was eagerly awaited by impatient European 'Great Powers'. In the west, the Spanish and Portuguese empires were equally as decrepit. Spain was in turmoil, riven by insurrection, and on the other side of the Atlantic in the Americas, Creole nationalists had all but broken the despotic tyranny of the Spanish Crown.

Although the Spanish East Indies lay on the liminal eastern margins of the empire, the explosive emergence of 'Creole' nationalist movements in the Americas radicalised many young Filipinos. But what was a Filipino and what language should he or she speak? That question was addressed by the Austrian scholar and citizen of another European empire, Ferdinand Blumentritt, who worked as a teacher in the little Bohemian town of Leitmeritz. Blumentritt was fascinated by the cultures of the Spanish Empire – and by 'Las Filipinas'. From his assiduous pen would flow more than 200 essays, papers and books about the many different ethno-linguistic groups of the archipelago and their culture. He recovered what the Spanish had hidden or destroyed. In 1885, a young Filipino called José Rizal set out from Manila on a pilgrimage to meet the sage of Leitmeritz. Like many young self-conscious Filipinos, Rizal was fascinated by the early history and ethnography of the Philippines – he wanted, as Benedict Anderson puts it, to 'discover the glorious past hidden behind a humiliating present'.

Poet, novelist, ophthalmologist, historian, doctor and political dreamer José Protasio Rizal Mercado y Alonso Realonda was born on 19 June 1861 in Calamba, a small town about 37 miles south of Manila, the capital city of the Spanish Philippines. His father, Francisco Mercado, was a gentleman farmer, who owned a large estate and had numerous servants. Teodora Alonso, José's mother, was the cultured daughter of another prominent family, who would raise her many children to believe in the value of a good education. The family embodied the entire tangled colonial history of the archipelago, with Chinese, Spanish, Japanese and native Tagalog ancestors dotted about the branches of the family tree. Teodora was devoutly Catholic and before José was born had made a pilgrimage to the Marian shrine in Antipolo City to ask the Virgin for a son. She read to her son in Castilian Spanish and Tagalog. José was educated by private tutors, then from 11 at the Jesuit school Ateneo Municipal in Manila. It was here that he witnessed at first-hand the brutal way the Spanish friars treated the native Filipinos.

Rizal was a reluctant revolutionary nationalist. He repudiated the revolutionary 'Katipunan' movement led by Andréas Bonifacio but his two novels *Noli me Tangere* and *El Filibusterismo* became the manifestos of Filipino nationalism. The Spanish regarded Rizal as a menace. But on 15 December 1892, in what would be his last political manifesto, he condemned the radicals and their 'savage insurrection, plotted behind my back, which dishonours the Filipinos [...] I abominate its criminal procedures.' The Spanish military judge-advocate general was not impressed. He immediately ordered Rizal's arrest for sedition and treason. He was tried by a military court and sentenced to death. The Spanish locked up the condemned man inside Fort Santiago, which had been built by the Conquistador Miguel López de Legazpi, to await execution. When Rizal was handed the death warrant, he noticed it described him as Chinese. Rizal spent his last hours writing his celebrated poem 'Mi último adiós' – My Last Farewell. Its penultimate stanza proclaims:

> My idolised Country, for whom I most gravely pine,
> Dear Philippines, to my last goodbye; oh, harken
> There I leave all: my parents, loves of mine,
> I'll go where there are no slaves, tyrants or hangmen
> Where faith does not kill and where God alone doth reign.[13]

'Mi último adiós' was the first great Asian hymn of national self-determination. At dawn on 30 December 1896, José Rizal was taken from his cell to a bleak open space called the Bagumbayan on the western edge of Manila overlooking the South China Sea. He was dressed in black tie and suit with well-polished black shoes. A bowler hat was jammed incongruously on his head. A small crowd had gathered. Rizal refused a blindfold and asked to face his executioners, a squad of native Filipinos attired in Spanish uniforms. This was refused. Traitors must be shot in the back. A Spanish lieutenant barked an order and Rizal fell face forward into the dirt. He was 36 years old. His last words had been fatalistic: '*consummatum est*': it is over.

In one sense Rizal was right. As Filipinos rose against their Spanish masters, the Americans declared war on Spain and seized the Philippines with the rebels' assistance. President William McKinley prayed for guidance, and God, it turned out, favoured annexation: 'there was nothing left for us to do but to take them all, and to educate the Filipinos and uplift them and civilise them and Christianise them [sic], and by God's grace do the best we could for them, as our fellowmen for whom Christ also died …'. A new imperial power was on the righteous path of war. From the American point of view, grabbing the Philippines made a lot of sense. They envied the British base at Singapore and McKinley had taken note of German ambitions in the Pacific: the kaiser longed for more colonies to spite the hated British and, the Americans feared, he might seize his chance by laying claim to some of the old Spanish possessions. It was essential to block the German advance. The English poet Rudyard Kipling dashed off a famous piece of doggerel urging the Americans to 'take up the white man's burden'. Senator Albert J. Beveridge from Alberta had, like McKinley, sought advice from the Almighty: he 'made us adepts in government that we may administer government among savage and senile people.' Acquiring the 7,108 islands of the Philippine Archipelago and their 7 million inhabitants cost the American government a trifling $20 million. Yankee imperialism quashed the nationalist dreams that had been given a voice with such eloquence by José Rizal, the 'First Filipino'.

The Dutch did not create modern Indonesia but they defined its borders and provided the intellectual loam that nourished the idea of a nation. The so-called 'Ethical Policy' that the Dutch adopted in 1901 even as the mercenary armies of Joannes Benedictus van Heutsz rampaged across Aceh was partly rooted in the bad consciences of the Dutch colonial class. Many of these were well-educated men and women and found it increasingly difficult to dismiss the shocking gap between their gilded lives in the grand mansions of Batavia and the grinding poverty they knew existed in the countryside and plantations. This disquiet was expressed as early as 1860 in a novel: *Max Havelaar: Or the Coffee Auctions of the Dutch Trading Company* was written by a former colonial administrator, Eduard Douwes Dekker, under the pseudonym 'Multatuli', from the Latin 'I have suffered or seen much'. Multatuli used the story of his eponymous hero to indict the venality of colonial

rule and the penury of native peoples. *Max Havelaar* had a remarkable impact.
The great Indonesian novelist Pramoedya Ananta Toer liked to say that it was the
book that 'killed colonialism'. But it would be naive to think that Dutch colonial
rule changed overnight or that mercenary calculations had no role to play. The
wealth of the Indies had enriched the Dutch and stimulated the economy of the
Netherlands. Industrialists began to realise that the Indies were a huge potential
market for their goods. But this could only happen if living standards were raised.
In the Outer Islands, Dutch speculators saw new opportunities in the extraction of
raw materials, above all, oil. As in British Malaya, the rubber boom was sucking in
a great army of workers. In short, ethics joined hands with profiteering. The result
was the 'Ethical Policy' – the midwife of Indonesian nationalism. In 1908, the
government established a printing press, called the *Balai Pustaka*, to print textbooks,
grammars and novels in the approved common language. Now 'Indonesians' had a
way of talking to each other – thanks to the Dutch.

The authoritarian imposition of Malay as a common language would ferment
an entirely new national consciousness. In colonial classrooms Indonesian pupils
sat and worked beneath wall maps and opened the pages of atlases that proclaimed
a single colonial state, an imagined community embracing a territory that
extended from the northernmost island of Sabang off the coast of Aceh to the tiny
military outpost of Merauke in New Guinea. It was this evocative geographical
span that the great nationalist leader Sukarno would adopt as a political slogan.
He demanded *merdeka* (independence) 'from Sabang to Merauke'. The cord
that connects the classroom to the nationalist rally is woven from many threads.
The idea of nation evokes a conceptual and emotional landscape that is spatial,
linguistic and psychological. Its energies derive from imagined geographies,
languages and thoughts. For the colonial power, this is a dangerous mix. The head
of Royal Dutch Shell, Hendrikus Colijn, sneered that '[Indonesia] is completely
a creation of the Netherlands. And if there shall ever emerge, through an inner
consciousness of togetherness, a "People of Insulinde", this people will be just the
foster mother of that Indies political process …'. But that 'inner consciousness of
togetherness' was now hard to deny and impossible to repress.

Numerous political parties emerged in Indonesia before and during the First
World War and in 1924 the first Communist Party in Southeast Asia was formed:
'Partai Komunis Indonesia' (PKI). The spectre of communism had at last risen in
the Far East. Indonesian radicals soon fashioned the PKI as an Indonesian party.
They ousted the Dutch radicals and, instead of Marx and Lenin, evoked the past
glories of Śrīvijaya and Majapahit, the lost kingdoms of Java. The party heroes
were the men who resisted Sir Stamford Raffles in the Java War. For colonial
governments, the lesson of reform, however half-hearted, was that it threw open a
door to the radicals. Soon that door would be slammed shut.

It was this political maelstrom that shaped the thinking of a young man born
Kusno Sosrodihardjo in Surabaya in 1901. After surviving a life of threatening

childhood illness, the little boy had been given a new name that meant 'good karma' in Javanese. Kusno Sosrodihardjo became Sukarno. In the course of a remarkable political life, Sukarno would be idolised, denounced, hated, reviled and adored. He would become the first president of an independent Indonesia – the Father of Independence. He would come to dominate Indonesian political life and struggle to reconcile nationalism, communism and Islam until he was deposed by a foul and murderous dictator. He, more than any of his contemporaries, believed in an eternal Indonesia.

In the mid-1920s the overheated Indonesian political world raced towards boiling point. The colonial government struggled to slam down the lid on the volatile genies that had sprung like dragons' teeth from the loam of nationalism. The Russian Revolution had terrified the Dutch – and the colonial security apparatus came down hard on the Indonesian left. The innately fragile 'Ethical Policy' that had been adopted to placate the new movements began to fray. Nationalists were soon at each other's throats. In Surakarta, Haji Misbach claimed that Islam and Marxism were one and the same: the 'Red Haji' was soon locked up in a Dutch prison cell but other radicals took up the cause of 'Islamic Communism'. Angry Muslims set up an 'Army of the Prophet' to punish these blasphemers while anti-Muslim Javanese retaliated with a 'Committee for Javanese nationalism'. The Dutch colonial government had exploited native mercenaries to smash the Acehenese rebels; now the administration turned a blind eye to a wave of rural violence perpetrated by *sarekat hijau* (Green Union), gangs of thugs and renegade police, who attacked and murdered communists. The PKI leadership, under unrelenting government assault, was provoked beyond endurance. In December 1925, rejecting warnings from Soviet Comintern agents and the charismatic communist Tan Malaka who was exiled in Singapore, the PKI began planning for a general uprising. In January 1926 the government launched a renewed attack and locked up numerous communist leaders. On 12 November 1926, the Indonesian revolution exploded with the force of a dud artillery shell. A single European was killed; government forces reacted promptly, decisively and without mercy. The first Indonesian revolution was all over by the following January. It signalled the end of the 'Ethical Policy' and the start of the most repressive period in the history of the Dutch East Indies. Few could have foreseen the shattering events of January 1942, which would bring Dutch rule to an end.

The Late Developers

As Indonesians staged a revolution, all was calm in British Malaya. The Dutch had dethroned the Javanese rulers, but the British had transformed the sultans of the Malay states into proxy governors. Since the Malays owed allegiance to their courts, nationalist stirrings were gentle tremors. Or so it seemed. When

the Malayan communist Abdullah C.D. reflected on why he had chosen such
a politically radical path, he remembered two great influences. There was
Mr Lewis, his English teacher at the Clifford School who had lent the bright
schoolboy books by Karl Marx: 'very interesting'. The second mentor Abdullah
recollected was a rubber tapper called Pak Inu, who lived near Kuala Kangsar.
Mr Lewis was an unusual teacher and Pak Inu was no ordinary rubber tapper. A
revolutionary fighter from across the Malacca Strait who had taken part in the
1925 uprising against the Dutch, he escaped to Malaya with his wife and son.
He too lent young Abdullah many thought-provoking books from his kampong
library. Some were by the famous Indonesian communist, Tan Melaka. In 1939,
Abdullah told his friend that he wished to join a new Malay organisation called
the 'Kesatuan Melayu Muda' or KMM, the Young Malays Union. Pak Inu was
already a KMM member and he welcomed Abdullah 'with open arms'. After the
Japanese invasion, Abdullah never saw Pak Inu again. But the Indonesian rubber
tapper had an overwhelming impact on the young teenager, who would become
a Malay nationalist and a communist.

But Abdullah's path would be a lonely one. At the Clifford School he was
ostracised by his classmates – and beaten up by some of the young princes who
attended the British school. Only a tiny minority of Malays had even heard of the
KMM. Many Indonesian radicals who had taken refuge in Singapore and Malaya
despaired of the Malays. The British ruled over competing ethnic communities
that had all, for different reasons, failed to develop an idea of nationhood. This
apparent passivity suited the British, to be sure. There had not been a revolution
in British Malaya. But it also reflected the resilience of the old *Kerajaan* idea
of a monarchical community and the way Muslims identified not with nation
but a globalised Islamic community: the 'Ummah' or, as the Koran says, 'the best
nation brought out for mankind'. Likewise the Chinese and Indian communities
in British Malaya struggled with the concept of a putative 'Malayan' identity.
Their struggle was with the Japanese in mainland China and the British in India.
We shall have a lot more to say about this shared conundrum later but we need
to have clearly in mind the paradox of imperial history. Colonial rule begat a
national consciousness that would become the principal political challenge to the
colonial powers. Nationalism means understanding and opposing alien rule as an
enforced denial of nationhood. In British Malaya the different racial communities
would follow their own tangled pathways to different kinds of national revolt.
The idea of the nation was just one competing identity among many other – and
this would shape the battle for independence.

Above all, Malay political consciousness was shaped by fear. For Abdullah, the
Malays had become more and more stupid because they were ruled by oppressive
and ignorant rajas. He wanted the 'bangsa' to become 'great and clever'. He
believed that if they worked hard *all* Malays could 'live like rajas'. Abdullah's
purpose was a reform of consciousness. At the dawn of the twentieth century,

this mission was taken up by the Malay journalist and editor, Mohammed Eunos Abdullah.

Eunos has been traditionally dismissed as the 'loyalist Malay'. The first newspaper he edited, the *Utusan Melayu*, was owned by an English publisher, William Makepeace, and produced in Singapore, a British colony under watchful British eyes. In the 1920s Eunos led the Singapore Malay Union, which devoted a great deal of time and energy to celebrating the coronation of King George VI. (The very first edition of *Utusan Melayu* printed a congratulatory epistle in Malay from Sir Frank Swettenham.) And yet *Utusan Melayu* was the first Malay language daily newspaper published in British Malaya, and Eunos insisted that it would carry news not just of 'Malay lands' but of other continents. He looked forward to the Malay race possessing 'knowledge and skills which cannot be bettered by other races in any aspect of modernity'. Read in coffee shops and schoolrooms all over the peninsula, *Utusan Melayu* was a landmark publication. Eunos believed that bangsa was not a given: it had to be forged. Munshi Abdullah despised the decadent and cruel Malay rulers. But in a groundbreaking essay Eunos asked what the rajas could do *for* the bangsa. Bangsa must take precedence over the ruler. In other writings, Eunos tentatively nudged the idea of bangsa towards 'nationhood' but in a tepid way that avoided issuing a direct challenge to the colonial power: as a member of Singapore's Legislative Council, which was of course a tool of colonial rule, Eunos exalted the Malay's 'rightful place in the sun as a happy and contented citizen of the British Empire'. This has the distinct odour of submission. But no sultan would ever imagine referring to his subjects as citizens. Eunos spoke to those Malays who had raised their game under British rule. His position was not much different from the Straits' Chinese leaders like Tan Cheng Lock who were Anglophilic in outlook. Tan Cheng Lock insisted in a speech made in November 1924 that 'I can assure [the Straits Legislative Council] we are animated by a sense of loyalty and duty to serve this empire and Throne to whom we owe allegiance …'.

Like every Malay nationalist who would come after him, Eunos also spoke the language of racial chauvinism and ethnic anxiety. Malays, according to scores of articles and editorials in the *Utusan Melayu*, were in danger of being 'driven from their own land by other races'. The Chinese were hard-working and already feared across Asia, Australia and in the Americas. The 'yellow peril', Eunos warned in an astonishing phrase, could create an emergency. He lamented that 'the places where the Malays used to fish are ruined; the rice fields have been plundered; the jungles have been cut down and the rivers ruined'.[14] To blame – the Chinese.

The same tone of 'bangsa anxiety' runs through the work of a later nationalist, Ibrahim Yaacob. An alumnus of the Sultan Idris College, Yaacob was, like Eunos, a journalist. When he was sacked by the editor of *Majilis*, he embarked on an investigative grand tour of the peninsula to observe the conditions of Malays under colonial rule. He was inspired, of course, by the example of Munshi

Abdullah who had made a similar journey more than a century earlier, but it would be interesting to know if he had read George Orwell's *The Road to Wigan Pier*, published in 1937, which explored the plight of the English working class during the Depression years. The result of Ibrahim's wanderings was *Surveying the Homeland*, published a year after he was thrown off the editorial board at *Majilis*. He described his short, sharp book as a 'gift' to the Malays: a 'service to my bangsa'.

The tone of Ibrahim's prose is, from the first pages, distinctly secular, irreverent and snappishly alert. He offers no preliminary obeisance to Allah nor does he include a single quotation from the Koran. In his acknowledgements he thanks instead 'the Tengkus, Rajas, Datuks, Tuans, Inchis, friends and comrades': here Ibrahim seems to have had his tongue firmly in his cheek for his exact and unsparing critique is directed not just against the British and the 'Residents' but also the Malay rulers whom, he believed, displayed a callous disregard for the common people. It is clear from his book that Ibrahim regarded the rulers, as much as the British, as a drag on political progress. Like Munshi Abdullah, Ibrahim attacked the Malay rulers' obsession with ornament, ceremony and status. He deplored the Sultan of Perak's insistence on innate inequality, expressed in the homily that 'the hornbill must fly with the hornbill, the sparrow with the sparrow' or as the English hymn has it: 'The rich man in his castle, / The poor man at his gate, / God made them high and lowly, / And ordered their estate.' Ibrahim believed that inequality weakened the bangsa.

Ibrahim was in some senses a socialist. But he was also, like many Malay nationalists, a chauvinist. Ibrahim criticised the Sultan of Perak for toadying up to wealthy Chinese 'towkays'. He was shocked to discover that the state council building in Johor was decorated with Chinese writings in honour of the 'praiseworthy services' of rich Chinese to the raja. He was appalled that in Kelantan the sultan had bestowed a Malay honorary title on a Chinese merchant. For Ibrahim, the power of Chinese wealth was part and parcel of colonialism. The flow of foreign capital exercised more power than any British Resident. Ibrahim saw the Malays 'jostled' by the forces of foreign capital, foreign goods and foreign labour. Everywhere, Ibrahim reported with dismay, 'new styles' were eroding Malay culture: 'Bedsteads replace mats; and the custom of the people is no longer to sit cross-legged but many rent tables and chairs.' Ibrahim warned that the erosion of Malay custom by the malign forces of global capitalism meant that 'good character' would be damaged and that everyone 'follows his own wishes'. So what was to be done?

To answer this question Ibrahim began by looking back at Malay history since the fall of Malacca. He describes a world that had since forgotten its bangsa and became preoccupied instead by narrow localised identities and riven by dynastic squabbles and petty warfare. The way out was for all Malays to embrace and 'love their bangsa'. They had to become 'sedar' – aware. It was not enough to be merely 'loyal to the Raja' to be a true Malay. The idea of 'Raya Indonesia' was a logical next step. Malays, he told his readers, consisted not just of 2½ million people in Peninsula Malaya but also of the 65 million in the Indonesian Archipelago.

Ibrahim's bangsa was in this sense inclusive. It could accommodate many different ethnicities so long as they acknowledged they were Malay. Less explicitly, Ibrahim dismissed the arguments of Muslim radicals, who advocated unity in the global Muslim community. This rejection of a globalising politics could take on a racial significance, which was spelled out by another influential journalist, Abdul Rahim Kajai, who insisted that 'bangsa nationalism' should not be contaminated by 'foreign' Arab or Indian Muslims. Kajai sneered at the many Malays who were known or suspected to have 'foreign blood'. Ibrahim was less rabid, but his passionately expressed devotion to the bangsa necessarily implied fear of other races – the Chinese and Indians. 'Bangsa mindedness', which was frequently expressed in English as 'pride in race', was more closely aligned to colonial ways of thinking than Ibrahim would have wanted to admit. This was why he and other Malay nationalists began to exalt the Malaccan Empire as an emblem of bangsa-consciousness and pride. When the sultan 'ran from Malacca' the consequences were not only 500 years of civil war between rival dynastic houses but also the intrusion of foreigners. Loving the bangsa implied knowing who could *never* belong: the flocking 'birds of passage', who forced Malays to 'retreat' in their own country.

2

THE OTHER SIDE OF HISTORY

Chinese Malayans?

The great paradox of anti-colonial nationalism in British Malaya is that the movement was led by the Chinese. Yet divided as they were by dialect and status, the different overseas Chinese communities in Malaya could only very rarely agree about their own identity and destiny. Some, like Tan Cheng Lock and the wealthy 'Baba' Chinese, relished their prestigious status as British imperial subjects. This meant nothing to impoverished Chinese 'guest workers', who had come to Malaya to work in the mines and plantations and remained staunchly attached to the world they had left behind and to which they hoped eventually to return.

Few politically conscious Malays could admit the Chinese or Indian inhabitants of British Malaya to their 'imagined community'. Likewise, when a nationalist consciousness began to emerge in the Chinese communities in Malaya, its ideological and emotional core was in China. The political evolution of the Chinese communities in Malaya was shaped by what was happening in China much more than developments in the colonial world of Southeast Asia. The British had a great deal to do with this deflection of political attention. In 1889, the colonial government brought in the 'Societies Ordinance' which banned the old secret societies, forcing them underground into drug-pushing, organised crime and extortion. Community power passed to new voluntary associations, called 'Huay Kuan', which soon proliferated to meet the social, cultural and recreational needs of the 'Laukeh' community in Malaya. The most important of the 'Huay Kuan' were the 'Chinese Chambers of Commerce' (CCC). These were generously supported by the Manchu government as part of a campaign to promote both commerce and pan-Chinese nationalism. The first CCC was formed in Singapore in 1906 and others sprang up in Kuala Lumpur, Penang, Malacca, Ipoh and Seremban. The CCC were not political parties. But since they were not aligned to specific dialect groups or clans, they soon became vehicles of an emerging political consciousness. The Chinese in Malaya began to think of themselves as members of a transnational community that extended far beyond the borders of colonial Malaya where they had made their homes.

With political awareness came discord. The important figure here was Sun Yat-Sen, the Chinese nationalist leader who had founded the 'Revive China Society' in Honolulu, Hawaii in 1894, which was dedicated to overthrowing the Qing dynasty and the founding of a Chinese republic based on the 'Three Principles of the Power' – the first of which was 'Mínzú', or national consciousness. The following year, Japanese armies humiliated the Chinese forcing the Qing to renounce all claims to Korea and to cede Taiwan and other territories. The death rattle of the Qing dynasty was loud and clear. Sun rarely stayed in one place for very long. His was the unrelieved peripatetic life of the exiled revolutionary. He liked to spawn revolutionary societies wherever he alighted. In 1905 Sun was in Tokyo. It was here that he founded the revolutionary secret society, the 'Tong Meng Hui', or 'Chinese United League'. At the beginning of December 1907, Sun returned to China to launch a botched uprising at the Zhennanguan Pass on the Chinese border with Vietnam. Loyalist troops swiftly routed the rebels and Sun was forced to flee to Singapore. Here he forged ties with Chinese businessmen, who promised to back a renewed attack on the Qing. Sun moved on to Penang, where in 1910 he organised a conference to appeal to the Straits' Chinese community for funds. Shortly afterwards, the British expelled Sun for 'anti-colonial agitation' and he took refuge in the United States. In China, anti-Manchu feeling reached boiling point and Sun was still in exile when, in 1911, the revolutionary Huang Xing overthrew the Qing, bringing to a climactic end 2,000 years of imperial rule in China. In Beijing, Sun was hailed as the 'Father of the Revolution' but rapidly fell out with the other nationalist leaders and war lords. The new republic plunged into chaos. The Chinese revolution would be prolonged and bloody. Sun was much preoccupied with the successor organisation to the Tung Meng Hui, the 'Kuomintang' (KMT). The first KMT lodge was established in Singapore in 1912 – and branches sprang up all across Malaya. The founding of a Chinese republic enthralled the overseas Chinese community. Many of its richest members responded with lavish donations. They would follow events with rapt attention.

Sun Yat-Sen died in 1925. Power passed to Chiang Kai-Shek, who was superintendent of the 'Whampoa Military Academy' and commanded the loyalty of the army. The 'Generalissimo' hugely admired Sun – but he was no revolutionary. While Sun had been influenced by Western radical thought, Chiang Kai-Shek's 'New Order' movement was a hybrid of traditional elitist Confucianism, Christian Methodism and Italian-style fascism. Under Chiang, Nationalist China was reactionary and authoritarian. In the overseas Chinese community, many KMT members held fast to Sun's revolutionary ideals. Chiang Kai-Shek broke with the Chinese Communist Party (CCP) in 1927 but many communists had joined or infiltrated the KMT in the early 1920s. In Malaya these communists set up a semi-autonomous 'Malayan Revolutionary Committee' loosely allied to the KMT. In 1930 this would become the Malayan Communist

Party. The traditional Chinese leadership – the Straits' Chinese, the Chinese Chambers of Commerce and the wealthy 'towkays' in Singapore and Ipoh – backed the republican KMT to the hilt. They mounted fundraising efforts for flood, famine and refugee relief activities in China, arranged memorial services for Chinese statesmen – and after the Japanese invasion of China in 1937 set up and co-ordinated anti-Japanese campaigns in Malaya. The Chinese community leaders valued their strong ties to the British and European business world and so stifled the anti-colonial sentiments of their members. The Chinese nationalist government, for its part, had no interest in stirring up anti-colonial emotions because it needed Britain as an ally in the war with Japan.

Both the Malayan KMT and MCP sprang from a Chinese ideological parent – the nationalist Kuomintang. The two movements were united by their preoccupation with the fate of the Chinese Republic and the military threat of Imperial Japan. Nevertheless, the most progressive and subtle analysis of the Malayan communal dilemma emerged from within the Straits' Chinese community and its lobby group the 'Straits Chinese British Association', which had been founded in Singapore and Malacca in 1900 and was dominated by English-educated professional men and wealthy merchants. The Anglophile Tan Cheng Lock, though he professed loyalty and devotion to 'Empire and Throne', was among the first to advocate 'a true Malayan spirit and consciousness'. He questioned the nature of colonial tutelage and communal stereotyping. He looked forward to a 'united self governing British Malaya' – a 'Malaya for Malayans and not only for one section of the people [but] for the people who have made Malaya, who are loyal to the country, to the Empire and to the King …'. In these words we have, almost submerged in loyalist protestation, the revolutionary idea of a national community of 'Malayans'. To be sure, Tan Cheng Lock was a radical conservative. He reviled communism as a 'poison' spread by domestic servants, and backed the colonial government's efforts to contain the KMT. This imagined community of 'Malayans' had, as yet, very little resonance for the most radical Chinese.

Voices of Revolt

The Communist International, or Comintern, which held its first congress in March 1919, was slow to recognise the significance of the turmoil rippling across the colonial world at the end of the First World War. That same year a 29-year-old native of French Indochina called Nguyen Tat Thanh entered the Palace of Versailles in a hired morning suit. He was clutching a tattered document that bore the title 'The Demands of the Annamite [Vietnamese] People'. It was addressed to the American President Wilson and signed Nguyen Ai Quoc – Nguyen the Patriot. 'The Demands …'. had been inspired by the president's celebrated speech about the 'Fourteen Points' and a vague promise of 'absolutely unmolested opportunity of autonomous development …'. The document Nguyen pressed into the hands of the president's senior advisor called rather modestly for political autonomy and equal rights for the peoples of French Indochina. It was not, as such, a demand for independence. The advisor promised that he would draw the president's attention to the document but Nguyen Ai Quoc would hear nothing more. The disappointed young man was soon radicalised. In 1922 he helped found the French Communist Party and the following year travelled to Moscow to study at the 'Stalin School' – the Comintern school for Asian communists. Not long afterwards, Nguyen the Patriot took on a revolutionary *nom de guerre* as Ho Chi Minh, 'he who enlightens'.[15]

Ho had realised early on that the end of the European war would shatter the deeply rooted complacencies. There had been revolutions in Russia and Germany. The British Empire, already tarnished by the Boer War, was under assault. There had been anti-colonial rebellions in Egypt, Afghanistan and Waziristan (now Pakistan). Irish republicans had won a landmark victory and, in India, Gandhi had launched a campaign of civil disobedience. The empire had been engorged by victory, snapping up the German colonies, but was beginning to look vulnerable. Japan, a British ally since 1902, had declared war on Germany in August 1914 and seized German territories in Micronesia in the Pacific and in the Shandong province in China. For the Chinese this was ominous. Japan was now a world power. Its representative, Prince Saionji Kinmochi, had sat alongside the 'Big Four' at the Paris Peace Conference and Japan was a member of the League of Nations. But for the most intransigent Japanese nationalists it was not enough. At the Paris Conference, Saionji had argued that 'racial equality' should be enshrined in the basic tenets of the League of Nations. But the European powers, fearful of stirring up their colonial subjects, refused. It would be much too dangerous to concede equality to their millions of colonial subjects. That would never do.

Japanese ambitions were focused on China. For its part the Chinese government resented what they saw as betrayal by the Entente Powers, who had supplied Japan with a strategic foothold in Shandong. In 1915, the Japanese had, with British connivance, forced the Chinese to accept a series of humiliating territorial concessions. When news reached China of the Treaty of Versailles and the loss of Shandong to Japan, tens of thousands of students from Peking University gathered in Tiananmen Square on 4 May 1919 to denounce the European powers and deplore the spineless behaviour of their own government. Versailles hardened nationalist sentiment in China – and at the same time stimulated Japanese ambitions in Asia. Nationalists in Japan resented any attempt by Western powers to curb their imperial aspirations, which they interpreted as a racial slur. An Asian people had just as much right to claim an empire as a 'white skinned' one. In 1924 the American government capped Asian immigration into the United States – a vindictive gesture that deeply offended many Japanese. After the accession of Emperor Hirohito in 1926 Japan lurched sharply towards a bellicose and imperialist stance that threatened China and the old European empires in the East.

For the European elites in Southeast Asia, Japanese ambition seemed to be less of a menace to their hold on power than the spread of communism from Soviet Russia. We can more easily understand the emergence of nationalist ideas in Asia as a political energy field sparked into life between the poles of Japan and the Communist International. The reality of modernising Japan and the dream of communism were equally inspirational. After the betrayal of Versailles, Asians admired both the Soviet Union and Japan as anti-Western powers. In 1920 the Soviet government burnished its reputation among Chinese intellectuals by repudiating all Russian claims to Chinese territory. Although there was much talk of liberating China from centuries of enfeebling elitist tyranny inspired by the philosophy of Confucius, Soviet-style communism offered some of the same values. Like Confucianism, communism offered ways and means to perfect behaviour. Both were philosophies that in practice, if not in theory, exalted order, hierarchy and strict moral codes. Ho Chi Minh proposed, in his *Road to Revolution*: '… let us [Vietnamese] perfect ourselves intellectually by reading the works of Confucius and revolutionarily by reading the works of Lenin'.

Communism had a much less abstract allure for many Asian radicals. The European empires ruled through proxy collaborating elites like the Malay sultans and the Indian princes. It made sense to argue, as Lenin had done, that domestic inequality was the reverse side of the imperial coin. The communist case was strengthened by the fact that the Bolshevik revolution had happened in backward Russia, on the eastern margin of Europe, with its vast peasant masses and small, embryonic working class. Josef Stalin was himself a Georgian, who had stepped rough-hewn from the Russian periphery and who became 'Bolshevik Commissar of Nationalities' in 1917. Later, Stalin would quash any kind of self-determination for the Soviet minorities – but in the immediate aftermath of the revolution he backed the cause of the anti-colonial movement. The second Comintern congress was held on the threshold of Asia in the town of Baku in the Caucasus, and many non-European delegates attended to debate the 'colonial question'. The congress brought into focus a problem that would come back to haunt the Malayan communists during the Emergency. When Lenin addressed Asian delegates at the congress, he urged them to adopt a 'Popular Front' strategy – by which he meant bonding with bourgeois nationalists and radical peasants to overthrow the colonial powers. Socialism could wait. It was well known that Lenin had always and vehemently opposed the idea of 'Popular Fronts' in Europe, but now believed they would work in backward Asia. Lenin was astonished when the Indian nationalist Narendra Nath Bhattacharya, who called himself M.N. Roy, stood up and denounced the Russian leader's speech. Roy had been in Berlin in 1919–20 and witnessed the collapse of the German revolution. He had concluded, he told the Comintern delegates, that the Western proletariat could not hope to capture power until imperialism had been weakened by the revolt of the colonial peoples. In short, it was the duty of Asian communists to open a second front. Responding to Lenin's advocacy of a 'Popular Front', Roy argued that the bourgeois nationalists were much too closely attached to the colonial rulers. He laughed when Lenin praised the 'revolutionary' Gandhi.

Roy may have been right to see Gandhi as a reactionary cultural revivalist, but he and other Indian communists grossly underestimated the determined resistance to the communist ideas they would encounter in India. Roy made no bones about the horrors of caste, but his frequent diatribes about its iniquities led many Hindus to spurn communism as an alien intrusion. This was not a mistake Gandhi would ever have made. The nationalist Congress Party fused soft-pedalled anti-modern socialism with Hindu traditions. It was the Congress Party that would bring the Raj to its knees – not the Indian Communist Party. The Comintern had great hopes for Japan, which by the early 1920s had become the most heavily industrialised country in Asia and so, according to Leninist theory, ripe for revolution. But the Japanese proletariat never acted according to the theory. In China, however, a handful of communist students had much greater success, even though many of them were sceptical about the Chinese peasantry, which was, in the words of communist Chen Duxiu, a 'partly scattered, partly stupid people possessed of a narrow-minded individualism ...'.

Fault Lines

The Chinese communists appealed directly to Moscow for help. When the Chinese Communist Party (CCP) was founded in Shanghai in July 1921, it was a joint venture between Chen Duxiu and the Comintern representative Grigorii Voitinskii. The Comintern agents who went to China were disconcerted by the Chinese communists. They appeared undisciplined and indecisive. For their part the Chinese resented the high-handed manner of some of the communist officials. Especially disliked was the Dutchman Hendricus Sneevliet, who had set up one of the first communist organisations in Indonesia. He had, it was said by one Chinese communist, 'the habits and attitudes of the Dutchman that lived as colonial masters in the East Indies ...'. When Chinese communist students travelled to Moscow to study at the 'Communist University of the Toilers of the East' they found disconcerting their teachers' insistence on aggressive 'study sessions' and 'self criticism' to discourage 'bad thoughts'. The bigger problem for the Chinese communists was reconciling revolutionary demands with the deteriorating situation back home in China. The high hopes of the revolution and fall of the Qing in 1911 had soon evaporated. Sun Yat-Sen was ousted by the commander of the most powerful Chinese army Yuan Shikai, who abandoned social reform and declared himself emperor. He ruled as a despot. After Yuan's death in 1916, power fell into the hands of military cliques – known as 'warlords'. In the 'warlord era' the new Chinese republic was broken asunder. How then could the Chinese communists talk of opening another front by waging class war? What did Moscow think?

The Comintern proposed a gradualist solution. China would have to be united by a national bourgeois revolution before the CCP could hope to seize power. On the basis of this theoretical conclusion the Comintern backed both horses – the CCP and Sun Yat-Sen's Kuomintang. The grand plan was for the CCP to become a bloc within the Kuomintang as a 'United Front'. Soviet advisors arrived to negotiate terms and Red Army officers trained Kuomintang and CCP soldiers together at the Whampoa Military Academy. Since the CCP was a branch of the Comintern the Chinese communists had very little ideological room to manoeuvre. The Comintern's word was law. The 'United Front' was a shotgun wedding arranged in Moscow that rapidly began to fall apart. As the Chinese elites, the rich merchants and landowners who supported the Kuomintang, began to resist social reform, the CCP moved to the left. The leadership backed strikes in the cities and peasant uprisings in the countryside against the hated and avaricious landlords.

This assault on the rural gentry and merchant classes was a direct challenge to the Chinese Nationalists. It was the old Chinese elites, whom the communists denounced as the main obstacle to national unity, that bankrolled the Kuomintang. Chiang Kai-Shek had once professed great admiration for the Soviet Union. He had even enrolled one of his sons in the communist youth league, the Komsomol. He respected the Red Army advisors who trained his young men at the Military Academy. Now, it seemed, the communists had shown their true hand. Chiang Kai-Shek had never been much interested in reform; he was, to be sure, no revolutionary. As the CCP turned leftwards and began challenging the 'selfish' elites, and conspiring against his leadership, Chiang Kai-Shek turned against the 'United Front'. In 1926 he launched the 'Northern Expedition', a military campaign that he proclaimed would unite China and defeat the warlords. His real purpose was to smash the communists. Chiang's 'National Revolutionary Army', which had been financed and trained by the Soviets, rampaged through China's eastern provinces. They defeated some warlords but many more joined forces with the Kuomintang – swelling the ranks of Chiang Kai-Shek's army with well-armed legionaries who hated communism. As the National Revolutionary Army closed in on Shanghai, the communists organised an uprising of 200,000 workers and deposed the local warlord. Their triumph was short-lived. In the spring of 1927 the Kuomintang army descended on Shanghai and smashed the 'United Front'. Chiang Kai-Shek turned on the communists. Backed by the Green Gang Mafia, city magnates and the international police, Kuomintang murder squads embarked on a killing spree to liquidate the communists and their sympathisers. The warlord General Bai won a macabre and deserved reputation as the 'Hewer of Communist Heads'. Tens of thousands of communists were murdered. The massacre inspired the epic novel *La Conditione Humaine* by the French '*homme engagé*', André Malraux, which, in true Gallic style, exalted heroic death in a noble cause. Bitterly denounced by the old guard of the Chinese nationalist movement, cut adrift by the Soviets, 'Generalissimo' Chiang Kai-Shek retreated to Nanjing. China's civil wars were not over. Nor had the Japanese abandoned their imperial ambitions. In 1931, the Japanese Kwantung army stormed into Manchuria and after a brutal campaign established a militarised client state called Manchukuo under the puppet ruler Pu Yi. After 1931 there was near continuous fighting between Chinese and Japanese armies. In July 1937, a skirmish at the Marco Polo Bridge in Beijing provoked a full-scale invasion by the Japanese Imperial Army. It was the beginning of a long and brutal war that would blight China and its peoples for nearly fifteen years.

These convulsions in mainland China generated violent shockwaves across the entire 'Nanyang' world of overseas Chinese. For many Asian nationalists who had no ties with China, Japanese aggression was conclusive proof that an Asian nation could compete with the other global powers. They brushed aside reports of grisly massacres in Nanjing and elsewhere and dismissed the lamentations of Western journalists – and writers like W.H. Auden and Christopher Isherwood, whose book *Journey to a War* published in 1939 exposed the horrors of the Sino-Japanese war: 'And maps can really point to places/Where life is evil now: Nanking. Dachau.' This was not an arbitrary juxtaposition. The Meiji oligarchs had taken Prussia as a model nation state. Although Adolf Hitler despised all 'yellow skinned' Asian peoples, Japan, which had left the League of Nations, signed the 'Anti-Comintern Pact' with Germany in 1935 – and in 1940 would become a fully fledged member of the 'Axis'. The world was now divided between two competitive imperialist power blocs and Japan was on a collision course with the colonial powers of Southeast Asia – Britain, France and the Netherlands.

Here then is the core paradox of anti-colonial nationalism in Asia. Japan behaved as a bellicose imperialist power by invading and occupying Manchuria and mainland China. The consequence was that all the many different Chinese communities and economic classes in Malaya and Indonesia were united in their hatred and fear of the Japanese. And yet for many Asian nationalists who had no ties to China it was Imperial Japan that still held out the best hope of ousting the European colonial powers. In Singapore and British Malaya even the most astute Malays were indifferent to what was happening in China. The Japanese rampage in China galvanised the Nanyang world of overseas Chinese communities. The sparks fell on well-primed tinder.

As early as June 1913 Lenin had noted the spread of a 'revolutionary democratic movement' to the Dutch East Indies. He looked forward to an alliance of the European proletariat with the 'young democracy of Asia'. Lenin, as we noted earlier, clashed with the Indian communist M.N. Roy at the Second Congress of the Communist International – and the Comintern ideologues in Moscow frequently misread 'Oriental communism'. For example, Lenin in his 'Thesis on the National and Colonial Questions', which was adopted at the Second Congress, deplored the 'reactionary medieval influences of the clergy' – coded reference to

pan-Islamic movements. At the Fourth Comintern Conference held in Petrograd
and Moscow in December 1922, the Indonesian representative Tan Malaka raised
the question of pan-Islamism once again, arguing that it was a popular movement
for national independence and merited support. He was shouted down. The
polarisation between radical Muslims and the PKI was an important reason why
the Indonesian uprising in 1926 was such an ignominious disaster.

Nevertheless, a number of communist parties sprang up in many regions of
Southeast Asia – in the Philippines, French Indochina, Malaya, Thailand and
eventually in Burma. The Comintern, however, still tending to view Southeast
Asia as an appendage of China, sent six cadres of CCP recruiters to Malaya and
Singapore in 1923 and, in the spirit of the United Front, funnelled supporters
to the Malayan branch of the KMT. This first wave of Chinese proselytisers
established a 'South Seas Committee' that brought together a broad church of
radical movements – or national revolutionary organisations – to harmonise
activities across Southeast Asia.

The ideologues in Moscow were frequently at odds with the Asian communists.
Following the disastrous PKI uprising in 1926, Moscow tried to impose a policy
of regional discipline through the 'South Seas Communist Party': the 'Nanyang-
kung-ch'an-tang'. Ho clearly understood that there could be communist
revolution without national liberation. This implied a 'broad front' assault on the
colonial powers. Stalin concurred. His Comintern spokesman, Dmitri Manuilsky,
criticised the PKI leaders for 'losing control over the national liberation
movement which passes into the hands of native nationalist elements'. As we will
see, it was an alliance between communists and 'national liberation movements'
that most alarmed the colonial powers. In British Malaya, the communal divisions
between Malays, Chinese and Indians would make any pact between communists
and nationalists well-nigh impossible to achieve.

In 1921, a young communist called Mak Chau had settled in Kuala Lumpur,
where he established the 'Nanyang Critique Society'. Ostensibly an education
debating society it was in fact the first communist organisation in Malaya.
Communists competed with the Malayan Kuomintang to find converts in
Chinese schools, which enjoyed considerable autonomy from the colonial
government. Since the Chinese schools were financed by the conservative 'Huay
Kuan' and the Chinese Chambers of Commerce, the KMT had most success.
During the United Front period, when the CCP and the KMT freely co-operated,
Malayan communists had a much bigger impact. On the night of 28 February
1926, the Special Branch raided a meeting at the 'Chi Min Night School' in
Blair Road, Kuala Lumpur and arrested local members of the 'Nanyang Public
Bodies Union' and a number of visiting delegates. The Special Branch seized
communist pamphlets in such profusion that they concluded, wrongly, that they
had stumbled on a hitherto unknown Malayan Communist Party. After the failed
Indonesian revolution a number of PKI members, like Tan Malaka and Alimin,

sought refuge and began proselytising in Singapore and Malaya. They had most success among the Hainanese. According to Malaysian historian Koo Kay Kim, this was because communism had secured an early and pervasive hold on Hainan Island, and because in Singapore and Malaya Hainanese speakers had a low social and economic status compared to other Chinese dialect groups. So it was that Hainanese trade guilds and unions of rubber tappers developed a precociously radical consciousness. In 1924 the Comintern – which effectively meant the CCP – established the 'Nanyang General Labour Union' to organise labour in Southeast Asia. By the end of the decade the Comintern was still struggling to repair the fallout from the Kuomintang purges in China that had splintered the labour movements in Southeast Asia. It was not until early April 1930 that Ho Chi Minh, as Comintern agent for Southeast Asia, brought together representatives of the main 'Nanyang' labour organisations in Malaya to formally open the first congress of the 'Malayan Communist Party'. It remains uncertain precisely when and where this momentous congress took place, but on the evening of 29 April Special Branch agents raided a house at 24 Nassim Road in Singapore and arrested a number of the new party's Central Committee and confiscated incriminating pamphlets and plans for a May Day rally. All eight arrested at the meeting were sentenced to two years in prison for 'illegal activities'. The colonial state was sharpening its claws.

The Birth of a Secret State

Colonial British Chinese policy was traditionally a muddle of grudging respect, envy and bewilderment. But in the aftermath of the Bolshevik revolution in Russia, attitudes to overseas Chinese in Asian colonies hardened. The British, Dutch and French colonial powers had no doubt that communism had emerged as the main threat to their empires. The founders of the communist movement had denounced imperialism in no uncertain terms. Karl Marx saw the impact of British colonial rule in India as 'palpable and confounding ... – the Hindus [sic] must throw off the English yoke altogether'. Lenin wrote in 1915: 'If tomorrow Morocco were to declare war on France, India on England, Persia or China on Russia, and so forth, those would be "just", "defensive" wars, irrespective of who attacked first, and every socialist would sympathise with the victory of the oppressed, dependent, unequal states against the oppressing, slave owning, predatory "great" powers.'

In Singapore and Malaya the British fretted that Chinese communists were plotting the downfall of their empire. Even in its halcyon days the British colonial world was saturated by fear. Colonial unease focused on the Chinese and Indian communities. Malays were supposedly docile; the Japanese were allies. The consequence of fear was a colonial police state dominated by the Special Branch. This secretive organisation had been founded in London by the Metropolitan

Police to stop a wave of attacks by Irish 'Fenians'. The Special Branch was from its inception an imperial police force. An Indian section was set up in 1909. Its brief was to command and control the empire and vanquish its enemies whether they were Irish republicans or Indian nationalists. In February 1915, as Chinese New Year celebrations reached a climax in the streets of Singapore, Indian troops of the 5th Light Infantry mutinied at the Alexandra Barracks. The mutineers were mainly Rajput Muslims. They seized rifles and stocks of ammunition and took over the Tanglin barracks. Here they discovered German prisoners, captured when the light cruiser SMS *Emden* had been sunk in the Cocos Islands, and tried to persuade them to join the mutiny. Preferring the security of their cells, the Germans refused. One group of sepoys laid siege to the bungalow of the much-disliked commanding officer Lt Colonel E.V. Martin. He and a handful of other British officers, reinforced by members of the Malay States Volunteer Rifles, held out until the morning. In the meantime, sepoys roamed the streets of Singapore firing at Europeans. The British governor general was forced to call for assistance. Some 600 Japanese volunteered and a small flotilla of French, Russian and Japanese warships steamed into Singapore. A combined operation proceeded to crush the mutiny. The survivors fled to Johor, where they were arrested by the sultan's bodyguard. In the following weeks 200 sepoys were court-martialled and forty-seven executed by firing squad. It was all thoroughly alarming. The Court of Enquiry, established in the aftermath of the mutiny, made much of Lt Colonel Martin's incompetence. The 400-page report the commission issued blamed 'local factors'. There was, Lord Crewe reported to Parliament, 'no bigger picture'. This was complacent nonsense as Governor General Arthur Young knew very well: 'I am afraid that it is due to something much more serious.' The Special Branch in India had indeed been picking up garbled reports about Indian 'Ghadr' nationalists in Singapore and Muslim imams. Special Branch agents had targeted a wealthy Indian Muslim merchant called Kasim Ali Mansur, who was fervently pro-German and, it was believed, well known to the Sepoys of the 5th Light Infantry. Also under surveillance was Nur Alam Shah, an imam at a mosque in Kampong Java Road – a 'very seditious and fanatical man', it was said. Some of the mutineers had visited Alam Shah's home, it was alleged, and he seems to have stirred them up with information about a fleet of German warships that was expected imminently in Singapore. Whatever the value of this information, the scandalous fact was that the Indian Special Branch had not troubled to inform their counterparts in Singapore.

While the British were still struggling to fathom the cause of the Singapore mutiny, trouble erupted in Pasir Puteh about 30 miles south of Kota Bahru in the northern Malay state of Kelentan.[16] Few Europeans lived in this remote area, so it came as a shock when the British advisor W. Langham-Carter sent an urgent message to Singapore that he was under attack. It turned out that the leader of the uprising was Haji Mohd Hassan bin Munas, better known as To' Janggut – a Silat martial-art master who sported an impressive, chest-length beard (*janggut* means beard in Malay). At the time the colonial authorities interpreted the trouble as a 'tax riot'. The British had indeed imposed a very unpopular new land tax in the state. These were hard times. In April 1915, To' Janggut had organised protests against the levy and the district officer, an unpopular fellow of mixed Malay and Indian ancestry called Che Latif, had been killed. When local police tried to arrest To' Janggut he escaped and a mob sacked the Pasir Puteh District Office and began burning the bungalows of the few European plantation owners who lived in the area. In Singapore, Governor Young, already unnerved by the sepoy mutiny, did not hesitate to act. He despatched two Royal Navy warships to Kota Bahru, which landed a force of 300 troops backed by Malay policemen and Malay State Guides. To' Janggut's insurgents fought a hit-and-run war – often frustrating the government troops. But on 23 May, a brigade of Malay State Guides cornered the rebels and slaughtered them all. To' Janggut had told his followers that he could not be killed by infidel bullets but there could be no doubt about the identity of the 'venerable bearded man' discovered lying behind a hedge next to an elephant gun. To' Janggut was stone dead. He showed signs of having suffered from elephantiasis. As news spread that the mighty warrior was mortal after all, his surviving followers lost heart: the Kelantan Uprising was over. This little-known skirmish was the first counter-insurgency campaign fought by British troops in Malaya. In a macabre foreshadowing of modern counter-insurgency tactics, the body of the rebel leader was used to make a point. To' Janggut's corpse was hauled to the bank of the Kelantan River and nailed upside down to a wooden frame as a grisly warning. The rotting corpse was not taken down for many days: a calculated affront to Muslims, who are required to bury the deceased as soon as possible after death. It is almost certain that British officers ordered the post-mortem humiliation of To' Janggut but a report by local police officer A.G. Morkill, whose photographs of the dead rebel leader can be viewed at Rhodes House in Oxford, suggests a different explanation. Morkill claimed that it was the Sultan of Kelantan who ordered the body to be publicly hung by the feet 'for four hours'. He did this, so the report suggests, to prove his loyalty to the British. The sultan may well have had something to hide. In the aftermath of these bloody events, Acting Colonial Secretary William Maxwell noted that 'His Highness the Sultan [of Kelantan] has ever since the Singapore mutiny believed that the downfall of the British Empire was at hand …'. The Turkish Ottomans were German allies. When war had broken out in 1914 the caliph had declared a 'Jihad' against the Entente Powers. The proclamation reverberated across the Muslim world – as far as the devout Malay state of Kelantan. Even in this remote, rural and sparsely populated corner of Malaya malevolent forces appeared to have been plotting the downfall of the empire.

For the British in Singapore, 1915 had been a troubling year. Violence had exploded in their midst like a tropical storm. Special Branch agents, it seemed, had acquired troubling information about various nefarious characters in Singapore but had chosen not to alert the authorities in Singapore. There seemed to be an intelligence black hole that threatened the Far Eastern bastion of the empire. Something had to be done. It would be a gruff, puritanical young Scot who would begin to repair this hopeless state of affairs. Born and educated in granite Aberdeen, David Petrie joined the Indian Police and Criminal Intelligence Department after leaving university in 1900. He was tough, forbidding and clever. In November, Petrie was despatched to Singapore to begin a root-and-branch reform of intelligence operations. His most far-reaching proposal was that there should be a dedicated department of intelligence that would not be burdened by mundane police work and could devote all its resources to ferreting out enemies of the colonial state. There were many of these, it seemed. The new 'Criminal Intelligence Department' (later renamed Special Branch) began work in 1918. Its director was René Henry de Solminihac Onraet, a former police officer and an alumnus of Stonyhurst College in Lancashire. He made the task of the reformed Singapore Special Branch very clear: it was to defend the peninsula from the deadly infection of radical political ideas. He had first made his mark in Penang, where he had defeated a gambling syndicate. Onraet was an avid reader of cheap spy novels and learnt some useful tricks from his fictional heroes. He often alluded to 'The Hidden Hand' to sensationalise the threat of communism. Under his dogged leadership Special Branch agents targeted left-wing printing presses and offices. His most celebrated coup was a raid on a purported bomb-making factory in the Balestier Road, central Singapore, where his agents discovered a cache of seditious leaflets with titles such as 'How to Carry out a Revolutionary Movement in the South Seas'. The Singapore Special Branch would obsess about the 'Red' threat to British Malaya until the moment a Japanese army stormed onto the beaches of Kota Bahru in December 1941. The colonial security had been looking in the wrong direction.

Three Lives

That the ethnic caricatures and communal identities imposed by the colonial government in British Malaya were profoundly damaging both to Britain and its subjects cannot be doubted. Recently a number of autobiographical narratives have emerged that illuminate the Asian experience of British rule and Japanese conquest. These include *My Side of History* by the Malayan communist leader Chin Peng that challenges many conventional accounts of the 'Emergency War'. Just as revealing are the memoirs of Malay nationalist Mustapha Hussain, one of the founders of the KMM, which were compiled and edited by his daughter, Insun Sony Mustapha. These political lives have much to tell us about the ferment of ideas that smouldered in the schools and kampongs of British Malaya on the eve of conquest. At the same time, we have learnt a great deal more about the treacherous Secretary General of the MCP, Lai Tek, whose astonishing career as a triple agent would poison the communist movement in Malaya and render its war with the colonial powers ultimately unwinnable.

Sometime in 1935, a stocky, dark-skinned Asian with a narrow face and a thin slit of a mouth strolled into a Chinese grocery store in Hong Kong owned by one Wu Si Li. Soon the stranger would become notorious as Lai Tek.[17] His real name was probably Pham Van Dac and he was as protean and treacherous as his many identities. That day, Lai Tek presented himself as an agent of the Comintern. Wu Si Li's store was a front used by both the CCP and the Malayan communists and Lai Tek was provided with funds to purchase a boat ticket to Singapore. As soon as he arrived he made his way to the Kongsi house of the Singapore Vegetable Growers' Association, another MCP front address, where he met someone calling himself Chen Liang. Lai Tek boasted that he was a 'senior Comintern liaison officer from Hong Kong' who had been sent to Singapore as a troubleshooter to ginger up the communist movement. He had, or appeared to have, impressive credentials. He had, he claimed, studied communist theory in France and Russia and had been a member of the Shanghai Town Committee of the CCP. He also claimed to be close to Ho Chi Minh. There was no one in Singapore who could disprove Lai Tek's account – and his rise to the top of the party was swift. In March 1937, Lai Tek took centre stage when the MCP backed striking miners at the Batu Arang coal mine in Selangor. The miners set up a 'Soviet' – the first ever in Malaya. The strike and the 'Soviet' swiftly collapsed but Lai Tek had made a powerful impression. Not long afterwards, he was elected secretary general of the party. His appointment was a spectacular coup – not for the Comintern, but for the British Special Branch. For Lai Tek was a double agent. When the Japanese occupied Malaya he would sell his political soul once again.

To understand how the Special Branch engineered the appointment of their agent to the very top of the banned MCP we need to go back to Lai Tek's first steps on the political stage of Southeast Asia. We now know that he was born Pham Van Dac in or near Saigon (then the capital of the federated French colony of Indochina) in 1903.[18] His father was Vietnamese, his mother Chinese: so he would have been called a *métis*, or, in Vietnamese, *minh huong*. It would seem that Pham Van Dac became politically active in his early twenties and began calling himself Lai Rac, the first of at least thirty-eight different aliases. What we do know for certain is that in 1925, when Lai Tek had just turned 22, he was arrested by the 'Sûreté Générale Indochinoisie' – a bureau of the French colonial secret service. Somehow Lai Tek was persuaded to work as an informer. The motivation may simply have been greed: Lai Tek liked to live high on the hog. In colonial Southeast Asia, French, Dutch and British security forces shared a fear of communist subversion and sometimes worked together. In the early 1930s, René Onraet, the head of the Singapore Special Branch, paid a cordial visit to his opposite number in the Sûreté Générale in Saigon. There is no evidence that Onraet was himself introduced to Lai Tek, but what seems most likely is that, for whatever reason, Lai Tek was no longer considered to be useful by the French and so was 'offered' to the British. In the meantime, Ho Chi Minh sent a number of Vietnamese communists, including Lai Tek, to Moscow to take classes at the Communist University of the Toilers of the East. The fact that Ho trusted Lai Tek enough to send him to this Comintern nerve centre suggests that he had acquired impressive skills passing himself off as a loyal and dedicated party member. This sojourn at the Comintern university in Moscow would provide Lai Tek with immense authority in faraway Malaya. He was the 'Comintern's man' and his word was law.

There is no extant documentary evidence to show how and when Lai Tek began developing a relationship with the Special Branch in Singapore. In May 1931, Onraet sent an invitation to George Nadaud, Controlleur Générale de la Sûreté Générale Indochinoise, to attend the trial in Singapore of the French Comintern agent Joseph Ducroux. They would have shared other information – and perhaps discussed how to make further use of Lai Tek. So it is likely that when Lai Tek walked into Wu Si Li's grocery store in Hong Kong in 1935 he was already working as a British agent. We do know that shortly after his arrival in Singapore Lai Tek secretly made contact with Onraet. The details of their meetings have never come to light, but the Special Branch chief must have seen the value of this new 'asset' because he assigned one of his top agents F.I. (Innes) Tremlett, who spoke fluent Cantonese, to act as Lai Tek's case officer. Lai Tek now became, for Special Branch purposes, 'Mr Wright'.

It was Tremlett who exploited the Batu Arang strike to establish Lai Tek's reputation as a political firebrand thus propelling him to the top job in the MCP. Very soon after Lai Tek was appointed secretary general, Special Branch agents arrested a number of Malayan communists and deported them to China. This was tantamount to a death sentence because the Kuomintang was now engaged in a ruthless and bloody civil war with the CCP. There can be no doubt at all that Lai Tek contrived these arrests to eliminate rivals and anyone who suspected his loyalty to the party. These were purges carried out with British connivance.

As Lai Tek clambered his way to the top rungs of the Malayan Communist Party, a bright schoolboy called Ong Boon Hua was dreaming of liberating the Chinese motherland from the hated Japanese. A few years after finishing school, Ong Boon Hua would be fighting the Japanese in the jungles of Malaya. By then he had adopted his *nom de guerre* – Chin Peng. He would eventually take on the might of the British Empire, becoming one of the most feared guerrilla leaders in the world. Chin Peng would not give up the cause of armed revolution in Malaya until 1989. As I was completing this book the old revolutionary was lying mortally sick in a hospital room somewhere in Bangkok. For more than two decades the Malaysian government rejected Chin Peng's many appeals to be allowed to return home. Bygones, it would seem, could never be bygones. He would always have been the spectre at the Malaysian feast.

The boy who would take the name Chin Peng was born on 21 October 1924 in a two-storey shop house on Jalan Kampong Koh in Sitiawan, a small seaside town in southern Perak. His father, Wong Sing Piaw, had been born in the coastal village of Jiang Dou in the Fukien province not far from Amoy. Orphaned when he was very young, Wong Sing Piaw came to Singapore to stay with an uncle when he had barely reached his teens. His uncle found him work as an apprentice with the Chop Ban Hong Leong company which sold bicycle and motor car spare parts. Wong Sing Piaw did well and quickly learned both Malay and English. Then, after an arranged marriage to locally born Kwan Nan Yong, whose father owned a rickshaw company, he left Singapore to manage a rubber plantation and bicycle shop for his uncle in Telok Anson in Perak. Soon afterwards the business expanded into nearby Sitiawan.

Like many ambitious 'new men' Wong Sing Piaw made good use of his old village connections, providing his growing family with a reasonably comfortable lifestyle in this quiet Malayan backwater. He was a successful businessman and a community leader: he was elected President of the Fook Ching Huay Kuan, a clan association, and served as chairman of the local primary school board. Chin Peng was the second son. He had two sisters and five brothers. For much of their childhood the children enjoyed a reasonably comfortable middle-class life. As he grew up Boon Hua walked 1 mile each way to the Hua Chiao Primary School (the Sitiawan Overseas Chinese Primary School). His family was Buddhist, but he recalled a Pastor Shi persuading him to join a Methodist youth club where the Chinese boys all sang 'Onward Christian Soldiers' in Hokkien. They played near the local Planters' Club, which was closed to non-Europeans. The British education authorities censored school textbooks removing any pejorative references to 'imperialists'. But Boon Hua and his schoolfriends soon learnt about the catastrophe overwhelming China. He was on the brink of adolescence when the Japanese invaded Manchuria and then attacked Shanghai. Political discussions were banned in Chinese schools but the shattering news from the motherland filtered through Chinese literature classes and was heard in the gossip of adults. At the same time, the Depression had a devastating impact on the fortunes of Ban Hong Leong. Like many hard-pressed Malays Boon Hua's father was forced to borrow money from Indian moneylenders, known as *Chettiars*. He also tried, without success, to set up a brokerage business selling smallholdings to the big rubber estates. This quixotic enterprise took him away from home for long periods of time and forced Boon Hua's mother, who could neither read nor write, to take over the spare-parts business alone, teaching herself a crude but effective method of bookkeeping. She made a great success of the business and became an agent for the big tyre-makers Dunlop, Goodyear, Firestone and Michelin. Boon Hua's brother, Boon Eng, had an aptitude for mechanics: he could take apart and repair any bicycle or motorcycle. Boon Hua, the future communist guerrilla leader, had few practical skills. Instead, he totted up his mother's takings at the end of every week and trotted nervously down to deposit them at the local Chartered Bank.

Sitiawan appeared on the surface to be a provincial backwater of small businesses and shop houses. But the Chinese community was highly politicised. Most shop houses displayed a photograph of Sun Yat-Sen, who had once taken refuge in Penang, and the Kuomintang leader Chiang Kai-Shek. On certain days, many Chinese wore black armbands to commemorate the tragic incidents of recent history. All over Southeast Asia, Japanese aggression against China galvanised Chinese communities. The Chinese in Malaya were preoccupied by what was happening in their old homeland and were deeply divided among themselves. Few knew much about Mao Zedong and the communists who had fled to escape the Kuomintang. It was not only the Chinese working and lower-middle classes in Singapore and Malaya that were drawn to the Chinese struggle against Japan. A handful of wealthy entrepreneurs became just as committed as young Boon Hua and his schoolfriends in Sitiawan. A most intriguing case is that of Tan Kah Kee, the 'Henry Ford of Malaya', who was a Singapore legend. But when he died in Beijing in 1961 this frail rather scholarly looking man, who had made and lost immense fortunes in colonial Singapore and Malaya, would be given a state funeral in communist China attended by Chou En Lai and Marshall Chen Yi.

Tan Kah Kee's is one of the most remarkable of all twentieth-century Asian lives. Although he never completely mastered the language of the colonial power, Tan Kah Kee was one of the king's most favoured subjects in the Straits Settlements. He was born in 1874 on the shores of the South China Sea in the village of Chi Mei in the Fukien province. He and his brother, who was much younger, saw their father, Tan Kee Peck, only on very rare occasions, when he returned from Singapore where he managed a thriving rice business. Father and sons appear not to have got on well. When Tan Kee Peck sickened and died in 1890, the 17-year-old Tan Kah Kee was ordered to proceed to Singapore and help manage the family business. 'Short, slim and frail looking' with a queue and half-shaven head to signify Manchu subjugation, Tan Kah Kee proved himself a gifted businessman. In 1904 he branched out into rubber; by 1911 he was a millionaire; at the end of the First World War, a multimillionaire. He owned a German Daimler car and three enormous mansions at 42 Cairnhill Road. These were important symbols of wealth and prestige. But Tan Kah Kee was an unstintingly generous philanthropist. Although both his English and Malay were rudimentary he was passionate about literacy. He was a founder of Amoy University and in 1924 established a library at the Singapore Ee Ho Hean 'Millionaire's Club' in Bukit Pasoh Road. He spent most of his spare time ensconced there reading, thinking and planning. He had a vast network of contacts. Tan Kah Kee dreamt of uniting the overseas Chinese to free their homeland from the Japanese oppressor. At the end of 1939, Tan Kah Kee decided to go back to China to find out what was happening on the ground. He took the train north to Rangoon in Burma and then boarded a rickety little aircraft bound for Chungking, Chiang Kai-Shek's new capital.

Tan Kah Kee was not impressed when he met the self-centred, petty-minded 'Generalissimo', and – he was something of a puritan – dismayed by the antics of the idle and hedonistic Kuomintang leaders. So Tan Kah Kee travelled on overland to find Chiang Kai-Shek's hated rival, the Communist leader Mao Zedong. He eventually tracked him in the caves of Yenan on the edge of the Gobi Desert in northern China where the communists had taken refuge after the 'Long March'. Mao's austere stronghold was the antithesis of Chiang's Chungking. He had a series of meetings with Mao and his comrades in a dank and claustrophobic cave and became convinced that the egalitarian, single-minded communists could defeat Chiang Kai-Shek's dilettante adventurers. When Tan Kah Kee returned to Malaya this unimaginably wealthy old man embarked on a national lecture tour to persuade the Chinese community that the future salvation of China lay in the hands of Mao and the communists. He insisted that he himself was not a communist. He was simply being realistic. His fervent advocacy of the Chinese communists provoked a storm of abuse and suspicion but he inspired many young Chinese men, and thousands volunteered to fight in China. Some toiled, and died, on the Burma Road. Others made the arduous journey to Yenan to learn guerrilla tactics at the feet of Mao. The Japanese followed the wealthy and untouchable Tan Kah Kee's activities with frustration and anger.

At the Anglo-Chinese Continuation School in Sitiawan, which was run by the Methodist Church, the young Ong Boon Hua – the future Chin Peng – was getting involved in politics. In 1937, the MCP set up the Anti-Enemy [Anti-Japanese in some references] Backing-Up Society (AEBUS) with branches all over Malaya. The British harried the AEBUS, well aware of its connections to the banned MCP – but this did not deter passionate young men and women, who hoped to fight for their motherland, joining up. Boon Hua was not yet a communist. His schoolfriends were all obsessed with an older student called Fung Shou Yi, who had managed to reach China and join the air force. (After the war he became a successful entrepreneur and anti-communist.) Boon Hua fervently wanted to join the nationalist Kwangsi Nan'ning Infantry Academy, but his parents rejected the idea. It is not entirely clear why the young Chin Peng abandoned his commitment to the Kuomintang.

In his memoir *My Side of History*, Chin Peng tells us that when he turned 15 he began devouring Mao's 'Protracted War'. If we are to believe his account, the AEBUS was just as preoccupied with the injustices of British colonial occupation as Japanese aggression in China. Young Boon Hua had impressed the local members of the MCP, one of whom was his Chinese literature teacher, Chen Jin Yun. When he left the school at the end of 1939, an old friend called Du Lung San called on Boon Hua and explained to him the way in which the MCP had established the 'Anti Backing-Up Societies' to co-ordinate support for the

Chinese nationalists. He wanted Boon Hua to take over from his teacher and lead political operations in the Sitiawan district. It was a heady opportunity for the 16-year-old. He was now a probationary member of the Communist Party. It was January 1940. Six months later, Boon Hua was forced to leave the Anglo-Chinese Continuation School to devote himself to the revolutionary cause. He had become Chin Peng.

Mustapha Hussain was a founding father of Malay nationalism. He would seem to have little in common with the communist Chin Peng. They took divergent roads to freedom. And yet both cared passionately about freeing Malaya from the colonial yoke and both endured years of isolation and denigration. After the war, the British arrested Hussain and denounced him as a collaborator. He took to cooking and selling food from a street cart in Kampong Bahru, the Malay village in central Kuala Lumpur. The food and Mustapha's conversation became famous. But this clever, sensitive man never completely recovered from the way he had been disgraced by the British – and by his fellow Malays. Many years later, after a long silence, he was asked to give a talk about Malay nationalism to an audience of Malaysian students. He wrote: 'bitter and gruelling experiences' flooded back: 'as a Malay Fifth Columnist leader, detained in several British lock-ups and prisons, taunted and jeered by Malays who saw me hawking food on the roadside, humiliated by people who slammed their doors in my face [...] even labelled as the Malay who brought the Japanese into Malaya ...'.

Mustapha Hussain was born the fourth in a family of ten children in Matang in Perak on 21 August 1910. It was dusk, he tells us, and the Prophet's legendary 'Night Journey' the 'Lailat al Mi'raj' was being noisily celebrated at the village mosque. The family had roots in northern Sumatra: a distant ancestor was Sultan Alam Shah of Batu Barain, who was a 'Nakhoda' or 'trader captain'. 'Thankfully', the egalitarian Hussain remarks, his ancestors 'did away' with their titles when they crossed the straits to find a new life in the peninsula. Hussain grew up with a strong sense of Malay history and tradition, but he also had a natural route to the radical Malay intelligentsia that sluggishly emerged in the first decades of the twentieth century. His father, Haji Hussain bin Haji Aminuddin, worked as a surveyor for the colonial government and had taught himself to speak English, which was despised by many kampong folk and traditional religious teachers as 'the language of hell'. He also tried to introduce the new Malay newspapers to the kampong – with little success. For his pains he was branded as 'Satan'. But Mustapha's father was a resourceful man, who supplemented his regular salary with earnings from a rubber smallholding.

At the beginning of the last century Matang, Mustapha's home town, was a colonial crossroads on the railway line that linked Port Weld, with its 'tanned Chinese smugglers', and Taiping, which, like Kuala Lumpur, was a city made by tin. Matang was where the British located their government offices (like the district police station) and it was where the first Malay Teachers' College was established before it was moved to Tanjung Malim and became the Sultan Idris Training College. Hussain learnt that it was to the Ngah Ibrahim Fort in Matang that the 'patriots' accused of murdering the 'impatient, unrefined' British Resident James Birch were brought to be hanged in 1877. For Hussain and his brothers, Matang symbolised 'Malay valour and gutsy defiance'. But its recent history demonstrated too the dangers which, according to the *Utusan Melayu*, now imperilled Malays. The 'Tin Wars' drew many Chinese 'mercenaries', as Hussain puts it, to the Larut region. Many decided to stay; the Chinese population swelled. Then the building of the new railway to Port Weld brought in thousands of Tamil labourers. Matang was no longer a Malay stronghold. Chinese entrepreneurs took over Malay shops. Hussain bitterly recalls an Indian Muslim shopkeeper who deviously out-competed Malay traders. Many Chinese, Hussain tells us, suffered from rashes and enjoyed spitting. Their mosquito nets smelt of opium. They even used toothbrushes! In short, the Chinese were different. As the number of migrants coming to Malaya grew, the British began replacing Malay workers with cheaper Indian labourers. The plantation manager opened a 'toddy shop' where Indian workers spent their wages on alcohol, which inevitably led to tense encounters between drunken workers and Muslim Malay villagers.

Hussain tries to demonstrate in his memoir the many ways in which his people were disadvantaged by the colonial economy. Malays disappeared from the rubber estates, displaced by cheaper Indian labourers. Malay entrepreneurs were denied investment. The British, he insists, wanted Malays to remain poor and thus docile. Hussain deeply resented the ubiquitous Indian moneylenders known as '*chettiars*'. These men were 'loathsome' he tells us. Malays were spellbound by rites and traditions. These had to be observed properly. This was expensive. So a wedding or festival usually required a demeaning visit to the local *chettiar* who usually charged exorbitant interest rates. The only collateral most Malays could offer was land, which the *chettiar* was entitled to take possession of in the event that the debt could not be repaid. The cost of observing tradition was a frittering away of property.

During Mustapha's childhood, the Hussain family was immune to these depredations. His father, Haji Hussain, could afford to employ two Tamil labourers, full-time, to do odd jobs on their estate. The Hussains' relative prosperity meant that Mustapha could enrol at the Matang Malay School when he was just 5. He was carried to and from the school by one of his father's odd-job men. This was a devout community. Every afternoon Mustapha attended the Islamic Religious School to prepare, as his mother put it, 'for the next world' by reciting and learning the Koran. In his memoir he provides a vivid account of the *Khatna* – circumcision – a rite of passage for Malay boys usually carried out with a razor blade or bamboo knife. Hussain offers us useful advice on ways to deal with unwanted erections when recovering from circumcision.

When he turned 11, Mustapha won a place in the Special Malay Class at the King Edward VII School in Taiping. Every day at 4.30 a.m. Mustapha and his brothers Osman and Yusuf rode the mangrove-burning Port Weld–Taiping train to get to their new school and enter its big, black, wrought-iron gates. Although Mustapha disparages this 'British experiment' in education, it is telling indeed that the emergence of an intelligentsia, the seedbed of nationalism, however fragile, was the gift of a colonial railway and a colonial school. Mustapha tells us a revealing story about the Malay College. His ambitious father hoped to get at least one of his sons a college scholarship. But the Malay College, 'the Eton of the East', was established to educate the Malay aristocracy, with provision for only a tiny handful of 'commoners'. Mustapha's father would need to call in some favours and he was certain he knew just the person: his exalted cousin, Mohd Hashim bin Datuk Panglima Nakhoda Taruna, was on nodding terms with the even more exalted Raja Sir Chulan. Togged up in a samarinda sarong from the Celebes, a five-buttoned white coat, a red velvet fez and shining pump shoes, Datuk Mohd Hashim called in on Raja Sir Chulan to seek Mustapha's passport to privilege and power. The astonished Datuk was summarily dismissed. No explanation was offered. Clearly the Hussains, descended though they were from Sumatran sultans, were regarded as infra dig. It is said that when a British educationist proposed raising the allowance for the 'commoners', a Malay prince asked: 'Why so much, Tuan? Malays [i.e. Malay peasants] eat only rice and chillies. Just a little will do.'

'Just a little' would never do for Mustapha. He was often rebuked by his teachers but he 'could not stop [...] everything was political'. But when Mustapha appealed to the tiny narrow-minded Malay elite, groomed by the Malay College and rewarded with a job in the MCS, it was, as he nicely put it, 'like drawing water out of a stone'. (Blood was out of the question.) This emerging Malay 'bourgeoisie' played tennis, took dancing lessons and visited cabarets: they had not a care in the world. They had become their masters like the pigs in Orwell's *Animal Farm*.

But in Kuala Lumpur, Mustapha found a secretive network of radicals, many of them Indonesians and probably under surveillance by the Dutch. One of the dissidents who had washed up in Kuala Lumpur was Sutan Jenain. He was older than most of the Malays he drew to his evening meetings in Kampong Baru, the 'Malay Agricultural Settlement' set up by the British in the heart of Kuala Lumpur in 1900. This Malay village set in the midst of a modern Asian city founded by Chinese tin mine owners was a refuge for Indonesian political refugees and the heart of the Malay nationalist movement. (It was in Kampong Baru that the post-independence race riots exploded on 13 May 1969.) 'Old Man Sutan' came up with a resonant analogy: 'A nation is like a fish. If we are independent, we can enjoy the whole fish – head, body and tail. At the moment we are only getting its head and bones. *We* of course meant Malays. Sutan explained:

Every person in a colony, except those in the good books of the colonial masters, lives in misery, poverty and humility.[sic] Who are the poorest people in Malaya? Are they not Malays? In Indonesia it is the Indonesians, except for those feudals [rulers] groomed by the Dutch: they are nothing more than horses the colonial masters ride on.

It was from Sutan Jenain that Mustapha first heard of 'Melayu Raya', or 'Indonesia Raya', a 'Greater Malaya' that, as it were, put back together the old 'Malay Land' that had been filleted by the colonial powers. Although Sutan Jenain warned his young Malay disciples that Indonesia was at a very different stage of political development, 'Greater Malaya' had a heady appeal for Mustapha and his new friends.

Divided We Stand

For many Malays, and certainly for the rulers and the datos, the heady thoughts of radicals like Ibrahim Yaacob and Mustapha Hussain emitted the bad odour of heresy and treason. Radical though they were, nationalists like Hussain and Ibrahim Yaacob developed their ideas inside the communal fences built by the British. The evils of colonialism impacted, it appeared to them, on just one of the races: the Malays. Overthrowing the British meant liberating Malays – giving *them* 'the whole fish'. For his part, the future communist leader Chin Peng admitted in his memoirs that before the war he and his fellow converts had no sense at all of being 'Malayans'. Few Chinese and Malays shared a common language. In the mosques, imams preached that communism was an evil doctrine. The Malay rulers had a phobic hatred of any whiff of egalitarianism. The British, too, did their best to thwart any communal rapprochement. The Director of Special Branch in Singapore, René Onraet, smacked down any effort by Malay radicals to join forces with the communists. A number of Malay delegates had been invited to the inaugural meeting of the MCP in April 1930. They never turned up – but not because of Malay 'laziness' or indifference: the British had intercepted the Malays on their way to the meeting and thrown them in Pudu Jail.

One evening in April 1938, Ibrahim Yaacob, Mustapha Hussain, and a handful of young Malay radicals met secretly at a house in Kuala Lumpur. That night, they formed the first Malayan anti-colonial nationalist organisation – the 'Kesatuan Melayu Muda', the Young Malay Union. Membership was open, as Hussain tells us in his memoir, 'to Malay youths, with Malay fathers, who practised Malay cultures and were Muslims'. The KMM would be the political saviour of '*nusa dan bangsa*' – nation and race. Its founders espoused a profoundly chauvinist national project. The KMM manifesto asserted the natural rights of Malays to possession of the *Tanah Melayu*, the Homeland, conferred on them by God. The KMM detested the way the British 'allow[ed] tens of thousands of "others" into Malaya'. To win a free Malaya for Malays, Ibrahim Yaacob would barter his soul to another imperial power, the Japanese.

3

TENNOUHEIKA BANZAI!

I Cannot Get Over Singapore

When wartime British Prime Minister Winston Churchill heard that Lt General Arthur Percival, the commander of the Singapore garrison, had surrendered unconditionally to the Japanese on 14 February 1942 he famously lamented that the loss of Britain's Far Eastern stronghold and commercial emporium was 'the worst disaster and the largest capitulation in history'. Churchill's doctor, Lord Moran, observed that the prime minister was 'stupefied'. The loss of Singapore, he wrote in his memoir, 'left a scar on his mind'; 'I cannot get over Singapore,' Churchill confessed months later. Nor it seems can British historians 'get over the loss'. The 'worst disaster' has been picked over, dissected and argued about for seventy years. Churchill knew very well that Singapore could never have been adequately defended from attack by a determined enemy. The Japanese Imperial Army was just such a foe.

Churchill, of course, fought the war as the prime minister of an imperial nation. After the Germans had broken through the French defences in May 1940, he spoke on the radio of 'a solemn hour for the life of our country, of our Empire, of our Allies and, above all, the cause of freedom'. Here was the rub. Churchill could never bring himself to offer liberty to the subjects of the empire he loved. It was remarked once that: 'If talking about a chip shop in Salford, Churchill would find a way to mention how important its chips were to the Empire.' By 1941, as Japan prepared its assault on Southeast Asia, Churchill was greatly preoccupied with America. In August, he had met Roosevelt on the US cruiser *Augusta* and the British battlecruiser *Prince of Wales* – that would be torpedoed and sunk off the coast of Pahang a few months later – and had to bite his tongue as Roosevelt used the opportunity to promote an anti-imperialist agenda. Point 3 of the Atlantic Charter insisted that Great Britain and the United States 'respect the right of all peoples to choose the form of government under which they will live ...'. and the restoration of rights to 'those who have been forcibly deprived of them'. This was clearly intended by the Americans as a rebuke to the British and a signal of intent. Leo Amery wrote that: 'We shall no doubt pay dearly in the end for all this fluffy flapdoodle.' Churchill, on his return to London, tried to backtrack on the implications of the 'Atlantic Charter'. But the nationalist cat was out of the bag. In October, U Saw, the Prime Minister of Burma, arrived in London to demand that the charter be applied to the Burmese. Churchill bluntly refused – and had U Saw arrested on his way home for allegedly promising, in conversation with Japanese diplomats, to lead an anti-British revolt. The irony of all this was that Churchill's mind was almost entirely focused on Europe and persuading Americans to come onboard. The Australian premier, Robert Menzies, had no success trying to persuade the British to reinforce Singapore and the naval defence of the Far East. Churchill's military assistant secretary, Sir Ian Jacob, admitted that 'Winston has never really understood the Far East problem and had deliberately starved Singapore in favour of home and the Middle East …'. In the longer run, Churchill knew that what mattered most was not Singapore but Washington. The great island base was worth the sacrifice. Churchill could not have foreseen the treacherous Japanese attack on Pearl Harbor, but he knew that Roosevelt could not stand idly by if the British were driven out of Asia. For the Americans there was too much at stake.

Even if Churchill had resolved to defend this glittering jewel of imperial trade and power, Singapore was doomed. Its defences were in chaos and the majority of the island's English residents thought only of ring-fencing their comfortable and segregated lifestyles as if nothing else mattered. Few of them took the distant war seriously until it was much too late. They were too foolish to fear the Japanese. We read again and again in reports and memoranda blithely disparaging remarks about 'short-sighted little men', who could not see well enough to shoot straight or fly an aircraft. The Japanese were 'gangsters'; they were little yellow men who could be easily 'brushed off'. This entrenched racism amplified the shock of capitulation. The *Daily Mail* cartoonist Leslie Illingworth depicted a simian Emperor Hirohito sporting a plumed colonial-style hat emblazoned with the word 'Singapore'. The caption: 'Fun while it Lasts'.

The *Mail* got it wrong. The conquest by the Japanese of British, Dutch, French and American colonial territories in Southeast Asia in 1941/2 was an event more resonant and decisive than the fall of Malacca to the Portuguese in 1511. It altered for ever the balance of power, both political and emotional, between the European powers and Asians. The Japanese electrified Asian nationalists and held up the beacon of self-determination to the oppressed peoples of Asia. The Japanese had no intention of granting such freedoms to other Asians, but the conquest of British Malaya and the Dutch East Indies released long bottled-up energies. Even if we take into account the weakness of France and the Netherlands, which had been occupied by Nazi Germany, and the beleaguered position of Great Britain, the speed and territorial reach of the Japanese advance was astonishing. In a matter of months, Japan seized a Southeast Asian empire which it had taken Europeans five centuries to complete. The Japanese dealt a savage and lasting blow to British imperial prestige that had been obsessively upheld ever since Sir Stamford Raffles had rolled out the red carpet for Sultan Hussain in 1819. As the Japanese Army raced across Johor and British troops fell back across the causeway connecting the island to the peninsula, students at Raffles College heard a tremendous explosion. A young man called Lee Kuan Yew explained to a fellow student: 'That is the end of the British Empire.' As historian Brian Farrell put it: 'the manner of this defeat was its worst consequence'.

Conquest

In June 1940, the Netherlands and then France fell to Germany. Long frustrated by the failure of the military campaign in mainland China, the Japanese began to look south. They signed an agreement with Phibunsongkhram's government in Thailand and then secured an agreement from the new Vichy regime in France to make use of ports in Indochina. In April 1941, the Japanese joined the other Axis powers in a ten-year tripartite pact, but with impressive foresight reasserted its neutrality agreement with Moscow. By the end of July, the Japanese had to all intents and purposes occupied French Indochina and secured rice, rubber, coal and other minerals from its territories. All this manoeuvring in Asia dismayed the United States and Great Britain, who applied diplomatic pressure and blockade to try and hold back the Japanese advance. All the while, Japanese army and navy planners prepared for operations in Southeast Asia. Then in October, the Minister of War, Hideki Tojo, replaced the more liberal-minded Prince Fumimaro Konoye as Japanese premier. Japan was by now under tremendous pressure from the Allied blockade. Its international prestige was wearing thin. Tojo feared that if he waited the United States might come to the aid of the British and Dutch. So at the beginning of November, Tojo's government decided on an early military strike into Southeast Asia. During the night of 7–8 December, the Japanese fell on Pearl Harbor, the American naval base in the Pacific, British Malaya, the Philippines and Hong Kong.

The Japanese onslaught on Malaya began on 8 December 1941 with simultaneous landings in neutral Thailand at Songkhla (Singora) and Patani, and at Kota Bahru in the northern Malay state of Kelantan. In the course of a shattering *Blitzkrieg*-style campaign, which Lt General Tomoyuki Yamashita called the 'driving charge', Japanese forces punched through every defensive line that the retreating British threw in vain across the peninsula. On 12 December, Japanese troops marched into Alor Setar, the capital of Kedah. In the meantime, the US Pacific Fleet had been crippled, and half of the American air force destroyed, at Clarke Field in the Philippines. On 10 December, Japanese aircraft sank the British capital warships HMS *Repulse* and HMS *Prince of Wales* off the coast of Pahang. Japanese bombers rained fire and terror on Pahang, the oldest British colony in Southeast Asia. The British fled, leaving their Asian subjects to fend for themselves. Within days, the Japanese had effective control of the air and sea. By 28 December, they had swept into Ipoh, in Perak; Kuala Lumpur, the colonial capital of the Federated Malay States, fell on 11 January. The last British line of defence collapsed. By the end of January, Yamashita's armies had reached Kluang in the southern Malay state of Johor, where he was warmly welcomed by Sultan Ibrahim. From the vantage point of the sultan's Bukit Serene Palace, Yamashita could now look out across the narrow straits towards the great prize of Singapore. From the British naval base a thick pall of black oily smoke rose from burning fuel tanks high into the cloudless sky: the funeral pyre of empire. Comfortably ensconced inside Sultan Ibrahim's state secretariat building, Yamashita and his general staff began planning the invasion of Singapore.

The end came quickly. On 15 February, the British commander Lt General Arthur Percival surrendered unconditionally. The British rulers of Malaya had been vanquished in just sixty-eight days. By then, Japanese troops had captured Manila and Cavite in the Philippines. From Thailand, Japanese troops struck at Burma – and the Thai government formally declared war on the Allies.

General Yamashita, the 'Tiger of Malaya', had not yet fulfilled his solemn promise to the emperor. The Japanese blitzkrieg now fell on the other side of the Straits of Malacca in Sumatra. The Japanese navy smashed the Dutch fleet in the Battle of the Java Sea and Yamashita's troops captured the Dutch colonial capital of Batavia on 6 March. By early May all the Dutch possessions in the vast Indonesian Archipelago had fallen. The colonial map had been torn apart. The new empire that the Japanese called the 'Co-Prosperity Sphere' was complete. Singapore had been officially renamed Syonan-to, the 'Light of the South'; Malaya became Malai. The rising sun had reached its zenith.

After the surprise Japanese attack on Pearl Harbor, President Roosevelt declared war on Japan. In Berlin a 'delighted' Adolf Hitler rallied to the Axis cause. He was certain that the Americans would now be tied down fighting the Japanese in the Pacific and that the loss of Britain's Asian colonies would fatally weaken its capacity to continue the war. Four days after the attack on Pearl Harbor, Hitler declared war on the United States. Churchill was as equally exhilarated by the news of Pearl Harbor as Hitler, believing that now America had at last joined the war victory would be inevitable. But history is not a narrative of inevitabilities. The events of the next three years would confound most prophecies and many hopes. In Southeast Asia, none of the many different ethnic and political communities could have any certain view about the possible outcomes of the Japanese invasion and the sudden collapse of colonial rule. Centuries of foreign rule had been abruptly brought to an end. The Japanese military earthquake shattered the colonial landscape. Old ties and bonds had been ripped asunder. The cartographic palimpsest of the Malay world would be redrawn once again. What would emerge from its ruins was – at the time – anyone's guess.

The Fujiwara Plan

It is ironic, then, that the Japanese accepted the British view of the Malays as backward and politically quiescent. In fact, the Malay courts had long-standing connections with Japan, and many Malays were fascinated by Japanese culture and commodities. In modern Malaysia, the somewhat mythologised tale of 'Raja Harimau' or 'King Tiger' still possesses much allure. Many Japanese came to Malaya in the colonial period to open barber shops. Some were spies. Tani Yutaka was the son of a Japanese barber who settled in the northern state of Terengganu. He apparently grew up to love Malay culture and usually wore traditional *baju malayu* and *songkok*. Then in the early 1930s his sister Shizuko was killed by Chinese rioters. Supposedly a British court freed the perpetrators and Tani Yutaka fled into the mountains where he formed a Malay bandit gang, which, according to legend, was 3,000 strong. The gang seems to have assisted the Japanese 25th Army. Tani Yutaka was struck down by malaria in either Johore or Singapore, and was buried with full military honours in the Japanese Cemetery Park. He was mythologised by both the Japanese and by Malays.

Japanese consular signals show that well before December 1941 Tokyo began planning widespread subversion and propagandist activities in Southeast Asia. This intensified at the beginning of 1941 and targeted Indian soldiers who were the backbone of British colonial defence. More than half of British troops in Malaya were Indian. To achieve the 'New Order' in Asia, as well as seize the oil resources of the region, the Japanese Minister of Foreign Affairs urged that clandestine networks in Singapore and Batavia accelerate 'agitation, political plots, propaganda and intelligence'. A telegram to the Japanese Consul General in Singapore referred to 'Native sponsored anti-British, anti-rebel and anti-Russian movements' and exploiting 'religious and social problems'. In April, Japan sent Major Iwachai Fujiwara to Thailand, which had a substantial Indian community, to investigate ways of fomenting dissent among Indians in Malaya and Singapore. The Japanese Army general staff set up an office in Bangkok, which made contact with Pritam Singh of the Indian Independence League. It has become clear that these contacts, and the intense Pan-Asian propaganda directed at Indian troops in Malaya, had, for the British, disastrous consequences, not entirely appreciated at the time. As early as May 1940, the 'Hyderabad Regiment' was riven by unrest and the Argyll and Sutherland Highlanders were on standby in case of a full mutiny. As Japanese troops surged ashore at Kota Bahru, the commander of the 1st Battalion, Lt Colonel C.A. Hendricks was shot dead by one of his men. The Hyderabads disintegrated. During the campaign, Japanese aircraft dropped thousands of pamphlets emphasising that they were fighting only the white man. Indian troops were being used as cannon fodder while their British officers hid. Any Asiatic soldier who gave himself up would not be harmed. This aerial propaganda bombardment was very effective. And the Japanese made good on their promises. At the end of December, Fujiwara met with Captain Moham

Singh, a disaffected officer of the 14th Punjab Regiment, who proposed forming an Indian liberation army to fight the British. The idea was backed by Pritam Singh. By the time the British surrendered, the Japanese had more than 50,000 Indian troops in captivity. Many would throw in their lot with the Japanese and join the Indian National Army, the INA. Earlier that year, the radical Indian nationalist Subhas Chandra Bose had escaped British captivity and embarked on a perilous journey to Kabul in Afghanistan. Here he had sought to make contact with the Soviets, but had been passed onto the Germans – the Nazi-Soviet Pact had not yet been broken by Hitler. When the Japanese failed to take advantage of the 'Quit India' movement in 1942, relations between Singh and the Japanese deteriorated. Many Indians now looked to Bose to save their cause and send the INA into battle against the British. But he was comfortably ensconced in a luxurious Berlin villa with a fine view of the Tiergarten, courtesy of the German Foreign Office, and not yet inclined to return to Asia. The embittered officers of the INA would have a long wait.

A Malay Fifth Column?

Malay journalist Ibrahim Yaacob, whose book *Surveying the Homeland* was discussed in the previous chapter, was also fascinated by the Japanese. He was one of the founders of the first Malay nationalist organisation, the Kesatuan Melayu Muda, the Union of Malay Youth, the KMM. Like Lai Tek, Ibrahim tried to play the British and the Japanese off against each other, claiming that he was authorised by the Malay rulers to contact the Japanese, while letting the British think he was 'theirs'. Ibrahim appears to have been addicted to clandestine thrill seeking. A month before the invasion, on 20 November, the British intercepted a message from the Japanese Consulate in Singapore to Tokyo that referred to a fifth column organisation called 'Kame' (Japanese for tortoise), which was composed of both Japanese and Malays, that planned to create panic and carry out unspecified acts of sabotage. This provoked the British, who on 4 December began rounding up anyone suspected of links to 'Kame' – and that included members of the tiny KMM. Ibrahim's dealings with the Japanese have puzzled many historians. The recently published memoirs of Mustapha Hussain have cast a great deal of light on these murky events. For a long time after the end of the war Hussain was puzzled by Ibrahim's relations with the Japanese. It would take him more than thirty years to find out the truth. At the end of the Japanese occupation, Ibrahim fled to Indonesia and never returned. In the 1970s he began corresponding with his old comrades in Malaysia. Hussain implies that this provoked him to dig deeper into Ibrahim's past. He discovered that in 1938, when the KMM was founded, Ibrahim, who was editor of the daily paper *Majilis*, had accepted funds from the Japanese Domei News Agency to buy the Warta Malaya Press. In a complicated arrangement, the money was 'laundered' through connections in Taiping and returned to Singapore – unnoticed by Special Branch. Then, on the eve of the invasion, Ibrahim met with a Japanese 'Kame' agent in Bukit Besi in Terengganu. An arrangement was made for Ibrahim to meet the Japanese Consul General, Ken Tsurumi, in Singapore. Another large sum was handed over. Ibrahim bought a Morris 8 saloon car and some expensive suits and had himself photographed haranguing crowds of Malayans. It was essential to give the impression that he was a serious political power broker. Ibrahim had in effect sold the KMM to the Japanese.

Hussain knew nothing of Ibrahim's dealings with the Japanese when he heard news of the Japanese landings. At the time he was in Kuala Lumpur Malay Hospital being treated for a nervous disorder. He had suffered some kind of breakdown caused by stress. As he lay in his hospital bed, Hussain listened to his fellow patients discussing the war. Many appeared to believe that the British would have no difficulty defending Malaya: 'Don't worry! You know how clever the British are! What do the Japanese have? They have slit eyes: how can they aim at targets accurately?' When he was discharged, Hussain drove his Hillman sports car to his parents' house in Temoh Station, near Tapah in Perak. He was accompanied by his wife and three children. It was here that he heard of the invasion. As the Japanese began bombing Ipoh the family fled to their hometown of Matang. It was soon evident that the Japanese would not be easily beaten off. Taiping fell – and Hussain watched as waves of confident Japanese soldiers poured along the fine British-made roads of Perak towards Kuala Lumpur. Hussain observed the Japanese troops closely, noting their curious web-toed rubber boots and long, frightening swords. Many Japanese were on tyreless and very noisy bicycles, which they often tried to barter for British-made Raleighs – or simply grabbed them and sped off. At the end of the month, Hussain was reflecting on the fate of 'hapless Malays' (presumably not the Chinese who the Japanese were raping and murdering) when several motor cars pulled up in front of his parents' house. They brought a party of KMM members, including Onan Haji Siraj, accompanied by fearsome looking Japanese officers. Onan informed Hussain that the British had arrested himself and Ibrahim in Singapore – but that Ibrahaim had convinced the British that Onan was not a KMM member and he was released. Ibrahim was released soon afterwards. Onan now told Hussain that KMM was codenamed 'Kame' – 'an animal that does not know retreat'. This was a rather garbled account of Japanese fifth column activities but the upshot was that KMM were now expected to seek out 'Kame' units with their secret hexagon symbol enclosing an F for Fujiwara. Since Hussain was the KMM vice president, the Japanese insisted that he travel with them to Taiping to meet Fujiwara. Hussain protested that he was still recovering from a nervous disorder but the Japanese offered to carry him.

So it was that at the Raja Rest House in Taiping Lake Gardens, Mustapha Hussain met Major Iwaichi Fujiwara, who was chief of the 'Fujiwara Kikan' – a Japanese intelligence unit that comprised officers, interpreters and assistants, including former barbers, schoolteachers and owners of photography studios. Hussain was now informed that Ibrahim had guaranteed KMM assistance to the Japanese. He also appears to have boasted of a huge membership that the Japanese now expected to join their campaign. A few hours later he and a number of other Malay KMM supporters found themselves heading south towards the Perak capital Kuala Kangsar on the Perak River, proudly wearing F Kikan armbands. As the Japanese advanced, many Malays inscribed an F (for Fujiwara) on their front doors to prevent looting by soldiers. In Kuala Kangsar, the Japanese ordered Hussain and a Japanese photographer called Suzuki to track down Sultan Abdul Aziz, who had fled his palace. It turned out that this Suzuki was already on good terms with the sultan, who had granted him a state hunting licence, which he made good use of to survey and map the region between Kuala Kangsar and Grik. Since he doesn't tell us, we have to assume that Hussain found the sultan. The Japanese understood that it was politically useful to keep the Malay rulers 'inside the tent'. When the Japanese moved on to Ipoh, Hussain and the KKM followed. Major Fujiwara had handed over command of the F Kikan volunteers to a Lt Yonemura, who now began organising basic training. These were heady times. He recalled: 'At the time, I felt as if Malaya was already in the hands of the Malays.' He could not have been more mistaken. For years after the war, Mustapha Hussain was tormented by guilt about his relations with the Japanese. Very few other prominent Malays shared his anguish. He was a sensitive – even vulnerable – and decent man. He was tricked, to be sure, by the mercurial and opportunistic Ibrahim Yaacob, but it is hard to duck the fact that he allowed the Japanese to exploit young KMM members. Hussain *did* collaborate, and the rather frequent emphasis in his *Memoirs* on Malays as victims and the Chinese as obsequious collaborators is repugnant.

It was when the Japanese reached the colonial capital Kuala Lumpur that Hussain's naive hopes would finally be dashed. The Malay F Kikan arrived in the city on 11 January. If there was any doubt that British Malaya was finished then the empty litter-strewn streets of the capital city of the Federated Malay States would have confirmed the fact a hundredfold. Columns of Japanese troops and military vehicles rumbled along the Batu Road, the city's main thoroughfare. British forces were retreating south towards a last line of defence in Johor; Kuala Lumpur had been declared an open city. At the prestigious Selangor Club in Lake Garden, one of the symbolic institutions of a soon-to-be vanquished Malaya, Hussain and other KMM members gathered to discuss how to deal with the Japanese. They began by writing a 'national anthem' to prove that the KMM really was a nationalist movement:

> Japanese troops have arrived
> Let us assist them …
> They came to liberate us …

(The other verses were not much better.) This foolish ditty failed to impress. The Japanese had doubts about the nationalist credentials of the KMM. The new song confirmed that impression. After this first rebuff Hussain had a second meeting with the commander of the Japanese Political Bureau. He insisted that KMM actually meant *Independent Malaya Union* – and they wanted independence, *merdeka*. The Japanese asked, perfectly reasonably: 'Where is your national flag, national anthem and constitution?' He then made the enigmatic comment: 'Let the Japanese be the father. Malays, Chinese and Indians live like a family. However, if the Malay child is thin, and needs more milk, we will give him milk.' So ended the first independence negotiations in Malaya: with a demeaning promise of racial favouritism. When Hussain arrived in Singapore, he finally ran the duplicitous Ibrahim Yaacob to ground. He was immediately reprimanded for discussing independence with the Japanese: you could have been beheaded, remonstrated Ibrahim. Hussain had already observed several summary decapitations and the prominent public impaling of human heads in Kuala Lumpur *pour encourager les autres*.

Hussain and the other KMM fellow travellers arrived in Johor Bahru on 8 February. Relations with the competitive Onan Haji Siraj had reached breaking point. They rowed frequently about who should lead the KMM. Onan was, it seems, hoping that Ibrahim, still languishing in a British jail, would be killed during the Japanese assault on Singapore. This began a few days later with a spectacular bombardment. The Japanese swiftly rebuilt the causeway across the straits – and Hussain followed the 25th Army into the city. As he landed on the island on 13 February, he scooped up a fistful of soil and offered a prayer that the land would be returned to its rightful owners, the Malays.

On 15 February, Hussain heard that the British had given up the fight. The Malays scented victory. At about 5 p.m., a white oval-shaped balloon was observed floating above the British-controlled sector of Singapore. 'Banzai Banzai Banzai' bellowed Japanese soldiers – 'We have won' shouted the KMM men. 'I was a Malay privileged to watch a moment of humiliation,' recalled Hussain. He was also preoccupied with the fate of captured soldiers of the Malay Regiment, who had fought a courageous rearguard action as the British retreated across the straits. When Hussain approached the tall, smiling, 'gentle, considerate and humane' Major Fujiwara to seek their release, he was rebuffed. The Malays, Fujiwara reminded him, had killed many Japanese soldiers. The Japanese would execute hundreds of Malay soldiers after they refused Hussain's proposal that they join the Japanese.

Hussain did not attend the surrender ceremony. Japanese officers searched high and low for him, but for reasons he does not explain they failed to track him down. The F Kikan was represented instead by his student Johar bin Kerong, who was kitted out with a *boshi* military hat adorned with a yellow star, a khaki tunic, breeches, boots, puttees, and a leather belt with empty holster. He was allocated a position some distance from the negotiators: a naïve bit part player in an absurd and demeaning piece of political theatre. In the days following the surrender, young Johar was hard to control: with another KKM man at the wheel, he took to driving around the battered city, which was littered with stinking corpses, in an 8-cylinder Chevrolet, looking like a 'Japanese master'. It was only when Johor and his 'driver' collided with two Japanese soldiers on a motorbike, causing severe injury, then driving away, that Hussain could get rid of this ridiculous peacock. Such was the Malay nationalist movement at the beginning of the Japanese occupation.

The Temptation of Nippon

The KMM leaders were inept to be sure – but we should take care before making too harsh a judgement. Ibrahim Yaacob was no Vidkun Quisling or Marshall Pétain. The sudden emergence of modern Japan as a virile Asian power inspired many other anti-colonial nationalists. In Burma, Thakin nationalist Aung Sang had fled the British police to Amoy in China to seek assistance from the nationalist government. He was intercepted by the Japanese who persuaded him to come to Tokyo. After receiving training, he returned to Southeast Asia at the end of 1941 to form the Burma Independence Army (BIA) in Bangkok. When the Burmese capital Rangoon (Yangon today) fell to the Japanese in March 1942, Aung Sang helped form a puppet administration which ruled Burma with the Japanese military administration. On 1 August 1943, the Japanese declared Burmese independence. By then, Aung Sang had realised that Japanese commitment to the Burmese cause was, as he put it, 'half baked'.

Japanese exploitation of Asian nationalist movements played out differently in the Dutch East Indies. The consequences would be far-reaching indeed. The Dutch colonial government had harassed the nationalist firebrand Sukarno throughout the 1930s. He and Mohammad Hatta closely followed the Japanese attack on China and believed that war would come to Southeast Asia sooner or later. When Yamashita's forces invaded Sumatra in February 1942, the Dutch kidnapped Sukarno, who had been exiled to Bengkulu, to keep him out of Japanese hands. When the kidnap party reached Padang, Japanese troops began closing in and the Dutch abandoned their Indonesian prisoners and fled. The Japanese onslaught and the complete collapse of Dutch defences that resulted plunged Indonesia into chaos. Anti-colonial factions seized the chance to attack Dutch troops and civilians, compelling thousands of desperate and homeless people to seek refuge in Japanese internment camps. Yamashita was dismayed. He had a war to win. Sukarno was well known to the Japanese – and now they turned to him to calm his fellow Indonesians. He had no doubts: 'Independent Indonesia can only be achieved with Dai Nippon!'

Sukarno always insisted that he was anti-fascist. He was not especially consistent. He denounced Nazi Germany but tended to rationalise Japanese 'excesses' in China as 'self defence'. He was convinced that Indonesia could be freed in the maelstrom of imperial conflict. He had other reasons for accepting Japanese political largesse. For many Indonesians Sukarno was a genuinely charismatic figure and his speeches were saturated with coded references to Javanese mythology. He and the crowds he addressed were fascinated by the Hindu Javanese king, Ratu Joyoboyo (or Djajabaja) of Kedini, who was believed to be the mythic 'Ratu Adil', or 'Just King' reborn. King Joyoboyo was famous for making prophecies which he had declaimed by court poets. When he reached old age, King Joyoboyo abdicated and lived as a hermit recluse in the village of Menang, which is still a pilgrimage site today. One of King Joyoboyo's prophecies foretells that: 'The Javanese would be ruled by whites for three centuries and by yellow dwarfs for the life span of a maize plant prior to the return of the Ratu Adil: whose name must contain at least one syllable of the Javanese Noto Negoro.' Sukarno may not have literally believed in this nonsense but he certainly understood the mythic appeal of the king's famous oracles to ordinary Indonesians. So too, as it happened, did the Japanese. When the Japanese landed in Java in March, they shrewdly appropriated the old Djajabaja myths, claiming that they had come to fulfil the old prophecies and liberate Indonesians from the slavery of the Dutch: 'So look for the yellow skins!'. The 'Djajabaja plan' was remarkably effective. As the Japanese armies swatted Dutch resistance aside, crowds of Indonesians responded with 'a frantic atmosphere of welcome', in the words of a Japanese naval officer. Many people now wondered if Sukarno could be the reincarnated 'legendary Ratu Adil: whose name must contain at least one syllable of the Javanese Noto Negoro'. Would the victorious Japanese now appoint him 'King of the Archipelago'?

The immense fervour of the Indonesian welcome – *Banzai dai Nippon*! – took the Japanese Saiki Shikikan (Highest Commander) General Hitoshi Imamura by surprise. His political advisor, Count Hideo Kodama, a veteran of the Japanese Foreign Office, urged him to play political softball with the people of the 'Southern Regions' – at least to begin with. Imamura described his 'Senjinkun' policy thus: 'to allow these obedient people to bathe in the genuine imperial graces [...] to share happiness with the Japanese'. Imamura would become one of Sukarno's most influential supporters. But Indonesians would be bitterly disappointed.

Japanese imperial ambitions never included genuine political independence. They wanted the oil wells of Borneo and Sumatra. So, not surprisingly, Japanese treatment of the nationalist question was muddled. Imamura's superior, the Commander of the Southern Army, Count Hisaichi Terauchi, rebuked him: this 'happiness sharing' policy was 'too lax'. He warned that if Imamura supported the 'secessionist' Sukarno and his ilk, he would risk being 'bitten by one's own pet.' Terauchi set about dismembering the Dutch East Indies. He broke up 'Indonesia': the core of nationalist aspiration. This was a bitter blow. The 16th Army was allocated control of Java; the ultracompetitive Japanese Navy took Celebes,

Borneo and the eastern region of the archipelago; Sumatra was severed from the rest of the Indonesian Archipelago and yoked together with the Malayan Peninsula under the command of the 25th Army, headquartered in Singapore. Under Japanese occupation, Indonesia ceased to exit. This brutal occupation policy would offer Indonesian nationalists nothing more than crumbs from the table of the 'Greater East Asia Co-Prosperity Sphere' – the euphemism for empire. What would Sukarno do? Would he spurn the Japanese offer or climb onboard? According to a memoir by Indonesian nationalist Sutan Sjahrir, Sukarno detested the Japanese as 'pure fascists' – but, he argued, since the Pacific war would last for at least ten years 'we must use the most subtle counter-methods to get around them, such as making the appearance of collaboration …'. Is the 'appearance of collaboration' that much different from collaborating? Sjahrir himself refused to follow the same path.

On 17 March 1942, Colonel Fujiyama summoned Sukarno to a meeting at Bukit Tingi, where the 25th Army had set up headquarters. He took a specially arranged train. As the train steamed across Sumatra it became known that Sukarno was onboard and big crowds assembled at points along the line to bless his journey. In Bukit Tingi, Fujiyama had taken over a mansion which had once belonged to a wealthy Dutch merchant. It overlooked the famous Ngarai gorge, which cuts between the mighty Merapi and Singgalang volcanoes. The encounter between the Japanese colonel and the Indonesian nationalist would be as dramatic as the setting. In his *Autobiography*, Sukarno describes 'my famous meeting' at some length. He quotes Fujiyama:

> You see, Mr Sukarno […] I am an administrator. You are a nation [sic] with layers of Javanese, Balinese, Hindu, Moslem, Buddhist, Dutch, Malaysian, Polynesian, Chinese, Filipino, Arababic and other culture, breeds, religions […] My assignment is to marshal this area into good running order quickly. The most efficient method is to keep the populace quiet …

Fujiyama claimed that the emperor wished fervently to liberate fellow Asians from their European oppressors. So does that mean, Sukarno enquired, that the ultimate goal of Japanese rule would be a free Indonesia? Fujiyama paused. 'Yes, Mr Sukarno. Perfectly correct.' Sukarno did not hesitate. He accepted Fujiyama's offer to 'keep the populace quiet'. He knew he was taking a tremendous risk: he feared that he would be remembered as 'the Indonesian Quisling'. But in his mind, hatred of the Dutch loomed larger than fear of Japanese intent. Collaboration was the road to freedom.

In Indonesia, the Japanese occupation released and shaped the political passions of an entire generation known as *pemudas*. The Japanese opened a Pandora's box that Sukarno would never completely control. This clandestine revolution had a lot to do with style: *pemudas* insisted on simple dress, wore their hair long, and spoke in a contrived idiolect comparable to estuarine English. It was the first punk revolution – and found its most characteristic voice in the words of the poet Chairil Anwar.

In a time of revolution Anwar lived fast and died young: 'No more of the old farts! No more gentle breezes of *that* kind!' He was the archetypal *pemuda*: as a friend recalled he was 'a thin, pale youngster, he stabbed, cut and smashed old notions, unaware of custom, a kind of bandit […] to influence his slower friends into revolutionary ways.' Anwar dedicated 'Siap Sedia', 'We're Ready' to his own generation:

> Everything's burning!
> Everything's burning!
> Friends, oh my friends,
> We'll rise up full of purpose,
> We'll stab the new light deep under its skin.
> Friends, friends,
> We'll swing our swords at the bright world …[19]

In the political crust of colonial Southeast Asia, a fault had begun to slip.

At the beginning of the Japanese campaign in the peninsula, the British had not taken much notice of rumours about the activities of the KMM and the 'Fujiwara Kikan'. In the aftermath of surrender, the humiliated Tuans began to wonder if they had been stabbed in the back. According to historian Cheah Boon Kheng, this perception of Malay treachery marked the beginning of British disillusionment with the 'sons of the soil'. It is unclear how much, if anything, the British knew about Ibrahim's murky dealings with the Japanese, but the fact that Malays had shown political *initiative* and thrown in their lot with the invaders struck down the hoary caricatures of the gentlemanly native or simple-minded kampong farmer. The 'docile' Malay of myth was not quite what he or she seemed.

From the Malay point of view the rapid collapse of the British colonial edifice was an epochal and shattering betrayal of trust. As Japanese bombers rained down death on Penang, the British slyly made sure Europeans escaped the onslaught but callously ignored Asians. At the docks, armed volunteers cordoned off the quayside as Penang's pale-skinned elite barged its way onto ferries. This ignominious departure was, as one British memsahib admitted, 'a thing which I am sure will never be forgiven or forgotten'. As Penang burned, the Japanese jeered 'How do you like our bombing, you English gentlemen? Isn't it a better tonic than your whisky soda?' (A reference to an iconic colonial pick-me-up.) The tradition-minded Malays had come to accept, albeit grudgingly, the British as protectors. That unwritten contract was reduced to ashes in the inferno of Penang. The Japanese invasion capsized traditional roles. The British appeared fainthearted, incompetent or both. Their feet of clay had not just been exposed, they had been washed away. At the same time, the fickle antics of the sultans and the supposed treachery of the KMM began to untangle the bonds between the British and the people they once regarded as 'nature's gentlemen'. The repercussions of this mutual disenchantment would play out at many different levels when the British reoccupied Malaya in 1945. On the long and twisted road to independence, the British and the Malays would come to resemble an oddly matched couple who would not speak of their differences openly but engaged in mutual recrimination behind their hands.

Massacre and Resistance

Since their first incursions into the Malay world, the British had never completely trusted the many different Chinese communities, and Singapore Special Branch had devoted much time and effort to clamping down on the Chinese-dominated Malayan Communist Party. It was the threat of communism that frightened the British colonial administration, not the seemingly more remote menace of the Japanese. This blinkered misconception was very hard to shift. In 1940, the British government in London set up the Special Operations Executive (SOE) to, in Churchill's words, 'create and foster the spirit of resistance [...] [and] establish a nucleus of trained men who would be able to assist as a "fifth column" in the liberation of the country concerned'. German-occupied Europe dominated SOE planning and strategy. But both the War Office and the Colonial Office urged the government not to forget Asia. At the end of 1940, the SOE agreed to set up an SOE group in Singapore. On 24 January 1941, the SOE sent a memorandum to the Governors of the Straits Settlements (Sir Shenton Thomas) and Hong Kong (Sir Geoffrey Northcote) formally setting out the tasks of the 'Oriental Mission' and assigning command to the Commander-in-Chief Far East, Air Chief Marshall Sir Robert Brooke-Popham. The 'Oriental Mission' had a mind-boggling operational brief: to set up operations in free and occupied China, Manchuria, the Philippines, the Japanese Empire, Siberia, French Indochina, the Dutch East Indies, Burma, Malaya, Hong Kong, Borneo, Sarawak and 'other British, French, Dutch and Portuguese possessions in the area'. This was immensely ambitious. But the British failed to recognise the special problems that would arise in any Asian theatre of war. In occupied Europe, the majority of resistance movements fought a common enemy, namely the Germans. This applied even when the internal resistance was divided, as it was in the former Royal Yugoslavia and in Eastern Europe. But in Asia the identity of 'the enemy' would never be clear-cut. Was it the invading Japanese or the ousted colonial power or other Asians? In Burma, for example, the SOE would develop a successful guerrilla organisation among the hill tribes such as the Karen, Chin, Arakanese and Kachin, who were more enthusiastic about fighting the Burmese than the Japanese, and professed little loyalty to the British. British agents sent to Asia faced a problem that their counterparts operating behind enemy lines in France or Yugoslavia rarely had to deal with: as Europeans, they were instantly recognisable. This meant that covert operations completely depended on Asians. 'The crux of the matter,' reported Colin Mackenzie, commander of the 'India Mission', 'is after all the agent or operator. For the great majority of our projects natives are essential. By and large there is little patriotism [sic] from which to recruit.'

The other problem was the colonial establishment in Singapore, above all its military branch. This is surprising because the SOE fished its staff from the same pool of public school types as the Colonial Office: the first head of the Oriental Mission, Valentine Killery, was an old Etonian who had spent many years working for Imperial Chemical Industries in the Far East. When Killery arrived in Singapore on 7 May 1941, he predicted that it would take at least a year to get the operation properly up and running, *assuming* he had the full co-operation of the civil and military colonial authorities. This he never achieved. He planned to divide Malaya into six operational zones under the command of a local European, who would recruit 'gangs of tough and reliable natives' as 'stay-behind-parties', who would be trained in the dark arts of irregular warfare. When the General Officer Commanding (GOC), Malaya, Lt General Arthur Percival, got wind of Killery's plans, he took offence and complained loudly to Brooke-Popham. Killery characterised Percival as 'a completely negative person with no vigour, no colour, and no conviction'. At a meeting with Sir Shenton Thomas (the Straits Governor) and Killery, Percival complained that SOE operations would waste resources and damage morale. Faced with Percival's vehement hostility to his plan, Killery offered to resign. Brooke-Popham refused to let him go and all parties continued to bicker until the eve of the Japanese attack.

The other stumbling block, from the British point of view, was the Malayan Communist Party. In July, after the German invasion of the Soviet Union had torn up the Nazi-Soviet Pact, the Secretary General of the MCP, Lai Tek, proposed a deal. He proposed that in return for political rights (the MCP was still banned) and the promise of a future 'Malayan Democratic Republic' the MCP would suspend its anti-imperial struggle and help defend Malaya against a Japanese attack. That July, the British brushed aside the MCP offer, but as the Japanese 25th Army swept relentlessly south towards Singapore the British executed an abrupt volte-face that would have far-reaching consequences. In December, Lai Tek used his Special Branch contacts to send a clear signal that the July offer was still on the table. Communists openly backed the leftist entrepreneur Tan Kah Kee, who was calling for Chinese mobilisation. Then, quite suddenly, the governor ordered the release of a number of communist prisoners. Events now moved swiftly – hardly surprising given the devastating speed of the Japanese advance. On 18 December, just as the MCP leadership had given up hope, the British replied positively to the offer of assistance. On the same day Lai Tek met a British delegation at a safe house in Geylang, Singapore's red light district, led by Major Freddy Spencer Chapman and Captain James Tremlett. The latter knew Lai Tek very well: he was his Special Branch control. Chapman had arrived in Malaya three months before the Japanese invasion. At the time, in mid-1941, the British authorities had forbidden discussion of so-called 'stay-behind-parties' – that is, irregular forces trained in jungle warfare, who would operate behind enemy lines in the event (considered unlikely, of course) that Japanese forces overran all or part of Malaya. In August, a detailed 'stay-behind' plan had been proposed to the Commander in Chief (C. in C.) and Governor Sir Shenton Thomas, but after much humming and hawing and paper shuffling it had been turned down. One reason was that the plan smacked of defeatism. The other was that the planners envisaged recruiting well-informed 'Asiatics' and that surely meant arming the communists. At the Geylang meeting, at which Lai Tek and the other communists insisted on a comedic *rigmarole* of secrecy and arrived hooded or wearing dark glasses, agreement was swiftly reached. Richard Broome and John Davis, who were both Chinese-speaking civil officers, were appointed to co-ordinate training at the 101 Training School. For the MCP, this U-turn was an astonishing stroke of political luck. On 23 December, Chiang Kai-Shek in Nanjing appealed to Chinese nationals in Malaya to support the British, and Shenton Thomas reciprocated by lifting the ban on the Kuomintang and the MCP, which joined forces as the 'Overseas Chinese Mobilisation Council'. Young volunteers like Chin Peng had long dreamed of forming guerrilla bands on the lines of Mao Zedong's 'Yenan Way'. SOE reports refer to their 'fanatical eagerness to fight the Japanese'. From the start there was tension between the communists, who had taken the lead, and Kuomintang volunteers: they could not be accommodated together at the training school. The British focused on training and, crucially, arming the MCP volunteers, to the dismay of Chinese officers despatched to Malaya by Chiang Kai-Shek. The SOE justified privileging the MCP on the grounds that the communist recruits were tougher. By the New Year, Broome and Davis had established sites for arms and supplies caches and led the first 'graduates' into action to infiltrate behind Japanese lines in Perak. They assigned other units to operate in Selangor and Johor.

In Singapore, the British persuaded, with some difficulty, the tycoon and philanthropist Tan Kah Kee – who had lost his rubber plantations in Perak to the Japanese – to head a 'Chinese Mobilisation Council' to co-ordinate labour recruitment to build defences for the city. At the first meeting, members of the Chinese Chamber of Commerce rubbed shoulders, uneasily, with recently released communists. When communist Ng Yeh Lu demanded that the British arm the Chinese in Singapore, Tan Kah Kee vehemently opposed him. But Shenton Thomas, who pointedly shook the hand of every communist he had just released, agreed. He appointed Special Branch officer Lt Colonel John Dalley to take charge of the Chinese irregulars, which would become famous as 'Dalforce' (or 'Dalley's Desperadoes') though the volunteers themselves referred to it as the 'Singapore Overseas Chinese Anti-Japanese Volunteer Army'. Some 2,000 strong, the volunteers were kitted out in blue uniforms with a red triangle. The Indonesian communist, Tan Malaka, who was working as an English teacher in Singapore, threw himself into organising recruitment. He wondered whether the British had a plan to eliminate *both* the communists *and* the Japanese – but such anxieties did not stop the volunteers fighting ferociously, even recklessly. Many women volunteered – one was the elderly Madam Cheng Seang Ho, who had fought the Japanese with her husband in China. Her heroic death fighting at Bukit Timah earned her the title of Malaya's *La Passionaria* (after the Spanish communist leader Dolores Ibárruri). Her husband, who survived that battle, was later tortured and killed.

The Japanese conquest consumed a bonfire of colonial myths and prejudices. General Yamashita's 'driving charge' that secured Singapore in sixty-eight days obliterated the old stereotype of the inferior Japanese. The British RAF was no match for the lethally skilled pilots of the superbly designed Japanese Zero fighters and bombers. The soldiers of the 25th Army, many battle-hardened in China, were remorseless warriors. This was not a gentle people. In the aftermath of victory, the Japanese proved to be merciless and brutal occupiers. Their ruthless treatment of the British and European prisoners of war is infamous. But the Japanese onslaught on the ordinary peoples of occupied Southeast Asia was unimaginably crueler and would provoke bitter communal resentments that would blight Southeast Asia for many decades. The British colonial administration had created the *conditions* for chronic intra-racial conflict – but it was the Japanese occupiers who turned conflict into civil war.

From the moment the 25th Army landed in Thailand and northern Malaya, Japanese soldiers had looted and raped with ferocious abandon. To be sure, the fanatical strategist Masonobu Tsuji, who, it will be recalled, had renounced sexual intercourse until the end of the campaign, raged against the larcenous behaviour of his men, but he had little real impact. Officers turned a blind eye to rape as it seemed to enhance their men's determination to win. In a memoir *This Singapore: Our City of Dreadful Night*, written after the war, we discover that 'some [Japanese soldiers] did it [raped] sadistically and brutally, booted and belted as they were; some did it indifferently as men answering calls of nature [...] The victims steeled themselves to accept the inevitable ...'. Most at risk were paler-skinned Chinese girls: many dressed as Malays and artificially darkened their appearance to evade attention. Native bodies were abused in many ways. As the Imperial Army marched south, they left in their wake a gruesome trail of severed heads, often displayed on pikes with placards inscribed with homilies such as 'This is an example for those who disobey the Japanese Imperial Army'. In Singapore, Charlie Cheah was brought up short by 'two heads on these stools, raised stools, opposite the Cathay Cinema'. Many survivors of the Japanese occupation commented on this lurid juxtaposition of one of Singapore's great entertainment emporiums with these dumb exhibits.

The Japanese military police, the 'Kempeitai' (which means 'Military Police Corps'), has deservedly acquired the same kind of notoriety as the German Gestapo (part of the SS), but was in fact modelled on the French *gendarmerie*, a branch of the armed forces. Founded in 1881, the Kempeitai was deployed as a semi-colonial force in Korea and Manchuria (where it was commanded by future wartime prime minister, Hideki Tōjō) and answered to the Minister of War. Like the German SS, the Kempeitai was an elite paramilitary organisation of volunteers that strictly controlled admission to its ranks. According to an American military report:

> This policy of selection and education has produced in the Jap MP an individual of much higher caliber than the average Japanese soldier. But though the I.Q. of *Kempei* men is higher than that of the rest of the Jap Army, it in no way has decreased their cruelty, or their devotion to the Emperor, as the residents of Jap-occupied territory will certify.[20]

In Malaya, Kempeitai units recruited local spies and informers to track down stolen goods and dispense summary lethal punishment. After the British surrender, this vindictive cruelty became more systematic.

General Yamashita set up temporary headquarters at Raffles College, the symbol of enlightened colonial rule. Yamashita had no intention of staying there long – the bulk of the 25th Army would soon cross the Straits of Malacca to Sumatra leaving behind a garrison force in Singapore. In the next ten weeks Japanese forces rampaged through Sumatra, Java and Borneo; they seized the strategic base of Rabaul between New Guinea and the Solomon Islands; Japanese aircraft bombed Darwin in northern Australia; they overran the Philippines and laid siege to the fortress island of Corregidor, forcing American General Douglas MacArthur to flee to Australia; the Imperial Navy destroyed Allied naval forces in the Java Sea; the Combined Fleet, now based in Singapore, ventured into the Indian Ocean, forced the British Eastern Fleet to withdraw, and attacked bases in Ceylon. In India, the Japanese threat inspired Congress to launch the 'Quit India' movement. The rays of the rising sun were now cast across one-sixth of the earth's surface. But conquering Southeast Asia would prove a lot easier than holding on to this territorial windfall. By as early as May 1942, the Japanese rampage was beginning to falter – the Battle of the Coral Sea stymied the push to Australia; in June, the Battle of Midway ended Japanese ambitions to seize Hawaii; in August, the Americans landed at Guadalcanal in the Solomon Islands and after protracted and ferocious fighting expelled the Japanese in February 1943, and from that moment on had the initiative in the Pacific War. This relatively swift reversal of military fortune would have a profound impact on occupation policy and on the attitudes of Asians to the Japanese.

Yamashita had been shaken by the scale of Chinese resistance, and on 17 February ordered a 'mopping-up operation' – *genju shobun* in Japanese, meaning 'severe disposal' – directed against 'anti-Japanese elements'. The precise nature of Yamashita's instructions and the organisation of what became known in Chinese as the 'Sook Ching', or 'purification by elimination', remains unclear. We know that the master strategist Tsuji drew up a plan, the 'Dai Kenso', or the 'great inspection', and that the commander of the Singapore garrison, Major General Kawamura Saburo, passed the 'severe disposal' order to Lt Colonel Oishi Masayuki of the Number 2 Field Kempeitai Group: to be carried out according to 'the letter and spirit of the military law'. It is not clear what this clause implied. One Japanese officer, who left a short memoir of his experience in Malaya and Singapore as 'Mr. Nakane', refers to 'cruising' the streets of Singapore to see how 'the personal examination is being carried on': he casually alludes to 'those who were to be killed'. Yamashita gave Tsuji and Masayuki two days to conduct the 'great inspection'. But the Sook Ching would turn into a month-long bloodbath that engulfed Chinese communities in Singapore and then the Malay Peninsula.

The Kempeitai had clearly defined targets: British colonial personnel who had avoided detention; Chinese 'Dalforce' volunteers (who had been issued with distinctive uniforms); civil servants and others who had worked for the colonial administration; members of the Kuomintang and MCP; secret society members (who could be easily identified by their signature tattoos); members of various anti-Japanese organisations. Like the German SD *Einsatzgruppen* murder squads, the Kempeitai used membership lists of proscribed organisations to identify individuals they judged to be security threats. Top of the most-wanted list was Tan Kah Kee, who had already fled to a mountain hideout in Japan. Was the Sook Ching comparable to the German 'Final Solution' or incidents of 'ethnic cleansing'? The Japanese never conceived a plan to liquidate an entire ethnic group, as the Germans did, so in that sense any direct or implied comparison to the Holocaust would be inappropriate. Nor did the Sook Ching significantly resemble incidents of ethnic cleansing (defined as 'the planned deliberate removal from a specific territory of persons of a particular ethnic group, by force or intimidation, in order to render that area ethnically homogenous') that took place during the late twentieth-century Balkan wars. Nevertheless, the prosecution of General Yamashita's 'severe disposal' order fits with at least three of the UN criteria of genocide established by the 'Rome Statute' of the International Criminal Court:

> … any of the following acts committed with intent to destroy, in whole or in part, a national, ethnical, racial or religious group, as such:
> (a) Killing members of the group;
> (b) Causing serious bodily or mental harm to members of the group;
> (c) Deliberately inflicting on the group conditions of life calculated to bring about its physical destruction in whole or in part;
> (d) Imposing measures intended to prevent births within the group;
> (e) Forcibly transferring children of the group to another group.

Lt Colonel Oishi Masayuki commenced operations by dividing Singapore into five operational sectors that were allocated to different Kempeitai officers. On 16 February, the sector heads spread out across Singapore to find suitable sites to use as screening centres. Lt Colonel Oishi, for example, selected the Supreme Court building; Major Satroru Onishi took over the Victoria School. Other commanders took over police stations and hotels. Most of the centres were located near the main Chinese communities in the city. The Sook Ching was a daunting task: the Chinese population numbered at least 600,000 people. Shortcuts would be inevitable. The Sook Ching would be a joint Kempeitai/army operation. Two divisional commanders were assigned to help out, and 1,000 infantry assigned duties as Kempeitai auxiliaries. Soldiers with loudspeakers, notices and posters soon appeared all over central Singapore ordering the Chinese men aged between 18 and 50 to present themselves at the screening centres. Information was confusing. Some were told to bring food, others not; sometimes women and children turned up for screening as well as men. Kempeitai agents searched private houses and clubs and accumulated a mass of evidence – mainly in the form of thick folders of names. These ever-lengthening lists drove the Sook Ching, forcing Lt Colonel Oishi to order a second and then a third round-up. Heng Chiang Ki remembered what happened at the screening centre in Victoria Street: 'Thousands were lining up to get clearance […] They had a long table there: high ranking Japanese officer […] and maybe one or two Chinese or Malays who were either informers or in the police force …'. After a brief interrogation Chiang Ki was 'chopped' (i.e. stamped) and allowed to go.

When the selections had been completed, Japanese soldiers, wearing Kempeitai armbands, drove parties of terrified men who had not been cleared and chopped to execution sites, which were situated often, but not always, in remote areas like Changi, Punggol and Bedok. A man who lived in the Sims Road area remembered that 'for almost a week, you could hear machine-gun sounds going through the night …'. The Japanese often chose to use beaches for mass executions: an ebbing tide would wash away the dead. Hundreds were taken out to sea in launches, shot, then dumped in the water. Some of the beaches were close to residential areas. There was no systematic effort to conceal what was happening: sometimes local people or even British POWs held nearby were forced to clear away the bodies. The British generally refused; locals had no choice. The Japanese were, in short, in a hurry. In early March, Colonel Tsuji ordered the Kempeitai squads to extend their campaign from Singapore to the peninsula. Here, too, they set up 'concentration centres' to screen Malayan Chinese. K.L. Chye remembers:

> … in every exit, there were masked men. And as we made to pass, if we are not wanted, we can go straight home. Don't turn back and look around. So many were stopped and asked to sit down on the field:, they are the ones who were eventually all executed …[21]

Japanese troops rapidly occupied rural areas in Malaya. It was in the villages and hamlets of the peninsula that the 'severe disposal' order became an excuse and opportunity for indiscriminate mass murder of Chinese civilians. Seow Boon Hor was 6 years old in March 1942:

> By four or five in the afternoon they still did not give us any food. We saw four army trucks carrying Japanese soldiers drive in. We were made to line up and follow them into the jungle and we were separated into groups. There were four Japanese soldiers standing in front of me. There was a young man who was afraid, he panicked and he ran. One of the soldiers ran after him and stabbed him. Everyone started to panic when they saw this and began to beg […] Help […] please don't kill us […] They ignored our cries, then the other three soldiers started to take out their bayonets and started stabbing people. My mother was next to me and she realised that something was wrong. She grabbed me and pulled me down. I could not see anything else after that. I was stabbed on my sides and I lost consciousness.

Some time later, as dusk fell, an elderly man came to the killing site and found little Boon Hor:

> He saw that I was still alive and still lying under my mother – so he pulled me out. My body was covered with blood, my mother's blood mixed with mine. My mother's eyes were wide open. I pulled her and said, 'Mother, wake up, let's go … wake up …'. But the old man said, 'your mother is dead […] we have to leave now.' My father was lying nearby, my younger brother was underneath my father. My youngest brother was stabbed and killed. My whole family perished …

The Japanese killed nearly every person in Boon Hor's village. Chang Loy was also 6 when the Kempeitai soldiers arrived in his village:

> They lectured us but we did not understand a word. Then they separated us into groups and led us away. They asked us to kneel down. My mother was on my left and she was carrying my youngest brother. The soldier grabbed my younger brother, threw him up in the air and bayoneted him through his stomach. My brother fell to the floor, his guts spilled out – but he was still alive and crying. I was stabbed from behind and the knife pierced through my body. The soldier then stepped on my back and pulled the knife out and I fell over. I then received two more stabs and I fainted.

In the 1970s, a documentary film-maker interviewed some of the Japanese soldiers who took part in the massacres in Malaya. 'Miyake' confessed:

> We went by lorry from Kuala Lumpur to a rubber plantation. There was a [Japanese] commander and 400 Chinese people standing before 60 of us soldiers.

The commander said, 'I'm issuing orders.' And what do you think the primary order was? 'Kill these Chinese people now.' We had no enmity against these people. We had no desire to kill them, because they're people too. And so, to drive us to kill, what do you think the officer said? 'Now, By order of His Imperial Highness, kill them.' The officer used their sword to cut off the heads of two men. I saw it happen. I saw a head fall and a pillar of blood rose 2 meters, or 3 meters, into the air. We buried 400 people in a hole in the ground [...] I think that around half of them hadn't died yet. They were buried alive.

The Japanese Sook Ching operations claimed tens of thousands of victims in Singapore and Malaya. In modern Malaysia, burial sites are still being discovered and investigated. To this day, it has proved impossible to quantify the exact number of victims: unlike the German SS, the Kempeitai did not compile meticulous records of specific operations. Estimates of the death toll have ranged from 6,000 to above 40,000. It is likely that the numbers were much higher. Unlike the German genocide in Europe, the Sook Ching operations came to an end after a period of several weeks: the Japanese regarded their race as an elite but there was no master plan to liquidate other races. How could there be? On 2 March the Japanese Army set up the Malayan Military Administration, the MMA. The MMA took a different tack: they rounded up prominent Chinese, such as Dr Lim Boon Keng and the Shaw Brothers, who were notable film producers, and incarcerated them at Kempeitai headquarters. They were tortured and threatened with death. Under extreme pressure the prisoners agreed to form the Overseas Chinese Association, whose purpose would be to atone for Chinese 'crimes' – namely, anti-Japanese activities. The Japanese split the Chinese into two groups – the Malayan born (or Straits Chinese) and the China born. Each group was assigned a different 'minder'. In the case of the China born this was a Taiwanese called Wee Twee Kim, who had worked as a storekeeper in Singapore and now worked as an informer for the Kempeitai. The Japanese made clear that the purpose of the OCA was to raise M$50 million as compensation. Dr Lim, the Shaws and other putative OCA leaders were forced to extract contributions from the Chinese communities according to their known incomes. The MMA ingeniously provided the OCA with copies of property reports from the Land Registry and Income Tax Offices to make sure no one cheated by under-declaring their wealth. But the chronic disruption that followed the Japanese invasion made the collection of the sum demanded extremely difficult: only M$28 million had been declared by the end of June. A Japanese expert on Chinese affairs, Takase Toru, then proposed that the OCA raise a loan from the Yokohama Specie Bank (later the Bank of Tokyo) at 6 per cent interest to be repaid within a year. The M$50 million gift was presented to General Yamashita on 25 June, who accepted the money as atonement. The ransacking of Chinese wallets was a breathtaking example of fiscal skulduggery. Military occupations are invariably hothouses of treachery and betrayal.

4

FIGHTING BACK

Into the Jungle

In the chaotic period before the fall of Singapore, the Malayan Communist Party had indulged in an orgy of hero worship focused on their enigmatic secretary general, Lai Tek. Banners were unfurled outside MCP headquarters in Singapore celebrating 'Lai T'e […] our able leader […] the most loyal disciple of Stalin …'. For many leading Malayan communists the future of the party depended on Lai Tek, who was, it will be recalled, a Special Branch informer. This personality cult would have a tragic outcome for its most fervent advocates. After the British surrender, Lai Tek, who was at the time calling himself Wong Kim Gyock, fled into hiding. But in March he was arrested and taken to the Kempeitai headquarters at the YMCA building in Stamford Road, Singapore. Cheah Boon Kheng discusses a number of theories that try to explain how and why the cunning and resourceful Lai Tek was caught. He may have been carelessly using a wireless transmitter; he was 'pointed out' by a Chinese former Special Branch detective. These are completely plausible theories. But according to Major R.J. Isaacs, who interrogated the Kempeitai officer Sartoru Onishi after the war, on 26 March, a Malay and a Chinese 'helped' Sgt Mitsuo Nakayama arrest a man called Wong Show Tong. At Kempeitai headquarters, Wong Show Tong confessed that he was an executive member of the Communist Party. Major Onishi was impressed by what the prisoner had to offer – presumably information that only a high-ranking communist would know about – and made sure he was provided with decent food and cigarettes. In the next few weeks the bond between captor and captive deepened. Finally, 'Wong Tong Show' confessed that he was none other than Wong Kim Gyock, the top man in the MCP, and entrusted by the party to control the entire organisation in Singapore and Malaya. A bargain was struck. 'Wong Kim Gyock', alias Lai Tek, would be released, with a substantial reward, if he turned over the names of the MCP top brass.

For the Japanese, Lai Tek's treachery was a marvellous gift. Onishi was assigned as his case officer. He would make contact through a café on Orchard Road or the home of Lee Yem Kong, a Chinese photographer who had been 'turned' before the invasion and worked for the Japanese as an interpreter. Now Lai Tek had to spin a convincing yarn to his admiring comrades in the MCP, who knew that he had been arrested by the Kempeitai. It would seem that he had developed a simple cover story. He had been arrested riding his red bicycle and accused of being a Kuomintang agent. After vigorously protesting his innocence he was released. Lai Tek's party admirers fell for this story because it chimed with his other apparently miraculous gifts as a leader. They had no desire to lose their charismatic general secretary. But Lai Tek was not yet in the clear. Communist Li Ying Kang had also been arrested by the Kempeitai and somehow got word to party leaders about Lai Tek's treachery. To deal with this, Lai Tek arranged with the Japanese for Li to be released – then had him buried alive, and the truth about Lai Tek's treachery along with him. He also took up with Li's wife. But Lai Tek was not yet safe. For other communists had also got wind of Lai Tek's dealings with Major Onishi or his subordinates. (Only four Kempeitai officers knew about Lai Tek's new role.) Although he must have been under considerable strain, Lai Tek either had his potential betrayers arrested and executed by the Japanese or denounced them as traitors to the MCP. He exploited, in other words, Japanese anxiety about the threat posed by the Chinese communists and traditional communist paranoia about enemies within. With Lai Tek's assistance, Onishi was able to draw up a detailed MCP organisational chart that provided an almost complete picture of communist activity in Singapore and the peninsula.

Lai Tek's strategy was a high-wire act. He risked discovery at any moment. But from now until the end of the occupation he used the Japanese to weed out literally hundreds of rivals and thereby safeguard and enhance his position as the MCP's top dog. The Malayan communists, naturally, had no idea who was behind the plague of arrests and executions that afflicted their party during the occupation. Lai Tek continued to report to his Special Branch control and yet did not hesitate to inform the Japanese about the comings and goings of British 'Force 136' officers – that is until it became clear that the Japanese would lose the war. It was a political 'hedge' scheme – and Lai Tek played it with amoral virtuosity. It is not surprising that Lai Tek baffled and intrigued anyone who worked with him: he was a puzzle wrapped in an enigma. Spencer Chapman recalled a 'young-middle-aged Chinese [sic] of great charm, considerable intelligence, and quiet efficiency. He had a large mouth and perfect teeth and when he becomes animated his eyes grow round and his eyebrows rise about an inch and a half ...'. John Davis was remarkably forgiving:

> I personally find a character like that – a person who has spent the whole of his life as an informer or traitor, or whatever word you like to use, for one side or the other, then doubly, develops a strange sort of character. You can't dislike a man intensely just because of that – you've got to look behind and understand a certain amount about it. And I don't think Lai Teck let us down, we couldn't have got anywhere without him.

But Richard Broome, a Malayan civil service official who served with Force 136 concluded Lai Tek was 'devious' – a nice understatement.

Lai Tek proved his worth to the Japanese occupiers time and again. In May, he passed on the identities of the Singapore MCP committee, who were all rounded up or killed by Kempeitai squads. Next it was the turn of the Johor State Committee to be liquidated, then those of Malacca, Negeri Sembilan and Selangor. In August, Lai Tek called a full meeting of the Central Executive Committee. It would take place on 1 September at Sungai Tua, a village close to the Batu Caves, a Hindu holy site and popular picnic area not far from Kuala Lumpur. The purpose of the meeting was to review the current situation and resolve future strategy. In the last week of August local people noticed a number of Japanese 'tourists' apparently relaxing on the Padang near Sungai Tua. They played games, danced and sang songs – and took an unusually keen interest in the village and its surroundings. The committee members arrived on the night of the 31 August with a small party of bodyguards. There was no sign of Lai Tek, and the Penang committee member Xiao Zhong took charge of proceedings. On the following day at about 1 a.m., Japanese troops noiselessly surrounded the village. They attacked at daybreak. In the fierce gun battle that followed, twenty-nine Central Committee members were killed as well as many of the MPAJA regimental 'Commissars'. For the handful of survivors there was one consoling fact: Lai Tek had survived. When he met distraught party officials, Lai Tek told them that providentially his car had broken down on the way to the meeting. At Kempeitai headquarters in Singapore there was much rejoicing: 'you would have been astonished,' Major Isaacs revealed, 'for Onishi was toasting none other than the leader of the MCP, Lai Tek himself.' Lai Tek's 'purge' continued unabated for the next year. As a fighting force the MPAJA was bleeding, battered – and increasingly paranoid. The 5th Regiment in Perak formed a 'killer squad' to eliminate 'traitors', and as Spencer Chapman's memoir *The Jungle is Neutral* reveals, jungle executions of anyone suspected of disloyalty became everyday events. The near continuous erosion of the MPAJA leadership favoured just one party member – Lai Tek himself. He was like the flint inside the chalk. By the spring of 1943 he was a virtual dictator. And yet the MPAJA did not evaporate. When Kempeitai officer Onishi was interrogated by Major Isaacs after the war he had no doubt that Lai Tek knew what he was doing: 'He realised that Japan would not win the war,' Onishi said, 'he did nothing to damage the real war effort.'

It was precisely because Lai Tek was so highly valued by the Kempeitai that he was able to function as an efficient party leader. He built up an intricate network of contacts up and down the peninsula and drove everywhere in a Morris 8 HP Saloon, supplied by the Japanese. On the communist side no one appeared to find Lai Tek's freedom of movement in any way unusual or suspicious. It merely added to his allure. Thanks to the personality cult that he had cunningly promoted before the Japanese occupation, he had assumed the mythological character of one of the old Malay heroes, like Hang Tuah, in modern form. Lai Tek was reputed to be able to fly aircraft, drive tanks, speak countless languages and, of course, pass through Japanese checkpoints without being questioned. He travelled in style, often accompanied by his Vietnamese mistress – and was a regular at the Coliseum Hotel in Batu Road in Kuala Lumpur. From here, Lai Tek would drive 12 miles north on the Ipoh Road to a mill where he would meet MPAJA representatives to discuss the military situation in Selangor. Then he would drive on to Perak where he would meet Chin Peng, who was known as Lai Tek's 'little boy'. According to Chin Peng's memoir *My Side of History*, Lai Tek had first summoned him to meet at a hilltop bungalow south of Kuala Lumpur. For Chin Peng this involved a perilous journey from his secret base in Perak. He immediately noted the secretary general's strange Vietnamese accent – 'He didn't look Chinese; he didn't sound Chinese. To me looked almost Eurasian. He was dark and quite small [...] he looked ill.' Lai Tek's young new disciple would be his nemesis.

The Rape of the Dream People

Almost a year to the day after the Japanese conquest of Southeast Asia, an unusual encounter took place deep in the Malayan jungle. It was a meeting between very different minds and cultures that would have unexpected and bloody consequences both during the Malayan Emergency and the American war in Vietnam. On a river bank in northern Perak, a British anthropologist called Pat Noone introduced the aboriginal tribe he lived with and studied to a party of communist guerrillas who were engaged in a life and death struggle with the Japanese occupiers. The bond that soon developed between the tribal peoples of the peninsula, now known as Orang Asli, and the guerrillas would have a tragic outcome for Pat Noone and change for ever an ancient way of life.

Herbert Deane Noone, always called Pat, was a British anthropologist who had a First in Archaeology and Anthropology from Corpus Christi College, Cambridge.[22] Pat's father was the splendidly named Herbert Vander Vord Noone, who made such a pot of money in India that he happily retired at 44 and returned to England. The Noone family subsequently enjoyed a somewhat peripatetic family life. Pat and his younger brother Richard grew up in Dymchurch on the Kent coast and across the channel in Saint-Jean-de-Luz in the Basque country of south-west France. 'HV' had great ambitions for his sons, most of all his eldest. Richard always said his brother seemed to be 'blessed'. For one thing, Pat was a strapping lad who had inherited his mother's famous blue eyes and colouring and was much admired as a teenage Adonis. He excelled at sports and passed exams effortlessly. He was, from his earliest years, unusually confident and assured. After coming down from Cambridge in 1930, he was offered a job by Ifor Evans, the curator of the Perak State Museum in Taiping, as a field ethnographer, and gladly accepted.

At the time, Taiping was a charming up-country town. Evans (Charterhouse, Clare College) had come to North Borneo in 1912 as a cadet district officer, then turned to anthropology and archaeology. He had been in Taiping since 1912. In the jungles of Perak, Evans fell under the spell of Malaya's aboriginal peoples, then referred to by Malays as 'Sakai', which means 'dependent' or 'slave' in Malay. Evans took early retirement in 1932 and he evidently passed on his passion to his young protégée. Pat could already see that the region of central and northern Malaya that Sir Hugh Clifford had called the 'aboriginal block' was contracting very rapidly as the British cut new roads and railways through the pristine jungle, or *ulu*. But Noone discovered that between the Cameron Highlands and Gunung Noring, a high point in the Main Range, there was an unmapped and apparently 'empty' *ulu* region that had so far escaped the encroachment of the modern. Here, he sensed, was a pristine world of rocky, jungle-clad peaks, riven by deep, plunging ravines, laced with foaming rivers and streams, and permanently shrouded in mist. It was a realm, so it was said, haunted by malevolent spirits and stalked by bloodthirsty cannibals. 'Nonsense, of course' concluded a 'vastly intrigued' Pat Noone.

At the beginning of the 1930s, the aboriginal peoples of this mysterious *ulu* region were not completely unknown to anthropologists. There is a patronising description in Sir Hugh Clifford's 1897 book *In Court and Kampong*:

> A curious group to look upon we must have been could any one have seen us: I, the European, the white man, belonging to one of the most civilised races in the Old World; the Malays, civilised too, but after the fashion of unchanging Asia; and, lastly, the [aboriginal] Sĕmangs, squalid savages, nursing no ambitions save those prompted by their empty stomachs, with no hope of change or improvement in their lot, and yet representing one of the oldest races in the world: a people who are doomed to speedy extinction, and who, never since time began, have had their day or have played a part in human history.

These attitudes persisted for a long time. A few years before Noone arrived in Taiping, the German anthropologist and theologian Father Paul Joachim Schebesta had referred to people known as the 'Northern Sakai' in his book *Among the Forest Dwarfs* published in 1927. Like their neighbours the Semai, the Temiar speak a Mon-Kher language known as Senoi and have lived for millennia in the upland areas of Kelantan, Perak and northern Pahang. They practice 'swidden' or 'slash and burn' farming of cassava and hill rice supplemented by hunting, fishing and trading of forest products. The Temiar have no written history and for millennia successfully kept the modern world at bay. Malays interacted with Orang Asli communities in much more exploitative ways – raiding their camps for slaves. Over time, Malays pushed many Orang Asli groups ever deeper into the remotest regions of the Main Range. The precarious world of these aboriginal peoples would be even more deeply eroded in the nineteenth and early twentieth centuries by European colonialists and then, after 1941, by the Japanese. British census reports estimated that some 27,000 aboriginals inhabited scattered and remote forest communities in British Malaya. Of that number, more than 24,000 lived in a single state – Perak – although territoriality meant very little to these wary forest peoples.

In July 1931 Noone set up camp at the confluence of the Telom and Cherkok Rivers in the deep jungle. He had chosen this location because he knew that a Semai camp lay on the other side of the Cherkok, but when he attempted to cross over the women and children fled into the forest. A surly group of men confronted him brandishing spears and made it all too clear that they did not want him to stay anywhere close to their camp. It looked very much as if Noone's second expedition would achieve as little as his first. The Semai simply did not want to be 'studied'. As Noone moped about in his little camp, his Malay cook, Puteh bin Awang, who Noone recalled had 'all the instincts of a gentleman and an amazing delicacy of manner', told him that he had discovered a young Semai girl alone in a small hut just half a mile away. She was covered in wart-like sores, and seemed to be dying. She was, Puteh told Noone, suffering from dreadful thirst. It turned out that the Semai girl had been abandoned by her people: no one was permitted to go near her until she had died. Noone had a rudimentary knowledge of tropical diseases. He examined the stricken girl, made a careful note of her symptoms and sent a runner with an urgent letter to the British medical officer in the nearest village, which was Tapah. He and Puteh brought the girl to their riverside camp, where she was nursed. The runner soon returned from Tapah with a diagnosis and medicine. The girl had tertiary yaws, a horrible tropical disease caused by a spirochete bacterium. Today yaws is treated with antibiotics, but these were unavailable in 1931. There was no certain cure but whatever it was that the medical officer in Tapah sent to Noone's camp worked. The little Semai girl was soon recovering, and her sores were fading.

This unplanned sequence of events completely changed Noone's standing among the previously hostile Semai. The stricken girl, it now turned out, was the daughter of the headman Batu, who showed off his white-skinned medicine man to other village chiefs and promised to take him deeper into the jungle to find the Temiars. In the meantime, Noone, in a state of elation, began working with the Semai, mapping their settlements and making notes on kinship networks and ritual. It was an exhilarating time but cut short all too soon. After a nasty bout of dengue, or 'break bone' fever, Noone, stricken with a temperature above 105 degrees and in very severe pain, was forced to return to Tanah Rata and then Taiping.

In March 1932 he set out again, following the Telom River and its tributaries. Many weeks later Noone reached the tiny settlement of Kuala Rening, where the Rening River roars down from a narrow, rocky gorge. It was here that a group of young Temiar warriors, armed with blowpipes and festooned with feathers, stepped boldly out of the jungle and gathered in front of the mysterious white man who had searched for them for so long. Richard Noone later described Kuala Rening as a 'haunted place'. For it was here that his brother began his journey into the world of the Temiar and where he would find love and eventually his own violent death.

Noone 'went native'. When Richard travelled to Malaya in 1935, Pat invited him to spend time with the Temiar. He was astonished to discover that Pat had married 'a jungle girl' called Ajang. Was she just 'a floozie on the side' a shocked Richard wondered? No, Pat insisted – they were married 'in the sight of God and the law'. But it was going to be 'damned hard' to explain Ajang to the family. A British planter who got to know Noone well called him 'Lawrence in a loincloth'. He was, to be sure, one of the last romantic anthropologists. Noone came to admire the Temiar as Rousseauesque 'Noble Savages': he saw them as jungle quasi-socialists – gentle pacifists who shunned violence. His idealistic conviction would turn out to be a literally fatal error.

Noone's ideas may have been muddled or misguided but he was a staunch defender of 'his' Temiar and its rights. He was also a professional anthropologist and returned to Cambridge in 1938 to complete his PhD. (He also introduced a fellow student to noisy Temiar-style tribal dancing, fuelled by Scotch, to the astonishment of the local constabulary.) When he was in Malaya, Noone, who had taken over from Ivor Evans as curator, worked for some of the year at the Taiping Museum, where he lived with Ajang. Temiar friends camped in the gardens. Noone was greatly preoccupied with the fraught issue of Senoi land rights, which were, of course, customary and had no legal basis. Although Temiar *ulu* lands lay deep in the Main Range he feared that civilisation would soon encroach. By 1938, Noone had persuaded the British colonial authorities to establish a new post of 'Protector of Aborigines' in Perak, which, naturally enough, he took on himself. As 'Protector', Noone campaigned for legislation that would protect the rights of the Temiar to preserve their culture, and proposed establishing land reservations where Orang Asli communities would be free to follow their own laws and traditions.

Then in December 1941 the Japanese 25th Army rampaged through Perak and the world of the Orang Asli would be turned upside down. It is a tragic irony that Pat Noone was the unwitting agent of this despoiling, which dragged the 'Dream People' into the jaws of a global military conflict. Many Orang Asli would form bonds with the MPAJA guerrillas and then, after the war, with the communist insurgents. The British would counter-attack by isolating the Orang Asli in jungle forts and forming their own aboriginal fighting units. The architect behind this plan was Richard Noone. At the end of the 1960s Noone would start arming Montagnard tribal groups to fight the communists in Vietnam.

After the fall of Singapore, many of the Chinese fleeing the ravages of the Sook Ching, including members of the MCP and the embryonic MPAJA, fled into the jungle, where they set up small self-sufficient settlements growing fruit and vegetables. Legally they had no right to the land they occupied and were called 'squatters'. For a long time the MPAJA relied on the Chinese squatters and would become even more dependent on them when they fought the British after the war. The Japanese were well aware of these illicit MPAJA supply lines and the Kempeitai focused a great deal of effort trying to block them, just as the British would a few years later. In the deep jungle of Perak the MPAJA regiments found that it was a lot more difficult to fodder their camps. At the end of 1943, Noone and his Temiar friends would provide the MPAJA with a solution to their dilemma.

The last European to see Noone alive was Robert Chrystal, known to his Malay friends as 'Tuan Tinggi'. Before December 1941, Chrystal had managed a rubber estate at Sungai Siput in north Perak. Although, as Chapman unkindly remarked, he was 'the wrong side of forty five' and suffered from duodenal ulcers, he gamely volunteered to join a 'stay behind' party after the Japanese landings. He ended up spending more than a year in an MPAJA camp. It was there that he met Chin Peng and another guerrilla leader called Low Mah. Coincidentally, Chin Peng had attended the middle school on the boundary of Chrystal's estate. At the end of November 1942, one of the MPAJA political leaders handed Chrystal a note. It was from the 'legendary' Pat Noone. He had, it seemed, been in Kelantan on the other side of the Main Range and had recently returned to Perak. He wanted to meet the 'Europeans' he had heard lived in the MPAJA camp. By then Chrystal was disillusioned with the MPAJA, having witnessed numerous 'traitor killing sessions', and secretly hoped that Noone might be able to rescue him from their clutches.

But Pat had other ideas. Shortly afterwards, as Chrystal and his MPAJA comrades celebrated the building of new *atap* huts with speeches and songs, Noone walked into the camp unannounced. His appearance was startling: he was naked save for pair of shorts and a black cummerbund in the Temiar- style, his hair was severely cropped and he was armed with a gleaming jungle knife, or *parang*. He was accompanied by a personal bodyguard of a dozen or so Temiar 'braves' armed with *parangs*, blowpipes and quivers full of poisoned darts. His entry into the MPAJA camp was a theatrical statement and it made an immediate and favourable impression on the MPAJA. Noone had strong views about both the Malays and the Orang Asli peoples. Low Mah and the other communists plied him with questions about why Malays were so resistant to ideals and whether their Muslim faith could somehow be diluted. Chrystal rather sourly remarked that the MPAJA leaders were overawed by Noone's academic credentials; they fancied themselves as intellectuals too. The former planter and the Cambridge anthropologists were worlds apart. Noone was just as impressed by these earnest young men who had sacrificed so much to fight the Japanese. In a long, passionately delivered speech he made a case for an alliance with the Temiar: 'With the squatters being exterminated by the Japanese in a determined effort to starve you out, your only hope of surviving in the jungle [is] with the help of the aborigines […] They are kind, unselfish and understanding …'. He promised that in the remote Temiar lands a 'Shangri La' laced with beautiful valleys and streams awaited them. Noone's speech had a tremendous impact.[23]

Smitten with a new cause, Noone sent out messages to the Temiar tribal leaders to get them to back the MPAJA guerrillas. He organised tours of their settlements and staged riotous parties to introduce the MPAJA fighters to the Temiar. Noone's crusade was a brilliant success. The headmen readily agreed to do whatever their Tuan Tata (Noone) proposed. Until the end of the Japanese occupation, the Senoi peoples helped the MPAJA survive the most dangerous periods of their struggle against the Japanese. They divulged their deep knowledge of the forest and its secret resources; they showed the MPAJA how to locate the best sites for their camps. Above all, they taught the guerrillas how to use bamboo. 'To describe the material culture of the Temiars,' Noone wrote, 'is to tell the uses to which bamboo may be put. Bamboo is indispensable for houses, household utensils, vessels, tools, weapons, fences, baskets, water pipes, rafts, musical instruments and ornaments …'. With their bamboo huts, the MPAJA camps increasingly resembled transient Temiar settlements. For the benefit of the MPAJA the Temiar transformed their once hidden *ulu* world into an academy of guerrilla warfare.

By mid-1943, the MPAJA leaders had learnt for themselves how to exploit the Temiar and the jungle. They had no further need for Pat Noone. That summer, dismayed by the way the MPAJA exploited his precious 'Dream People', Noone broke with the MPAJA. According to Chrystal he was suffering from a nasty bout of malaria. His wife Ajang seemed to be devastated. Had Pat fallen into the hands of the Japanese? It was odd, though, that she was now sharing the same long-house mat as Noone's tribal 'blood brother' Udu. Pat Noone was never seen again, alive or dead. The mystery would remain unsolved until Richard Noone returned to the jungle more than a decade after his brother's disappearance to recruit the Orang Asli – to fight the communists.

Merdeka?

The Malayan communists and the MPAJA guerrillas both saw their war against the Japanese as a first step to securing independence for Malaya. But what kind of Malaya? Between the political aims of the Malay nationalists and the Malayan communists lay a turbulent gulf. The 'object of the communist struggle', as one wartime manifesto proclaimed, was a democratic republic which offered equality and justice for all races, freed from the yoke of empire.

Ibrahim Yaacob, leader of the Kesatuan Melayu Muda (KMM), was just as committed to independence – *merdeka* – but on Malay terms. He and his small group of like-minded nationalists saw the solution to the Malay demographic dilemma in a union with an independent Indonesia. Yaacob dreamed of creating a Melayu Raya or Indonesia Raya – Greater Malaya or Greater Indonesia. Although the communists, like Lai Tek (Secretary General of the MCP) and rising star, Chin Peng, favoured collaboration with the British to defeat the Japanese, Yaacob hedged his bets. He knew very well, as he said on 17 February 1942, that 'Japan's victory is not our victory'. It may come as a surprise to discover that Yaacob had frequent wartime meetings with MCP representatives to formulate a united front strategy against 'Japanese fascism', while simultaneously holding out hope that the Japanese might at some point resume independence discussions with the KMM. In 1942 the Japanese repeatedly dashed Yaacob's hopes. Although KMM members had, as we have seen, assisted the Japanese 'Kame' organisation as the 25th Army rampaged towards Singapore, their inept attempts to persuade the Japanese to declare Malaya independent had come to nothing.

Nevertheless, the Japanese treated KMM supporters well and implied at least that they would adopt a pro-Malay policy. They continued to consult Yaacob on various matters and gave him access to a radio, which was, of course, strictly controlled. In Malay villages the Japanese turned to KMM members to gather information and recruit manpower. This perversely elevated the status of the KMM in Malay eyes. Its membership list expanded rapidly. Japanese patronage meant that KMM members had privileged access to information, food rations and other perks, which meant that they in turn could become much envied patrons in their own right. In other words, the Japanese turned the KMM into a collaborating elite. This brought them into conflict with the Malay aristocracy and the British-trained MCS bureaucracy. This worsened when the KMM were given powers of arrest and interrogation, which they used against any rival for power. A future Malaysian High Commission recalled that 'KMM officials swaggered about in villages and in government offices, throwing their weight around …'.

The days of KMM swaggering soon came to an end. In June, the Japanese administration ordered Yaacob to dissolve the KMM. Although the Japanese had become nervous about preening Malay nationalists, the main reason for this fresh humiliation was practical. The KMM was incompetent. Its core membership comprised schoolteachers and low-level government employees. The old colonial order, the Datuks and the princes, was soon back, and happy to slap down KMM upstarts, who had challenged their power and status under the Japanese. By the end of 1942 the tainted glory days of the KMM were over. Mustapha Hussain refused to have anything further to do with the Japanese, as did another leftist Malay, Ahmad Boestamam. But after the dissolution of the KMM, Captain Ogawa, who was secretary to General Wataru Watanabe, head of the Malay Military Administration (MMA), invited Yaacob to accompany the director general on a tour of 'Malai': he eagerly accepted. At the end of the tour, over dinner, Ogawa offered Yaacob a government post as advisor on Malay affairs. Once installed, Yaacob became a familiar voice on radio urging Malays to co-operate with the Japanese, hinting that if they behaved well they would be rewarded with independence. He gave his closest and most loyal associates

jobs on the *Berita Malai* and other publications, which all cleaved to the KMM
line. The phantom KMM was riven by bitter disagreements between Yaacob's
privileged inner circle and those on the outside like Hussain and Boestamam,
who had come to despise their leader's autocratic style. The Japanese for their
part adroitly kept the Malay nationalists on the hook of future promises. In
June 1943, Prime Minister Tojo toured Southeast Asia and announced in the
Diet (Japanese parliament) that the Philippines and Burma would become
independent in the very near future. He offered somewhat fragile hope to the
'Indonesian peoples' of Malaya, Sumatra, Borneo and Java.

This tepid non-committal announcement was welcomed by the Malay press.
At the end of July, Yaacob was invited to take an eight-person Malay delegation
on a three-month tour of Japan, which was enthusiastically reported by the
Japanese Domei news agency. The Japanese mission was to 'rouse Indonesians,
including Malays, from the stupor into which they had fallen during the Dutch
and British regimes ...'. A new gospel of co-existence and co-prosperity had
been brought to Malaya! Within days of Yaacob's return to Malaya the Japanese
dealt him an unexpected blow. Concerned that allied Thailand was becoming
increasingly restive, Japan ceded the northern Malay states Kedah, Kelantan, Perlis
and Terengganu – restoring in effect the old Siamese suzerainty discussed in
Chapter 1. This was devastating for Malay nationalists, who dreamt of a Greater,
not lesser, Malaya. Mustapha Hussain mourned that 'Malaya to me was a fish
the Japanese had cut into two [...] presented to the Siamese on a silver platter.'
The loss of the northern states was a stinging political slap. It was also a blow to
the Malay stomach because what the Japanese had 'presented' to the Thais was
Malaya's 'rice bowl': the consequences would be dire.

It is quite astonishing that Yaacob still refused to give up hope that Imperial
Japan would deliver. As he was grieving the wrenching loss of Malaya's northern
states, Watanabe proposed that he help form volunteer militias, the Giyu Gun
and Giyu Tai, to defend against Allied attacks and 'keep order'. The MMA had
already set up the Heiho (Auxiliary Servicemen) to provide labour services.
Yaacob would himself take part in military training exercises. Inevitably these
volunteer militias would be dominated by Malays and they would be deployed
not only against the British or Americans but anyone hostile to the occupying
power. Tame Malay journalists on Yaacob's payroll at *Berita Malai* indulged in an
orgy of banner waving, celebrating the Giyu Gun and its commander, Ibrahim
Yaacob. 'The Giyu Gun is a genuine Army that will consist only of Malays ...'.
declared Ishak Haji Muhammad: 'within the breasts [of volunteers] flows the
blood of Hang Tuah [the legendary Malay warrior] who once reminded us [sic]
"The Malays shall not vanish in the world."' Warming to his theme, he declared
that 'the Malay *Kris* demands blood ...'. Yaacob allowed the Japanese to control
recruitment and training, which undermined his claim that the Giyu Gun would
become a Malay army. An Indonesian nationalist called Mas Parjo denounced

him: 'Don't let the Japanese pick the men for the Giyu Gun. Bung [brother] – you must pick them yourself.' Yaacob had yet again shown himself to be a master of political miscalculation.

Yaacob's antics reflected Japanese vagueness about Malays and Malaya – or 'Malai' as it was now called. Their occupation policy was generally inconsistent and contradictory. The reason for this was simple. The Japanese had never developed a plan for Malaya. In strategic terms the peninsula was merely a stepping stone to the oil fields of the Dutch East Indies. For this was fundamentally a war about oil. From the moment the Meiji oligarchs embarked on their plan to transform Japan into a global power they faced a tremendous disadvantage. Japan was poor in raw materials and depended on foreign imports to feed its people, factories and armies. In the late nineteenth and early twentieth centuries, tens of thousands of impoverished Japanese fled their homeland to California, Hawaii, Peru and Southeast Asia. The solution was territorial expansion first into Manchuria, then China. Japanese adventurism troubled its former allies in the First World War. Modern armies, navies and air forces depend on oil. In 1938, the Americans imposed an oil embargo to check Japanese ambitions in China, cutting off at a stroke 80 per cent of its supply. The Dutch rejected Japanese pleas to increase exports from their oil fields in the Dutch East Indies. Over the course of the next two years the Americans tightened the screws, forcing the Japanese to think beyond China. To the all-powerful Japanese generals, it was clear that victory in China depended on tapping the rich oil resources of Southeast Asia. It was this desperate need that forced the Japanese to take on the European colonial powers. Liberating other Asians was expedient political flim-flam. This was veiled from the Asian nationalists like the Burmese Aung Sang, the Vietnamese Phan Boi Chau and the Indian Rash Behari Bose, who turned to Imperial Japan to seek political liberation from the hated colonial powers. For the Japanese, backing nationalist Asian movements was a rhetorical patina.

That this was indeed the Japanese plan became all too clear as soon as the European regimes had been ousted. Instead of liberating Asians, the Japanese murdered them and exploited millions as forced labour. In Malaya, as we have seen, the Japanese toyed with the naive KMM – but dropped the hot potato of independence as soon as the British had surrendered. It is telling that the Japanese military administration under Wataru Watanabe yoked together Malaya, Singapore *and Sumatra* as a 'Special Defence Area', which was considered to be part of Japan. General Yamashita, the 'Tiger of Malaya', openly referred to the people of the 'Special Defence Area' as 'Japan's subjects' – a slip which provoked the wrath of the Japanese Prime Minister Tojo, who exiled the 'tiger' to Manchuria. While the Japanese persecuted the Chinese in Singapore in Malaya, they cultivated the Malays. As we have seen, they looked down on Malays with the same condescending contempt as the British. For their part, many Malays had hoped that the Japanese occupation would lead to a flood of cheap imports to alleviate Malay poverty. They would be bitterly disappointed. Japanese needs and occupation policy had little to do with Asian nationalist aspirations.

Rather than indulging Malay aspirations the Japanese sought to 'Nipponise' compliant Malays. Clocks and calendars were switched to Japanese time; people were forced to bow in a north-easterly direction towards the emperor in Tokyo, which was, of course, problematic for Muslims because it meant facing away from Mecca. Mosques were also required to offer special prayers to the emperor, which was even more offensive to Muslims, whose faith rested on the assertion that 'There is no God but Allah.' The Japanese insistence on Tokyo time scrambled the ritual observance of sunrise and sunset for daily prayers and fasting during Ramadan.

For children, occupation meant that the old British schools were replaced by 'Nippon Go' schools. Mr Lingham recalls that: 'We all had to assemble at the field, and first we had to sing the [Japanese] national anthem the "Kimigayo" and raise the Japanese flag and everybody saluted and after that we went through the physical exercises …'. Seventy years on, the late Datuk Zainal could still remember verses of the 'Kimigayo': 'We were young at that time […] 12 years old is easy to pick up the Japanese language and the characters: and you have to sing all the Japanese patriotic songs: *miyoto kaino, sorakete, kyoka jitsu takaku, koga yageba/tenji no sei ge, hatshu ratshu to, kibora o do ru, oyashima* …'. Zainal has no doubt what the Japanese plan was: 'They have got one thing in mind. They have got *sheisin*: they have got spirit. They wanted to embed it in us. They don't want us to be lazy. The Japanese never like idle people and you have to be punctual, you have got to be strong in your behaviour. They call it *sheisin* …'.[24] The Japanese had their own 'myth of the lazy native' and believed that supposedly innate Malay indolence would be cured by a good dose of scholastic discipline, or something worse.

Malays were, however, not exempt from labour service. The treatment of British POWs on the 'Death Railway' is an emblematic symbol of wartime Japanese brutality, but many tens of thousands of Asians were also enslaved, and in much worse conditions. In Malaya, the Japanese used biddable kampong elders to lure young men into slave labour. Mohamed Salleh, who lived in the little village of Buluh Kasap, was lucky to survive. He remembers that 'the assistant village elder was always looking for people to work [for the Japanese]. He said we would be working in a town in Siam [Thailand]: the food is easy and there is lots of rice, he said, so I followed him. We were happy and twenty-four of us went …'. The 'volunteers' boarded trains that took them hundreds of miles north across the Thai border: 'We worked building the train road, day and night, we took it in shifts, there were many of us, Indian, Chinese, Malays, a real mixture. The whites wore underpants, they did not wear clothes, it was terrible working with the Japanese, we were not workers, we were slaves.' The work was back-breaking and the Japanese guards provided only the most basic food for the workers: 'Twenty, thirty, sometimes forty died every day […] We dug a big pit and they were thrown into the hole. They did not allow us to bury them individually. So many of our people died there …'.

Arming the Natives

The Japanese administration was aware of growing Malay disaffection. As the Japanese Empire began to crumble, this did not bode well. The formation of the Giya Gun under Ibrahim Yaacob was one response to this anxiety. At the same time, the Japanese authorised the establishment of Sangi Kai, regional councils for Singapore and the Malay states, that gave at least the semblance of self-government albeit by aristocrats and reliable civil servants. Chinese, too, served on these new councils. This reflected the fact that after the loss to Thailand of the northern states, *non-Malays* became the demographic majority. This is an important, and often overlooked, development that deepened Malay anxieties. It certainly reinforced Ibrahim Yaacob's commitment to the Giyu Gun. On New Year's Day in 1944, he made a new appeal to young Malay men to join up to 'serve their country'. By early summer, Lieutenant Colonel Yaacob and some 2,000 recruits had finished their training in Johor Bahru. Then in July the Japanese sent the Giyu Gun into action against the MPAJA near Kota Tinggi, where they killed twenty-five guerrillas. In Perak, however, Giyu Gun men refused to attack MPAJA camps – and the Japanese withdrew the unit to Singapore. 'Arming the natives' is always tricky. Ibrahim was promoted to colonel but effectively stripped of power. By now he had fallen out with many of the other KMM leaders. Hussain, it will be recalled, had long before retreated back to his home in Perak. After the Giyu Gun debacle even Yaacob's staunchest supporters deserted him. In September the ground shifted again. As the Japanese retreated across the Pacific the Tojo cabinet fell and General Kuniaki Koiso replaced him as prime minister. On 9 September, Koiso announced that the former Dutch East Indies would be prepared for independence. This astonishing development appeared to vindicate the 'collaborationist' policies of Sukarno, who had adopted the pro-Japanese slogan '*Amerika kita setrika, Inggris kita linggis*' ('Let's iron America, and bludgeon the British') and, like Yaacob, had helped recruit pro-Japanese militias – the 'Pembela Tanah Air' (PETA) and 'Heiho' (Indonesian Volunteer Army). By mid-1945 some 2 million Indonesians had volunteered to join Sukarno's army to repel any Allied attempt to take back Java.

Yaacob closely followed what was happening on the other side of the South China Sea in Java. Sukarno's success renewed his interest in the idea of 'Raya Indonesia' and reinforced his delusion that collaboration was the road to *merdeka*. The American onslaught in the pacific also focused Japanese minds. In May 1945 a Japanese academic called Yoichi Itagaki and his superior Professor Kaname Akamatsu, who headed the 'Chosabus' research bureau in Singapore, which studied Malayan life and culture, contacted Yaacob and urged him to rally his supporters. At a meeting at Yaacob's home in Tanjong Katong, Itagaki claimed that 'independence for Malaya is coming'. The Japanese chief of staff, he went on, had proposed that Ibrahim 'function as leader of the Malay nationalist movement'. This was of course thrilling news. Since the KMM was a thoroughly spent force, Yaacob suggested calling the new nationalist movement KRIS. This has variously been said to mean 'Kesatuan Rakyat Indonesia Semenanjung' (Union of Peninsula Indonesians), or 'Kerajaan Ra'ayat Indonesia Semenanjung' (Government of Peninsula Indonesians), but in any case a *Kris* is, of course, a Malay ceremonial dagger and the acronym fitted perfectly. The Japanese referred to KRIS as Hodosho. Ibrahim had an important condition. He insisted that he could not 'start anything' without the involvement of Mustapha Hussain, who had consistently refused to kowtow to the Japanese since his experiences in Singapore in February 1942. He had been ousted from the Malai Giyu Gun (he had been a major) for various acts of insubordination such as refusing to bow to the sun and saluting all Japanese soldiers whatever their rank. Hussain had written a memo proposing the integration of all the Japanese-sponsored Malay militias, like the Hei Ho auxiliaries and the Gun Po, under the umbrella of the Giyu Gun. For the Japanese this would have been a step too far towards a national Malay army. Hussain had been bitterly disappointed by the loss of the northern Malay states to Thailand and was ambivalent about the idea of 'Raya Indonesia': he was happy with what God had already allocated to Malays. Hussain's honourable intransigence was, of course, precisely the reason why Ibrahim wanted him onboard. Itagaki, too, seemed to understand how vital it was to secure Hussain's blessing: he was the Hatta to Ibrahim's Sukarno; he was the incorruptible Malay. His endorsement was beyond price. KRIS needed Hussain.

There are at least two versions of what happened next. According to Cheah Boon Kheng, Professor Akamatsu and Itagaki travelled to Perak accompanied by General Yoshijirō Umezu of the Japanese 29th Army to try and persuade Hussain to come onboard. This was a high-level delegation and Hussain was flattered. With impressive cunning General Umezu confessed that Japanese policy had been wrong and that now they would 'do their best' to get Malays what they wanted. Such disingenuous 'honesty' won over the decent open-hearted Hussain and he pledged his support to KRIS. Was this *merdeka* at last? Hussain's own version is that he was summoned to meet a Japanese delegation in Taiping. He agreed with great reluctance. He feared for his life but was aware that many Malays suspected he was an informer. At the Japanese administrative headquarters in Taiping, Hussain was led into an office where he was greeted 'like a long lost brother' by a Japanese officer and – to his astonishment – by one of the founding members of the KMM, Dr Burhanuddin bin Muhammad Nur al-Hilmi, commonly known as Burhanuddin al-Helmy, who had been employed by the Japanese as an advisor on Islamic custom. Although Dr Burhanuddin was not at all comfortable with his devious Japanese colleague, he explained the purpose of KRIS and urged

Mustapha to pledge his commitment. Hussain promised to consider the matter and returned to his farm. That night Dr Burhanuddin came alone to Hussain's home to 'coax him to join'. They spent the night praying and sobbing. The following day Hussain agreed to 'give the Japanese another chance'. It was a few days later, when Hussain rushed to Taiping to attend the first KRIS meeting at the Nurses Hostel, that he met and argued with Major General Umezu and Professor Itagaki. It was at this meeting, according to Hussain's memoir, that Umezu apologised and secured his agreement to join KRIS. According to Hussain, Umezu returned again and again to the same point: the Malays had not fought for their independence. It could not be handed to them on a plate. Although Hussain protested that this was untrue, referring to his petulant demand for independence in January 1942, Umezu had a point. After that first meeting at Taiping, Hussain and Dr Burhanuddin spent the next several days drafting an 'Independent Malaya Constitution'. When Yaacob arrived, accompanied by a Giyu Gun adjutant, he and Dr Burhanuddin insisted that the new 'Constitution' made no reference to reincorporating the lost northern Malay states: as Hussain pointed out, both men were employees of the Japanese military administration and their hands were tied. As Hussain bitterly acknowledged later, this rather farcical constitution performed, in effect, the 'last rites on a dead Malaya'.

Freedom Fighters

In Malaya, ruthless Japanese exploitation of their most prized intelligence asset, the MCP Secretary General Lai Tek, had crippled the MPAJA as an effective guerrilla force. Scattered across the jungles of the peninsula, MPAJA regiments were starved, badly trained and poorly equipped to fight a guerrilla war. The MPAJA fighters struggled to survive. Those who did developed exquisite jungle warfare skills that a few years later they would turn against their former colonial masters. Freddy Spencer Chapman describes how 'very embarrassing' it was to live and fight with people who had lost 'every shred' of faith in the British. That would take a lot of hard work to restore.

In his memoir Chapman describes a typical MPAJA hideout. His guides followed an unmarked path that wound between untouched jungle and the detritus of abandoned tin mines overgrown with bracken and rhododendrons. The little party turned aside to follow a spit of dry stony sand that, thankfully, took no footprints. They struggled uphill, plagued by mosquitoes and enormous leeches, until they came upon a grove of bamboos split by a narrow path. This led to a deep, narrow trench that had been cut into the ridge line, and led to a chamber just 10ft square that had been excavated from a bank of red clay and covered with an *atap* roof. Sleeping benches were cut into the walls. In front of this man-made cave, a natural palisade of bamboos concealed any smoke or other signs of life. Here Chapman feasted on sticky rice, fried salt fish, aubergine stew and coffee. A few days later he spotted a tiger as it slipped silently between the trees. From this hideout Chapman organised the occasional sortie to attack the railway line that ran to the nearby town of Tanjong Malim. But for a long time this was a campaign of hit-and-run skirmishes: a pinprick jungle war. Chapman's memoir *The Jungle is Neutral*, published in 1949, provides an enthralling account of his experience. But read attentively the book shows how very little Chapman and other stay-, or, more precisely, *left*-behinds were able to contribute to the jungle war. He is dismissive of the British soldiers who inadvertently found themselves trying to survive in a menacing world of man-eating tigers, deadly fevers, venomous snakes and scorpions, natives armed with poisoned darts and a 'host of half-imagined nameless terrors'. Some saw the jungle as a moveable feast of animals, fish and fruits, there for the taking. Both were myths. That is why Chapman described the jungle as neutral: survival depended on mental discipline. Not giving up, or lying down to die ... Many of the British soldiers he encountered *expected* not to survive.

Chapman is just as disparaging about the MPAJA guerrillas. At the end of 1942, he describes how the MPAJA unit he was attached to was much harried by Japanese patrols and decided to move to a more remote location. After an arduous journey the MPAJA unit reached the Pertang River, which was in flood. One of the women was nearly washed away. The new camp was 1,000ft above sea level at the headwaters of the Sungai Menchis. It was, Chapman realised, 'most unsatisfactory' since it was exposed to the fierce winds, called 'Sumatras', that periodically blow across the Straits of Malacca. As the MPAJA men and women struggled to make camp, trees and branches crashed down around them. One man was decapitated. It was here that Chapman had his first experience of the punitive MPAJA 'traitor killing' regime. Three Chinese 'informers' were dragged into the camp and beaten almost to death with rattans, then bayoneted. The third man was held alive overnight for further interrogation, but managed to escape. The MPAJA had to shift camp at once.

Late in 1943, Chapman was taken to a MPAJA hideout 5 miles or so outside Ipoh, close to the junction of the Raja and Senju rivers. It was the temporary home of about twenty men whose mission was the 'systematic and ruthless elimination of informers – a job they carried out with remarkable energy, enthusiasm and success'. They told Chapman that they had killed more than 1,000 such 'traitors'. Their policy was strictly ecumenical. They disposed of Chinese, Sikhs, Malays and Tamils. The 'traitor killers' patrolled in small close-knit groups and possessed a formidable arsenal of weapons, including Bren guns, shotguns, grenades and an agricultural implement called a changkol, which was used to beat victims to death. Chapman wrote later that he enjoyed the company of these 'traitor killers': they were more efficient and less 'boy scoutish' and earnest than the more high-minded MPAJA fighters. He got to know one 'traitor killer' well. This man boasted that he had personally despatched more than 150 individuals.

What motivated him? Chapman wondered. It was not mere bloodlust, it seemed. During the Sook Ching massacres, the Japanese had killed his parents, his wife and his children. 'Killing Japs and traitors' was now his obsession.

In mid-1943, there was a change of mind on the British side about the strategic value of the MPAJA. This change of heart reflected a revolution that was quietly under way in the Allied intelligence services. In Whitehall it had been broadly agreed that the British Secret Intelligence Service (SIS) needed root and branch reform after a succession of failures and the collapse of its European networks. There was little love lost between the Foreign Office, the chiefs of staff and the SIS, which tended to cultivate their own intelligence gardens behind high and impenetrable hedges. Allied intelligence was simply not very intelligent. It was hard to avoid the damning conclusion that the catastrophic loss of Singapore and Malaya was to a significant degree a failure of intelligence. As the Axis powers consolidated their grip on Europe and Southeast Asia, Prime Minister Winston Churchill became an advocate of reform. Instead of centralising intelligence operations, as common sense might have suggested, Churchill proposed in July 1940 a new organisation dedicated to 'sabotage and subversion' as well as 'black propaganda' – the Special Operations Executive (SOE), which would become the fiefdom of the Minister for Economic Warfare Hugh Dalton. The recently appointed head of SIS, Stewart Menzies, known as 'C', was not consulted – guaranteeing SIS hostility. Churchill had not troubled to keep the Foreign Office and the chief of staff in the loop. Dalton himself remarked that he had been tasked to 'set Europe ablaze', but the inferno was so far confined to the corridors of Whitehall. On the other side of the Atlantic, in June 1941, President Roosevelt approved the formation of a centralised intelligence service, the Office of Strategic Services (OSS) under General William 'Wild Bill' Donovan, America's most highly decorated soldier, who had been urging Roosevelt to establish a co-ordinated intelligence service since the Japanese attack on China in 1937. Although American historians might disagree, the OSS depended for some time on British expertise. On the eve of the surprise Japanese attack on Pearl Harbor, the British set up a secret service training centre in Canada that was staffed by OSS and SOE agents. Many hundreds of trainee American operatives passed through 'Camp X' between 1941 and 1944, including the future CIA head, Richard Helms.

The SOE had strong imperial ties. Sir Frank Nelson, the first director, had been President of the Associated Chambers of Commerce in Bombay in the 1920s. His successor, Colonel Sir Charles Hambro, was a merchant banker. Sir Colin Gubbins, who took over when Hambro was ousted in 1943, had fought the Irish Republican Army. Soon after the SOE was formed, Dalton agreed to set up an Oriental Mission in Singapore. It was in the nature of British bureaucratic style that the SOE clashed with the other colonial power bases and individuals. SOE played a leading role in the development of plans for Operation Matador, and

numerous SOE operatives had infiltrated southern Thailand, occasionally clashing
with Japanese military spies, who took rooms in the same hotels. Brooke-Popham's
failure to implement 'Matador' led to much resentment. The SOE philosophy
of 'setting ablaze' Axis-occupied territories by backing local insurgents deeply
worried the colonial establishment: for a long time they blocked attempts to 'arm
the natives'. This internecine bickering crippled the formation of 'stay behind
parties' – and delayed acceptance of the MCP 'July offer'.

Although the Allied powers agreed on a 'Germany first' policy to win the
war, both Churchill and Roosevelt fretted that if the Asian war was sidelined
Japan would build up such a formidable momentum that it would prove hard to
dislodge. At the Casablanca Conference in January 1943, Roosevelt and Churchill
agreed to increase the proportion of their resources devoted to winning the war
against Japan from 15 per cent to 30 per cent. Although the two Western Allies
sharply disagreed about the *future* of British imperial possession in the East, they
agreed to a joint South East Asia Command (SEAC) to co-ordinate the war on
Japan. In August 1943, Churchill appointed Admiral Lord Louis Mountbatten as
Supreme Allied Commander Southeast Asia and accepted the American General
Joseph 'Vinegar Joe' Stilwell as deputy commander. It would be a distinctly
uneasy alliance. In October, Mountbatten set up headquarters at Kandy in the
Central Highlands of Ceylon. From his operational headquarters at the Royal
Botanical Garden in Peradeniya, Mountbatten would dominate the war in
Southeast Asia. He made no bones about what he intended: 'to return to the
attack in Asia and regain our lost Empire'. Resented by many of his staff, who
believed his royal connections had led him to be over-promoted, Mountbatten
surrounded himself with teams of advisors and specialists – whose huts inexorably
multiplied and spread across the pristine green lawns and hills of Peradeniya to
accommodate more than 7,000 staff. Immensely vain, but often insecure, 'Dickie'
Mountbatten was an inconsistent manager of people: he was fixated by detail
and wanted to be seen to have a finger in every pie. His chief of staff complained
that Mountbatten was never so happy 'as when designing a badge, arranging the
seating for a conference, or worrying over some question of flying a flag …'. For
Mountbatten, meddling and fussing was a form of relaxation. It is no wonder that
many suggested that SEAC stood for 'Supreme Example of Allied Confusion'.
But Churchill may, in this case, have known what he was doing. SEAC would
not be undertaking any major military operations. It was much more important
to combat and overturn the perception that Britain had lost its Southeast Asian
empire through indolence. Mountbatten had charm, energy and glamour in
spades – the spirit that made, not lost, empires. And in any case, the Americans
admired his style and dash.

Mountbatten had a schoolboyish passion for special forces and covert ops. He
was, it was said, sympathetic to 'funnies'. This often got him, or rather the men
he sent into action, into hot water. When Mountbatten was given command of

SEAC his enthusiasm for 'special ops' would turn the Malayan MPAJA into an effective fighting force. In 1943, SEAC had begun planning for the invasion of the central west coast of Malaya, to retake the peninsula and Singapore. To prepare, the SOE organised support for the Malayan resistance. That would mean backing the communist MPAJA. The SOE Malaya section was staffed by former Malayan policemen and civil service officials, who had fought long and hard against the Malayan communists before 1941. But by 1943, after a year of Japanese occupation, many had become convinced that the MPAJA could be 'of vital use'. Neither the Malays nor the Tamil Indian community, it was realised, had much to offer. There remained a fragile hope that any surviving European and Chinese 'left-behind-parties' might still be able to play a part directing resistance operations, but very little was known about what had happened to them. The bickering between SOE and GOC Arthur Percival had meant that many had been thrown into action far too late. When the war ended it would be discovered that most of the forty or so European 'stay-behinds' had been killed in action or by disease, executed, or captured. By mid-1943, just four Europeans were still alive and at liberty in Malaya. One indomitable survivor was, of course, the legendary Freddy Spencer Chapman who, unknown to SOE, was stranded in Pahang without a radio: less 'stay-behind' than 'left-behind', as his friend Chin Peng remarked. No one in the British camp had any idea if he was dead or alive. Chapman spent his time dodging Japanese patrols and organising training sessions for the young men and women in the camps. He was forced to move frequently. Occasionally Chapman led attacks on trains or Japanese patrols. He would have been the first to admit he was doing little of great military consequence even though the Japanese had put a high price on his head. He was bored, frustrated and often laid low by malaria. The SOE had no idea if Chapman was alive or dead (they assumed the latter). Their plans to set Malaya on fire would remain theoretical until contact was made with a resistance group. This was daunting because Malaya was beyond the range of any available aircraft. The other option was submarines – but these were in very short supply.

In the meantime a Singapore businessman and nationalist called Lim Bo Seng had escaped from Singapore through Chongqing in south-west China. Born in China in 1909, Lim had come to Singapore with his family as a teenager. He was academically gifted, studying at Raffles College and passing the Senior Cambridge Examinations in 1928. He went on to study at the University of Hong Kong. Lim was a fervent nationalist and when he returned to Singapore to launch a career in business he became director of Hock Ann & Co., which was linked to the Brick Selling Agency. At the end of 1941, Lim took a leading role mobilising thousands of Singapore Chinese through the Civil Defence Corps – many of these passionate young recruits would later be killed by the Japanese. Lim managed to escape Singapore through Chongqing, Chiang Kai-Shek's provisional capital. Here he was interviewed by the head of the SOE, Lt Colonel Basil Gerritsen Ivory, who was very impressed by the young Singaporean. Since Lim's wife, Gan Choo Neo, and their seven children remained in Singapore, he was provided with a cover: he became agent No BB 192, as well as a number of aliases. SOE only referred to Lim as 192.[25] Gerritsen Ivory sent his promising new agent to Calcutta where he was reunited with his brother and met the head of the SOE 'Malayan Section' Basil Goodfellow. With Goodfellow's backing, Lim returned twice to Chongqing, where he used his nationalist contacts to recruit Malaya-born students for a Sino-British espionage unit codenamed 'Dragons'. They would be trained by the SOE in Poona (in India) by Davis and Broome and sent back into Malaya. One of the new recruits was another Singaporean, and champion badminton player, called Tan Chong Tee, who was secretly sending reports back to Kuomintang contacts about SOE plans. In May 1943, Lim began working with Major John Davis, a former police officer who had organised the first 'stay-behind' parties with Freddy Spencer Chapman before the fall of Singapore. Davis and a senior civil servant, Richard Broome, had escaped from Singapore on 3 February 1941, sailing to Bagansiapiapi on the Sumatran coast, from where they planned to rescue stranded British soldiers being sheltered in Chinese villages. On 16 February, Davis and Broome had tried to cross back over the Straits but had been forced to turn back. Davis, Broome and eighteen other British survivors reached Ceylon after many weeks sailing on a leaky Malay prahu.

A year later, Davis prepared to return to Malaya with Lim. They hatched up a scheme, which they codenamed 'Gustavus', for a series of sorties into occupied Malaya to contact guerrilla forces and track down any survivors of the 'stay-behind' mission. On 24 May 1943, Davis, Captain Broome, and five Chinese agents left Ceylon on the Dutch submarine, the *O-24*. Once the submarine entered the Straits of Malacca on the evening of 24 May, the team transferred to three folding kayaks, known as 'folboats'. The plan was to rendezvous with a Chinese junk, but the crew refused to assist so Davis had no choice but to proceed with a blind landing on the coast of Perak. At midnight the team battled through heavy surf to the beach near Tanjung Hatu, between Dindings and the island of Pangkor. They hid the folboats near the beach and headed inland and found a hideout on a rubber plantation near Bukit Segari. The Chinese agents made contact with local Chinese sympathisers and discovered that there was an MPAJA camp located near Sitiawan. Davis then returned to Ceylon and prepared the next stages of the operation. When he returned to Perak he and Broome made contact with the MPAJA guerrillas at Sitiawan and heard that Chapman was still alive. By September, Lim and the Chinese SOE agents had ingeniously established themselves in the Ipoh area. One found work in a coffee shop; another set up a fishing business. Most importantly, a communist member of the group Tham Sien Yen had made contact with the MPAJA.

Traitor of Traitors

On 30 September, a young MPAJA representative walked into Davis's camp at Bukit Segari. He called himself Chen Chin Sheng – it was Chin Peng. To the dismay of KMT agent Tan Chong Tee, Davis and Chin Peng formed an immediate bond, which was to last for many years. One of the other Chinese SOE agents recalled that Chin Peng's 'vast knowledge and far-sightedness won us over'. He spoke with passion and power: 'it had all of us spellbound'. It was not entirely clear to Chin Peng what the SOE unit had to offer the MPAJA. But he had no doubt that Davis and Broome could not stay much longer at Bukit Segari. It was only a matter of time before a Malay policeman or a Japanese patrol stumbled on their hideout. Chin Peng insisted that Davis move inland – deeper into hiding somewhere in the limestone vertebrae of Malaya's mountainous spine. At the time, the area between Sitiawan on the coast and the Main Range was occupied by a vast area of swampy jungle. Chin Peng took the SOE party south to the mouth of the Perak River, where they requisitioned a boat and sailed upriver in broad daylight while Chin Peng took another route overland. At Jenderata, Davis rendezvoused with a party of MPAJA carriers. Chin Peng in the meantime had gone down with fever and Davis was forced to rely on the carriers, who proceeded to blunder their way towards Blantan Mountain, where Chin Peng had prepared a camp. The MPAJA 5th Regiment was stationed not far away in the Cameron Highlands. By the time they reached the camp, Broome had fallen very sick – as had two of the Chinese, including the radio operator. Davis knew the area well: he had served nearby in the small town of Bidor before the war. The camp was a long hard trek through rough terrain from the main road. But from their new camp on a clear day they could see the twisting Perak River and a hazy blue sliver of sea 80 miles distant. Chapman was still in Pahang.

Because Broome was so ill, it was Chin Peng who had to make the next rendezvous with the SOE agents who had arrived off the Perak coast by submarine. Chin Peng refused point blank to escort the British officers ashore but agreed to admit a Chinese agent calling himself 'Tan Choon Lim': it was Lim Bo Seng. Chin Peng also took possession of a new radio. The one Davis had brought was absurdly heavy and underpowered. One of the SOE officers Chin Peng snubbed was a former policeman called Claude Fenner. After the war Fenner would be appointed chief of police in Malaya – and wage war on Chin Peng's communist guerrillas. Lim Bo Seng accompanied Chin Peng back to the camp at Blantan, where he was reunited with Davis and Broome. It was inevitable that, as a Kuomintang supporter, he would not find the MPAJA camp congenial and Lim would soon return to Pangkor Island to try and resuscitate the nationalist anti-Japanese networks. As a cover he played the part of a dissolute playboy and took up with a 'taxi dancer'. As it would turn out, the KMT network was as leaky as a sieve. This would have fatal consequences for Lim – and for the KMT resistance.

In June, Lai Tek summoned Chin Peng to a meeting near Kuala Lumpur. This would be the first time they had met face to face. Chin Peng travelled south to Kanching, where he met a female party messenger. She escorted him to an *atap* hut, where he spent the night. As a red hot sun set over the limestone crags of the Main Range, Chin Peng could see a two-storey bungalow on the other side of the valley that overlooked the road from Kuala Lumpur to Ipoh. It was in this house that Chin Peng first met Lai Tek the next day. The party leader was accompanied by a male secretary. The meeting was conducted in Mandarin. It was at this first eyeball to eyeball encounter that Chin Peng noted Lai Tek's Vietnamese accent, and how ill he looked. The meeting lasted two days, with Lai Tek and his entourage returning to the Coliseum Hotel in Kuala Lumpur before the curfew began. Lai Tek was impressed by Chin. Three months later he appointed him 'State Secretary' for Perak. Then at the end of December Lai Tek travelled north to Perak to meet the British. Ever since their arrival at Blantan, Davis and the other SOE agents had urged Chin Peng to arrange a meeting with a 'ranking MCP official'. Chapman had finally reached Blantan on Christmas Day. It had taken him two months to cross the Main Range. Now at last that meeting would take place. On 31 December, Chin Peng rendezvoused with Lai Tek near Bidor at a village controlled by the MPAJA close to the forest track that led up to the Blantan camp. He had driven from Singapore in a black Austin 10 supplied by the Kempeitai. Lai Tek was starved and sick: during the long climb he had to resort to using crutches and frequently halted, panting hard.

When they reached the camp at last, Lai Tek insisted on resting for more than an hour: he had no intention of being outmanoeuvred. Chapman, Davis and Broome waited impatiently. Shortly before the appointed time they heard a rumble of thunder and soon drenching rain was pounding the *atap* roofs of the MPAJA huts. Lai Tek was still indisposed, and by the time the soaked British party made its way to the meeting a blazing sun was sending up plumes of warm steam from the saturated undergrowth. The British SOE men and the communists gathered round a rough-hewn table. Chin Peng sat opposite Davis: the MPAJA guerrilla leader and the former British policeman got on well. Broome was still very ill. They all spoke good Malay or Cantonese but 'Tan Choon Lim' acted as interpreter.

As Lai Tek entered, Chin Peng introduced him as Chang Hong. For John Davis this was a supremely challenging moment. Here was the Special Branch's top agent suddenly in their midst. He could not afford to betray how well he knew the man calling himself Chang Hong. When Chin Peng discovered many years later how much Davis had known about Lai Tek's treachery he would feel profoundly betrayed. The meeting that followed was a strange game of smoke and mirrors, and it is still not completely certain who knew what about whom. Lai Tek may have recognised 'Tan Choon Lim' as 'Lim Bo Seng' and he may have reported his presence in Malaya to the Japanese. Had he already decided to spurn the Japanese and bond with the British? Nothing is certain about that meeting on a hill in the jungle of Perak except that the two parties reached an agreement which, as Chin Peng put it, 'embedded' the seeds of 'eventual armed struggle against the British'. More than a decade later it would be Davis who escorted Chin Peng to a meeting with the British-backed Malay leader Tunku Abdul Rahman. On that occasion Chin Peng had few cards left to play: he returned to the jungle empty-handed. But on New Year's Eve 1943, it was the Malayan communists who had the best hand and Chin Peng knew it: 'The British badly needed our assistance.' As Davis had made all too clear, the British wanted a deal. At the end of 1943 a Japanese defeat was not by any means a foregone conclusion and SEAC would need help dislodging the occupier and retaking Malaya. The MPAJA wanted British arms and supplies but they had no intention of agreeing to let the British simply walk back in and establish the *status quo ante bellum*. Although both sides skirted around what would happen after the Japanese had been ousted, 'Chang Hong' quibbled over the precise terms of the agreement: the British wanted the agreement to refer to 're-occupying' and 're-occupation' and he astutely insisted on the word 'retaking'. Finally, at the beginning of 1944, the two sides signed what became known as the 'Blantan Agreement' – scribbled on a scrap of paper torn from a school exercise book and dated 31 December 1943. The British would provide training, arms and ammunition and monthly payments of 50–70,000 Straits dollars.

At a conference in 1999, the elderly Chin Peng was evidently reluctant to discuss his relationship with Lai Tek. His reticence is not hard to understand. The swathe Lai Tek cut through the MCP and MPAJA cadres, which began at the Batu Caves, benefitted those who survived – most of all Chin Peng himself. Lai Tek smoothed Chin Peng's rise to power. Many potential rivals were arrested or killed by the Kempeitai. That is not to imply that Chin Peng was not a persuasive, determined and charismatic young man. He impressed SOE agents like Chapman and Davis, who reported that the young communist was 'able, sensible and likeable'. The SOE teams *depended* on Chin Peng: 'it is almost entirely due to him,' Davis's report admitted, 'that we have in Malaya today nearly 30 patrols armed and ready to strike at Japanese communications and that excellent friendly relations exist between AJA [Anti-Japanese Army, i.e. the MPAJA] patrol leaders and the British Liaison Teams …'. From the outset Broome and Davis had tried to persuade Chin Peng that the MPAJA forces should be 'conserved' until the Allies were ready to 'retake' Malaya. They should not 'go it alone'. The communists understood that this was official SEAC policy to keep the lid pressed firmly down on the communist resistance. British support for the MPAJA was entirely pragmatic. They wanted to expunge the memories of February 1942 and that meant Malaya and Singapore had to be seen to be taken back by British forces, not Malayan communist ones. The MPAJA leaders understood this perfectly well. They had their own agenda. In the short term the agreeable Chin Peng was training 'secret mobile squads' that the British knew nothing about. The MPAJA used these squads to liquidate

collaborators or 'special services people', meaning locals allegedly employed by
the Kempeitai. In 1945, the MPAJA would take the idea of a 'secret army' a lot
further – to prepare for a war against the British.

End Games

Behind the scenes, the British SOE was fighting a turf war with Donovan's OSS,
which had begun taking an interest in Malaya. An OSS officer attached to SEAC
had come up with a scheme to make contact with a group of old Dutch and
Portuguese 'burger' families, who had intricate connections with local Malay and
Singhalese notables, and establish intelligence networks. The Americans were also
interested in stirring up revolt in Thai-occupied Kelantan – even though the OSS
also backed the 'Free Thais', who were opposed to the pro-Japanese dictator Field
Marshal Plaek Phibunsongkhram but suspicious of Malays. The OSS proposed
encouraging an alliance between the 'Free Thais' and Kelantan Sultan Ismail
Ibin Mohamad IV. These schemes never reached fruition but they troubled the
British – especially since a number of old Malayan hands in the Colonial Office
hoped not only to retrieve the northern Malay states from the Thais but push
the colonial Malayan border northwards into Patani. They had always viewed the
Malay–Thai border as a temporary expedient. Edward Gent, head of the Eastern
Department of the Colonial Office, who would become the first post-liberation
governor of Malaya, was very active in promoting SOE projects and fending off
the OSS – with some success. An OSS agent complained that the British always
insisted on making first contact with any group and so only 'permit us to enter
on their terms'.

The secret role of the India Mission and Force 136 in Malaya is one of the most
celebrated aspects of the war in the Far East. Freddy Spencer Chapman's memoir
The Jungle is Neutral is a classic. The truth is that the British had very little *military*
impact on the guerrilla war, as a careful reading of Chapman's book makes all
too clear. Backing the resistance in Malaya, which was dominated by the MPAJA,
had political, not military, significance. In early 1945, the SOE endorsed and
supported an armed organisation dominated by Chinese communists. This would
significantly shape post-war conflict in Southeast Asia and was in rational terms
inimical to British interests. The same point might be made about Greece and
Yugoslavia. The fact is that in all theatres of war it was the communist guerrillas
who proved themselves the best and most resilient fighters.

In Burma, the British faced a very different problem. Anti-colonial nationalists,
like Aung Sang and other 'Thakins', had to begin by allying themselves with
Japan. In 1941, the Burma Independence Army, one of whose commanders was
future dictator Ne Win, marched into their colonised homeland in the vanguard
of the Japanese advance. But by the end of 1944 it was clear to Aung Sang and the
Burmese nationalists that the Japanese were finished. Early in 1945 he adroitly

began negotiations with the British. Many old Burma hands were appalled by the idea of dealing with the 'collaborator' Aung Sang: 'sheer madness' they warned. But Aung Sang discovered that he had a powerful ally in the shape of Lord Mountbatten, who quashed all objections and backed Aung Sang's plans for a national revolt in March. He pointed out that 'we shall be doing no more than has been done in Italy, Roumania [sic], Hungary and Finland.' He did not refer to Yugoslavia although arguably Aung Sang was the Asian Tito. The Burmese uprising took the Japanese by surprise. On 26 March, Japanese soldiers cheered as troops of the 'Burmese Defence Army' (BDA) marched out of Rangoon to fight the British 14th Army, which was advancing from the north against stiff Japanese resistance. This was an elaborately planned ruse, for the following day Burmese BDA troops launched co-ordinated assaults on Japanese positions near Rangoon. By May, the Burmese were fighting alongside British troops as the Japanese occupation regime collapsed. For many British this was anathema. But General William 'Bill' Slim – who met Aung Sang in May and admired him – acknowledged that the BDA played a vital role liberating Burma. The Burmese puppet ruler Ba Maw fled to Tokyo. Aung Sang became a national hero as Mountbatten had anticipated.

Events unfolded very differently in Malaya. Since the humiliation of February 1942, Churchill had been obsessed with retaking Malaya and Singapore: this was, he insisted, the 'supreme British objective in the whole of the Indian and Far Eastern theatre. It is the price that will restore British prestige in the region.' SEAC began laying plans for an amphibious invasion of Malaya's west coast in 1944, codenamed Operation Zipper. Air strikes would be mounted against Japanese bases, while infantry divisions landed near Port Dickson and Port Swettenham. Mountbatten was convinced that Malayan resistance forces could play a vital role softening up the Japanese prior to launching Zipper. As in the case of Burma, the idea of backing anti-Japanese militias was divisive. Many British policymakers were thinking in terms of neutralising, not supporting, these compromised and potentially troublesome patriots. They were sensitive to the dangers of the 'Chinese' claiming final credit for defeating the Japanese. This would inevitably stoke up political expectations following Japanese surrender. For that reason the SOE had organised an all-Malay resistance group, led by Tun Ibrahim Ismail, that had infiltrated the east coast state of Terengganu in October 1944. A Malay chief had betrayed Ibrahim's team to the Japanese. Mountbatten and those who supported backing the resistance argued that by sending British SOE officers to work with the guerrillas, they could 'get to know the whole of the organisation and its policy'. It was also realised that if the British refused to supply the insurgents they would steal arms from the retreating Japanese. So SOE support for the Malayan resistance was about surveillance, control and, in the longer term, constraint. It was also about propaganda and the fraught relationship with the Americans, who were determined to dismantle the empire. Mountbatten sent a prescient and astute memorandum to Colonial Secretary Oliver Stanley, which is well worth quoting at length:

> Presumably, we have not previously found Colonial Subjects rising to fight on our behalf when we were about to occupy their territory, and the fact that they are doing so today seems to me a wonderful opportunity for propaganda to the world in general and to the Americans in particular, at a time when we are being accused of reconquering colonial peoples in order to subjugate them.[26]

The British had very little room for manoeuvre in any case. SOE agents acting on behalf of SEAC had signed the 'Blantan Agreement' with Chin Peng and party boss Lai Tek at the beginning of 1944, which bound both parties until the Japanese were defeated. The Malay contribution to the resistance was negligible and the communist MPAJA had steadily won its own internal war against the KMT resistance groups. The Japanese had unwittingly helped reinforce the MPAJA. As we have already noted, Chinese farmers had begun opening up new land in Malaya for cultivation and taking over plantations abandoned in 1942. The Japanese took a hands-off position. Two years later some half a million Chinese settlers had taken over 70,000 acres of plantation land and cleared 150,000 acres of forest reserve. They kept pigs and ducks, grew hill rice and a few cash crops like tobacco, and even developed fish ponds. Even though the Chinese had no legal right to the land, and were referred to as 'squatters', their settlements soon took on the character of real village communities. These tiny 'republics' usually grew up close to the edge of the forest, which was the fiefdom of the MPAJA. It did not take long for the Chinese 'squatters' and the MPAJA fighters to forge close ties based on mutual dependency. The MPAJA needed food, supplies and information; in return they offered the 'squatters' protection. Communal assistance like this had deep roots in the world of the overseas Chinese, though the MPAJA had no hesitation resorting to force.

By mid-1944, the MPAJA dominated the resistance to the Japanese. By then the Axis powers were in headlong retreat on every front. There could no longer be any doubt that the Allied powers would win the war. In October 1944, Lai Tek again summoned Chin Peng to a meeting of senior cadres to discuss future strategy. He and another MPAJA leader called Liao Wei Chung, or 'Itu', walked all the way from the MPAJA camp in Perak to Serendah, just north of Kuala Lumpur. It took them two weeks using secret jungle paths: they dared not even use bicycles. Lai Tek spoke to MCP leaders from Johor, Pahang, Selangor and Perak: he anticipated an Allied invasion 'imminently'. He was wrong on both counts. The British would not reoccupy Malaya for many months, and by then the Japanese would have surrendered. There would be no 'invasion'. Lai Tek revealed that he had made an agreement with the British, as Chin Peng, for one, already knew, and that they would supply weapons and finance to the MPAJA. To deal with this he proposed a Machiavellian new strategy. The MPAJA would be split. Some MPAJA units would fight openly alongside the British. But others would form a 'secret army' that would later 'take the fight to the British'. 'As Allied troops splashed ashore our guerrillas should be ready to seize as much territory as possible.' Smaller townships would be captured, and banks, post offices, and railways stations seized. Occupying bigger towns like Ipoh and Kuala Lumpur was ruled out. Chin Peng realised much later that Lai Tek had, with characteristic slyness, accommodated both his British masters and the younger MPAJA firebrands, who were longing to take the fight to the British. They would be siphoned off into this new 'secret army'.

Chin Peng and the other delegates returned to their states and began organising their secret armies, the 'Mi Mi Tui'. In Perak it was essential to conceal these preparations from Davis and Broome. Little over a month later, Davis finally managed to establish radio contact with SEAC headquarters in Ceylon, which meant that the year-old 'Blantan Agreement' could at last be implemented. RAF Liberators would soon begin supply drops to Malaya and the MPAJA. The first drop took place successfully on 26 February. On 16 April, another meeting was arranged with 'Chang Hong'. It was a bizarre affair. Chin Peng was recovering from another bout of malaria; the skeletal Broome was so ill he had to be carried by Chapman and Davis; the ailing Lai Tek refused to walk any further than the road where he parked his Austin 10. He was taking, it seemed, a terrible risk. Nevertheless, the meeting between the British and their MPAJA allies was cheerful, optimistic and 'accommodating'. No one, it seems, spoke of the unfortunate KMT leader Lim Bo Seng, who had been imprisoned and murdered by tha Japanese. The British insisted that a liaison officer and a platoon of Gurkhas would be parachuted into Malaya and attached to each company-sized MPAJA unit. 'Chang Hong' happily agreed to all the British conditions.

Debacle in Kuala Lumpur

In Malaya, Ibrahim Yaacob's KRIS movement struggled to keep pace with rapidly unfolding events. Ibrahim now set about rallying disillusioned KMM supporters and sent representatives to Sukarno to seek a promise that Malaya would be included in a future independent Indonesia. Both Sukarno and Mohammad Hatta backed a 'Raya Indonesia' that comprised the former Dutch East Indies, Malaya, New Guinea, North Borneo and the Portuguese Timor. Perhaps Ibrahim's gift of Malaya seemed too good to be true? Events now moved rapidly, but not, as it turned out, rapidly enough. KRIS had the bit between its teeth. Yaacob made plans for a big All-Malaya Pemuda Conference in Kuala Lumpur for 18 August. He drew up plans for an interim 'cabinet' that would include the sultans of Perak, Pahang and Johor, Tunku Abdul Rahman, who was the son of the late Sultan of Kedah, and Datuk Onn bin Jaafar. He had meetings with General Umezu in Taiping, though he may not have mentioned the idea of the cabinet.

On 6 August, Colonel Paul W. Tibbetts took off from the North Field American air base in Tinian, Guam in the B-29 *Enola Gay* (named after his mother) bound for Hiroshima. In its specially modified bomb bay was the 'Little Boy' atomic bomb. Three days later, another B-29 (*Bockscar*) dropped 'Fat Man' on Nagasaki. In Tokyo, Emperor Hirohito presided over a stormy meeting of the Supreme Council.

On 12 August, Sukarno and Hatta arrived in Taiping to meet Yaacob, General Umezu and the KRIS delegation. Reports of what happened are contradictory. Some of the Indonesians, possibly Hatta, had no sympathy for including Malaya in an independent Indonesia. They had never much respected the Malayan nationalists. In any event, some sort of agreement was reached and preparations for the big *pemuda* meeting at the Station Hotel, Kuala Lumpur – a monument of British rule – proceeded at a feverish pace.

Sometime on 13 or 14 August, Emperor Hirohito made a phonograph recording of the 'Imperial Rescript on the Termination of the War' in the Imperial Palace in Tokyo. A handful of diehard militarists heard that the recording had been made and tried to storm the palace to prevent it being broadcast. The phonograph had to be smuggled out concealed in a laundry basket. On 15 August, the Japanese people and soldiers listening on short-wave radios all over East Asia heard, many for the first time, the high-pitched voice of the emperor speaking in stilted classical Japanese that was muffled by crackling background noise: 'the war situation has developed not necessarily to Japan's advantage […] it is according to the dictates of time and fate that We have resolved to pave the way for a grand peace for all generations to come by enduring the unendurable and suffering what is unsufferable. [sic]' Many Japanese had dreaded what they might hear the emperor, who personified the nation, say. It was a royal prerogative to demand mass suicide to protect the dignity of the nation. Instead the emperor's eccentric address marked the end of the Second World War. The 'Jewel Broadcast' heralded the birth of a new Japan.

As Yaacob and Itagaki drove into Kuala Lumpur together to prepare for the conference, they tried to digest the devastating news and its implications. Ibrahim was flustered. 'Please get me a plane in Singapore!' he pleaded, 'I want to escape to Java.' At the Station Hotel, the Malay nationalists were locked in debate about what to do. There were shrill calls to resist the British. It was agreed that Yaacob would leave immediately for Singapore to rally the Malay Giyu Gun to defend the homeland from the former colonial power. On Friday 17 August came another blow. At 10 a.m. that very day, Sukarno had declared independence in Batavia. The Indonesian leaders had troubled to inform the Malays. The men and women who had gathered at the conference were dazed. Many wept openly. Delegates were still arriving in Kuala Lumpur – but when they heard what had happened and saw the traumatised confusion in the face of their comrades many simply turned around and went home. KRIS was dead in the water. In Singapore, Yaacob tried to contact leaders of the MPAJA. But for reasons we will return to in the next chapter, Lai Tek had made a decision not to resist the British – in the short term. In the meantime, members of the Malay Giya Gun seized arms from the bewildered Japanese to fight the 'Chinese'. On 19 August, Ibrahim Yaacob boarded a plan in Singapore and flew to Jakarta. He would never return to Malaya.

The Pacific war was over. Oceans of blood had been spilt. The Japanese 'Co-Prosperity Sphere' that had brought death, suffering and misery to the peoples of Southeast Asia had gone the way of every other empire. For a short time the guns fell silent across the imperial crescent. More than three years of Japanese rule had primed the fuses of a new war – an internecine conflict that would be fought across the charred ruins of empire and define the future shape of Southeast Asia.

PART THREE

MALAYA ABLAZE

1

ON THE BRINK

The Sham Invasion

At the end of August 1945, Chin Peng arrived in Kuala Lumpur for discussions with Force 136 officer John Davis, who had become a close friend. The British rolled out the red carpet for the MPAJA heroes. SEAC had commandeered bungalows in the well-heeled Kenny Hill area of the city – and one had been allocated to MCP officials, with cars and drivers on hand. One day in early September, Davis knocked on the door of the main MCP bungalow. Would Chin Peng and the other comrades like to witness history in the making? A few days later Davis and Chin Peng 'stood side by side in companionable silence' – as he recalled later – close to Morib Beach some 60 miles from Kuala Lumpur. Davis knew this part of the west coast well. He had enjoyed family holidays here in pre-war days. Now, he remembered later 'somewhere out at sea, in the darkness, we heard the sound of marine engines […] At first light, we saw the fleet. The horizon was filled with ships large and small, all shapes and sizes …'. As the lights of the fleet twinkled off shore, a flotilla of landing craft crunched onto the beach and began debouching their cargoes of Indian troops, lorries and small amphibious DUKWs. As he watched the spectacle with Davis, Chin Peng overheard 'exuberant words of congratulation […] expressions of praise and jubilation …'. He wrote later:'I must have thought: we are letting them back unimpeded to reclaim a territory that they have plundered for so long …'. It was 9 September 1945.

Operation Zipper had been conceived as an invasion. In July, SEAC supremo Lord Mountbatten had flown to Berlin where he was appraised of plans to drop atomic weapons on a Japanese city. Churchill advised him that the Japanese would surrender imminently. Mountbatten instructed his staff to reconfigure Zipper for reoccupation. The British would not return as invaders. Although Chin Peng ruefully noted those 'expressions of praise and jubilation', Zipper did not go according to plan. The reoccupation force was on Ceylon time and arrived off the Malayan coast on a receding tide. A number of vessels were left stranded. The tranquil beach rapidly became a scene of confusion and disorder as Indian troops struggled ashore alongside lumbering vehicles carrying bulldozers and heavy plant equipment. Studies of aerial surveys had concluded that Morib was a perfect landing spot. But the data was now shown to be flawed. Beneath a crust of hard sand were layers of soft and viscous silt. Scores of vehicles became immobilised. A report admitted: 'As soon as vehicles drove off [...] the under-surface of the beach collapsed and vehicles bogged down on their axles.' Away from the beach, tanks became trapped in ditches. The heavy vehicles that successfully moved forward from the beachhead destroyed road surfaces causing a massive tailback. What Chin Peng had interpreted as a triumphant return was a farce. It was fortunate indeed that the Japanese had already surrendered. As a British report put it: 'the invasions forces [sic] would have been very roughly handled.' Zipper would have been a bloodbath. Although British troops marched into Klang and Port Swettenham the next day, Zipper was a calamitous opening to a new era – and beyond the beaches, the British had only the most fragile control of the rest of Malaya.

For more than 500 years Europeans had ceaselessly reconfigured the region of the world we now call Southeast Asia. The capture of Malacca by Afonso de Albuquerque on 24 August 1511 was the beginning of five centuries of plunder. Portuguese, Spanish, Dutch, English and French adventurers rode roughshod over the old regional polities and turned their peoples into the subjects of a globalised colonial economy. The patchwork of colonies, usurped monarchies and protectorates that the Europeans wove together across the vast equatorial crescent stretching from the eastern extremities of British India, through Burma and the Malay Peninsula and spanning the 18,000 islands of the Indonesian Archipelago was not only a ravenous emporium that fed on spices, tin and rubber. Colonialism gave rise to a *psychic* remapping within the expedient borders that had been slashed through ancient rainforests and across the shimmering surfaces of equatorial oceans. From this colonial cartography frothed up the heady brew of nationalism. The nation was an idea of immense potency that would eventually be turned against the same Europeans who had invented it and the dynastic courts that could barely conceive what it meant. Asian nationalism was, like the rubber tree, seeded from the disordering rapacity of the 'Empire Project'. At the end of 1941 an Asian power, the Japanese, took just ten weeks to rip apart colonial Southeast Asia. From this violent and wrenching assault would come yet another cataclysmic remapping embroiled with convulsive cycles of turmoil and murder. The Japanese occupation would prime an anti-colonial struggle that was inextricably entangled with internecine civil wars.

After the Japanese surrender, the old colonial masters returned to Burma, Malaya and the Dutch East Indies. But the tsunami of war and occupation had swept away the creaking edifices of the colonial states, leaving in its wake a shattered, torn and bewildering new landscape. The Allies had won the war against the Axis. For the British the taste of victory had very bitter undertones. Churchill was a staunch and bigoted defender of the empire. His desperate efforts to persuade the government of the United States to join the war against the Axis powers had forced him, at the very least, to acknowledge that his American allies possessed a vehement, if hypocritical, contempt for imperialism – or rather *British* imperialism. The upshot of that peculiar and unequal 'special relationship' was that Britain would take back its former Southeast Asian possessions, like Burma and Malaya, but on American sufferance. Reoccupation would be a prelude to a process of decolonisation that would be enforced by the world's biggest superpower. Churchill's beloved India would be sacrificed almost immediately. But as renewed global conflict ripped apart the Grand Alliance that had crushed Germany and Japan, American strategists realised that a British presence in the old outposts of empire, Malaya and Singapore, could be very useful for a long time to come.

This is not to say that Britain regarded the recapture of its purloined Asian possessions in purely strategic terms. Reoccupation was the only way to wipe clean the national slate of humiliation. In London, planning for eventual reoccupation began very soon after the loss of Singapore: a Malayan Planning Unit (MPU) was soon busy hatching up plans for reshaping 'British Malaya'. The MPU had drafted a plan for a future Malaya that would harmonise the awkward patchwork of colonies and Malay states in a new 'Malayan Union'. The MPU planners also envisaged overturning the traditional privileges of the Malays and granting citizenship rights to many more Chinese and Indians. The Union plan would prove bitterly divisive.

For Asian intellectuals, like the future prime minister of Singapore Lee Kuan Yew, who was a student in 1942, the Japanese capture of Singapore heralded the end of the British Empire. For Britain's colonial mandarins the catastrophe of conquest was a chance to start afresh. Historians usually interpret the two decades after 1945 as a period of 'decolonisation'. This is the judgement of hindsight. The new Labour government insisted, in a pamphlet published in August 1946, that 'British Imperialism is dead, insofar as it ever existed, except as a slogan used by our critics …'. But the new prime minister, the famously modest Clement Attlee, was a pragmatist. Old style 'Imperialism' was buried. But Attlee was firmly committed to protecting British overseas interests to generate recovery and fend off the Soviets. The Minister of Defence was clear: post-war policy would be reshaped to resist the 'onrush of communist influence' and improve the 'standard of living of our own people at home'. This did not mean merely 'carrying on'. The world had been rocked by war, and Britain was grossly overextended – troops were deployed across the world from the West Indies to Kuala Lumpur. British garrisons were stationed in West Germany, Gibraltar, Malta, Libya, Cyprus, Greece, Turkey, Egypt, Palestine, Aden, the Persian Gulf, India East Africa, Singapore and Malaya. There were expensive naval bases to maintain in the West Indies, Gibraltar, Simon's Town, Aden, Singapore and Hong Kong. Somehow the British would need to both retrench and adjust. No one expected that to be easy. In Malaya, they would confront the bitter energies of civil war.

Terror in Malaya

Historical understanding begins with chronology. Knowing what happened *when* is necessary to knowing *why*. The conventional historiography of post-war Malaya goes something like this. After the Japanese surrender and before the arrival of British forces, Malayan communist guerrillas emerged from their jungle strongholds and imposed a reign of terror. They seized towns and villages, set up kangaroo courts and slaughtered Malays and Indians. The events of the 'Interregnum', the power vacuum that followed the Japanese surrender, injured communal relations for many decades. That Malaya was brought to the brink of bloody revolution cannot be doubted. The violence that engulfed Malaya in August 1945 is not a myth. But the Interregnum provides modern Malaysia with a clutch of useful legends: a warning, above all, to future generations that might be tempted to challenge the communal status quo. Implicitly, the myth of the Interregnum enshrines chauvinist racial mythologies that represent Chinese Malayans as the 'threatening other'. Months *before* the MPAJA guerrillas emerged from their jungle refuges, Malay Jihadists had launched a campaign of violence and intimidation directed at Chinese villages. To explain why this happened we need to step back and look at the fraught relations between the Allied powers at the end of the war. At the beginning of 1945 no one could be completely certain how long the Japanese would continue to hold out in Southeast Asia. The end of occupation may well have seemed certain in the long term but how the collapse of the Japanese Empire would play out was anybody's guess. We should also remember that the Japanese effectively controlled news and propaganda and very few in occupied Malaya dared listen to or even possess a radio. Rumour took on the aura of fact. At the end of July, Harry S. Truman, who had become American President after the death of Roosevelt on 12 April, flew to Potsdam near Berlin to discuss with Stalin, Churchill and Clement Attlee the future administration of defeated Germany. (Attlee succeeded Churchill as prime minister when the Labour Party won the general election while the Potsdam Conference was still in session.) Chinese nationalist leader Chiang Kai-Shek was also in Potsdam. On 26 July, the Generalissimo signed an agreement with Churchill and Truman – not Stalin since the Soviet Union was not then at war with Japan – setting out the terms for a Japanese surrender. The Americans had by then successfully tested an atomic bomb and Truman was confident the new weapon would end the war. In Malaya, Chiang Kai-Shek's attendance at this global summit of victorious powers provoked a cloud burst of frightened speculation. Many Malays feared that the Chinese National Army would soon be marching across the Thai border into Malaya to oust the Japanese and impose 'Chinese rule'. A Singaporean recalled that 'we Malays thought that the Chinese troops would land on the island. Some of my Chinese friends expected this to happen. Many Chinese suddenly became quite chauvinistic and arrogant …'. The communist MPAJA too had no desire to see a Kuomintang force taking over the peninsula. Fear of these phantom Chinese armies spread like wildfire.

Since the beginning of the nineteenth century, Islamic holy men known as *kiyai*, or *tuan guru*, had provoked and led anti-colonial uprisings in the Dutch East Indies and British Malaya. Although the matter remains contentious, the spread of Islam in Southeast Asia coincided with the flourishing of the mystical Sufi movement in the Middle East – and Sufis played a significant role as Muslim proselytisers in the Malay world. Sultans often had their own Sufi teacher, or shaykh. By the end of the eighteenth century, on the eve of colonial conquest, the semi-secret Sufi *tarekat* (orders or brotherhoods) had started to attract a mass following in Aceh, Kedah, Perak, Minangkabau and even among the Malays of Cape Town, South Africa. In its Malay form, Sufism fused older semi-magical beliefs with a cult of physical invulnerability. Since the European powers that had forcefully entered the Malay world possessed and did not hesitate to use superior firepower, the promise of this magical kind of protection was naturally hard to resist. In 1819, in Palembang in southern Sumatra, which had recently been occupied by the Dutch, groups of men dressed in white worked themselves into a frenzy to the accompaniment of *dhikr* drums; then, convinced that they could not be harmed, fearlessly threw themselves against colonial troops. The consequence was entirely predictable. Sufi teachers took part in anti-colonial rebellions – in Banten, West Java in 1888, on the island of Lombok a few years later, and in East Java in 1903. In each case rebels performed spiritual exercises that supposedly conferred physical protection. To' Janggut, the *nom de guerre* of Haji Mohd Hassan bin Munas, who led the 1915 Kelantan rebellion in Malaya, was reputedly blessed with such powers and was immune to bullets. He was, of course, shot dead. Another charismatic peasant leader inspired a revolt in Terengganu in 1928. The rise of nationalist movements in Indonesia and later in Malaya led to a decline in Sufi-inspired rebellions. But in early 1945 the increasing visibility of the MPAJA, as well as tales of mythical Chinese armies, led many Malays to feel powerless and unprotected, let down by their sultans, the KMM and the Japanese-recruited Giyu Gun, and the Malay police. This unease inspired the emergence of charismatic holy men ready to declare Jihad against invading unbelievers. The most prominent of these Malay Jihadists was the leader of the Sabilillah, or Holy War movement, Kiyai Salleh. Sabilillah was especially active in the Batu Pahat district of Johor, where Indonesians – mainly Bugis, Acehnese and Javanese – outnumbered indigenous Malays. They had brought with them millenarian and Sufist traditions.

Kiyai Salleh Abdul Karim was born in Parit Jawa, a small fishing village in the Muar district of Johor. According to Dr Syed Naguib al-Attas, the leading Malaysian authority on Sufism in the region, who interviewed Kiyai Salleh, he was short and dark complexioned with striking beady eyes that could 'glow with boyish mischief' or 'strike terror into the hearts of his enemies'. He was a disciple of Shaykh Kiyai Haji Fadil, who was the *pawang*, or magician, of Sultan Ibrahim. Despite his spiritual aspirations Kiyai Salleh was a gang leader before the war and had spent time in prison. In May 1945, Muslim groups such as the Barisan Islam (Muslim Front) unleashed violent and chaotic attacks on Chinese villagers in Batu Pahat. By then, Kiyai Salleh had acquired notoriety as a charismatic and devout leader, and many urged him to take command of the disorganised local Jihadists. He needed little persuasion. By June, his *Tentera Sabil Selendang Merah*, 'Holy War Army of the Red Bands', had pulled together the various Muslim bands and declared a holy war. His recruits were mainly Javanese and Banjarese. They wore armbands made of red cloth; Kiyai Salleh issued his commanders with a red cummerbund. They armed themselves with traditional Malay weapons like the *parang panjang*, a long-bladed sword, the *kris*, *pedang* and *tombak*. This was a peasant army armed with the weapons of the kampong. MPAJA fighters had automatic weapons, supplied by SOE, but a frenzied attack by a Red Sash band could do frightful damage. Most Chinese villagers were unarmed.

There are conflicting reports about how the violence unfolded. Malay accounts stress that MPAJA units had begun abducting and murdering Malay villagers – compelling Malays to defend their communities. There is no hard evidence to support these claims. The situation on the ground was much less clear-cut. A surviving Japanese report describes a mass meeting called by the MPAJA in Seri Medan on 15 February. The MPAJA spokesmen announced the introduction of various taxes, and, it was said, attacked local mosques. No one was murdered. Attacks on the mosque enraged local Malays. According to some Chinese accounts, which were later collected by an official of the British Military Administration (BMA), the Japanese actively incited Malays to attack Chinese villagers – 'to stir up holy war against the pig eaters'. On 10 May, a Malay gang stopped a car on the Batu Pahat–Pontian Road. The Chinese driver was immediately killed and the car set on fire. A passenger managed to get away and reported the incident to the local Malay police. They blamed the attack on communists and refused to investigate. This angered the Chinese but also triggered another wave of Malay assaults. This confusing rumour-saturated wave of 'attacks and massacres' (the words of historian Cheah Boon Kheng) rapidly engulfed the Batu Pahat district. Malay policemen often took the lead in attacks on Chinese villagers, or covered for Malay killers if there was any chance that armed MPAJA units would intervene. Malays broke into Chinese homes, brandishing long swords, daggers and sharpened bamboo spears and screaming like banshees. They slashed and hacked to death men, women and children. They robbed and burnt Chinese shop houses. Massacres of Chinese took place in Parit Gumong, Parit Raja, Parit Kecil and Parit Kali. The Malay bands slaughtered hundreds of people in some Chinese villages. Many of those who died had been reluctant to flee their homes. Others took refuge in the larger towns. A Chinese source tells us:

> Because the Chinese were tied down by their families and love of property, they were not united together to resist the Malays and therefore suffered great losses

in lives. On the other hand, the Malays abandoned their occupations and turned into murderers, all led by headmen in each district …

The Chinese nationalist government was horrified by the bloodbath in Malaya. A report was sent to the British Consul in Nanjing on 7 February 1946:

In May, 1945 at Batu Pahat, Johor the Malays, instigated and variously armed by the Japanese, started an attack on the Chinese residents of the place. Chinese being taken unawares, between 15,000 and 20,000 Chinese inhabitants including women and children were killed and rendered destitute and homeless. The Japanese authorities treated the incident as a mere disturbance of the peace …

Kiyai Salleh and the 'Army of the Red Bands' (or Red Sashes) clearly provided a focus for Malay anger. His fast emerging legend as a Malay hero with supernatural powers stoked the inferno of hatred. A British report on the Red Band movement commented on the way in which Malays fervently believed that in the tradition of To' Janggut, Kiyai Salleh 'cannot be killed by bullets'; he could walk across rivers 'dryshod'; 'he can burst any bonds'; his voice could 'paralyse his assailants'; even if his Chinese enemies were to throw him in boiling water he would emerge unharmed. This kind of mumbo jumbo may seem laughable but in May 1945 its consequences were deadly. In parts of Johor and Perak the Sabilillah movement attracted huge crowds of credulous Malays who collectively recited verses of the Koran, several hundred times it was said, to become invulnerable. Red Band warriors pierced and slashed their arms with 'delimas' or charms, usually gold needles or sharpened stones. Magical potions that had been blessed by an imam, or Kiyai Salleh himself, were consumed. In these turbulent months before the Japanese surrender, the Sabilillah movement exploited Malay anxieties about the end of Japanese rule, and the weakness of their rulers to bolster self-confidence and fend off the communist MPAJA. Since it was useful to confuse 'the Chinese' with the guerrillas, the 'Red Sash' insurgency turned into a religious crusade to kill Chinese Malays without discrimination. Force 136 officers attached to MPAJA regiments, like John Davis, despatched urgent reports about the massacres to SEAC headquarters in Ceylon. The news thoroughly alarmed the supreme commander, Lord Louis Mountbatten. Air drops of propaganda leaflets were organised urging Malays to *Jaga Baik-Baik* – take heed. Mountbatten carefully blamed the Japanese for inciting outbreaks of communal violence and warned that 'the day of repayment will come'. British threats deepened the anger of many Malays. In Johor the violence did not abate. The Japanese refused to intervene – and in mid-June Japanese army units backed by Malay policemen launched a massive new attack on the MPAJA 4th Regiment to finish it off for good. This would turn out to be the last major Japanese counter-insurgency operation in Malaya, for on the international stage events were moving rapidly towards denouement.

A World Gone Mad

The Japanese surrender was not openly acknowledged in Malaya for nearly a
week. Readers of the *Syonan Shimbun* in Singapore would have enjoyed stories
about Allied losses and been warned not to listen to foolish rumours. An editorial
condemned the use of a 'super bomb' against Asiatic peoples. On 20 August, Prince
Kanin Haruhito, who was a cousin of the emperor's wife, arrived in Singapore to
deliver the message of surrender to Japanese commanders. All military activities
would be suspended from 25 August. On the same day, the *Syonan Shimbun*
published the 'Imperial Rescript', which emphasised Japan's humanitarian
decision to spare the peoples of Asia further suffering. There was no admission
of surrender. Japanese soldiers swallowed this mendacious rationalisation hook,
line and sinker – with traumatic consequences for the peoples of Southeast
Asia. By the time the Japanese emperor had made his infamous 'Jewel' broadcast,
communal relations in Malaya and across Southeast Asia had been fractured
and poisoned by more than three years of occupation. The collapse of Japanese
power would bring Malaya to the very brink of revolution. It would be a time of
revenge and retribution, a chance to settle scores. 'It was a world gone mad' one
Malay policeman recalled.

The 'madness' of the Interregnum would be the violent first act to a 'long,
long war' in Malaya that would not end until 1989. In the summer of 1945, the
Pacific War was not yet over and Britain and the United States began planning
a final assault on Japan. From the British point of view it made strategic sense
to recapture their former colonial possessions in Southeast Asia as a springboard
for an invasion of the Japanese islands. Japanese military planners had by this
stage of the war developed a last-stand mentality. To defend Malaya they began
transferring troops to Thailand and reinforcing their divisions in Singapore. They
seized complete control of French Indochina. At his headquarters in Saigon, the
Commander of the Southern Expeditionary Group, Count Hisaichi Terauchi,
was confident that his forces could hold out for at least another twelve months.
In May 1945, General Bill Slim's 14th Army finally reached Rangoon in Burma.
Mountbatten ordered SEAC planners to begin drafting plans for the invasion of
Malaya and Singapore. They proposed seizing Phuket Island ('Operation Roger'),
then Penang ('Operation Jurist') and finally the west coast of Malaya: 'Operation
Zipper'. The attack on Singapore, 'Operation Mailfist', would provide a climax.
British intelligence was aware that the Japanese were busily reinforcing Malaya:
SEAC planners anticipated 'formidable opposition'. In May, the British plans were
thrown into disarray when the British wartime coalition government was dissolved
in preparation for a general election, and tens of thousands of troops and personnel
were withdrawn from active duty. This reduced by an entire division the forces
available in Southeast Asia. Then, at the beginning of August, the Supreme Allied
Commander General Douglas MacArthur confided to Mountbatten's American
deputy, Lt General Raymond Wheeler, the astonishing news that the Americans

had the means to end the war within weeks: he was, of course, referring to a 'new weapon of unusual destructive force' – the atomic bomb.

For the British, the possibility – indeed, it seemed, the *likelihood* – of imminent Japanese surrender had perplexing implications. A bloody and protracted struggle to seize Malaya and Singapore from a fanatical enemy would no longer be necessary. This was surely to be welcomed. How then was Mountbatten to reassert imperial prestige shattered by the surrender of Singapore in February 1942 to an army of myopic midgets? At the time, a British soldier had famously quipped 'never had so many been fucked about by so few'. That raw and humiliating loss of face had to be undone. But how, if the foe threw in the towel, as the Japanese duly did in August?

His lordship's solution to the dilemma would be to stage a kind of ersatz invasion of Malaya and Singapore. SEAC strategists completed the new plans in four days, stressing that the occupying forces must 'arrive as quickly as possible and in the maximum possible strength for the maintenance of law and order'. Start of operations would be 'X-Day' – the seizure of Penang, where it was expected that the Japanese would formally surrender. The military occupation of Malaya, 'Operation Zipper', and Singapore, 'Operation Tiderace', would follow. Mountbatten and his planners now faced another difficulty. The vain and arrogant MacArthur, who had himself fled the Philippines when the Japanese invaded in 1942, forbade any Allied forces commencing surrender negotiations with Japanese commanders in Southeast Asia until after he had personally conducted the main surrender ceremony in Tokyo. Meanwhile President Truman was anxiously monitoring the relentless progress of Soviet armies in the Kuril Islands and urged MacArthur to hurry. A repetition of Soviet success in Eastern Europe had to be avoided at all costs in the Far East. The surrender was eventually scheduled to take place onboard USS *Missouri* in Tokyo Bay on 2 September. MacArthur repeatedly altered the surrender timetable, and 'X-Day' had to be postponed no less than three times until it was finally set for 21 August. These delays set off a disastrous chain reaction as SEAC planners scrambled to keep pace. As a consequence, British convoys would not reach Malayan waters until 2 September and Singapore would not be retaken until 5 September; 'Operation Zipper', the reoccupation of Malaya, would be delayed until 9 September. The period of 'phoney surrender' as it has been called, would last nearly four weeks – and this Interregnum would have dire consequences for many Malayans.

The unexpected, and at the time *unexplained*, power vacuum that followed in the wake of the announcement of the Japanese surrender handed the Malayan communists a unique historical opportunity. This surely was the dawn of a Malayan republic. But the revolution never happened. What we now know is that the MCP's treacherous secretary general, Lai Tek, had very different ideas. In his memoir, published in 2003, Chin Peng tells us what happened. In August, a mood of 'fevered expectancy and high morale' swept through the camps of the MPAJA. On 16 August, Chin Peng chaired a routine meeting of the MCP's Perak state committee in Ayer Kuning near Kampar. Soon after midday his secretary burst into the meeting room with the astonishing news of the emperor's speech, which he had picked up on the All-India broadcasting network. Chin Peng recalled: 'I promptly switched our meeting's agenda to a review of how best to implement Lai Te's [sic, alternate spelling] previous October Directives.' The message of these directives, it will be recalled, was that in the aftermath of a Japanese defeat, the MPAJA would launch a new struggle against the British. The MPAJA commanders had been busy transforming the MPAJA into a 'national liberation movement'; now with the stunning news of the Japanese surrender, it was a matter of 'tidying up loose ends'. The next day a courier arrived with a message from Lai Tek ordering Chin Peng to travel immediately to Kuala Lumpur for a meeting. He took the next available train and reached the new party headquarters in Selangor on 19 August. The MCP had abandoned the Sungai Buloh leper colony and moved to a British estate manager's bungalow nearby. Chin Peng now discovered that Lai Tek had already returned to Singapore – so was briefed instead by the Selangor state secretary Yeung Kuo. This 'bright, energetic and committed' young man was in a state of shock. He told Chin Peng that the previous day Lai Tek had made a speech at Sungai Buloh to a small hastily convened group of communists. His message was simple, and utterly bewildering: 'Support Russia, China, Britain and America in a new organisation for world security ...'. As Chin Peng put it: 'I realised the programme amounted to nothing more than a vapid move to appease the incoming British.' It was nothing less than a '180 degree turn'. Instead of armed revolution, the MCP must now focus on the organisation of labour and infiltration of unions. It is no wonder that Lai Tek had decided not to confront his protégé face to face – though it is likely that his hasty return to Singapore was also to do with his resurrected relationship with the Special Branch. Chin Peng was also troubled by another decision that Lai Tek had communicated to the comrades at Sungai Buloh. He had set up a new 'Central Military Committee' to co-ordinate the Three Star Army under his command. He appointed Chin Peng to serve as his No. 2. This was his reward for compliance. Lai Tek left instructions for Chin Peng to arrange a meeting with John Davis as soon as possible.

As Chin Peng tells us in his memoir, Davis was thoroughly confused by his friend's new role: he had always assumed he was a liaison officer with the MCP Central Committee, rather than the MPAJA military commander he really was. In any event, when the new No 2 in the MCP Military Command met Davis in Serendah, the SOE officer proposed that Chin Peng come with him to Kuala Lumpur to assist with the handover of power from the Japanese to the British. This was clearly a stratagem to keep the MPAJA 'onside', and Chin Peng refused. He had important business in Perak. This was an understatement. He now had to sell the new party line to impatient military commanders, who wanted to take the fight to the colonials. When he got back to Perak, Chin Peng discovered that his deputy, Ai Tek, had already begun negotiations with the Japanese commander in Taiping, who made his position very clear: 'If you choose to fight on, you can rely on our support.' Now Chin Peng had the unenviable task of telling his comrades that the Malayan revolution had been cancelled. In fact a few hundred Japanese soldiers preferred to join the MPAJA rather than surrender. The communists had been divided about how they should deal with the Japanese: the ideal of 'Pan-Asian unity' retained a powerful allure to many on both sides. We have to understand that in August 1945 the MPAJA was poised to wage war on the 'white colonial intruders' with backing from at least some Japanese. Lai Tek's new directive slammed shut the gaping door of insurrection. Why then did Chin Peng accept the new appeasement policy with barely a murmur of dissent? The explanation demonstrates the fundamental weakness of all political movements that defer to charismatic leaderships and top-down policymaking. Lai Tek, the 'Asian Lenin', spoke with the authority of the revered Comintern. He was the Comintern's man; to challenge or disobey him would be to challenge Moscow. These young Malayan communists like Chin Peng had been confined for more than three years in isolated jungle camps with almost no contact with the world outside except through their SOE contacts. Stalin had abolished the Comintern in 1943. Lai Tek was not the 'Asian Lenin' but the Malayan 'Wizard of Oz' expertly conjuring a completely false reality from behind a silken curtain.

What makes this pivotal moment in Malayan history even more remarkable is that on 21 August a 280-strong Giya Gun unit that had been sent from Singapore to Kuala Lumpur by the Japanese ran into MPAJA forces in northern Johor. Chin Peng: 'The Malays made their position quite clear. If we were willing to go ahead and continue the fight against the British they were willing to join us.' Now it was the communists who had to tell the Malays in the Giya Gun that repelling the British was no longer on the agenda. In the Sungai Siput district in the Kinta Valley in Perak, another group of MPAJA guerrillas had also been tentatively forging links with INA units, and in Kuala Lumpur two meetings had taken place between MCP and INA representatives at the Sri Maha Mariamman temple. At the end of August all the MCP representatives involved in these negotiations abruptly fell silent. There were no more meetings. A potential anti-colonial coalition of Chinese, Malay, Indian and Japanese forces was nipped in the bud – thanks to Lai Tek. As we will see shortly, the Japanese surrender had put Lai Tek in a perilous position. He had very good reasons to ingratiate himself anew with the British.

The SOE had never had any illusion that they were playing with revolutionary fire by backing the communist and Chinese-dominated MPAJA. John Davis and his fellow Force 136 officers had all served in Malaya before the war and understood, as far as any European could, the communal tensions that had been stoked by colonial administrators for more than nearly a century. To be sure both the SOE agents and the MPAJA commanders understood that their alliance was expedient and temporary. Hostilities would at some point be resumed. In negotiations with the British SOE representatives Lai Tek and his subordinates like Chin Peng had not tried to disguise their intention to take on the British colonial power after the war was over. There was a tacit recognition on the British side, reinforced after the Labour Party's electoral victory in May, that independence in some form was on the far horizon but that in no imaginable circumstance would Britain hand over Malaya to the communists. The fundamental weakness of Malay resistance, the virtual collapse of the Chinese nationalist KMT and the bad odour of collaboration that clung to the Malay KMM meant that the SOE never had any alternative to working with the Malayan communists. To all intents and purposes the MPAJA *was* the Malayan resistance. It is not often appreciated that a few of the SOE Force 136 agents had genuine friendships with some of the leading MPAJA guerrillas. In this pivotal time after the Japanese surrender, Davis was very much on the side of the MPAJA. In August he sent a strongly worded telegram to Force 136 headquarters pleading the cause of the MPAJA. It is worth quoting at length:

> Controlled AJUF [MPAJA] are soldiers under command of SACSEA [Mountbatten, Supreme Allied Commander South East Asia]. They expect and await specific orders and not vague directives. I am satisfied that they will obey such orders provided they are reasonable. Orders for them to remain half starved in the hills while the Allies leisurely take over the administration from the Japs [sic] will not be reasonable …

And then the crucial sentence:

> AJUF must be given full share in the honours of victory […] The alternative to all this is chaos and anarchy which may take decades to eradicate. The matter is very urgent. There is serious risk of a disastrous anti-climax.

Mountbatten concurred. He too regarded the MPAJA guerrillas as allies and appears to have known enough about the history of Malaya to sympathise with the Chinese. In May he had written that 'the best chance of military action against the Japanese lies in my supporting the largely Chinese movement known as the Anti-Japanese Union and Forces [MPAJA]. The political implications of this are governed by the fact that the Chinese in the greater part of Malaya did not in the past enjoy equality of status …'. Mountbatten staunchly backs the cause of the Malayan guerrillas, insisting that 'we owe them a special debt' and arguing that the 'Malayan Union' plan, which offered more rights to non-Malays, might in the long-term 'wean' the Chinese from communism. He pointed out that the Chinese nationalists who were aligned with the KMT were preoccupied with the future status of China. Only the communists had a sense of themselves *as Malayans*. This was an astute insight.

The Colonial Office refused to publicise the 'Malayan Union' as Mountbatten had suggested. The MPU planners, like Sir Edward Gent (who would become the first High Commissioner of Malaya), realised that the Union plan would need very careful handling. They knew that neither the Malay rulers nor the Malay nationalists would welcome their proposals to liberalise citizenship rights. Some rather forceful persuasion would, it was realised, be required. Mountbatten and even the 'men on the spot' like Davis and Chapman had a limited understanding of the pent-up political energies that would be unleashed on Malaya like a ferocious tropical storm. At a meeting convened on 21 August, Mountbatten discussed the matter of the MPAJA with SEAC top brass: the august gathering included General 'Bill' Slim, the victorious though rather embittered former commander of the 14th Army, Commander of Force 136 Colin Mackenzie, and the head of the Political Division, Captain G.A. Garnon-Williams. It was a tense and acrimonious occasion. Garnon-Williams backed the proposals made by Davis that the MPAJA should be given specific and 'honourable' tasks by British forces to avoid any sense of anti-climax and a collapse of discipline. Above all, the MPAJA should be very actively diverted from attacking surrendered but still heavily armed, Japanese troops. Slim had greatly profited from the intervention of Aung Sang's rebel army during the latter part of the Burma campaign but he now vehemently disagreed with any plan to support the rebels. The MPAJA should not be given any chance to act independently; they would need to be integrated into the reoccupation forces. Mackenzie pointed out that this would be immensely difficult to carry out. The MPAJA units were very widely scattered, many were starving and many guerrillas had begun to exhibit 'refractory attitudes'. It was questionable indeed whether a handful of Force 136 officers could effectively control their guerrilla friends for much longer. Nevertheless, Slim's views prevailed. After all, Ceylon was a long way from the steamy jungles of Malaya and the world Davis knew so well. As Mountbatten impatiently waited for MacArthur to conclude arrangements with the Japanese government in Tokyo, SEAC reinforced Force 136 units in Malaya to keep the lid held firmly down on the communist guerrillas. Freddy Spencer Chapman was parachuted back into Pahang, where it had been reported that MPAJA guerrillas were openly hostile to the British. By now SEAC had appointed Ralph Hone to begin organising the 'British Military Administration' that would take charge of Malaya and Singapore in the immediate aftermath of reoccupation. Hone, too, reported that the 'jungle communists had every intention of taking over Malaya'.

The British strategy to deal with the MPAJA problem was thus hopelessly confused. It was now proving very difficult indeed to 'honour' the heroism of the communist resistance and simultaneously control the MPAJA guerrillas. It was a case of giving with one hand while taking away with the other. The 'Davis Plan', had it been followed through, might well have worked. In the event it was fudged. On 25 August, SEAC began short-wave radio broadcasts to the Malayan resistance, informing them that they should move into regions that the Japanese had already left. They should not seek confrontation with any Japanese troops. Their first duty would be to keep order, prevent burning, looting and stealing, to secure bridges, roads and railways from attacks by 'bandits or collaborators'. They should continue to follow orders given by their British officers: 'see that life in your district goes on smoothly'. The SEAC broadcasters then turned to future plans. The BMA would help the MPAJA guerrillas retake their place in Malayan society; provisions would be made to support wives and families. A few days later, thousands of copies of a newsletter (in Malay, English and Chinese) were airdropped across Malaya. Davis had urged SEAC to work through the MPAJA leadership – in short the Malayan Communist Party. This was anathema to the British. In a few minds at least the Cold War had already begun. The new propaganda blitz was a deliberate and insulting attempt to bypass the MPAJA top brass. None of the leaflets referred to the MPAJA guerrillas as 'SEAC troops' – another slur that would never be forgiven. History is, of course, awash with such tantalising might-have-beens.

In Malaya, rumours of Emperor Hirohito's 'Jewel Broadcast' had been circulating since 10 August and were confirmed by Allied radio broadcasts a few days later. Many Japanese soldiers and their commanders refused to accept that the war was over. For many soldiers, the emperor's weasel words were confusing. Many, such as General Seishiro Itagaki, insisted they would fight on. But Count Terauchi summoned the rebel Japanese commanders to his headquarters in Java and made it clear that the emperor must be obeyed. The war was over. So Itagaki flew back to Singapore and ordered all Malayan language newspapers to print the emperor's speech. At the Japanese military headquarters in Raffles College he told his officers that 'we must lay down our arms'. Many were distraught: a rebel group fled to Aceh in Sumatra to continue the war. Other Japanese officers are believed to have contacted the Malayan Communists to propose a pact to fight on against the British. A good number of Japanese soldiers did join up with MPAJA units – and, according to Cheah Boon Kheng, two Japanese were reported to be serving with the communist MNLA on the Thai border as late as 1977. The main force of Japanese troops stationed in Singapore and Malaya were soon on the move. The overall plan was to maintain control in the big cities like Kuala Lumpur, Taiping and Ipoh, and to begin concentrating the various divisions in specific designated areas to prepare for evacuation. The Japanese commanders wanted to avoid revenge attacks on their men and did as much as they could to remove them from public sight. The Japanese plans for withdrawal shaped the strategy of the MPAJA.

As Japanese soldiers vanished from the smaller towns and villages in Malaya, MPAJA units moved in – ostensibly to maintain law and order. They all wore caps with three red stars: the Tiga Bintang. The traditional Malay administrations and police in the rural areas had by and large complied with Japanese rule. They lost protection overnight. Now they were vulnerable and frightened. There was no sign of the British. The single authority in some areas was the MPAJA. The consequences should have been predicted. Many guerrillas who had lost families in the Japanese Sook Ching massacres thirsted for revenge. Many of them meted out brutal punishment to people they regarded as informers and collaborators. Vengeful energies were directed especially at Malay policemen. 'It was a world gone mad,' recalled a survivor: 'a world turned upside down. Suddenly people seemed to remember every little wrong I did ...'. Wherever the Axis powers had been defeated revenge was the order of the day. All over Europe the defeat of Nazi Germany provoked vengeful attacks on collaborators and informers. Public humiliation was meted out to women who were alleged to have collaborated 'horizontally'. In France it is believed that at least 9,000 alleged collaborators were executed without trial during the *épuration sauvage* (the wild purge) that followed the Liberation. Revenge was sexualised. Between 10,000 and 30,000 French women endured the grotesque punishment of public head shaving. They were known as *les tondues*. Vengeance is the bitter aftertaste of occupation. In Malaysia, communist violence has become a founding myth of nationhood. But anecdote is not history.

It is very difficult to even estimate numbers of victims. And not all the victims were Malays. During this Interregnum, there were at least three different phases of violence that unfolded over a relatively short period of time. To begin with, local people, both Chinese *and Malays*, enacted summary justice against neighbours and strangers, both Malay and Chinese. Looting and theft were widespread. Then as the MPAJA units tightened their grip on many towns and villages, they set up so-called 'People's Courts' as a paralegal system that judged accused individuals and meted out punishments. As Tan Sri Kamarul Ariffin recalls bitterly today, these MPAJA courts dealt out very rough justice. When the MPAJA arrived in his village in Pahan, Kamarul's father was immediately arrested and put on trial. Summary execution was the most likely consequence. For the family, this was a time of terror, not justice – and the experience inspired Kamarul to take up law as a profession.

This period of semi-legal violence provoked in turn a communal war that had been simmering since the eruption of the Jihadist Sabilillah (meaning in Aarabic 'the cause of Allah'), or Red Band movement, in May. These phases of the Interregnum overlapped in different districts of Malaya. The energies of one fed the others since the MPAJA was perceived to be a *Chinese* movement and many Chinese saw *Malays* as collaborators.

J.J. Raj was loafing about Taiping in August 1945. He has never forgotten what happened when the MPAJA came to town:

> I watched their kangaroo courts [...] You go, you wait, a lot of people are assembled. And then you have somebody in uniform, this Tiga Bintang. He sits there. And others don't have a table la. So the fella's so-called prosecutor and all

standing there you see. So they have a long list and they call out one man. So
the fella is brought in. These are so-called traitors, so-called people who fought
against the Tiga Bintang. Thirty or forty of them were brought in. One by one
they are brought in and the so-called prosecutor reads out the various offenses
this man has committed …

According to Raj, these MPAJA 'people's courts' also acted as conduits of public
rage, rather than being simply an instrument of communist brutality:

> Then the standing officer looks at the crowd and say, 'What do you do?'
> Somebody in the crowd say, 'Kill him!' Then the whole lot says: 'Kill! Kill! Kill!'
> So he says kill. So immediately the man was taken away. Later I saw what was
> happening la. So similarly the others one by one, almost every case the crowd,
> they just say, 'Kill! Kill!' Just say, 'Kill kill!' So everyone that came out has to be
> killed. Pretty straight forward, they tie the person up on a tree and they just stab
> him in the heart. And then he dies on the spot.[27]

As in liberated France, women who were suspected of having had 'horizontal'
relationships with the Japanese occupiers often became hapless targets of
vengeful fury:
J.J. Raj:

> … they get hold of these girls who supposed to have committed offences. So
> they are punished lah, you see. So they hair they, they shave all the hair. Tie the
> person up la you see. And tie them on to a tree or to a hammock la. And under
> the hammock you have a small fire burning only smoke coming up you see. And
> on top of that, some more they bring these red ants and put it on the head of all
> these poor girls there you see all those ladies la […] The person screams, screams
> […] A person is tied up, her head is bald and full of red ants all over the body and
> you can't move at all. Then I really don't know what happens to them after that.

Such 'atrocity stories' saturate memories of the Interregnum period. The problem
is that such anecdotes are often imprecise about who was doing what to whom
– and why. Singapore resident Lee Kip Lin described the situation as: 'totally out
of control. There were murders everywhere and I knew some of the people who
had been collaborators had been murdered. A lot of personal vendettas went on.
You done me wrong. I don't like you. Now is the chance.'[28]

Chaos. Anarchy. Violence. Revenge. It is convenient to attribute the most
egregious outrages to the MPAJA. In national memory the communists are
villains of the Interregnum. There is no doubt that the MPAJA had developed an
internal culture of suspicion, violent revenge and 'traitor execution' during the
Japanese occupation, like most insurgent organisations. It is equally true that many

MPAJA leaders made efforts to control an unstable situation. When the MPAJA emerged from the jungle the priority was to seize control of the apparatus of local government as the Japanese pulled out. According to one estimate the guerrillas took over 70 per cent of small towns and villages in Malaya – and had the most significant impact in Johor, Selangor, Negeri Sembilan, Perak and Pahang. According to a report made by Chapman in October, the local population in Kuantan, Pahang was 'absolutely under the thumb of the Seventh Regiment [...] they barricaded the main roads and stopped inter-district road travel.' This does not sound especially 'anarchic' – or violent for that matter. Chapman continued: the MPAJA 'took over every department of Civil Administration and occupied most of the large buildings from the Chinese Chamber of Commerce to the police station. They were in complete and absolute control ...'. Based on his experience in Pahang, Chapman concluded:

> It must be admitted that the AJUF [Anti-Japanese Union Forces] did an extremely good job [...] Though the government rice stocks disappeared in an unaccountable manner and there was the usual 'bumping' off of collaborators after a mere mockery of a trial, they certainly kept order and prevented looting. Their methods did not tend to restore confidence to the Malays ...

It would be easy to discount Chapman's report as being biased. He had spent a great deal of time with MPAJA units and was on good terms with many of the regimental leaders. The SOE and Force 136 had their own reasons to show their communist allies in the best possible light. Chapman, as we know, had spent time in the MPAJA's jungle execution camps: he was no starry-eyed 'fellow traveller'. The MPAJA saw the punishment of 'traitors and running dogs' as necessary to maintaining security, the task they had been given by SEAC. As J.J. Raj's experience implies, the punishments handed down by the 'People's Courts' were condoned or even encouraged by public reaction.

The tragedy of the Interregnum is that Malays bore the brunt – or rather *believed* that they did. A Malay district officer lamented that 'eight days of rule by the MPAJA was worse then three and a half years under the Japs'. It is important to point out that the MPAJA 'justice' was not solely directed at Malays. Many Chinese also suffered. When the MPAJA crossed the causeway into Singapore they brought what local Chinese called the 'whispering terror'. Wealthy 'towkays', who had blithely conducted business as usual under occupation, were especially vulnerable, as were the Chinese or Eurasian mistresses of Japanese officers. In Chinatown, criminal gangs exploited the culture of retribution to carry on old feuds under a revolutionary rubric, and gangs such as the 'Exterminate Traitor Corps', the 'Blood and Iron Corps' (shades of a Prussian influence?) and the 'Dare to Die Corps' ran riot. Ordinary people were anxiously ambivalent. Low Ngiong Ing recalled that: 'We could not find it in our hearts to condemn this wild justice, which we were too squeamish to mete out ourselves. Indeed, we were thankful to our guttersnipes for doing it for us.'

No one knew, of course, about General MacArthur's injunction against 'local' surrender negotiations that had paralysed SEAC. The apparent failure of the British to restore order in Malaya led many Malays to assume that the 'Chinese communists', who had fought with the British against the Japanese, had tacitly been given a free hand. *They* would become the new masters of Malaya and Singapore just as Malays had always dreaded. It was time to fight back.

In Johor, inflamed Malay passions galvanised Kiyai Salleh's 'Red Band Army' and the Sabilillah movement. The Jihadists had begun attacking Chinese villages before the Japanese surrender in the Batu Pahat district. In a bloody explosion of violence, Kiay Salleh's murder squads now launched a fresh wave of ferocious attacks that targeted MPAJA men and women as well as any Chinese who had the bad luck to be in the wrong place. Fired up by their fanatical leaders the 'Red Band' men 'came down like a wolf on the fold', chanting, lashing out with their long parangs, bamboo spears and iron rods inscribed with verses from the Koran. As the Red Band Holy War rippled angrily across Johor, Sultan Ibrahim, who had been expelled from Bukit Serene just before the Japanese surrender for insulting an officer, called on Kiyai Salleh to meet him at the crown prince's palace at Pasir Pelangi. The sultan's *pawang* Kiyai Fadil, it will be recalled, was Kiyai Salleh's religious guru. The sultan and the rebel leader embraced and sat down together to a lavish meal. Kiyai Salleh called on Ibrahim to 'guard our country'. Sultan Ibrahim had always been a fickle ruler. Now he appeared to embrace Kiyai Salleh as the saviour of the Malays.

There was one Malay nationalist who became uneasy of the consequences of the Sabilillah Jihad against the Chinese. Dato Onn bin Jaafar, the 'father of Malay nationalism', had once been close to Sultan Ibrahim. Now he would openly criticise the sultan's reckless support for Kiyai Salleh. Dato Onn – who would become for a short period the most influential of the Malay nationalist leaders – was of mixed Malay and Turkish parentage. His father had served as the first 'Menteri Besar', or chief minister, of the Johor court. His son received an elite education in England and at the Malay College in Kuala Kangsar. For some time Sultan Ibrahim took a paternal interest in the bright young man but with unusual independence of mind Dato Onn bit the royal hand and criticised the sultan's treatment of Orang Asli. For this impertinence, Dato Onn was exiled to Singapore where he remade himself as a campaigning journalist who reported on Malay grievances under colonial rule.

Dato Onn played a somewhat ambivalent role in the KRIS debacle. He was one of the prominent Malays chosen by Ibrahim Yaacob to serve on his proposed 'cabinet'. But Dato Onn was no one's stooge. On 17 August he was the single voice of dissent at a KRIS reception attended by General Itagaki and the 'Malay experts' Yamada Hideo and Ono Seizaburo in Kampong Bahru, the Malay district of Kuala Lumpur. Itagaki made a speech regretting that the emperor's decision had disrupted progress towards independence. Dr Burhanuddin had then made a blustering speech insisting that KRIS must carry on the struggle. Dato Onn quietly poured cold water on his friends' impatient passions. Malays were not ready for independence. When Dato Onn returned to Singapore the sultan asked him to take over as district officer in Batu Pahat, the epicentre of the Red Band violence. At first he was reluctant, perhaps frightened. But when he found out about the British reaction to the Malay Jihad – his son Hussein was serving with the Indian Army – and read the implied threats of retribution, he decided to take on the job. It has been convincingly argued that with the collapse of KRIS and the flight of Ibrahim Yaacob to Jakarta, Dato Onn had a clear view of the road to political power – once the British had returned. It was imperative to purge Malay politics of the wild men of Johor.

On 21 August, the MPAJA was struggling to retain control of the Batu Pahat district and the nearby town of Muar. Kiyai Salleh and the Sabilillah Army of Red Bands planned a new attack on Parit Jawa and a number of other, mainly Chinese, villages. Led by Kiyai Salleh himself, more than 1,000 Red Band warriors gathered in Kampong Bagan and for much of the night recited mass prayers to inspire the slaughter of defenceless people. At dawn the following day, Kiyai Salleh led massed columns of Red Band men in the direction of the Chinese villagers … Dato Onn had no doubt that the Red Bands could do irretrievable damage to the Malay cause. He decided to stop the violence. The accounts of what happened next are, like so many other events in the Interregnum, obscured by myth. Suffice it to say that Dato Onn persuaded Kiyai Salleh to agree to a truce with the local MPAJA to bring the cycle of killings and reprisals to an end. The aristocratic Dato Onn won over the surly, hot-tempered and wild-eyed Jihadist. The deal was signed at the beginning of September on Hari Raya Puasa, the Muslim Festival which ends the fasting month of Ramadan. (It is, incidentally, followed by Syawal or Shawwal, the month of forgiveness.)

The cherished legend of Dato Onn Jaafar as the peacemaker of Johor should not be taken at face value. Jihadists were potential voters. In the aftermath of the peace negotiations, Dato Onn and Kiyai Salleh developed a close political attachment. When British forces returned to Malaya on 3 September and BMA officers arrived in Johor a few days later, they launched an investigation of the Batu Pahat incidents and made plans to arrest Kiyai Salleh. But Dato Onn, with the sultan's support, put a decisive end to British plans. He insisted to the BMA: 'Salleh has now been accepted and acknowledged as leader of every Malay in the Simpang Kiri [district north of Batu Pahat] …'. Arresting Kiyai Salleh, he was implying, would lead to more disorder. Dato Onn, it would soon become clear, saw the charismatic Jihadist as a future vote winner. The following year, when he formed his own political party the Pergerakan Melayu Semenanjung (Peninsula Malay Movement, PMS), Dato Onn appointed Kiyai Salleh president of its Simpang Kiri branch. When Dato Onn transformed the PMS into UMNO, the United Malays National Organisation, Kiyai Salleh devoutly transferred his allegiance.

The near disaster on Morib Beach was a shambolic beginning to reoccupation. In Singapore British and Commonwealth troops arrived on 5 September under a dull and thundery sky. An American officer reported that 'enthusiastic and cheering crowds massed at the pier' but sensed that this had more to do with relief that the Japanese had gone than pro-British feelings. That evening clocks were turned back from Tokyo time to Malayan time and a solitary Union Jack was hoisted over the Cathay Building. The Japanese surrendered officially a week later. On 12 September, the SEAC Supreme Commander Admiral Mountbatten and his American deputy General Wheeler were driven through Singapore in an open-topped car. A former prisoner of war was at the wheel. Royal Marines lined the streets. The Padang and the rooftops of nearby buildings were packed. Union Jacks flew alongside Kuomintang flags. Victory belonged to both the British and to China. At the grand Municipal Building a surrender party of Japanese generals and admirals awaited the victors. The Japanese delegation looked, Mountbatten wrote in his diary, 'villainous, depraved and brutal ...'. When they 'shambled out' to surrender their swords he thought they resembled 'a bunch of gorillas with great baggy breeches and knuckles almost trailing the ground ...'. The same kind of racial contempt provoked the Japanese to humiliate the British in 1942. The Japanese Colonel Tsuji noted, when he left Singapore, that the famous bronze statue of Sir Stamford Raffles had been replaced on its podium near the harbour. It appeared to have faded. Had it, Tsuji wondered, 'lost confidence in the principle of government by force'?

For some of the British the return to Singapore was sweet, but many Asians had not forgotten or forgiven the abject surrender and flight of their colonial masters three years before. Lee Kip Lin was disgusted by the arrogance of many of the British officers strutting around the Padang:

> It's the same old arrogance you saw before the war. And you felt very annoyed because these swine who were beaten by the Japs and were coming back here without having to fire a shot were still wearing that same arrogant face ...

The reason why the mask of arrogance had been so quickly put back on would soon become clear. The British had embarked on another imperialist crusade in Southeast Asia.

2

INFERNOS

Holy War

The Holy War did not end. The racial clashes did not abate. The British Military Administration (BMA) was now responsible for law and order in Malaya and Singapore and was much too overstretched to damp down the fires of communal hatred and fear. Batu Pahat in Johor remained tense. 'Red Band' squads were still active, burning villages and killing, while ordinary Malays were reported to be terrified of the MPAJA. In the northern state of Kelantan, Kuomintang units had taken control of Kota Bahru and were said to be massing for an attack. Interracial clashes were reported in Malacca and Senggarang in Johor. Malay attacks on Chinese escalated in November. Early on the morning of 6 November, a party of Malays armed with parangs and krises rampaged through the Chinese settlement at Padang Lebar near Kuala Pilah. They were led by another Jihadist, Kiyai Selamat, supposedly a disciple of Kiyai Salleh's. The Malay gangs killed hundreds of Chinese including women and children. A witness to some of these incidents was the former head of the Chinese Protectorate, Victor Purcell, who had returned to Malaya with the BMA. On 8 November, Purcell toured the area near Padang Lebar to reassure terrified Chinese refugees that British troops would soon restore order. Purcell watched as a British colonel made a speech to an assembly of Malay headman 'with several references to their own proverbs, that they had lost in one day the reputation it had taken years to build. He rebuked them as cowards and criminals, who had slaughtered innocent women and children ...'. Purcell observed that a number of Malays in the crowd were clutching parangs. The reports of the Padang Lebar massacre horrified the Chinese community in Singapore. Kuomintang leaders sent telegrams to the newly elected British Prime Minister Clement Attlee, deploring the loss of so many Chinese lives after the Japanese surrender. They blamed the BMA. The Padang Lebar massacre had a different significance for Malays. The somewhat exaggerated horror stories in Singapore newspapers gave the inadvertent impression that Malays were winning: according to a BMA report 'any movement designed to rouse Malays [...] is sure of support ...'. In December, the BMA began supervising the disarming of

Malayan anti-Japanese units – this applied not only to the communist MPAJA but also the KMT units and the tiny Malay 'Wataniah' resistance. With Malay Jihadists still on the rampage many Chinese veterans were reluctant to give up their weapons.

Malay attacks on Chinese persisted until at least March 1946. The violence was cyclical, with Chinese gangs launching reprisal raids on Malays, which would be followed by inevitable revenge attacks. When a British patrol entered Kampong Gajah, north of Telok Anson on the Perak River, they discovered that a crowd of Malays had armed themselves with spears and parangs, and publicly hacked scores of local Chinese to death in the market. A despairing BMA official reported on the cycle of violence:

> … there were outbreaks in various parts of the country, especially in lower Perak […] and in the Raub district of Pahang, where on the 11th of February, the Malays made a sudden attack on the Chinese and killed thirty […] on the 2nd of March […] seventy-six Malays were massacred in a surprise attack …

The Shabby Comeback

Then in March the rampage abruptly fizzled out. One reason was that the BMA persuaded many of the sultans to take a stand against violence in their states. The other reason was that Malays faced a new threat – not from the Chinese alone but the British. Plans were afoot for a complete reorganisation of the old patchwork of colonies and protectorates that would turn Malaya into a single colony and offer rights to non-Malays. For Malay nationalists like Dato Onn bin Jaafar these proposals were a red flag to an already infuriated bull. The KMM leaders Mustapha Hussain and Ibrahim Yaacob had scorched their political reputations by openly collaborating with the Japanese. Hussain was humiliated and Ibrahim fled to Jakarta. Dato Onn had kept his hands clean – and his prestige was untainted. Early in 1946 Dato Onn Jaafar called an emergency meeting of the 'All-Malay Congress' at Sultan Suleiman's Club in Kampong Bahru in Kuala Lumpur, the Malay heart of the colonial capital. He called for a new political organisation to lead a crusade against this new foe: the British proposal for a 'Malayan Union'. The new party he proposed would be officially formed on 11 May – and be called the 'United Malays National Organisation' (UMNO). Dato Onn would, before too long, lose his way politically to a much more conservative political class of Malay nationalists led by Tunku Abdul Rahman. The founding of UMNO would be the zenith of his career. The Malays had brandished a bloodied parang in the face of the British. Now they would do battle for the future of Malaya.

There was a fundamental though unspoken weakness in the British position. They had not 'won back' Malaya and Singapore. There was no military feat won in 1945 that might have wiped out memories of the abandonment of Malaya and the unconditional surrender of Singapore. The French and Dutch colonial administrations were in an even weaker position since both France and the Netherlands had been defeated and occupied by the Germans. This innate weakness was compounded by the manner of reoccupation. Events would have turned out very differently had the British Military Administration (the BMA) acted fairly, competently and efficiently instead of becoming, as historian Anthony Stockwell put it, a 'shabby scramble'. 'Joyful welcome' rapidly gave way to 'disgust'.

The BMA had a calamitous impact on the tarnished relics of British colonial prestige. Lee Kuan Yew was eloquently scathing about the 'education in unfairness' provided by the British officials:

> The men in charge – majors, colonels, brigadiers – knew they would be in power only until they were demobilised, when their wartime commissions would vanish like Cinderella's coach. The pumpkin of civilian life to which they would then be reduced was at the back of their minds ...

This was corrupting. The BMA was more commonly and contemptuously referred to as the 'Black Market Administration'. Many – not all – of the BMA officers took greedy advantage of the desperately needed supplies they controlled, selling them to black market dealers for lavish kickbacks. Even the British would be forced to admit later that losses from racketeering amounted to at least $15 million. But even if Mountbatten had appointed the most virtuous to run the BMA they would have faced a monumental, many-sided task of reconstruction. Although the British had not had to fight their way into Malaya against enemy opposition, the peninsula had been wrecked by the war. The BMA made a bad situation worse. They abolished the wartime currency, the so-called 'banana money', wiping out savings and driving up inflation. Rice was thirty to forty times its pre-war price. To try and make ends meet the BMA restarted the import of opium, becoming, as Mark Frost puts it, 'the island's leading drug dealer'. No doubt the drug was a relief for many. Food was generally scarce and water supplies unreliable or fouled. Everywhere desperate people grabbed unoccupied land to grow tapioca. In many areas, the landscape was despoiled by these dilapidated rough-and-ready farms that were worked by severely malnourished women and children. The BMA needed a vast army of labourers for reconstruction and was not scrupulous about how it was recruited. The sight of Japanese labour gangs became a familiar sight. But even ordinary Malayans and Singaporeans were press-ganged by contractors. Wages were below pre-war levels. If this wasn't bad enough, the behaviour of many British and Commonwealth soldiers and officers was grossly insensitive. Although we talk of the British 'coming back' to Malaya and Singapore, many of the new invaders were not 'old Malay hands'. Someone like Victor Purcell, who was a veteran of the Chinese Protectorate and spoke all the Chinese dialects fluently, was a rarity. Rape, belligerent drunkenness, the trashing of shops and stores – this was the face that Tommy turned to the East. They now treated Malaya and Singapore as conquered territories.

Reinventing Empire

At the Potsdam Conference in July 1945, a decision had been made to divide responsibility for the territories of the imminently defunct Japanese Empire between the Chinese Kuomintang nationalists, the Americans and the British. The Americans would control the Philippines and Korea, and manage the temporary occupation of Japan. We should remember here that President Roosevelt and his successors in Washington had drawn far-reaching anti-imperialist (meaning anti-British) lessons from wartime events in the Philippines. In 1941, Filipino troops fighting alongside American forces had stubbornly resisted the Japanese onslaught for many months. When the Japanese finally triumphed, very few Filipinos had heeded the siren call of collaboration. For Roosevelt and Truman their loyalty had a straightforward explanation: America had always dealt fairly with the native people of the Philippines. The former Spanish colony, purchased by the United States after the failed revolt at the end of the nineteenth century, had become a self-governing commonwealth in 1935 and full independence was firmly inscribed on the American agenda. The Philippines, Roosevelt believed, offered 'a perfect example of how a nation should treat a colony or dependency'. He made it clear to Churchill on many humiliating occasions that the British, Dutch and French could make no such claim about *their* Asian fiefdoms. In August 1941, after the signing of the 'Atlantic Charter', Roosevelt proclaimed that 'I venture to think that the Allied declaration that the Allies are fighting to make the world safe for the freedom of the individual and for democracy sounds hollow so long as India and for that matter Africa are exploited by Great Britain.' The president's speechwriter, Robert Sherwood, went further: it would not be long before 'the people of India, Burma, Malaya, and Indonesia were beginning to ask if the Atlantic Charter extended also to the Pacific and to Asia in general'. This was, of course, a reasonable conjecture. Desperate to get the Americans into the war, Churchill tended to sidestep the imperial problem – much to Roosevelt's annoyance. He would never let the matter drop. The president later told his son: 'Don't think for a moment that Americans would be dying in the Pacific tonight if it hadn't been for the short-sighted greed of the French and the British and the Dutch.' Ironically, perhaps, it was the French colonial regime in Indochina that most provoked Roosevelt's ire. He was disgusted by the abrupt French military collapse in 1940 and scorned its colonial government as decadent and unfit for purpose. The French and British were surely right to detect the whiff of humbug. The American revulsion about the imperialism practised by other nations was expedient and therefore adaptable. After the defeat of Nazi Germany the wartime bond between the victorious allies unravelled. With the demise of fascism Soviet communism reassumed its menacing part as the principal threat to global peace and prosperity. Roosevelt, who had frequently sided with Stalin against Churchill during the war, was dead. Under his successor Harry S. Truman, American foreign policy would be overhauled and the anti-imperialist note would not be played so loudly. In the new world order France would be reinforced as a strategic European bulwark against Soviet ambitions – and that meant shoring up its position in Indochina. Communism clearly threatened not just Europe, but Asia. During the Cold War that followed the defeat of the Axis, the old colonial powers would serve the global interests of the American imperium.

This meant that SEAC would be assigned the job of a proxy imperial police force. Before the Japanese surrender, Mountbatten's administrative empire incorporated Burma, Thailand, Cochin China (South Vietnam), Sumatra, British North Borneo, Malaya and Singapore. On the day that the people of Japan heard Emperor Hirohito admit that 'the war situation has developed not necessarily to Japan's advantage', MacArthur imperiously handed over to SEAC responsibility for half a million square miles of the former Dutch East Indies, warning 'Lord Louis to keep his pants on or he will get us all into trouble'. Across the daunting ruins of the Japanese 'Co-Prosperity Sphere', SEAC was charged with the care and evacuation of hundreds of thousands of prisoners of war, the repatriation of surrendered, but not defeated, Japanese troops and the restoration of law and order. The British government had been bled dry by the world war, and in a troubling echo of the debacle of 1941 could not afford and deploy sufficient men, arms and political muscle to reassert power in the fractious, volatile new world of Southeast Asia. Tremendous, superheated political energies were already bubbling up through fractures opened up by the Japanese occupiers. As the chief civil affairs officer of the BMA, Major General Hone, struggled to police Malaya and cope with chronic food shortages and the fraught introduction of an unpopular new currency to replace Japanese 'banana money', British troops would embark on the first 'savage wars of peace' in Southeast Asia to refurbish the power and prestige of former colonial rivals, the French and the Dutch. Both France and the Netherlands had been defeated, occupied and humiliated by another ferociously imperialist power – Nazi Germany. Both European nations needed to retrieve their lost Asian empires to rebuild credibility. SEAC forces would now become their proxy conquerors.

In the last months of 1945, British troops fought the first 'small wars' that would define the post-war world. The soldier Mountbatten despatched to Saigon, Major General Douglas Gracey, had one vital qualification for the job. He was a political naif but commanded the complete loyalty of the 20th Indian Division. In a time of imperial crisis, this counted for a great deal. In the long shadow of Subhas Chandra Bose, few British officers could confidently rely on their Indian troops as Gracey could. During the Burma campaign, 'Chacha' (uncle) Gracey and his Indian soldiers had fought with reckless courage at Mandalay and Meiktila, earning the approbation of the grumpy General Bill Slim: 'a magnificent division, magnificently led'. But the loyalty of the 20th Indian was about all Gracey could offer SEAC. He despised politics as 'ideas and waffle' and knew very little about Indochina. This would endear him neither to the French nor the Vietnamese people – and he probably could not have cared less. The famous French war correspondent and photographer Germaine Krull watched Gracey's men fly into Saigon:[29]

> The transport planes carrying British troops arrived in Saigon at one o'clock [...] We had left Rangoon at three o'clock that morning. I was the only woman and one of the three correspondents to accompany these handsome, impeccable Gurkhas – like over-grown children – and their Scotch commanding officer ...

The airport, Krull observed, was still 'serviced entirely by the Japanese', who followed British orders punctiliously. As the party of journalists followed Gracey's troops into Saigon, they noticed 'sullen, stormy-eyed Annamites [Vietnamese] and Chinese ...'. As they entered the city, banners and slogans festooned walls and official buildings: 'Down with French imperialism!', 'Vive les Alliés!', 'Down with the colonials!', 'The era of colonisation is over!' Flags were everywhere – British, American, Chinese, Russian – and the Viet Minh's big red one with a yellow star. In the city, Krull walked along the Rue Catinat, 'the heart of it' – the elegant street was teeming with French families, a few Chinese – but not a single Annamite, 'not even a rickshaw'. A British captain contemptuously described a 'feeble WOG [i.e. Viet Minh]' party that was expecting the British to 'confirm their independence from the wicked French'. The latter were 'all rather futile and vaguely Vichy ...'. The British war in Vietnam was a disaster. Krull's last report pulls no punches:

> I left by plane on the next day, the 25th of September. Saigon was in flames as we flew away. The last ten days in Saigon proved to me that the French population understood nothing of the situation and knew nothing of the outside world; that it consisted of people who would not tolerate the least infringement upon their comfort and who also were incredibly cowardly. Never have cause and effect been so closely linked. The events of the 22nd of September determined the issue of the conflict. Everything which happened thereafter can be directly traced to that date – women captured and mistreated, men and children assassinated, Dutch, English and American officers killed, shooting, burning factories, mysterious disappearances, all these and more happened. The French, terrorised by the lack of foresight and motivated by avarice [...] are responsible for what happened.

There was revolutionary upheaval too in Burma and Indonesia. Nationalist Aung Sang and the Burmese National Army had helped the British defeat the Japanese but the Burmese made it very clear that they wanted independence and soon. The situation was even more complicated in the Dutch East Indies. The Netherlands had been occupied by the Germans during the war and in peacetime the country was in desperate straits. The Dutch government needed to restore the flow of treasure from its former overseas domains. Mountbatten had little choice but to assist with the restoration of Dutch rule – though he had few illusions about its long-term viability. The Indonesian revolution that erupted with Japanese connivance had released cataclysmic political energies that few could control – not even the charismatic nationalist figurehead Sukarno. The revolutionary impetus came from young Indonesians known as '*pemudas*'. Benedict Anderson writes:

> The central role of the 'Angkatan Muda' (Younger Generation) in the outbreak of the Indonesian national revolution of 1945 was the most striking political fact of that period. For the returning Dutch and their British allies, as well as for the Eurasian and Chinese communities, the once innocent word *pemuda* (youth) acquired an aura of remorseless terrorism [...] On the Indonesian side, a whole literature of glorification attests to an exultant consciousness of the sudden emergence of youth as a revolutionary force ...

The British campaign reached a bloody climax in Surabaya, the great industrial port known as 'The City of Heroes'. The consequences of the British onslaught were eloquently expressed by the poet 'Idrus':

> ... from people's mouths came the moans of death. The air stank of cordite and human and animal carcasses [...] Now and then an explosion could be heard, followed by black smoke billowing up into the sky. The rain was full of a dirty black dust which hurt the eyes and heart alike ...

The British eventually abandoned the Dutch to try and restore colonial rule. But their victory was short-lived. In December 1949, the Dutch conceded independence. Sukarno became the first president of the Republic of Indonesia. By then, India was already independent, as were the Philippines. The British relinquished Burma in 1948. The French grimly hung on in Indochina. Seismic shudders had begun to splinter the old colonial domains. But in British Malaya, the imperial sun was dipping close to the horizon – but it would not set for some time to come. There was too much at stake.

3

THE EMPIRE REBORN

A New Colonial State?

The swift crumbling of the Japanese Empire in Southeast Asia after August 1945 brought British colonial minds hard up against the brute fact of Asian nationalism – that it was poised to wrest India from British hands. In Malaya, the grandees of the BMA watched the Indonesian revolution unfold with increasing concern. There had to be lessons here but no one was quite certain what they might be. The infection of revolutionary fervour might of course spread. Trade, goods, people and ideas had flowed back and forth across the Straits of Malacca and the South China Sea for many centuries. There was no reason to suppose these great migrations would dry up any time soon. Against a background clamour and much wailing and gnashing of teeth from Tory diehards, led by wartime Prime Minister Winston Churchill, the new Labour government was resigned to the setting of the imperial sun in Africa and Southeast Asia. Nationalist aspirations, voices, dreams, demands, could not be brushed aside for much longer. There could be little doubt that in the medium or, preferably, long term these churning energies would prove irresistible. The point was to somehow ensure that the way the empire was wound up served the interests of the departing power. The new owners of Britain's overseas properties had to be the right sort of people.

So the challenges for the custodians of Malaya were nettlesome ones. What kind of independent Malaya would suit the strategic interests of Britain and America in Southeast Asia? How long a preparation would Malayans need? A decade? Two? What indeed *was* Malaya? Was there any such person as a *Malayan*? Should Singapore be included along with the peninsula and Sabah and Sarawak, the crown colonies in northern Borneo? These questions would take a long time to resolve. The independent Malaya that eventually emerged from the end of empire was the peculiar distillation of a long-term experiment conducted in a laboratory of conflict. The Malayan wars began with the idea of a 'Malayan Union'.

It is natural to view the Japanese conquest of Malaya and the British unconditional surrender of Singapore in February 1942 as the beginning of the end of British imperial rule in Southeast Asia. Once more, hindsight deceives.

The loss of Singapore was traumatic and led to much recrimination and soul-searching. British prestige was in shreds. But the official documents of the period, however, rarely reflect much sense of an imminent imperial apocalypse. On the contrary, the ousting and enforced exile of Malayan colonial administrators and planners led to an immediate rethinking of colonial rule, not its abandonment. The likelihood of self-rule shimmered on the far horizon.

The development of 'British Malaya' from the mid-nineteenth century was a by-product of globalisation. Profit underpinned British colonial acquisitions just as it did French and Dutch interests in Indochina and the Indonesian Archipelago. In a remarkably short period of time the human landscape of most of Southeast Asia was transmuted when Chinese and Indian workers flooded into Malaya to work the tin mines and plantations that fed a rapidly enlarging world market for raw materials. As the British tightened their hold on the Malay states, their natural resources and their rulers, the great tide of coolie labour sucked into the maw of the colonial economy appeared to threaten the indigenous rights of Malays – whose ethnic identity was shaped by a mythic sense of territorial entitlement. Malays, too, had once been migrants. For many decades it suited the British colonial administrators to enforce and reinforce the communal or racial divisions of colonial Malaya. The conceptual world of colonial administrators in Southeast Asia was shaped by new theories about racial difference that had first emerged in France and Germany and seemed to conform to Charles Darwin's theory of human descent through natural selection. These ideas found their administrative expression in the institution of the colonial census which with increasing rigour defined the different Malayan races – the Malays, the Chinese and the Indians. The British believed they were obligated to respect the 'natural rights' of Malays. As High Commissioner Sir Hugh Clifford insisted in 1927: '[Malay states] are, and they must remain – unless our duties, our obligations and our engagements to the Rajas [rulers], the Chiefs and to the people of these countries [sic] are to be wholly ignored or forgotten – *Malay* states' (emphasis in original). This was not high-mindedness or charity: from the British point of view, the supposedly docile Malay sultans were proxy colonial rulers. The problem for the British was that Malay rights, enshrined in the individual rulers of the different states, resulted in territorial fragmentation. From the 1920s on, various attempts were made to centralise the political administration of the Malay states, which invariably foundered on Malay resistance since it appeared to imply a further loss of royal power. There was an untidy feel to British Malay, with its three crown colonies, its federated states and unfederated states. Colonial administrations no doubt prefer to rationalise their fiefdoms. But the main issue in Malaya was not merely a fastidious concern with neatness. Territorial unity promoted economic efficiency.

Even before the Japanese invasion, British officials had begun to suspect that their vested interest in the 'traditional apprehensions of the Malay sultans' had become a 'barren policy' that prevented Malays 'standing on their own feet' –

and rode roughshod over the interests of other races. These were the words of
Sir Edward Gent, who had accompanied W.D. Ormsby-Gore, the Parliamentary
Under-Secretary of State on a 'fact-finding' tour of Ceylon, Java and Malaya in
1928. After the fall of Singapore in February 1942, Gent would become one of the
leading advocates of a new deal for British Malaya. The British had manufactured
the fractured communal landscape of Malaya. Now it would seem they had a bad
conscience about the repercussions.

It was in Palestine that the fallout from communalism had the most poisonous
impact. After the First World War, the collapse of the Ottoman Empire made
Britain the dominant power in the Middle East. Various territorial settlements
made after the Paris Conference in 1919 allocated Palestine to the British as
a mandate. The French took Syria. The British struggled with little success to
balance the interests of rapidly increasing numbers of well-organised Zionist
immigrants, who regarded Palestine as a future 'homeland', and the Arab peoples
of the protectorate. The Arab leadership became ever more intransigent: 'We will
push the Zionists into the sea or they will push us into the desert!' Although
many Arabs living in the mandate benefitted from the arrival of hard-working
Zionist immigrants, by the mid-1930s emotions were running very high. In 1936
the grand mufti of Jerusalem, Haj Amin al-Husseini, provoked a mandate-wide
campaign of strikes, civil disobedience and violence targeted at the British, Jews
and other Arabs. An Arabic slogan of the time proclaimed: 'the British into the sea,
the Jews into their graves'. The Arab Revolt impressed on the minds of Colonial
Office mandarins an acute fear of communal conflict. The more enlightened of
them had no illusions that British colonial rulers had played a not insignificant
role fermenting the conflict. The Peel Commission appointed in 1937 to address
and solve the Palestinian problem recommended partition and population transfer
as a means to lance the boil. A large number of Arabs, about 225,000, would be
transferred out of the 'Jewish area' and about 1,250 Jews would be transferred
from the 'Arab area'. As we will see, more than a decade after the Arab Revolt
an ambitious plan of population transfer would be an integral aspect of British
counter-insurgency strategy in Malaya. The Peel Commission report justified its
proposal by referring to the population transfers that were agreed in 1923 after
the Greco-Turkish war:

> A convention was signed by the Greek and Turkish Governments, providing
> that, under the supervision of the League of Nations, Greek nationals of the
> Orthodox religion living in Turkey should be compulsorily removed to Greece,
> and Turkish nationals of the Moslem religion living in Greece to Turkey. The
> numbers involved were high—no less than some 1,300,000 Greeks and some
> 400,000 Turks. But so vigorously and effectively was the task accomplished that
> within about eighteen months from the spring of 1923 the whole exchange
> was completed [...] Before the operation the Greek and Turkish minorities had

been a constant irritant. Now Greco-Turkish relations are friendlier than they have ever been before.

This was a grotesque misrepresentation of the actual consequences of the 1923 transfer which was, in practice, a series of forced deportations. In any event, both Jews and Arabs rejected the commission's proposals.

The wartime 'reformers' in the Colonial Office were equally as preoccupied with the imminent independence of India. Only Churchill and his circle of unrepentant imperialists refused to acknowledge that this was inevitable. While the Raj maintained its position as the 'jewel in the crown', Malaya was on the imperial periphery as a staging post between India and China. The heart of empire beat in Delhi. But if India had to be given up – as seemed likely – then Britain's Southeast Asian possessions would have proportionally greater significance in both strategic and fiscal terms. To prepare for this adjustment, the British government set up the 'Malayan Planning Unit', the MPU, in July of 1943 in offices near Hyde Park Corner in London. The MPU was headed by 'Chief Planner' Major General Herbert Ralph Hone, who had a Colonial Office background and was a former head of civil affairs in the Middle East. (He was also a 'Grand Officer' of the Grand Office of the Rose Croix branch of the Freemasons.) Hone started work with six military officers. By 1945, MPU staff had grown to 162 officers supported by 127 civilians and lower-ranking military personnel. Their task was to prepare a 'Key Plan' for the military administration of Malaya and a set of future policy directives. The result of their deliberations was the 'Malayan Union' plan. Judging by the correspondence in the National Archives, many discussions about the future of Malaya were dominated by Gent. He is the main author of the most important policy discussions and directives.[30]

The 'Malayan Union' was conceived as a decisive break with the colonial past. Its purpose would be to reconfigure the plural societies of what the MPU planners called the 'Malaysian region'. A separate planning unit was responsible for the future of the British colonies in Borneo. The MPU planners, who were working 6,000 miles from Malaya in London, struggled to reconcile progressivism with hard-nosed practicality. This was succinctly put by a Mr Ashley Clarke: 'we must be prepared to give up non-essentials to maintain the really important things.' The idea was to create a new 'Malayan' endowed with a 'Malayan consciousness' who could be entrusted at some future time with the tasks of governing a new Asian nation. At the same time it was assumed that the erasure of the old communal identities – Malay, Chinese, Indian – would 'streamline' the Malayan economy. Standing in the way of this grand project was entrenched Malay 'parochialism' and 'dynastic pride'. One of the MPU officers put it like this:

The Malays cherish a definite loyalty towards their Rulers and this feeling conflicts with the development of any allegiance towards a larger unit than the state. There is no widespread conception among the Malays that they are 'Malayan' with common duties and problems: and this is the first problem that must be faced in Malaya if the country is to advance towards nationhood and self-government within the British commonwealth.

The Malays, in other words, would have to be weaned from their old loyalties. No one in the MPU thought this would be easy to accomplish. From the British point of view the idea of the Union was rather like prescribing strong, not very palatable medicine to promote political well-being in the future. The 'Malayan Union' challenged the traditional status of the Malay states as the dominant framework of Malay political activity and loyalty. The traditional privileges of Malays would be at the very least qualified and new rights of citizenship offered to Chinese and Indians. The peoples of the 'Malaysian region' would, in theory, become 'Malayans'. This would mean confronting the Malay rulers because, as we read in one MPU report, 'the Malay rulers have always set their faces against any proposals to recognise as their subjects any persons not of the Malay race or Mohammedan religion.' The British had once *reinforced* the status of the Malay rulers in order to rule through them. Now they proposed – or appeared to be proposing – abolishing the Malay *ancien régime*. It would have been hard to predict in 1945 that, in just over a decade, the British would bequeath to independent Malaya a 'unified monarchy' and a chauvinist Malay governing class.

The three key elements of the 'Malayan Union' plan were:

1. A centrally governed peninsula union comprising the nine Malay states, Penang and Malacca, but not Singapore.
2. A common citizenship scheme for all who regard Malaya as their home.
3. The nine Malay states abrogate their powers to the crown.

The MPU planners understood that each one of these proposals was potentially explosive. The Malay rulers had resisted any proposal of centralised rule for more than half a century. Malays staunchly refused to accept Indian and Chinese 'birds of passage' as equal citizens. How then could Malay rulers be persuaded to give up what little the British had left them of their traditional powers? It was readily acknowledged that the sultans and their Malay subjects would need a great deal of persuading. When Mountbatten became involved in discussions about the future of Malaya he emphasised that the Union idea was virtuous and progressive:

I cannot help feeling that in the long run nothing could perhaps do more to perpetuate sectional antagonisms [...] than the giving of special recognition to one race [...] If we can make a start in this way by getting people, whether Malays, Chinese or Indians, to combine together as citizens (and not as racial communities) [...] we may hope that one day they will come to look at the wider problems of Malaya in the same light ... (29 July, 1944)

The Secretary of State for the Colonies Mr Stanley of the MPU replied to Mountbatten a month later:

... you have much to say about the rousing of communal antagonism. On this point I think we have a satisfactory answer. For a long time at any rate, we must expect that the natural [sic] China and India ties [sic] of the Chinese and Indian domiciled communities will tend to be stimulated by the nationalist policies of those two countries. Our pre war experience offered hardly a sign of any conception amongst the three peoples that they were Malayans. Our plan is to proceed both from the top and the bottom in fostering the growth of such a conception ... (21 August, 1944)

After the Japanese conquest and the beginning of the occupation, British valuations of the different Malayan races began to change. There was widespread distrust of 'traitorous' Malay nationalists like Ibrahim Yaacob; Malay submission to Japanese rule was contrasted unfavourably to Chinese defiance. Many Malays, too, had resisted the Japanese; some wealthy Chinese tycoons had profited during the occupation. Historian James Allen cites in his book *The End of the War in Asia* (1976) the impact on MPU thinking of 'an anti-Malay atmosphere', 'anti-Malay whispers' and 'anti-Malay sentiments'. As we have seen, SEAC supremo Mountbatten admired the mainly Chinese anti-Japanese guerrillas – and insisted that they must be honoured and rewarded as co-partners in victory. They, and not the Malays, had fought 'for Malaya' and were, by implication, true Malayans. There is a remarkable document in the National Archives, dated 3 September 1945, commenting on the MCP August 'declaration of aims'. Mr M.E. Dening admits that:

The sentiments expressed in this document are irreproachable. It will be seen that the Communist Party have rather stolen our fire [i.e. the 'Malayan Union Plan'] and that we have lost that element of surprise for our progressive policy which would politically have been so valuable [...] the very reasonableness of it makes it all the more important that the speediest and fullest practicable publicity should be given to our own plans ...

The 'Malayan Union' might therefore be seen as both punishment and gift. It rebuked the Malays and their rulers and reimbursed non-Malays with the promise of citizenship. As it would soon become clear, the idea of the 'Malayan Union' would satisfy neither Malays nor non-Malays.

The reoccupation of Singapore and Malaya started and got worse. The BMA caretaker government was soon broadly despised. Historians have judged its record harshly. This is thoroughly deserved. The BMA was expediently organised, corrupt, understaffed, and eventually vindictive and reactionary. This dismal record of failure is not the whole story. In its first few months, as the British officials struggled with food shortages, a worthless currency, and the chaotic collapse of the Japanese administration, the BMA inadvertently brought forth a thrilling and short-lived 'Malayan Spring': a time of cultural exuberance and breathtakingly liberated political discussion. Might the political history of Malaya have taken a different turn after the war? The 'Malayan Spring' inspired a tantalising meeting of minds and hearts that has been largely expunged from Malaysian historiography.

Take, for example, Ahmad Boestamam: the stormy petrel of the Malay left and the leading political activist of the Malayan Spring. He spent long periods of time in detention both under British rule and after Malaya became independent and wrote an engaging political autobiography called *Merintis Jalan ke Punchak*, which means 'Carving a Path to the Summit'. 'Perjuangan' means struggle in Malay – and for Boestamam it was a way of life. He was born Abdullah Sani b. Raja Kecil in a village near Tanjung Malim in southern Perak in 1920 and educated at the Anderson School in Ipoh. At the time, this was one of the leading English language schools in British Malaya and had many Chinese students. Its enlightened cross-communal atmosphere had a profound impact on the young boy from the little Malay kampong. He instinctively shunned the narrow-minded chauvinism of other Malay nationalists. Evidently a talented writer, Abdullah Sani became a journalist and a frequent contributor to *Majilis* and the old *Utusan Melayu* in Singapore. He was rebellious and impulsive by nature, and a few days before the Japanese invasion of the peninsula he and other KMM members were arrested by the British and thrown into Changi Prison. The British were of course deeply suspicious of the Malay nationalists. Boestamam and the other KMM people were released by the Japanese in February 1942 and thereafter pursued a strategy of 'above ground cooperation' with the Japanese and 'underground resistance'. Boestamam himself had a job with the Japanese Propaganda Department in Ipoh, where he worked as a censor, and in 1945 became a second lieutenant in the Japanese-sponsored 'Giyu Tai', a kind of Home Guard. In his political autobiography, Boestamam says that he had no sense of shame or mortification about this at all. He was after all a passionate admirer of Sukarno who had shown few compunctions about accepting Japanese political largesse.

Boestamam's account of the period after the Japanese surrender, when the British tried to impose the 'Malayan Union', is revealing. One of the enduring mysteries of the Malayan Spring is the identity of a political activist who called himself Moktaruddin Lasso, or sometimes 'Lang Lang Buana' ('the traveller' in Javanese). Boestamam describes the day Moktaruddin walked into the editorial office of the new Malay-language *Suara Rakyat* ('Voice of the People'). Boestamam wondered if their visitor was Special Branch: Moktaruddin smoked English-made Craven A cigarettes. On the contrary, Moktaruddin told the

Malays he had come from the headquarters of the MPAJA and was 'just out of the jungle'. He told Boestamam that he liked the new paper and wanted to help fund it. No strings, he insisted. 'You are given complete freedom …'. According to a British intelligence report, Moktaruddin was a former schoolteacher who had spent time in Moscow and was a disciple of Sukarno. Was he perhaps Tan Malaka? Moktaruddin disappeared just before Tan Malaka made a comeback in Indonesia. We will never know for certain. In any event it was Moktaruddin who, once the funding matter had been solved, introduced Boestamam to other Malay radicals, such as Rashid Maidin and Abdullah C.D., who would be the core of a the first Malay political party to be formed after the Japanese occupation, the 'Partai Kebangsaan Melayu Malaya' – the Malay Nationalist Party, or MNP. Moktaruddin had proposed calling the new party the 'Partai Socialis Malaya' but the Boestamam camp persuasively argued that while 'they did not disagree with socialism' – the purpose of the party was to fight for independence. He won the argument. In his autobiography, Boestamam is at pains to point out that the MNP was 'not continuing the struggle of the KMM'. It was not, he was saying, a communal party.

On 30 November, the new MNP held its first congress in Ipoh. This event has been eclipsed in Malaysia's national story by the foundation of UMNO the following year – and UMNO has, of course, dominated Malaysian politics since independence and has a vested interest in concealing the 'path not taken'. That congress can now be understood as Malaya's lost future. The MNP was a broad front nationalist party – and in Ipoh many shades of leftist opinion were openly represented. Even the Sultan of Perak had been invited to attend though, not surprisingly, he declined. Chen Tian Wah represented the MPAJA 5th Regiment. Abdullah C.D. urged unity to fight colonialism – a sentiment echoed by most of the speakers, who warned against a narrow-minded i.e. a communal politics. In his main speech to the congress, the new party leader Dr Burhanuddin al-Helmy reiterated the ideals of 'Raya Indonesia'. There is a revealing analysis of Dr Burhanuddin's subtle political thinking in Farish Noor's *The Other Malaysia*. Noor writes that:

> The broad based nationalism of Dr Burhanuddin was one that was not anchored solely on the essentialist categories of race or a politics of authenticity. He regarded national identity and cultural belonging as historically determined and to be evolving categories that needed to be developed on a sounder foundation that was provided by religion and ethics [...] Rather than focusing on the difference between Islamists, Nationalists and Leftists, Dr Burhanuddin preferred to stress the chain of equivalences that bound their projects together.

Recognising a 'chain of equivalences' and 'evolving categories' would always be anathema to the feudal-minded Malay elite that would dominate UMNO – and independent Malaysia. In 1965, the same Dr Burhanuddin would be the second member of the Malaysian parliament to be arrested under the notoriously illiberal 'Internal Security Act' (ISA). In prison his health collapsed and he died soon after his release.

Battle Is Joined

On 3 September 1945, the British War Cabinet had agreed proposals for 'the establishment of a Malayan Union with a central legislature'. After a great deal of acrimonious debate, Singapore had been excluded from the Union and would henceforth pursue a different course. Union amounted to legal annexation. To begin with, opposition was rather muted. The MNP leadership had broadly supported the idea of the 'Malayan Union'. This too had proved hard to stomach, especially for Malays. This was a clear sign of trouble ahead. It was not unanticipated. The BMA already treated Malaya as a single administrative entity. This was merely expedient, for the 'Malayan Union' plan envisaged a *permanent* unitary state. This would require the British to renegotiate their treaties with the sultans. How was this to be achieved? For the MPU in London, success depended on an element of surprise. It was essential to move as quickly as possible. Speed, they hoped, would outflank and weaken opposition. The key to their compliance was the sultans. If the rulers could somehow be persuaded that Union was best for Malaya, then Malays would surely come onboard. This would prove to be a seriously flawed calculation.

Persuasion would be laced with a strong dose of coercion. The diplomat chosen by the Colonial Office in London to make the long-gestated Malayan Union a reality was Sir Harold MacMichael, whose tenure as the High Commissioner of Palestine and Transjordan had ended in the autumn of 1944. He seems to have understood his task with unflinching clarity. According to a cabinet minute:

> Sir Harold, ever since he was provisionally appointed for this task, has been very anxious to know how far he can go in making it clear to individual Sultans that H.M.G. intends to bring the policy into effect, not withstanding possible resistance by any or all of them.

Mountbatten had pointed out that there were now different 'categories' of Malaya sultan:

1. Pre-invasion sultans still in office.
2. Puppet sultans known to be disloyal or otherwise unsuitable whom the Japanese have placed in office by deposing the legitimate sultan.
3. Sultans who have assumed or been appointed to office during the Japanese occupation ...

It was made clear to MacMichael that the compromised position of some of the Malay sultans offered him the gambit of: 'rejection of individual Sultans in favour of other claimants who would be ready to co-operate'. Evidently MacMichael received from H.M.G. the guarantees he had requested. He was given the right to use *force majeure*. This was not exactly gunboat diplomacy but in spirit the difference was just a hair's breadth.

On 27 September 1945, MacMichael flew from London to Colombo, where he boarded HMS *Royalist* on 7 October. A few hours after the British government announced its intention to carry out constitutional reform in Malaya on 11 October, MacMichael disembarked in Port Swettenham on the west coast of Malaya. By then the sultans had already been 'softened up'. All through September Brigadier H.C. Willan had toured the Malay courts to investigate the roles played by the rulers during the Japanese occupation and to assess their fitness to rule. Willan's fascinating and occasionally amusing reports provided MacMichael with potentially incriminating information about whether or not the different rulers might kick up a fuss when it came to signing on the dotted line. Of the sultans appointed before the Japanese invasion, five remained in office: the sultans of Johor, Selangor, Perak, Pahang and the Yam Tuan of Negeri Sembilan. The Japanese had been as manipulative of dynastic succession as the British had. They had, for example, deposed the Sultan of Selangor Tunku, Sir Hishamuddin Alam Shah, because he was a British favourite and replaced him with Tunku Musa-Eddin, who had been debarred. Sultan Musa-Eddin became the most enthusiastic royal supporter of the Japanese during the occupation and backed Ibrahim Yaacob. The sultans of Perlis and Terengganu had both died during the occupation and the Japanese had directly intervened in the succession. Much the same happened in Kedah and Kelantan. A flavour of Willan's negotiating style comes over in his account of a meeting with Sultan Ibrahim in Johor Bahru. Accompanied by a Colonel Hay, Willans arrived in town at 5.25 p.m. and was informed that the sultan was in residence at the Pasir Plangi Palace. Here Willans found Ibrahim relaxing with his Romanian wife, Marcella Mendl, in a generously proportioned lounge. The sultan was overjoyed, or so he said, to see the two British officers, and offered them bracing whisky *stengahs*. The sultan, Willans said, 'needed no prompting to talk': he insisted that he hated the Japanese who had compelled him to make pro-Japanese speeches. It was all nonsense. A Japanese general had even stolen his jewellery. Willans concluded that Sultan Ibrahim would be perfectly willing to serve *under* (a word he stresses in his report) the British. There is a Gilbert & Sullivan feel to all this. The sultan was 'delighted' that the British had come back and hoped he would be permitted to attend the Japanese surrender in Singapore. Later, Willans sent a telegram to SEAC and to the Colonial Office apologising for missing out a detail of his conversation with Sultan Ibrahim. The sultan was 'very nervous about Chinese resistance forces in his state': 'He said that if the BMKA would authorise him he would arm 20,000 Malays to quell the Chinese ...'. Sultan Ibrahim was not quite as genial as he appeared.

Willans ran into more serious trouble in the northern state of Kelantan. Here the old Sultan Sir Ismail had died in June 1944. The Raja of Kelantan, Tunku Ibrahim, the regent and brother of the sultan, was installed on the same day with the approval of the Thai government. The Japanese apparently took against the raja and later ransacked his palace. Although Willans was convinced by Ibrahim's protestations against the Japanese, he was required to inform him that because he had been appointed during the occupation he could no longer be considered sultan until he was formally recognised. He must immediately remove his flag. This must have been grossly humiliating – but the sultan's only anxiety at the time appeared to be whether or not the British would keep up his allowance and how much it would be. As soon as he had been reassured on these points he 'cheered up'. At the end of the month Willans' report about his findings was reassuring. He was certain that the majority of the rulers would agree to sign the new treaties with the possible exception of the Sultan of Perak, who had been 'difficult'.

In the aftermath of Willans' mission it was not only the sultans who felt bruised. For the British, collaboration was a simple moral issue. You had been either for or against; no nuance was conceivable. Collaborators were traitors. The net of innuendo and open accusation spread inexorably. Willans warned Sultan Ibrahim that he would 'enquire into the conduct of Government servants and State notables [...] Their continued employment would depend on whether they had collaborated with the Japanese ...'. The Malay police, which had indeed co-operated with the Japanese occupiers, now suffered near complete moral collapse. In the troubled district of Batu Pahat in Johor, Major A.J. Blake reported that 'the feeling against Malays here was so strong that I had to make a plunge [sic] and do something about it ...'. The taint of collaboration spread like a bad smell. The 'Field Security Section' of the BMA began arresting members of the KMM: Mustapha Hussain was briefly taken into custody but released when former members of the Malay Regiment, whose lives he had saved in Singapore, protested. Ibrahim Yaacob had already fled to Jakarta; other former KMM and KRIS campaigners disappeared. A colonial police state was quietly being reassembled. This at least was a job the BMA could perform well.

In October, MacMichael followed Willan's trail with due pomp and circumstance. Willans had, he hoped, prepared the way: it was now his job to get the new treaties signed. But the sultans had had time to think over what the British were proposing, and in a few states MacMichael ran into serious resistance. The first engagement would take place in Johor. On 18 October, MacMichael was driven from Government House in Singapore across the causeway to the Pasir Plangi Palace. Much depended on the encounter with Sultan Ibrahim. The British were certain that once he signed, the other rulers would follow suit. His agreement was critical. The sultan was, as before, expansively agreeable (though he was 'obviously suffering from gout') and invited MacMichael's party to take tea. After some desultory conversation, MacMichael presented the sultan with the English and Malay versions of the proposed treaty. He read over the English version 'very slowly' and asked some unnervingly astute questions. If he agreed to join the 'Malayan Union' would Johor be obliged to bail out the poorer states? To be sure, MacMichael replied, the rich would help the poor – to their mutual benefit. By the end of the meeting the sultan seemed agreeable. 'These are all right by me,' he declared, gesturing airily at the documents, but he wanted more time to think matters over. A disappointed MacMichael agreed to a delay of two days, but no longer. A second meeting was scheduled for 20 October. This time tea was postponed until business matters had been 'cleared off'. But this time 'there was no hitch or awkwardness,' MacMichael reported. Sultan Ibrahim signed the treaty.

And thus MacMichael's mission proceeded, state by state, teacup by teacup. In Kedah the sultan agreed to sign the treaty, but then:

> ... delivered, standing, a short speech [...] He said that this was the most distressing and painful moment of his whole life. Henceforward, he would lose the loyalty, the respect and the affection of his subjects, and he would be pursued with curses towards his grave by the ill-informed. He called upon Allah to witness his act and protect him for the future ...

By the end of the year MacMichael had secured or compelled the agreement of all the Malay rulers. He had embarked on his mission in the certain knowledge that the British government '*intends to bring the policy into effect*'. Negotiation meant in reality forceful persuasion. The treaties *would* be signed. Behind the chink of tea cups MacMichael was overbearing and insistent. Although he had no prior knowledge of Malaya before he had stepped ashore at Port Swettenham, he embodied the spirit of the new imperialism with punctilious dedication. In the wake of his progress from Johor Bahru to Kota Bahru he left behind bruised Malay emotions – that would in very short order scupper British plans.

Open opposition to the Malayan Union was being vented not only in the royal courts of Johor or Selangor. It swept though the narcoleptic world of London's exclusive clubs, old colonial boy networks and well-upholstered drawing rooms. When the government published the 'White Paper' proposals in January 1946, old Malay hands were enraged. The hated new Labour government was, it seemed, trashing everything that they had built up with such selfless dedication. They had taken up the white man's burden. Now it was being thrown back in their faces. On 26 February, Sir George Maxwell, former chief secretary to the Federated Malay States (FMS), and two former high commissioners, Sir Cecil Clementi and the nonagenarian Sir Frank Swettenham (b.1850), confronted the Secretary of State in his lair at the Colonial Office and made their feelings very clear. Swettenham died the following year – but in a new edition of his book *British Malaya*, a paean to supposedly benevolent colonialism, he had pointedly regretted that the 'early practice of making real friends of the Malay rulers, their chiefs and also their people, seems to have been abandoned'. An army of retired civil servants and businessmen led a vigorous parliamentary and extra-parliamentary campaign to crush this brutal abrogation of the principles of benevolent colonial rule. What angered the anti-Unionists was the abandonment of the Malays, embodied in the proposal of equal citizenship for the Malay races. The underhand strategy of secret planning followed by swift implementation blew up in the faces of the MPU and the Colonial Office. Soon, aggrieved letters sent to London by a number of Malay sultans were read out in the House of Commons.

MacMichael's high-handed treatment of the sultans galvanised Malay opinion. The force of their reaction caught the British on the back foot. The docile Malay, it seemed, had become extinct. Nature's gentlemen were behaving like tigers. The British government stood its ground. Sir Edward Gent, one of the main architects of the plan, made preparations to leave London to be installed as the first governor of the new Malayan Union when the unloved BMA bowed out, appropriately enough, on 1 April 1946. The British had not just provided a focus for Malay protest, they had put the rulers back at centre stage. Even those Malays who had despised the sultans as despotic relics of a feudal past who had no place in a democratic Malaya understood that they were a last defence against the long-feared incursion of non-Malays through the breach of citizenship. If the sultans caved in and signed away their sovereign rights this would fatally undermine the status of all Malays.

It was Dato Onn bin Jaafar, the aristocratic journalist who had stood up to the 'Red Band' Jihadists in Johor, who now stepped forward to seize the leadership of the campaign against the Union. It is important to grasp here that Dato Onn's campaign did not merely set out to defend the rulers. He had come to believe that the traditional bond between the sultan and the people, the *rakyat*, would have to be overhauled. He expressed his idea in a famous slogan: 'the *rakyat* have become the raja, the raja have become the *rakyat*'. This implied that *bangsa* had priority over the ruler; the ruler embodied the *bangsa* but did not stand above it. The sultans should be regarded as custodians of the Malay nation, its servants, not its beneficiaries. Dato Onn's rescripting of Malay nationalism was simultaneously radical and reactionary. His political formula made the sultans servants of the people, but in the same breath reaffirmed the rulers' integral place in Malay political life. The British did not immediately perceive the danger Onn posed to their plans. When he was confronted by Special Branch agents, he eschewed not just the Malayan communists but 'Indonesian interests'. Malays, he inisted, were not 'ready' for independence:

> My plan is to get Malays to put their own house in order and to keep away from communists and Javanese [Indonesian nationalists]. Their affairs are no concern of ours.

The Sungai Remok Estate 2013. This is where the kongsi huts in which the plantation workers and their families lived were located in December 1948.

The road to the murder site on the Sungai Remok Estate near Batang Kali.

The Batang Kali claimants' lawyer Quek Ngee Meng in the cemetery at Hulu Yam Bahru where the murdered workers are buried.

Quek Ngee Meng locates the place where some of the plantation workers were shot dead.

The Scots Guards took groups of plantation workers to the bank of the river.

The dead bodies of the twenty-four plantation workers were brought to this police station in Ulu Yam Bharu.

The dense jungle along the Main Range – the battlefield for the Malayan Emergency.

On 11 December, 1948 a Scots Guards platoon set off from this army camp in Kuala Kubu Bharu.

The British High Commissioner Sir Henry Gurney was assassinated at this turn in the road to Fraser's Hill by MNLA guerrillas led by Siew Mah in October 1951. For many on the government side this was the low point of the war.

Confirmed as Inspector - 1.12.52
$240 per month Basic. Total $340

The young Yuen Yuet Leng, one of the first Chinese police recruits. He was denied Malayan citizenship until he had been 'wounded twice' fighting the communist insurgency. (Tan Sri Yuen Yuet Leng)

Aircraft equipped with loudspeakers to broadcast propaganda to communist guerrillas. (Ministry of Information Communications and Culture (KPKK)

Special Branch officer Tim Hatton inspected the Batang Kali killing site the day after the shootings. He realised immediately that the twenty-four dead men were not communist guerrillas, but plantation workers. He took photographs of the victims and wrote an angry report about what he had discovered. Neither Hatton's report nor the photographs he took have been seen since. (Novista TV)

Malay communist Hassan in a Thai 'Peace Village', 2010.

Malay communist leader Abdullah CD photographed in 2010. He was the leader of the much feared '10th Regiment' that recruited Malays to fight the British.

Left: The classic image of Sir Gerald Templer, who was both High Commissioner and Director of Operations. PM Winston Churchill promised Templer 'more power than Cromwell'. (National Archives, Malaysia)

Below left: Tan Cheng Lock, Straits Chinese leader and once a proud subject of the British Straits Settlements.

Below: Sir Edward Gent, the architect of the disastrous Malayan Union and the first British High Commissioner after the war.

IN AN ENGAGEMENT 22 C.Ts, INCLUDING 3 WOMEN, WERE KILLED BY ½ GURKHA RIFLES SOUTH OF LABIS, JOHORE IN 1949.

The government security forces were obsessed with photographing communists killed in battle, for both propaganda and identification purposes.

Dato Onn bin Jaafar, the leading Malay nationalist after the war until the rise of Tunku Abdul Rahman, and a bitter opponent of the Malayan Union proposal.

Malays campaigning against the Malayan Union in 1945. (Muzium Negara, Kuala Lumpur)

The High Commissioner Sir Henry Gurney was attacked in this Rolls Royce.

Sir Harold Briggs, the author of the 'Briggs Plan' which proposed the forced eviction of more than 1 million Chinese 'squatters'.

A guerrilla brigade during the Second Emergency 1969–89. (Museum Chulaborn)

Guerrillas in a jungle camp in the 1950s.

Chin Peng, the MCP General Secretary meeting Mao Zedong in Beijing after his escape from Malaya.

Chin Peng returns to the Thai Malaysian border during the Second Emergency.

One of the new villages built to accommodate Chinese 'squatters' evicted under the 'Briggs Plan'. Conditions in these camps were often very poor. (Miles Templer)

Roy Follows joined the colonial police in search of adventure. (Roy Follows)

Gus Fletcher when he joined the police in Malaya in 1948. Gus would prove himself an accomplished linguist during his time in Malaya. (Gus Fletcher)

The flamboyant propagandist and PSY-OPS expert C.C. Too with his MG sports car. (Anthony Too)

A wounded terrorist being held at gunpoint after his capture. (IWM)

A Douglas Dakota CI leads a Percival Pembroke CI, Scottish Twin Pioneer CCII and Scottish Aviation Pioneer CCI over a river winding its way through the Malaysian jungle. These aircraft are probably from 209 Squadron, Royal Air Force (RAF), which operated all four types during the Malayan Emergency. Indiscriminate bombing raids on the Malayan jungles may have killed some 5,000 Orang Asli.

This was fine music to British ears. But with the Union plans on the table, Dato Onn would rapidly turn into the most vociferous critic of the Malayan Union – and be the main architect of its demise. Dato Onn saw straightaway that the Union offered him a unique *casus belli* – and a way to bring Malays together to defend their rights and rulers. Immediately after the 'White Paper' was published, he proposed calling a conference of all Malayan associations to settle their differences and oppose the White Paper.

But Malay political emotions were already running ahead of Dato Onn. At a meeting at the Abu Bakr Mosque in Johor Bahru on 1 February, Dato Abdul Rahman bin Mohamed Yassin publicly censured Sultan Ibrahim for signing the MacMichael treaty. His action contravened, he argued, the Johor Constitution of 1898 that expressly forbade the sultan from surrendering the state to any other power or country. This was just what the new White Paper now proposed! There were loud cries of 'Down with the Sultan!' – probably the first time that the words '*down*' and '*sultan*' had ever been heard in the same utterance. Dato Onn was appalled but Sultan Ibrahim, rattled by this unprecedented attack by his Malay subjects, now wrote to the British government claiming that MacMichael had forced him to sign an illegal treaty.

It was in the aftermath of these events that Dato Onn proposed establishing a new party to defend Malay rights – the United Malays Nationalist Organisation, UMNO. So it was that a large number of anxious British officials arrived at the Sultan Suleiman Club in Kampong Bahru in Kuala Lumpur on 1 March 1946 to observe proceedings at the 'Pan Malayan Malay Congress' that had been called by the troublesome Dato Onn. The congress was opened by the Sultan of Selangor, Tengku Sir Hishamuddin. As described earlier, Dato Onn used the congress to announce the formation of the new party. UMNO was the first mass political movement in Malayan history: it was, as Cheah Boon Kheng emphasises, supported to begin with by all the key Malay groups – the rulers and princes, those Malay leftists who had spurned the MNP, Islamic groups, civil servants, police, ex-servicemen, as well as the village Malays, whom no one had imagined could ever be stirred into taking political action. Now they had. Dato Onn had, it will be recalled, cleverly courted the 'wild eyed' Jihadist Kiyai Salleh and his legion of followers. The momentum generated by the establishment of UMNO overwhelmed the more hesitant MNP. The baton had passed to the new party – and would never be given up.

Judging by British reports made in March – less than a month before Gent was due to arrive in Kuala Lumpur to take up his post – there was little sense of the body blow UMNO would shortly deliver to British plans. A report on the Kuala Lumpur congress acknowledged that many delegates were hostile to the idea of the Union: but 'given time and patience, the bulk of opposition could be won over'. Uneducated Malays, the intelligence report concluded, probably had no idea what was in the White Paper – but had been swayed by 'propaganda with a religious tone'.

Over the next few weeks, British alarm rose in pitch. On 23 February 1946, H. T. Bourdillon, head of the Malaya Department at the Colonial Office, referred to 'Malay revulsion' – 'in almost all reactions from popular bodies,' he went on 'it is citizenship which is attacked …'. Giving non-Malays a stake in Malaya was more repellent than the loss of prestige and power by the sultans. Major Hone began to fret that the 'citizenship proposal' might have 'cast its net too wide'. The British had, in short, offered too much to non-Malays. Replying to this, Mr Bourdillon stressed that Gent was certain that any 'concessions or delays' to implementation of the reformed citizenship rules would in turn arouse antagonism from the Indians and Chinese – he did not think that they were at all indifferent to the matter. Gent had got this round the wrong way. For non-Malays the British proposals did not go far enough. It was all very well promising, as one cabinet memorandum put it, 'full political rights in the Malayan Union to all those of whatever race, who regard Malaya as their true home and object of their loyalty' but what did these fine words imply in practice? Would it mean giving up their Indian or Chinese citizenship? While the Malays feared that the reforms would reduce their status to that of Palestinian Arabs or American 'Red Indians', many non-Malays, with the exception of the older Straits communities, appeared to be disinterested in the reforms.

In the early hours of the morning of 31 March 1946, the aircraft carrying Sir Edward Gent, the 'father of the Malayan Union', touched down in Kuala Lumpur. He was driven to King's House where he began to prepare for the ceremony of inauguration. Soon this rather drippy looking fellow was attired in all the ornamental finery of British colonial power. The sultans had in the meantime gathered at the Station Hotel, that lovely Moorish confection near the Padang. On the same day, the 'Pan Malayan Malay Congress' called an emergency meeting and empowered Dato Onn to request that the rulers refuse to attend the ceremony. He was very persuasive. That afternoon the rulers sent a telegram to King's House informing Gent that they would not participate in the inauguration ceremony. The Sultan of Perak took the lead. He assured Gent that no disrespect was intended. But the British proposals, even if they were watered down as Gent implied they might be, represented an unacceptable diminution of their position and prestige. They would, they suggested, accept federation but not union. The sultans insisted that they could not participate in any ceremonies or even to meet Gent publicly because this would imply that they recognised the Union. They emphatically did not. The sultans then adjourned to discuss Gent's suggestion of future consultations but were, as the Sultan of Perak informed Gent, 'unable to vary their discussion'. Gent reported to London that he believed that the rulers were 'embarrassed' and in a 'difficult' position because they had 'put themselves in a position of responsiveness to the new political Malay organisation known as Malay Congress [the embryonic UMNO] …'. The attitude of the Congress (i.e. UMNO) was, he admitted, 'not at all promising'. Mr Bourdillon made it clear that:

... the Sultans are more than ever united in an attitude of polite but categorical [sic] non-cooperation and, secondly, that there is a large measure of unanimity [...] amongst the more thinking Malays ...

The 'Malayan Union' had provided an invigorating shot in the arm for the Malay nationalist movement. By bullying and embarrassing the sultans and, worst of all, making rash promises to non-Malays, the British stiffened up, albeit inadvertently, a chauvinist national movement tied closely to the traditional rulers. The sultans now found themselves holding most of the cards. Their agreement to any reforms was essential. By the end of the month Governor Gent was holding talks at the palace in Kuala Kangsar to try and find out what concessions would satisfy the sultans. Now talk was of federation, not union. The situation was, for now, deadlocked. Gent was unwilling to sacrifice his political baby. The sultans and their political allies in UMNO regarded it as an abomination.

The English poet Alexander Pope coined an aphorism that British colonial administrators took to heart: 'For forms of government, let fools contest/what e'er is best administered is best.' 'May there not be wisdom,' wondered Sir Gilbert Laithwaite in 1953 'in *not* laying down any general constitutional rules?' Pragmatism was preferable to misguided idealism. As Gent flapped about in King's House, the Colonial Secretary in London began to explore ways out of the impasse. So too did another British power broker: Sir Malcolm MacDonald, the Governor General designate in Singapore. MacDonald was unimpressed by Gent and the way he seemed to believe he could rescue the Union by tweaking a few details. He urged him not to proceed 'piecemeal'. He could see that Gent's cherished idea was in its death throes. The sultans had thrown a lifeline by talking about federation – MacDonald had few doubts that it should now be seized. After all, federation was in effect a kind of union but the idea implied a level of state integrity that might satisfy the rulers. The British had been surprised by the co-ordinated, well-organised Malay opposition – and the intransigence of the rulers whose arms they had got so used to twisting. The breach with the Malays needed to be healed. To understand fully the Emergency war that erupted two years later we need to keep that point firmly in mind.

As the Union fracas grumbled on, violence exploded in the British mandate of Palestine. At the Colonial Office, a Mr Hall linked the worsening crisis in the Middle East to the dire consequences of alienating the Malays. On 11 May, Governor Gent finally deciphered the writing on the wall and threw in the towel. On 24–25 July, he and MacDonald held secret talks with the Malay rulers and UMNO representatives. The British agreed to reaffirm their commitment to the rulers' sovereignty and the special position and rights of Malays. The contentious matter of non-Malay citizenship was hurled far into the long grass. The Malay delegates gave some ground. They accepted the need for a strong centralised government to ensure efficient governance. A working party was set up to work out the details of a 'Malayan Federation' – and to bury the 'Malayan Union' without honour. MacDonald noted that:

> Malay opposition is roused as never before. By itself, this is not a bad thing for it is highly desirable that Malays become politically conscious so as to prepare themselves to play appropriate part [sic] in developing self-governing institutions. But it will be extremely unfortunate if this awakened political consciousness and interest gets rail-waded [sic, railroaded?] into extremist and anti British channels ... (21–22 June)

UMNO and the sultans had won the first round. Or so it seemed. Privately, the British patted each other on the back, confident that the new Federation of Malaya still gave them '90 per cent of what they had wanted'. The losers were the Malayan radicals and the unfortunate Sir Edward Gent. His status had been hobbled by what was perceived as an inept response to the Union crisis.

The long-term consequences of the battle of the 'Malayan Union' would be an uneasy rapprochement between the British and the conservative Malay elites. The colonial power now embraced the most reactionary and chauvinist defenders of Malay rights – and it was this united front that would wage war on communism and forge the political identity of an independent Malay. In Malaysian historiography, the bond cemented between the colonial power and the Malay elite is seen in hindsight as a natural alliance. It was in reality the outcome of a fiercely contested struggle that saw the extinction of less well-adapted political ideas. Malay opposition compelled the British to abandon the 'Union' and its promise of broader rights of citizenship. In the future any concessions made to the other Malayan races would have to be on Malay terms. The idea of the Malayan Union was simultaneously a belated attempt to reform inequalities manufactured by the pre-war colonial administration and an instrument of a new imperialism. This freakish anatomy rendered it unviable.

4

THE COMMUNIST DILEMMA

Rewards

On 6 January 1946, crowds gathered in Singapore's Padang witnessed a remarkable spectacle. Eight former commanders of MPAJA regiments, among them the young Chin Peng, departed the once opulent Raffles Hotel, where they had spent the night, and were driven in a gleaming sedan, flanked by motorcycle outriders, to the Municipal Hall. On the grand staircase that swept up to the main entrance, they stood to attention in front of a podium draped with British flags. A band of the Royal Marines played 'Abide with Me'. The young Chinese communists, all in their MPAJA uniforms, waited patiently. Chin Peng recognised a few KMT men, three Malays and a Chinese veteran of Dalforce. The Royal Marines launched into 'See the Conquering Hero Comes' as a line of military vehicles turned into the Padang and headed towards the Municipal hall. Lord Mountbatten, the Supreme Allied Commander, sprang from the lead vehicle, and, smiling broadly, strode towards the flag-draped podium. The ceremony began. Mountbatten spoke warmly of the MPAJA's contribution to the Allied victory. Then he stepped away from the podium and walked down the line of 'Three Star' MPAJA fighters and spoke a few words to each in turn 'thanking him for his selflessness and courage', as Chin Peng remembered. Mountbatten returned to the podium. The names of the medallists were called out and each MPAJA man gave a clenched fist salute as he stepped forward to accept his medals: the Burma Star and the 1939/45 Star. That evening the MPAJA medallists attended a gala cocktail party at Government House. Mountbatten circulated with patrician grace thanking the young communists in mandarin. He wore a glittering decoration on his chest that had been presented to him by the Chinese nationalist leader Chiang Kai-Shek. It was an evening of many ironies. There was, of course, no sign of the British double agent 'Mr Wright' – known to his comrades in the MCP as comrade Lai Tek. He was the all-powerful secretary general of the party.

The Bubbling Pot

As Malays organised to boycott the British proposal for a 'Malayan Union' the communists struggled to reboot their campaign. It was a confusing time for young men like Chin Peng. Mountbatten and the BMA's new 'Chief Chinese Affairs Adviser', the scholarly Victor Purcell, were, in their paternalistic fashion, liberals. They preached tolerance with fervour and practised it with restraint. Purcell was a convinced advocate of Chinese rights and interests (from his service with the 'Chinese Protectorate') and Mountbatten remained in thrall to the Malayan wartime resistance. But when the Malayan communists threw off their roles as war heroes to become obstreperous political nuisances, Purcell's empathy would soon be boiled off in the heat of confrontation.

The history of the MCP in this period is confusing. The official records and Chin Peng's memoir throw only the faintest light on what was happening behind the scenes. Secretary General Lai Tek pursued a policy of appeasement though there is no record of him having significant contact with the British before the beginning of 1946. He could not in any case completely control the political energies released with the end of the war. The MCP was a legal party. It was natural for its members to take advantage of the climate of immiseration, corruption and injustice that the BMA had brought in the wake of reoccupation. The heroic status conferred on the MPAJA by Mountbatten was intoxicating. Since the 'Bintang Tiga', or Three Star, MPAJA warriors had fought and died in the cause of a free Malaya, many communists now spoke confidently as *Malayans* and saw Malaya as the stage of a future revolution that would oust their former British allies. In the Happy Valley amusement park in Singapore, huge crowds gathered to celebrate Gandhi's birth on 2 October 1945. 'Long live Gandhi!' they shouted. But the Mahatma would not have approved of all the raucously proclaimed slogans of the evening: 'Long live the Communists in India! Long live the Malayan Communist Party!' A week later, even bigger crowds paraded round the city on China's National Day. On this gathering tide the MCP founded its first newspaper, *New Democracy*, and began calling for immediate independence. From the beginning, the MCP insisted on a broad front, non-communal strategy, which is why the party poured funds into the Malay language newspaper *Suara Rakyat* ('Voice of the People') and backed the MNP.

A crucial test was the obligatory disbandment of the MPAJA. In September, Force 136 officer John Davis, on behalf of the British 14th Army and the BMA, presented the MPAJA with a detailed schedule of demobilisation. Lai Tek swung the MCP behind the proposals but protracted negotiations, mainly conducted through Davis, proved tough. The most contentious issue was to do with the payment of gratuities to 'retiring' guerrilla fighters. It took until the beginning of December to get this resolved – and the MPAJA formally ceased to exist. As the complicated process of relinquishing arms and ammunition began in earnest, British supervisors noticed that only older types of weapons were being handed in. They suspected, rightly as it turned out, that newer weapons parachuted in at the end of the war by the SOE had been held back and hidden in jungle caches. It will be recalled that in 1944 Lai Tek and Chin Peng had hatched a plan to keep a covert MCP militia in play. That plan appears to have been carried through, though to what extent is hard to assess. In the spring of 1946, British intelligence found out that two MPAJA regiments, one in Perak and the other in Johor, had never demobilised. Then at an old MPAJA hideout near Bekor in Perak, British troops stumbled on a big jungle camp that was still flying a red flag. Uniformed men were busy drilling on an extensive parade ground. The MPAJA did not vanish overnight. Instead it secretly turned into a clandestine insurgent militia: a ghost army in waiting.

In Singapore, the BMA had inspired widespread discontent. A Eurasian, English-educated intellectual called Gerald de la Cruz established a radical non-communist party, the Malayan Democratic Union, headquartered in a corner of the 'Liberty Cabaret' on the North Bridge Road. He called for 'full democratic government for a united Singapore and Malaya in the British Commonwealth'. Though de la Cruz and his co-founders started the new party with a few chairs and a table, by January 1946 they had, with communist backing, gathered enough clout to lead a general strike of more than 150,000 workers. 'We admired the communists for standing up to the Japanese,' admitted de la Cruz. He said in striking contrast to the Malay leaders: 'There was an extraordinary sense of tolerance in that time because what we wanted was [to] all work together in the same direction for self-determination.'

On the other side of the causeway, the MCP seemed to be in hibernation. Chin Peng married his wartime comrade Khoon Wah and though he was 'too busy' to attend the small wedding dinner himself, the couple moved into a comfortable bungalow on Ampang Road in Kuala Lumpur. It came complete with a Japanese piano. Chin Peng wanted this decadent accoutrement removed – but Lai Tek explained that he needed him to resemble the perfect Chinese bourgeois: an 'up-and-coming businessman'. At a local grass-roots level, a younger generation of party activists were showing signs of impatience. As Sukarno and Hatta had found to their cost, party leaders could not always stay on top of their youthful cadres.

As this new generation jostled for a role in the future of Malaya, pressure was mounting on Secretary General Lai Tek. It is notoriously difficult to dislodge communist leaders and Lai Tek had impressive survival skills. There was a murmur of rumours and allegations about his wartime relationship with the Kempeitai, but since the sources of the accusations were usually MCP members who had themselves been forced to 'work with' the Japanese, the dirt failed to stick, even though it was other 'collaborators' who were most likely to know the truth. In September 1945, Lai Tek had been denounced by Ng Yeh Lu in a Chinese newspaper published in Penang. The article had little impact until it came to the attention of Yeung Kuo, the clever young head of the Selangor committee, who

had met Chin Peng at party headquarters back in August when he had delivered
the text of Lai Tek's 'appeasement' strategy. Chin Peng grudgingly complied with
the revised programme but Yeung Kuo objected – and, when he heard about this
heresy, Lai Tek banished him to Penang, which is how he stumbled on Ng Yeh Lu's
'J'accuse'. But Yeung Kuo faced daunting obstacles. Lai Tek was still the revered
'Comintern man'. Denouncing him was tantamount to questioning the wisdom
of Moscow even though Stalin had abolished the Comintern. So Yeung Kuo was
left fuming in Penang. But grave anxieties about the loyalty of the MCP secretary
general were revived when the exalted remains of Lim Bo Seng, the celebrated
SOE agent who had been tortured to death by the Japanese, were disinterred
from Gajah prison in Ipoh and solemnly reburied in Singapore. There were many
KMT supporters who were convinced that Lim had been betrayed – and his
posthumous beatification inspired a tsunami of recrimination that threatened to
engulf the most likely suspect.

The commotion around Lai Tek caught the attention of British intelligence.
The pieces of the 'Mr Wright' puzzle had at last come together. Had 'Chang
Hong', the all-powerful 'Plen' who had negotiated the 'Blantan Agreement' with
SOE agents at the beginning of 1944, been Special Branch's most valuable pre-
war human asset 'Mr Wright'? Before the Japanese invasion, Lai Tek's case officer
had been Frederick Innes Tremlett, who had later become a lieutenant colonel
in Force 136 and head of the 'Malayan Country Section'. On 21 August 1945,
Tremlett sent a report to SEAC referring to:

> the Sino-Vietnamese known by the pseudonym of Lai Te [sic], who took over
> the Communist Party of Malaya. Lai Te arrived Singapore late 1932 and became
> Communist Party of Malaya Secretary General 1938. The British identified him
> as ethnic Vietnamese as well as CPM's [MCP's] most secret agent and revered
> personality. He is a shrewd and clever man but no fanatic.[31]

A few weeks after sending that report Tremlett was killed when the RAF
Liberator flying him back to SEAC headquarters in Kandy in Ceylon went down
in the Bay of Bengal. Tremlett took with him the secret of 'Mr Wright'. In the
period after the Japanese surrender, the case of Lai Tek flickers in and out of focus.
On 24 September, Victor Purcell and other BMA officials met a man called 'Chan
Hoon', who promised to use his influence with the communists and MPAJA. At
a subsequent meeting he introduced BMA officials to a local MCP leader whom
he called Wu Tian Wang. Purcell was impressed by the co-operative attitude of
both. Then 'Chan Hoon' disappeared again. At the beginning of 1946, as Secretary
General Lai Tek emerged from the shadows of the MCP, the 'Malayan Security
Service' (MSS) evidently concluded that it was high time loose intelligence ends
were tied up. Was this Lai Tek the old 'Mr Wright'? A new investigation was begun
under the aegis of Major R.J. Isaacs. He soon began sounding alarm bells. Isaacs

confirmed once and for all that 'Mr Wright', 'Lai Tek' and 'Chang Hong' were one and the same person. He had, it might be said, found his Mr Wright. But then came another strange and unexpected turn of events. One of the key informants Major Isaacs had been interrogating committed suicide. Isaacs immediately got in touch with Major Blades of the MSS and Victor Purcell. Isaacs was terrified that if an inquest was required he would be obligated to show his hand. Frustratingly the documentary trail goes cold at this point – and Isaacs' investigation vanishes in a puff of archival dust.

As Isaacs puzzled over the mystery of Lai Tek, grumbling anger with the BMA burst into the open. On 10 October, tens of thousands of Chinese Malayans celebrated 'National Day' with processions and mass meetings orchestrated by the communists. In such a febrile atmosphere, a single incident can take on unexpected resonance and shape future developments in unintended ways. On 12 October, the RAF police arrested a prominent communist called Soong Kwong and charged him with intimidation and extortion. It was alleged that at the beginning of September – the date was important – Soong Kwong had abducted a rich Chinese merchant called Chan Sau Meng, a notorious collaborator, and demanded $300,000 on pain of death. To save his life the terrified gentleman had written a *promissory* note for the sum demanded and handed over jewellery and cash worth some $32,000. But he had then reneged on the deal and gone to the police. Soong Kwong was immediately arrested. He was no Robin Hood and the story was pretty sordid. But in the eyes of many Chinese the kidnapping was natural justice. The supposed victim was a traitor: he deserved, it was thought, much worse. All this had happened *before* 12 September, the date on which the BMA had officially taken over and agreed to a kind of statute of limitations concerning offences committed during the Interregnum. Soong Kwong should never have been arrested in the first place. The case became a cause célèbre.

On 15 October, the MCP organised a mass protest in central Kuala Lumpur to demand comrade Soong Kwong's release. In Perak, a crowd of at least 3,000 demonstrated in Ipoh. There was a wave of strikes and stoppages. The most serious incident took place in the small town of Sungai Siput, the 'worm river', in northern Perak. On 21 October, 5,000 people gathered in the 'New World' amusement park and then marched to local government offices. This was protected by a small platoon of British soldiers. When the crowds refused to disperse they began firing – killing one man and wounding a number of others. Three years later, communist squads killed three British plantation managers on estates not far from Sungai Siput: the first shots of the 'Emergency war'. Chin Peng has always maintained that the war really began that day in Sungai Siput.

The Soong Kwong case kept the political stew bubbling. The ideological gloves were slowly being pulled off. Chinese newspapers denounced the arrest as a typical colonial injustice. The complainant, Chan Sau Meng, had, it was alleged, been an agent in league with the much-feared Japanese Kempeitai chief in Selangor. 'Is the confiscation of the property of traitors and Japanese underlings extortion?' demanded an editorial in *Min Sheng Pau*.

For Malayan nationalists the arrest and prosecution of Soong Kwong showed that British liberalism was a sham. For Lai Tek the abrupt darkening of the political mood was alarming. It strengthened the hand of the party radicals, the very people who had denounced him as a traitor. The old pretender had not yet given up the fight, and he was well adapted to tight corners. He was still respected by many in the party's old guard. This was demonstrated at the end of 1945 when Lai Tek's devotees organised a campaign in the Chinese-language press that celebrated his political feats and slandered his accusers as 'fascist remnants'. The campaign was well orchestrated. A consortium of influential Chinese associations sent a joint telegram to MCP headquarters lauding Lai Tek as the saviour of the 'five million people of Malaya [...] your life and health are of deep concern to us all [...] we request you give us more guidance.' Lai Tek was happy do so. His comeback campaign was a resounding success. He soon had a chance to show he had no reason to let go the reins of power. At the beginning of 1946, the 'Eighth Enlarged Plenum of the Central Working Committee' of the MCP met in Kuala Lumpur. This was Lai Tek's chance to seize back the leadership of the party and outflank his young critics. And it is hard not to be impressed by his consummate political skills. He made a long speech that cleverly nodded to impatient militants:

> During these past few months in Malaya, there has been an outbreak of strikes, demonstrations and economic struggles of the 500,000 peasants, workers, youths and intellectuals, manifesting their desires and demands for a democratic system and a better livelihood [...] The Malayan people are under colonial rule. The struggle of the Malayan revolution remains: complete liberation and complete independence of the nation [...] We the MCP must carry on a 'New Democratic Movement' ...

Lai Tek reaffirmed the 'United Front' policy of seeking alliances and building up mass organisations, trade unions and youth movements. He insisted, to loud cheers, that 'Malaya's revolutionary movement is preparing conditions for a high tide of anti-imperialism ...'. At the end of the plenum, Lai Tek was near unanimously re-elected as Secretary General of the MCP. He had quashed his critics – for now.

For the British, the reappearance of 'Mr Wright' was of great interest. Could he be persuaded to cool once more the simmering Malayan cauldron? The wave of strikes and demonstrations showed no sign of abating. As soon as the business of the plenary meeting had been concluded the MCP Central Committee called a general protest strike for 29 January under the auspices of a new 'Pan Malayan General Labour Union'. As the Malayan radicals prepared for this first great trial of strength, the Soong Kwong case was approaching its climax in a military courtroom presided over by a British judge and two Malay 'assessors'. Soong Kwong had already been tried twice. The British judges had sought a guilty verdict with dogged persistence but had twice been overruled by the 'assessors', who recommended acquittal. This was intolerable. At a third and final trial, the assessors were dismissed on the grounds that they had been intimidated, and were replaced by two military judges. Now the matter was settled quickly without fuss. Soong Kwong was pronounced guilty and sentenced to four years imprisonment. As he was led away he hurled his prison issue slippers in the direction of the judges. The conduct of the trial by the British was unashamedly vindictive. But Malayan radicals had a new hero. The BMA now turned on the people Lord Mountbatten had decorated. A troop of British soldiers broke into the offices of a number of Chinese associations and ripped down pictures of Chiang Kai-Shek. At least thirty other former MPAJA heroes were now locked up in Pudu Gaol. A cloud of brooding fury descended on Malaya and Singapore: political lightning flickered on the horizon.

Mountbatten was now headquartered in Singapore. He was no friend to British colonial judges. He was dismayed by the way in which the BMA had pursued Soong Kwong and he contemplated ordering his immediate release. It was at this moment, as Mountbatten pondered, that tens of thousands downed tools or left their workplaces. Markets froze; factories and harbour wharfs fell silent; great masses of demonstrators poured through the streets to the Padang. The MCP called for a general strike. Mountbatten could not afford to appear to be intimidated, so Soon Kwong stayed locked up in his cell. Then, quite suddenly, on the eve of Chinese New Year the great wave of protest ebbed. The general strike was called off. The new labour unions claimed victory – but the sudden collapse was puzzling. Support had been ebbing, to be sure, but had 'Mr Wright', some wondered, pulled a few strings?

Mountbatten now ordered the release of Soong Kwong. His release could look like a gesture of mercy rather than fear. But it seemed to many that the communist barbarians were at the gates of empire. Some counselled compromise: 'if force were to be used, it would be disastrous for here and for the Empire as a whole.' But many demanded tougher measures. The powerful planters' associations made their views clear: they wanted 'more flogging and hanging'. Richard Broome, the former Force 136 officer, openly denounced the MCP claiming that he knew well how they thought: 'the great majority of the leaders are after nothing else but trouble, and gratification of the lust for power …'. he ranted to Mountbatten. The MCP was not cowed for very long. They proposed commemorating the date of the British surrender, 15 February, as 'National Humiliation Day' – a taunt that was too much for Mountbatten. His paternalist style of liberalism had limits and they had been breached. There was a widespread sense that a crisis point had been reached. Victor Purcell did not pull any punches:

It cannot be disguised that the Forces in Malaya [the BMA in other words] are at present very unpopular with the people [...] in Singapore, the rudeness and high handedness of some of the officers, the careless way in which vehicles are often driven, and the ill discipline of many troops are common subjects of conversation [...] It is very hard for a newcomer to detect this attitude among a population who are masters of restraint – indeed self repression – until they explode in uncontrolled hysteria [...] It may seem too ungrateful that the natives [sic] should feel in this way towards the Army that has liberated them. But they do not look at it like that.

There had to be ringleaders. Could they be persuaded to back down? The MSS had only the vaguest idea of the identities of party leaders. What role was the MCP playing? What *was* the MCP? Who was in charge? Was anyone? So when Lai Tek staged his comeback at the plenary meeting it was if a light had at last been switched on at the top of a dark staircase. The Special Branch re-established contact with 'Mr Wright'. Although the documentary evidence is sparse and inconclusive, Lai Tek now seems to have resumed his role as 'Mr Wright'. Throughout 1946 and well into 1947 he was periodically debriefed, probably by Major Isaacs. The British hoped to use Lai Tek to counter the militant elements in the MCP, described in an intelligence report as 'hot headed youth elements'.

'Mr Wright', however, seemed to have lost his way. He seemed incapable of reining in the radicals. The jittery BMA hardened its position – and the 'hang-'em-and-flog-'em' party now had Mountbatten's ear. British wrath fell most heavily on the Chinese. On 13 February, the BMA issued public warnings that anyone interfering with the 'due course of the law' by calling strikes would be 'repatriated to the country of their origin or their citizenship'. This was aimed at Indonesian radicals as well as Chinese. The proclamation had an immediate impact: the big demonstration was called off. But on 15 February a smaller protest was organised close to the centre of Singapore. British police and troops fell on the little group armed with that traditional colonial tool, the lathi. An 18-year-old student called Lin Feng Chow was killed. The next day, 5,000 mourners attended his funeral. The BMA stubbornly held the line. Repatriation heralded a new phase of open repression. All over Malaya, British troops struck at strikers and demonstrators.

In Singapore, the SEAC supremo dithered. As Major Hone, the tougher-minded head of the BMA, realised, poor Mountbatten wanted to be remembered as a liberator not a represser. The communists were really just decent chaps: he had given them some nice shiny medals. It was Purcell, the former Protector of Chinese, who expressed the new spirit most forcefully. He had been shocked when his Chinese servants had refused to serve him on the day of the general strike. He concluded: 'we must prevent them [sic] taking charge of the country or abdicate'. He reserved his most vitriolic analysis for his journal:

The ideal human being boils down to the moronic: the adenoidal, the unwashed, the scrofulous, the naked, the illiterate, the dumb and above all the passive and the victimised: until Malaya produces her own leaders and her own sense of civic responsibility (which sometimes seems a thousand miles away) we must continue to accept the responsibility of governing ...

Purcell left Malaya soon after writing that entry. He had not quite washed its tropical soils from his shoes: he would return a few years later to excoriate the conduct of the British Emergency war.

The Downfall

Although Lai Tek had inveigled himself back into power, a lot of thick and dirty smoke continued to swirl around the secretary general inside the party. It was hard to believe that there was not a fire. Yeung Kuo was convinced that Lai Tek had been a traitor – and could well be still working hand in glove with the British. But Chin Peng was reluctant to make a move against the man who had propelled him to the top ranks of the party. Then a respected party member called Huang Yeh Lu sent a letter to the Central Committee that denounced Lai Tek and offered detailed and convincing evidence of the secretary general's dealings both with Special Branch before the war and the Kempeitai during the occupation. Was Huang's evidence reliable? Who *was* he?[32] It turned out that Huang had himself been betrayed and forced to work as an 'analyst and translator' for the Kempeitai. He spoke and read Japanese. In the course of his duties Huang had come across a story in a Japanese police magazine about a Kempeitai agent who was a top-level communist. From telltale details in the article, Huang deduced that this individual could only be Lai Tek. Still, Chin Peng was not entirely convinced. Huang was a somewhat tainted witness; he too had been 'turned' by the Japanese. But if the scales had not yet fallen from Chin Peng's eyes, they were loosening.

In mid-October, Chin Peng's father, Wong Sing Piaw, arrived in Kuala Lumpur on his way to Penang. He suggested that his son accompany him. He surely needed a break. It was a chance to get to know each other again. Another lure was that Chin Peng's wife, Khoon Wah, and their new baby daughter had recently moved to Penang to stay with her mother. So he borrowed the MCP's Austin 8, confiscated from the Japanese, and drove north with Sing Piaw. Chin Peng was not in a relaxed frame of mind. Lai Tek was very much on his mind. His doubts came to a head when he met up with a Yeung Kuo and the two comrades took a bus to Tanjong Bunga on Penang's north-eastern coast. As they sipped iced coffee by the beach, Yeung Kuo blurted:

'He's an international spy.'

'What proof do you have?' demanded Chin Peng.

'He worked for the British before the war. He was a Japanese agent during the occupation. I know that. Now he's back working with the British again.'

Yeung Kuo's evidence was certainly disturbing. Look at how often Lai Tek had evaded police raids. After one swoop, when he had been picked up, he had been released without being questioned. Why? What about the Batu Caves massacre? Lai Tek should have been at the meeting. His car had broken down. Convenient! The two young men fell silent. The sun pounded down on the glittering white sand of the beach. Chin Peng finally spoke: 'We have to expose him.'

That conversation took place in October 1946. Chin Peng seems to have vacillated. But his old mentor was feeling the pressure. The tightrope he had trodden for so long was at last fraying. In December, Lai Tek called a Central Committee meeting in Kuala Lumpur at a house on Ampang Road. Chin Peng and the other committee members sat at a long table wondering what their leader would have to say. Was he about to confess? His announcement astonished everyone. Lai Tek declared that he planned to 'take a holiday': he was ill and needed time to 'improve his Chinese'. He heaped praise on Chin Peng and said he would leave the party in his capable hands while he was on vacation. Chin Peng lost his temper: 'Stop praising me! I don't measure up to these words.' Astonishingly, Lai Tek burst into tears. This lachrymose response got him off the hook, though he was clearly at breaking point and Chin Peng was reprimanded. And he had, of course, blown his cover. Lai Tek made his excuses and left. None of the delegates at the Ampang meeting that night would ever see him again.

And yet the denouement came with glacial slowness. In late January 1947, the MCP Central Committee summoned Lai Tek to appear at a special meeting. It was time to confront the inferno of rumour. Even now Chin Peng fully expected that the secretary general would turn up and somehow explain everything away. On the appointed morning, Chin Peng and the other delegates began assembling at the safe house on Ampang Road. They waited a long time. At the head of the meeting table, Lai Tek's chair was mockingly empty. A decision was eventually made to track down the missing secretary general. Perhaps he had been involved in an accident? Lai Tek still spent a lot of time in Singapore but the party had provided him with a modest bungalow in Gombak near Kuala Lumpur – which was, with unintended irony, not far from the Batu Caves. He lived there with his Chinese 'wife', Jang Sueh Yong, who at the time was pregnant. She had been the 'messenger' who, four years before, had escorted Chin Peng to his first meeting with Lai Tek in that hilltop villa. Chin Peng and Ah Dian, a Central Committee member who remained stubbornly loyal to Lai Tek, drove to the Gombak bungalow to find out what had gone wrong. When they got to the house, a very surprised Jang Sueh Yong told them that at least an hour earlier her husband had taken breakfast and then driven off in the direction of Ampang. She was surprised that he had not turned up. Chin Peng's first thought was that he must have betrayed them all to the British Special

Branch. They could all be arrested at any moment. Now, as in a classic detective story, Chin Peng had a breakthrough.

A few months earlier, a party of Viet Minh communists had come to Kuala Lumpur on their way to a meeting in Singapore with none other than Lai Tek. He had helped them recruit more than 600 volunteers in Singapore, set up three secret weapons caches along the coast of Johor and arranged a boat with a full crew to get them back across the South China Sea to the Ca Mau Peninsula. Shortly after Lai Tek's baffling disappearance, the Viet Minh party returned to Kuala Lumpur. They had found out that the landing site arranged by Lai Tek was swarming with soldiers. It seemed very likely that the whole deal was a sting and they, too, very much wanted to talk to the secretary general. Chin Peng was forced to admit that neither he nor anyone else in the party knew anything about Lai Tek's whereabouts. He suspected that he had been kidnapped by the Special Branch. The Viet Minh delegation laughed loud and long. They did not think this was very likely. Perhaps Chin Peng had seen too many movies? They told Chin Peng that there was a comrade in Singapore who could tell him everything that he needed to know about Lai Tek.

We have no idea who this man was – Chin Peng just tells us that he was a middle-class intellectual. But whoever he was, he was more than willing to talk. He revealed that long before the war Lai Tek had worked for French intelligence agencies in Indochina and, threatened with exposure, fled to Singapore. He was an incorrigible turncoat. The informer confirmed that Lai Tek had become an agent for the British Special Branch and then, after the Japanese invasion, for the Kempeitai. Chin Peng was introduced to other Vietnamese who knew much more. The puritanical young man was shocked to discover that Miss Jang was Lai Tek's *fourth* wife. Lai Tek was using party funds to rent an apartment in the Hill Street area of Singapore, where he had installed a mistress. Not content with this arrangement Lai Tek had settled another woman in a third party-funded love nest. He was also, it seemed, a profligate gambler and bon vivant. No wonder Lai Tek had experienced so many difficulties reaching the MPAJA camp at Blantan.

When he was summoned to the Ampang bungalow Lai Tek had long realised that the game was up. Some weeks before, he had ordered the party 'State Secretaries' to send all their surplus funds to the main office in Kuala Lumpur – to himself in other words. The MCP was hoarding a fortune. The British had handed over a small fortune in gold bars and sheets and more than 100,000 Straits dollars. Then, after the Japanese surrender, the MPAJA had appropriated a vast tonnage of raw rubber that had been stockpiled by the Japanese and sold it on at a huge profit. From this gold and rubber windfall, Lai Tek pocketed at least 1 million Straits dollars. When he fled Kuala Lumpur, he took with him the entire contents of the party coffers.

Lai Tek had smoothed Chin Peng's rise to power. So it is surprising that instead of being tainted by his mentor's crimes, Chin Peng was elected as the new secretary general. He was just 23. But the Lai Tek crisis was not over. The MCP needed those purloined funds. At a meeting on 6 March, the new politburo agreed that the newly elected party leader, Chin Peng, should lead the search for Lai Tek. In early July, Chin Peng took the train from Kuala Lumpur to Butterworth, where he changed onto the Bangkok line. In the Thai capital, Chin Peng found a cheap hotel and began contacting local communists. His plan was to stay two weeks and if he found no trace of the renegade he would fly on to Hong Kong. As Chin Peng was coming back from the Cathay Pacific office on a trishaw, he noticed a short gentleman in the shadows on the other side of the hot, crowded street. He was buying cigarettes and had his back turned. But there was something familiar about the squat posture and the delicate way the man took the packet with a delicate gesture ... Could it be Lai Tek? Chin Peng shouted at the trishaw man to stop. The man in the shadows turned and lit up, blinking in the acrid smoke. It seemed as if he was looking directly at Chin Peng. There could be no doubt. It was the fugitive, standing just yards away. Chin Peng ordered the trishaw driver to turn round. But his quarry had leapt into a motorised tuk-tuk that roared off in a cloud of oily smoke. Chin Peng rushed to the offices of the Vietnamese Communist Party in Sukhumvit and told the comrades about his sighting. He was certain it was Lai Tek. It would be hard for any Vietnamese gone to ground in Bangkok to avoid detection. Still, Lai Tek had vanished once again.

What happened next has become clear only recently. For years afterwards the fate of Lai Tek remained a mystery. Some intelligence experts claimed that the British Special Branch had whisked him off to Hong Kong and provided him with a 'new identity'. One historian suspected that he was still active in 'Siamese Communist circles'. It was only in 1998 that Chin Peng, by then exiled in Bangkok, finally revealed to Chinese newspaper reporters the fate of the 'Lenin of Asia'. Lai Tek had bowed out of history not with a bang but a muffled whimper. A Viet Minh hit squad had tracked him down to a squalid hotel that backed onto a rubbish-filled stream. Lai Tek had put up quite a fight. One of the Vietnamese agents awkwardly strangled him. The traitor of traitors was dead. At the back of the shop house the assassins found a few lengths of hessian. They bundled up the corpse in these rags and then waited for dark. As soon as night fell, they heaved the still warm body of Lai Tek, enshrouded in hessian, into the Chao Praya River. The bundle of rags floated away into darkness – and out of history.

The Inheritance of Betrayal

So ended the remarkable life of one of the most enigmatic and, it must be said, *influential* secret agents in twentieth-century intelligence history – the puppet master of Malayan communism. Lai Tek had done sterling clandestine service for French, British and Japanese intelligence agencies and government. He had a significant impact on the wartime strategy and identity of the Malayan communists and the MPAJA. It is odd that Chin Peng did not accompany the squad to positively identify Lai Tek and confront him about his betrayal. Perhaps it was he who strangled Lai Tek. He will take that secret to his grave. We have no idea at all why the British Special Branch abandoned their 'Mr Wright' to his fate. No one ever discovered what happened to the fortune that Lai Tek stole from the party coffers. Perhaps General Fang Fang knew more. Years before, Freddy Spencer Chapman summed up his impressions of Lai Tek:

> I personally find a character like that – a person who has spent the whole of his life as an informer or traitor, or whatever word you like to use, for one side or the other, then doubly, develops a strange sort of character. You can't dislike a man intensely just because of that – you've got to look behind and understand a certain amount about it. And I don't think Lai Teck let *us* down, we couldn't have got anywhere without him.

Lai Tek served the British well but he grievously wounded the Malayan communist movement. His betrayals cut a murderous swathe through the ranks of the best and the brightest. As Chin Peng bitterly recalled in his memoirs, it was Lai Tek who in August 1945 snatched away an historic chance to form a broad alliance of Malayans to strike at the returning colonial power. Imagine for a moment that Lenin had pulled back from the brink in October 1917 and then been exposed as an agent of the Tsar's secret police. The course of Russian history would have flowed in a very different direction. But Lai Tek was no Lenin. The difficulties faced by the MCP leadership following his exposure and flight reflected less tractable weaknesses in both the organisation of the party, its doctrine and its place in Malayan society. The Chinese communists had failed to solve the nationalist issue. In his memoirs Chin Peng states that he became committed to forging a Malayan republic. We know that in the aftermath of the Japanese surrender tentative links were made with Malays and Indians. The evidence suggests, however, that the MCP had not made the leap to a fully mature nationalism. This failure was reflected, in part at least, in the way the MCP was perceived by the British and Malays as a *Chinese* party. This perception undermined the MCP's efforts to build a political united front. In short, they had an image problem. But the image reflected reality.

The different Chinese communities in Malaya were torn between very different perceptions of national identity. This is why some British commentators incorrectly concluded that the Chinese were 'indifferent' to the idea of the Malayan Union. Under the new non-racial citizenship proposals some 80 per cent of the Chinese in Malaya would have qualified for a political stake in the Union – and a future independent Malaya. This raised troubling questions. Would Malayan citizenship weaken bonds with the Chinese nation or *guojia*? Was there a distinctly Chinese Malayan identity? For many, the simple question was whether or not it would be permissible for 'Malayans' to hold more than one passport. But the Chinese press, which had been reinvigorated when the Japanese occupation ended, became an arena of often feverish philosophical debate. The powerful Chinese business community preached pragmatism. Forget about being 'Overseas Chinese' and focus on winning freedom in Malaya. Some argued that the Chinese reform themselves: that 'the foundation of an interracial unity for all races lies in the unity of the Chinese themselves ...'. In other words, if the Chinese communities remained divided among themselves what hope was there for a racially unified Malaya? Some argued that the Chinese had written a 'testimony in blood' under the Japanese and not only deserved recognition for that but would dominate a future Malayan People's Republic: Malays after all were migrants from Indonesia. In Singapore the MCP tried to influence the debate through the Malayan Democratic Union (MDU) – the founding party of the All Malayan Council of Joint Action (AMCJA) that campaigned for a united Malaya, including Chinese-dominated Singapore, based on common citizenship. Under the veteran Straits Chinese leader Tan Cheng Lock the AMCJA reached out to radical Malays like Ahmad Boestamam, who were troubled by the exclusive racial doctrines of UMNO. But UMNO leaders very effectively smeared the Malays aligned with the AMCJA by accusing them of 'selling out' to non-Malays. Most beat a hasty retreat to form yet another nationalist party, the Pusat Tenaga Rakyat (PUTERA). UMNO may have provoked the split, but the short-lived alliance foundered on very different ideas of the nation and community.

The fissiparous state of Chinese nationalism made it very difficult for the MCP to grasp the nationalist baton. Contrariwise, Malay nationalists had, by the end of the occupation, outpaced the Malayan communists. This might sound like an historical truism. It was in fact a surprising outcome. Before December 1941, the KMM was an obscure Johnny-come-lately in the nationalist landscape of Southeast Asia. Its leadership had proved too immature and inept to exploit the Japanese as cleverly as Sukarno had done in Indonesia. Following the debacle of the aborted declaration of independence in August 1945, KMM leaders like Mustapha Hussain and Ibrahim Yaacob fled the scene. The collapse of the KMM and the KRIS movement cleared the way for a charismatic new national leader to emerge in the shape of Dato Onn bin Jaafar. After proving himself in the confrontation with the Johor Jihadists, Onn seized on the Malayan Union plan to focus and define Malay nationalism and rally Malay nationalists and Malay rulers – the sultans and the people. The formation of UMNO as a Malay nationalist mass movement was in effect a civil *coup d'état* that decisively outflanked the Malayan communists. The upshot was that in the aftermath of the Malayan Union struggle it was the MCP that looked like the new kids on the nationalist block: the Malays had streaked ahead. In the next decade the MCP would fall even further behind as the conservative Malay leaders of the UMNO behemoth exploited the Emergency to tar *all* radical movements with the brush of the 'communist menace'. The new UMNO leadership that emerged under Kedah aristocrat Tunku Abdul Rahman at the beginning of the next decade deftly wielded the draconian laws and regulations of the colonial security apparatus to buttress the Malay elites. The radical Ishak Haji Muhammad saw this coming:

> You must know that according to these gentleman, we are all communists and agents of Uncle Stalin. This red baiting against the progressive movement is part of the attempt to pave the way for the suppression of the progressive movement in the name of 'public interest and security'.

5

THE ROAD TO REVOLT

The Uneasy Federation

As the new Burmese prime minister, Thakin Nu, celebrated independence in Rangoon, the sultans of the nine Malay states gathered in their pomp at King's House in Kuala Lumpur. A long procession of luxury automobiles purred through the gates and crunched across the immaculate gravel drive. The Malayan Union was dead: long live the Federation! Governor Gent was now High Commissioner of the Federation of Malaya. The sultans' glittering display of pomp asserted – or so it seemed – the old Malay order. The inauguration ceremony was a triumph of ornamentalism, enhanced by techniques borrowed from Hollywood. There was just one hitch. The Sultan of Perak insisted that the signing be completed by midday. The sultan had, it transpired, a horse running in the 5.30 race. The high commissioner's staff only just made the deadline. This is how Gent blithely reported the proceedings:

> We had tremendous fun and games here yesterday with the signing of the State and Federation agreements [...] with everyone dressed up to the nines and the Malays looking most magnificent and myself a picture of purity in my white uniform. The whole show was accompanied by a Hollywood atmosphere of brilliant lights and movie cameras [...] The temperature in the room here at King's House finally was about 150 degrees, what with the filming lights and the natural atmosphere in this part of the world in the afternoon [...] We all had our fingers crossed in case Dato Onn [...] should turn sour on any particular point [...] However, it went with a swing before he had time to raise his usual series of grouses [...] He maintains a barracking on every conceivable action of this government, mostly fruitless and childish, but he is very alert for any possible ground for offence.

The truth was that a new generation of Malay leaders led by UMNO leader Dato Onn bin Jaafar was asserting newfound powers behind the scenes. Dato Onn was still haggling for further concessions to Malay rights right up to the last minute, and Gent, the new high commissioner and architect of the 'Malay Union' plan, had not been forgiven.

Unite and Quit?

Gent had been humiliated by both MacDonald and UMNO but the British government was not altogether dismayed by the awkward demise of the 'Malayan Union'. The long-term plan was to 'unite and quit', leaving behind a successor state that would continue to sustain the globalised economy of empire. The Union debacle had not moved the goalposts very far. The same game was being played and, as the devious Commissioner General MacDonald smugly observed, the Federation was a victory of sorts. The grand plan simply had to be tweaked. The British had been forced to concede to a Malay national movement that had always been defined by fear of Chinese dominance and extinction of the bangsa. The 'idealistic' ingredients of the Malayan Union scheme would need to be modified. They would not be ditched. British anxiety about communal conflict, which had already afflicted Palestine and India and which threatened to derail the entire 'unite and quit' project, meant that some kind of reconciliation was still regarded as desirable – indeed necessary. The population of Singapore was dominated by the Chinese, and the global plans of both Britain and the United States depended on maintaining this Southeast Asian fortress. So the Chinese could not be ignored, but in Malaya their interests would have to be clearly subordinated to those of Malays. This would mean purging the Chinese community of its most radical elements so that Malays would eventually accept some kind of alliance. The upshot of this calculation was that the British would have to take on, sooner or later, their one-time ally – the Malayan communists.

In the short term, anxiety about communal conflict could be exploited to justify staying put. 'Divide and rule' is a cliché of imperial history. The case was made very clearly by Churchill in February 1940 who:

> ... said that he did not share the anxiety to encourage and promote unity between the Hindu and Moslem communities [in India]. Such unity was, in fact, almost out of the realm of practical politics, while if it were brought about, the immediate result would be that the united communities would join in showing us the door. He regarded the Hindu–Moslem feud as a bulwark of British rule in India.

Later it was noted that 'Winston rejoiced in the quarrel that had broken out afresh between Hindus and Moslems, said he hoped it would remain bitter and bloody ...'. The reformers of the 'Malayan Planning Unit' did not completely share Churchill's grisly views but they recognised the expediency of communal quarrelling as a justification for holding onto their most valuable colonial possessions. With the loss of India, Malaya was without any doubt the top imperial performer.

Ever since the foundation of the East India Company in the early seventeenth century, European colonial conquest had been driven by profit. Imperialism had manufactured a globalised market whose profits flowed into the coffers of the European powers in London, Paris, Berlin and The Hague. In Britain, the collapse of the East India Company after the great uprising in India led to a moral reconfiguration of colonial enterprise. Empire builders talked of bringing good governance to native peoples. The new imperialism was not entirely bogus, but good governance was principally a mechanism to streamline the flow of native labour and profit. Colonial reform was driven by hard-headed fiscal calculation. It has become a cliché of British history to say that 'we won the war but lost the peace'. The defeat of the Axis powers had, of course, mainly been the achievement of the Soviet Union and the United States. Britain was wounded by victory. The new Labour government was committed to a programme of expensive domestic reform as it staggered under the unrelieved burden of five years of war. Post-war colonial policy reflected the severely weakened state of the British economy. The battle with the Indian nationalist movements could no longer be afforded. Independence at least in part was a consequence of fiscal realism. For the United States, the war had been highly profitable. Britain had become a debtor nation and the American dollar had replaced sterling as the most powerful global currency. Since Britain had exhausted its foreign currency reserves there was a desperate need to accumulate dollars. In a telegram sent to 'all Colonies' on 20 August 1947, the Colonial Secretary spelled out what had to be done:

> … our present financial position is one of comparative, though we believe temporary, weakness. But against that weakness can be placed the underlying permanent strength which can be drawn […] from the natural resources and people of this country and those its overseas connections.

So Britain demanded the 'whole-hearted co-operation of the Governments and people of the Colonies …'. India could no longer be afforded, but Malayan tin and rubber had the potential to earn the dollars Britain needed so desperately. The new Federation, however compromised, would streamline the economy and new investments worth at least £86 million would gush into Malayan rubber estates and tin mines. For Asian nationalists, including the leaders of the Malayan Communist Party, it was evident that the failure of the 'Malayan Union' had no impact at all on the determination on the old colonial power to tighten its iron grip on Malayan resources for its own ends.

The Plan to Revolt

On the very same day that the Malay sultans and their sycophantic attendants paraded into King's House to inaugurate the new Federation, Chin Peng and the MCP Central Committee were locked in debate at their Klyne Street headquarters. As British guns fired round after celebratory round on the Padang, sending flocks of startled pigeons clattering and wheeling into the warm and curdled tropical air, one of the more articulate politburo members rose to his feet: 'I feel we have tried our best [...] We have used every peaceful means to further the cause of the masses [...] Yet we have had no impact whatever ...'. For the Malayan communists, who had refused to support the 'Malayan Union', the new Federation was a political nadir: the Malay–British alliance was in the ascendant. They had decisively lost the first round. Protest, strikes, demonstrations – these tactics had all failed. The struggle had to be ramped up. Many frustrated Asian nationalists had come to the same grim conclusion.

In 1948, violent uprisings exploded across Southeast Asia in Indonesia, Burma and Vietnam. The Labour government in London, as well as a later generation of historians, interpreted this chain reaction as evidence of a Soviet plot: the fuse of revolt had surely been lit in Moscow. British foreign policy was now dominated by the imperatives of anti-communism. In the minds of Prime Minister Clem Attlee and Foreign Secretary Ernest Bevin, the idea that Asian rebels had received instructions from agents of the Cominform made sense. In March 1946, the former prime minister, Winston Churchill, had sonorously warned:

> From Stettin in the Baltic to Trieste in the Adriatic an iron curtain has descended across the Continent. Behind that line lie all the capitals of the ancient states of Central and Eastern Europe. Warsaw, Berlin, Prague, Vienna, Budapest, Belgrade, Bucharest and Sofia, all these famous cities and the populations around them lie in what I must call the Soviet sphere, and all are subject in one form or another, not only to Soviet influence but to a very high and, in some cases, increasing measure of control from Moscow ...

It was, many feared, only a matter of time before the Soviets threw that iron curtain as far as Asia. According to a Colonial Office memorandum:

> [T]here is a distinct danger that, as measures are developed for the security of Europe and the Middle East, pressure [from the Soviet Union] upon South East Asia will increase. Conditions there are generally speaking favourable for the spread of Communism, and if the general impression prevails in South East Asia that the Western Powers are both unwilling and unable to assist in resisting Russian pressure [...] eventually the whole of South East Asia will fall a victim to the Communist advance and thus come under Russian domination.

The spectre of Bolshevism once more stalked Britain's fragile empire. It lurked in the jungles of Malaya and on the harbour wharfs of Singapore. A former director of operations in Malaya, Lt General R.H. Bowen, succinctly expressed this mounting sense of disquiet:

> The Malayan Communist Party campaign is part of a wider Soviet-inspired drive to obtain control of what is strategically and economically one of the most important areas of South-East Asia. [...] In June 1948, on the instructions of the Cominform issued at two conferences in Calcutta four months earlier, the MCP started a campaign of murder, sabotage and terrorism designed to paralyze the Government and develop into armed revolution.

It would be surprising if Asian communist parties such as the MCP were *not* *influenced* by Moscow. But influence is not the same as an issued directive. A great deal of new information about the origins of the revolutionary movements in Southeast Asia has provided a more nuanced picture. Stalin had abolished the Communist International, or Comintern, in 1943. As former allies, the Soviet Union, the United States and Great Britain fell out after the defeat of Nazi Germany; Stalin established the Communist Information Bureau, or Cominform, as a counterweight to the American 'Marshall Plan'. The secretive founding conference of the Cominform was held in an isolated Silesian village called Szklarska Poręba in September 1947: at the very centre of a ruined Europe. According to historian Robert Service:

> The purpose was to instruct communist parties to adopt a more aggressive posture. In eastern Europe this was to involve switching to a campaign of rapid communisation on the Soviet model; in western Europe it would mean a reinforced campaign against the Marshall Plan and a shift to more militant opposition to the existing governments.[33]

At the conference Andrei Zhdanov excoriated Polish delegates for timidity. He attacked the French and Italian communist parties for holding to the discredited path of peace and compromise. Zhdanov insisted that with the end of the war 'two camps' now vied for power on a global scale. On the one side was the Soviet Union and the peace-loving, progressive Eastern European democracies. They confronted a hostile American-dominated camp that was politically reactionary and imperialist. It was the duty of all communists to resist the onslaught of the reactionary West with every means available, including armed revolt. The time of compromise was over. Zhdanov's famous 'two camps' speech, published in the Cominform newspaper in November as 'For a Lasting Peace, For a People's Democracy', had great resonance for Asians who endured under the yoke of the European colonial powers. At the 'Conference of the Youth of Southeast Asian

Countries' that took place in Calcutta in February 1948 and was attended by leftist youth organisations from twenty-five counties, the 'two camps' idea had an electrifying impact.[34] Zhdanov was saying that compromise with the old colonial powers was a political dead letter. The imperialists must be ousted once and for all through armed revolt. The conference was dominated by the Indian Communist Party – but there was one Malayan delegate, a young man called Lee Siong, who the MCP had chosen because he spoke the best English. At the end of the Calcutta conference, Lee travelled on to Rangoon where he pitched up at the 'Congress of the All Burma Peasants Union'. He finally returned to Singapore on 22 March – missing by one day the MCP's crucial fourth plenary meeting. So Lee was likely to have conveyed to the MCP the Moscow line since he was at sea. It was at this meeting that, as Chin Peng describes in his memoir, the MPC Central Committee passed a resolution to *prepare* for armed insurrection. There was no actual call to arms. The 'Fourth Plenary Conference Paper on the Current Situation' is strikingly tentative:'... it is impossible to avoid or do without the armed struggle (the people's revolutionary war). That is why the armed struggle has its particularly important significance.' To sum up, the 'line' from the Cominform directive to the MCP resolution to prepare for revolt is not a straight one. There was no direct contact at all between Cominform agents and the MCP.

If we want to find a 'Cominform messenger' there is a more convincing candidate than young Lee Siong. Soon after the Youth Conference finished in Calcutta, the Indian Communist Party had its second congress. This was a meeting of 'professionals', not youthful hotheads. One of the most prominent of the revolutionaries who came to Calcutta for the CPI Congress was Lawrence 'Lance' Sharkey, the president of the Australian Communist Party. Sharkey was a devout and uncompromising Stalinist. En route to Calcutta, Sharkey stopped off in Singapore and called in at the MCP headquarters in Queen Street. Chin Peng describes his encounter with the bluntly spoken Australian at some length in his memoir. He 'spoke with Sharkey for several hours on matters of general interest.' The two got on well it would seem. When the CPI congress wrapped up in Calcutta, Sharkey returned to Singapore in time for the last day of that crucial plenary meeting in March. He was, it was said, a 'rugged and forceful speaker'; he was fiercely dogmatic, frequently devious and had a fondness for strong liquor. But Sharkey had a talent for explaining tricky ideas in a simple way. He no doubt clarified the Cominform line and told the Malayans that the Indian communists were set to embark on a confrontational strategy with the new government of Jawaharlal Nehru. (Gandhi had been assassinated by an extremist Hindu in January.) Then this exchange took place:

MCP committee member: 'Comrade, how do you Australians deal with strike
    breakers?'
Sharkey, leaning back in his chair: 'We get rid of them.'

MCP:'You mean you eliminate strike breakers, comrade […] Kill them?'
Sharkey:'But not in the cities. Only in the outlying areas. The rural areas. The mining areas.'

There is a twist to this story. Sharkey left the meeting soon after that exchange and returned to his room at the Raffles Hotel. One he was gone, the same committee member who had asked about strike breakers now delivered a bombshell. An Indian comrade who worked as a printer in a Federation government office in Kuala Lumpur had come across a draft proposal of new legislation to clamp down on the labour unions. He had secretly copied the document and passed it on to a more senior party member. The proposal, Chin Peng and the committee members suspected, was the first step to banning the party itself. Sharkey was forgotten. It was the stolen document and what it revealed about British intentions that most powerfully impacted on the developing strategy of the MCP: in short, to take up arms against the new Federation at some time in the future. The next Central Committee meeting was convened in northern Johor on 5 May. Discussion now focused on the 'implementation of armed struggle'. At the end of the meeting an historic decision was taken to set up 'guerrilla force nuclei' in all the Malay states and to retrieve wartime weapons and ammunition from secret jungle caches. When this decision was made the MCP was still a legal organisation. Chin Peng had indeed taken a decisive step in the direction of armed revolt. The party had been pushed in this direction not so much by Moscow 'directives', but by the aggressive plans of the colonial government. Communists were simply not compatible with profits.

The End of the Malay Radical Movement

The Malayan communists had a surprising advantage. It was not just that they were former allies of the colonial power – but that the British intelligence agencies knew very little about what they were up to and what they might be planning. A year before the Emergency began it was the Malay radicals that troubled the sleep of the high commissioner. The biggest threat to Malaya appeared to be not the MCP but a now forgotten youth organisation called the 'Angkatan Pemuda Insaf' ('Generations of Aware Youth') or API – which means 'fire' in Malay. Note that word '*pemuda*'. After the split with UMNO the Malay Nationalist Party had brought together congeries of organisations to agitate for independence – the All-Malaya Council for Joint Action (AMCJA), 'Pusat Tenaga Rakyat' (Centre of People's Power), or PUTERA, and the Malayan Federation of Trade Unions. These had jointly organised a general strike, or 'hartal', in October 1947. At the centre of this anti-colonialist and nationalist cauldron was Ahmad Boestamam – talking, speechifying, writing – and drilling. Since his schooldays at Anderson College in Ipoh, where he had joined the cadet corps, Boestamam had demonstrated a weakness for militias and delighted in the '*pemuda*' values that exalted action and rebellion. He wanted to inject the MNP with the soul of '*pemuda*' revolt. This was the purpose of the API, which was formed on 17 February 1946 on the six-month anniversary of Sukarno's declaration of independence in Jakarta. The API was, in a sense, the armed wing of the MNP and it was Boestamam's pride and joy. He provided his young recruits with uniforms, armbands and marching songs. He set up training camps, where they drilled and paraded. The API slogan was 'Independence through Blood'. They marched under a red and white Indonesian flag. Boestamam was consciously provocative. His *pemudas* wore old Japanese boots, which caused deep offence to all who had suffered during the occupation. The API, with its aura of violence, troubled the MNP president Dr Burhanuddin, and at the party's second congress he cut ties between the MNP and the API. Boestamam himself was excluded from holding any party office, though he remained an active party member.

The API frightened the Federation government. But in the aftermath of the Union fiasco the British hesitated before striking at a Malay organisation. While Dato Onn insisted that Malays were not yet ready for independence, Ahmad Boestamam, Dr Burhanuddin and the MNP revelled in the tradition of the mythic Malay rebel 'Hang Jebat', who was killed by the loyalist 'Hang Tuah' for defying the throne. At the next MNP conference, held in Malacca at the end of 1946, Dr Burhanuddin proclaimed that 'there is no space for any narrow communalism' – a clear snub to UMNO chauvinists. He recited a verse:

> On the ruins of Malacca Fort
> We build the spirit of independence.
> Unite! Malays of every stock,
> Uphold the rights of our just inheritance.

'Malays of every stock' – we must assume that Dr Burhanuddin meant *Malayans*. The growing influence of the MNP was a headache for the Federation government. Mustapha Hussain had emerged from self-imposed internal exile to campaign for the MNP, and one day overheard a British policeman referring to Dr Burhanuddin as 'the Gandhi of Malaya': this was not intended to be complimentary. 'Gandhi' stood for dangerous nationalist firebrand, Churchill's 'half naked fakir'.

In early 1948, on the eve of the Emergency, the British struck at the Malay radicals. The API was quashed under an ordinance that banned public marching and Boestamam was arrested, for the second time. He would spend more than seven years behind bars, completely cut off from every form of public life. He was released on 29 July 1955 – the day after polling ended in the first federal elections. The summit was in sight but it was not the peak *he* had hoped to reach.

6

THE MEANING OF EMERGENCY

You Say You Want a Revolution?

Few wars have neat, chess-like openings, let alone immaculate finales. In Malaya, violence had been pervasive from the moment the British imposed power by exploiting communal mentalities. The Japanese sharpened and deepened these communal antagonisms. As historian Anthony Stockwell points out: 'violence had been a constant factor in post-war Malaya, sometimes waxing sometimes waning, but never disappearing altogether.' The crucible of violence was in the Malay state of Perak.

In 1942, the Japanese Sook Ching massacres had driven many Chinese Malayans to flee towns and cities and take refuge in the countryside. Here they joined the many thousands of Chinese who already illegally occupied land. They would become known as 'squatters'. During the Emergency, British counter-insurgency strategy was directed as much against the squatters as the armed guerrillas. The word is pejorative, with connotations of indolence and untidiness, but most Chinese squatters in Malaya were hard-working agriculturalists with families, who took over parcels of land of widely different acreages that had been abandoned by fleeing European mine and plantation owners. Some of the squatters ended up farming on land that was unused but 'reserved' for Malays. Many Chinese lived cheek by jowl with Malays in kampongs. In some areas well-organised squatters carved out much bigger terraced farms to grow rice. Others tapped and sold rubber. The world of the Chinese squatter was diverse, usually productive and, for Malays, distinctly unnerving. By the end of the Japanese occupation, the numbers of 'Chinese squatters' had swelled. At the end of the war the total population of the Kinta Valley was about 282,000 and at least 94,000 of these were classifiable as squatters. Most were resourceful and adaptable. They had to be. Some at least were militants. Some 15,000 squatters clustered in small settlements close to the Batu Arang coal mine in Selangor. They grew their crops and took work in the mine when it was available. If union leaders called a strike or stoppage, many of the mine workers could rely on their smallholdings to survive a period without work. Squatters helped make Batu Arang a flashpoint for industrial militancy.

For a short period after the war, the British allowed many Chinese squatters to stay put by issuing temporary permits on condition they grew crops to help deal with chronic food shortages. The infamous squatters prevented Malaya starving. A typical Chinese agriculturalist could work miracles with just a handful of acres. In February 1949, Harry Fang wrote a report on the squatter economy for *The Malaya Tribune*. He estimated that an astonishing 95 per cent of Malaya's population had come to depend on the output of Chinese smallholdings for supplies of rice, vegetables, meat and eggs. Fang could see that many squatters had put down roots. Their social relations had been deepened by the suffering many had experienced under the Japanese. Trouble came when the new colonial government believed that the Chinese squatters had outlived their usefulness. As the legitimate Malayan economy was slowly brought back into operation, European companies lobbied for mass evictions to free up land. Malays piled on the pressure – they wanted the squatters evicted from their 'reservations'. It was claimed, wrongly, that the larger-scale terrace farms were damaging Malaya's timber reserves. It was not long before the British started arresting squatters without residency permits. These clearance operations began in the Kroh Forest Reserve in Kinta and then moved on to the Sungai Siput area in Perak. Near Kuala Kangsar, bailiffs took on some 2,000 Chinese farmers to force them to abandon their land and homes they had built and lived in ever since the Japanese invasion. At a time of worsening economic hardship, land clearances were a bitter experience. Many squatters were radicalised. As unrest spread, eviction took on a political purpose: it was a means to forestall a Malayan 'peasants' revolt'. Clearances were met with violent protest: 'pa kung mor!', meaning 'beat up the red head' [sunburnt European]. In early 1948, the Indian communist R.G. Balan, an MPAJA veteran and organiser of the 'Rubber Workers Union', began secretly touring estates to organise protest. A wave of strikes struck at the mines and rubber plantations of Perak.

Viewed in this longer perspective, Malaya was almost continuously 'at war' from the time of the Japanese invasion to 1989 when the Malayan communists finally capitulated. This long war can be understood as a sequence of smaller-scale conflicts that reshaped the relationships between the Malay political associations and the MCP, and between these competing nationalist parties and the British colonial government. The Federation had the power to reward compliance with political independence. This long Malayan war moulded and defined the postcolonial national state and unfolded in a broader arena of armed revolt in Burma, Indochina, the Philippines and Indonesia. The new global superpowers that had emerged from the ruins of the Second World War struggled with varying degrees of success to influence and shape the outcome of these civil wars. After 1945, British colonial policy had to accommodate American strategic interests. The language of counter-insurgency was saturated with anti-communist rhetoric. There is no hard evidence that the Malayan communist guerrillas ever received aid, either financial or military, from external powers such as Communist

China or the Soviet Union. The impact of the global communist movement was in a way counter-instinctual. It did little for the Malayan communists, but Mao Zedong's seizure of power in 1949 and the flight of Chiang Kai-Shek to Taiwan persuaded many 'Overseas Chinese' to embrace more tightly Malaya as a homeland in preference to one ruled by a communist party. In the early 1950s, spending on the Korean War enriched the Malayan economy, providing the Federation government with the means to ramp up spending on counter-insurgency strategies. The global conflict between the superpowers and the proxy small wars fought in Asia thus hastened the defeat of the Malayan insurgents.

These reversals of fortune could not have been foreseen by the Malayan communists in 1948. With the liquidation of Lai Tek, the MCP could begin abandoning its much-resented strategy of appeasement. A communist organiser called Tan Kan made precisely this point:

> Our policy, since the time of the anti Japanese campaign, has been a wrong one. We seem to have fallen into the doctrine of the rightists [...] Human beings are born to struggle [...] To yield to hateful favours and endure will not do any good, it is the road to death. The way out is to stand united and to fight.

For a young Malay communist called Hassan Saleh the issue was simple:

> Our homeland has a lot of tin, gold and timber. This belongs to us. They take it all and take it back to England. Our wealth is taken to England. The prosperity is there not in our homeland.[35]

Violence, in other words, was a logical rejoinder to the avaricious new imperialism pursued by the British government after the war. The exploitation of Malayan resources was enforced through violence. It was British troops who fired the first lethal shots in Sungai Siput and Taiping in October 1945. Post-war colonial policy was driven not only by the patrician liberalism of the 'Malayan Planning Unit' but the near bankrupt British government's desperate need to exploit Malaya's resources. The colonial government was determined to crush any kind of subversion, plot or strike that threatened the profits of Malaya's mines and plantations. It would be in Malaya's industrial heartland, the Kinta Valley, that the Emergency war would first erupt. But the lurch to armed revolt would take Chin Peng completely by surprise.

The Accidental Spark

On the northern edges of the Kinta Valley in the district of Sungai Siput, the little town of the same name straddled the trunk road that led north towards the Thai border and south to Ipoh. From Sungai Siput a web of unpaved roads and paths radiated out to connect the tin mines and rubber plantations that nourished the colonial economy and fed the coffers of empire. At the northern end of town the Lintang Road cut through the jungle for twenty or so lonely miles until it came to a dead end. On each side of the road marched regularly spaced lines of rubber trees seemingly without end. They belonged to the Sungai Siput and the Elphil Estates – two of the biggest plantations in Perak. It was here on the morning of 16 June 1948, that communist hit squads murdered British plantation managers Arthur 'Wally' Walker, John Allison and a trainee called Ian Christian. The assassins had reassured the Indian estate clerks: 'We are out only for Europeans. These men will surely die today: we will shoot all Europeans.'

The Sungai Siput murders in June 1948 have an iconic significance in the history of the 'Malayan Emergency'. Few historians trouble to mention the murders of a Chinese foreman on the Senai Estate near Johor Bahru and a Chinese contractor near Taiping that happened on the same day. The murders are conventionally viewed as the decisive spark that ignited a twelve-year-long war. It would be more realistic to see the murders as a tipping point. Since the end of the war, the European owners of the Perak plantations had pushed down wages on their estates, provoking a succession of strikes and stoppages. The powerful associations of rubber planters and miners in Kuala Lumpur complained incessantly to High Commissioner Sir Edward Gent (who was widely perceived as a kind of socialist) to 'do something' – to 'govern or get out' as an infamous newspaper headline insisted. The Europeans clamoured for Gent to declare martial law. The killing of the three white Tuans on a single day was a gift to these vociferous hardliners. As enraged and frightened British planters and their representatives ranted at their clubs, Gent made a decision. He declared a state of emergency in Perak, which was extended to the whole of the peninsula two days later. In July, Gent's proclamation was replaced by a 'Federal Emergency Regulations Ordinance', which defined the terms of engagement for the next twelve years. Under the ordinance, the British banned the MCP and other hostile political parties. The war without a name had begun.

Why did Gent and the high commissioners who followed him so staunchly resist calls to declare martial law? The most frequently cited reason is that the Emergency 'label' protected insurance claims made by the European owners of tin mines, plantations and other private colonial businesses, for loss or damage to property, which would have been forfeit under martial law. In conditions of war, responsibility for financial compensation would have fallen on the impoverished British government – and Prime Minister Attlee was most unwilling to shoulder this future burden. This is true as far as it goes – which is not very far. Before the Second World War, British soldiers who took part in counter-insurgency operations usually did so with the sanction of a declaration of martial law. But according to a 1934 document, 'Notes on Imperial Policing', martial law:

... is in reality not 'law' at all [...] it denotes the suspension of ordinary law and its suppression by military rule during the war or rebellion, and amounts merely to the exercise of the will of the military commander ...[36]

This admission that martial law was 'not "law" at all' reflected a great deal of unease about its application and consequences. This was, in part, humanitarian. Martial law often led to considerable loss of life. It was in many cases a licence to kill. Much depended on the will of the military commander – as the 1934 document pointed out – 'upon whom has fallen the task of ensuring the safety of the State ...'. Although martial law was used against 'domestic riots', it was mainly an instrument of colonial rule. In the British colonies, martial law was resorted to on numerous occasions: Barbados in 1805 and 1816; Demerera in 1823; Jamaica in 1831–32 and 1865; Canada in 1837–38; Ceylon in 1817 and 1848; Cephalonia in 1848; Cape of Good Hope in 1834 and 1849–51; and the Island of St Vincent in 1863. The problem was well put in a legal judgement in 1831:

Now a person, whether a magistrate, or peace officer, who has the duty of suppressing a riot, is placed in a very difficult situation, for if, by his acts, he causes death, he is liable to be indicted for murder or manslaughter, and if he does not act, he is liable to an indictment on an information for neglect; he is, therefore, bound to hit the precise line of his duty ...

How precisely would that line be drawn? A century later, historically informed soldiers feared that they might suffer the humiliating fate of Governor Edward John Eyre, who had used a declaration of martial law in 1865 to crush a 'negro revolt' in Jamaica: a Royal Commission recorded that 439 people were put to death by being shot on the spot or hanged after court martial, 600 men and women were publicly flogged, and more than 1,000 native cottages razed. In Britain there was tremendous outrage. Governor Eyre had powerful defenders, but the 'Jamaica Committee', led by MP for Westminster J.S. Mill and supported by liberals such as Charles Darwin and Thomas Huxley, demanded his indictment for murder. Eyre was chastised and removed from office. Unease about the application and consequences of using martial law deepened when, in April 1919, Brigadier General Reginald Dyer ordered Gurkha troops to open fire on unarmed Indian civilians, who had gathered in the Jallianwala Bagh in Amritsar, resulting in massive loss of life. For British soldiers, the most troubling issue was not so much the appalling loss of life, but the subsequent treatment of Dyer by the government. He had been 'thrown to the wolves'. Even Churchill condemned the massacre as 'monstrous'. Under martial law there was no indemnity for military commanders who were judged to have used excessive force – and not 'hit the precise line of [their] duty'.

So, for the military commander, a declaration of martial law carried formidable risks. It was also very expensive. This was demonstrated in Palestine in March

1947 when the British mandate government declared martial law in Tel Aviv and parts of Jerusalem. The army shut down all public services, closed post and telegraph offices, telephone exchanges, and customs and railways facilities. The result was economic meltdown. Government revenues dried up while the Zionist and Arab insurgents continued attacks outside Tel Aviv. The experiment was abandoned after two weeks. The chief secretary to the mandate at the time was Sir Henry Gurney, who would become the second British High Commissioner of the Federation of Malaya. In May 1949, he reflected on his experiences in a report to the Colonial Secretary: 'The withdrawal of the civil power and the substitution of military control represent the first victory for the terrorists. Unfriendly propagandists paint the picture of political failure and of resort to force and repression.'

The trick, as Gurney had discovered, was to mask 'force and repression' behind a facade of civil legality. Such a device had been hatched in October 1896: the 'Order-in-Council' that conferred on colonial governors of so-called fortress colonies like Malta and Gibraltar the power to issue a proclamation giving them control of all property and persons in the colony. This was extended to other colonial territories, including Palestine in 1937, and consolidated as the 'Emergency Powers (Colonial Defence) Order-in-Council' in 1939. After 1945, these 'Emergency Orders-in-Council' would provide the legal basis of British counter-insurgency wars in Malaya, Kenya, Cyprus and Nyasaland. The fundamental point about Emergency ordinances was that they handed the civil governor of a colony the power to make such regulations he believed 'necessary or expedient for securing the public safety, the defence of the territory and the suppression of mutiny, rebellion and riot …'. Emergency Regulations provided the governor with the right to amend or suspend 'the operation of any law and for applying any law …'..

Power stayed in the hands of the civilian authority; it was not subordinated to the military. In Malaya, the civil administration would co-ordinate the operations of the police and the army. This meant that the British colonial governments could put on the mask of legality while employing as much or as little violent coercion as seemed necessary in different circumstances. It is telling indeed that, in 1938, Prime Minister Neville Chamberlain had hesitated to introduce the new Orders-in-Council in Parliament because he feared such draconian legislation would be thrown out. He resorted to using the royal prerogative. A Colonial Office official, Sir John Shukburgh, admitted that the new legislation 'must be kept a secret […] It is a Prerogative Order, publication of which is not necessary.'

What this added up to was that Emergency powers could, if necessary, have the force of martial law but not be subject to the kind of censure that had brought down Dyer and Governor Eyre. There is another point we should make here. Since the Emergency was never, officially, a war, the insurgents were merely 'bandits' or 'terrorists': and since they did not have the status of enemy soldiers they were not protected by the Geneva Conventions. During the Malayan Emergency the communist MNLA guerrillas were robbed of their humanity by that ubiquitous abbreviation, 'CT' = communist terrorist. Noel Barber's book *The War of the Running Dogs*, which was published in 1973, uses 'CT' as if it was a simple descriptive term, impartial as 'Jap' or 'Kraut' or 'Charlie'. It is lethally derogatory. During the Second World War, the German Army and SS police used the same polemical tactic against resistance forces or partisans in the Balkans and in the occupied territories of the Soviet Union. German situation reports never referred to 'partisans': this was considered to be excessively ennobling. The enemy was always a 'bandit' not worthy of honourable or humane treatment. Civilians who were assisting, or were believed to be assisting, partisans fell into the same category. The war on bandits sanctioned the killing of unarmed civilians. British counter-insurgency in Malaya and other colonial territories adopted the same semantic strategy.

There was another aspect to this demonisation of communist insurgents. The British government did not want to be seen to be violently repressing a nationalist revolt. That would not go down well in Washington. So the communist MNLA had to be, as it were, 'denationalised'. The new Colonial Secretary, Arthur Creech-Jones, wrote that: 'Malaya, after all, is the only colonial area in Southeast Asia where no genuinely anti-European movement has emerged since the war …'.

This is a remark of spectacular ignorance. He continued:

> I would say, emphatically, particularly in view of the vilification of Britain – the wilful lies in regard to the Malayan situation which have been put across from Moscow – that we have not here at all the emergence of a nationalist movement which Britain is engaged in putting down. This is not a movement of the people of Malaya. It is the conduct of gangsters who are out to destroy the very foundations of human society – orderly life.

On the Back Foot

The Emergency declaration took Chin Peng and the MCP leadership by surprise. If the communist assassins had been paid by the British government or an agent of UMNO to throw the Malayan revolution off course from the very start they could not have done a better job. The MCP was, as Chin Peng revealed in his memoir, planning to take up armed struggle at least eight years down the line. It was with this distant deadline in mind that the MCP 'State Committees' had tentatively commenced preparations at the very moment the Emergency was declared. There was no MCP plan for full-scale mobilisation in mid-1948.

At the very moment the Chinese murder squads were cycling into the Elphil Estate, Chin Peng was 40 miles away at the opulent hilltop home of a Chinese businessman called Lee Tong Ching, whose family owned the Tong Fatt tin mine near Kampar. He was there for a surprising reason. Tong Ching's elder brother had been an MPAJA commander during the occupation. After the Japanese invasion, the family business had been ruined. In 1945, the MCP was flush with money from rubber speculation and Tong Ching begged Chin Peng, who during the war had become close friends with both brothers, the ardent capitalist and the communist guerrilla, for help. Chin Peng persuaded the Perak state committee to invest some of its surplus funds in the Tong Fatt Mine in return for a percentage of the profits. Soon after the mine was brought back into operation, a new tin seam was discovered – and Tong Ching began making big profits. The MCP knew all about this – but Tong Ching doctored his accounts and refused to honour the deal. After 'some persuasion', as Chin Peng puts it, the 'capitalist saw reason'. That was why Chin Peng was relaxing on a rattan lounge chair at Tong Ching's sprawling bungalow on the morning of Wednesday 6 June, the day that changed Malayan history: he had come to collect the first instalment from his old friend. He wiled away the hours reading *The Straits Times*. Commissioner General Malcolm MacDonald had just returned from China, where he had held talks with Chiang Kai-Shek. There was rapidly growing unrest in Burma, which had become independent earlier in the year [...] As it grew dark that evening Chin Peng heard the rumble of trucks approaching Tong Ching's bungalow. He had no doubt that these were military vehicles. Leaving behind his passport and two expensive suits he had bought during the pursuit of Lai Tek, Chin Peng fled into the twilight. It was not long before he realised that he had lost the advantage in the struggle with the British. He was inadvertently at war.

The Malayan planters were traumatised and angry. They complained bitterly about Gent. In Singapore, Governor General MacDonald was deviously talking down the high commissioner to the Colonial Office. 'One of the reasons for our friend's [? Omission] not only in recent weeks but during much of the two years, was his inexperience in practical administration ...'. was typical of his barbed complaints to Creech-Jones in London. Gent was suspected of weakness by all sides: the planters and the conservative Malays. Accused of 'Fabian' (meaning soft socialist) sympathies, Gent was on the defensive. But he feared, reasonably, that the response the planters wanted would be tantamount to decanting gasoline into a brush fire. Whatever his personal or administrative failings, Gent was pursuing a perfectly rational strategy. He would not openly declare war on the Malayan communists but would batter away at their legal rights. He hoped they would show their hand – and, of course, they did. Gent does not deserve his reputation as a 'Fabian' ditherer: it was his draconian treatment of the Malayan labour movement that slammed shut the door on non-violent protest – and forced the MCP to make a sharp turn towards violent revolt. Colonial documents show that the Federation government was bitterly divided between conciliators and the 'hang-'em-and-flog-'em' types, who wanted a more aggressive and pre-emptive strategy. Ignorance nourished disagreement. As in 1942, on the eve of the Japanese invasion, the Federation was blighted by an intelligence vacuum. During the occupation, the Japanese had seized, and made good use of, the Malayan Special Branch and Malayan Security Service (MSS) records of communism. This was a disaster. Before the war, the Special Branch had used Lai Tek to virtually run the MCP. In 1947, the Special Branch no longer had access to its pre-war records – and Lai Tek had vanished. The 'Mr Wright' operation had been so successful before 1942 that the British had grown complacent. They had not – as far as the records show – recruited any other undercover communist agent. The Malayan Security Service was groping for insight. The Colonial Office in London had a sense that Malaya was at the mercy of communist hordes 'burrowing like moles' or scurrying hither and thither on 'mischievous errands' (the words of one J.B. Williams). Both the British and the communists were like wrestlers circling each other warily in an unlit ring.

7

THE WAR WITHOUT A NAME

Prelude in Palestine

On 15 May 1948, the Union Jack was lowered for the last time on the rooftop of the British High Commission headquarters on the Hill of Evil Counsel in Jerusalem. The hurried, shamefaced ceremony marked the end of British rule in the mandated territory of Palestine. A huge convoy of military vehicles rumbled along the main road that led from Jerusalem to the narrow coastal plain towards the port city of Haifa. The road took the great convoy past the ruins of biblical Megiddo, and the Valley of Armageddon. Thousands of British soldiers and policemen were jammed uncomfortably inside trucks, jeeps and armoured cars. A few sniggered as the last British high commissioner, Sir Alan Cunningham, swept by in an armour-plated Rolls-Royce Daimler. As the early morning sun beat down on parched, stony pastures and abandoned olive groves, an 18-year-old police constable called Gus Fletcher clung to the tailgate of a crammed truck. He had completed two years of national service in Palestine and was wondering about his future. He had as yet no inkling that he would soon be defending the empire in the jungles and plantations of British Malaya.

For three years the British had been struggling to resolve the future of the Palestine mandated territory. Palestine was not, of course, a British colony. It had been 'entrusted' to Britain by the League of Nations in 1923. Reckless promises had been made to both Arabs and Zionist Jews. At the end of the war, with Jewish survivors of the Holocaust still trapped in displaced persons (DP) camps in liberated Europe, Zionist terrorists turned their guns on the British and Arabs. Arab nationalists like the Grand Mufti of Jerusalem Haj Amin al-Husseini, who had spent the war in Nazi Germany, laid plans to resist the coming of a Jewish state. Shortly before the outbreak of the Second World War, Colonial Secretary William Ormsby-Gore had appointed a new high commissioner to try and bring an end to the communal conflict that was threatening to drown Palestine in a tide of blood. The new man was Sir Harold MacMichael, the same aloof diplomat who would, a decade later, strong arm the Malay rulers to sign up to the 'Malayan Union' over a cup of tea. Back in 1938 in Palestine, Sir Harold promised to 'never waver, never forgive', but by the end of the year Arab forces had seized control of much of Galilee, forcing MacMichael to cede power to the British Army, in effect declaring martial law. This failure was seared on the minds of colonial administrators like the first High Commissioner of the Malayan Federation, Sir Edward Gent.

In Palestine, the British Army developed many of the techniques of counter-insurgency that would be used against the Malayan communists (and for that matter by the Israeli army against Palestinian civilians after 1948). They attacked and razed Arab villages, blew up houses and corralled thousands of refugees into camps. But the fury of the Arab revolt compelled the British to make concessions. The result was the notorious 'White Paper' published in 1939. Its architect was Malcolm MacDonald, then Secretary of State for the Colonies. MacDonald informed Zionist Chaim Weizmann that since nearly half a million Jews had now settled in Palestine the British mandate government had fulfilled its old promises. Weizmann, who was outraged, said of MacDonald that he was 'so anti-Semitic as to be almost demented'. The German destruction of European Jewry would soon make such British drawing room anti-Semitism look grossly irresponsible.

The ageing Lloyd George said in 1943: 'The revolting treatment of the Jews by the Nazis has made any other solution than a Jewish state in Palestine unthinkable.' The Americans, who had done as little as the British to rescue Jews in German-occupied Europe, had swung round to the Zionist cause. The new British foreign secretary, Ernest Bevin, a rough-tongued former trade unionist, insisted that a Jewish state would be unjust to the Arabs and the empire now depended on Arab oil. Under pressure from the Americans and facing domestic outrage about murderous attacks by Zionist terrorists, British strategy was foundering. Hugh Dalton, the beleaguered Chancellor of the Exchequer, lamented: 'you cannot, in any case, have a secure base on top of a wasps' nest ...'. He also noted that the conflict was 'breeding anti-Semites [in Britain] at a most shocking speed'.

In April 1947, Bevin 'threw in the towel' (the words of Dean Acheson, the American Under-Secretary of State) and referred the Palestine issue to the United Nations to find a solution. The UN proposed a two-state solution. Arab leaders vehemently opposed partition, just as they had in 1937, since it implied acceptance of Zionist territorial claims. Ben-Gurion, the president of the Jewish Agency, clearly saw that compromise would unlock the iron gates of statehood. His Arab opponents demanded everything and came away with nothing. In the immediate aftermath of the UN vote, Britain had to govern a land that was descending ever deeper into the mire of communal strife. The last high commissioner was obliged to remain 'neutral' – which, in practice, meant he stood back as Arabs and Jews killed each other. Israeli historian Ilan Pappe has estimated that as many as 750,000 Arabs fled Palestine or were expelled in this period. The Chief Secretary of Palestine, Sir Henry Gurney, who in October 1948 would become the second British High Commissioner of the Federation of Malaya, deplored this enforced neutrality, comparing it to sitting on the branch of a tree while industriously sawing it off. He spent many hours improving his tennis game. In the eyes of Americans and Jews the British government was losing its grip on empire. There was much hand-wringing, too, on the British side. The Chief Justice of Palestine decried 'walking out and leaving the pot we placed on the fire to boil over …'. Leo Amery, a close friend of Churchill's, lamented 'throwing over the work of thirty years and washing our hands of all responsibility for either Jews or Arabs …'. On 14 May 1948, Ben-Gurion proclaimed the establishment of the new State of Israel. The Zionists had won against formidable odds. The following day, the last British soldiers and policemen embarked on their dismal exodus from the Holy Land. Gus Fletcher was part of the great caravanserai that set off for Haifa where troopships waited in the harbour.

At a press conference on that final humiliating day of British rule, the chief secretary of the British administration, Sir Henry Gurney, was asked to whom he intended to leave the keys to his office. Gurney replied:

'To nobody. I shall leave them under the mat.'

Policeman in Malaya

Young Gus Fletcher landed in Southampton still in police uniform and unsure what he could do next. He went to stay with his parents in Somerset. He had an itch for adventure. Not long afterwards he spotted a press advertisement calling for British police, needed 'to serve in Malaya to counter a Communist terrorist jungle war, their object being to have a Communist-led Government take over Malaya from the British'. He immediately applied to the Crown Agents in London. He was issued with a rail-ticket voucher and travelled up from Southampton for an interview. He was asked to return a few days later and was given a medical examination. Mustered at a barracks in Hounslow with forty or so other young men, Fletcher, not yet twenty, would be despatched 6,000 miles to another colonial front line. On a balmy night in July, Fletcher boarded an Argonaut aircraft bound for Changi airport in Singapore – and the front line of another 'war of peace':

> … the aeroplane, to my amazement, was stripped down: it was a four engine propeller plane. It could carry about 48 to 50 passengers. We were all given numbers: from the beginning of the alphabet, and I was F for Fletcher and my number was 19. So there were a few others in front of me. The aeroplane was just an aluminium shell in order to get more people in: all the seats had been replaced with two strips of canvas to sit on. So as my neighbour got up, I went down, as I sat down, he went up, and it was like a yo-yo. We were on that plane for two and a half days.

As the Argonaut flew closer to the equator the temperature inside the packed aluminium tube rose uncomfortably. As the men sweated, Fletcher realised that they had distinguished company:

... Our new Commissioner of Police [Colonel Nicol] Gray, CMG, DSO no less was sitting there in a full 'Guard's undress': a black jacket, trousers, bowler hat and a striped weskit. As the plane got hotter and hotter and hotter, his language became, I could hear him where I was sitting, became [...] very military. It was wonderful to hear. And he first of all divested himself of his jacket, and then his weskit, then his trousers [...] but he kept his bowler hat on. We stopped about 6 times, 8 times, and each time he got off, he puts all of his clothes back on again. To keep up appearances! Finally and thankfully, Singapore slid under our wings and we landed at Changi at about 3 a.m. They let us sleep until 6 a.m. – three hours – at the Nee Soon Barracks then woke us up, then showed us the stand gun, ammunition 3 magazines, our camp, bed, a floating camp bed, car keys, our jungle brim [tea making] equipment and then off to the train, to Kuala Lumpur, which was a very long journey [...] At the station, there was Gray again. He had flown up a lot more comfortably on one of Malayan Airways two DC3s. He told us where we would be assigned. Pahang as it turned out ...

Fletcher arrived in Malaya just weeks after Gent had declared a state of Emergency – first in the Ipoh and Sungai Siput police districts of Perak and parts of Johor, then across the rest of the country. The regulations brought in that June were simple compared to the complex police powers that would be introduced later. The police now had powers to arrest, detain or exclude people from designated areas. Anyone arrested could be detained for an entire year, though they retained the right to appeal to a reviewing committee. The police could search anyone at will, as well as their houses or business premises, without obtaining a warrant. They could close roads, paths and waterways. They could requisition buildings, vehicles and boats. The Emergency Regulations also gave the police powers to seize allegedly seditious documents and anything that might be used as an offensive weapon. Anyone caught with unauthorised firearms or ammunition would be executed.

The declaration did little to satisfy the angry and frightened planters and mine owners on the front line. This stiff-necked community had come to despise the conciliatory Gent. They regarded him as a lily-livered 'Fabian' type like the new prime minister in London. *The Straits Times*, which customarily spoke for the establishment, printed a notorious headline aimed at Gent: 'Govern or get out ...'. The Emergency has been called a 'revolt on the periphery' – and to begin with the conflict was confined to Malaya's plantations and mines. The communists waged war on planters and mine owners. The estates and mines soon bristled with armoury: by 16 June, every estate manager in Perak and Johor had police or Gurkha escorts. All leave for police officers was cancelled; officers taking holidays were recalled; the British Army formally accepted a request to assist the civil power and began issuing guns and ammunition to the police. For the average city dweller in Kuala Lumpur or Johor Bahru, the Emergency seemed remote and confusing. According to veteran reporter Harry Miller people 'stared unbelievingly' when grim-faced planters or plantation owners strode into hotels in Kuala Lumpur like characters out of a Wild West film with revolvers tucked in their waists or grasping formidable looking rifles. In King's House, Gent and his staff were just as much in the dark.

Warring Parties

We last encountered the young MCP General Secretary Chin Peng as he fled the opulent bungalow home of Chinese tin-mine owner Tong Ching just seconds before a British military patrol roared up the drive to arrest – as it turned out – his absentee host. As he slipped away through the tropical twilight, Chin Peng knew nothing of the bloody events at the Elphil Estate and Singei Siput Plantation. 'Quite unknown to me,' he recalled, 'the very worst possible scenario I could have envisaged was being enacted by party elements barely 40 miles north …'. He was referring to the attacks on the plantations near Sungai Siput. Chin Peng has often insisted that the murders carried out by impetuous comrades in Perak and Johor that day were a 'serious mistake'. He explained: 'The executions pre-empted our plans and undermined our efforts to withdraw our cadres into a well-organised underground network and our guerrilla army to secret jungle bases.' It was not murder as such that Chin Peng objected to – it was the fact that the comrades had killed *Europeans*. At the MCP plenary meeting in Singapore the year before, the Australian communist Lawrence Sharkey had recommended 'getting rid' of strike breakers and 'running dogs'. Communist gunmen had been busily doing just that for many months: liquidating scores of 'collaborators'. Most were Chinese or Indian. There had been no order to murder Europeans. Chin Peng realised that the Sungai Siput murders were an unwelcome game changer. Battered by Lai Tek's years of betrayal, the MCP was forced to lurch into war. Chin Peng (who had by now received an OBE for his contribution to the war effort) would have to take on the might of the British Empire on the enemy's terms.

Chin Peng and other communist leaders had no way of knowing at the time of the Sungai Siput murders that the British colonial establishment was crippled by internal strife and had been since the end of the war. The new Federation was riddled with fault lines held in precarious equilibrium. (It's when a fault slips that an earthquake occurs.) By abandoning the Malayan Union, the British had won over the Malay conservatives. They had cracked down on dangerous Malay radicals like Ahmad Boestamam. The Federation government in Kuala Lumpur was under attack from the Malayan business community. These tough, staunchly reactionary, no-nonsense men and women knew that they kept the motor of the Malay economy running and expected proper protection. The government (the Malayan Union) seemed helpless or, worse, unwilling to defeat the plague of lawlessness – and sedition. Banditry and industrial unrest spawned from the same communistic nest. And yet Governor Gent and the mandarins in King's House were still preaching moderation and caution. Gent's difficulty was inconsistent intelligence reports. John Dalley, who had set up the 'Singapore Overseas Chinese Anti-Japanese Volunteer Force', or 'Dalforce', at the end of 1941, estimated, alarmingly, that the MCP had already called up more than 5,000 fighters and organised nearly a quarter of a million supporters. Commissioner of Police H.B. Langworthy was sceptical: he told Gent, correctly, that Dalley's figures were exaggerated. Langworthy's was the more convincing opinion and Gent, quite reasonably, kept his powder dry.

The End of Gent

MacDonald struck the first blow when he travelled to Kuala Lumpur for a meeting with Gent on 22 June. The purpose was to discuss how to deploy government forces in Malaya and to try and read the mind of the enemy. As well as Gent and MacDonald, the Governor of Singapore, Sir Franklin Gimson, the GOC Malaya, Lt General Galloway, and heads of the police and intelligence services, all gathered in the opulent teak-lined conference room. Hot sunlight cut through the thick blinds. A demure Indian boy served tea and biscuits. A thick pall of cigarette and pipe smoke hung in the warming air. The atmosphere was tense. It would soon turn combative. On 4 July, the Federal Executive Council had been informed secretly that there was no prospect that any reinforcements could be sent from abroad. To defend Malaya's mines and plantations Galloway had ten infantry battalions, though at least two more would be transferred from Singapore. They comprised two battalions of the Malay Regiment, the Seaforth Highlanders (who had seen action in Java), the King's Own Yorkshire Light Infantry and six Gurkha Rifle Battalions. Squadrons of Spitfires and Sunderland flying boats (the latter of some antiquity) were also stationed in Malaya. The Photographic Reconnaissance Squadron flew a few Austers. Police strength was around 6,000 men. The government had already decided that it was vital to present a show of force across the entire Federation and so these meagre resources were spread very thin. To begin with the discussion was nervously complacent. No one expected the Emergency to last longer than a few weeks – perhaps a couple of months at the outside. It was the acerbic MacDonald who changed the tone. After listening to a succession of inconclusive exchanges between Gent and Galloway he waded in, insisting that the priority *had* to be Malaya's mines and plantations. It was vital to restore the confidence of the business community and this could be achieved only by stationing troops or police at all the estates and mines, wherever they were situated and whoever owned them, European or Asian.

This was a startling proposal. No one at the conference had bothered to do the maths beforehand, but a back-of-an-envelope calculation showed that this would take up most of the available police and require the use of troops. The discussion now became acrimonious. For the GOC it was anathema to have British soldiers on 'static guard duty'. Gent insisted that it would be simply impossible to protect every mine and plantation. The only realistic strategy, he proposed, was to go on the offensive and neutralise the small number of communist ringleaders. Keep the enemy on the run, concurred Galloway. MacDonald was not perturbed. He insisted that the priorities had to be national morale and the economy. He then delivered a stinging attack on the lack of preparedness and co-ordination and proposed forming a new central planning committee to co-ordinate operations and liaise with Singapore. On paper these proposals sounded sensible, even innocuous, but Gent exploded. MacDonald was trespassing onto his patch:

> ... full responsibility remained with him [...] So far as he was concerned, the measures he had in view would be put into operation and could not be dependent on the consent of or the direction from the [British Defence Co-ordination Committee in Singapore] ...!!!

Gent's outburst sealed his fate. Pressure had been mounting for some time to appoint a new high commissioner. MacDonald had already informed Gent that he was looking for a suitable candidate at the beginning of May. On the same day that MacDonald arrived in Kuala Lumpur, a delegation of 'Malayan interests', led by the Rubber Growers' Association, met the Colonial Secretary in London to bemoan Gent's failure to 'handle the present situation'. He had 'completely undermined their confidence'. *The Straits Times*, which had published the infamous 'Govern or Get Out' front page, kept up a steady patter of fire. At the end of June, MacDonald complained to London that Gent was the stumbling block in the way of quick, effective action. His list of complaints was long indeed: the high commissioner had ignored warnings from the Malayan Security Service; he had delayed taking emergency powers and then declared them without sufficient, or any, planning or co-ordination; he openly admitted that the police could not cope but he had done nothing to remedy the defect. The avalanche of criticism was now pouring in from every quarter. Dato Onn wanted him gone; so too did the Commander-in-Chief General Ritchie and Air Marshal Lloyd. Gent, who had won the DSO at 23, was 'a good staff officer but certainly no regimental officer'. Gent had, it seemed, few friends left. On 26 June, he received a telegram from the Colonial Office summoning him to return to London for 'health reasons'. Gent understood, naturally, that he was being sacked. His last defiant gesture was to insist that the public announcement refer to 'consultations'. Lady Gent stayed on in Singapore.

On 28 June, the high commissioner left King's House in Kuala Lumpur for the last time. He flew to Colombo, where he was delayed for twenty-four hours. He transferred to an Avro York freighter aircraft and took off for London. Just before 3 p.m. on 4 July, the York was cleared to descend to 4,000 feet as it approached

RAF Northolt near London. The weather was nasty and visibility poor. As the York rumbled through thick cloud, it collided with a Scandinavian Airways DC-6 bound for Stockholm that the Northolt tower had just cleared to ascend. The starboard wing of the Swedish aircraft smashed into the side of the York and tore off the tail unit. Both aircraft plummeted into woodland and exploded. The York was completely destroyed. Not a single passenger in either aircraft survived. The unfortunate Gent was incinerated. Only his gold cigarette case survived the inferno.

Gent's grisly demise was cruelly symbolic. He had become a spent force. The only Malayans who mourned his passing were Chinese moderates like Tan Cheng Lock, who undermined MacDonald's oft-repeated slur that Gent did not get on with Asians. In a message sent to London on 4 July, a 'dumbfounded' Tan Cheng Lock accused 'European vested interests' of perpetrating an 'act of gross injustice': that accusing the former high commissioner of not 'nipping things in the bud' was a 'false show of wisdom'. In an angry letter to *The Straits Times* his son Tan Siew Sin (who would become finance minister in independent Malaya) celebrated Gent's 'courage and determination to obey his conscience in his dealings with the local-born communities.' Tan provoked the colonial establishment:

> In the eyes of the majority of his own countrymen, he committed the unpardonable sin of treating Asians as if they were human beings and their grouse against him was [as a *Times* editorial writer had written] 'the living refutation of the poisonous slander upon British colonial policy and objectives in Malaya'.

Gent had been crippled by the Union battle, hung out to dry by MacDonald and Dato Onn, and roasted by the planters.

8

KNOWN UNKNOWNS AND UNKNOWN UNKNOWNS

Dithering

The death of the high commissioner should have been an opportunity for the Federation government to regroup. Instead the British dithered. The high commissioner had been killed but would not be replaced until early October. There was institutional inertia. The entire Federation government was an administration in suspension. Sir Alex Newbolt was acting high commissioner; there was an acting chief secretary; an acting attorney general; an acting financial secretary ... Commissioner of Police Mr H.B. Langworthy had been ill for some time and resigned in June shortly after Gent declared the Emergency. He would be replaced some two months later by the cantankerous Colonel William Nicol Gray, who had been inspector general of the Palestine police. There was to be sure a permanent general officer commanding (GOC) in the shape of Major General Charles Boucher, who had acquired experience of counter-insurgency when British troops, mainly Indians transferred from Italy, intervened disastrously in the Greek civil war. The British had eventually been forced to seek American assistance to end the war – and bequeathed to the people of Greece a ruined economy, a bitterly divided society and a weakness for authoritarian governments. It was Boucher who, when he was transferred to Malaya, bragged: 'I can tell you this is by far the easiest problem I have ever tackled. In spite of the appalling country, the enemy is far weaker in technique and courage than either the Greek or Indian Reds.' Since the British intelligence services in Malaya were so ignorant of what was happening on the communist side, Boucher's boast is perhaps understandable. He would not be allowed to forget his remark. In June 1948, the acting Federation government was struggling both to develop a strategy and to build a decision-making apparatus.

Although the governor general in Singapore, Malcolm MacDonald, had blithely accepted the collapse of the 'Malayan Union', the British now had to fight a counter-insurgency war through a Federation of Malay States. Administrative disarray was rooted in a weak and divided government apparatus. The withdrawal of the offer of new citizenship rights to the Chinese predisposed many of them to at least sympathise with the rebels, if not join them – and the new federal constitution that made each Malay state a protectorate ruled by a sultan vitiated the formation of a centralised government that might have acted more decisively when the first communist attacks were launched. A federal arrangement weakened a system of rule that had always been a kind of confidence trick. Since the birth of the empire, the British spread its administrative cadres very thinly. This made the imperial system more cost-effective but fundamentally weak. This is why the British depended on the Fourth C of colonialism – collaboration. Collaborators with any colonial regime have to please both the imperial power that invest them with power and the people they ruled and exploited by proxy. To police this inherently unstable system, the colonial powers had to rely on police forces that were generally small, under-equipped and poorly trained, with sometimes the shallowest understanding of the human terrain they had to negotiate. After the Second World War, and with the onset of colonial revolt, these police forces became paramilitary units.

The 'Palestine Police' led the way. This 2,000 strong force was equipped with small arms and trained, in effect, as light infantry. The crucial difference was that the police were cheaper than soldiers. This reflected the new British aversion to martial law. Police could appear to be acting for the civil authority, not as an autonomous army. Like occupying armies, however, the colonial police was obligated to stand outside and above the communities they controlled. Colonial policemen were, as one constable assigned to Palestine complained, 'piggy in the middle'. The same tactic was applied in Malaya, where 400 ex-Palestine police ended up serving after 1948. But here the Malay rulers, who had been newly empowered by the federal constitution, made sure that few Chinese Malayans served in the police, a disequilibrium that would be remedied by the British many years after the onset of the Emergency. Senior ranks were filled by Europeans. This was of course to ensure some kind of order, but in Malaya, as British officials acknowledged, the newly imported officer class had no local experience or knowledge, could not speak local languages, or understand local customs. As military historian David French points out, the command cadres of the Malayan police were 'inexperienced, inadequately trained, poorly disciplined, and prone to take bribes and extort money.' The problem was that in the post-war period the empire had to pay its way, and in almost every case it was only after the declaration of an emergency that deficiencies in policing were noticed and acted on – and then inadequately. In 1959, the Inspector General of the Police Department of the Colonial Office reflected on the fact that he and his colleagues had time and again made three basic recommendations for adequate numbers, better training and higher pay, which were ignored in all but the better off colonies. Even in Malaya, which was one of the better-off colonies, it took a long time to reform the police. The same point has already been made about the intelligence services in Southeast Asia, which had been badly damaged during the Japanese occupation. In June 1948, the Malayan Security Service (MSS) was working at half its pre-war strength. Only a tiny handful of Special Branch officers could speak any of the Chinese dialects: a crippling disadvantage given that the counter-insurgents were mainly Chinese. The burden of gathering information fell on Chinese, Indian or Malay junior policemen, who, it was assumed, would not call attention to their job when they mingled with crowds or attended local political meetings. They were in constant danger and since taking notes in public could result in a lynching, reports were always verbal – and probably inaccurate 'Chinese whispers'. Reform of intelligence gathering would be agonisingly slow. Sir Hugh Foot, a senior official who served in Palestine and Cyprus, pointed out that 'sledgehammer tactics' like mass arrests, mass detentions and collective punishments 'do more harm than good' by alienating general opinion. What was needed, he contended, was a 'selective drive against the terrorist leadership undertaken by small numbers of skilled forces acting intelligently …'. That was the theory. But if the intelligence service had no idea who the terrorist leaders were, let alone the enemy's order of battle, the only option was to wield the dim-witted sledgehammer.

The deployment of the British Army in colonial counter-insurgencies was bedevilled by many of the same kinds of problems. The weakness of the colonial police meant that colonial governments ran to the Colonial Office in London to beg for military assistance. Many beleaguered colonial governments were no doubt put in mind of getting blood from stones. After the end of the Second World War, the Chief of the Imperial General Staff (CIGS), Field Marshall Bernard Montgomery, now 1st Viscount of Alamein, launched a fundamental reorganisation of the British Army. The mission of this 'New Model Army' – which came into being with the passage of the 'National Service Act' in 1947 – was to deter and, if necessary, fight a hot war against Soviet aggression in Europe or the Middle East. By March 1951, 429,000 soldiers served in the British Army: 63,000 were stationed in West Germany, 45,000 in the Canal Zone and 35,000 in Malaya. The most parsimonious allowance was made for colonial garrisons. Montgomery's master plan was grossly short-sighted. The abrupt surge of colonial revolts in 1947–48 made the 'New Model Army' obsolete. Montgomery's successor as CGIS at the War Office was Sir William 'Bill' Slim, who had led the 14th Army to victory in Burma. Slim was forced back to the drawing board. For the next two decades the War Office improvised a succession of reserve brigade deployments to the hot spots of a contracting empire, as well as the European front line of the Cold War, in Malaya, Hong Kong, Korea, the Canal Zone, Kenya and Cyprus. At the beginning of the Emergency, there were just thirteen army units stationed in Malaya. By March 1953 that number had doubled. These figures disguise a long-term battle to supply sufficient men and materiel to fight the small nasty wars of decolonisation. The cupboard of the War Office was often bare. The solution was a tried and tested one. After 1947 the British lost control of that remarkable asset of empire – the Indian Army. But the Colonial Office still had access to huge human reservoirs in Africa, Southeast Asia – and of course in Nepal. The British had negotiated a deal with the Indian government that permitted the recruitment of an Anglo–Gurkha division. The Indian government retained, however, power of veto as to where the Gurkhas would be used. Manpower would be sought in the colonies. The military forces that Britain deployed in both Malaya and Kenya during emergencies included a very high proportion of colonial troops. In Malaya that proportion was between 42 per cent and 44 per cent of the garrison between 1950 and 1956, rising to 50 per cent the following year, when Malaya was made independent. During the 'Konfrontasi' war with Indonesia, which broke out after the abolition of national service, the British would deploy even higher numbers of colonial troops. Behind this strategy were two callous calculations. Colonial troops were cheaper, and British voters were unlikely to mourn their fate if they were killed in action in some faraway jungle. The decision to recruit in the last colonies did not end the War Office's dilemma. The troops had to be paid for – and since they were merely 'natives' British officers had to be supplied to lead them in the appropriate manner. As the wave of small wars of empire showed no signs of ebbing, the War Office put enormous pressure on colonial governments to pay for their garrisons. But no colonial governor was prepared to completely underwrite the cost of military operations on their territory, and so the British colonial armies were perennially strapped for cash. Tricky decisions had to be made about deployment. Germans did not want dark-skinned Nepalese stationed on the Rhine.

The Federation government could not escape the consequences of communal antagonism. Federal committees also needed to deal with sometimes troublesome new 'State Liaison Committees'. The UMNO leader, Dato Onn, who was also the 'Menteri Besar' (Chief Minister) in Johor, was frequently vocal in his criticisms. He complained that the British continued to distrust Malays and threatened to withdraw from the Federation. He never did. In fact, the raising of the special constables, which was dominated by Malay volunteers, in the first months of the Emergency war was a notable success. By the end of September, 24,000 Malays had enrolled. Their training was rudimentary. It was only when veterans of the Palestine police like Gus Fletcher arrived in Malaya that training improved. The majority of special constables were Malays. Their loyalty impressed the European colonial administrators and the business community. Their sole task was to protect Malaya's estates and mines. Chinese Malayans looked on anxiously as the British, egged on by Dato Onn, appeared to be arming the Malays just as the Japanese had during the occupation and for the same purpose. Sir George Maxwell, the former chief secretary, had in fact urged the government to arm Malays alone: 'If they were provided with ordinary shotguns, the change in the internal security of Malaya might be almost instantaneous.' This communal disequilibrium was compounded by the fact that special constables were rarely assigned to guard

Chinese-owned estates. According to a government memorandum: '… some Chinese mine or estate owners are paying protection money to the communists […] to leave them without protection would almost certainly result in a further lowering of Chinese morale …'. This was precisely the consequence. The only way that Chinese managers could win protection was by informing on the communists – and for many that was too much of a risk. From the Federation point of view 'arming Chinese' was judged to be hazardous.

The Nature of the Insurgency

The Malayan Emergency began with both sides knowing almost nothing about the strengths and, most significantly, the *weaknesses* of the enemy. The declaration of the Emergency had caught the communists with their pants down. It would be months before the MNLA was ready to take the fight to the British. Neither Chin Peng nor his adversaries, like General Boucher, knew that their opponent was hamstrung by circumstance. It would be some time before the Malayan security services even identified Chin Peng (who had by now been awarded an OBE for his contribution to the war effort) as the military commander of the MNLA. The Emergency would very slowly evolve into a war that used intelligence, the acquisition of knowledge of the enemy, as an equal partner to force of arms and bodies in uniform. The Emergency would be a war of skirmish and attrition. It would be won by starvation and the cultivation of disloyalty. There would be no climactic confrontation: no jungle Waterloo. Victory was a continuously receding mirage. It is instructive to compare the unfolding of the Malayan Emergency with the First Indochinese War. Between March and May 1954 the Viet Minh general, Vo Nguyen Giap, decisively smashed French forces at the Battle of Dien Bien Phu, forcing the French government to seek peace. The irony of Dien Bien Phu is that the French commander, Henri Navarre, had developed a strategic master plan to entice the elusive Vietnamese guerrillas into fighting a pitched battle that he assumed he could win. He was unaware that under General Giap the Viet Minh insurgents had evolved from strike and run guerrilla bands to become a well-equipped, well-lead and disciplined army that was capable of delivering a knockout blow. An American military analyst summed up the lessons of Dien Bien Phu: 'At every level of war the French seem to have violated the principle of mass while the Viet Minh did just the opposite.'[37] The overconfident French leapt headlong into a trap.

In Malaya no such set-piece battle would ever be fought. The MNLA did not have the means to follow the same evolutionary path as the Viet Minh. Nor was there a communist military strategist equal to General Giap. In his memoir, Chin Peng ruefully admits that 'the rush of events would determine the details of our strategy'. It was a matter of 'trying to make sense of the chaos'.

The First Phase

So, too, was the Federation government. Even the alarmist John Dalley had reported on 14 June, two days before the wave of murders in Sungai Siput, that 'there is no immediate threat to internal security in Malaya …'. He warned, though, that 'the position is constantly changing and is potentially dangerous'. It is not altogether surprising that Gent had no idea quite how to respond. 'We are groping in the dark,' complained MacDonald, who distrusted information passed down from Kuala Lumpur. In the aftermath of the Sungai Siput murders, Gent was in a sense lashing out – with the declaration of the Emergency and then police raids on MCP offices followed by large-scale arrests on 17 June. On 23 July, the Federation declared the MCP, the AJA Ex-Service Comrades Association, and the New Democratic Youth League, to be illegal.

We now know that the MCP was scrambling to mobilise. It had to transform from a legal political organisation to a guerrilla army that would need rice, weapons and ammunition. It was, as Chin Peng acknowledged, improvised and chaotic. The MCP had, of course, lost the element of surprise. Although the abrupt and unintended escalation of hostilities plunged the MCP into disarray, Chin Peng and the other military commanders clung to the classic Maoist schema of insurrectionary war. To begin with, Mao spoke of seven discrete steps:

1. Arousing and organising the people.
2. Achieving internal unification politically.
3. Establishing bases.
4. Equipping forces.
5. Recovering national strength.
6. Destroying enemy's national strength.
7. Regaining lost territories.

Mao later boiled seven stages down to three: In phase one the guerrillas win the population's backing by circulating propaganda and undermining the organs of government. In phase two intensifying attacks are launched against government forces and institutions. In phase three the guerrillas adopt conventional military tactics to seize cities, overthrow the government, and assume control of the country. In Mao's vision, the most important first step was the liberation of zones and the establishment of secure bases. To achieve this essential task rebel forces had to win the hearts and minds of peasants: the 'sea in which the guerrillas needed to swim'. Counter-terrorism expert David Kilkullen makes this point:

> … insurgent operational art remains fundamentally a matter of aggregating dispersed tactical actions by small groups and individuals, and orchestrating their effects into a strategically significant campaign sequence. Similarly, the operational art of counterinsurgency remains fundamentally concerned with

displacing enemy influence from social networks, supplanting insurgent support within the population, and manoeuvring to marginalise the enemy and deny them a popular base. Thus, at the operational level counterinsurgency remains a competition between several sides, each seeking to mobilise the population in its cause. The people remain the prize.

For the MNLA that 'prize' would be formidably hard to grasp. As far as we can tell, the MCP adapted the Maoist schema to fit the situation in Malaya. The first objective would be disruption of the economy and the Federation government. Terror would force the European managers of the estates and mines to flee, as they had in 1941. The estate and mine workers would embrace the guerrillas and supply rice, information and moral support. In the meantime, assassinations of government officials and 'running dogs', that is to say collaborators, would demolish effective government. Tax revenue would dry up and the country would become ungovernable. The MCP could then seize control of the state and eliminate British and local armed forces. Malaya would be a free republic. Such a revolutionary plan was not unfeasible. For good or ill, communist guerrillas would seize power in China, Vietnam and Cambodia. In *My Side of History*, Chin Peng wanted to explain why the MCP insurrection failed in Malaya. He devotes many pages to what went wrong and why. So preoccupied is he with explaining why the MCP failed, that the war appears unwinnable. He did not believe this at the time. Reading between the lines of his account, Chin Peng was often optimistic, most of all in those bloody and tumultuous months between June 1948 and the end of 1951. The MCP suffered from chronic frailties as it prepared to take on the colonial government. In the light of these inherent strategic weaknesses it is remarkable how much damage the communist guerrillas managed to achieve during the first two years of the Malayan Emergency. A point to emphasise is that the MCP Central Committee conceived of mobilisation in discrete stages, beginning with the destruction of party records and disposal of property and preparations to evacuate from towns and cities. This would be followed by actual mobilisation, first of hard-core MPAJA veterans followed by apprentice revolutionaries. The message, as suggested before, was to prepare for revolt. The rhythm of the entire process depended on how the Federation government decided to act. This was perhaps a fundamental error. It explains why Gent was able to take the MCP by surprise in June.

With hindsight it is clear that the MCP Central Committee soon made another mistake. In May and early June they ordered a vanguard cadre of semi-professional MPAJA veterans to disappear and form 'Special Service Corps', or 'Lau Tang'. These were, in short, murder squads. Since Central Committee had tenuous control of the 'Lau Tang', we have to conclude that it was one or more 'Lau Tang' gangs that killed the plantation managers in Sungai Siput, thus provoking the declaration of the Emergency. This would explain why Chin Peng was taken in by what happened on 16 June and was unprepared for its consequences.

In a very short space of time, the MCP had to undergo a radical transformation from a semi-legal political party based in towns and cities, to a clandestine guerrilla force that would depend on a ghost army of supporters. Right from the start of the war, the communists faced a daunting task of building links between different organisation levels and establishing supply lines that linked scattered settlements on the margins of the jungle to the MNLA bases on the flanks of the Main Range. The communist guerrillas would depend on compliant Chinese squatters and the produce of their smallholdings. As Spencer Chapman always insisted: the jungle is neutral. It gives nothing. The MNLA also took money from the squatters and expected them to actively gather information about the whereabouts of security forces. It was this umbilical bond between the MNLA guerrillas and the Chinese squatters that the British would move heaven and earth to break.[38]

We can imagine hovering a few hundred feet above the long, green jungle spine of the Malay Peninsula in July 1948 as the Malayan communists begin to organise. It is, of course, extremely difficult to see very much through the dense and tangled jungle canopy to the forest floor. The guerrillas have in any case taken great pains to conceal the camp from the air. Let us take poetic licence and in our mind's eye drop down to the forest floor. We would pick out an intricate network of secret paths and tracks linking the MNLA camps to the squatter communities. Many of these camps are old MPAJA strongholds brought back into service. Any camp that once had a British Force 136 officer in residence would be avoided. A typical MNLA camp can be built in a few hours. The bigger ones, with parade grounds, lecture halls and so on, took longer. Guerrillas returning with supplies of rice from a squatter settlement would follow a carefully concealed path that snaked through swampy *lalang* jungle. After a mile or so this would give way to thick *beluka*. The trail climbs steeply up a hillside. There is as yet no sign of any camp. It is difficult to move without making a lot of noise: dry sticks have been placed along the path. After climbing and scrambling up 600ft or so you come on a hidden sentry post, which overlooks the path and is built inside a clearing, or 'rentis'. A couple of hundred yards further on is a second sentry post. Then, 100 yards further on is the camp – an MNLA jungle fortress.

Camp construction is a job for experts. This one has accommodation for more than 100 guerrillas – simple lean-to huts made from *atap* and bamboo. The raw materials have been cut and collected from across a wide area so that any signs of a clearing are invisible from the air. A great deal of cunning has gone into the positioning of these simple huts. They are built on a sloping surface and separated by undisturbed strips of jungle vegetation. Any aerial observer would see only a number of isolated huts. A kitchen has been built inside a hollow and covered with *atap* to conceal smoke from cooking fires. Hollow bamboo pipes bring water to the camp from a nearby stream. Situated high above the main camp is another sentry post with an uninterrupted view of the entire valley. The camp is well concealed in the deep *beluka*, but is just a mile or so from the nearest squatter settlement. This proximity is deceptive. Government forces would be hard put to locate the camp – let alone mount a surprise attack. They would need to find some unfortunate 'traitor' to show them the way. Tropical jungles are hot, dark labyrinths. These MNLA camps were not fortresses. In the event of an attack it was normal practice for the sentries to fire a few shots to hold up the attackers while the rest of the guerrilla brigade fled. The camp would not be defended. Most were discovered abandoned. A typical MNLA camp, like the one described here, was a complex ecology of defiance and subterfuge.

In the first few weeks of the Emergency, the MNLA stumbled towards a pattern of attack. The first 'Combined Intelligence Staff Summary' of 15 July reports a few apparently random murders (a Chinese schoolteacher and a gardener) but only two large-scale attacks. The desultory character of the first weeks of the MNLA campaign is confirmed by Chin Peng's memoir. He describes, for example, an attack launched by a fifty-strong MNLA unit at Kulai, 20 miles north of Johor Bahru on the main road to Kuala Lumpur. The guerrillas were after weapons, but in Kulai they found none. A few Chinese villagers were killed. 'Mere adventurism' concluded Chin Peng. Malacca and Negeri Sembilan were quiet. This suggests that, in 1948, guerrilla mobilisation reflected the strength of the MPAJA in different areas during the occupation. The Japanese had mainly driven the MPAJA units out of Negeri Sembilan and Malacca.

The MCP raised the stakes on the morning of 13 July. Five guerrilla groups converged on the Batu Arang coal mine in Selangor. This was Malaya's only coal mine, but it had enormous symbolic importance. It was located in the capital state and had been the scene of violent labour disputes before the war. It was during one protracted strike here that Lai Tek had demonstrated his fitness to lead the party – with the collusion of the Special Branch. The attack that began that morning was a well-co-ordinated assault on a symbol of colonial power and exploitation. The MNLA attackers cut telephone lines and set up road blocks. The different units then split up: one entered the town, another attacked the police station, another the mine itself. A number of KMT men, including a mine superintendent, were killed immediately. They had evidently been 'pre-selected'. When the train from Kuala Lumpur steamed into Batu Arang station, some forty or so guerrillas boarded the coaches, herded terrified passengers onto the platform and seized any valuables. They seized a first-aid box at the station. A bus was stopped at a roadblock and the driver shot and wounded. A lorry was set alight, mining equipment damaged. No attempt was made to hold the Batu Arang area. When the guerrillas pulled out they took thousands of detonators with them. Other attacks were reported the same day, at Ulu Yam and Kajang.

There could no longer be any doubt that Malaya was at war again. But what kind of war? This was not entirely clear. On 16 July, a police squad surprised a number of guerrillas, including six women, in a hut about 3 miles from Kajang, 13 miles south of Kuala Lumpur in Selangor. The detectives attacked and killed two of the guerrillas and captured the rest. As they took stock a second MNLA unit struck, but the police aggressively counter-attacked, killing at least six guerrillas, including five of the six women. One of the dead was identified as Liew Yau, who was a member of the MCP Central Military Committee and president of the MPAJA Ex-Comrades Association. What was MCP top brass up to in Kajang? The British journalist Harry Miller was convinced that a plot was being hatched to capture Kajang and turn the town into a headquarters – a base, in other words. This is surely implausible. Many Chinese who lived and worked in the big coffee estates that clustered around Kajang were probably sympathetic to the communists but the area is much too close to Kuala Lumpur, the centre of colonial power. If capture of Kajang was the plan, which seems unlikely, it failed. But the MNLA would achieve a more impressive success when they struck at the little railway town of Gua Musang in south-east Kelantan 200 miles to the north.

This was, at least in theory, a cleverly chosen target. Anthony Short, in his classic study of the Malayan Emergency, suggests that the Gua Musang district was 'ripe for liberation'. What happened there in July 1948 would, for the MNLA leadership, offer a bitter strategic lesson. The 'base' idea was very hard to make work in Malaya. China is, of course, at least thirty times more extensive than the Malay Peninsula. In the early 1930s, the Red Army had been forced to retreat some 3,700 miles northwards by Chiang Kai-Shek's nationalists: the famous and much mythologised 'Long March'. The CCP eventually took refuge near Yenan in the Shaanxi province, which was a long way from any nationalist stronghold. The simple fact that Mao could find a territorial sanctuary with only the most rudimentary communication links to the KMT heartlands was essential to the CCP's long-term strategy – and spectacular success. Shaanxi could be 'liberated' with little interference from the centre.

The MCP would learn the hard way that the Malay Peninsula could not offer a long-term refuge. British Malaya had good communications, especially along the west coast, which meant that, in theory, government forces could respond quickly to guerrilla activity. This severely limited the guerrillas' room for manoeuvre. And building bases meant that the MNLA guerrillas had to leave their network of jungle lairs, which was always risky. But for the MCP in 1948, the Maoist ideal of the liberated area was a matter of faith. Chin Peng and the other politburo leaders made a decision early on to concentrate on three main areas: the Betong Salient on the Thai border; Tasek Bera, a region of freshwater swamp in Pahang; and the Gua Masang district in the Kelantan-Pahang-Perak watershed. Each one had advantages and disadvantages.

Clinging to the edge of a vast area of ancient rainforest, the town of Gua Musang clings to the edge of the Nenggiri River beneath steep, limestone crags. In 1948, the town was the last stop on the old East Coast Railway that came up from Kuala Lumpur. The railway meant that government forces could reach Gua Musang quite quickly. But access from Kota Bahru, the nearest big town, was a good deal more arduous. The road from the north ran out at Kuala Krai and the journey had to be completed by river, which could take up to ten hours, then by foot along an abandoned railway track. This hardly provided for even the most determined military assault. The railway was the problem. Undeterred, Chin Peng argued at the time that the Gua Musang area, including the nearby hamlets of Bertam, Pulai and Meraph, was 'the best opportunity for a major lunge at the British'. It would seem that Gua Musang was a kind of MCP 'Shangri La'. They certainly had form there, for during the Japanese occupation the MPAJA had often occupied the town for months at a time. They had even built a small mosque there. By 1948, the local people were mainly Chinese, with just a handful of Malays. The small band of police constables in Gua Musang and Bertam were poorly resourced and demoralised: they rarely troubled to put on uniforms. They had no access to wireless. On balance, it is not difficult to understand how Gua Musang could look like an opportunity rather than a trap.

The 'major lunge' commenced in a rather confusing way. At the beginning of July, the *penghulu*, or headman, of Pulai, who was Chinese, cycled (since there was no wireless) to Gua Musang with news that a large number of armed insurgents had been spotted in the area. The police post was reinforced, but the men were completely unnerved. On 17 July, MNLA commander Kim Siong led a 100-strong guerrilla force, backed by villagers from Pulai armed with parangs, into Gua Musang. From the precipitous limestone cliffs above the town, guerrillas rained down a barrage of grenades. The police put up token resistance, then surrendered. They were rewarded with $20 and a cup of coffee. The attack, which may not have been authorised by the Central Committee, was something of a confidence trick. The *penghulu* himself took part in the attack. It turned out that he had been informed by Kim Siong that Gua Musang was the last city still held by government forces in Malaya: Kuala Lumpur had already fallen to the communists. It came as a nasty surprise when RAF Spitfires roared in from the rocky crags and began strafing Gua Musang a few days later. The communists claimed the aircraft were Chinese come to liberate Malaya. A relief force, led by a Major Shaw, was sent up from the south, but was ambushed near Merapoh. 'Shaw Force' was wiped out. Clearly, something more spectacular was needed to dislodge the insurgents. A bigger relief force was organised, backed by RAF fighters, which soon reached the outskirts of Gua Musang. The game was up and Kim Siong did not put up much of a fight. He and his men vanished back into the jungle. After five days, the Gua Musang base was no more. The reason for this failure was simple. The MNLA could not deploy sufficient manpower to back up Kim Siong's units and thus secure the liberated area. Nor for that matter did Kim Siong's guerrillas do much to win over the hearts and minds of local people. The MCP, however, seemed to have been encouraged. It was around the time that Gua Musang was in guerrilla hands that the 'Malayan People's Anti-British Army' was renamed as the 'Malayan National Liberation Army'.

It is tempting to see the Gua Musang debacle as foreshadowing the failure of the MNLA campaign. But in this first phase of the war the MNLA was attacking and the Federation was reacting. It was Chin Peng's war. In northern Johor and Perak the MCP could often muster large numbers of guerrillas, sometimes up to 400, for attacks on the hated mines and estates. They used roadside ambushes to pick off estate managers and members of their families. In the more remote areas, the MNLA seized a number of plantations. There was an exodus of Europeans from these remote areas. The advance into the estates made ideological sense. Communist propaganda put out by the 'Lenin Publishing Press' rammed home the message that ruthless British imperialism was 'sucking dry the blood of Malayan people'. The British owned all the big mines, estates, trusts, business concerns, factories, communications, harbour wharfs, naval and military bases – and controlled it all through 'oppressive inducements and violent oppressions'. The imperialists came back to Malaya after the war thanks not to any martial prowess but to lucky breaks, and snatched the fruits of victory from the Malayan people. The British were puppets of the Americans; they hatched plots with 'Fascist accomplices', like the reactionary Kuomintang, Malay royalty, and capitalists, to rebuild their 'Fascist colonial state'. The British were slaughtering workers and peasants; farmers were turned off their land; trade unions banned; thousands of comrades arrested and banished. The MNLA fighters, the party propagandist insisted, were the very best of people: brave, intelligent and self-sacrificing. Propaganda like this was not the only inducement to back the Malayan revolution. The MCP appealed to unenthusiastic MPAJA veterans by pointing out, with good reason, that if the British sent them back to China the Kuomintang would murder them as soon as they stepped ashore. Why not join former comrades and win independence in Malaya? The MCP had less savoury persuasion strategies. Assassinations of 'running dogs', which usually meant Chinese who assisted the government, would be resorted to throughout the period of the Emergency. Corpses would be dumped in markets and other public places, complete with a charge sheet. The pamphlet pinned to the body of the unfortunate Pho Tee Lai denounced him as a 'rotten staff of the people': he 'protects unwholesome elements and becomes their informer. He is not loyal to the local people. We must exterminate this evil and running dog for the people whose rights and privileges he sells to the British imperialists.'

By September, the British 'Combined Intelligence Service' reported confusing movements of MNLA units across northern Johor and Perak and into Kelantan. It was hard to see a pattern. It was increasingly evident that the MNLA insurgents tended to muster in areas close to Chinese squatter settlements or where security forces were thin on the ground. Evidently the MNLA depended on a lifeline – the squatters. The British would become ever more obsessed with breaking this bond.

In this early period of the Emergency, Chin Peng was continuously on the move between jungle camps. His role as the MCP military commander was as yet unknown to the British. Nor did they know that security forces had killed the ablest communist commander, Liew Yao, one of the MPAJA heroes who had been invited to the Victory Parade in London two years earlier. As Chin Peng describes in his memoir, he was still struggling to define clear lines of command. The grand plan of waging nine separate insurgencies in the different Malay states was clearly unworkable. Chin Peng's peripatetic life at this time was a desperate attempt to rationalise the structure of the MNLA. He was frequently in great danger. On one occasion he was hidden in the back of a biscuit delivery van and driven to an old MPAJA camp at Ayer Kuning in Negeri Sembilan that had been constructed on swampy ground close to the Sungai Manik river. The British had funded a rice planting scheme here and the area near the camp was latticed by narrow irrigation ditches. The MNLA camp was separated from a nearby Malay village by one of these channels. When he reached the camp, Chin Peng immediately called members of the Perak State Committee to a meeting. He wanted to discuss establishing two main MNLA camps in the north and south of the peninsula. They all huddled inside a tiny squatter's hut that was hidden in the *lalang* jungle just behind the main camp. Suddenly a squadron of Spitfires whined low across the Sungai Malik and began strafing the camp. As Chin Peng stumbled out of the hut, he heard the ominous rumble of a Dakota spotter plane circling overhead. As the Spitfires soared away to the south a British patrol began advancing through the padi. They made slow progress. The Ayer Kuning camp had to be abandoned. Chin Peng now fled north to the Cameron Highlands in Perak. It would be here that, months later, he would hear of a British 'action' at a rubber tappers' village called Batang Kali.

Prelude to a Massacre

In December 1948, veteran reporter Harry Miller cheerfully informed his readers that 'Britain was fastening on Malaya's armour.' In August, three regiments of the Guards flew into Changi: the Coldstream Guards, the Grenadier Guards and the Scots Guards. Their arrival caused great excitement: they had a proud history and famous rites and traditions. But the Guards had no experience at all of jungle warfare. They had won only 'old world' glories. An American correspondent wryly commented: 'Well, Britain's pride of the palaces are just one more bunch of boys in the basha-huts of Malaya.' Although the aura of the Guards regiments conjured up images of bearskins and faultless parade ground drills, many of the soldiers were callow young national servicemen. After undergoing very limited jungle training, the Scots Guards set up headquarters in Kuala Kubu Bharu in the Malay State of Selangor. In December, according to a Far Eastern Land Forces British Army (FARELF) report, MNLA guerrillas launched a series of attacks in the Kuala Kubu Bharu area: 'bandits destroyed a railway station at Umu Yam Kala'; attempts [by MNLA unit] to burn down police station frustrated'; 'bandits fired on a police party in K Kuba Bahru wounding one'; on 11 December, two special constables were ambushed and wounded; later on the same day a police jeep was attacked on the Kajang Seninyeh road: 'three police killed, two specials wounded.' The wounded policeman was Captain Harnum Singh. He claimed later that a number of British soldiers had been killed in the attack that was not reported by FARELF or by a newspaper. It would appear that at the Scots Guards barracks in Kota Kubu Bahru feelings were running high. On 11 December 1948, a fourteen-man army patrol from the 7th Platoon, G Company of the 2nd Battalion Scots Guards, set out for the village of Batang Kali on the Sungai Remok rubber estate. According to another FARELF report: 'Vigorous patrolling by mixed Army–Police detachments continues in the areas in which bandit activity has been reported and several clashes have taken place.'

It would seem that on the British side feelings were running high.

9

A VERY BRITISH MASSACRE

An Exemplary War?

An insurgency has been succinctly defined by the historian David French as 'a contest between the insurgents and the colonial state to win political legitimacy in the eyes of the civil population.' Between 1945 and 1967, the British fought anti-colonial insurgents in Palestine, Malaya, the Canal Zone, Kenya, British Guiana, Cyprus, Oman, Nyasaland, Borneo and Aden – and for a short period in 1948 the Gold Coast. Counter-insurgency procedures, which were honed by the British between 1945 and 1967, 'laid the foundations,' historian Andrew Mumford writes, 'of a counter insurgency paradigm that required the concomitant utilisation of military, intelligence and political means to ensure an eventual defeat of the insurgents'. Counter-insurgency wars are invariably fought 'amongst the people'. They blur the distinction between insurgent and civilian. Armies that take on insurgents always face the moral risk of collateral damage: the killing of civilians. Since the Second World War, the British Army has been praised for developing more sophisticated and gentler counter-insurgency methods. This idea was enshrined in Sir Robert Thompson's *Defeating Communist Insurgency*. Thompson had served in Malaya as a senior government official and was closely involved in the development of security policy. His book argues that British security forces waged war in Malaya according to strict legal guidelines that insisted on the application of minimum necessary force. They refrained from abusing and terrorising the local population and relied on sophisticated intelligence to pick off the enemy leadership. The 'innocent many' were moved into protected encampments, or 'New Villages', that prevented them being intimidated by insurgents. Thompson stressed that the British way in counter-insurgency was compatible with liberal notions of right and wrong and could lead to the foundation of a just society. The hero of Thompson's book was Lt General Sir Gerald Templer, who, when he took charge in Malaya as high commissioner and director of operations in 1952, insisted that the war on communism must be won 'in the hearts and minds of the people'. Thompson's analysis of the Malayan Emergency as a 'paradigm' has been broadly applied to other counter-insurgencies. In his book he argued that British success fighting the small wars of decolonisation had depended on the continuous and critical analysis of campaigns so that the civil and military organisations responsible for prosecuting any conflict could absorb the lessons of experience. British counter-insurgency, as David French puts it, was praised by Thompson and his followers as a 'virtuous learning cycle'.

Thompson's glowing report on the genius of British counter-insurgency was enormously influential. His book flattered the historical record of British decolonisation. The retreat from empire was not, as some liberals and left-leaning historians claim, a chaotic and bloody retreat. Thompson gave it coherence and moral decency. Sir William Jackson, a former quartermaster general, bragged that the last act of empire 'never became a rout nor did it cost as much blood and treasure as the French, Dutch, Belgian and Portuguese withdrawals, or as the humiliating American fiasco in Vietnam'. *We* did it better. The 'Ideal Type' of British counter-insurgency continues to be taught at the Royal Military Academy at Sandhurst. The Malayan Emergency is admired as an exemplary case study in numerous British and American military text books. This rose-tinted version of post-war history is now under increasing pressure from both historians and soldiers on active service. The 'Malaya doctrine' may no longer be relevant to the global insurgencies that erupted after the destruction of the World Trade Center on 9/11. Some intelligent young British officers have come back from Afghanistan convinced that the war in Central Asia will not be won by what one called a 'stretched version of the Malaya campaign'. A more fundamental question is whether Thompson got right what happened in Malaya. Does the 'Malayan Paradigm' stand on strategic feet of clay?

It is certainly a puzzle that British forces in Malaya took more than a decade to quash a guerrilla army that had no outside support whatsoever – and that the 'defeated' communists were capable of renewing their assault a few years after the victory was celebrated. The debate about the 'Malayan Emergency' is only a matter of perceived success or failure. It also raises urgent moral questions about the role of violence by colonial security forces. Historians and lawyers acting on behalf of survivors have relentlessly uncovered the cruelty of British counter-insurgency practice in Kenya and Cyprus. The British counter-insurgency record in Malaya appeared for a long time to offer a benign counter-example. It was a 'good thing'. We had united conflicted communities and departed. The Emergency war surely was all about winning hearts and minds, not beating, torturing and killing unarmed civilians. This is a fable. We have already seen that Emergency Regulations permit a discrete and flexible application of violence. The Emergency war in Malaya was a nasty and brutal business that had unintended consequences which punish and divide the people of Southeast Asia to this day. Violence was integral to 'the British way in counter insurgency'. To be sure, counter-insurgent violence had different forms. It did not only mean shooting down unarmed villagers and burning their villages. In Malaya, the British undertook the forced transfer of more than half a million Chinese civilians and their incarceration behind barbed wire. Colonial officials described this policy as protection. As we will see, population transfer carried out during the Malayan Emergency was punitive by both design and effect.

The role that would have to be played by violence was admitted to by both the high commissioner and the GOC General Boucher at the time. Early on, the British positioned 'the Chinese' at the crux of the problem. The documentary evidence is fragmentary – but suggestive. In November 1948, a police officer based in Pahang told the commissioner of police apropos responsibilities of police and army officers:

> I am afraid we shall have a lot of trouble regarding this question of burning down of buildings by the military [...] [Officers Commanding Police Districts] are the only people allowed to seize and/or burn down buildings, and the military know this [...] General Boucher mentioned the fact that it was not proposed to obey this law ...

High Commissioner Gurney confessed that it was not possible to fight the Emergency 'within the law' and that the army and the police had 'to break the law everyday'. A Colonel X, who had spent just seven days in Malaya, is quoted in a police report: '[he] is fully prepared to deal with the present situation which he considers can only be met by fire and slaughter ...'. Situation reports document many shootings of men running out of buildings or huts and failing to stop when challenged. In many cases no arms or ammunition were discovered. Some police commanders were troubled by such incidents: 'I can find no legal justification for the shooting ...'. admitted the CPO Johor when he studied the evidence in one case. The perception was that the British had become convinced that the Chinese supported the communist insurrection and the Malays opposed it. This perception was assiduously cultivated by Malay political leaders like Dato Onn. This meant that Chinese villagers and workers living in plantation settlements were consistently targeted.

The destruction of Chinese villages had become accepted counter-insurgency practice from the very beginning of the Emergency. There is reliable documentary evidence about the destruction of Kachau village in the Kajang District of Selangor – not far from where a party of high-ranking communist guerrillas had been surprised and shot by police in July.[39] There is no question that this district, not far south of Kuala Lumpur, was deeply 'penetrated' by MNLA guerrillas. Kajang was known as 'Little Yenan' alluding to the refuge established in the Shaanxi province by Mao Zedong. Attacks on mines and plantations were frequent. An 8-year-old English boy had been killed in a guerrilla attack. Early on the morning of 2 November, a 'jungle police squad' razed the village of Kachau. This action followed an attack on a coffee plantation and there seems to have been some official concern about the destruction of an entire village. Official reports insisted that the unnamed police officer in charge had acted 'on his conviction and information' that the villagers 'harboured bandits'. The report concluded that the burning of Kachau was 'a hard blow' that nevertheless had a 'most deterrent effect'. A few of the homeless villagers had courageously made claims for compensation. These were dismissed as 'sheer impertinence'. The villagers, it was said, had made the mistake of 'backing the wrong horse' – the communist guerrillas. The tone of the report is defensive. We can detect the odour of discomfort. The possibility that the police squad had crossed a line was confirmed two weeks later when the Federation promulgated two new Emergency Regulations, 18A and 18B, which retrospectively gave police commanders powers to 'destroy buildings or structures', though not their moveable contents. A large number of the villagers' personal possession had gone up in flames when the police burned Kachau. The facts of the case troubled an experienced assistant police commissioner, Charles Thomas Winston Dobree. We don't know a great deal about Mr Dobree. He was educated at Westminster School and came to Malaya before the war; his wife was called Kathleen. He took part in setting up the Kedah 'Boxing Board of Control'. He was interned by the Japanese … Dobree was evidently a decent man and he was not prepared to accept that defensive official report about the burning of Kachau. Some details didn't ring true, so he began making enquiries. He discovered that at least two of the villagers had provided assistance to security forces, not the communists. Dobree kept digging. He was unable to interview the police officer in charge, who had left the force and was referred to as 'Mr X'. Witness testimony was consistent and persuasive. Here is what he discovered – and reported to the police commissioner. At 2 a.m. on the morning of 2 November, guerrillas had attacked the smoke house and rubber store at the Dominion Estate. Kachau village was half a mile from the estate. At 5 a.m., police commander 'Mr X' entered Kachau with his squad. He gave orders that the villagers should be awakened and instructed to leave within thirty minutes. Many villagers had insufficient time to gather their possessions. Personal property that was removed was dumped near the railway line. 'Mr X' then 'gave the order to set fire to the village'. 'Nothing was left of the village when the flames subsided …'. The piles of household goods and furniture left at the station also caught fire. The people of Kachau were then 'left to their own devices'. They were abandoned.

There is no suggestion in Dobree's report that 'Mr X' had any evidence at all that the villagers of Kachau had supported the MNLA guerrillas. The proximity of the village to the Dominion Estate implies, and the timing of the raid a few hours after the guerrilla attack strongly implies, that the police action was spontaneous retribution. The burning of Kachau was, in short, a reprisal – and a criminal act.

History in the Court Room

Subterfuge was integral to British counter-insurgency. The colonial power cannot afford to appear weak, but nor must its hands be too bloody. Blood spilt must be cleaned up: the inheritance of Britain's small wars is disavowal and cover-up. In 2013, the British Foreign and Commonwealth Office resolutely continues to defy any and every effort made to investigate and hold open public enquiries into acts of alleged criminal violence by British servicemen or police that took place during the period of decolonisation. British lawyers Martyn Day, Danny Friedman and John Halford (the latter backed by a Malaysian team led by Quek Ngee Meng) have taken on the Foreign Office with impressive determination. In 2011, after a protracted legal campaign, Mr Justice McComb agreed that 'ample evidence exists that there may have been systematic torture of detainees during the [Mau Mau] emergency [in Kenya]'. The government had argued that since Kenya was now a sovereign state, responsibility for the 'systematic torture' now lay with the Kenyan government.

The same brazenly disingenuous defence was made again in May 2012 by government barristers during the 'Batang Kali' trial at the Royal Courts of Justice in London. In this case Halford and Friedman and their Malaysian associates were acting on behalf of surviving relatives of the twenty-four men killed in the plantation settlement near Batang Kali at the beginning of December 1948 by a platoon of Scots Guards. The two judges appointed to hear the case did not accept this defence, though the outcome of the trial is unresolved at the time of writing. The purpose of the trial was to determine whether or not the defendants, the Foreign and Commonwealth Office, had been justified in denying that they had an obligation to hold an enquiry into the killing of twenty-four rubber planters in the village of Batang Kali near Kuala Lumpur in December 1948.[40] The government's legal team argued that since the killings took place in a British protectorate, the Malay State of Selangor: 'It follows that the Scots Guards were, like other members of the local police force, *acting as agents of the Ruler of Selangor*, a legal authority independent of the United Kingdom' (author's emphasis). This was a brazen case of buck passing – and was rejected by the two judges hearing the case, Sir John Thomas and Mr Justice Treacy.

In 2012, the publicity generated by 'Mau Mau' torture claims and the Batang Kali massacre trial forced the government to release a tranche of secret 'colonial' documents that had been locked away for many decades in the vaults of Hanslope Park. They had never been made available to researchers and historians. Hanslope Park is one of the government's most secretive and little-known establishments set deep in the Buckinghamshire countryside and surrounded by 16ft-high security fences topped with razor wire. The secret archive guards the reputation of empire. When the colonial files were released with much fanfare at the National Archives in Kew in 2012, the disappointment in the reading room was palpable. In the case of Batang Kali there was not a single relevant document – no paper smoking gun.

The implications were troubling. Either the paper trail had been obliterated – or the government had filleted the most damning evidence. In May, the Batang Kali trial began in London. As we have noted, the trial was not a public enquiry – but a proceeding to determine whether or not such an enquiry should and could be undertaken. We would be taken to the threshold of a secret history and no further. It was moving to see that vulnerable group of elderly Malaysian 'claimants' entering the intimidating gothic pile of the Royal Courts of Justice. They had waited to hear the truth about the fate of their relatives for nearly seven decades. Asking for a true account of what happened in Batang Kali and why it happened would not seem to be too much to ask. The claimants had no interest in prosecution and punishment of guilty parties. Truth is all. For two days their lawyers presented to the court the hard evidence of what they had discovered about the events that took place in Batang Kali. The 77-year-old Tham Yong, who died before the trial in 2010, spent decades fighting for a full public enquiry: 'after so much time, it still hurts me every time I talk about it, I remember it just like yesterday [...] I'm still angry because these were innocent persons but labelled as bandits and communists [...] My advanced cancer means I will not be around much longer, but I hope people remember what happened here so that those who were killed here are never forgotten ...'.

The account that follows is based on records submitted to the court in 2012.[41]

Exposing Britain's My Lai

On 11 December 1948, a patrol of fourteen British soldiers of the 7th Platoon, G Company of the 2nd Scots Guards Battalion struggled through the semi-cultivated fringe of the Malayan rainforest 45 miles north-west of the colonial capital of Kuala Lumpur. They had set off some hours earlier from their barracks in Kuala Kubu Bharu. The target was a small settlement of Kongsi huts that had been built in a clearing on the Sungai Remok rubber estate. For the platoon the march would have been a stressful experience. The young men, who were all doing national service, had received only the most rudimentary training in jungle warfare. It was fiercely hot and humid. They would have been tormented by mosquitoes and other biting insects. The platoon was led by two lance sergeants, Charles Douglas and Thomas Hughes. Among the men they commanded were William Cootes, Alan Tuppen, Robert Brownrigg, George Kydd, Victor Remedios, Keith Wood, Roy Gorton, George Porter and James Fern. A quarter of a century later, four of these men would make sworn statements about what they did and witnessed on the rubber estate. The platoon was guided by a Malay special constable called Jaffar bin Taib and accompanied by Detective Sergeant C.P. Gopal and a Chinese detective Chia Kam Woh.

In Malaya the British faced the classic problem of many counter-insurgency campaigns: uncertainty about the identity of the enemy. As a consequence of more than a century of colonial rule Malaya was a racially divided society. A significant proportion of the MNLA and communist leadership was Chinese. The MNLA was backed by a mysterious 'Masses Organisation', the Min Yuen. There is no hard evidence about the numbers of 'Min Yuen' in Malaya at any one time – or even a precise sense of what membership required of them. There was a pervasive sense that the 'Min Yuen' were everywhere. Anyone you met could be a 'Min Yuen'. So it was all too easy for government forces to suspect that *any* Chinese Malayan was a 'bandit' or 'bandit supporter'. Unusual behaviour by Chinese individuals could be construed as threatening, with deadly consequences. The brutal and indiscriminate tactics of some members of the British security forces assigned to Malaya was already a cause of concern by the end of 1948. The chief police officer of Johor, the southernmost Malay state, was unhappy about the number of reports he received about 'suspects being shot while attempting to escape,' and had heard rumours of 'rounds of ammunition planted on bodies to justify the shootings'.

By the time the Scots Guards platoon left their barracks that morning in December 1948, the Emergency war had settled into a bloody pattern of terror and counter-terror. According to a 'Memorandum by the Colonial Office on the Security Situation in Malaya' from April 1949, the number of fatalities since June the previous year included 386 civilians and 197 members of the security forces; bandit strength was estimated at between 3,000 and 5,000. However, security forces had killed or captured '800 of the enemy' and an astonishing 10,000 people had been 'arrested, detained or deported'. Of these, 4,000 would be deported to China. In Selangor, where the Scots Guards were based, guerrilla violence appeared to be escalating. At the beginning of December, a fifty-strong unit from the Eighth Regiment of the MNLA marched brazenly into Rawang and fired some 2,000 rounds at the police station, coffee shops, private houses and the ticket office of the local railway station. The Malayan Emergency has been described as a 'war on the periphery'. But this kind of audacious display of MNLA strength in Selangor was frighteningly close to the colonial capital. Everyone was on edge.

The young men marching towards Batang Kali were all 'virgin soldiers'. The commanding officer at the time explained that 'the requirements of the Emergency overrode the unpreparedness of the national service soldiers on the ground, and resulted in officers and men finding themselves on patrol and on active service the day they arrived.' The implication, of course, is that what happened in Batang Kali was a consequence of inexperience or incompetence rather than strategy. These may well have been factors in what happened, but all the evidence we now have points to the strategic murder of unarmed civilians. Orders were given and acted on.

There is abundant corroborating evidence that the slaughter was premeditated. In his testimony, William Cootes said that 'Men were angry [about the guerrilla attacks that took place prior to 11 December] and we were unofficially told we were going to wipe out the village …'. Alan Tuppen recalled that Captain Ramsay clearly said that their objective was to wipe out the village and everyone in it because they were terrorists or supporting terrorists. Victor Remedios also referred to Ramsay's briefing: the villagers were feeding the terrorists and every one of them had to be killed. When Ramsay himself was interviewed by journalists in 1969, he denied issuing these orders. But he made this very revealing comment:

> As a matter of fact we had often been criticised before the incident because of our inability to hit moving targets. Up to that day our bag of terrorists had been very poor indeed.

If Ramsay intended the Batang Kali operation to 'improve' his kill rate, as this surely implies, he succeeded.

The patrol arrived at the settlement in the late afternoon of 11 December. They discovered about fifty unarmed adults and a few children who lived together in the Kongsi huts. The plantation clearing was bordered by jungle on the east side and a small stream ran nearby. It was the permanent estate workers who lived here in the plantation. The 'day tappers' lived in the nearby village of Ulu Yam Bahru and were brought to work by lorry. They were not squatters. The people of Batang Kali were all well known to the owner of the estate, Thomas Menzies, who spent most of the time in Kuala Lumpur. He was chairman of the Selangor Estates Owners' Association and a well-known figure in the planters' community. He had a good relationship with the plantation manager, Lim Chye Chee, and both men later vouched for the good character of the workers. Lim had nothing bad to say about any one of them.

From the moment the Scots Guards platoon entered the plantation village they all appeared to act with calm deliberation. One group of soldiers immediately separated the men from the women and children. In counter-insurgency wars, this is a typical preamble to the execution of suspected male insurgents. When Victor Remedios was interviewed on the BBC *World this Weekend* in 1970, he said this:

> 'We were told that we were to […] we was to wipe out the village.'
> [The interviewer Roger Blythe] asked him, 'So the Sergeant told you that the men who had been separated from the women were going to be shot, there and then, and if you did not want to take part you need not?'
> Remedios: 'That's it.'

The platoon then locked the two groups inside different Kongsi huts. According to Emergency regulation 24(3), the soldiers should have taken any person suspected of being an MNLA guerrilla or an active communist sympathiser to the nearest police station, in this case at Kuala Kubu Bharu, for questioning. Instead, members of the platoon began the interrogations straight away. The two patrol commanders Lance Sergeants Hughes and Douglas took the lead. According to Cootes' testimony the atmosphere changed when Sergeant Hughes struck a female villager. According to statements made to the Malaysian police in the 1990s, Hughes then searched a young man called Loh Kit Lin and found a piece of paper in his pocket inscribed with Chinese writing. This seemed to be incriminating. Another villager tried to explain that the piece of paper referred to an agreement made with local Orang Asli to supply durians. But Hughes was convinced that it was a list of goods to supply to the terrorists. The accounts of what happened next are confusing. A few minutes later, Loh Kit Lim had been shot by Lance Sergeant Douglas a short distance along the road leading out of the plantation. There is some suggestion that Loh Kit Lin had been ordered to run. In any event, Hughes walked towards the wounded man and finished him off with a shot to the head. Hughes later told a journalist that:

> he saw the top of the man through the bushes and he seemed to be running. Douglas had shot him, but another guardsman discovered that he was not dead and informed Hughes. Hughes shot the man in the head as 'a humane act'. He could not say if anybody told the man to run: 'I was surprised at the shooting in the circumstances.'

What is most likely is that Loh Kit Lin was simply led away and shot.

That night, Cootes alleged, Douglas and Hughes called the soldiers together and told them they planned to 'execute the entire village'. Sergeant Hughes and Cootes then began questioning some of the villagers. The soldiers must have been frustrated. They fired shots close to the villagers' head to simulate an execution. A man called Choi Loi was so traumatised that he collapsed. The interrogations continued throughout the night. It would seem that Hughes and Douglas assumed that communist guerrillas would come to the village under cover of darkness to pick up supplies. None did.

Early on the morning of 12 December, the lorry from Ulu Yam Bahru that brought in the 'day workers' rumbled into the village. The soldiers gathered together the women and children and herded them onto the lorry. Choi Loi, the villager who had become ill under interrogation during the night, was forced to join them. But Lam Tin Shui, the *kepola*, or manager, who was in charge of the day workers and lived in Ulu Yam Bahru, was detained. As the lorry drove away from the settlement, Sergeant Hughes addressed the patrol. The men and boys must be shot, he told them. Anyone too 'squeamish' should take one pace forward and fall out. Alan Tuppen stayed put. James Fern and Victor Remedios both opted out and Hughes ordered them to stand guard on the road. In the meantime, police officers Gopal and Woh had taken Cheung Hung to the village store to continue questioning him. According to Cootes, Hughes then ordered the rest of the patrol to shoot the villagers, 'or they would be shot themselves'. The men were split into groups and led away towards the river. Cootes:

> We still hadn't fired and we were still looking at each other. Then we heard shooting from one of the other groups so instinctively almost, we opened fire. Once we started firing we seemed to go mad. The old man died immediately from one bullet. The one that was furthest away at the time took about seven bullets before he finally stopped crawling [...] I remember the water turned red with their blood. The incredible thing was that none of them spoke. They didn't shout or scream or anything [...] The man who kept crawling we shot in the head at point blank range. The man's brains spilled onto my foot ...'.

Robert Brownrigg:

> I don't know whether someone shouted an order but suddenly firing started and all the villagers started running [...] I fired to miss them, but within a minute or two all the male villagers were dead. Some tried to escape in a stream but were shot.

This is the only witness statement that refers to the villagers 'trying to escape'. It might seem to support the government version of events. But Brownrigg clearly states that he started shooting *before* any of the villagers bolted. What he is describing is a perfectly natural flight response. The Scots Guards took less than ten minutes to shoot all twenty-three villagers. As the shooting stopped, Gopal and Woh returned with Cheung Hung. They had been away for fifteen minutes. Hughes informed them that the villagers had tried to make a run for it and his men had been forced to shoot. He then showed Gopal fifteen rounds of Sten gun ammunition that he had found, he claimed, in one of the Kongsi huts. This was odd since searches conducted the day before had turned up nothing. It was the same kind of ammunition supplied to the Scots Guards.

The only male villager to survive was a teenager called Chong Fong. His different accounts are not completely consistent. One of the British soldiers – it is not known who this was – then told Cheung Hung to hide. He ducked into a patch of yams behind a chicken house. From there he heard bursts of gunfire, and caught glimpses of the slaughter by the river. He recalled that when the British soldiers returned, they 'seemed very pleased, they were talking to each other and smiling [...] but not all.' He later told the Malaysian police a rather different story. He too had been led away towards the river, but fainted on the way. Then he said: 'I recovered and saw three or four bodies with blood stains. I ran for my dear life.' He managed to reach Ulu Yam Bahru, where he hid in his father's coffee shop.

Twenty-four men now lay dead on the banks of the Sungai Remok. The platoon set fire to the Kongsi huts and returned to their base at Kuala Kubu Bharu. At least one of the platoon, Private Fern, was described by a soldier who had not accompanied the platoon as 'pale, nervous and distressed'. Captain Ramsay called the men together on the same evening, 12 December. In his BBC radio interview, Remedios claimed:

> *Remedios:* We were told by the sergeant after the incident that if anyone said anything we could get 14 or 15 years in prison. We were more or less threatened by the sergeant.
> *BBC:* So you got together and conspired to fabricate a story?
> *Remedios:* Yes, more or less.
> *BBC:* All the platoon?
> *Remedios:* More or less, yes.

In 1970, a journalist challenged the former Sergeant Hughes:

> *Journalist:* How can you be sure the men were terrorists?
> *Hughes:* How can you be sure? But we thought they were. I sensed danger in the village. I can always sense danger. It is better to be safe than sorry.

He then made this chilling confession:

> If the women and children had made a break for the jungle, I would have given the order to fire. That's natural in war.

The witness statements quoted above were all made by members of the platoon long after the events. But back in December 1948, a British police officer had already uncovered the horror of Batang Kali. Timothy Hatton, aged 80, told his story in 2011:

> … the CPO [Police Commander] rang me up and said, there has been a frightful incident, No, correction: there has been a wonderful victory, we've killed twenty communist terrorists, the biggest group killed in the Emergency so far and I want to congratulate the security forces for doing it. Could you find the details and I will write to them? It was outside my district: a good way out. I had a map of all the Chinese estates which nobody else had. And I find this one [Batang Kali]. I went there and there were two lorries, opened lorries. In the back were men, dead as door nails. All dressed in singlets and pants. They clearly weren't bandits of any kind who were usually very dark and tall and bigger and more energetic looking.

Hatton had no doubt at all that the dead men had not been 'bandits'. He was disturbed 'to see how white were the palms of their hands [...] They were not at all like the [communist] Gombok Armed Work Force, whose hands were dark and rough.'

> ... So I went along, [to Ulu Yam Bahru] and there was this one woman who managed to escape and she said it's the army who's done this. It's nothing to do with terrorists. We have got nothing to do with terrorists. It's sheer murder. My son's gone and my husband's gone. Nobody's going to keep me and I'm pregnant with my next one. It will be very difficult for me. And I'm on my own, twenty have gone and I have left.

There were claims that ammunition had been stored in the Kongsi huts. Hatton was not convinced:

> Another Chinese came up, someone next door and said, yes they were communists in there, definitely. They hid their arms and ammunition in the roof, attic roof. And when it burned, you could hear the 'pop', the ammunitions going off, quite definitely the communists were using that place. So I said, do you see that little out-house there with an attap roof? Lets burn it. So we burned it and it went 'pop pop pop', and he said yeah that's the ammunition. I said, no it isn't, it's the bamboo, it's the male bamboo which when you burn it, the air expands and breaks the bamboo and it goes 'pop'. So that was the end of that little exaggeration. Anyway, I reported all this to my chief police officer who absolutely couldn't believe it at all: 'I think there probably is something funny about this!' So I said, its not something funny about it, its sheer murder of twenty people and it's a complete disgrace. From then on, the government hid it, covered it up, wouldn't say anything ...[42]

Hatton took photographs and submitted a report to his senior officer expressing his concern about the incident. Both the report and photographs vanished. They have never been found. The day after the killings High Commissioner Sir Henry Gurney sent a confidential telegram to the Colonial Office: '26 [sic] bandits shot and killed by police and military action in the Kuala Kubu area of Selangor.' Gurney's account was reiterated in a FARELF situation report a few days later: 'bandits attempted mass escape [...] twenty-five killed. One recaptured.' To begin with the British tried to spin the Batang Kali operation as a success – and a very impressive one. In any counter-insurgency it is very rare for the government forces to eliminate such a large number of the enemy in a single action. Guerrilla fighters are by definition elusive. At this stage in the Emergency, war success stories were desperately needed. Harry Miller dutifully reported in *The Straits Times:* 'the biggest success occurred in Batang Kali [...] Scots Guards numbering 14 shot dead 25 Chinese who they surprised yesterday morning ...'. Details had been 'flashed by radio from the jungle'. Miller clearly did not visit the scene. It is revealing that he does not even bother to stigmatise the dead 'Chinese' as 'bandits'. The villagers are referred to as 'Chinese' throughout the article. The crucial ingredients in the British 'success story' are carefully laid out in the article. The platoon had encountered two 'armed Chinese in uniform' en route to Batang Kali. Ammunition was found hidden in one of the Kongsi huts. 'One of the Chinese attempted to escape and was shot dead.' Even the arrival of the lorry with the day workers and food supplies was made to look suspicious. And finally: 'Suddenly the 25 men made a break in all directions. A police officer said: 'The Guards had been well placed and the running men just ran into their guns. Every man was killed.' Miller was not the only offender. The British had repeatedly described the killings as 'the biggest success achieved in one operation in Malaya since the Emergency began …'.

The Story Collapses

The 'successful operation' story began to crumble remarkably quickly. A small party of surviving villagers had managed to reach the Chinese Consulate in Kuala Lumpur and told their horrifying story to Consul General Li Chen. He held a press conference on 21 December. The following day the British owner of the Sungai Remok Estate, Thomas Menzies, issued a statement that 'All those killed by the Scots Guards had been employed by the plantation contractor Lim Chye Chee, with whom [he] had been associated for 20 years.' Menzies had clout in the British planting community and his intervention was bad news for the government. Menzies identified one of the dead as his plantation *kepola* and another as his estate clerk. He emphatically denied that the lorry driver from Ulu Yam Bahru had any connections with the communists. The food he had brought was for the plantation workers. By 24 December, *The Straits Times* was calling for a public enquiry into an incident that caused 'serious concern among all communities'. The Chinese Consul General spoke out again on behalf of the bereaved families, insisting that the military authorities address 'the circumstances in which the men were shot' and 'the wider question of the instructions under which troops and police operate'. These were the right questions and they have never been answered.

By the end of the year the British seem to have realised that they had a problem. Their response was to accept the need for an enquiry, which is, of course, a characteristic holding action. The gentleman appointed to lead the enquiry was the colonial attorney general, Sir Stafford Foster-Sutton. He told *The Straits Times* that 'a full enquiry was in hand'. In 2012, historians and researchers hoped that the formerly secret colonial papers released by the government to the National Archives would include evidence submitted to a 'Foster-Sutton enquiry'. We were bitterly disappointed. If Stafford Foster-Sutton carried out a 'full enquiry' in 1949 he left no trace of his activities. We have instead a single statement that the attorney general had 'carefully considered the evidence' and visited Batang Kali. He had concluded that no further action was required. A supplementary statement released to the press and dated 3 January includes a crucial change of tack. The government now refers not to 'bandits' but to 'occupants of the kongsi houses'. They, the statement claimed, had been interrogated and disclosed that 'armed bandits were in the habit of visiting the area'. On the morning of 12 December, the statement goes on, the Chinese men were released from the hut: 'one of them shouted and they thereupon split up into three groups and made a dash for the three entrances to the jungle …'. When a Scots Guards officer called out the Malay word for 'Halt!' the escapees continued running and 'the soldiers opened fire'.

It would seem that since Harry Miller had made his 'extremely accurate' report – which had been commended by General Boucher – Stafford-Sutton, or someone else involved with the 'enquiry', had noticed gaping holes in the official story that had first been concocted by Sergeant Hughes and was desperately trying to plug the gaps as best he could. The official statements made in January no longer refer to the dead plantation workers as bandits; the nonsense about finding ammunition has mainly disappeared – and there is no further suggestion that the lorry was bringing food supplies for the communists. Instead, the statement shores up the 'shot trying to escape' narrative, and stresses that the members of the Scots Guards platoon issued clear warnings. There is a notable discrepancy between the original claim that the escaping villagers ran *into* the platoon's field of fire and the new story that they were running *away* into the jungle. A simple examination of the dead men would have settled that question but one was never carried out. The 'full enquiry' was, as far as we can tell, bogus. When interviewed on *The World at One* in 1970, Stafford-Sutton admitted that 'no enquiries were made of inhabitants' [i.e. the women and children] on the grounds that they would have lied or been afraid to tell the truth. Nor did he seriously investigate the statements made by Detective Sergeant Gopal and Detective Woh. Both contradicted the official version of events. If the members of the Scots Guards platoon made official statements to the 'enquiry', these are no longer extant.

The Colonial Office in London could not completely disguise the bad odour that hung over the events at Batang Kali. At the end of January, a communist MP called Philip Piratin rose in the House of Commons to insist that the Colonial Ssecretary, Arthur Creech-Jones, fully account for the actions of the Scots Guards. By now the government version was firmly entrenched – and in fact has never changed. Creech-Jones informed Piratin that an 'enquiry by the civil authorities' had concluded that 'had the security forces not opened fire, the suspect Chinese would have made good an escape, which had obviously been pre-arranged …'. This has been the 'government line' ever since.

The 'enquiry' into a 'necessary but nasty operation' quashed the debate about the Batang Kali killings – until that bitterly cold day at the beginning of December 1969, when former national serviceman William Cootes, who had served in the Scots Guards, made his confession to the *People on Sunday* newspaper. He had been one of the fourteen Scots Guardsmen who had entered

Batang Kali that day in December 1948. In the aftermath of *The People* story 'Massacre in an Unnamed Village', and the furore that came in its wake, the Secretary of State for Defence, Denis Healey, referred the matter of Batang Kali to the Director of Public Prosecutions (DPP) on 13 February 1970. At the end of the month DPP lawyers recommended that further enquiries should be conducted by the Metropolitan Police, much to the dismay, as we can see in the official documents, of the Foreign Office. DCS Frank Williams was appointed to lead an investigative team. All the former members of the Scots Guards platoon who had testified to *The People* were interviewed again, this time under caution – and Williams learnt of at least four witnesses, including Woh, DS Gopal and Cheung Hung, who remained alive in what was now independent Malaysia. He made plans to fly to Kuala Lumpur to continue with their enquiries. Then on 18 June 1970, the Labour government was ousted by the Conservatives – and just weeks later the new attorney general, Sir Peter Rawlinson, halted the Batang Kali enquiry 'with a view to upholding the good name of the Army'. This pattern of revelation followed by denial and cover-up was repeated after the broadcast of a BBC *Inside Story* documentary, *In Cold Blood*, that was transmitted in 1992. Peter Dale's powerful film had an equally powerful impact as the original story in *The People*. The programme makers carried out distressing interviews with a number of key witnesses – and with Ron Dowling, the police officer who had been scheduled to go out to Kuala Lumpur, who complained bitterly: 'We could have got to the truth, which is what I wanted to do …'. The documentary proved conclusively that a number of reliable eyewitnesses should have been contacted and interviewed in 1970. This time a *Malaysian* police enquiry was launched, and then stopped without explanation. Documents referred to in court revealed that the Batang Kali massacre remains a highly sensitive issue for British governments. To this day the official line remains unchanged: 'shot trying to escape'.

Not the End of the Road

At the beginning of September 2012, the High Court rejected the claimants' demand for a public enquiry. Sir John Thomas, the president of the Queen's Bench Division, and Mr Justice Treacy, concluded that it was 'very questionable' that 'much can be learnt'. They stated: 'All in all, it would appear to be very difficult at this point in time to establish definitively whether the men were shot trying to escape or whether these were deliberate executions. Nor, in our view, would it be any easier to determine whether the use of force was reasonable or proportionate.' John Halford, the solicitor who has fought so long and hard on behalf of the Malaysian claimants, has won the right of appeal against this verdict. The verdict was disappointing. But it was a breakthrough. For the first time, British judges refused to accept the moth-eaten 'shot trying to escape' story that has been spun by the British government for more than six decades. During the trial, the claimants' barristers had set out '10 key facts'. Of these, the High Court accepted that: '[t]here is no evidence, sixty-three years later, on which any of the 10 key facts relating to what happened at Batang Kali can seriously be disputed.' These 'key facts' included:

- the inhabitants of Batang Kali (not 'bandits', but 'families' of 'civilians' who 'had no weapons') were subjected to 'simulated executions to frighten them'.
- the next day women and children were taken away in the only available vehicle.
- the village hut where the male villagers were held 'was unlocked'.
- within minutes, all of the twenty-three men were dead as a result of being shot by the patrol.

The judges agreed that 'there is evidence that supports a deliberate execution of the 24 civilians at Batang Kali'. *Evidence of a deliberate execution*: these were momentous words. A moral victory had been won.

As well as forcing the Foreign and Commonwealth Office onto the defensive, the Batang Kali trial in 2012 brought to light a significant volume of new evidence about British counter-insurgency tactics in Malaya. We now know that Sir Stafford Foster-Sutton, the attorney general in Malaya in 1948 who carried out that first sham enquiry, was privately convinced that 'there was something to be said for public executions as a legitimate means to demoralise those involved in the insurgency.' On 22 January 1949, the Federal government of Malaya quietly introduced a new Emergency regulation, 27A(6), to legalise past as well as future cases of 'using force to secure an arrest if this was resisted, or to prevent escape' as long as a warning or challenge was issued. The actual words of the regulation read as follows: 'Any act or thing done before the coming into force of this regulation which would have been lawfully done if this regulation had been in force, shall be deemed to have been lawfully done under the regulation.' The killers of the villagers of Batang Kali were retrospectively found innocent of any crime. According to a document presented to the court in 2012, Sir Alex Newboult in the high commission summed up the lessons for the government of the Batang Kali affair as follows. His words encapsulate perfectly the British way in counter-insurgency:

One of the difficulties of this situation is that we have a war of terrorism on our hands and are at the same time endeavouring to maintain the rule of law [...] Rightly or wrongly, we feel here that we must be conservative in our criticism of the men who are undoubtedly carrying out a most arduous and dangerous job [...] Moreover, we feel that it is most damaging to the morale of the security forces to feel that every action of theirs, after the event, is going to be examined with the most meticulous care.

10

ADVANTAGE CHIN PENG

Defenders

After landing at Changi Airport in Singapore, former Palestine policeman Gus Fletcher and the other exhausted young police recruits, who had endured an arduous succession of uncomfortable flights across half the world, boarded trucks to begin the long drive north across the causeway towards Kuala Lumpur. Since leaving London, the young men had had just three hours' rest. But they wouldn't stay long in the Federation capital. One party continued on towards the town of Raub, not far from Fraser's Hill. Fletcher's unit drove east across Malaya's rocky spine into Mentakab in Pahang:

> We went to Mentakab, six of us – and the hotels, the rest house were all full up. We camped out on the verandah of the plantation we had been assigned to – and the manager introduced us to the 'Stengah'. We had never heard of a 'Stengah' before. In England there's a beer called Stinger, but 'Stengah' – we didn't know about it. A siren went off. There was shooting [...] a building on fire. We went out in our civilian clothes, which I thought was stupid because we were all wearing white shirts. We picked up the dead body of some poor Chinese manager. We came back hours later: it was 3 a.m. but before we can get to bed, another one, another attack, we go off to different direction, to another plantation. This time we brought back a dead body of a CT [communist guerrilla] because some Home Guard chaps shot him [...] Then a few minutes rest, and we are off again. Another fire ...

The planters he was defending had developed a siege mentality:

> Because of the huge number of CT regiments, and independent platoons around that area of Mentakab, a curfew was in operation. Nobody could move. Now at night, you will see lights moving, and then they [MNLA] start shooting. So you hit the floor and press one switch which put off the electric lights in the manager's house. Another would put on the flood lights outside. Bump, bump, bump, all night long. And one night, I suppose it was one in the morning, the guard down below said he could see lights. And there was indeed – two lights

out in the blackness. I picked up the guard's rifle and said: 'let me have a go'. And I fired and with the second and the third shot, the light went down. And we waited for the attack. Oh, it was tiring. We waited, nothing happened. Then in the morning, a young man appeared. It turned out that I had shot his father – a poor Tamil rubber tapper. A weeder: and he had been going out getting some 'Samsu' [alcohol] for his daughter's wedding. And I shot him. He was taken to a hospital. What he was doing was strictly speaking illegal, of course but I asked that he should not be prosecuted. You know the poor fellow had been punished enough. He was in the hospital for about a week. And when he recovered, he came up to the bungalow with a basket of fruits. And an invitation to his daughter's wedding. I accepted the fruits but not the invitation, not the way I felt. I was very embarrassed at shooting the father of the bride.

On 6 October, a new high commissioner arrived in Malaya. Sir Henry Lovell Goldworthy Gurney had no experience in Asia. He had presided, as chief secretary, over the shambolic and shaming British abandonment of Palestine. The governor general in Singapore, Malcolm MacDonald, who had engineered the ousting of the first high commissioner, Sir Edward Gent, feared that Gurney was not well known enough. The people of Malaya, he complained, were hoping for a 'big hitter' who would fly into Kuala Lumpur and 'get the job done'. Gurney would need careful 'building up'. For UMNO leader Dato Onn bin Jaafar, Gurney's appointment was unwelcome for a different reason. He was concerned that the new high commissioner would administer Malaya *as if it was Palestine*. What he meant by this was that Gurney might adopt an even-handed approach to the Malayan communities as the British had tried – and failed – to do in the Middle East. In Dato Onn's view, the British could not view the Malayan races as having equal rights. In the event the boycott was averted. All but the Sultan of Johor attended Gurney's inauguration. He would have more intractable problems dealing with his own staff – and with the devious MacDonald.

By the time Gurney was settling down at King's House, there was a deepening recognition that intelligence was crucial but deficient. The trickle of information about the MNLA leadership and order of battle was clearly inadequate. This constipated system of intelligence gathering was exacerbated by the civil war between the GOC General Boucher and the new commissioner of police, Colonel Nicol Gray. Who was in charge? The army or the police? This was a tricky question because the strategic philosophy of the Emergency was that the army was 'assisting the civil power'. Since martial law had not been imposed and never would be, the campaign against the communist insurgents would be led by the civil government. The Emergency thus favoured Gray to the discomfort of Boucher. So Gurney's first task was to knock heads together. Gray would never be an easy subordinate. But Gurney never doubted that the police would have to bear the brunt. This meant that colonial police took on ever-burgeoning powers. British Malaya became a police state – and even after independence the extraordinary powers allotted to the Malaysian police were not rescinded.

Gurney brought in new Emergency Regulations that had been tried and tested in Palestine. By December 1948, the security apparatus had become a great deal more formidable. The police acquired untrammelled powers of search, detention, curfew, and control of the movement of persons and traffic. Anyone suspected of being a 'terrorist' or assisting the communists could be detained for ever-lengthening periods of time. The carrying of arms became a capital crime. By the end of 1948, at least 5,000 Malayans had been arrested and were in detention at centres and camps. The 'Printing Presses Bill' – which still remains in force – compelled newspapers to obtain a permit from the chief secretary. These would not be granted to those applicants not considered to 'share our ways of life and thought'. If reporters and editors refused to toe the line, the all-important permit would be rescinded. Reporters accompanying army or police patrols had to submit their copy for approval and there was a great deal of bullying to make sure they filed the right sort of story. These Emergency Regulations worked hand-in-hand with a policy of national registration. This was a means of bonding loyal subjects to the government and excluding potential malcontents. Registration drew a clear line between honest card carriers and doubtful types without the necessary documents. Registration was a socialising process and, like the old colonial census operations, reinforced racial division. Most Chinese Malayans used more than one name, or had variant spellings of the same name. These variations were referred to pejoratively as 'aliases' – and offended the colonial sense of order. The new identity cards known as ICs were limited to just one name. For most Chinese, registration was demeaning.

For the MNLA, national registration was a dire threat. The IC cards threatened to divide the people of Malaya into law-abiding IC holders, and non-card holders who could be stigmatised, isolated or arrested. The MNLA warned Chinese villagers not to register, and if they already had usually forced them to tear up their ICs. MNLA hit squads targeted the teams of administrators and portrait photographers sent out to make the new policy work.

According to K.L. Chye:

> … all photographers who take pictures of these civilians and so on, many were taken away by the communist in the dead of the night, they were tortured and then left dead.

A communist called Shung Sheng explained why:

> The implementation of identity cards caused a lot of inconveniences. We were free without identity cards because they could not identify who was a communist. Those without identity cards were arrested, so the CPM went around the villages and confiscated all the identity cards …

Another communist called Ah Hai admitted that: 'We confiscated the identity cards and this affected the people. They got into trouble without identity cards.'

Policeman J.J. Raj remembers that a favourite tactic was to ambush buses that were crammed with Chinese peasants: '... these Communists tried different methods [...] they stop the bus and collect all the ICs and burned them [...] they take these people into the jungle and murdered them ...'.

By the end of the first year of the Emergency the number of guerrilla attacks had begun to fall. As the new high commissioner took stock, the mood in the colonial clubs and estate offices, in King's House in Kuala Lumpur and at Government House in Singapore was surprisingly buoyant. The fuss about the Batang Kali incident had been successfully dealt with and there was a sense on the government side that a corner had been turned – and that the storm was receding. But this time of self-congratulation and all-round back slapping would not last long.

Gurney was no liberal. This was made abundantly clear on 10 January 1949 when he brought in a raft of new 'Emergency Regulations' that had been tried and tested in Palestine, the most notorious of which would be '17D'. This gave the police unprecedented powers to detain suspects without bringing them to trial. An Indian member of the Federation Legislative Council, Mr R. Ramani, who was also a member of the Bar Council, denounced this 'new despotism of the executive and the newer despotism of the police'. His most caustic barbs targeted the hated new Regulation 17D. On what grounds, he asked rhetorically, might a detainee appeal?

> He is supposed to state the grounds of his objection without knowing a word about why he has been detained: and then what happens? [...] the Advisory Committee [...] go on to say sapiently these magic words: 'the grounds for making a detention order against you were that you were suspected of having recently acted or – mark these words – of being likely to act in a manner prejudicial to the public safety or good order.

'Being likely to act' is one of these all purpose pseudo-legal tricks, typical of repressive regimes. Over time Regulation 17D grew into an illiberal monster. The significance of 17D is that it handed the high commissioner the power to order *collective detention*: this meant that entire districts could be declared 'bad' or 'black' and all or any of the people living inside their borders could be detained. The regulation spelled out the high commissioner's rights with draconian thoroughness. He could order mass detentions if any of the residents of the district or area: aided, abetted, harboured, or consorted with persons who had acted or intended to act in a manner prejudicial to public safety or order; suppressed evidence of offences; failed to give information; failed to take reasonable steps to prevent the escape of any person they knew or had cause to believe was a person who intended to act or had acted in a manner prejudicial to public safety or order. Those detained could later be 'removed' from the Federation, which meant deportation to Communist China. Only British or Federation citizens had any right of appeal. Regulation 17D, to sum up, provided the security forces with the sanction to 'cleanse' 'certain specific areas' judged to be 'bad' or, in the words of Nicol Gray, the commissioner of police, 'uncooperative'.

Gray was a staunch advocate of Regulation 17D. Even before Gurney announced the new regulation he had ordered police to draw up lists of 'dangerous areas' so that they could act immediately, 17D came into force. On 11 January, police arrested 564 persons at Sungai Jeloh, near Kejang in Selangor: 'mainly women children and some old men' who were all 'medically examined and detained'. Between January and October, sixteen raids under 17D led to the detention of no fewer than 6,343 detainees in Selangor, Negeri Sembilan and Kedah. That February, the police herded more than 1,000 former detainees onto two ships and sent them to face an uncertain fate.

The Chinese press in Malaya protested vigorously against this collective punishment. That was to be expected but so, too, did a handful of Federation officials, including the deputy chief secretary to the Secretary of Defence, Edgeworth David, who had recently spent time in Hong Kong. He warned his colleagues that British tactics in Malaya had begun to resemble, for many influential commentators, the mass population transfers that had caused so much suffering across Europe at the end of the war. David's blistering memorandum denounced both the conduct of the '17D raids' and their rationale. The Federation had only been concerned with 'denying the particular area to the bandits and not with the fate of the wretched people who are being transplanted from their home and forcibly removed for ultimate dispatch to China where the majority arrive in a state of destitution …'. He emphasised that:

> … to all intents and purposes, these people who have in many instances spent years building up their small livelihood and establishing their homes are at a moment's notice evicted from their homes (which are destroyed behind them and deprived of all their property […] They may have lived in Malaya for twenty years, they may be Malayan born, they may have personal and business interests which they cannot wind up at a moment's notice …

Collective detention was indeed cruel and punitive. Repatriation was not merely callous, but absurd. The vast majority of people banished to China were women and children; they reached their destinations in states of complete or semi-destitution: many were left to starve – 'there is no question,' David concluded, 'that these operations involve a very severe degree of hardship and inhumanity which is very difficult to defend'. Gray was forced to defend his application of '17D' at a meeting called by the high commissioner at the beginning of June. His defence was robustly crass: 17D worked. He dismissed the criticisms as the machinations of a 'Chinese scholar' (i.e. David) who, regrettably, had to 'deal with the human problems in detail'. This, naturally, clouded his judgement. Gray convinced his old friend the high commissioner. There would be no second thoughts.

The Front Line

As the Scots Guard platoon marched towards Batang Kali on 11 December, Chin Peng was once again on the move. At the MNLA camp in the Cameron Highlands, he had organised a 'North Malayan Bureau' to bring some order to the communist campaign in the north, in Kedah, Penang and Perak. He still favoured the idea of a liberated zone in Kelantan, though the Gua Musang fiasco was hardly a good omen. To tackle the chaos in the south, Chin Peng called a meeting of the Central Committee at a jungle camp near Titi in Negeri Sembilan, on the border with Selangor and Pahang. It was soon apparent that he could not possibly reach Titi in time – so he delegated to Yeung Kuo, who, it will be recalled, had helped plot the undoing of Lai Tek. In the meantime, Chin Peng organised a fresh assault on Kelantan, sending three units, each one between 100–200 strong, back into the Gua Musang area. Deploying and supplying these bigger detachments was a formidable logistical task. Communications depended on hundreds of Min Yuen supporters who carried messages back and forth between drop spots on bicycle or on foot.

At the end of the year, Chin Peng abandoned the MNLA camp in the Cameron Highlands and headed south with a small party of bodyguards. Their first destination was Kuala Lipis, on the Sungai Jeli in Pahang, where they hoped to make use of the tangled network of rivers and streams that flow into the Sungai Pahang. The long first part of the journey would need to be made on foot on forest pathways. Public roads were much too dangerous. From Kuala Lipis the party planned to head towards Raub but the way there was now said to be heavily patrolled. Chin Peng, now accompanied by an entire brigade, was forced to make a long detour to the east before plunging south again in the direction of Mentakab, where Gus Fletcher had experienced his baptism of fire back in July. His destination was the 'Ten Milestone Village'. Chin Peng's journey ended up taking him five months: he left the Cameron Highlands camp at the end of December and reached 'Ten Milestone Village' in May 1949. From there, Chin Peng was escorted to an MNLA camp, which he tells us was 'half a day's trek from the road' and located on a steep jungle hillside. Here he was greeted by MNLA commanders, Yeung Kuo, Lee An Tung, Siao Chang and Ah Dian. They were the politburo elite.

Chin Peng's narrative of this gruelling jungle trek gives us a good idea of the immense logistical difficulties faced by the MNLA – and shows how government patrols by government forces had an impact on the guerrillas' plans even when they failed to engage a guerrilla unit. Low rates of 'contact' frustrated soldiers and policemen. British soldiers may have blundered noisily about the jungle, to find a few abandoned guerrilla camps – but at the beginning of 1949 they forced the military commander of the MNLA to waste an astonishing amount of time just getting from one camp to another just 80 miles away. So it was that in June 1949, a year after the Emergency war had begun, that Chin Peng was able to 'settle down to our first wartime politburo meeting'. His account of this tells us a great deal about the mood in the MNLA in mid-1949.

There was thrilling news from China. As Chin Peng was stumbling through the forests of Pahang in January 1949, CCP forces moved to encircle Beijing. The Nationalist commander defied Chiang Kai-Shek and capitulated. Standing in the back of an American truck, Mao led the jubilant Red Army into the future Chinese capital. The capture of Beijing was a brilliant propaganda coup that shattered nationalist morale, but the Chinese civil war was really won in the countryside. Here the CCP forces had, as Maoist military doctrine insisted, 'mobilised the people'. At the climactic battle fought with Kuomintang armies in the Huai-Hai region north of Nanjing, the nationalists sent in their armoured corps, which had been held in reserve to deliver a crushing final blow to Mao's peasant army – but CCP cadres (one led by Deng Xiaoping) organised literally millions of peasants to excavate a great ring of tank traps that threw the Generalissimo's last throw of the military dice into confusion. The Generalissimo would not concede defeat until December, when the Red Army overran Chengdu. But by the time Chin reached 'Ten Mile Village' in Pahang, a communist victory in China was assured. It was a stunning coup for an army of former cave-dwelling insurgents.

The great drama of Mao's triumph emboldened Chin Peng and his politburo comrades: 'We were on the right track'. He should have reflected more deeply on the lessons of Mao's feat. CCP strategy depended on mass mobilisation of 'the people'. Despite the determination of many 'Min Yuen' supporters, this level of popular mobilisation would be formidably hard to achieve in Malaya. The MNLA leadership did itself few favours. It is telling that it was not until after his journey south that Chin Peng discovered that a poisonous ideological row had erupted among comrades in Malacca. Siew Lau (Phang Yi Foo), a respected MPAJA veteran who had been critical of the MCP leadership, called a meeting of the working committee of the MNLA military sub-district that covered Malacca and part of northern Johor to promote some new thinking – and above all to criticise the leadership style of the politburo. Siew Lau was very well versed in communist theory and argued that Chin Peng and the other Central Committee members had completely misunderstood Mao's 'New Democracy'. He accused the MNLA of using terrorist methods: destroying ID cards, slashing rubber trees, shooting at trains and so on – all these bad habits 'alienated the masses'. He derided the Central Committee as 'horse communists' driving the party to its doom. Siew Lau would never be forgiven.

At the new camp, the politburo made one important strategic decision spurred on by the news from China. The majority of attacks launched by the MNLA had so far used mainly platoon-sized units of guerrillas. These may have been sufficient to assassinate a few planters and estate managers but to ramp up the assault on the colonial power Chin Peng argued that they must now build bigger company-sized attack forces. Why not try an experiment? A large number of MNLA guerrillas had marched into Ten Mile Village shortly after Chin Peng's arrival. So the politburo despatched the Johor company to capture a police station a few miles south of Mentakab. As it turned out, the police station was strategically sited on a hilltop and well defended by rings of trenches. A little band of Malay policemen easily repelled the attack. Not long after this wasteful setback, British security forces launched an attack on the MNLA camp. A warning came just in time and Chin Peng and other politburo members packed their bags and fled deeper into the jungle.

Soon after the attack on the camp in Pahang, a bitter dispute broke out between a regional committee member called Lam Swee and politburo member Ah Dian. Lam Swee accused his superior of cowardice because he often refused to carry a gun. A furious row erupted. In the end, both Lam Swee and Ah Dian were admonished. Lam Swee took this very badly. He defected the following year. We know a great deal about why Lam Swee made this decision, because he wrote a pungent little booklet about his experiences called *I Accuse*. This notorious defection and the row with Siew Lau would have calamitous consequences for the MNLA and its leadership.

Federation intelligence had only the cloudiest idea what was going on in the minds of the MNLA leaders. We know now that the politburo was not a thoughtless rabble of bloodthirsty killers. They spent a lot of time arguing about strategy and obsessively analysing failures. It was clear to Chin Peng as early as the summer of 1949 that the MNLA was having minimal success 'liberating areas' and building 'bases'. The politburo fell back on a diluted version of insurrectionary doctrine that depended on reinforcing the 'Masses Organisation', the Min Yuen. This new strategy was explained in a typically longwinded 'Supplementary opinions of the Central Politburo on Strategic Problems in the Malayan Revolution' published in December:

> ... the Min Yuen work would be expanded with increased activities, radiating spearheads into enemy-held territories, so that an intermeshing of territories would be the result [...] the further enlargement of the points of the spearhead would bring about entanglement and encirclement of the enemy ...

Behind this convoluted rhetoric the MCP was acknowledging a weakness of fundamental significance. The hope that the MNLA might become a liberation army of all Malayan races was taking its last breath. Very little is known about the shadow army of the 'Min Yuen' even today. But we can be sure that the

'Masses Organisation' was predominantly Chinese. By focusing attention on the Min Yuen, the MCP was struggling to deal with the brutal fact that the colonial device of divide and rule had prevailed.

The Spectre of the 10th Regiment

For the Federation and its conservative Malay allies, the risk that the contagion of insurrection would spread from the Chinese communities to the supposedly docile Malays was the stuff of nightmares. The GOC, General Boucher, made this clear in the crassest terms: a dead Malay 'terrorist', he said, was worth seven or eight Chinese 'kills'. In 1949, the spectre of Malay insurrection began stalking the kampongs of Pahang when the Malay communist Abdullah C.D. (Cik Dat bin Anjang Abdullah) began recruiting the '10th Regiment' in the Temerloh area. Abdullah C.D. ties the old Malay radical movement to the Malayan revolution. With Dr Burhanuddin, Ahmad Boestamam and Ishak Haji Muhammad, he was one of the founders of the Malay Nationalist Party. He was a committed and sophisticated communist whose deeply felt ideas had been nourished by childhood tales of Malay rebels like Maharaja Lela, who had struck against the British. But he shared with other Malay radicals a hatred of the feudal Malay states and their rulers. He regarded them to be as guilty of impoverishing Malay peasants as the British. Poverty blighted the riverine settlements of Pahang. In the Temerloh district, communists, both Chinese and Malay, had been preaching revolution – and many kampong people listened. There was also a sizeable number of people in the area who had settled there recently from Indonesia. Security forces rarely patrolled in Temerloh and the custom-minded village headmen had lost influence. Temerloh was ripe for revolution. In May 1949, Abdullah C.D. and another veteran communist, Rashid Maidin, recruited a small band of like-minded Malays. They called themselves the '10th Regiment'. Another recruit, whose autobiography has been translated into English, was Shamsiah Fakeh. She was the head of 'Angkatan Wanita Sedar' (AWAS), which joined forces with Ahmad Boestamam's 'Angkatan Pemuda Insaf' (API) as flag bearers in the demand for independence from the British. Her collaboration with Boestamam inspired quite a number of Malay youths to take up arms. Soon afterwards the district oficer was complaining about a sudden escalation of 'banditry' – which he interpreted as more to do with thievery than ideology. These *were* very poor guerrillas.

To begin with, the security forces were unsure how to deal with the threat. The Malays did not act like the Chinese guerrillas. The ecology of insurrection was very different in the kampong world of Temerloh. They stayed close to home. Abdullah's men did not build jungle camps, but battened onto the kampongs, where they usually ate and slept. They were hard to identify, let alone winkle out. By the end of the year, the district officer was complaining that Temerloh was now the region in Malaya worst hit by banditry. The security forces were having no success, as the advisor in Pahang lamented: 'We are trying to cut our gold green with a scythe rather than a small, fine mowing machine.' The solution was to 'set a fox to keep the geese'. A Malay special ops unit was formed – some fifty or so loyal Malays, who swore their oaths of loyalty on a Koran. The leader of this Malay special ops unit was the founder of the Pahang anti-Japanese 'Wataniah', Yeop Mahidin bin Mohamed Shariff, who happened to be Abdullah C.D.'s cousin. Mahidin knew the Temerloh kampongs and their people well. Insider information meant that his men could target the Malay guerrilla leaders – and by the end of 1949 the 10th Regiment had been eviscerated. The leadership fled across the Thai border. For the Federation, Yeop Mahidin's successful campaign had immense symbolic value. He had exorcised the spectre of Malay communism in short order. But his success was made much easier by the fact that the hard core of the 10th Regiment completely depended on Muslim Malay villagers, who had no real interest in communism. Their short-lived rebellion may well have been, as the district officer suspected, a reaction to chronic poverty, not political ardour.

Fortunes of War

For many of the British and ordinary Malays the fury of the Emergency seemed to be unabated. From mid-1949 until early 1950 MNLA attacks averaged some 200 every month. This fell to 100 a month in 1949 but the MNLA quickly recovered with attacks hitting a bloody peak in September 1950. For Special Branch officer Tim Hatton, the continuous battery of attacks on railway lines and trains, villages and estates was demoralising:

> The first five or six months were difficult and nasty and the communist side were doing these ambushes all around the countryside and people thought they were beginning to win the war.

For the soldiers and policemen like Tim Hatton on the front line it was the jungle that seemed to be the guerrillas' most effective ally. To them the jungle did not appear to be at all neutral. As Thambipillay, a Malayan police officer, puts it:

> The jungle was the terrorists' first home. They knew the jungle inside out because they were involved in fighting the Japanese: they had already prepared themselves, they had dumps, food dumps, arms dumps deep in the jungle: they were at a great advantage in the initial stages.

A Malay communist called Mamat concurred:

> The jungle is our world. When they [government forces] entered the jungle, it's akin to a deer entering a village. They just don't know which way to go. Their

life in the jungle is dependant on the compass. Which way to go? Which hill? Which river? They used a compass and a map – to only one direction, the rest of the area they don't know.

Roy Follows remembers the jungle battleground as a baffling maze:

> You have got to try and navigate through [the jungle], which has no landmark for you to see because you are enclosed by [it]. All the time, you are sweating and falling over, ripping your uniform [...] You come to a big river and sometimes it's not on the map. Constantly, you were lost ...

For many young and often untrained British national servicemen jungle fighting could be traumatising, as a Chinese Malayan police officer, Leong Chee Woh, who later served with the Special Branch, noticed:

> In the jungle – life was very harsh [...] I was leading a patrol of national service people who were shanghaied from the schools at the age of 18 [...] They really suffered [...] They were not trained in the tropics and suddenly they're thrown into a jungle [...] and at night you can hear the boys crying (laughs) ...

The journalist and historian Neal Ascherson did his National Service with the elite Royal Marines in Perak and Selangor in 1951–52. He remembers a frustrating war of energy-sapping jungle patrols punctuated by bewildering bursts of violent action. He rarely encountered the enemy. This was a conflict of shadows and skirmishes. On one occasion,

> ... a young marine had left his patrol to wash in a forest stream. He suddenly found himself facing a group of Chinese guerrillas led by a slim woman with a pistol. The woman looked at the naked boy for a moment, and then lowered her gun. She said: 'My name is Lee Meng. Go and tell your comrades that we do not murder helpless men.' Then she and her companions vanished back into the trees.

The story, Ascherson admits, may be apocryphal. Lee Meng became one of the most celebrated or infamous Malayan communists when she was captured, tried in a colonial court and sentenced to death. Lee Meng was a striking looking young woman and her trial caught the attention of the world. On another occasion, Ascherson and his commando section were waiting in ambush when a small MNLA unit suddenly walked out of the trees. Both sides hesitated for a few seconds, then opened fire. A number of guerrillas were killed. One young man, who had not been hit in the first fusillade, ran back to help a wounded comrade. He was shot dead. Ascherson recalls that he could not help thinking of the verse from St John: 'Greater love has no one than this, that one lay down his life for his friends.' And yet these young men were supposed to be heartless killers and torturers. Ascherson's unit, '42 Commando', was stationed at Jelapang, a small town in the Kinta Valley that has since been absorbed by the northern suburbs of Ipoh. Some six months after arriving in Malaya, Ascherson was no longer the gung-ho young commando who had come to fight communist bandits for king and country. He had an 'urgent feeling' that the Emergency was 'mistaken' and 'unjust'. It was, he sensed, being fought to protect British businesses from a Chinese working class. The war was, he realised, discriminatory. When he was sent south to Selangor he could no longer keep silent. He wrote an angry letter to a well-known politician called Nancy Yap, decrying the war. She never replied: a letter like this from a British soldier could have been a trap. He wrote next to a family friend, the Tory MP Cedric Drewe, who *may* have shown his long passionate 'J'accuse' to Anthony Eden … But the war did not end. When Ascherson returned from Malaya, he went to Cambridge to read history. His teacher was the Marxist Eric Hobsbawm. At a social gathering, Ascherson remembered:

> Eric inspected me. A specimen, indeed. 'What's that medal affair you're wearing?' 'It's my national service campaign medal. For active service in the Malayan emergency.' Eric pulled back and took another look at me. Then he said, very sharply but without violence: 'Malaya? You should be ashamed to be wearing that.'

The Emergency war would not be won or lost in the jungle but in the world of the Chinese squatters. It is to this other war that we must now turn.

11

THE WAR ON THE SQUATTERS

Communal Conundrums

The roots of the Emergency war in Malaya reached deep into colonial history and the antagonistic communal politics the British had cultivated for nearly two centuries. The problems Britain faced after 1948 were of its own making. British rule, in its various forms, had for a long period of time failed to uphold the rights of the Chinese and Indian peoples who had come to Malaya to serve the interests of European colonial power. The consequence was that this counter-insurgency war would be fought against a communist guerrilla movement that was dominated by Chinese communists. Since the Malayan communists were intimately rooted in many of the Chinese communities in Malaya, the Federation government was faced with a conundrum. The Emergency should not appear to be directed at Malayan Chinese as a whole but at the communists. The problem was how to winnow the chaff from the grain. We see in document after document from this period that the political allegiances and sympathies of the Chinese communities preoccupied the British colonial administrators. Were they for us or against us? The implication was that the Chinese communities would have to be purged or, as one administrator put, 'politically conditioned' or, to use the euphemistic language of the colonial state, they would require 'protection'. If the British were ever to 'unite and leave', the strategies of their counter-insurgency war had to be carefully calibrated to maintain at least a semblance of communal unity. The colonial army and police could not appear to be fighting on behalf of a narrow communal faction, the Malays, but had to be seen as defenders of a cross-communal Federation.

The experience of the Japanese occupation had for a short period readjusted the balance of power between the Chinese and Malays. When the British returned to Malaya and Singapore, they were no longer prepared to concede to the traditionally privileged Malays political *carte blanche*. For a number of reasons, not least the well-publicised role played by MPAJA guerrillas fighting the Japanese, they proposed offering new rights to Chinese Malayans, who made up nearly 45 per cent of the population. But fierce Malay opposition, whipped up by the charismatic Dato Onn bin Jaafar, and backed by a lobby of ultraconservative former colonial administrators like Sir Frank Swettenham, hobbled the 'Malayan Union' – forcing the British to back down. The Federation of Malaya that emerged from the ruins of the Union reasserted communal Malay rights and left some 90 per cent of Chinese out in the cold as non-citizens. The battle over the 'Malayan Union' advanced an aggressive new kind of Malay nationalist, and a new party – UMNO – that would fight their corner for the rest of the century and beyond. As the 'Union' was consigned to the dustbin of history, the Malayan communists (and a handful of Malay radicals) launched a political assault on the British colonial government to demand independence. These demands were tied to a wave of strikes and stoppages that posed a direct threat to the colonial economy. British intransigence in the face of workers' demands forced the Malayan communist to embark on a long-term plan for armed revolt that was unintentionally ignited in June 1948. Since the insurgents were mainly Chinese, the British found themselves with the communal conflict they had dreaded. Such a war was unaffordable.

I have reiterated this argument here to make better sense of how the British and their Malay allies understood the conflict. It was a war, in short, fought to exterminate – a word used repeatedly by British high commissioners – Malayan communists and bring other Chinese communities to heel: 'the hard core of armed communists in this country are fanatics and must be, and will be, exterminated' proclaimed Sir Gerald Templer, who would be appointed high commissioner and director of operations in 1951. The Emergency war had to be waged on many fronts at the same time. Police and army patrols could sweep the jungle to 'exterminate' the guerrillas. But that hard core of fighters depended, as we have seen, on a complex ecology of supporters known as the 'Min Yuen' and communities of Chinese agriculturalists known as 'squatters'.

By the end of 1948, British minds had focused on what they disparagingly called the 'squatter problem'. The squatters were the sea in which the guerrilla fish swam and breathed. The solution the British came up with would be one of the most radical examples of colonial social engineering since the Boer War. Resettlement, as it came to be called, forcibly relocated more than half a million Chinese Malayans and dumped them in 'resettlement areas'. They would become known as 'New Villages'. The military purpose of resettlement was to destroy the capacity of the MNLA to regenerate, which, it was believed, depended on recruits, supplies and intelligence drawn from the well of the rural Chinese communities. The same brutal device would be used in Kenya: the notorious 'Operation Anvil', for example, was conceived to cut off 'Mau Mau' insurgents from their logistical bases in Nairobi. Resettlement was social engineering for military ends: and it would be done at gunpoint. The political aim was even more ambitious. This was, as one discussion document puts it, to 'educate the Chinese into accepting the control of government'. Another word used in official documents was 'conditioning'. The purportedly 'lawless' squatters would be dragged kicking and screaming into the realm of government. The squatters' world was Malaya's last frontier. It would be tamed. Let's not forget the economic imperative. Resettlement would generate an orderly pool of cheap labour for the mines and rubber estates. The British spoke of 'protecting' the Chinese squatters. To be sure, many MNLA guerrillas extracted money and food from squatter communities at the point of a gun. This does not alter the fact that resettlement was coercive.

One of the first enthusiasts for resettlement was UMNO leader Dato Onn, who wrote in the following terms to High Commissioner Gurney on 6 November 1948:

> There is in my view one answer only and that is that the police and Military take the line which has, I believe, been followed elsewhere, e.g. Palestine and N.W. Frontier etc. [sic] of burning out squatters and leaving them to work out their own salvation, i.e. by going into settled areas, towns and so on, or into other and temporarily less objectionable squatter areas, or best of all, slipping over the Siamese border ...

Dato Onn was referring to a spate of evictions of Chinese squatters that had taken place in the state of Kedah. He was worried that evicted squatters might end up on land reserved for Malays. From his point of view eviction and resettlement should be used as a means of ethnic cleansing: 'This government [of Kedah] is anxious that [...] Kedah remains a genuinely Malay state ...'. Dato Onn unashamedly hoped that the British police and military would drive 'squatters', i.e. non-Malays, across the border into Thailand.

Squatter is of course a profoundly derogatory term – and the negative charge is emphasised in 'the squatter problem'. Defining who and what a squatter was, precisely, was not straightforward. At a conference of Perak district officers in February 1947, 'squatter' was defined to include three forms of land occupation:

1. illegal occupation, without any title or licence whatsoever;
2. legal occupation of state land;
3. legal occupation of land alienated for mining.

'Legal' here implied possession of a licence. So squatting might be legal or illegal in different circumstances. An equally important point is that squatting was not a whimsical lifestyle choice, but a consequence of colonial exploitation. From the end of the nineteenth century, Malaya's tin and rubber industries sucked in a vast mobile army of Asian workers or 'coolies'. These industries were vulnerable to long bouts of boom and bust, which turned Southeast Asia into a vast human bellows, alternately sucking in and then spewing out this labour force as needed. By the late 1920s the cycle of recruitment and repatriation was becoming difficult to sustain, for reasons explained at the time by the Under-Secretary of State for the Colonies W. Ormsby-Gore: 'Whereas formerly only a certain proportion of the Chinese remained in Malaya [...] nowadays the tendency is for the Chinese to remain in Malaya.' In other words, Chinese migrants were becoming 'Malayans'. This was clearly indicated by the statistical fact that fewer Chinese men now came to Malaya alone. Many were bringing their families with them. They wanted to settle.

This change of outlook did not pass unnoticed. It thoroughly alarmed Malays but a British administrator admonished Charles Vlieland, the superintendent of the 1931 Census, for continuing to see the Chinese as 'mere sojourners': 'surely,' he wondered 'a larger number would have accepted the offer of repatriation?' Since they hadn't, this implied that they had begun to see Malaya as home, in the German sense of 'Heimat'. Many Chinese put out of work now chose 'cash cropping' to survive in preference to repatriation. Their so-called 'market gardens' began to flourish near the plantations and mines as a way to deal with the cycles of employment and unemployment. European owners, of course, always tried to keep wages at subsistence levels even in good times. Some of these 'market gardeners' were issued with 'Temporary Occupation Licences', or TOLs, and it was the TOL system that made the 'squatter'. For the Chinese, getting a TOL only very rarely resulted in permanent legal occupancy. For their part, the Malays feared the encroachment of these resourceful Chinese farmers, while mine and plantation owners were unwilling to 'alienate' land for cultivation for long periods of time. A boom in rubber or tin prices would force them to take back the land handed over to the Chinese agriculturalists. So many of them had to 'squat' under the official radar and many did so with great success. A report from Ulu Kinta in Perak in 1927 noted 4,000 dwellings occupied by Chinese 'vegetable gardeners', who had 5,000 acres of state land under cultivation. This was by no means an isolated example. In 1929 an inspector of agriculture stumbled on 100 acres of 'vegetable gardens' that was being diligently cultivated by Chinese families. Many of the men also took work when it was available in the nearby mine. These farmers, the inspector went on, had built fine new houses and the whole area had a 'sense of permanence'.

After 1942, these pioneers of the wild east were joined by many thousands of urban Chinese escaping persecution by the Japanese and, later, food shortages and price inflation. By 1943, the Japanese had been forced to promote rice production by Chinese farmers in Malaya although this had minimal impact and many were forced to adopt tapioca as a replacement staple. From the beginning of 1944, the now rather desperate Japanese Military Administration embarked on large-scale transfers of Chinese and some Eurasians to deal with the problem of the MPAJA guerrillas. 'Resettlement colonies' sprang up, mainly in Johor and Negeri Sembilan. The Japanese encouraged Chinese farmers to occupy unused Malay reservation land in areas of Perak, near Grik and in the Dindings district. Since the Japanese had no interest in Malayan tin and rubber, they turned a blind eye to illegal occupation of mining land and plantations. A consequence of the occupation was thus a huge increase in the number of Chinese squatter communities. As noted earlier, it was the Chinese squatters who ameliorated the impact of food shortages for every community in occupied Malaya. The squatters saved Malaya from mass starvation.

The ordinary Chinese market gardener, or cultivator, turns into a 'squatter' in official language when he and his family pose a threat. When the British returned to Malaya in 1945, they could see that there might be a 'squatter problem'. For at least a year the British Military Administration (BMA) brushed aside calls from Malays, land offices and mine owners to launch large-scale evictions. They took the opposite course and distributed thousands of TOLs. The reason for this was simple: the squatters were still feeding Malaya. This generosity ended in 1947 when the post-war permits ran out and were not renewed. Even then it was mainly Malays who led the crusade to evict squatters from their reserved land. Many British officials had a lot of sympathy for the squatter communities and hesitated to begin evictions. Many squatters fought back and some had very good lawyers. As the Emergency war intensified in 1949, the Federation government abandoned any pretence of benevolence. Now the talk was all of the 'squatter problem'. The Chinese rural communities were represented as human swamps that bred and above all *fed* revolt. The realm of the squatter was lawless, uncontrollable and beyond the writ of Federation power. If the law could not be brought to bear on the wild frontier of the squatters' world, the squatters would have to be herded into the realm of government in concentration camps.

This might seem to be an inflammatory way to refer to one of the most admired aspects of British counter-insurgency in Malaya: 'Resettlement'. It is completely appropriate. The idea of the concentration camp was invented almost simultaneously by the Germans and British in the same region of the colonial world: in southern Africa. Johann Chapoutot points out (in the *Online Encyclopaedia of Mass Violence*) that it was the invention of barbed wire in France in 1865, followed by its mass production in the United States after 1874 to restrain cattle, that inspired the construction of vast, cheap internment camps. In the Second Boer War (1900–02), Lord Kitchener led a pitiless 'scorched earth' campaign to flush out Boer insurgents – burning their farms, slaughtering their livestock, destroying their crops, poisoning wells and evicting their families. By sweeping the country bare, Kitchener would starve the Boers into defeat. The British herded at least 150,000 refugee women and children into hastily improvised internment camps – enclosed by mile upon mile of barbed wire. Kitchener called this empire of barbed wire thrown up on the Veld 'camps of refuge'. It was his critics, such as the liberals C.P. Scott and John Ellis, who first used the term 'concentration camp'. The term stuck. In 1904, German Chancellor Bernhard von Bülow ordered General Lothar von Trotha to erect '*konzentrationslager*' in German south-west Africa to intern the African survivors of the Herero War. Thanks to campaigns led by Emily Hobhouse and Millicent

Fawcett, the abysmal conditions in the South African camps, which killed at least 25,000 Boer and African civilians, shamed the nation – signalling the terminal moral decline of the 'British Empire Project'.

The British, closely followed by the Germans, showed that the forcible 'concentration' of large numbers of civilians could be used to weaken and/or demoralise an insurgent army. In South Africa this army was the Boers. We now associate the concentration camp almost exclusively with the German Holocaust, although *internment* camps like Dachau, Sachsenhausen and Bergen-Belsen had a different function from the specialised extermination centres built in occupied Poland like Sobibor and Auschwitz-Birkenau. Precise language is among the first casualties of war. In Malaya, 'Resettlement' referred to the enforced removal of Chinese squatters to new settlements that would later be called 'New Villages'. This mealy mouthed lexicon is window dressing. The Malayan settlements were identical in design and purpose to concentration camps built in South Africa half a century earlier.

By 1949, banishment or repatriation was no longer an option. Mao Zedong slammed the door shut. The British had negotiated repatriation agreements with the Kuomintang government. On 1 October 1949, Mao proclaimed the founding of the People's Republic of China in Beijing. Mao's spectacular victory belated the Malayan communists and brought the British policy of deportation to an end. The solution to the 'squatter problem' would have to be worked out in Malaya.

British advisors had, as they were obliged to do, been seeking the views of the Menteri Besars: the chief ministers of the Malay states. From the Malay point of view the solution to the 'Chinese problem' was not complicated. The British advisor in Negeri Sembilan reported that the Menteri Besar there had been frank: 'These people [Chinese squatters] have made nuisances of themselves. Why should we give up good Malayan land for occupation by them, when such land is likely to be needed for future expansion by the Malays? The only sensible method is to deport them …'. As the troubling implications of the Communist victory in China sank in, all sides realised that this was no longer an option. The 'Chinese squatter', that much abused and rather mythological ogre, would not disappear overnight on a slow boat to China. Resettlement leapt to the top of the counter-insurgency agenda. The Chinese would be 'deported' – but within Malaya.

The Man with a Plan

At the beginning of the new decade the British remained pessimistic. The number of guerrilla attacks had risen and would reach a bloody peak between September 1950 and October 1951. The mood in the MNLA camps was buoyant. A Perak guerrilla wrote to a relative: 'If the reactionary KMT in China have failed although they enjoy the aid of the American imperialists […] how can the British imperialists be victorious?'

How indeed! General Sir John Harding, commander-in-chief of FARELF, complained that mediocre intelligence gathering meant that 'an enormous amount of military effort is being necessarily absorbed on prophylactic and will o' the wisp patrolling and jungle bashing …'. There was a pervasive fear that the Federation could be seen as confused and on the run and that it could 'lose face'. A psychological miasma seeped into British colonial minds. Sinews would have to be stiffened and, crucially, *seen* to be reinforced.

It was no secret that in London the Labour government was dismayed by lack of progress in Malaya. The Emergency was costing too much and had begun to look unwinnable. Something had to be done. So it was that the first 'Man with a Plan' flew into Kuala Lumpur on 3 April 1950 to take up a freshly minted job as 'Director of Operations'. Lt General Sir Harold Rawdon Briggs has been called the 'Ike' of Malaya, referring to America's soldier president, Dwight D. Eisenhower, who had been forced to take on the burden of post-war reconstruction in Europe and the new Cold War. Briggs was, as Anthony Short writes, in the 'anomalous position of a soldier who was a civilian, directing military operations in support of a civil power'. He was 'the general in a Trilby'. Born in 1884, Briggs was a competent enough soldier who had command experience in Asian theatres of war. He had fought in Burma and was appointed GOC there following the Japanese surrender. Between 1945 and 1948 Briggs had co-ordinated counter-insurgent operations against Burmese communists. He seemed to have all the right qualifications. Briggs had been strong-armed by his old boss, Field Marshall Slim, who said of him: 'I know of few commanders who made as many immediate and critical decisions […] and I know of none who made so few mistakes.' The problem was that the 66-year-old Briggs was dying and knew he had very little time. So for 'important private reasons' he refused to stay longer than eighteen months. In that short time he would become the architect of resettlement.

It is a myth that Briggs 'invented' resettlement. As we have seen, the British had already experimented with small-scale transfers before Briggs' arrival, usually with dismal results. Resettlement would be only one aspect of the broad solution he proposed that became known as the 'Briggs Plan'. But it was he who grasped the war-winning significance of 'spatial control': the Emergency could be won if the human sea that fed the guerrillas was bled dry. As soon as he arrived in Kuala Lumpur, Briggs embarked on a lightning tour. A week later he met Gurney to present his main recommendations. The tour must have been cursory and, in many respects, Briggs fed back to the high commissioner what he knew already: the communists were sustained by 'uncontrolled squatter areas, unsupervised Chinese estates and smallholdings, estate labour lines and timber kongsis'. This had an obvious implication. If the ties that connected the guerrillas to the Chinese peasants could be severed, the war would be over. The 'Briggs Plan' was an expanded version of this first, hasty report. This 'Federation Plan for the Elimination of the Communist Organisation and Armed Forces in Malaya' was presented to the British Defence Co-ordination Committee on 24 May 1950. It was not just about population transfer. Briggs proposed creating a new 'Federal War Council' that would streamline the wasteful administrative pile-ups that had stymied effective operations. The War Council would comprise a small committee that would focus policy and provide the required resources. Briggs could see – or he was told – that intelligence was still patchy. The main communist leaders remained shadowy figures. That fact alone was thoroughly dismaying. So the War Council would be backed by a 'Federal Joint Intelligence Agency'. Briggs was perfectly right to focus on intelligence. The Emergency would become an information war. Execution of policy, the waging of war in other words, would be the responsibility of 'State and Settlement War Executive Committees': these would comprise the Menteri Besars of each state, as well as police and military commanders. Briggs understood that the Chinese must 'commit to our side': but his language often has a distinctly anti-Sinitic tone: 'The Chinese population is generally content to get on with its business, even if it entails subsidising the communists […] They are vocal and promise a lot, yet do nothing …'.

Even if we accept, as many historians still do, that Briggs had put on the table the means of beating the communists, few would dispute that the Briggs Plan was on a very slow burn: and it was not intended to be. He pushed for a 'steamroller' military operation that would liquidate the MNLA units on a state by state basis. This would, he proposed, commence in Johor and Negeri Sembilan in the south and 'roll up' the MNLA northwards towards the Thai border. Here Briggs paid the price of that rushed tour of inspection. He had failed to appreciate that the MNLA was strongest in the southern states and Perak. Here its grip on the local people was concomitantly tight. By the end of Briggs' first year as DOA there was no sign of any 'rolling up' and the flow of intelligence was still clogged. Briggs was described as 'a man of immense charm, the best kind of soldier and gentleman …'. He charmed government officials, to be sure, but hit a human brick wall when he tried to win over the stubborn commissioner of police. Briggs and Gray did not hit it off. The commissioner of police had in fact seen off many other hapless colleagues. He fought any military encroachment on *his* police force and resented the way that Briggs' plans placed such a heavy burden on his men. As he had with Boucher, Gray doggedly waged a rancorous turf war with Briggs until the end of the year when an exasperated Gurney sacked him.

Even with Gray out of the picture, Briggs needed to fight every inch of the way through a tangled web of jealous and protective Federation and state fiefdoms. He was often frustrated by the insouciant high commissioner's hands-off manner: Gurney was far too concerned with 'social questions', Briggs complained. He had a war to win. The 'Briggs Plan' has had a good press from historians, but it was nothing less than ruthless. Resettlement may have been a long way down Briggs' list of proposals but it would define his reputation. He knew that badly organised half-hearted transfers had not worked. The time had come to be completely ruthless. Resettlement had to be all or nothing. It was not a social welfare plan: the purpose of resettlement was to 'destroy the bandits'. Only later would the British talk of 'protecting the squatters'.

When Briggs left Malaya, he believed that he had failed. It would be rather too easy to conclude that Briggs himself – 'quiet of speech and of manner', 'patient, courteous and understanding' – was not steamroller enough to weed out complacent colonial dross and fight a proper war. He was too avuncular. More to the point: he was mortally ill. So does the human factor explain the initial failure of the Briggs Plan? Not really: the main problem was that Briggs took on an administration mired in entropy. Historians who stress Briggs' character defects probably have in mind the impact of Sir Gerald Templer, the next 'Man with a Plan'. But the Malayan problem had improved fundamentally by the time Templer stormed into King's House.

Before he finally left Malaya, Briggs struggled to speed up resettlement. From late 1950 the numbers of people ousted from their smallholdings and resettled beyond the reach of the guerrillas increased: by January 1951 some 117,000 people had been moved to eighty-two resettlement areas. Speed was of the essence. It is astonishing to discover that Gurney hoped to end the Emergency *by the end of 1951*. He was under immense pressure from the Labour government, which was facing a very tough election. Haste made the Briggs resettlement plan a human disaster. An eye witness was the Catholic Belgian-Chinese novelist and doctor, Han Suyin. In her autobiography *My House has Two Doors* (1982) and a semi-factual novel *And the Rain my Drink* (1956), she wrote searing accounts of the lives of the 'resettled'. These caused such a fuss at the time that her husband, Special Branch officer Leon Comber, was sacked. The couple later divorced. Han Suyin points out that resettlement buttressed the division between the Malayan races: 'Whole villages, in some cases villages established for a century or more, in which Malays and Chinese had lived peacefully together, were now sundered, the Chinese taken away and put in "new villages" behind barbed wire.' A wire barrier now descended between the rural Chinese and other races – as well as the rest of the Chinese communities. Conditions for the uprooted squatters were often dire. The first hastily established 'resettlement areas' would not become 'New Villages' for some time. Han Suyin describes visiting a resettlement camp with a Mr Winslow, who was 'in charge of resettlement'. (I could not find any other reference to this gentleman; Han Suyin may well have changed his name.) Whoever he was, Mr Winslow was proud of what had been achieved. It took four hours by jeep to reach the new settlement, the little party bumping along a new road slashed through the jungle. The first sign that they had reached their destination was a great barrier of barbed wire and a police post at the edge of a fetid mangrove swamp. Outside the wire was the 'sombre menace of the jungle'. The new houses spread into the swamp:

Four hundred beings, including children, huddled there: foot deep in brackish water. There were some atap huts with rusty zinc roofs [...] I shall never forget the pale, puffy faces: beri beri or the ulcers on their legs. Their skin had the hue of the swamp. They stank. There was no clean water anywhere. Mr Winslow, standing on a box [...] admonished them sternly in Malay: a Chinese interpreter translated in Techew dialect. The villagers had been guilty of passing food to the bandits and so they had been transported here. Now they must work hard to redeem themselves ...

Han Suyin also observed comparable levels of poverty in Malay kampongs. Some Malay peasants were probably worse off than the resettled Chinese. These resettlement areas would eventually prosper, thanks to both government investment and Chinese communal ethics. From the Malay point of view, the Chinese squatters were unfairly pampered. And yet long-term investment in Malay rural development has had paltry results.

Confronting Defeat

By the time Briggs died less than a year after he left Malaya, the MNLA onslaught appeared to be unrelenting. A murderous pattern had been perfected. The standard guerrilla tactic had been taught by Force 136 officers: stage an incident then ambush the relieving force. For obvious reasons, a huge volume of police and military traffic flowed along Malaya's roads and highways. Trucks, jeeps and entire convoys provided an almost continuous procession of suitable targets. The physical geography of Malaya increased the vulnerability of government forces. North of Kuala Lumpur, the road network twisted and turned through the highlands, with frequent uphill bends that forced drivers to slow down to below 15mph. Road bends became 'kill boxes' and MNLA units armed with automatic weapons (like Bren guns) could do a great deal of damage. They usually killed or incapacitated the driver to immobilise the vehicle, then picked off the rest of the party before they could 'debus', regroup and fire back. Resettlement made matters worse: thousands of Chinese had to be moved, then protected. The pressure on government forces was enormous and showed no sign of ever falling. With hindsight we can see that the Malayan war reached a peak level of violence in 1951: in April, August and October the security forces suffered their heaviest losses, as did the MNLA. There was no reason at the time to imagine that the line on the graph would not continue to rise. A member of the Legislative Council lamented: '... the number of troops pouring into this country has been creating a feeling of suspicion on the part of the masses. They think and are probably justified in thinking that the signal for a bloodthirsty war is what they are seeing.'

12

THE LOWEST EBB

Assassination

For the British in Malaya it was the worst of times. By early 1950 the MNLA had not just come through the first full year of the war relatively unscathed but had managed to retrain and regroup. Morale had been lifted by the establishment of the People's Republic of China on 1 October 1949 and the ignominious flight of Chiang Kai-Shek and his followers to Taiwan. In Korea, tension was mounting along the 38th Parallel that divided the peninsula between the communist north and the American-dominated south. For Chin Peng and the party leadership this was a time of optimism. Still, the Emergency remained a war of 'incidents' and skirmishes. From the middle of 1949 official reports show a steady rise of guerrilla attacks reaching a peak in September 1950. For the European and Malay populations this was unnerving. Civilian morale was in free fall. But the pattern of guerrilla attacks revealed weaknesses as well as strengths.

Many 'incidents' were hit-and-run road ambushes. Attacks on mines and estates were very rarely pressed home. The MNLA was better organised but desperately short of firepower. Many 'incidents' seem to have been organised with the sole intent of securing weapons and ammunition. The 'Joint Intelligence Advisory Committee' estimated that the main force of the MNLA was between 3,000 and 3,500 with unknown numbers of reserves on the other side of the Thai border. But guerrilla losses were believed to be running at 25–30 per cent, with new recruits joining the MNLA regiments at much lower rates of 5–10 per cent. The problem for High Commissioner Gurney was that the national mood and morale did not reflect the intricate implications of the Emergency statistics. In February, Gurney sent an alarming report to London that thousands of Chinese communists had landed in southern Thailand and begun infiltrating across the border from an area known as the Betong Salient. The newly formed Malay Regiment was despatched to northern Malaya to deal with the threat. The 'Chinese invasion' was a false alarm. Gurney's reaction exposes not just inept intelligence work, but that a pessimistic malaise was afflicting the Federation. The communists seemed to be winning. The commissioner of police, Nicol Gray, pointedly forwarded to

Gurney a letter written by a tin miner in Batu Gajah not far from Ipoh in Perak. 'Kampong talk', the miner reported:

> ... goes like this: 'The government is getting weaker and weaker – Communism which is to liberate us all is triumphant in China and will shortly be the same in Siam and then here [...] This government is terrified and has recognised Communism in China and will shortly hand over to Communism here ...

One evening at the beginning of October 1951 High Commissioner Gurney sat at his desk beneath a steadily pulsing overhead fan in King's House reflecting on the 'Chinese problem'. He began writing a note to vent his exasperation. What troubled him most was that the 'whole vast scheme of resettlement' was in danger of failing. The MCP 'are trying hard to penetrate' the new settlements and 'are succeeding'. He excoriated the Chinese for letting the communists get away with it: '... the Chinese themselves have done absolutely nothing to help their own people resist Communism [...] The British government will not be prepared to go on protecting people who are completely unwilling to do anything to help themselves [...] These people live comfortably and devote themselves wholly to making money ...'. Gurney never finished the letter. But the message was all too clear. The language is positively venomous: 'These people live comfortably and devote themselves wholly to making money [...] They can spend $4 million on celebrations in Singapore but can spare nothing for the MCA anti-communist efforts.' Two days after he wrote this embittered lament Gurney was killed. His violent death would plunge the British into hand-wringing despair and elate the communists. But this spectacular coup – the assassination of the British high commissioner – was not quite what it seemed.

Two days after penning his exasperated invective against the Chinese, Gurney decided to escape Kuala Lumpur to spend the weekend at Fraser's Hill, the hill resort near Raub in Pahang. Lady Gurney was not in good health and seemed to benefit from the cooler world of the old British resort. Soon after dawn on 6 October, the high commissioner's black Rolls-Royce, with its eye-catching Union Jack pendant, sped out of King's House escorted by a Land Rover, an armoured scout car and a police wireless van. About 8 miles from Fraser's Hill the wireless van broke down. Gurney refused to wait and the Rolls sped on ahead towards Gap Road, which led up through thick jungle to Fraser's Hill. His escort lagged far behind.

For two days, MNLA leader Siew Mah, which means Little Horse, had been camped above the long twisting road that leads up towards the turn-off to Fraser's Hill with a platoon of thirty-six guerrillas. His plan was to ambush a convoy and seize arms and ammunition. Siew Mah was a short, fit man who at the end of 1941 had been trained by the British at the 101 STS in Singapore to fight the Japanese. Using the skills he had learnt then, he had set up a 'killing box' on the

Gap Road close to the 57th Milestone (the distance from Kuala Lumpur) where a hairpin bend forced any vehicles approaching or departing Fraser's Hill to slow to a crawl. His men had dug into three firing positions, armed with Bren guns and rifles. Behind them waited the 'charging squads' that would race down to plunder the hoped-for convoy when its drivers had been 'immobilised'. Two days later not a single truck had entered Siew Mah's 'killing box'. By then, food was running out. His men were hungry. At midday on Saturday 6 October Siew Mah made a decision to pull out in two hours.

An hour later, at 1.15 p.m., Siew Mah was suddenly alert. He could hear the grinding clunk and whine of strained gears as a big vehicle began to negotiate the tight bend at the 57th Mile. A Land Rover came into sight packed with armed police followed by a gleaming black limousine. Siew Mah had to make a decision. He gave the order to fire. Further on, guerrillas hauled a felled tree across the road. The hail of bullets tore into the open back of the Land Rover hitting all but one of the Malay policemen inside as well as the high commissioner's driver behind them. The Rolls lurched to the left and came to a halt at the precipitous edge of the road. Inside, Lady Gurney and the high commissioner's private secretary, D.J. Staples, crouched, terrified, on the floor. The volley of firing reached a crescendo. Then something unexpected happened. A tall gentleman in a light tropical suit emerged from the back of the Rolls, stepped into the road and began walking away from the car towards the other side of the road. The astonished guerrillas directed their fire at his upper body and head. The tall man fell forward into the deep drainage ditch at the side of the road. In a terse report the chief secretary, Sir M.V. del Tufo, described what happened next:

> … Lady Gurney and the Private Secretary remained in the car until the firing eased when they crawled out and found Gurney's body in the ditch on the right side of the road. The Officer in charge of the Scout car returned about twenty minutes later on foot with reinforcements from the Gap Police station, bandits having felled a tree across the road above the site of the ambush. Armoured vehicles from Kuala Kubu arrived on the scene about 2.15pm and engaged in follow up operations.

But Siew Mah was long gone.

Reacting

The killing of Sir Henry Gurney shattered morale. If the high commissioner could not be protected, who, then, was safe? Royal Marine Neal Ascherson was on a troopship approaching Singapore harbour when he and 44 Commando heard the news. 'We suddenly understood that something serious was going on …'. The lethal ambush at Fraser's Hill, a bastion of the old pre-war Malaya, badly dented the reputation of the security forces. Entire battalions were drafted in to pursue the guerrillas in the Raub area near Fraser's Hill, rampaging through the jungle like enraged elephants.

In the MNLA camps, the killing of the British high commissioner was a cause for celebration. MNLA veteran Shun Sheng remembers: 'I was happy! It was great news because he was a British High Commissioner who probably holds higher power.' The jubilant mood would be short-lived. The British had no idea that the 'Briggs Plan' was already beginning to dent the Malayan revolution. Chin Peng's guerrillas were feeling the first pangs of the hunger that would defeat their cause. As High Commissioner Gurney tumbled dead into the ditch on the Gap Road, the insurgent tide had already begun to ebb. The rebel leaders had once again been forced to rethink their strategy at the most fundamental level.

On the British side, ignorance of the souring mood in the jungle camps of the MNLA fed despair. This coincided with the election of a Conservative government in London and the return to power of the elderly Winston Churchill. In the Colonial Office, Mr R.H. Scott warned the incoming foreign secretary, Anthony Eden, in plain terms:

> ... the pinning down of British forces in Malaya weakens our position throughout the world; the disturbed condition of Malaya makes it difficult to move forward with any assurance in planning with other interested powers for the defence of Southeast Asia in war; and the threat to Malaya's export trade is a factor of great importance to the sterling bloc.

It is now almost forgotten that Clement Attlee's battered Labour government was re-elected in 1950 with a small majority. Urged by the king, Attlee went back to the country eighteen months later hoping to bolster his frail majority. This was a fatal miscalculation. This time the Conservatives won, and at the end of October 1951 Churchill strolled into 10 Downing Street for the second time. Labour had polled a quarter of a million more votes but the quirks of the British electoral system delivered a majority of sixteen seats to the Conservatives, who immediately began to unpick the achievements of their predecessors. Conservative governments would now preside over the bloody end of empire.

Winston's Emergency

We must return to Malaya's political battlefield. For now, we should keep in mind that as Churchill's new Conservative government began to take stock of the Emergency, communal antagonisms in Malaya showed every sign of becoming a lot more poisonous. Churchill accepted the basic commitment made by Attlee (in April 1949) to the Malayans: self-government, but no premature withdrawal. Even after three years of a communist insurrection, Malaya remained the principal dollar earner for the whole of the Commonwealth. Although communist attacks barely dented the flow of treasure, the outlook for the Malayan economy was stormy and cast doubt on whether the Federation could afford to wage war for much longer. By 1951, the Emergency was costing an eye-watering £56 million every year – which put immense pressure on Malayan reserves. It was often said that 'Malay is as rubber does' and the prognosis for the two industries that underpinned Malayan wealth was troubling. Gurney acknowledged that 'the solution of our difficulties [...] is going to be concerned very closely with finance.' Fiscal worries sharpened minds. In December, Churchill sent the new Colonial Secretary, the suave aristocrat Oliver Lyttelton, on a reconnaissance mission to Malaya. Lyttelton was considered an expert on Southeast Asian matters mainly because he had been a director of the 'London Tin Corporation' and its Malayan subsidiary 'Anglo-Oriental'. He certainly appreciated the economic value of Malayan raw materials as dollar earners. The outgoing Secretary of State, James Griffith, confessed to him that Malaya had 'become a military problem to which we have not been able to find the answer'. Lyttelton, with Malaya's rubber and tin firmly in mind, appreciated the likely repercussions if this 'troubled and tender' part of the world was lost to communism. So it was that at the end of that grim year the people of Malaya wryly observed the progress of yet another British eminence as he sped back and forth along the highways and byways of their embattled homeland. During his peregrinations, Lyttelton quizzed politicians, army officers and policemen, tappers and miners, people in resettlement villages and schoolchildren. On the horizon, promised Lyttelton, was a free Malaya. What is delaying progress he asked? This was his reply: '... the answer is Communism. The answer is the terrorists. The answer is the Min Yuen and those who, partly from fear and partly from sympathy, create a passive but no less serious obstacle to victory.' On them, he promised, would fall the 'full severity which their betrayal merits'. Privately, Lyttelton was even less sanguine. The situation, he concluded, was 'appalling': 'I have never seen such a tangle as that presented by the government of Malaya.' On his return to London a few days before Christmas, Lyttelton called on Viscount Montgomery. There was speculation that the hero of Alamein was about to be offered the job of sorting out Malaya – or that he was lobbying for a colonial appointment. Neither was true. By then Montgomery, who was an inept politician, had fallen out with the British military establishment and was a cantankerous has-been in search of a role. After talking to Lyttelton about the Malayan dilemma he wrote a now famous letter:

Dear Lyttelton, Malaya. We must have a plan. Secondly, we must have a man. When we have a plan and a man, we shall succeed: not otherwise. Yours sincerely (signed) Montgomery (F.M.)

This terse and rather comical advice was singularly insensitive to the first 'man with a plan', Sir Harold Briggs, who had just left Malaya for good, disillusioned and mortally sick. Lyttelton had no idea, it would seem, that in the MNLA jungle camps the 'Briggs Plan' had already begun to bite.

Screwing Down the People

The 'Briggs Plan' had been presented to the Federation Council in mid-1950 and encountered very little opposition. The colonial government became responsible for funding and managing resettlement – but the operations to evict and move people far from their homes would be handled by the army. The squatter problem was first and foremost a security issue. It is perhaps not appreciated that the Briggs Plan divided squatters into two groups. Squatters on estates, mines and near towns would be 'regrouped' into controlled settlements situated no more than 2 miles from their existing holdings. In normal circumstances, district officers toured the area to give the communities due to be resettled locally prior notice. The second, much bigger, squatter group in Briggs' plan lived on the jungle fringes and foothills: they would be moved to new settlements located far away from the existing community. These families would be forced to abandon their holdings, crops, houses and way of life. Everything would be destroyed.

Many of the Malay 'Menteri Besars' pushed for much more ruthless solutions to the 'squatter problem': one proposed 'burning out squatters and leaving them to work out their own salvation'. But the strategy and practice of resettlement should not be seen as a softening or liberalisation of British counter-insurgent strategy. It was in fact a *radicalisation* of the war. When Briggs presented his plan to Gurney, he referred to a successful application of similar operations in pre-war Burma '… it was proved […] that if these areas are dominated to such an extent that food, money and information were denied the enemy, or even diminished, the task of security troops would be easier […] the initiative then becomes ours.' Once the guerrillas had been cut off from their suppliers, they could be lured into carefully chosen 'killing grounds' to be captured or killed.

In Malaya, the army played a major role in resettlement operations. These were secretive and ruthless. An hour or so before dawn, British troops would encircle an entire squatter area. As mentioned above, the villagers would have received no warning that their lives were about to be turned upside down. The reason for secrecy, of course, was to prevent any MNLA units in the area disrupting the operations. Then Chinese-speaking police entered the village and went from door to door ordering the villagers to gather together all their moveable belongings. As people stumbled bleary-eyed from their homes, a long convoy of trucks came rumbling down the main road. Soldiers began herding women and children and the frailer villagers into the open cargo beds. The more robust would have to walk hundreds of miles to their new homes. For many, the experience was traumatising. One British official admitted that 'we had to use a good deal of forceful persuasion to get some of them to move. If you [the squatter] would not dismantle your own house and bring it along and rebuild it in the new village we will just pull it down, and we did.' Once all the squatters had been moved out, the soldiers set fire to houses and Kongsi huts. K.L. Chye recalls:

> The whole place is surrounded by the police and the military to prevent any of the villagers from running away […] There's be a lot of crying […] or some of them were cursing me. They say, 'You're a running dog!'

Resettlement subjected the Chinese people of Malaya to a massive demographic dislocation that would have a critical impact on the course of the Emergency war. The fact is that resettlement *worked*. But this 'success story' has made it very easy to forget that hundreds of thousands of people suffered compulsory eviction from farms and homes that many had occupied productively for decades. The figures are astonishing. By March 1950 – that is, *before* the arrival of Briggs – 6,861 people had been resettled in the whole of Malaya. Two years later, in June 1952, the total had leapt to 470,509. In 1954 a government survey showed that by the end of the operation 532,000 people had been resettled. Later these figures had to be revised upwards: according to K.S. Sanhu, 572,917 people had been resettled in 480 'New Villages' by the end of 1954. That was the number of people who had been relocated significant distances. It did not take into account the 650,000 squatters living near plantations and mines who were 'regrouped': which meant being moved into camps near their places of work. All in all, the Briggs Plan impacted on 1.2 million people – one-seventh of the entire Malayan population according to the 1947 census. Over 56 per cent of the 'resettlement villages' were located in Johor, Selangor and the Kinta Valley in Perak.

The *experience* of resettlement is a lot more difficult to get a feel for now. Military historians who present the Malayan Emergency as a textbook counter-insurgency argue that resettlement shielded Chinese squatters from predatory MNLA guerrillas and won them over to the side of the Federation. As we will see shortly, resettlement would hit the MNLA guerrillas hard. But that is a different matter. Government propaganda dehumanised the squatters, and their suffering has never been taken seriously. Resistance to eviction was explained away as an irrational response to communist propaganda. Policeman J.J. Raj:

> The communist terrorists started all out propaganda and they really went to town and the squatters believed them. They said now look, 'In Germany and all, the millions of Jews who were sent to the concentration camps were killed. You now, the government is taking you to the camp and all will be killed.' As a result of that, quite a lot of people resisted, mostly the elderly people, the ladies, wives and children, they all resisted. So they have to be forcibly brought out on to lorries and taken there.

These people may simply have not wanted to be thrown out of their homes. Did they really know anything about the German camps?

When the evicted villagers arrived at the resettlement camps the reality was more often than not a nasty shock. In a chapter of her novel *And the rain my Drink*, poignantly entitled 'No Fruit but Thorns', Han Suyin evokes a frightening new world where 'barbed wire is incorporate to the land, another vegetation':

> It encloses the resettlement areas, where six hundred thousand ex farmers now live. Thickened to triple height and depth, it bristles with the watchtowers of detention camps, loops around the police posts, straggles up and down labour lines and factories, dodges the jungle to enclose the forests of rubber with their managers' bungalows, special constables' quarters, and machinery sheds.

Han Suyin's fiction was closely based on real experience. She had worked as a doctor in a resettlement camp in Johor. She was not the only voice to raise an alarm. In April 1952, the Malayan branch of the British Medical Association published an alarming report on the resettlement villages. The British Medical Association warned that insanitary conditions blighted many of the camps and were a serious threat to public health. There was a serious risk of infectious epidemics. Medical services were overstrained and sometimes grossly inadequate. The British Medical Association accused the Federation of giving little or no thought to public health. In early May, a resettlement supervisor based in Kuantan, Pahang sent a bitter report from his district, as damning as Han Suyin's novel:

> The general location of sites is bad, with indication that water supply, agriculture and permanency were apparently never considered. These failings have caused the local inhabitants to be, in far too many cases, grouped, regrouped, settled and resettled. This [...] has provoked a sullen subjection to the changing whims and fancies of successive powers with the appalling result that East Pahang natives are very definitely anti-government, and uncooperative in all issues ...

Early in 1952, government propagandists began calling resettlement camps 'New Villages' and boasted in newsreels and official reports that the resettled Chinese squatters now had their own schools, community centres, places of worship and roads, as well as water and electricity supplies and sanitation services. The reality was that in 1952 very few camps had such amenities. The idealised 'New Village' was a long way in the future. All in all, resettlement and 'after care' cost the Federation a great deal of money. It was affordable because of the Korean War boom. In 1951, the peak year of resettlement, the overall cost was just over $40 million. But the money was mainly spent buying land, constructing mile upon mile of fencing and access roads and on digging wells and latrines. Huge sums were lavished on new police stations and security gates. Just $2.4 million was spent on educational, medical and health amenities. By the end of 1952, only 8 per cent of the total allocation of $67 million was spent on 'after care'. A measly $1.35 million went to agricultural aid.[43] The priority was security, as Mr Chiaw recalls:

> *Mr Chiaw (New Villager):* The gates were guarded by soldiers. The gates are open at six in the morning. At three in the afternoon, everyone must leave their plantations and come back here. By five in the evening you cannot go out of your house until six the next morning. Can you imagine how difficult life was then?

Many former squatters had to work outside the camp perimeters in local plantations. Here they re-entered the domain of the guerrillas. J.J. Raj:

> The communist will wait for them in the jungle and when you are tapping rubber, they will come and say [...] Eh [...] where is the rice you promised? Where are the medicines? Where are the bandages and various other things? So if these people don't give everything they are told, when you next come and you don't bring, you will be killed.

Coercion by both communists and government remained a fact of life for many villagers. Mr Chiaw: 'You have to do it. People were forced. You are caught in the middle. You cannot avoid the communist. If the government finds out you will be arrested.'

Many villagers persisted in supporting the guerrillas.

> *J.J. Raj:* 'They had ingenious ways of hiding stuff: they put [rice] into a bicycle pump and their latex pail – they had false bottoms. They put rice there everything and they go …'.
> *Mr Chiaw:* 'The [MNLA] supporters will carry out faeces in big buckets. The faeces will be on top and they will hide things underneath to smuggle out.'

K.L. Chye was a liaison officer in one New Village: 'If you see women, women suddenly became pregnant, search properly, those with big bras, also search properly.'

For Briggs, resettlement would be a blunt weapon without the simultaneous application of rigorous food control. The typical resettlement camp was a hunger machine. Each camp was encircled by barbed wire with just two entrances, which were stringently patrolled. The district authorities purchased every kind of food supply in controlled quantities. Food was secured in silos and could be purchased only by holders of ration cards. Rice was rationed. Store holders were required to keep a meticulous record of every item sold. Foodstuffs arrived in the camps at strictly controlled times; supplies could not be moved at night. Lorries could only stop at regulated points – and had to use only the most direct route.

A few villagers tried to get round these regulations, as we have seen, to help MNLA units lurking near the camps. But in many districts, food controls throttled the guerrilla supply lines. When four MNLA men surrendered in northern Selangor in August 1951 they told interrogators that they had been forced to eat fruit seeds instead of rice. They all suffered from severely swollen legs and ulceration brought on by vitamin deficiency. It may be that the sudden and final upsurge of violence in 1951 was a desperate response to starvation. The worst, for the MNLA, was yet to come.

The Hunger War

Resettlement was neither philanthropic nor humanitarian. It was a means of waging war. Arguably resettlement *punished* rural Chinese communities just as the Scots Guards had punished the plantation workers of Batang Kali. The 'Briggs Plan' was a crushing blow to the MCP from which it would never recover. The impact of the 'Hunger War' became a lot clearer after the publication of *Dialogues with Chin Peng*, a record of a 'Workshop' held at the Australian National University in February 1999, and the communist leader's own memoir, *My Side of History*, in 2003. These and other accounts by former MNLA guerrillas added a great deal of depth to the narrative of the war. Chin Peng revealed that:

> … as more and more people were herded into the new villages with their high cyclone wire fencing, their barbed wire, flood lights, police guards, constant searches, frequent interrogations […] we realised we were facing nothing less than a crisis of survival.

As resettlement operations gathered pace, disrupting the communist supply lines as Briggs intended, the MNLA regiments were forced to move much more frequently. Chin Peng was now based near Kerdau in Pahang. The incessant moving, fighting, withdrawing, regrouping and fighting took a huge toll. The success of any insurgency depends on guerrilla units being able to decide when and where to attack and when to withdraw. By 1951 this was no longer an option for many MNLA regiments. They were forced to react, not act. Worse, in a frighteningly short period of time the guerrillas began to go hungry. Resettlement camps were now springing up in the same district, further eroding supplies. This forced Chin Peng to break up the bigger platoons into smaller units. Rice rations were cut and foraging parties despatched to nearby rivers to gather edible reeds. The soundtrack to the war was no longer gunfire but a rumbling stomach. It will be recalled that Siew Mah was about to withdraw just hours before the high commissioner's limousine appeared, because his men had run out of food. As we noted before, Gurney's murder coincided with a pervasive mood of defeatism on the British side. The chronic weakness of the Federation intelligence services meant that the damage being done to the MNLA by settlement was not apparent. Hungry guerrillas had assassinated the high commissioner.

The MCP politburo reacted to the onset of resettlement as aggressively as it had to registration. This is why the number of attacks and 'contacts' with government security forces rocketed in 1951. Like the attack on the Gap Road, the MNLA surge was a consequence of fear. As Briggs had predicted, the onslaught on the squatters' communities forced MNLA units into the open – into the 'killing zones'. The number of 'contacts' between the security forces and the guerrillas had risen, but so too had the numbers of insurgents killed. The Min Yuen had become almost as vulnerable. According to one courier, Lao Jiang:

> Everything was fine when we lived near to the people. But if the enemy attacked us [Min Yuen], we'd be forced to flee to isolated areas deep in the jungle. And then we'd be in trouble. We would survive by eating wild vegetables and animals – everything from rats to elephants.

But it was not only hunger that was starting to tear apart the MNLA. By the time the spectre of starvation stalked the jungle camps, the MCP was reeling from the fallout of ideological discord. Resettlement struck at a rebel army that was already riven by internal strife. It is conventional in Malaysian historiography to represent the communist guerrillas as amoral beasts devoted to brutal slaughter. It may come as a surprise then that the debate that divided the party and the armed movement at the beginning of the 1950s was about the problem of violence. At the end of 1950, the chairman of the Central Selangor District Committee, Hoong Poh, wrote to Central: '… if we insist on continuing our present policy [of terror] we will cause the enemy no disadvantage but create unpleasantness for the general public who will gradually withdraw from us …'.

Hoong Poh pointed to what he called the unlearnt lesson of the MNLA campaign against registration and ID cards. The government, he pointed out, had carried out the registration scheme within a very short period of time. Did that simple fact not suggest that the masses were happy to be registered?

> … if the masses have no desire to surrender their cards and we insist on taking them away then it will be a question of taking by force […] we would be committing something against the will of the public. I think that public opinion is against us.

Hoong Poh's argument should have been blindingly obvious to the Central Committee comrades. Had they understood nothing of Mao Zedong's philosophy of guerrilla warfare? Hoong Poh hedged his bets with a reference to Stalin's maxim that 'methods must be changed according to different conditions' but the implications of his letter were devastating. The politburo had been fighting the wrong war.

Hoong Poh's provocative letter was written in the turbulent wake of a succession of bruising arguments and defections in the party. These had coagulated around a prominent MNLA officer called Lam Swee who had defected and thrown in his lot with the colonial government. Chin Peng and the politburo hit back with a ponderously entitled pamphlet: *The incident of Lam Swee going over to the enemy and betraying the party*. Backed by the government propaganda apparatus, Lam Swee counter-attacked. *My Accusation, written against the blind struggle of the communist party* was published by the government in early 1951. There are few political passions as intense as those of the relapsed convert. Lam Swee focused his ire on the politburo. The communist leaders were corrupt and greedy. They had their own special weapons, their own bodyguards, access to good food and clothing, and often exploited their position to keep their wives, official and unofficial, at MNLA headquarters. Rank and file had no such privileges. Lam Swee was not finished. Members of the Central Committee, he went on, had never been elected; they were anonymous cowards; they disdained democracy. The shadowy power brokers of the politburo were cruel and incompetent. The rumbling anger in MNLA ranks that Lam Swee gave a voice to so powerfully in his vitriolic 'J'accuse' grew much louder later that year. In May 1951, Chin Peng ran out of patience with the independent-minded former schoolteacher, Siew Lau. When he tried to escape with his wife to Sumatra, Chin Peng had them intercepted and executed. The Malayan communists were turning on their own.

New Directions

The semi-judicial murder of one of the party's most admired and eloquent theoreticians did nothing to silence the barrage of criticism that was now being flung at Chin Peng and the Central Committee. Hoong Poh's letter had, as far as we can tell, a bracing impact. The popular chairman of the Central Selangor District Committee could not be so easily silenced or his comments dismissed. In October, a few days before High Commissioner Gurney set off for Fraser's Hill, the Central Committee issued new 'directives' which on paper at least overturned the 'hit harder' terror policy. A year later a copy of the 'October Directives' fell into the hands of the security forces and were on the desk of the Secretary of State for the Colonies, Oliver Lyttelton, in December.

The main argument made by the MCP in the 'October Directives' was that 'violent tactics which have antagonised peasants and workers' must be abandoned. The directives were quite precise. Comrades should no longer seize identity and ration cards; they must stop attacking resettlement villages, post offices, reservoirs, power stations and other public services; hand grenades must not be hurled indiscriminately into coffee houses … The comrades would now have to 'take care when shooting running dogs [collaborators] found mixing with the masses, to prevent stray shots from hurting the masses'; they must cease burning religious buildings, sanitation trucks, Red Cross vehicles and ambulances; and destroying rubber trees and attacking plantations. 'Stop' is the most frequently used word in the directives. A typical sentence: 'explosives and other methods shall not be used to capsise [sic] the relevant trains, for in doing so it might inflict casualties on the masses …'. An especially interesting point made in the 'October Directives' is that if the masses are treated as reactionaries, they will behave as reactionaries. Party strategy must henceforth focus on 'educating and convincing the masses': 'Our Party cannot compel the masses in the least …'. This was an astonishing concession to reality. Another crucial argument made in the directives is that 'the lives of the maximum number of trained Communists' must be preserved, i.e. not risked in combat, to carry on the tasks of education and persuasion. A practical consequence of that proposal was Chin Peng's decision to withdraw some especially well-educated and valued cadres to the Thai border the following May.

The language of the 30,000-word 'October Directives' may appear stiff and hackneyed, but the MCP had taken a remarkable and in many ways enlightened step in a new direction. This was publicly acknowledged by the correspondent of *The Times*, Louis Heren. General Sir Rob Lockhart, the deputy director of operations under Gurney's successor, Sir Gerald Templer, allowed Heren to read a translation of the 'October Directives' not long after they had fallen into government hands. 'The language,' he recalled in his autobiography, *Growing up on The Times*, 'was unusually obscure even for such a document, and the ideological jargon self-serving, but there was no doubt that the leadership admitted defeat […] the war had already been won …'. Heren was over-optimistic. More precisely, he was wrong. The MCP was not admitting defeat, but redefining their struggle.

PART FOUR

REMAKING MALAYA

1

WAR ON HEARTS AND MINDS

Chinese Dilemmas

After 1951, the Emergency war became less a task of crushing an insurrection than a way to forge a new independent Asian nation: one that would serve the interests of the former colonial power and the tame elite it had promoted. The great puzzle of the Emergency can be put very simply: Why did the war persist for so long? By the time the MCP politburo began drafting the 'October Directives' at the end of 1951, the MNLA had, as historian Kumar Ramakrishna argues, become a 'prisoner of terrorism'. What this implies is that the MCP could no longer speak for 'Malayans' as a nationalist organisation. This disaster was only in part the result of errors made by Chin Peng and the politburo. The British and their Malay allies drummed home the simple message that the communists were terrorists not nationalists. They had chosen to take the path of violence not the road to independence. Since the communists had lost the nationalist initiative, the MNLA would now become the stalking horse of national independence. The 'shooting war' that waxed and waned after 1951 truly became, to borrow Tim Harper's phrase, 'a war on the periphery'. The Emergency would now be exploited to browbeat the people of Malaya to choose political righteousness. The irony of the Malayan Emergency is that Chin Peng and the communists were enlisted as agents of nation building, but *in absentia*. The spectre of communism, like some demoniac figure in a 'Wayang Kulit' shadow play, acted to bind together the political fibres of independent Malay(si)a by consolidating and then conserving the powers of an anti-communist ruling class. The Emergency was the making of Malaysia.

The Briggs Plan showed that what military historians call the spatial control of a population could enfeeble an insurrection by tearing apart armed insurgents and their supporters. Mao Zedong warned his followers that guerrilla warfare 'basically derives from the masses [...] it can neither exist nor flourish if it separates itself from their sympathies and cooperation.' Luis Taruc, who led the 'Hukbalahap' revolt in the Philippines after the Second World War, insisted that a rebellion can 'hold out as long as it is supported by the masses ...'. General Briggs may not have read Mao. He could have learnt the same lesson by reading T.E. Lawrence. In *Seven Pillars of Wisdom*, his account of the Arab Revolt against the Turkish Ottomans, Lawrence concluded that rebels 'must have a friendly population, not actively friendly, but sympathetic to the point of not betraying rebel movements to the enemy'. The MNLA undermined the trust of the people with terror. Chin Peng and the politburo acknowledged this in their 30,000 word 'October Directives'. By the end of 1951, when the 'Directives' were sent out to MNLA regiments, the damage had been done. Resettlement would be the *coup de grâce*. By the beginning of 1952, the MNLA guerrillas resembled gasping fish flapping on the edge of a dried-up ocean.

Since the end of the nineteenth century, the many different communities of overseas or Nanyang Chinese had been powerfully influenced by the ideas of a new generation of Chinese nationalists. The great nationalist revolt against the decayed Qing dynasty was planned at the 1910 'Penang Conference' in Malaya. For a long time, the political ferment in the Nanyang world was focused on what was happening in China. In Malaya, communists and moderates joined forces to support their fellow Chinese against Japanese aggression. After 1942, the Japanese invasion dislocated these ties. The experience of occupation fractured the old Nanyang world, breaking the patron-client bond between the wealthy commercial elite, the 'towkays', and the wider community of workers and peasants and unpicking the close-knit communal bonds that had been woven over many decades. By the time the Japanese surrendered and the British returned, the Nanyang kaleidoscope had been shattered.

The British had created the racial topography of Malaya. Colonial administrators favoured Malays, and ruled through the sultans, but could not afford to ignore the Chinese. They made friends with tycoons. They respected the commercial dynamism of Chinese entrepreneurs but tried to control their famous clannishness. The Special Branch kept a close watch on subversive Chinese societies. The colonial government was expected to make sure that the Chinese stevedores, miners and tappers did as they were told and to enrich the empire. This was the task of the Chinese Protectorate, established by William Pickering in 1877 and headquartered in Singapore. The protectorate was staffed by some of the cleverest servants of empire. They were required to master the many different Chinese dialects spoken in Malaya and prided themselves on their intimate knowledge of every nook and cranny in the Nanyang world. The protectorate mandarins poked their noses into all aspects of Chinese life, gathering in a harvest of information that was sifted, collated and studied. The Chinese respected and resented the panoptic activities of the protectorate in about equal measure. When the Japanese captured Singapore in 1942, the staff of the Chinese Protectorate vanished. They were captured or fled home to Britain. In London, the Malayan Planning Unit began its deliberations. To Gent and his colleagues, the old 'Chinese Protectorate' looked like an anachronism. Their proposal for a new 'Malayan' citizenship that eschewed race was incompatible with a body devoted to the care and control of just one Malayan community. The MPU abolished the protectorate. At the stroke of a pen, the British unravelled their former ties with the Chinese. The now rather anomalous 'Secretary for Chinese Affairs' became, it was said, a 'head without a tail': the secretary had 'no face with the Chinese'.

For many young Chinese, the Malayan communists had tremendous appeal after the end of the war. The MPAJA fighters, who marched proudly through Singapore when the British returned, were the heroes of the anti-Japanese struggle. This radicalisation of a new generation of Chinese was intensified by the disastrous period of the British Military Administration and then the crackdown on the labour movement. There were many other Chinese who opposed or were indifferent to the communists – the 'towkays', the many supporters of the Kuomintang as well as well as ordinary shopkeepers, stallholders, taxi drivers and such who were all trying to make ends meet in desperate times. This other Chinese community had no single political voice: it was, to use Sun Yat-Sen's vivid phrase, 'like a plate of loose sand'. This estrangement explains in part at least why so many Malayan Chinese took so little interest in the arguments about the 'Malayan Union' and new citizenship rights. Few wanted to stick their necks out. It was only when vociferous Malay nationalists led by Dato Onn bin Jaafar and UMNO turned their guns on the Union that non-Malay communities began to mobilise. There was widespread anxiety in both the Chinese and Indian communities that the British had given in to the Malays. And, of course, they had. The battle to rescind the 'Malayan Union' had energised Malay nationalism; now opposition to the Federation that replaced it brought together non-Malays. Many Chinese realised too late that the Federation was a political betrayal. Above all, they feared the new citizenship rules that now excluded many Malayan Chinese – and made the Straits Chinese, often called 'King's Chinese', the subjects of the Malay rulers. This was a very hard pill to swallow – as was the fact that the new Federal Council would have a built-in Malay majority.

The legendary Tan Cheng Lock was still enthroned as the most renowned and influential representative of the Straits Chinese. His forebears had first settled and prospered in Malacca in the eighteenth century: if Tunku Abdul Rahman wanted to know 'who are these Malayans' this venerable old gentleman was a living answer to his question. Before the war, Tan Cheng Lock had rarely questioned the virtues of British rule. But the catastrophe of February 1942 changed his mind. In 1942, he had escaped with his family to India and seen at first-hand the high tide of Indian nationalism. He revered Gandhi. Tan Cheng Lock was no firebrand but in October 1947, on the eve of the inauguration of the Federation, he backed calls for a one-day 'hartal' or strike to harness non-Malay opposition. The Indian nationalists had used national stoppages to great effect: now India had won independence. Victor Purcell, who had served with the old 'Chinese Protectorate' and returned to Singapore in 1945 as an advisor to the BMA, reported that 'virtually all business and transport were at a standstill and Singapore was without buses, trams or taxis [...] the Chinese community of Singapore as a whole stayed at home.'

In a very short period of time, the British had bred a hornet's nest. A resolute new Malay nationalist movement gloated across a widening chasm at the splintered political world of the non-Malays. The 'Malayan Planning Unit' had ineptly tried to mend the internecine consequences of colonial communalism. The Federation had reinforced the barriers. The insurgency that erupted in June 1948 threatened not so much a communist takeover of Malaya as a prolonged sharpening of a communal civil war. If the British were to 'unite and leave' they had to find a way to put into reverse the headlong rush to a communal stalemate. Malaya must not be allowed to become another Palestine or partitioned India. By 1951, resettlement had begun to 'condition' the rural Chinese, and wean them forcibly from the communists. This left the matter of the other Chinese communities that Gurney had accused so bitterly of sitting on the fence. Could they be wound into the Malayan project and could the Malays be persuaded to let that happen?

The Korean Dividend

On 25 June 1950, the North Korean Army swept across the 38th parallel under a barrage of artillery fire. The Americans immediately pledged to back the South Korean government of Syngman Rhee against communist aggression. President Truman ordered General MacArthur to begin transferring US troops from Japan. The United Nations led by the United States voted to back a 'police action' to help defend the South. As UN forces pushed the North Koreans back across the border, Mao Zedong sent Chinese troops to reinforce his communist allies. As a member of the UN Security Council, Britain was soon drawn into the conflict. Labour Prime Minister Clement Attlee reminded a colleague who had doubted the wisdom of joining another war that Korea was: 'Distant, yes, but nonetheless an obligation.' More than 90,000 Britons, many of them national servicemen, would fight in Korea. By 1952, both sides had fought each other to a standstill. In the meantime, the war had generated massive demand for tin and rubber. The Malayan economy boomed.

One important lesson learnt early on during the Malayan Emergency was that counter-insurgency is expensive. In the first two years of the Emergency, the price of rubber had slumped and so too had the morale of the industry. Attacks and assassinations by MNLA guerrillas turned the job of managing a tropical plantation or a tin mine into a high-risk occupation. This was, of course, the MNLA master plan. Capital and European management haemorrhaged. But as the war in Korea drove up demand for natural rubber and other raw materials to equip the British and American armies, the global price of Malayan raw materials leapt and would stay high for a long time to come. The Korean War reversed the flow of capital. Profits meant bonuses for estate managers and ample funds to fortify their estates against terrorist attacks. In 1949, $4 million was being spent on defending European mines and plantations. By 1951, that sum had quadrupled. The big rubber company Dunlop alone spent $4 million acquiring seventy armoured cars and a company unit of professionally trained security officers. Another problem that General Briggs had confronted was that his plan, especially resettlement, was costly. After 1950, it was the Korean War dividend that made the 'Briggs Plan' affordable. Over time, the surplus would very slowly trickle down to the 'resettled' Chinese agriculturalists when the Federation government began to transform squalid resettlement camps into 'New Villages'.

The war boom generated tremendous demand for labour. This made it more difficult to find local police recruits. To overcome this, the government introduced the 'Manpower Regulations' in February 1951, which required young male residents to register with the government for service in the police force. This was, in effect, conscription and was resented by many Chinese who had the opportunity to earn better wages as the Malayan economy rebounded. Conscription meant that they and their families would lose out as the economy rebounded. Many Chinese men lodged appeals while others tried to avoid registration altogether. The consequence of this inept legislation was to undermine Chinese support for the Federation while reinforcing the hostility of both the British and Malays who habitually regarded the Chinese as fence-sitting shirkers. Tan Cheng Lock countered by pointing out that it was surely unfair to conscript for service in the police people who were aliens under the Federation rules of citizenship. The numbers show just how restrictive these were: in 1947, 3 million people qualified automatically for citizenship; of these 2.5 million were Malays; 225,000 were Indians, Pakistanis or Singhalese; *only 350,000 were Chinese*.

The Emergency war, as Tan Cheng Lock scolded the Federation government time and again, disproportionately punished the Chinese. Complaining about Chinese indifference was gross hypocrisy when it was Chinese civilians who suffered disproportionately from Emergency Regulations. Was it any surprise that the average Chinese rubber tapper, shop owner or mine worker was loath to walk into a police station to offer information about local insurgents if his or her action was likely to end with the informant locked up or murdered by vengeful guerrillas? There was another matter that troubled many Chinese. The killings at Batang Kali implied that British troops were careless at the very least with the lives of Chinese civilians. Although there had been no further incidents comparable to the savagery perpetrated by the Scots Guards, counter-insurgency operations often led to the incineration of villages and plantation Kongsi huts. Military commanders in Malaya continued to chaff at having to fight the Emergency as junior partners to the police. Some of them overcompensated by launching large-scale 'sweep' operations and calling in RAF bombers to pound the jungle. The consequences of this blimpish bravado could be deadly. In November 1950, a Lincoln bomber released its bomb load on a rubber estate killing at least twelve Chinese tappers; in October the following year, artillery fire inadvertently struck Chinese civilians in the Sungai Perangin resettlement camp. Tan Cheng Lock implored the government to 'build up an attitude of love, confidence and trust …'. But this was hard to achieve if, as happened throughout the period of the Emergency, the corpses of dead guerrillas, most of them Chinese, were paraded through towns and villages on the backs of lorries and then made into grisly exhibits in front of schools and public buildings. The British *Daily Worker* would embarrass the British government when it published gruesome photographs of British soldiers proudly holding up the severed heads of Chinese guerrillas killed in Sarawak. Who could doubt that the war was being fought against just one Malayan community?

Propaganda Wars

It would be useful here to remind ourselves what the British hoped to achieve in Southeast Asia after the Second World War. The frequently reiterated narrative of 'end of Empire' and 'decolonisation' has tended to obscure rather than illuminate British intentions. In many respects, decolonisation was an adjustment of British imperial power, not its complete abandonment. Moreover, empire ended in different ways in different parts of the world. The abandonment of Palestine and then India took place as plans were being laid at the Colonial Office in London to hang on to valuable territories such as Malaya and Singapore. In Southeast Asia, bankrupted Britain needed to maintain its grip on Malaya's dollar earning resources. Its dependency on American largesse meant that on a long-term basis the British would pay for a strong regional base in Singapore, buttressed by friendly local states purged of the communist virus. The former Allies looked at unpredictable Indonesia with its charismatic anti-Western president and huge communist party with deepening anxiety. If Malaya was to be granted independence as Attlee and his more reactionary successors had all promised, it was essential that the new nation respected the interests of the British and the United States and provided a counterweight to Indonesia. To retool Malaya as a kind of proxy regional power aligned with London and Washington meant that a lasting fix had to be found for the old Malayan dilemma: communal discord. The British could not afford to repeat Mountbatten's mistakes in India. Nor did they want 'another Palestine'. The Emergency war could not be won on the jungle battlefield alone.

Since the majority of the Malayan communists were Chinese, the prosecution of the Emergency war continually risked stoking the furnace of strife. The first, bloodless post-war political battle in Malaya had been fought with the Malays, but the abandonment of the Malayan Union and its replacement with the Federation had bonded the British with the Malay elites. As the military collapse of the MNLA became evident in the early 1950s, the British could turn their attention to 'squaring the Malayan circle' by creating a new 'imagined community' as the prelude to independence. The second phase of the Emergency would be a war on the mind.

There is an entire lexicon attached to this second chapter of the war: 'winning of hearts and minds', 'building confidence' and so on. Propaganda can be defined as *force applied to the minds of combatants*. The German theoretician of war Carl von Clausewitz wrote that: 'War is an act of violence intended to compel our opponent to fulfil our will.' This implies that the stronger the *feelings* of your enemy about, say, the justness of his cause, the harder he will be to defeat. Propaganda is an act of war aimed at the mind. An important point to keep in mind is that propaganda is not necessarily a matter of 'making stuff up'. Propagandists may not tell the whole truth but they feed on facts.

The notorious case of the 'German corpse factory' during the First World War shows this very well. In 1917, both *The Times* and the *Daily Mail* splashed on their front pages a grisly story about German soldiers boiling down their own dead to extract lubricants, glycerine for explosives, fats, soap, and bone meal for animal feed. The story spread rapidly around the world. The 'corpse factory' provided hard evidence of unspeakable German barbarity. There was no such 'corpse factory'. The origin of the story reveals the intermixture of fact and fantasy that nourishes propaganda. It turns out that a journalist called Karl Rosner had filed a report for the Berlin *Lokal-Anzeiger* that referred to a 'Kadaververwertungsanstalt' that he had 'smelt' while travelling near Reims. In German, a human corpse is *die Leiche*, but *der Kadaver* (or *die Tierleiche*) refers to an *animal carcass*. The German Army was, it seemed, boiling the cadavers of dead horses. Fact had been rendered into a useful fable. Wartime propaganda always tells a *story* that is useful for one side or the other; the propagandist uses fact, but is under no obligation to tell the truth. Propaganda is generated in the mutable gap between truth and falsehood.

For the first few years of the Emergency war, government propaganda had been confused and paltry. By the beginning of the 1950s, with the arrival of General Briggs, a root and branch reform of both intelligence gathering and propaganda was under way. Briggs repeatedly stressed the importance of breaking down communist morale through targeted propaganda. That was one side of the coin. The other was trumpeting success and that meant talking about kill rates. Remember how the murders at Batang Kali were first reported as the 'biggest success so far'. The gleeful celebration of 'bandit kills' helped restore the faith of Malays in the Federation. For many Chinese Malayans, the obsession with such statistics was filed with botched resettlement operations, deportations and 'collective punishments' as 'Chinese bashing'. In October 1951 – that cruellest of months – anger about resettlement reached an angry climax when the Mawai camp in Johor was attacked by the MNLA. More than 1,000 squatters had been dumped at the camp at the start of the Emergency in 1948. For three years, the evicted squatters had lived in jerry-built dwellings strung along a 2½ mile road that wound along the edge of the jungle. The camp had no fencing and was protected by a handful of disinterested Malay policemen. For three years, nothing was done to improve conditions. By 1951, Mawai was allegedly penetrated by Min Yuen cells and preyed on by local MNLA units. The camp was at last reinforced with the addition of four 'Specials'. They failed to stop the killing of four alleged informers and the abduction of thirty-six young men. At the end of the month, the government responded by ordering the closure of Mawai camp, to the great dismay of the villagers who had struggled to rebuild their lives in the face of immense hardship. Once again, Tan Cheng Lock protested with forceful eloquence: 'they are being treated like cattle and ordered to move their homes and their crops on a whim of the government ...'. The almighty row about Mawai camp added to the sense that the Chinese were being left out in the cold. It was no wonder that so many seemed unwilling to 'come off the fence'. The solution proposed in the dog days of the Labour government by Secretary of State James Griffiths was to send to Malaya an expert on psychological warfare and propaganda. The 'man with a propaganda plan' who was chosen for this task was the 'very tall, thin, bespectacled and shambling' Hugh Carleton Greene.[44]

Greene was supremely well qualified. A fluent German speaker, he had worked in Berlin as a correspondent for *The Daily Telegraph*. It may come as a surprise to discover that unlike the pro-Hitler *Daily Mail* and the resolutely neutral *The Times*, the *Telegraph* opposed the British government's appeasement policy with Nazi Germany and Greene was unflinchingly critical of the Hitler regime. His chilling accounts of the anti-Jewish pogroms that swept through Germany on 9 November 1938 enraged Propaganda Minister Josef Goebbels: Greene was expelled the following year. Soon after the war began in 1939, he was recruited by the BBC as head of its German Service. Churchill was sceptical about propaganda, which he described as 'killing Hitler with your mouth'. Like many Conservatives, he reviled the BBC which he decried as 'an enemy within the gates doing more harm than good'. Churchill's contempt reflected the fact that while BBC editors accepted that they had obligations to the national interest in wartime they remained staunchly committed to telling the truth as they saw it. The legendary BBC panjandrum Lord Reith insisted that broadcasters should 'help in stifling rumour and sensation by the presentation of fully authoritative and carefully presented news [...] No permanent propaganda policy can in the modern world be based upon untruthfulness.' During his time in Berlin, Greene had observed and indeed fought against the exaggeration and bombast of the German propaganda machine that shamelessly put out what Hitler called 'the big lie'. Greene and his colleagues in the BBC foreign language broadcasting department followed the Reithian axiom that truth made the best propaganda. When the BBC broadcast details of the fall of Singapore in February 1942, a

German who secretly listened to the BBC commented that 'if they can admit a catastrophe so openly, they must be terribly strong'. All over occupied Europe, and even in Nazi Germany, people secretly listened to the BBC because, as the former French prime minister, Léon Blum, said: 'in a world of poison, the BBC became the great antiseptic.'

After the war, Greene worked in occupied Germany and observed the Soviet clampdown in Eastern Europe at first-hand. This experience made him a convinced, if liberal-minded, anti-communist. When Major General Sir Ian Jacob, head of the BBC's Overseas Services, summoned him and asked 'Hugh, how would you like to go to Malaya,' a badly hungover Greene accepted with alacrity.

Greene arrived in Kuala Lumpur on 19 September 1950 and embarked on the customary whirlwind tour of the peninsula accompanied by an armed escort. He wrote home to his mother that he had soon 'fallen completely under the spell of Malaya'. When he reported back to the high commissioner, Greene made three fundamental recommendations: raise public confidence in the Federation government; demolish the morale of the MNLA by 'driving a wedge between the leaders and the rank and file' and encouraging defection; and 'create an awareness of the democratic way of life' and the threat of communism. Greene got on well with High Commissioner Gurney ('one of the greatest men I have ever met') and, backed by an equally enthusiastic General Briggs, began to lay waste to the creaking 'Department of Information'. Not everyone welcomed Greene's blitzkrieg. One bruised subordinate complained that he had the manner of a 'cold fish', 'unflappable and appeared domineering'.

Since the abolition of the Chinese Protectorate, the Federation had been afflicted by a shortage of Chinese and even Chinese-speaking staff. This deficiency had magnified the government's often insensitive treatment of even the most conservative Chinese Malayans. Greene had no Chinese nor was he planning to stay in Asia for long enough to learn very much, so he began putting in place a cadre of properly qualified staff. One of the new recruits was a brilliant young man called Too Chee Chew.[45] Greene was immediately very impressed by Too. He was, it was remarked, 'a clear and fast thinker, with photographic memory, magnetic gaze and oratorical skills'. The single quality that Too lacked was modesty. He had been born in the Federated Malay state of Selangor on 31 March, 1920. The family, who were Cantonese, were steeped in the Chinese nationalist tradition. His grandfather had been close to Sun Yat-Sen. Like Greene, C.C. Too was a clever man who rarely hesitated to advertise his genius. Two qualities above all made Too equipped to become an effective propagandist. He was a lucid writer and speaker in both English and most of the Chinese dialects, and above all he had himself flirted with communism. He understood the allure of idealism. We know very little about how Too and his family survived the Japanese occupation. He said later that he spent a great deal of time hiding out in the Kuala Lumpur Book Club – an English public library that the Japanese, for some unknown reason, never bothered closing – 'reading everything'. It was, he boasted later, an 'unusual and fateful exercise' that gave him 'the power of penetration and lucid perception'. This orgy of reading, he remembered, put him in an 'invincible position to tackle the communists later'. Be that as it may, Too was, like many other young Chinese Malayans, fascinated by the grizzled MPAJA guerrillas when they emerged from their jungle hideouts after the Japanese surrender. His memories of the Interregnum period before British forces landed at Morib beach were very different from the lurid tales told by Malays. He was astonished by the way the MPAJA fighters so swiftly penetrated every layer of Malayan society. He was impressed by their discipline and sense of purpose.

Too soon discovered that he had useful party connections. One of his friends from the Confucian School in Selangor was a member of the MCP Central Committee. At the time, the MCP suffered from an acute shortage of 'English educated personnel'. This was a disadvantage as the British set up the new military administration, the hated BMA. So Too was asked to help. He was invited to meetings, rallies and given free access to the MCP headquarters in Kuala Lumpur. He shadowed MCP leaders 'all over the place'. He took part in passionate debates and absorbed MCP syntax and phraseology. He came to respect MCP propaganda skills which drew on 'a very, very thorough knowledge of all the people on the ground level'. In the spring of 1946, the MCP asked C.C. Too to act as translator for the MPAJA veterans who had been invited to take part in the Victory Parade in London. He turned down that tempting offer, but a few weeks later attended a party at the MPAJA Ex-Comrades Association in Peel Road, Kuala Lumpur to welcome the heroes back home. It was here that he met the future secretary general of the party, Chin Peng. He liked him: he had a 'sort of scholarly presence which command[ed] respect'. Years later, Too brushed aside any suggestion that he had been a fellow traveller. The communists may have had 'pleasant manners and apparent sincerity', but he soon began to detect their 'naive syllogistic and contradictory theories'. For all their waffle about the will of the people, they were just 'cynical manipulators' and hungry for power and wealth. The Central Committee was:

> a gang of half-educated, swollen headed, power-mad adolescent demagogues trying to take over the country. I told them many facts which, as self-claimed leaders, they should have known but did not. What they were really trying to carry out boiled down to nothing but a gigantic swindle ...

Was he perhaps protesting too much?

A year or so after his encounter with the communist elite, Too began working for the Chinese Consul in Kuala Lumpur. He soon made a good impression. In 1947, Too and Wing Commander Robert Thompson negotiated the surrender of some KMT guerrillas holed up in the Betong Salient on the Malay–Thai border. Too liked Thompson who, he remembered, had few 'colonial airs and graces'. Not long afterwards, the British formally recognised the communist government of China and the consulate was closed down. Too lost his high-profile job. He moped about disconsolately for a few months before noticing that his old friend Thompson was serving on General Briggs' staff. So Too, hoping to call in a favour, applied for a job as an Emergency information officer in the same department. Thompson did not respond. When Too rang to find out what was going on, he was put through to a different plummy voiced Englishman who informed him that Thompson had recently left the department. In any case, the post had been filled. The Englishman, sensing that he was talking to someone of unusual personal qualities, suggested that Too drop by for an informal chat. He revealed that he was Hugh Carleton Greene, the head of the new 'Emergency Information Services' (EIS) that was based, appropriately enough, in Bluff Road in Kuala Lumpur.

For his part, Too liked the way that Greene was relaxed and 'unstuffy'. He was not a typical colonial type and dressed like a 'loafer' in a plain shirt and baggy trousers. Not long after he recruited Too, Greene brought the defector Lam Swee onboard. It was Too who translated Lam Swee's indictment of the MCP, *My Accusation*, into English. These 'Surrendered Enemy Personnel' (SEPs) who would come in from the cold in ever-increasing numbers would play a vital role in the Federation propaganda world.

Greene did not stay long in Malaya. But he set down the core principles that his successors would follow. Above all, propaganda must be credible. Any information should stand up to cross-checking. Many MNLA guerrillas, he suspected, were highly intelligent men and women who, though they were starved of news and information in their jungle camps, would take a hard look at government claims. Second, propaganda should be positive rather than threatening: Greene vetoed a proposed leaflet called 'Death to Min Yuen Workers'. Threats, he knew, would stiffen resistance. Propaganda should be spiced with entertainment. Here spoke a future Director General of the BBC. Greene broadcast radio shows such as *Spotlight on the Emergency* and *This is Communism* that mixed hard news with regular spots for a radio doctor and popular storytellers such as Lee Dai Soh. Finally, Greene insisted that propaganda had to draw on the most refined, up-to-date and precise market research, culled from meticulous examination of MNLA documents. Because of the shortage of Chinese-speaking staff in the EIS, enemy propaganda was an unknown unknown. With the arrival of C.C. Too and Lam Swee at the EIS, accurate up-to-the-minute translation became a vital tool in the war on communism.

Greene learnt from Too and other Chinese colleagues that government propaganda had to be exquisitely tailored to a culture that most valued information conveyed by word of mouth. This is, of course, how the communists worked: the Min Yuen went from village to village, town to town, talking up the MCP message. So Greene persuaded the government to invest heavily in the SEPs and in radio. He realised that the personal stories told by the SEPs like Lam Swee who had renounced the struggle could have a powerful impact. The problem was that some SEPs had 'blood on their hands'. To serve as government spokesmen they would have to be forgiven some pretty nasty acts. This was tricky. If an SEP went on the road, he had to have a clean record. It would lead to widespread revulsion if a star government turn was found to be a notorious killer. Nor was it a good idea for SEPs to know about other defectors who had been executed by the government. So Greene persuaded Gurney to show mercy to even those SEPs who had committed alleged atrocities, or at least keep very quiet about the ones who had been tried and hanged. The EIS organised Federation-wide speaking tours by mobile SEP units. The former guerrillas spouted carefully crafted moral homilies at big public gatherings. There was no doubt a degree of voyeuristic ogling to catch sight of these once feared but now humbled bandits. The SEPs were forced to travel in bulletproofed wagons, with convoys of armoured troop carriers and a dozen or so police.

Too became closely involved in the SEP campaign. He made sure they said all the right things. He was, in fact, overworked. As Chinese assistant to EIS, he was tasked with the analysis of captured MCP documents; compilation of summaries and synopses; providing advice on propaganda; responding to MCP propaganda; writing, editing and drawing cartoons for *New Path News* which had a circulation of 90,000; as well as chaperoning Lam Swee and other SEPs on their lecture tours, which could last as long as three months. He complained bitterly to whoever would listen that he was Lam Swee's 'bodyguard and driver rolled into one'. Too worked long into the night and most weekends and soon acquired a gastric ulcer. He was not a happy man.

Greene and his successors invested heavily in film and radio propaganda. As well as the SEP tours, mobile projection units toured Malay kampongs and resettlement villages showing films to a rural population that was still largely illiterate. Titles such as *The New Life: Resettlement in Johor, Rewards for Information* and *The Shame of Pusing, Communist Extortion Methods* give a good idea of the kind of productions that were shown on improvised screens all over the peninsula. Greene spread the jam of entertainment on the bread of government information. An SEP drama *Love in the Jungle* and a serial called *The Adventures of Yaacob* about a young man's derring-do escapades fighting 'CTs' in the jungle had great success. Home grown 'filums' were shown with imported old Tarzan epics. Greene loved radio and saw its potential in Malaya. Soon after his arrival, the government had invested in powerful new transmitters and Greene made sure that he was, as it were, radio editor in chief. He appointed Alex Josey as controller of Emergency broadcasting. Josey, 'a character of bohemian appearance and considerable wit', had been controller of programmes in the 'Palestinian Broadcasting Service', and then worked for 'Radio Malaya'. He was a maverick sort of socialist and some of his comments upset a few diehard planters who unleashed a barrage of abuse, forcing his resignation. But Greene liked Josey and recognised his talent. He procured generous funds to enable his protégé to develop a 'Community Listening Organisation' that transmitted in Malay, Tamil and the four main Chinese dialects. The shows were finely tuned to their audiences and their dialects and Josey made sure that not all the output was overtly 'political'. A regular show that became enormously popular was *Can I Help You?*, which answered questions sent in by listeners about ID cards, food control regulations, applying for resettlement grants and even marital difficulties. In Malaya in the 1950s, very few people in rural areas possessed a radio. So the colonial government sponsored setting-up transmitters and loudspeakers on estates, and in kampongs and resettlement villages. Hundreds of small battery-powered receivers were distributed to coffee shops and community centres. Radio embraced Malaya.

These aspects of Greene's innovative work focused on what the government called 'raising confidence': that is to say, convincing ordinary Malayans, whatever their race, that their future depended on supporting the Federation and whatever came after. News programmes like *This is Communism* reported on the iniquities of the Soviet Union and the tyrannous new regimes in Eastern Europe. Few Malays needed to be convinced that communism was a very bad idea. This was all about pushing the message home to the Chinese and the Indians. On another front, Lam Swee and C.C. Too developed ways of taking the propaganda war to the MNLA guerrillas. The EIS became a laboratory of psy-ops.

As well as radio, Greene was a passionate leaflet man. He introduced two simple but effective innovations. Propaganda leaflets would be waterproofed, so that they lasted longer in tropical conditions, and would be much more widely distributed. Like all good propaganda, the message of each leaflet had to win over the man or woman who found and read it in secret. The idea was to 'turn' the MNLA rank-and-file guerrillas by breaking down respect for their commanders and the MCP Central Committee. The MNLA fighters needed to be convinced that the government they had fought for so long was making promises to them in good faith. Surrender would be rewarded. Many might have wanted to follow in Lam Swee's footsteps but feared being punished, exploited or just quietly disposed of by the security forces. This was where credibility mattered most. Greene explained that 'the task of propaganda is to persuade a man that he can safely do what he already secretly wants to do because of disillusionment, grievances or hatred of life in the jungle, and to play on these feelings ...'. In his memoirs he recalled witnessing a surrender: 'one cheerful ruffian walked in from the jungle with a reward leaflet, carrying his commanding officer's Sten gun – and his commanding officer's head.' This traffic in human heads would be a gruesome signifier of the MNLA's slow decay.

Graham Greene visited his brother Hugh when he was in Malaya. He had been commissioned by *Life* magazine to write about the Emergency for the then princely fee of $2,500. Ensconced in Kuala Lumpur, Graham Greene was rather bored. He disliked the 'dreary' British colonies, much preferring their French or Spanish counterparts. He would, of course, spend a great deal of time in Vietnam. He perceptively said of the war in Malaya that it was 'like a mist; it sapped the spirits. It wouldn't clear.' For his *Life* assignment he managed to get himself 'embedded' with a Gurkha patrol and headed off into the jungle kitted out in a green uniform and rubber-soled anti-leech boots. He stumbled, slipped and slithered in the wake of the fast-moving Gurkhas and was quickly exhausted. Then the patrol stumbled on the mutilated corpse of a young Malay constable. The man had been stripped and beaten, then stabbed through the heart. 'I'm a bit off meat,' the squeamish Greene later wrote to his mistress Catherine Walston.

Hugh Greene's protégé C.C. Too became a master of psy-ops. He had an imaginative genius that let him reach out to the bored, hungry MNLA man or woman marooned in a decrepit jungle camp and desperate for any diversion that would distract from painful, suppurating leg ulcers caused by severe vitamin deficiencies and maddening insect bites. The new-style waterproof leaflets never judged the individual 'CT'. He or she had made an 'awful mistake': a mistake that could be remedied. There was news about comrades who had been killed or wounded. There were photographs of smiling and happy SEPs, with short messages addressed to their former comrades in the camps. The MNLA leadership always warned that the government executed any 'CT' who surrendered once they had been interrogated. So group photographs of SEPs were taken showing that even those who had given up months earlier were still alive and well. Lam Swee's *My Accusation* had lacerated the MNLA leaders who lived high on the hog while their comrades starved. This was a recurrent theme in C.C. Too's pamphlet bombardment. Historian and expert on terrorism Kumar Ramakrishna comments:

> In Malaya the Psychological Warfare Section led by the legendary Tan Sri Dato C.C. Too always tried to split the CPM rank and file guerrillas from their leaders. Psywar efforts focussed on highlighting and emphasizing very deliberately the precise ways in which the CPM leaders lived it up in the jungle at the expense of their foot soldiers. Deliberate care was also taken not to paint the rank and file as evil. The line taken instead was that the guerrillas were essentially honourable men who had been misled by the evil and nefarious CPM leadership.

C.C. Too was also aware that the *decision* to surrender could easily be undermined by the difficulties of getting out of the camps and then finding the appropriate government representative. So every single leaflet dropped on the jungle had a safe-conduct pass printed on the back that was 'signed' by the high commissioner. Batches of leaflets were printed offering 'how to' instructions. These must have been persuasive because many SEPs had these 'manuals' in their pockets. Greene's friend the Labour MP Richard Crossman had always preached that propaganda was useless if it was 'fired' at the wrong moment. Psy-ops had to, in Greene's words, 'prey on feelings' – and emotions were mutable. It would have been absurd to promise amnesties when the MNLA was riding high after the assassination of the high commissioner. The perfect psychological moment (Crossman's phrase) was more likely to be many weeks later when disillusion had crept back into the hearts and minds of guerrillas. Propaganda must be reactive. When MNLA leader Tan Guat of the 3rd Regiment surrendered after reading Lam Swee's *My Accusation* on 22 April 1951, he was swiftly processed, photographed and persuaded to put his name to a new leaflet that was air dropped, just forty-eight hours after he had stumbled out of the jungle, into the precise area where his regiment was stationed. Seizing the 'psychological moment' like this depended on close co-operation between the army, police and information services.

Propagandists exploited many different emotions. As well as fear, anxiety and despair, Greene targeted simple human greed. Greed, he believed, was more powerful than fear. The government had introduced a system of rewards for information long before Greene arrived. But he urged 'big increases' to secure the precious information that led to the killing or capture of guerrillas. By now the MNLA leadership was a lot better known and there was a sliding scale of rewards from $80,000 for the now much demonised Secretary General Chin Peng to $2,000 for a rank-and-file 'CT'. Rewards were another Korean War dividend. The government hoped that the increased sums offered for politburo 'trophies', above all Chin Peng, would induce MNLA rank and file to betray their leaders. The reward system had some grisly consequences: a severed head was a lot easier to offer as proof of death than a heavy corpse. Special Branch officer Tim Hatton (who had reported on the carnage at Batang Kali in December, 1948) describes a typical consequence of the reward system:

We all sat down and the leader of the [guerrilla] party produced a bag, a big green bag and dumped it on the table in front of me like that [...] and I said: 'What's that?' He said: 'It's the captain.' I said: 'It's a Captain?' And I looked more closely at it and I could see black strings of hair and bits of blood on the side. And I said: 'It's a human head, good God.' My inspector lifted it up by the hair: and there was Ah Koek, Central Committee member of the MCP grinning at me. His eyes were open. That was a shock.

Ah Koek had been the hitman sent by Chin Peng to 'resolve' the 'Siew Lau problem' in Malacca.

Towards an Alliance

As resettlement, government propaganda and the rewards system bit deep into support for the MNLA, the British felt confident enough to begin searching for ways to mend fences between the Malay nationalists and the Chinese. In this way, as even Tunku Abdul Rahman admitted, it was the Malayan communists that provided the catalyst for nation building, though, unlike real chemical catalysts, the MCP would be destroyed in the process.[46] Tunku Abdul Rahman admitted in 1983 that 'the struggle for the independence of this country [Malaysia] *was carried out by the communists alone* [...] [but] the communists of Malaya were not the indigenous people of this country and they were fighting to set up a communist regime which the believers in the faith of Islam [Malays] could not support ...'. (italics added). The British, who had 'manufactured' the antagonistic Malay 'races', now presented themselves as conciliators.

It was the slippery British Commissioner General for Southeast Asia Malcolm MacDonald who first stepped onto the long bumpy road of communal reconciliation. He pushed for new Chinese advisory boards to fill the gaping hole left by the abolition of the protectorate and actively sponsored the first post-war Chinese political party, the 'Malayan Chinese Association', the MCA. In 1949, MacDonald established the 'Communities Liaison Committee' to bring together Malayan moderates: it was in a sense a dry run for independence. He invited Dato Onn bin Jaafar, then the UMNO president, to meet and discuss with other communal leaders like MCA leader Tan Cheng Lock and the Singhalese C. Thuraisingam. It may be the case that MacDonald had lured Dato Onn, who had been staunchly antagonistic to non-Malays, with the promise of becoming prime minister of a future independent Malaya. Whatever the reason, Dato Onn went back to UMNO with a proposal to accept more liberal terms of citizenship for the Chinese and Indians. This betrayal, as many in the party interpreted conciliation, led to his downfall. Dato Onn had leapt ahead of his own party and paid the price. He left UMNO to form the cross-communal Independence of Malaya Party (IMP). MacDonald never lost faith in Dato Onn. As the founder of UMNO fell, so Tunku Abdul Rahman rose to power by seizing on Malay fears of any change in the racial status quo: 'This country was received from the Malays and to the Malays it ought to be returned. What is called "Malayans", it is not yet certain who they are; therefore let the Malays alone settle who they are ...'.

Tunku Abdul Rahman was a rather lazy epicurean who had a record of annoying the British. He had kidnapped his father, the Sultan of Kedah, to keep him out of British hands when the Japanese invaded. Now the British were deeply suspicious of this avuncular but wily Malay aristocrat. MacDonald detested the Tunku's famous rabble-rousing rants at UMNO congresses. But the Tunku was too interested in personal comforts to embrace the bracing political energies of the UMNO right-wingers. He had spent many years in Britain where he had won a reputation as a lover of fast cars, louche girlfriends, profligate betting and booze. He had finally passed the bar exams at the ripe old age of 46! Now in 1951, the Tunku discovered a new appetite for power and its trappings. As he surveyed the Malayan political landscape, he sensed that his new status was not completely secure. The threat came not from the Malayan communists or the Chinese party, the MCA, but from Dato Onn. The Tunku may not have known that the British still favoured his charismatic rival. He probably suspected as much. So he needed allies and he needed to ingratiate himself with the British.

In the aftermath of the Tunku's election to leadership of UMNO, Dato Onn had tentatively begun discussions with Tan Cheng Lock with the view of forming an alliance with the MCA. Predictably, the mercurial and hot-tempered Dato Onn failed to bond with the unflappable Tan Cheng Lock. Nevertheless, the Tunku seized his chance. In February 1952, he led UMNO into a strategic alliance with the MCA to contest the IMP at municipal elections in Kuala Lumpur. UMNO/ MCP won nine seats, the IMP two. If the Tunku was having problems winning over the chauvinist diehards in his party, a spectacular string of local election wins convinced the majority to formalise the relationship. The new Alliance Party, as this expedient union was now called, would decisively transform the political landscape of Malaya. Although, as the official records reveal, the British still hoped that Dato Onn would return to the fray, the formation of the Alliance was a seismic change. It offered Malayans – Malays, Chinese and Indian – a platform to demand independence and, to the Tunku's relief, accelerated Dato Onn's fall from grace. Above all, the Alliance showed that the more conservative Chinese would accept Malay political dominance in return for a big slice of the business pie. It was famously and cynically said by one prosperous businessman that the colour of the cow didn't matter so long as it could be milked.

From the British point of view, the new party offered a way to avoid the communal bloodbath they feared might overwhelm Malaya. For Malays, the Alliance was preferable to a genuinely multiracial party like Dato Onn's IMP. Malays and Chinese would stay within their own political realms. By rejecting the IMP and embracing UMNO, Tan Cheng Lock had accepted and ratified Malay dominance of the independence struggle. It would be the Tunku who would lead Malaya to *merdeka*. His Alliance partners would have the supporting roles. They would watch from the wings. The Alliance had smoothed over the political landscape of Malaya. It had not broken down any communal walls.

2

A TERRIFYING COMBINATION OF CRASSNESS AND VOODOO

More Power than Cromwell

Stories need heroes. The historical narrative of the Malayan Emergency offers that role to Sir Gerald Templer. There is a good reason for this. When he was appointed in 1952, Templer was given more power than any other British high commissioner before independence. He used his power to energise the war on communism and halt the long slide into despair. He set Malaya on course for independence. He won the battle for 'hearts and minds', a phrase he is wrongly credited with coining. Inevitably, doubts have been raised about whether or not Templer deserved such accolades. By the time Templer was appointed, much of the heavy lifting had been done. The communist threat was receding. There was a workable political alliance emerging between the main communal parties. And yet the conservative British government remained convinced that Malaya was an expensive and intractable problem. A highly visible solution was required. Templer took that role.

Few would question that Templer, the 'Tiger of Malaya', was a dynamic, incisive, strong-willed and rebarbative professional soldier who seems not to have had a single moment of self-doubt in his life. He was bluff, frequently downright rude and the word 'blustering' might have been invented for him. And yet his record was mixed. As director of civil and military affairs in occupied Germany, he had clashed with the future chancellor Konrad Adenauer. When Templer had inspected Adenauer's Cologne fiefdom, he had been appalled. The city 'stank of corpses'. There was no water, no drainage, no light, no food. Dr Adenauer's attitude was 'I am doing my best – if you don't like it, it is just too bad.' Templer sacked him for 'laziness and inefficiency'. Templer liked to boast that Adenauer, who presided over the miraculous economic rebirth of West Germany, bore him no grudge. The truth was that Adenauer hated the British, and Gerald Templer most of all.

To get to the bottom of the Templer puzzle, we need to go back to the time when the new conservative Secretary of State Oliver Lyttelton returned from his tour of Malaya. Lyttelton reported to the newly re-elected Winston Churchill that the situation was 'appalling'. Although he ended his report with a few sentences about low morale among loyal Chinese and Malays, his ire was mainly directed at the Federation government. 'There was divided and often opposed control at the top,' he complained. The civil and military powers had only the vaguest idea of their tasks; the commissioner of police was at loggerheads with the head of Special Branch. The civil administration moved at a 'leisurely, snail-like pace'; intelligence about the MNLA was 'scanty and unco-ordinated'. One of the servants at the high commissioner's residence in Kuala Lumpur was exposed as a communist spy. Here was the nub of the Malayan problem, Lyttelton argued. Briggs, the 'General in a Trilby', had run into difficulty because he had never been provided with the clout to cut through the sclerotic and fractious workings of the Federation government and the Malay state legislations. This is what Montgomery was hinting at when he wrote: 'When we have a plan and a man, we shall succeed …'. Montgomery was hinting at a power arrangement that was tantamount to a dictatorship. The 'man' he evoked would need to be – or have the qualities of – a soldier and the guile of a diplomat. He would, as Lyttelton now proposed, be a 'Supremo'. In practice this meant welding together the roles of high commissioner and director of operations.

Templer was not Lyttelton's first choice. He approached Bill Slim, now a field marshall, who insisted he was too old and put up three names. One was Templer's. Lyttelton met him, liked him, and on 3 January 1952 he sent a wire to Churchill, who was en route to New York, that he had 'hardened in favour of Templer'. By 11 January, Templer was on his way to meet Churchill, now ensconced at Rideau Hall, the governor general's residence in Ottawa. Their conversation has passed into legend. Churchill placed his hand on Templer's knee:

'I want you to go to Malaya […]'

'Yes, sir.'

'As you realise General, I may be sending you to your death. And I am an old man now – I may not see you again […] And I don't buy a pig in a poke.'

A tear or two ran down the Prime Minister's fleshy cheeks. After these bizarre theatricals, Churchill got down to business. Malaya's tin and rubber was vital, he told Templer:

'You must have power – absolute power – civil and military power. I will see that you get it. And when you've got it, grasp it – grasp it firmly. And then never use it. Be cunning – be very cunning …'.

General Templer was thus appointed director of operations *and* high commissioner. Templer had, as Churchill remarked, 'more power than Cromwell.' The question is – what did he do with it? For every historian who believes that (in the words of John Nagl) 'it is impossible to overstate Templer's role', there is another who decries the 'Tiger of Malaya' as an 'overenthusiastic Boy Scout', or worse, a 'military dictator'. Former police officer J.J. Raj, who served under Templer, has no such doubts:

> To my mind Providence had sent the right man, at the right time to the right place to crush the communist terrorists in Malaya. A lesser man would have failed. By the sheer force of his personality, drive, energy and determination, General Templer, in a short space of time was able to win over the hearts and minds of large masses of the population [...] [Templer] commanded enormous respect from the Police, the Armed Forces, and the Civil Service and more especially from people in the kampongs and the New Villages.

Historian Karl Hack has made the point that:

> ... the Emergency began to change in nature and direction as early as 1951–52 [before Templer was appointed] and that the necessary local and counter-insurgency ingredients were already in place by that time [...] The critical conditions had existed before Templer and 'hearts and minds', and that in the most important policies there was, and was always likely to be, continuity not change around 1952 ...

Hack's argument has upset a few historians. His argument, however, fits the evidence. Templer brought very few new ideas to the Malayan situation that had not been proposed already by Briggs and at least partially realised. The Templer myth is of course wrapped up with the larger matter of the British myth of the Malayan Emergency that was enshrined in Sir Robert Thompson's *Defeating Communist Insurgency*. Templer is the hero of Thompson's counter-insurgency manual. Wars fought against guerrillas are hard to win decisively and the Emergency was no exception. Like forest fires, insurgencies can fizzle out but then flare up again. So achieving victory is to some significant degree a game of smoke and mirrors. It is crucial – no, necessary – to be seen to win. And Templer was just the kind of 'man with a plan' who could play that to perfection.

The Templer Way

Templer flew out of London Airport on 5 February 1952, on a BOAC flight bound for Karachi. Flying with him was Donald MacGillivray, his deputy who was destined to become the last colonial high commissioner of Malaya. This was only the second time the two men had met. At Karachi, Templer and his party transferred to an RAF flight bound for Kuala Lumpur where he arrived on the afternoon of 7 February. After making a short speech at the airport, Templer was ushered by Federation General Secretary del Tufo into the high commissioner's limousine that still bore the scars of the fatal attack on the Gap Road. Templer was a professional soldier and had had no 'imperial' experience – unless we count his role in occupied Germany. The significance of this has perhaps been underrated. Like Hugh Greene, Templer did not 'know Malaya' and that was an advantage. When his Rolls drew up in front of King's House on that humid afternoon, Templer insisted on shaking hands with Malay members of staff, brushing aside del Tufo's muttered caution that: 'The British in this country don't shake Asian servant's hands.' Templer did.

Before he had left London, Templer had asked Churchill to define his objectives in Malaya: 'I am not at all clear,' he complained 'what HMG is aiming at from a political point of view. Is it a "united Malayan nation"? And if so what exactly does this mean? I must have a clear policy to work on.' It would seem that Templer was forced to come up with his own answers. He listed three tasks: to get a real grip and co-ordination of intelligence, to reorganise and retrain the police and to get the information services to tell the people what the Federation government was doing to win the war. Templer's plan reiterated proposals made two years earlier by Briggs. Templer had the power and the appropriate kind of personality to smash through the thicket of petty checks and balances that had, it was believed, stymied the war. He was a bully, but sensitivity has never been the most admired qualification for the kind of job he had been assigned. As his frequent public statements show, he was intelligent enough to see that the Emergency needed to be fought on many different battlefields and he was sufficiently cunning to find ways of doing so. Templer also had an instinctive respect for the theatre of power and an actor's talent for commanding the stage. He was often on tour in Malaya, as thousands of photographs show, and he was a lot more visible than his late predecessors had ever been. He knew how to project authority and determination. Templer's visibility dramatised the certainty of victory.

To be sure, Templer was more than just a symbol or figurehead. He galvanised a ramshackle administration and reformed the gathering of intelligence as Briggs had urged. Templer was an innovator in only one respect: he would take the war into the deeper jungle to the Orang Asli aborigines who became increasingly important to the MNLA. The widely shared sense that 'something had to be done' helped Templer get his way. There was, without any doubt, deeply rooted crisis of command. The shock generated by Gurney's assassination had not diminished; Lyttelton had delivered his damning report; Briggs had gone. But so too had Nicol Gray, the divisive commissioner of police, and Templer made sure that his successor, Colonel Arthur Young, took in hand the rickety system of police training. We should also bear in mind that Templer inherited security forces at peak numbers: 23 battalions, an SAS regiment, 67,000 police and 250,000 'Home Guards'. It was not fully appreciated that the MNLA was in poor shape. In 1952, Chin Peng was forced to abandon the camp in Pahang and return to the Cameron Highlands. When he arrived there, he was dismayed to discover that food was scarce and attacks by security forces frequent. The retreat north would turn out to be the beginning of the MCP's 'Little Long March' all the way to the Thai border and beyond.

Templer inherited, from his predecessors in King's House, their ambivalent, sometimes openly hostile view of the Chinese. At the end of March, just weeks after he had set up at King's House, Templer grasped an opportunity to signal his with brutal clarity intentions with regard to 'fence sitting' Chinese. On 24 March, MNLA guerrillas cut the water supply to the village of Tanjong Malim, which is about 43 miles north of Kuala Lumpur on the Perak border not far from the Sultan Idris Training College. The following morning, the assistant district officer, R.M.C. Codner, set off with an engineer and a small unit of policemen to repair the damaged pipes. The MNLA ambushed the party – killing Codner, the engineer and seven policemen, and seriously wounding five others. Templer seized the opportunity that this outrage offered to him. The resettlement village near Tanjong Malim was, in Emergency parlance, 'black'. There had been a number of ambushes in the area, rubber trees had been slashed, a train derailed, a Malay village attacked … Its people had a reputation for clamming up. Although the investigation into the most recent incident had barely got under way, Templer assumed that the people of Tanjong Malim would not offer up much information unless they were put on the rack. He had to act and be seen to act. Templer summoned acting Head of Information Services Yaacob Latif to King's House. He told him that he was going to the scene of the crime the next day and wanted all the newspapers to come and see what transpired: 'You get them. If you fail … You won't.' Early next morning, Templer flew in an Auster to Kuala Kubu Bharu (from where the Scots Guards platoon had set out for Batang Kali) and picked up an escort of armoured cars. This was all part of the act. He descended on Tanjong Malim in a way that made clear he meant business. The new high commissioner and DOO coming down on a Chinese village like a wolf in the fold was a wonderful photo op. The DOO had ordered the community leaders to gather in the local meeting hall. Templer marched in, bristling. 'None of this would have happened,' he ranted, 'if the inhabitants of this part of the country had any courage […] Are any of you communists? Put your hands up!' No one did, of course. Templer put on a fine show of theatrical outrage. 'All right, I shall have to take extreme measures!'

He was as good as his word. He imposed a twenty-two-hour curfew. Schools would be closed; the rice ration cut to less than half the normal allowance; no one would be permitted to leave the town. 'It does not amuse me to punish innocent people,' he proclaimed, 'but many of you are not innocent. You have information which you are too cowardly to give.' Since Templer had so publicly chastised and punished the people of Tanjong Malim, there were, as he must have anticipated, loud cries of pain from the Chinese and left-wing British journalists. In London, the following exchange took place in the House of Commons on 30 April:

Mr *S. S. Awbery*: asked the Secretary of State for the Colonies how far relief for the people of Tanjong Malim, Malaya, arising out of the curfew, has been left to charitable organisations and how far it has been undertaken by the Government; to what extent the supply of food is adequate; what attention is given to the villagers' cattle during the curfew period; and when the curfew will be lifted.

Mr *Lyttelton*: Local communal organisations provided relief for the poorer inhabitants of Tanjong Malim. It has not proved necessary for the Government to give relief. The supply of food is adequate ...

Mr *Awbery*: While it will give some satisfaction to right-thinking people that the curfew has been withdrawn for at least some period, is the Minister aware that the period of the curfew was for 22 out of 24 hours; that people live four and five in a room and were not allowed to leave their houses to go to an outside latrine, and were fined 50 [Malayan] dollars for so doing –

Mr *Lyttelton*: Useful information has been received but it is as yet too soon to assess the full results of the measures taken at Tanjong Malim. I have no intention of interfering with General Templer's reasonable exercise of the discretion entrusted to him to deal with the very serious situation in Malaya.

Templer was not at all dismayed. Liberal griping was grist to his mill. Tanjong Malim was a chance to reveal an iron fist and use it. The collective punishment of Tanjong Malim was, as Templer admitted, a way to 'cause a flutter in the dovecotes'.

Templer used this kind of collective punishment frequently from the time of his arrival well into the following year. In August, a Chinese resettlement officer was murdered in a coffee shop in the village of Permatang Tinggi on the main road between Butterworth and Parit Bantar. Once again, Templer and a military escort with eight armoured cars sped north from Kuala Lumpur. When he arrived at Permatang Tinggi, Templer went through his now customary routine: the village leaders were ordered to gather together and then harangued to name the killers. He gave them four days. When no names were forthcoming – probably because the murder was an inside job – Templer evicted sixty-two men, women and children and sent them to a detention camp in Perak. The village of Permatang Tinggi was destroyed.

It was this kind of action that won Templer his reputation as the 'Tiger of Malaya'. He was an 'absolute ace', as Secretary of State Lyttelton rejoiced. Templer's campaign coincided with the sharp fall in the number of guerrilla attacks: it looked as if the 'Tiger' was getting the better of the communists at last. It is no wonder that Templer was so angry when the contents of the MCP 'October Directives' were leaked by *The Times*. 'I'll shoot the bastard who says this Emergency is over!' he told the *New York Herald Tribune*. He continued: 'There are probably as many Communist terrorists in the jungle as there were two years ago.' So much for reforming intelligence!

Severed Heads

In Britain, the Malayan Emergency troubled the prime minister and the Colonial Office but stirred little reaction from the wider public. On 28 April, the communist newspaper *The Daily Worker* (now *The Morning Star*) slapped across its front page the photograph of a Royal Marine commando posing with the severed heads of two guerrillas that were proudly held aloft in each hand. The unnamed soldier is standing in front of a hut with two Dyak recruits holding rifles and was presumably taken in Sarawak on Borneo. 'This is War in Malaya' was the accusatory headline. The photographs severely embarrassed the government. A spokesman tried to claim that they had been faked. *The Daily Worker* responded a week later by printing a second photograph of British soldiers also brandishing heads. In the meantime, the Royal Marine in the first photograph had been identified and tracked down on leave. He readily confirmed that the photograph was genuine. Neal Ascherson informed me that the practice was standard. The only problem the British soldiers had was that the Dyaks took so long to perform appropriate rituals to placate the spirit of the dead man. On 7 May, the scandal of the severed heads came up in the House of Commons:

> *Mr Awbery*: Is the right hon. Gentleman aware that nearly all hon. Members on this side of the House desire to see Malaya achieve nationhood as quickly as possible, but we are also agreed that the methods suggested in the photograph are neither desirable for the promotion of that nationhood nor will help towards its accomplishment, and will he give definite instructions that such methods will not in the future be adopted for jungle warfare?
>
> *Mr Lyttelton*: In my answer I have already explained that definite instructions have been given that decapitation is not to take place. I am afraid I shall be in some difficulty in explaining what happened in April, 1951.
>
> *Mr Emrys Hughes*: Does the Colonial Secretary say that this was a genuine photograph, and is he definitely convinced that it is not a fake?
>
> *Mr Lyttelton*: Yes, Sir, it is a genuine photograph.

Templer was a great deal less conciliatory.

> It is absolutely essential that communist dead should be identified [...] War in the jungle is not a nice thing, but we cannot forego the necessity for exact identifications [...] The viewpoint of [critics] who have no possible inkling of an understanding of conditions or terrain [...] is not understandable to the Security Forces who have the task of tracking down armed communist murderers and producing evidence ...

As suggested in an earlier chapter, the display of 'kills' nevertheless had ingredients of Grand Guignol theatricals. When MNLA leader Liew Kon Kim, known as the

'Bearded Terror of Kajang' was hunted down and killed, his bloody corpse was stretched out on a rack fixed to the back of a lorry and toured for three days through some of the 'New Villages' in Selangor. The main exhibit was trailed by vans with loudspeakers that sermonised about the dead man's wicked past and how he had met his justified violent end.

Which Hearts? Which Minds?

The propaganda reforms set in motion by Greene and refined by C.C. Too focused on the Malayan Chinese either as terrorists or as real or alleged MNLA supporters. Although Templer was a professional soldier who had been sent to Malaya to break a military stalemate, he was also charged with preparing Malaya for independence. The British government, as Churchill had made clear to Templer in Ottawa, needed Malayan rubber and tin. So an independent Malaya would still need to serve the interests of the former colonial power. Reconciliation was as much about economics as politics. The worst-case scenario from the government point of view would be one in which the Malays defied the British, jumped the independence fence prematurely and pushed aside even the moderate Chinese perhaps into the hands of the MCP. The Emergency war, while it continued, made this unlikely. A future Malay government would not want to – and could not – take on a resurgent communist insurrection. As long as the country was at war, the Malays could be kept on side. At a reception, a Malay official was overheard saying to Templer: 'You know, the Malays don't really want the British to leave …'.

Templer worked hard to get on with the rulers, who had helped Dato Onn scupper the Malayan Union. He attended coronations, and dished out baubles and knighthoods. The sultans feared that they had a great deal to lose from independence. They knew that in India, Congress had turned on the privileged Indian princes after independence. They resented giving ground to democracy; they certainly did not want Chinese subjects, or to work with Chinese administrators. They resented being forced to give up land to resettled Chinese squatters. Feathers needed to be unruffled. Though Templer worked hard on the sultans, he failed to appreciate Tunku Abdul Rahman's devious manoeuvrings. The Tunku had a reputation as a time-wasting playboy who liked to fool about at Legislative Council meetings, much to Templer's annoyance. Like Gurney and MacDonald, Templer liked Dato Onn a great deal more. But the Tunku was unperturbed. He knew that UMNO wanted him to adopt a confrontational pose. '[Templer] objected to the speeches I was making in political rallies,' he recalled '"All right", I told him "put me in prison. It's your job."' Templer glared back at the Tunku: 'I wouldn't give you that satisfaction. I don't want to make a martyr of you.' For the Prince of Kedah, this was all shadow boxing. He knew that he could not afford to take the hard path that Gandhi had in India.

Templer had less tractable problems with the Chinese leaders. His relations with the MCA and Tan Cheng Lock hit rock bottom in August 1952. This particular crisis was provoked by the return to Malaya, at the invitation of the MCA, of Victor Purcell, who had retired from the Malayan Civil Service to take up a post at Cambridge University where he was writing a history of the overseas Chinese. He had last been in Malaya during the dog days of the 'British Military Administration'. At the time he had become exasperated by the communist-inspired strike and labour stoppages. Now, years later, he took up the cudgel on behalf of the Chinese. He toured Malaya telling journalists that Templer was a tinpot military dictator who was leading the country up a political blind alley. The Chinese, he declaimed, would be forced to accept Malay domination. They must stand up and fight. This was too much for Templer. He summoned Purcell and his colleague, Dr Francis Carnell, another Sinologist, for a dressing down. He took an instant dislike to Purcell: 'he did look like a fat white pig,' He told a colleague: '… I really am very angry at the whole business. It takes quite a lot of jockeying to keep inter-racial nonsense out of the vapourings of local politicians and others of the so-called educated classes. To have them stirred up by a creature of this sort [Purcell] from England is too much.' The general did not warm to the urbane and witty Cambridge scholar.

Historians have dismissed Purcell's attack on Templer's conduct of the war as *ad hominem* and misleading. Anthony Short devotes several pages to a rebuttal of Purcell's attack in his classic study of the Emergency. To be sure, it does Purcell no credit that he often praised Templer when he was in Malaya, then unleashed his most venomous attack when he was safely ensconced behind the ivy-clad walls of his Cambridge college. What cannot be doubted is his passion.

Purcell launched his campaign against Templer in *The New Statesman* in January 1953, and then the now defunct *Twentieth Century* in February and delivered his final onslaught in a short book *Malaya, Communist or Free?*. Templer's biographer John Cloake dismisses Purcell's attacks as 'tedious'. The old fool, he implied, had descended from his ivory tower to tilt at windmills. But should Purcell's apparently Quixotic views be so easily dismissed? His book on Malaya, published by Victor Gollancz in 1954, is a thorough and thoughtful study of the situation written by a highly intelligent and respected scholar. He points out that the Secretary of State had stated in December 1951 that the British position was: 'Complete military victory before self government.' He had subsequently been forced to modify this by agreeing to the creation of civil instruments of government in wartime. But, Purcell insists, these 'steps towards self government' were window dressing. Electoral statistics clearly show a strong bias against Chinese and Indians. Purcell concluded that 'Malaya early in 1954 is politically one of the most backward territories in the British Empire.' He pointed out that the best political minds – the Malayan Nehrus, Gandhis and Sukarnos – were all under lock and key, or in exile. Templer had argued that what was happening in Malaya was no different from what was happening in Indochina. The British were standing up to communism. If that was the case, Purcell argued, then the MNLA, like the Viet Minh, must 'really represent a national movement which the British are opposing'. In other words, the communist MNLA had as much right as UMNO to claim the title of nationalists. This was an argument of considerable subtlety. Purcell went on to point out that the nations that were most successfully *resisting* outside influence (i.e. communism) from East or West were the newly independent ones: India, Burma and Indonesia. This implied that the British were making Malaya *more* vulnerable to communism by throttling any advance to genuine self-government. The Templer regime was, Purcell thundered, a 'terrifying combination of crassness and voodoo ...'. It was devoid, he fumed, of political imagination, reliant on threadbare platitude and corrupt. He recalled George Orwell's first masterpiece *Burmese Days*, which had enumerated the 'Five Beatitudes of the Pukka Sahib', 'Keeping up Prestige', 'The Firm Hand (without the velvet glove)', 'We white men must hang together', 'Give them an inch and they will take an ell', and 'Esprit de Corps'. According to Purcell, these were the axioms of Templer's circle: the spirit of Stamford Raffles had been replaced by that of the reactionary Bulldog Drummond. Purcell believed that the Chinese had become the 'Jews of Malaya': in British minds 'all ills were due to the Chinese, ignoring the fact that a large proportion of them were native-born Malayans ...'. He quotes a piece of colonial-era doggerel:

> Another <u>Chinese</u> bandit gone below,
> Praise God from whom all blessings flow ...

Purcell had a splendid turn of rhetorical phrase. *Malaya, Communist or Free* is a very entertaining book. It is uncomfortable reading for those who want to see Templer as hero rather than as a dictatorial martinet whose orders had the sanctity of Holy Writ. Purcell was not the only vocal critic of the Templer regime. Writing for *Time* magazine, the American judge William O. Douglas referred to the 'General's thin lipped tigerish sneer [...] [a] smile like a soundless growl [...] upper teeth bared to the gums in anger ...'. According to Judge Douglas, Templer had a disquieting relish for the 'dog hunt' of jungle warfare – a trope passed on to his troops. 'I met an Irish officer of the Gurkhas,' the judge recalled 'who talked of the bandits exactly as if they were foxes – "that was a fine bandit, a damned nice run."' By then, killing or capturing Chin Peng had become an obsession for many. Templer had doubled the price on the communist leader's head from $60,000 to $120,000 – but to no avail. Chin Peng would never be captured or betrayed. Although Templer supported the use of big military sweeps and patrols, the success of the Briggs Plan had made it even harder to track down MNLA units that had fallen back from the jungle fringes. This forced Templer to launch operations into much deeper jungle areas – the subject of the next chapter.

Through the Chinese Ceiling

A clear sign of Templer's difficulties was the low level of Chinese police
recruitment. When Colonel Young, formerly the Commissioner of Police of the
City of London, took over from Nicol Gray, he proposed reforming the standing
of the Malayan police so that the average constable had the same benevolent
reputation as the London 'Bobby'. To this end, Young and Templer inaugurated
'Operation Service' to persuade ordinary Malayans that the force was with them.
Templer summed up the purpose of 'Operation Service' as showing that the
police was not an instrument of tyranny. This overhaul needed Chinese recruits.
The police in Malaya had to start looking Malayan. Gurney had visions of luring
up to 10,000 Chinese volunteers for regular police work. Templer rather more
realistically hoped for 2,000 recruits – but by the end of his first year in Malaya, a
piffling 800 out of 800,000 Malayan police were Chinese. One Malayan Chinese
who responded to the government call for volunteers was a young man called
Yuen Yuet Leng. He had grown up a passionate nationalist with a reverence for
British traditions:

> I used to read about the British heroes – Harold the Saxon, 1066, Lord Nelson
> 1805. I was quite influenced, especially by Lord Nelson, and how he gave his
> life for his country. So I had a lot of respect for British history and how their
> patriots sacrificed themselves when necessary. Not because I loved everything
> about the British, whether we like it or not, they were still colonialists. But they
> were good colonialists.

As a teenager during the war, Yuen was drawn to the many Chinese anti-Japanese
organisations. Like C.C. Too, he flirted briefly with communism. After the Japanese
occupation ended, Yuen won a scholarship to study in Shanghai. These were bitter
times in China. Civil war raged between the forces of Chiang Kai-Shek and the
Red Army. Yuen saw nationalist soldiers forced to beg on the streets. He returned
to Malaya thoroughly disillusioned. His future would not be in China.

> I was a clerk in the Malayan Railways who sponsored my scholarship. But later
> on I went to Seremban to be a teacher. It was 1949, and that was when the
> communists threw a grenade at Tan Cheng Lock in Ipoh. He didn't look very
> strong but he was a brave man [...] the communists were not happy especially
> when you call upon the Chinese to rally around the government because in
> those days, even between the British government, there were two schools of
> thought – whether to arm the Chinese or not to arm [...] But Tan Cheng Lock
> made the appeal, to the government, to take in Chinese ...

Yuen was one of the few Chinese who heeded Tan Cheng Lock's call and
discovered, through service, a 'Malayan' identity:

... Every morning we would do physical training, throwing logs on one shoulder and the other shoulder, and my God, being the shortest, the weight comes on you. I almost died but I survived.

Q: So the training was a mix of all races?

Yuen: Yes. You see, that's how the comradeship was built up – because of the threat of common danger. When the shooting starts, they don't care what race you are you know? You just want to survive. And you have to survive as you are trained, fighting in the coordinated manner. You find that your friend is pinned down by heavy fire, and you're ok and have a good defensive position, you open fire so that he can crawl somewhere else. And he does the same for you. So you save each other.

Yuen would go on to have a distinguished career in CID and then the Special Branch. When I met Tan Sri Yuen in Kuala Lumpur in 2013, he was sick and disillusioned. He told me bitterly that when he joined the police he was not a Federation citizen. He had to be wounded twice before he was considered to be a true 'Malayan'. He was, he admitted, pleased that Mao had won the war in China. Tan Sri Yuen was an original.

Templer's Troubles

Templer flew into heavy communal headwinds. He was buffeted by local turbulence until the day he flew out of Kuala Lumpur Airport. Like his predecessors, he found it hard to give up on Dato Onn. He could not quite bring himself to recognise that the excessively relaxed Tunku Abdul Rahman, with his princely pedigree, had a potent appeal to Malays. Under the Tunku's leadership, the Alliance was the future of Malaya – but was it a future the British wanted?

It would seem not entirely. Templer had pressured the British government to give Dato Onn a knighthood in the Coronation honours. His fawning acceptance sunk his political standing even deeper. He soon reverted to plain Dato. The British were reluctant to accept that Dato Onn had shot his bolt. They clung to his faded coat-tails for one reason only. He still believed that Malaya was not quite ready for independence. He was the local 'break man'. The dilemma that Templer had to somehow solve – and he never would – was that the UMNO/MCA Alliance was pressing hard on the Federation to speed up the pace of independence. Templer referred to the UMNO/MCA tie-up as the 'unholy alliance' and complained that the Tunku was backed by a 'a lot of bad hats'. He told Lyttelton:

A very few people realise the truth which is that the only political party which is properly organised in Malaya is the Communist Party and that even if the shooting did stop [after independence] (which it would not) it would only be a matter of a very short time before a great number of people in this country were put up against a wall and shot in droves.

The British had accepted that Malaya would become independent but worried about going too far too fast. As Templer's memorandum implies, the great fear was that an 'Alliance' government would be too weak to resist a subsequent communist *coup d'état*. In private, Templer doubted that many Malayans even wanted independence:

> I am now absolutely and firmly convinced that there is no desire for self-government in this country today in any community whatsoever. The desire is only in the minds of a very few tens of thousands [...] most of these are the left wing element, so to speak, and a few are the self seekers for power [...] our successors will have very considerable difficulty in inducing the country to accept the prize.

So by the time Templer began preparing to leave Malaya, he was forced to confront a perplexing situation. The MNLA had been battered into retreat. But the battle with the Malays and their conservative Chinese allies was intensifying. Templer and his likely successor Donald MacGillivray would have to work hard to contain energies released by the new Alliance Party. In February 1954, the British clumsily counter-attacked by boosting the new Party Negara (National Party). Onn was very much 'in it', Templer reported: he was, in fact, party president. Unlike the Alliance, the 'Party Negara' was truly multi-ethnic, but like Dato Onn's many other initiatives to build a third force to oppose the Tunku, this latest failed to steal a single spark from the flame of *merdeka*. For all the British efforts to sabotage the Alliance Party, it was the Tunku who would now determine the speed of change. As Templer put it in one of his final reports to London, 'the UMNO/MCA case is not properly answered and goes by default.'

In the months before Templer left Malaya, the battle with the Alliance escalated. After failing to get the level of representation in the Legislative Council that he had wanted, the Tunku demanded a meeting with the Colonial Secretary in London. Lyttelton refused but the delegation set off anyway. Under pressure from the Tunku's influential English friends, Lyttelton caved in. He refused to meet the delegation, but agreed to see the Tunku and Tan Cheng Lock in private. As it turned out, Tan Cheng Lock was forced to remain in Malaya – and on 14 May, it was Tunku Abdul Rahman, Abdul Razak and Mr T.H. Tan, the Executive Secretary of the MCA, who sat down face to face with Lyttelton. For the Tunku, the key issue was the Alliance demand for a three-fifths majority in the council. This was essential, he argued, if the party with the biggest popular vote (and of course everyone assumed this would be the Alliance) was to have a working majority. Lyttelton countered by pointing out that the Malay rulers had stuck at a much lower majority – no doubt fearing that a future independent Malaya might be too democratic. On 19 May, Lyttelton rejected the Alliance demands and the delegation returned from London with little to show for their efforts. So at a 'Round Table' meeting at the home of a Chinese member of the Alliance, they agreed to reject the Federation proposals. On 25 May, the Tunku presented the Alliance resolution at King's House. In six days, Templer would be leaving Malaya for good. When he had finished reading, he looked up: 'The pistols are out.' The Federation was at war with the Alliance.

There is a very striking eye witness portrait of Templer at the end of his time in Malaya that might give both his admirers and critics pause for thought:

> The problems of the Malayan Emergency were clearly telling on him, for I have never before or since seen a man under such manifest strain. He chain-smoked cigarettes incessantly with trembling hands the whole time he was speaking to us, and I wonder [sic] how long he could last.

Templer had not won or even ended the Emergency war, but the war to crush the MNLA would become secondary to the struggle with the Alliance. This is not to suggest that the jungle war had become merely background noise. The presence of communist guerrillas in Malaya would continue to cast its shadow across the political arena and the spectres of communism would now propel Tunku Abdul Rahman to power.

As Templer was departing Kuala Lumpur, the Viet Minh military commander General Vo Nguyen Giap crushed the French colonial armies at Dien Bien Phu. By the end of the year, the French had withdrawn completely from Indochina leaving behind a communist-controlled Democratic Republic of Vietnam. A domino had fallen. Ho Chi Minh and the Vietnamese communists had exploited advantages denied to Chin Peng and the Malayan communists. Vietnam, Cambodia and Laos all had porous land borders with the Chinese Republic and the Viet Minh guerrilla armies were well supplied with materiel and intelligence. Malaya was a peninsula with a single land border with Thailand. This offered Chin Peng and the MNLA refuge, but only the most paltry access to any materiel assistance. More profoundly, the Viet Minh could justifiably claim to be a national liberation movement. The Malayan communists had never broken through the communal barrier.

From the point of view of the American government, dismayed by the French collapse in Indochina, Malaya began to look like a success story in the global war on communism, and Templer did nothing to disabuse visiting Americans that the British domino would not fall. From the beginning of 1953, as Templer was making his mark on Malaya, there was a steady flow of distinguished observers from the Defence and State Departments to study the British way in Malaya. Glamorous foreign correspondents sent by American newspapers ventured onto the jungle battlefields. Templer himself glared belligerently from the cover of *Time* magazine. Presidential hopeful Adlai Stevenson toured Malaya, as did the Vice President Richard Nixon and his wife Pat, who visited a few kampongs and schools. Nixon was 'an extremely nice man in every way', Templer enthused. He introduced him to Dato Onn, H.S Lee and a handful of Menteri Besars – but not, it would seem, to the Tunku. Templer took Nixon on patrol with the Somerset Light Infantry 'during which time the young national service platoon commander shot a terrorist dead'. It was also convenient that a local communist branch committee member had just walked out of the jungle and surrendered. Nixon was 'tickled to death'. By the beginning of the 1960s, a steady stream of British 'counter-insurgency experts' would start flying over to Saigon to offer their services.

The Little Long March

In late 1952, the beleaguered MCP Central Committee headquartered near Raub in Perak made a reluctant decision to continue their 'Little Long March' northwards following a battering by the RAF. At the beginning of the following year, Chin Peng set up camp north of the Sungai Telom River in the Cameron Highlands – at the very same place where he had dreamt of founding a Malayan Republic nearly half a decade before. Now he had to confront the brutal reality that the communists 'held no territory, no liberated zones'. These were desperate days for the MNLA: the small band of guerrillas was hungry and the courier system had broken down. Early in March, Chin Peng read in a two-day-old local newspaper that Stalin had died. The state of Perak had once been the hub of the communist insurgency. Now local support had all but evaporated. Supplies had dried to a trickle. The plague of resettlement had got a grip even here. The next day, Chin Peng and his bodyguards set off once more. His plan was to head for the village of Grik in northern Perak that was just a few kilometres south of the Thai border crossing at Betong. For two gruelling months, Chin Peng and his comrades battled their way through some of the most impenetrable jungle in Malaya. Such was the communist threat in 1954.

At Grik there was more trouble. For more than a year, Shen Tien of the local state committee had been trying to identify a traitor. This was the only possible explanation for a series of thwarted raids and betrayals and the ransacking of food and weapons dumps. The most likely suspect was a middle-aged party member called Lian Sung. As soon as Chin Peng arrived at the MNLA camp near Grik, he ordered Shen Tien to arrest Lian Sung. He was body searched and a government cheque for the sum of $50,000 discovered in one of his pockets. This was remarkably careless of Lian Sung, who – he admitted – had somehow been successfully feeding information to the Special Branch for over a year. Chin Peng: 'He was, of course, executed immediately.' Lian Sung had done so much damage to the local communist organisation that it was impossible for Chin Peng to stay on in the Grik district for very long: and so the long, grimly demoralising retreat was resumed. In the next few months, Chin Peng would set up new camps in the Betong Salient and the Sadao region, both on the Thai side of the border with Malaya. It was the end, for now, of the 'little long march'.

3

MALAYA'S SECRET WARS

New Tactics

This was a time of evolutionary change in the British war on communism in Malaya. General Templer seized on Briggs' proposals and sharpened their impact. This was a significant achievement but he was not an innovator. He took credit for a decline in the number of MNLA attacks that was already under way when he flew into Kuala Lumpur in early 1952, and was in any case as much a consequence of an MCP tactical change of mind as more effective security. The Templer myth flourished because the uncontested 'Supremo' Templer could gallop roughshod through the dark entangled groves of Federation bureaucracy – and above all because he made himself and British power tangible to ordinary Malayans. Gent and Gurney had been diffident mandarins. Templer was confident power incarnate. This is not to suggest that the Templer effect was just bluff and bombast. In this chapter, we will look at the way Templer reformed the Malayan intelligence services and put the finishing touches to a colonial security state that would become his legacy to modern Malaysia. This secret war was fought alongside an equally clandestine push into the deepest realms of the jungle. Here British soldiers would turn the Orang Asli aboriginals against the beleaguered communist guerrillas and make them crusaders against communism in Malaya and later in Vietnam.

Under Templer, the Emergency war in Malaya became an instrument of state formation. This new state would be equipped with a steely authoritarian armour which even after independence it has never shed. The colonial Federation government was in some respects totalitarian. It was certainly not a democracy. To be more precise, the Federation was an authoritarian regime with features of totalitarianism such as a paramilitary police force, significant investment in propaganda and charismatic leadership, as well as a preoccupation with communal difference. The new colonial state groomed a new relatively compliant elite and excluded anyone who might oppose it. During the Emergency, information services, or propaganda to be exact, seized control of social, psychological and political realities by means of coded euphemisms such as 'resettlement', 'protection', 'New Villages', 'bandits', 'CTs' and so on. 'Winning hearts and minds' and 'building confidence' described a process of social and psychological reconditioning. In a semi-feudal society in which it was obligatory to revere rulers and princes, the role of a highly visible leader was crucial. This was Templer's most important contribution. There is a description quoted in Kumar Ramakrishna's study of *Emergency Propaganda* that gives a concrete idea how this worked:

> [Templer] would stride rapidly from place to place, looking into their [the rural Chinese] shops, their houses, their gardens [...] Then he would talk to the villagers – his cap on the back of his head, his hands on his hips – in that clipped harsh voice that could be so frightening (or exhilarating). As they listened to him, there would come a suggestion on their impassive faces [sic] that here was a man to whom it might be well to accord respect, even at some future date a measure of trust.

Templer himself admitted: 'Government extended right down the line into the lives of the simple people ...'. Although Templer rarely embraced the ingrained racism of colonial society, he understood that his most important task was bludgeoning the Chinese (he thought Malays were merely 'irritating') to renounce communism and accept a postcolonial state dominated by Malays.

Less than a year after Templer arrived in Malaya, the British became aware of the MNLA 'October Directives' and began pondering their implications. These were troubling. The MCP had, it was evident, profoundly rethought its tactical game plan. The politburo admitted mistakes had been made and that as a consequence of a kind of 'warlordism' they had antagonised the masses as well as the 'medium bourgeoisie'. They had not taken account of the interests of shopkeepers, entrepreneurs, teachers, taxi drivers, etc. even though this was the social world from which Chin Peng and many other politburo members had come. The new policy was to concentrate on winning over a united front of workers, peasants and petty bourgeoisie. Military units would be rested and retrained and encouraged to start growing their own food rather than relying on, i.e. exploiting the masses. Attacks would be more selective. Colonial officials would remain legitimate targets but not if innocent Malays could be caught in the crossfire. Sabotage of rubber trees and the destruction of IC cards would cease. The 'October Directives' took several months to reach some units but they were clearly having an impact by mid-1952, as Templer realised: he wrote to Lyttelton in September 'the number of bandit-inspired incidents except for such stupidities as lorry burning is at the moment down to practically nil ...'.

What troubled the Federation deeply was not just that the MNLA was regrouping but that its efforts would focus at least temporarily on infiltration and subversion. The implications for the future of Malaya, especially the loyalty of its Chinese and Indian communities, were frightening. Subversion would be much harder to fight and defeat than a few thousand hungry guerrillas. The war on the periphery could become a different kind of war in the centre. Communism would have to be contested as if it was a moral contagion. Once again the Chinese squatters were on the front line.

The forced eviction and resettlement of more than a million rural Chinese squatters and estate workers was an act of war intended to smash their bonds with the MNLA. Government propaganda represented this draconian population transfer as a way to protect Chinese squatters. It was also a means of adjusting the place of rural Chinese in the Malayan state and economy. This implied that it was not enough to simply incarcerate hundreds of thousands of people behind barbed wire fences. By 1951, the Federation government could no longer deny that, as one administrator put it, the resettlement camps were 'getting in a mess'. It was feared that security was lax and the camps provided not just supplies to the communists but supporters as well. The infection had to be stopped. When Templer arrived in Malaya, he focused on improving the physical security of the camps by, for example, electrifying perimeter fences and codifying a checklist to ensure a reasonable quality of life: a clean supply of water, decent sanitation, schools, community centres, temples and so on. Government propaganda films began to show life in the 'New Villages' as a kind of rural idyll, albeit lived behind barbed wire. The reality for many former squatters was demeaning. When tappers left the camp for work, they had to wait in long queues to be body searched by suspicious Malay constables. They were permitted to take with them only a jug of unsweetened tea: so they faced long, hard and hungry hours in the estates. They had to leave work in time to be back inside the camp at 7 p.m. The curfew lasted from 11 p.m. to 5 p.m. Rice was rationed. Every aspect of life was regimented. Life in a resettlement camp was as much punishment as protection. Over time, these conditions improved. In May 1952, Templer pushed through the 'Local Councils Ordinance' (note the terminology) which established elected 'Village Councils'. Resettlement camps slowly turned from punishing Chinese squatters to socialising them. Templer wrote encouragingly to the Colonial Office in July 1953:

> The Coronation celebrations throughout the Federation were amazing [...] It was amazing to see the efforts that were made in the New Villages and the kampongs. I heard of one Indian who was looking at a New Village all dolled up with its little decorations, who said that this was the end of communism in Malaya ...

Voices from Heaven

Propagandists needed facts on the ground. Templer saw propaganda as an instrument to convince people that 'everything the government does' is for their benefit. In the war on communism, it shored up the frontier of the mind.

Propaganda, the war for hearts and minds, is seen as one of the great success stories of the Emergency. During the short time Hugh Carlton Greene had spent in Malaya, he had energised the Federation information services and encouraged indigenous talents C.C Too and Lam Swee. Too had flirted with communism and was convinced that meticulous analysis of interrogations and captured MNLA documents would expose the fears and vulnerabilities of rank-and-file communist guerrillas. These could then be exploited to persuade them to give up the cause. By the time Templer arrived, Too was optimistic that his strategy was working. The evidence was in the transcripts of numerous interrogations of MNLA guerrillas who had come in from the cold.

Templer was not impressed. He became convinced that the information apparatus was another colonial muddle and in many respects he was right. Hugh Greene had not, in the short time he was in Malaya, come to grips with the organisational malaise that afflicted the information services as much as any other Federation department. The work of propaganda was messily split between autonomous fiefdoms: the 'Emergency Information Services', the 'Department of Information', the 'Malayan Film Unit' and 'Radio Malaya'. The whole shebang was plagued by strategic confusion, tangled lines of command and frequent duplication of tasks and responsibilities. Templer began casting around for someone who could restore order. He refused to consider a 'local' and Too took this very badly.

Templer wanted to firmly embed information in the war on communism. Propagandists would have to learn and apply the dark art of psychological warfare, or psy-ops. The man he eventually chose to take on the new post of 'Director General of Information Services' was, in 1952, the headmaster of Adams Grammar School in Shropshire. But Alec Peterson was a master of the black arts. He had been in charge of 'black propaganda' for the SOE Force 136 and seconded to Lord Mountbatten's general staff as deputy director of political warfare. A useful website defines the different species of propaganda as follows:

Black	Propaganda which falsifies its origin
Grey	Propaganda which gives no clear indication of its origin
White	Direct Allied-sponsored propaganda
Strategic	Propaganda designed to make civilians take action favourable to the Allied Military operations (WWII)
Tactical	Propaganda aimed at reducing the enemy's combat strength by impairing morale and persuading the individual soldier to stop fighting (WWII).[47]

In his book *Black Boomerang*, Sefton Delmer, another celebrated wartime propagandist, provides a succinct definition of the black variety:

To stimulate the Germans into thoughts and actions hostile to Hitler [...] they would have to be tricked [...] A new weapon of psychological warfare was needed for this purpose [...] In analogy to 'Black Mass', 'Black Magic' and 'Black Market' my friends and I called this new psychological attack black propaganda.'

Outright deception was anathema to Greene and the BBC. Templer wanted to apply the black arts of psy-ops in Malaya and he was convinced that Peterson was the man for the job. He arrived in Kuala Lumpur in July and was astonished to read local headlines 'Templer's Mystery Man Arrives!' The idea was that Peterson would spend two months assessing potential for using psy-ops in Malaya and report back to Templer before returning home. When he read Peterson's report, Templer offered him a permanent job on the spot. A potentially tricky matter was the fact that Dato Onn, who was the Member for Home Affairs in the Legislative Council, was in theory head of information services. Templer would have to square Peterson's appointment with the prickly old man. As it turned out, Dato Onn was perfectly agreeable to hand over to an expert. In the meantime, Templer had ordered the construction of a brand new headquarters for the Information Department on Brockman Road in Kuala Lumpur. Thrown up in record time, the spanking new building was ready for occupation by the time Peterson returned to Kuala Lumpur on a two-year contract. Peterson's first task was to rationalise the cumbersome machinery of the old department. He followed a simple plan which was to weld together political warfare with military operations. He had emphasised in his report that this implied forging close bonds between the 'State Information Officers' and local military commanders. Both should have complete confidence in the other and, Peterson argued, this meant appointing Europeans. This was tantamount to abandoning the 'Malayanisation' of the colonial government. Templer knew that this could well cause ructions with the sultans and/or Dato Onn. So he sent Peterson on a tour of the Malay courts to curry favour for the new appointments. He must have been persuasive, for only the Sultan of Terengganu insisted that a Malay be appointed to the job in his state.

So Peterson transformed the culture of psy-ops. The British were firmly in charge and local initiative was reined in. He brought in a fresh cadre of British information officers, and expected C.C. Too and other Asian members of the new department to 'support' their work. The new director general and C.C. Too never hit it off. Too was demoted to 'Assistant Head of the Operations Section of Information Services' and would work under Major R.J. Isaac, the Special Branch officer who had investigated Lai Tek. For the proud and irascible Too this was galling indeed. He felt – and was – underappreciated and could not stomach Peterson's paternalistic management style. He resented what he saw as a mania for prizing British staff 'of the requisite experience and authority' and disdaining his own refined understanding of the communists' mental world. Too could never be a pliant subordinate. And he was upset. On 1 March 1953, C.C. Too resigned. His desk was taken over, he recalled later, by 'an old English professor' who spoke some Chinese but knew nothing at all about the Malayan communist movement. Too 'wandered about' for two years, and at one point tried to get a job at the Perak Museum in Taiping. When Major Isaacs was promoted to head the Psychological Warfare Section, he tried to persuade Too to return, as did Peterson's successor O.W. Walters. His first response was to tell them to 'go to hell'. The damage done to the Malayan information services when Peterson forced C.C. Too out of the department would not become apparent until he grudgingly returned to his desk in April 1955. His first job was to deal with an unexpected peace offer from the Malayan communists.

For many MNLA guerrillas, the sight and sound of the 'Voice Aircraft' as they throbbed ominously overhead was alarming. These 'voices from heaven' seemed to symbolise a surreal kind of aerial omnipotence. Some MNLA guerrillas referred to 'Voice Aircraft' contemptuously as 'dogs barking at chickens', but data culled from SEP interrogations show that so-called 'Voice Flights' could be an effective instrument of psy-ops. The idea of attaching loudhailers to balloons or aircraft is not new. During the Second World War, both the Germans and Americans experimented with such devices to demoralise enemy troops but with no success. Engine noise muffled or drowned out the voice recordings and so-called 'loudhailer aircraft' had to fly at slow speeds and keep to a low, fixed altitude and that made them 'sitting ducks'. When the Korean War began in 1950, the United States Air Force (USAF) took advantage of innovative new amplifier technologies to begin investing heavily in aerial broadcasting. On 5 October 1950 an adapted Douglas C-47 aircraft called *The Voice of the United Nations* took off from the Tachikawa air base in Japan, headquarters of the Far East Air Materiel Command, and made an experimental flight over a suburb of Tokyo. Onboard the C-47, American technicians had installed powerful 500 watt amplifiers and attached a bank of loudspeakers to the cargo door recess. The experiment was judged a success and five days later *The Voice* was in action flying along the north-east coast of the Korean Peninsula. A Korean student read out messages for forty-five minutes at 7,000ft, then for thirty minutes at 10,000ft. On the ground, the bizarre event caused consternation, but the content of the broadcast message was inaudible. The USAF pressed on. A second 'Voice Aircraft', *The Speaker*, was brought into operation and new experiments carried out with American soldiers as 'target listeners'. After a great deal of tinkering, both *The Voice* and *The Speaker* flew into action over North Korea with an escort of F-51 Mustang fighters at the end of May. A female speaker hammered home the message that:

-   The communist cause is illegitimate
-   Continuing to fight is synonymous with suffering and death

- It is safe to surrender
- The United Nations is fighting for peace and reconciliation.

The buzz around the new American technology thrilled General Templer. Some use had already been made of loudspeakers in Malaya, and a Brigadier Henniker had attached loudspeakers to captive balloons. This was all rather Heath Robinson and not, as far as anyone could find out, effective. Templer was fascinated by the buzz around the new American technology. He persuaded the USAF to loan *The Speaker* to carry out trials. He knew very well that well-targeted leaflet drops, sometimes 1 million at a time, had great success coaxing weary guerrillas to give up the fight. The idea of 'Voice Flights' promised a more 'personal' approach'. So experimental flights successfully took place near Kuala Lumpur and then across primary jungle in Malacca and Selangor. Messages were broadcast in many Chinese dialects by male and female speakers and the audibility was assessed from the ground. Tape-recorded messages worked better than live speakers who could be put off by turbulence. Templer sent an excited report to Lyttelton:

> We are carrying out trials over all types of jungle [...] the first day the whole thing put the fear of God into the inhabitants of Kuala Lumpur, who heard a voice repeating over and over again the words 'World Communism is doomed' from thousands of feet up in the air above the clouds [...] they thought it was all very spooky.

At the beginning of November 1952 a Dakota 'Voice Aircraft' flew across six target areas in southern and western Selangor broadcasting news that MNLA leader Liew Kon Kim had been shot dead and exhorting any guerrillas in earshot to surrender. They would be fairly treated. Six days later, two MNLA men surrendered and their voices were immediately recorded for further broadcasts. Two other guerrillas then handed themselves in. The 'Voice Aircraft' really could work. By the beginning of 1953, British technicians had developed and refined their own 'Voice Flight' aircraft using the Vickers Valetta transporter, equipped with 2,000 watt loudspeakers, and the little Austers which were small and light enough to operate over roads and on the edge of the jungle. The new 'Voice Flight' unit sent specialised crews to bases and airports in different parts of Malaya and co-ordinated their flights with planned ground operations. The Valettas, which were rather too noisy in action, and the little Austers circled over their assigned targets at about 3,000ft for hour-long bursts over the course of three or four days.

In the next few years, the 'Voice Flights' became increasingly sophisticated. When the last Valetta crashed, it was replaced by two much quieter Dakotas. Requests for voice operations were sent to the 'Voice Area Committee' which passed them on to the 'Joint Operation Centre' in Kuala Lumpur, which assessed their usefulness and co-ordinated the actual operation with the 'Air Control Centre'. In 1954 alone, the 'Voice Flight' unit flew 600 missions; in August that year, eighty-nine operations were flown over 400 targets in thirteen days to broadcast news about the Geneva Peace Conference. At the beginning of the year, Templer had taken a few lessons in Cantonese. When he was sufficiently proficient, he boarded a Dakota and was flown over the jungle. He announced, in basic Cantonese: 'This is General Templer speaking. To all members of the Malayan Communist Party. You need not be afraid and you can surrender. This is my personal pledge to you …'. At least one MNLA man responded. He told his interrogators: 'All the jungle men knew they could trust General Sir Gerald Templer.'

It was reluctantly recognised that the average 'CT' was thoughtful enough to make hard decisions based on many different issues. In August 1953, an MNLA commander called Kang Wei had given himself up with eight of his men. He told the Special Branch officers who debriefed him that many more lower-ranking guerrillas wanted to surrender but were too afraid. On the basis of this flimsy intelligence, the EIS launched 'Operation Bison'. This was an ambitious plan to incite mass surrenders by air-dropping no less than 18 million leaflets right across the peninsula. The leaflets promised an identity card and 'an immediate new life' to anyone below the rank of Central Committee member who brought out five other comrades at $500 per head. On the other side of the leaflet were photographs of happy, safe SEPs. Despite these enticements, only a handful of guerrillas surrendered. The hoped-for mass exodus from the jungle didn't happen. The failure of 'Operation Bison' showed that MNLA morale had not yet collapsed. The reason was that MCP propagandists had latched onto the French collapse in Indochina and claimed that Viet Minh troops would soon be marching down through the peninsula to liberate Malaya.

Templer lamented that 'the puzzle is why more of them don't come out …'. He told London that a new plan was afoot:

> We are starting to go in for a psychological interrogation of captured enemy personnel in a much more scientific way […] what I want to know the answer to is why these people went into the jungle in the first place and what eventually made them come out.

Templer needed better intelligence.

The Intelligence Wars

Intelligence is the lifeblood of propaganda. It was Templer's 'absolute top priority'. But during the bloodiest period of the communist uprising in 1950–51, Federation intelligence agencies possessed only a hazy idea of the enemy's leadership cadres and order of battle. The war was being fought 'through a glass darkly'. And yet according to Colonel Richard Clutterbuck, a doyen of counter-insurgency experts, the great lesson of the Malayan Emergency was that 'the soundest (and, in the end, the cheapest) investment against communist insurgency in any country is a strong, hand picked and well paid intelligence organisation backed up by the funds to offer good rewards.' The work of the Malayan Special Branch during the Emergency is admired as a counter-insurgency success story: the Malayan insurrection was crushed, many believe, by a barrage of intelligence. This is not a matter only of historical interest. The panoptic security state that the colonial government built has never been dismantled. The British colonial government bequeathed its intelligence apparatus to the modern state of Malaysia. Colonial-style intelligence is embedded in Malaysian culture, as the historian and social scientist Yin Shao Loong points out:

> Malaysian culture abounds with myths about the undead and other seen or half-seen spectres. Occupying a similar twilit space on the periphery of our senses are the secret police, the Special Branch, who serve as the eyes and ears of government. Like the ghosts and spooks, political police are part of the Malaysian milieu, appearing as figures of mystery, fear, and conspicuous undercover dress.

So if you seek Templer's monument, look around. It was typical of Templer to solve the intelligence problem by concentrating power in the hands of a single individual.

So it was that Guy Madoc, a passionate bird watcher, was appointed Director of Intelligence. Madoc told a revealing story about Templer's fascination with surveillance. On one occasion, Madoc let slip that he had a new toy. It was an unmarked van crammed with the latest devices for clandestine observation. The idea thrilled Templer, and Madoc suggested he try the thing out for himself. The driver parked outside a café with Templer installed in the observation post. 'Gerald was like a terrier at a rat hole', Madoc recalled, 'I just couldn't get him to give up. He wanted to go on looking; it was the first time he'd seen the Asian population behaving quite normally.' The colonial gaze!

How was an inept and disorganised intelligence operation transformed into a war-winning security apparatus? When Field Marshall Sir William Slim, Chief of the Imperial General Staff, arrived in Malaya on a tour of inspection in October 1949, he was dismayed by the mediocre quality of intelligence operations. He insisted that the Special Branch (which had taken over from the Malayan Security Services after the war) needed restructuring 'on modern lines', with a 'proper central headquarters'. His fiercest criticism was directed at the failure of Colonel Nicol Gray, the police commissioner to equip the Special Branch to 'deal with the Chinese'. There was a chronic shortage of British officers who spoke Chinese adequately, or at all; and just a tiny handful of Chinese officers served in the Malayan police. That this was a serious handicap was often pointed out. The call for 'Chinese to fight Chinese' was a leitmotif of Tan Cheng Lock's public pronouncement: 'the best man to catch the Chinese bandit [sic], communist agent or rebel is the Chinese policeman, Chinese spy or Chinese soldier.' Chinese recruitment was the nettle that no one with power seemed willing to grasp. Many Chinese Malayans were, to be sure, reluctant to join the colonial police. But the British too feared the consequences of creating a kind of Trojan Horse. It is ironic that the British Labour government's recognition of communist China in January 1950 threw up a new barrier to reform. Many anti-communist Chinese in Malaya still backed Chiang Kai-Shek's Kuomintang that had been crushed by Mao Zedong. So when Tan Cheng Lock proposed recruiting a 'large Malayan Chinese Secret Service', the British fretted about opening the door to a 'Third Force' of questionable loyalty. There were the usual grumbles about Chinese 'fence sitting'. The debate was heavily racialised. When the new Colonial Secretary, Oliver Lyttelton, toured Malaya in the panic-stricken aftermath of Sir Henry Gurney's assassination, he too lamented the poor performance of the Special Branch: he noted the confusion and duplication of command – and complained about the failure to widen and reform recruitment. It is telling that as late as 1953, in some Malay states there was not a single gazetted British Special Branch officer who could speak Chinese. Reorganisation and reform were constantly mooted and then deferred. Interdepartmental warfare was a root cause of this damaging pattern. The first true 'Director of Intelligence' to be appointed in Malaya, Sir William Jenkin, repeatedly clashed with the cantankerous commissioner of police, Colonel Gray – and Jenkin survived just eighteen months. He had, despite Gray's obstructive harassment, introduced a number of reforms. This should not be taken to imply that Jenkin was in any sense a liberal. He increased the number of Chinese officers, though not by much, and sent them into the squalid resettlement camps to trawl for information. He explained this strategy in the following semi-literate terms:

In these camps, the detenus [sic] are persons who have been arrested [sic] because they have been or have been strongly suspected of being guilty of political subversive activity [...] they should have in their possession information of much value to the Special Branch and the Government ...

The Special Branch had never been and never would be a liberal-minded body of men. It was first set up in London as a department of the Metropolitan Police in 1883 to combat a bombing campaign by the Irish Republican Brotherhood, known then as Fenians. When British Malaya and Singapore were rocked by riots, mutiny and revolt during the First World War, and the ripple of rebellion widened across the empire, the Straits government set up the 'Criminal Intelligence Department of the Straits Settlements Police': the Singapore Special Branch. Its second and most celebrated director René Henry de Solminihac Onraet was a brilliant linguist

– his Hokkien was said to be flawless – and a fervent anti-communist who saw his job as the defence of empire against foreign subversion. It was the Special Branch, of course, that 'ran' Lai Tek with such success. When Southeast Asia was invaded not by communists but by the Japanese Imperial Army, the intelligence services were caught on the back foot, if not with their trousers down. After 1945, recovery was slow and hampered, as we have seen, by the destruction of intelligence records during the Japanese occupation and the outing of Lai Tek.

Organisational reform was already on the agenda by the time Churchill sent Templer to 'sort out' Malaya in 1952. The culling of information from both MCP documents and its human agents was increasingly sophisticated. In 1950, the Special Branch had established a huge new 'Holding Centre', known as the 'White House', for captured guerrillas on 10 acres of land near the police depot on the outskirts of Kuala Lumpur. Hidden behind 10ft-high barbed wire fences, patrolled by armed guards and equipped with its own aircraft landing strip, this Malayan Guantanamo was a highly efficient information extraction factory. Very few people knew the real purpose of the 'White House' even in the Special Branch. Behind its walls was a dystopian world of custom-designed cells equipped with two-way mirrors and listening devices. In other rooms, staff worked feverishly translating MCP documents and opening intercepted mail. Down the corridor, boffins tinkered with gadgets designed for sabotage and destruction. The most effective were custom-designed battery-operated radio receivers of a type known to be relied on by the MNLA. Copies were manufactured at the 'White House' and made available at attractive prices in the shophouses that were suspected to be supplying MNLA camps. When the unsuspecting guerrilla took the radio back to his jungle camp and switched it on, it acted as a homing beacon for spotter aircraft. Special Branch officer Tim Hatton recalls a typical operation:

… it was terribly important [for the MNLA] when they sit on top of the mountain in the jungle to have their wireless on so that they could hear [news of the communist movement around the world]. When they asked for a wireless set we will get hold of our people in KL to make a new one and put false valves into it which give a signal and we alert the airplanes […] and we have a ground vehicle as well. So you got three lines going in: where they crossed, that is where the wireless would have been placed. So we bombed that particular place – and we killed nine people. One man escaped and when I went in afterwards I found him sitting by the river completely demoralized by all these bombs, the noise. He'd had a terrible time …

At the 'White House', MNLA defectors worked alongside British intelligence officers. Many MNLA documents were written in tiny characters on thin rolls of rice paper that could be easily hidden – a favourite place was inside the handlebars of a bicycle. Deciphering these was a specialised job that was best

handled by native Chinese readers. Accurate translation depended on people who
understood communist jargon. Just as intricate in a psychological sense was the
turning of MNLA guerrillas. The most effective persuaders were the defectors.
Some built up formidable reputations as interrogators. Most had been high-
ranking MNLA officers. William Chow Yong Bin, known to the Special Branch
as the 'Gen', had been the commander of the MPAJA 1st Regiment in Selangor
and was one of the small party that took part in the Victory Parade in London.
Wong Lin Hong had been the General Secretary of the Malayan Rubber Workers
Union. His MCP name was Chan Choong and Chin Peng bitterly describes his
defection in *My Side of History*. His Special Branch moniker was 'Hardy'. Very
little is known about Goh Chin Kim – but he was considered to be the most
effective interrogator at the White House: and was high on the MNLA's wanted
list of traitors. At the end of the Emergency, Goh was provided with a new
identity and emigrated to Canada. Chan Choong was murdered by unidentified
assailants in 1973: the MCP had a long memory.

Templer insisted that the Special Branch focused on identifying the communist
leaders. They had been shadowy bogeymen for the first two years of the war. Now
a price could be put on their heads. Special Branch officer Tim Hatton recalls:

> When we first started the Special Branch in about at the end of '48, we got
> instructions from MI5. How to do a dossier. We knew absolutely everything
> about a person. What his habits were: did he smoke, what his sex life was like,
> who his girlfriend was […] everything we could possibly think of. A list of about
> thirty or forty things per person and then you got a very good description: what
> sort of person: who if he came in [surrendered], or if he is captured or, if he was
> killed, you knew all about him, like reading about him as an old friend. We did
> this to every single 'CT' in the jungle: about 3,000 of them and the most of these
> were in the greatest detail. When Chin Peng went up North, I did a dossier for
> each of the persons going up so that everybody knew who they were …

Special Branch officer Jack Barlow described in a letter to historian Leon Comber
a series of interrogations that he carried out over a three-week period with the
assistance of Feng Yeh Kim, a Chinese police inspector. Barlow was astonished by
his subjects' 'total recall' which yielded very detailed confessions. He concluded
that the guerrillas lived for very long periods in a 'very enclosed and confined
environment': 'All those long days and nights in jungle encampments with
nothing to do but talk and talk and talk about their joint experiences. They must
have learnt a great deal about their comrades …'. These prisoners were walking
and talking 'Who's Whos'. One prisoner that Barlow interrogated provided no
less than 600 names, with very full details of their personal history in the MNLA.
This man was not just loquacious: the information he provided in such volume
tallied precisely with information from captured documents.

Special Branch officers like Barlow took great pride in their files. His 'pride and joy' was the 'file on Hor Lung' a Central Committee member who controlled the MNLA across most of southern Malaya. Barlow knew just about everything about Hor Lung – and on 5 April 1958, the man himself strolled into a police station near Segamat in northern Johor, unarmed, wearing khaki shorts, a ragged T-shirt and plastic shoes, and surrendered to the Malay police officer on duty. He wished, he declared, to take advantage of the '*Merdeka* Amnesty' that had recently been offered by the newly independent Malayan government. Hor Lung had, of course, heard about the amnesty from government leaflets. When he studied the leaflets, he realised that he could make a great deal of money, tax free, if he could persuade more MNLA guerrillas to surrender and renounce communism. Special Branch officers like Jack Barlow had built up a voluminous file on Hor Lung, which showed how important he was as a kind of lynchpin in the communist movement in Johor. A team of Special Branch officers set about exploiting his surrender and greed. Over the next few months, Hor Lung brought in no less than 160 guerrillas – which as Chin Peng admitted was a mortal blow to the MNLA in Johor. Hor Lung had no intention of merely coaxing his comrades to throw down their arms. Instead, he convened a series of meetings with small parties of MNLA fighters. He was accompanied by Special Branch officers disguised as 'CTs' and a handful of SEPs who had been roped into the operation. Hor Lung informed the guerrillas who had come to the meeting that the Central Committee had ordered them to stop fighting and come out of the jungle. Malaya was now independent; the war was over. Many of the guerrillas who surrendered were, according to Special Branch records, 'hard core'. By the end of the operation, Hor Lung had earned $500,000 – and a new identity. The communist diehard went into business.

The Bigger Picture

This all-seeing 'intelligence eye' was designed to research, document, analyse and then erode the MNLA support networks that had survived the shock of resettlement. Templer had a passionate, even obsessive interest in intelligence and surveillance but the factor that was driving reform was the establishment of the Southeast Asia Treaty Organisation (SEATO), following the signing of the Manila Pact in September 1954. SEATO emerged in the aftermath of the French collapse at Dien Bien Phu and the opening of the Geneva Conference in May and brought together the governments of Australia, New Zealand, France, Pakistan, Thailand, the Philippines, the United States and Great Britain. From the start, SEATO was riven by disputes between the British and Americans about how to deal with the French withdrawal from Vietnam and respond to the rise of communist China – but its purpose, in very simple terms, was to ring-fence Southeast Asia to stop any more dominos tumbling. A concomitant of this broader anti-communist strategy was internal security. For the British, regional anxieties focused on the Thai border, and the narrow Isthmus of Kra – which the Japanese had exploited to such devastating effect at the end of 1941. This was the very area where Chin Peng and the MCP Central Committee had taken refuge. With impressive prescience, Templer had anticipated the broadening of the anti-communist front with his top secret Director of Operations Special Directive No 21, issued in April 1952. In this remarkable document, Templer argues that the Malayan intelligence must be, in contemporary jargon, 'future proofed': the intelligence network, he argued, must remain 'alive whatever the MCP plans to do ...'. In other words, the communist threat was likely to evolve: to become, for example, 'a policy of secret selective killing and the fomentation of labour unrest ...'. British intelligence would take its secret war out of the jungle and into the lives of ordinary Malayans.

High Noone

As Chin Peng and the MCP Central Committee retreated north across the Thai border, other MNLA units withdrew into the jungles of Malaya's rocky green spine. Here the guerrillas began to reforge old bonds with Malayan aboriginals, known as Orang Asli which means 'original' or 'natural' people. During the Japanese occupation, MPAJA guerrillas were forced to take refuge with Orang Asli communities. This made them vulnerable to reprisal attacks by the Japanese. The war broke down the last protective barriers that had sheltered the Malayan aboriginals from the modern world. It was the most populous surviving Orang Asli group, the Senoi-speaking tribes, who found themselves on the front line of the Emergency war. (Senoi, incidentally, just means 'people'.) European anthropologists had romanticised the Orang Asli, especially the Temiar, as 'pacific peoples' who eschewed violence. And yet by 1960, the 'Head of Aboriginal Affairs' Richard Noone was able to boast that the Orang Asli paramilitary units he had recruited had killed more terrorists in a single year than any other counter-insurgency unit operating in Malaya. The Emergency wronged the Orang Asli, the only truly indigenous people of Malaya, and forced them to take up arms in a war they could not comprehend. This secret war would summon back the restless spirit of H.D. 'Pat' Noone, the British anthropologist who had vanished at the end of 1943, and bring British Cold War warriors to the highlands of Vietnam in the 1960s.

It will be recalled that H.D. 'Pat' Noone was a brilliant English anthropologist and archaeologist who had come to Malaya at the beginning of the 1930s. He had begun studying the Temiars in northern Perak and married a young woman called Ajang. Noone lived with her for long periods in what was then remote and unexplored jungle, studying the culture of the Temiars and listening to Elgar and Noel Coward songs on a clockwork record player in the evenings. When the British returned to Malaya in 1945, there was no trace of Pat Noone. He had vanished. No one was left to speak up for Malaya's indigenous peoples. A curator of the Raffles Museum in Singapore wrote in 1946 that: 'It is only a matter of time, perhaps a few years, before these primitives cease to exist.' The only people who did seem to care about the welfare of the Orang Asli were the communist guerrillas who had come to depend on their resources and skills.

Richard Noone was ten years younger than his famous brother. Like Pat he had studied at Corpus Christi College in Cambridge and followed his brother out to Malaya where he was introduced to the comely Ajang and to Pat's Temiar 'blood brother', Udu. Richard noticed the close bond that had flourished between the strikingly handsome Udu and Pat's Temiar wife. At the beginning of December 1941, Richard met his brother at a rest house in Kroh, a small village in northern Perak. The two brothers touched glasses to Pat's favourite toast 'Nong pai' – Temiar for 'new path'. Pat then climbed into his rickety pickup truck and drove away through the thickening twilight in the direction of Grik: 'So long, Dick, until next time …'. There would be no next time.

When the Pacific War ended, Richard was in Australia. With no word from Pat, he drew on every contact he could muster to track down his brother. For a while it seemed as if Pat might have survived. Hope soon faded. All the reports of Pat's movements dried out at the end of November 1943. After that – silence. Richard Noone's tireless detective work revealed tantalising clues about his brother's fate. He interviewed the planters Robert Chrystal and John Creer who had been marooned in Malaya and captured by MPAJA guerrillas. If Pat was dead, it seemed more than likely that he had been killed by the Japanese or executed in one of the MPAJA 'traitor killing camps'. Pat's father H.V. Noone tracked down MPAJA veteran Low Mah when he came to London for the Victory Parade in 1945: they met for tea at the Savoy. Low told Noone that his son had been last heard of somewhere in the Cameron Highlands. In the meantime, the prestigious Royal Anthropological Institute in London asked the Colonial Office to help recover Noone's research notes, photographs, and sound recordings, which had acquired legendary status as the final word on aboriginal culture in Malaya. At the Taiping Museum, there was no trace of this alluring anthropological cache, but Pat's former servant Puteh bin Awang suddenly reappeared with a story about thirteen boxes of notes and books that had been buried near a 'halting bungalow' in Kuala Temengor in the course of a forced march Pat and Ajang had taken to escape Japanese patrols. When the museum hunting party reached the tiny settlement the headman told them that the boxes had been discovered by a Japanese patrol and burnt. Pat Noone's work had gone up in smoke in a jungle clearing.

In 1948, a London court ruled that Pat Noone could be presumed dead and that he had died sometime in November 1943; his estate was wound up. There were some like H.T. Pagden, the Director of Museums in Malaya, who refused to give up hope. As Geoffrey Benjamin has pointed out, there are baffling references to 'Pat' in *The Straits Times* as late as September 1945. But Richard's plans for a search party fizzled out. What perturbed Richard and other friends and colleagues who had become obsessed with solving the mystery was that the Temiar who had once esteemed Pat now refused to mention his name. He had become taboo. The mystery deepened and darkened. In August, 1950 news came that seemed to promise a breakthrough. Pat's Temiar wife, Ajang, and his 'blood brother', Udu, had both emerged from the jungle near Kuala Legag where they were alleged to have been assisting the MNLA. They had subsequently been 'resettled' near Lasah on the north bank of the Plus River. But when Peter Williams-Hunt, the 'Advisor on Aborigines', tracked them down the following day, he saw that Ajang was dying. She had a severely ulcerated throat, and could no longer speak. It is most likely that she was suffering from TB and had been very ill for some time. Ajang died a few days later, taking her secrets to a jungle grave.

By the summer of 1953, Richard Noone had been drawn deep into the Emergency war as secretary to the Federation Intelligence Committee. One morning in early October, the telephone on his desk rang with, as it seemed to him, unusual urgency. It was the chief secretary: 'General Templer has asked me to inform you of your new appointment. You are to take over the Department of Aborigines.' That evening, Noone was summoned to King's House. Ensconced behind a long table in the conference chamber, Templer brusquely described the job: 'Noone, what I don't want is a desk man. Nor do I want a purely scientific type …'. Templer pushed back his chair and walked over to the big operational map displayed close to the desk. The 'map' was in fact a photographic blow up of one of Pat's old surveys of Temiar country. Templer continued: 'These jungle people have become the most serious problem of the Emergency, and something has to be done about it.'

The crisis had been building out of sight and out of mind for some time. Pat Noone's battle to secure land and other rights for the Senoi tribes had come to nought after the Japanese invaded, and after 1945 the British had little reason to reflect on the fate of Malaya's aborigines. Even before the war, many Chinese had dealings with the Orang Asli in civilian life as wild rubber tappers, tin poachers, shopkeepers, squatters and traders in jungle produce. After the Emergency war began in 1948, the majority of MNLA regiments relied on the rural Chinese and the Min Yuen. It was only in the Tasik Bera lake region on the Negeri Sembilan–Pahang border, where the communist Central Committee was headquartered, that the MNLA regiments made significant contact with local Orang Asli who used them as a kind of 'early warning screen' when security forces got anywhere near.

From the point of view of the Federation government the natural solution was resettlement: get the Orang Asli out of the hands of the insurgents. This panicky response was, according to John Leary, an expert on the experience of the Orang Asli during the Emergency: 'unco-ordinated, chaotic and misguided.' Resettlement was wrenchingly traumatic for many Orang Asli. Figures are disputed, incomplete and contradictory but 5,000–7,000 Malayan aboriginals may have died in this period. In August 1948, a Doctor Ramsay employed by the Social Welfare Department in Perak reported that his department had, without warning or preparation, taken on responsibility for a 180 'Sakai' who had been dumped near Morib 'for their own protection'. Conditions were so bad at Bukit Betong, near Kuala Lipis in Pahang that Williams-Hunt sent a letter to Federation Chief Secretary del Tufo warning that people were 'dying like flies'. More than 1,500 Semai were relocated to Bukit Betong, and at least forty of them had died between October 1949 and January 1950. Resettlement operations against Orang Asli settlements were carried out in much the same hard-headed way as those against Chinese squatters. In February 1950, two British policemen and a small party of Malay police fell on an Orang Melayu Asli group who were living on the jungle fringes near Ulu Langat in Selangor. The Malay-speaking headman testified later that 'In the hurry we only managed to remove half our belongings.' The police then burnt down all the dwellings. These resettlement operations were 'improved' in the next few years – but according to Richard Noone, who had now been appointed Protector of Aborigines (following the unfortunate death of Peter Williams-Hunt, who had fallen from a bridge and been impaled on a bamboo spike):

> Used to living at higher altitude, these unfortunates could not stand the heat of the plains. Their stomachs could not get used to the abrupt and complete changes from their staple diet of cassava and fresh meat and vegetables to rice and salt fish …

Even worse, in a longer perspective:

> After living a naturally energetic life, the men fishing and hunting, and the women planting and collecting wild fruits and tubers, they could not adapt themselves to a life of idleness.

John Leary concludes that the ad hoc resettlement of the Orang Asli was 'the most cumulatively lethal cause of indirect violence against the peoples of the jungle in the Emergency'. Both the MNLA and Federation security forces attacked and killed Orang Asli – who are often referred to as 'Sakai bandits' in official reports. The most destructive onslaught came from the air. According to counter-insurgency historian Richard Clutterbuck, offensive air strikes proved to be 'almost entirely unsuccessful'. But at the time, the RAF devoted vast recourses to launching indiscriminate raids across jungle areas: the strategy was analogous to dropping bombs in the sea in the hope of hitting a passing submarine. The Australian Air Marshall Frederick Scherger, who was descended from Prussian stock, took over as Air Officer Commanding Malaya in 1953. Scherger was keen to make use of some 20,000lb bombs (left over from the Second World War) to clear helicopter landing sites in jungle areas. These raids frequently killed aboriginal peoples who were unfortunate enough to be living in the target areas. It is not possible to establish precisely how many Orang Asli died as a consequence of the RAF and RAAF bombing campaign: the number is likely to exceed 5,000 people. The use by Federation forces of chemical sprays remains controversial. Even the staunchly loyal journalist Harry Miller confirmed that chemical sprays (mainly 2-4-D) were used to destroy crops being grown in jungle clearings by MNLA guerrillas. Since these chemicals were released from helicopters it was impossible for anyone living in a close vicinity to escape being poisoned. Between 1952 and 1954, Malaya Command, the War Office and the British chemical behemoth Imperial Chemical Industries (ICI) secretly discussed the subject of defoliating potential roadside ambush sites using 2-4-Dichlorophenoxyacetic Acid and 2-4-5 Trichlorophenoxyacetic – both ingredients of the notorious 'Agent Orange'. Experimental spraying was carried out in Malaya. To his credit, General Templer called a halt to any further experiments when he realised that ICI were clearly exploiting government subsidies for their own purposes – and the people of Malaya were spared the ghastly consequences of chemical warfare that would inflame such violent revulsion in Vietnam.

The communists were surprisingly slow to exploit this assault on the Orang Asli. But in September 1951 the MCP Central Committee issued instructions about relations with 'the masses of the nationality in the jungle.' It enjoined the MNLA to 'strengthen our links with them, propagandise and agitate among them, and call upon them to flee [from the resettlement areas] and return to the jungle to cultivate'. The tactical redirection of the armed conflict that slowly took shape after Chin Peng and the Central Committee promulgated their new directives through the battered MNLA courier networks, through the end of 1951 and into 1952, bewildered the Federation security forces. The most obvious symptom was the sudden drop in the number of attacks and 'contacts'. 'The Emergency is all pretty puzzling,' Templer admitted to Lyttelton shortly after he arrived in Malaya: '… their leaders and their brains [sic] are going deeper into the jungle, where they hope to be able to exist partly on jungle cultivation'. Templer seems to be referring here to the formation of 'Jungle Cultivation Corps' rather than the recruitment of Orang Asli. But the government clearly feared such a development. The Briggs Plan had severely weakened the old support networks: they clearly had to be rebuilt and in the deep jungle there was only one option. For their part, the MNLA leadership talked of 'serving' the 'masses of the nationality in the jungle areas'. They promised the Orang Asli headmen that if the MCP won the war against the colonial power the new republican government would protect their rights to tribal land. This reflected what they had learnt from Pat Noone in the early years of the Japanese occupation when he had forged links between the Temiar and the MPAJA: Richard Noone admitted that his brother had 'given the communists the key to the Senoi social behaviour pattern'. The MNLA leaders may well have spoken in good faith. But Templer's declared objective was to 'kill or capture Communist terrorists in Malaya' and the war in the deep jungle would disrupt for ever the world of the Orang Asli.

The MNLA guerrillas who entered the domain of the Orang Asli had made clever use of Pat Noone's ethnographic studies of aboriginal society. Some time at the end of 1951, some of the MNLA leaders began establishing 'Asal Clubs' among the Senoi tribes that Pat Noone had lived with and worked among in remote areas of northern Perak. 'Asal' is a Malay word meaning origin, root or source and was carefully chosen by the MNLA to contrast with the Malay term 'Sakai'. Although the Senoi tribes like the Temiar provided the largest number of recruits, MNLA recruiters were also active among the Orang Melayu Asli in the remoter regions of Negeri Sembilan, Selangor, Pahang and Johor – and in the Tasik Bera swamplands. There is some debate about which MNLA leaders took the main role: Richard Noone was certain that Low Mah, the man his father had interviewed in London shortly after the war, was the chief organiser. Special liaison teams were selected and trained. These Asal specialists usually had long experience of the Orang Asli as jungle traders, jelutong traders or tappers and spoke at least one of the Senoi dialects. Ah Soo Choi, an MCP state committee member in Perak, for example, was married to a Senoi woman and he was known to be frequently on the move between Perak and Kelantan in search of new recruits. Just as Pat Noone had done when he first sought out the Temiar, these MNLA recruiters arrived with gifts like axe heads, parangs, tobacco, cloth, salt and medicines. A number married into the tribal group. They came as powerful men with guns who promised good times in the future.

The MNLA recruiters did a very good job. Noone estimated that the MNLA had recruited at least 50,000 Senoi and Orang Melayu Asli by the end of 1953 and 'dominated all the deep jungle groups' as far as the Thai border. 'One can only view this achievement with wonder […] it was incredible,' he admitted. And he had no doubt that the lectures his brother had delivered to the MPAJA 5th Corps leaders back in 1942 had played a vital part unlocking the aboriginal door. The Asal organisation perfectly harmonised with the Senoi social system. Each 'club' or committee was set up on a 'saka' or clan basis under a 'Dato Pengerusi' who was usually a headman or shaman. John Leary conducted interviews with two Asal veterans called Bah Dek and Bah Sepidi who revealed a good deal about the workings of the Asal. Their platoon was quite heavily armed and controlled by two MNLA men who spoke the local Semai dialect. The MNLA issued the Asal with weapons and ammunition: a Bren light machine gun, shotguns, rifles, Sten sub-machine guns, and carbines. The MNLA also supplied khaki uniforms, but did not offer any kind of payment. Asal members all attended a compulsory weekly meeting where future strategy was thrashed out and propaganda dispensed. The MNLA naturally made a great deal of the disastrous resettlements and the bombing of the jungle ladangs. As Noone ruefully acknowledged, the MNLA offensive was very sophisticated. In his book *Rape of the Dream People*, he quotes a captured document that provides a good idea of the communist plan:

> All comrades engaged in the work of the Asal must take full responsibility in investigating and studying the habits of living, customs, traditions, rituals and other racial characteristics of the Asal. Information on the foregoing should be compiled for reference. This will help us improve our methods of work. Understand fully the Asal compatriots way of life. We should try to identify ourselves with them by adopting their way of living.

The MNLA used the Senoi as foragers, porters, guides and scouts. Asal units attacked government patrols on very rare occasions. Both the Asal leaders and the MNLA wanted to avoid damaging reprisal attacks. The Protector of Aborigines in Perak, Mr Corfield, told Leary that 'the aborigines exaggerated about their being so heavily armed. I never heard of any abos [sic] being armed with either Bren or Sten guns, and normally, if the CTs entrusted them with fire-arms, these were only shot guns …'. If there was any fighting to be done, this fell to the 'Asal Protection Corps'. A few Semai fighters achieved some notoriety.

'The aborigines,' Templer had told Richard Noone, 'hold the key to the deep jungle situation.' Noone would fight this war from a tiny backroom office in the Museums department in Kuala Lumpur. He inherited a typewriter and staff of three – including Pamela Gouldsbury, a 'bustling' South African – and Pat's former 'servant' Puteh who was now working with the department as an interpreter. As well as that typewriter, the Department of Aborigines possessed a wall map of Malaya and a telephone shared with the curator of museums. There was also a 'field staff' of five unhappy aborigines accommodated not far from Kuala Lumpur. Resources in the Malay states were even less impressive. Before Noone had the chance to petition Templer to bolster the department, he was summoned by the new GOC Malaya Sir Hugh Stockwell – a tall, thin man always accompanied by a loudly panting Alsatian dog – to assist with a new operation in the Cameron Highlands codenamed 'Operation Valiant'. A small patrol of paratroopers of 22 Special Air Services Regiment had stumbled on and killed an MNLA guerrilla who had been having a quiet smoke. The dead man had been stripped and buried. At headquarters, his surprisingly well-tailored clothes, and a recent laundry receipt in one pocket, immediately aroused suspicion. Could the dead man have been a member of the supposedly privileged MCP politburo? Did the jungle track where he had enjoyed his last cigarette lead to the new headquarters of the MCP Central Committee – the hideout of the now notorious Chin Peng?

Stockwell ordered Noone to get to Perak and contact any Senoi in the area who might know the whereabouts of the communist lair. Noone followed his brother's faded tracks into the Temiar heartland along the Telom River – this time with a flight of eight SAS helicopters. It was raining hard. At headquarters near Kuala Misong, the SAS had used explosives to fell some giant trees to create a helicopter landing site. The jungle itself was being violated. Patrols had rounded up a handful of aboriginals for Noone and Puteh to interrogate. One was the headman, Achok: Pat had stayed in his long house with Chrystal and Creer not long before he disappeared. Achok denied that he had seen any communists in the area. Noone also asked Achok about Pat. 'Have you heard any more about my brother?' he asked. Achong clammed up. 'I have not seen him since he and Puteh came to my father's lading. Puteh was then a boy ...'. Noone persisted but got nowhere. He and Puteh were certain that Achong was lying about the communists and about Pat. But why? A few days later, a wizened, betel nut chewing old man called Kerami Hondai turned up at the SAS camp. He had a parang thrust into his loin cloth and an imposing 7ft-long blowpipe. He was known as 'Clerk' Hondai because he always carried a battered leather notepad and pencil and appeared to be making notes whenever he talked with a European. When Noone sneaked a look at the notepad, he discovered that its pages were covered with long lines of squiggles. Just as Achong had done, 'Clerk' Hondai denied all knowledge of Pat. The atmosphere chilled when Pat informed him that Ajang was dead. 'I did not know Tuan Tata's wife,' Hondai lied. He had not seen Pat again after the Japanese came; he had fled to Kelantan.

Like Richard's quest for his brother, 'Operation Valiant' had achieved very little. Some 5,000 soldiers had thrashed about in the Cameron Highlands, but no trace of the MNLA camp had been found. There was no new evidence about Pat.

The strategy that would soon break the bond between the MNLA and the Orang Asli was a development of the cruel practice of 'influenced migration': meaning, of course, resettlement. Like the MNLA, the British had learnt many lessons from Pat Noone. In one of his reports he had pointed out that many different Temiar groups always assembled in certain well-established areas. He had reported that:

> In Legap, the Temiar from the furthest sources of the Plus [river] are continually gathering; it is a recognized rendezvous and of great importance therefore to the administration of the area, since one night on the way, at Kuala Temor, will bring any officer who forewarns into contact with all the headmen of the Plus valley, for the headwaters of the Plus open up like the fingers of an outstretched hand with the tips pressed against the Kelantan divide.

The solution the British eventually came up with was the construction of a chain of 'Jungle Forts' in these traditional meeting areas that would 'protect' the Orang Asli from the MNLA. But to begin with the British seemed not to have grasped this essential point. In April 1952, three squadrons of the 22nd SAS Regiment, backed by the 5th Malay Regiment and police federal jungle companies, had forcibly removed Orang Asli from the Jelai Kecil area of Pahang which had been infiltrated by a number of MNLA companies. A 'Voice Aircraft' circled the area for days to warn the local people in Malay and the local dialect that they must immediately leave their ladangs; to ram home the point, the RAF bombed and rocketed suspected MNLA camps. For the Orang Asli, the noise of these near continuous assaults was terrifying. The point was to demarcate a 'prohibited zone' in which, once the majority of the Semai had been persuaded to leave, any Orang Asli still in the zone would be classified as hostile and shot on sight. The Orang Asli who trickled out of the jungle then endured a five-day march to a resettlement camp set up at the 19th Mile on the Cameron Highlands Road near Tapah.

The camp had been built on an exposed and barren hillside, enclosed by barbed wire. This was 'Fort Jor'. The Semai built huts in this desolate place that were exposed to the full heat of the sun during the day, and freezing temperatures at night. It was impractical to grow tapioca, the staple crop; the men could no longer hunt and fish, so they became idle and miserable. Very little went right. When Templer visited the camp in September he 'was not impressed with the arrangements nor did he have a high opinion of the Aborigines …'. These Orang Asli had been completely deracinated. How then could they 'impress' Templer? They no longer cultivated the land, fished or hunted but eked out a desiccated life on parsimonious government handouts.

As the cruel fiasco unfolded at Fort Jor, an army officer called John West, who seems to have studied at least some of the surviving anthropological reports made by Pat Noone, proposed building a chain of forts at strategic points in the same region Noone had explored in the 1930s. The first 'Jungle Fort' would be sited close to the junction of the Legap and Plus rivers about 20 miles east of Kampong Lasah; the second at Kampong Temengor, a few miles east of Grik; and the third in the Blue Valley tea estate in the Cameron Highlands on the border with Pahang. The new forts would be built in areas with a dense tribal population – and on well-known local transit and trade routes. In August 1952, West and a small party of soldiers and police ventured into the Legap River valley to begin work on the first fort. Local Temiar people were roped in to help build huts and cut a dropping zone from the jungle. Although West's party was not attacked, he soon discovered from local informers that an Asal group was in the area. He set out with a small patrol, tracked down the communists and managed to kill all of them. He paid his informants $5,000 reward money, a gesture which brought a flood of new information. A small-scale propaganda war ensued. The communists threatened retribution and put it about that many big MNLA units would shortly be arriving in the area. West called their bluff. He boasted that he had a garrison force of more than 250 in and around the fort. For the Orang Asli, these were hard times. They had no ideological investment in either the government forces or the communists and were forced to make complex judgements about their own welfare. Many declared a plague on both houses and fled.

Fort Lagap would be the model for all the forts that would be built in the jungles of Malaya – in Perak, Kelantan and North Pahang. Each one was designed to symbolise government power in the first place and federal benevolence in the second. Fort Lagap cost a paltry 7,000 Malayan dollars to construct – labour and materials were supplied by the Temiar. Lagap was surrounded by barbed wire, punctuated by gun pits. Behind the wire were two atap-style barracks roofed with plaited palm fronds; officers' quarters made from bamboo; canteen, medical and administrative blocks; and a visitors' building for transient Temiar travelling through the Lagap valley. The forts were garrisoned by the Police Field Force (PFF). A big drop zone had been cut from the jungle – and fresh food and mail were delivered by helicopter every week. The arrival and departure of the noisy British helicopters provided another valuable show of force. By early 1954, a chain of seven Lagap-style forts had been built at strategic locations across the Temiar lands. Many of the later forts had landing strips as well as drop zones – and light aircraft flew in and out reinforcing or relieving the garrison, and evacuating or returning sick policemen, soldiers and Orang Asli.

The forts took some time to work. The Orang Asli had to be convinced that the garrisons were not fly-by-night: here today gone tomorrow. They feared that if they embraced the government side, severe retribution would follow when the soldiers and policemen flew out as swiftly as they had flown in. The British for their part remained ignorant about the mysterious people of the forests. As Noone discovered, many of the Orang Asli headmen – 'simple jungle folk' – were convinced that the communists would soon win the war. The communists explained to their Asal recruits that so many British soldiers were patrolling the tribal areas because they had been driven out of a place called Korea and so had to hide from the Chinese. To counter these MNLA stories, Noone bussed 100 Orang Asli headmen into Kuala Lumpur, where he showed off the military might of the empire. The headmen happily inspected infantry and police battalions; they were shown aircraft and helicopter fleets at the aerodrome; they stood on a hill and watched the Royal Artillery blasting away at some hapless *atap* huts. They got the point.

To get a grip on the Orang Asli 'in the wild', Templer ordered a reconnaissance operation to 'dominate aborigines in fort areas'. 'Operation Galway' was led by elite soldiers of 22nd SAS Regiment who were considered experts in jungle warfare. Their task was to work across the tribal lands that stretched across the Main Range between Grik in Perak and Fraser's Hill in Pahang to root out information about the local tribes and the MNLA units that relied on them. In the end, the MNLA could not hold out against the technology, manpower and money of the colonial government. The war in the deep jungle erupted as the Korean War boom brought immense profits to Malayan businesses that had become the most important dollar earners in the Commonwealth. This bonanza meant that spending on the Emergency leapt from $US 4.6 million in 1948 to $US 89.1 million in 1953. Money gushed into the coffers of the Department of

Aborigines – and the Federation could afford the lethal toys, like troop-carrying helicopters and aircraft, that Noone had showed off to the Orang Asli in Kuala Lumpur. It also meant that the Federation could splash out on building forts, providing garrisons – and flying in medicine and doctors. The Asal Clubs did not stand a chance.

It was now ten years to the day since Pat had gone missing but Richard remained obsessed with finding out what had happened. One evening he was working later. The telephone shattered his concentration. It was the duty office at the 22nd SAS headquarters: 'We've just had an urgent signal. I can't discuss it over the phone, but the colonel would like to see you straightaway.'

When Noone walked into the SAS ops room, he was greeted by Colonel Oliver Brooke who handed him a signal. A 'hostile group of fifty-four aboriginals' had arrived at Fort Telanok in the Cameron Highland, seeking protection. The following conversation ensued:

'The squadron commander's problem is feeding them,' Colonel Brooke said.
'They have abandoned their lading [sic] and they haven't a sausage.'
'Don't worry, we'll take care of that,' Noone promised.

The next morning Pamela Gouldsbury, who was first to reach Fort Telanok, sent a signal with more details. Noone was stunned: the 'hostile group' was led by a headman from the Upper Rening Valley called Angah whom Pat had lived with in 1942. Gouldsbury's next message was electrifying:

Angah […] has vital information concerning your brother but will not discloser to anybody except yourself stop …

Gouldsbury was at that moment on her way back to Kuala Lumpur with Angah.

Angah was a Semai who had married into the Temiar and then succeeded his father-in-law as headman. He was a solemn and dignified man who spoke slowly and ponderously. As soon as Angah arrived at Noone's home in Kuala Lumpur he fell asleep curled up on a rug. He did not wake up for three days. When he woke at last, Noone knew that he could not hurry the solemn old man. But he decided to take a risk:

'My brother used to say you were his good friend.'
Angah sucked on his cigarette but said nothing.
'My brother loved your people. "Tuan Tata" made your "saka" the first Senoi reserve. No man can take that land away from you … You know that don't you?'
Angah nodded.
'Then why don't you speak, Headman Angah? You have nothing to be afraid of … I give you my word.'

Noone remorselessly coaxed the story out of Angah. Pat Noone had not been killed by the Japanese; nor had he been murdered by the communists. The truth was tragic and banal. Uda, the handsome young Temiar, whose presence had troubled Richard when he had met Pat for the last time in 1942, Angah told Noone, had begun sleeping with Ajang:

'But your custom allows a younger brother to do this, Uda was like a brother to Tuan Tata.'

'Yet,' replied Angah, 'when Tuan Tata learned this he was very angry. He sent Uda away for some time and he was in disgrace. Later Tata forgave him [...] but Uda had no woman to sleep with and he was full of virility. He loved Ajang, and having already tasted her he dreamed of her ...'.

'How do you know these things?'

'Tuan, the whole of Telom Valley knows of Uda's dreams. He dreamed that Tata would take Ajang away from her people. He dreamed that Tata would make the Senoi fight the Japs ...'. Angah hesitated.

'Don't be afraid to tell me anything.'

'Tuan, it is the terrible secret of the Telom Valley. Your brother was murdered by Uda and [his cousin] Busu.'

So Pat had been killed by one of the 'Dream People', and by his 'blood brother' to boot. It was chilling news. But the taboo, it seemed, had been broken. Now there was a cascade of revelations. Pat, it turned out, had been blowpiped – a revelation that, Noone recalled, left him 'unable to move'. Angah had, of course, known this all along. He told Noone: 'I arrived to find Ajang weeping. Uda and Busu were there, looking very frightened. They had set out with your brother the day before, but now they were back – with his revolver. It lay at the centre of the longhouse floor ...'. Noone pieced together as many details of the tragedy as he could draw out from his Senoi contacts. The tragic story of what had happened to Pat was slowly but surely coming together.

Some time after these first encounters, Noone ran into a young man called Toris who owed him a favour. Noone had once supplied Toris with false teeth. The grateful Toris had also known Pat – and told Noone that he knew a Temiar man who might have more information. His name was Akob and he lived not far away in a jungle clearing with 'four young maidens'. Akob told Noone a tortuous story about his long ago search for a length of rare 'buloh seworr' bamboo that he needed to make 'the most wonderful blowpipe of all the Temiar'. He wanted it to be at least 'four times the length of his right arm' – about 8ft long. Akob had journeyed across the high mountains of the Ulu Perak 'towards the setting sun', but failed in his quest to find any 'buloh seworr' bamboo of the length he needed. Even on the steep slopes of the mighty Gunong Swettenham, the right kind of bamboo was elusive. Disheartened, Akob descended into the Telom Valley where he found shelter in the ladang of headman Ngah. Here he courted and married a young woman called Amoi. Akob had shrewdly collected many pieces of rare bamboo which he sold to pay Amoi's dowry. Shortly after his marriage, Akob met the strange white man who was living in a small hut not far from the ladang. The man had no luggage, Akob recalled, just a revolver and he enjoyed smoking the locally grown tobacco. Akob was struck by how well the man they called 'Tuan Tata' spoke the Temiar dialect. Pat explained to Akob that he had 'become a Temiar and lived like a Temiar'. Akob helped Pat repair the leaking roof of his *atap* hut. He described to him his long and fruitless search for the right length of bamboo. Pat told Akob about another young man he had known once who had found the right kind of bamboo on the slopes of Gunong Swettenham. 'But I have already looked there, Tuan!' Akob protested. 'Try again,' Pat advised, 'Try again ...'.

A few days later, headman Ngah asked Akob to collect maize seed for planting from Kuala Ta-nai. He was away for several days. When he returned, he discovered Uda and Ajang living in the *atap* hut where he had met Tuan Tata. Now Pat was nowhere to be seen. No one would tell Akob where he had gone. Days passed and Tuan Tata did not reappear. Then Akob stumbled on Uda's cousin Busu hiding away in a little hut in the jungle; he was clearly very frightened. Akob somehow forced him to talk. Tuan Tata was dead. Murdered. Akob returned to the Temiar settlement. He asked headman Ngah what had happened to his friend. The killing, he discovered, had been premeditated: Uda had dreamt that Pat would force the Temiar to fight the Japanese; they would all be killed. And everyone knew, Ngah said, that he did not want to share Ajang. So one day, Tuan Tata, Uda and Busu had set off into the jungle, leaving Ajang behind. Pat had no reason to be suspicious. He often accompanied Temiar hunting parties. Did Ajang know about Uda's dream and what he now intended? We will never know. The little party stopped at the Wi River to rest. Pat settled himself down by the little stream and lit a pipe. Uda and Busu began sharpening long staves of hard, thorny 'rakap' wood. Uda then approached Pat 'with a strange look on his face'. Alarmed, Pat drew his revolver – but Busu knocked it out of his hand with one of the 'rakap' staves. Pat fled back along the path towards the ladang. Uda 'loaded' his blowpipe and ran after him. The two men disappeared. Then Busu heard a piercing cry. He ran after Uda and found Pat writhing on the ground and vomiting profusely. A dart had penetrated his left eye. Busu watched as Uda raised his parang and brought the blade swinging down on Pat's skull.

Akob later followed Tuan Tata's advice and returned to Gunong Swettenham. And this time he was successful. He found just the right length of 'buloh seworr' bamboo he had craved for so long to make the 'longest blowpipe'.

Modern anthropologists have debated whether Pat Noone truly understood the significance of dreams in the culture of the Temiar people. It was a dream that was his undoing: a dream about the MPAJA.

The Second Rape of the Dream People?

How would Pat Noone have judged the British treatment of the Orang Asli during the Emergency? It is surely unlikely that he would have been impressed. Richard Noone's own account of his experience as Protector of Aborigines during the Emergency is called *The Rape of the Dream People*. For Noone, naturally enough, the rapists were the communist MNLA. But it was his idealistic brother Pat who, as we have seen, dragged the Temiar kicking and screaming into the savage world of modern warfare – and he must bear some at least of the responsibility for the 'rape'. Like the Chinese 'New Villages', the Jungle Forts slowly but surely untied the bonds that had been woven between the Orang Asli and the MNLA. Marine Roy Follows arrived in Malaya in 1952 – and was posted to Fort Brooke in the Cameron Highlands a year or so later. His account of his experience offers insights into the way the Forts worked in practice:

> You have to walk to these forts or get there by rafts or whatever: helicopter only available for a few places. I have to walk in and walk out. I walked over the Cameron Highlands to the Fort Brooke. Many areas were not marked on the map. Fort Brooke was about at about 2,500 feet, surrounded by barbed wired and sharpened bamboo sticks sticking out at a forty five degree angle. All the houses were made of bamboo with *atap* roof just above the floor. Water came down from the river; no electricity and isolated – and all the food have to be dropped in by air. Oftentimes, the parachute would not open and the stuff crashed into the ground. One occasion, my bottle of Whiskey was in it. When I got the broken pack, I can smell the Whiskey. Thank God it did not happen very often.

For many of the Orang Asli, the Fort was a culture shock:

> They didn't know a pair of scissors, matches or candles. I remember once I contacted a tribe who had never seen a European before and they came into the fort. I had my news on the radio: I am a news junky. When they heard the news coming out from a box, they were terrified and ran away. They had never seen or heard a radio before. I would give them magazines to look at and they looked at them upside down. They could not count and did not even know what day it was. I could not say to them like meet me at nine o'clock, because it was meaningless to them.

A number of Orang Asli that Follows met remained in thrall to the communists:

> I had a leading Aboriginal communist: Pangoy his name was and he was in charge of the Asal Organisation. He surrendered to me personally. Those in Kuala Lumpur from in the Aboriginal Department wouldn't listen to me: as

though he is safe for them and he is a good man. I was suspicious. I was ordered to give him food everyday. One day, I marked a sack of rice and handed it over to him. Four days later, a jungle patrol found the marked sack in an MNLA camp. I confronted with Pangoy about the sack. He did not know what to say and I told him never come to the fort again, which he didn't. So you see I could not trust them.

The solution was to 'seduce' the best-behaved aborigines with the usual trinkets of the colonial world:

They used to work at the fort, bringing food, collecting bamboos, *ataps*. I paid them with salt, beef and cheap tobacco. They were quite happy with that. Sometimes we gave them food as well. On two occasions, they put on a special dance for me which not many seen and I was privileged to witness it. The women came in with bamboo instruments which make rhythmic sounds and the men dance around in the circle and they kept on for almost two hours until they were all completely out. It was a very good experience …

The forts acted as fast-track instruments of colonisation, transforming the Malayan aboriginal peoples into Federation subjects for the first time. The logical next step was to recruit Orang Asli as paramilitary auxiliaries. This was the origin of the Senoi Pra'aq – Malaya's killer elite.

The Real Apocalypse Now

Richard Noone's rationale for forming the 'Senoi Pra'aq' (Fighting Senoi) was that he believed 'it was necessary for [the Senoi] to take an active part in repelling the intruders who had dominated and virtually enslaved them. They themselves must fight.' This was disingenuous to say the least. The Federation security forces could be regarded just as much intruders as the MNLA guerrillas. The record of the Senoi Pra'aq demolishes the old cliché that the Senoi tribes, such as the Temiar, are naturally peace-loving peoples. The killing of Pat Noone, who had created the myth of the 'Dream People', was perhaps a salutary lesson to his brother. The Temiar were as capable of cold-blooded murder as any European, MNLA communist or Malay.

There were precedents for Noone's plan. In the early years of the Emergency, a few Orang Asli had been recruited as guards, special constables and even Special Branch officers. The Perak Aborigines Area Constabulary (PAAC) had been established in March 1950, with Orang Asli making up some 10 per cent of its numbers; the rest were Malays – though some were Orang Asli who had converted to Islam. It is noteworthy that the Malays had been recruited under the 15 December Manpower Regulations while the Orang Asli were volunteers.

They proved themselves to be ferocious fighters capable of acting, as one military report admitted, 'independently and with flair and consummate bravery'. Peter Williams-Hunt had refused to arm any of his Orang Asli guides and in a short booklet written for the Federation security forces, *An Introduction to the Malayan Aborigines*, he stressed that aborigines did not 'like being fired on'. It was the Asal movement that proved Williams-Hunt's paternalist protectiveness to be nonsense. In January 1953, shortly before the arrival of General Templer, a new policy was promulgated in the Director of Operations Instruction No 17, 'The Control of the Aborigines in Malaya'. This directly linked the fort-building programme to the recruitment and arming of Orang Asli under the auspices of the SAS.

Richard Noone was convinced that the Orang Asli could do more to defeat the insurgents. His case was made more persuasive by the rising costs of eliminating MNLA guerrillas as the Korean War dividends began to decline. In July 1954, the War Office in London turned down Templer's request for a second SAS squadron to be posted to Malaya. This forced the Federation to look for a cheaper 'local option': and the Orang Asli were the last 'untapped' source of manpower to pit against the MNLA. To persuade the government, Noone experimented with a small corps of ten surrendered Asal fighters attached to D Squadron of the 22nd SAS Regiment. One of these volunteers was a Semai called Bah Tangga, who was reputed to have been one of the MNLA ambush party that had assassinated High Commissioner Gurney in October 1951. So it was fitting that *The Straits Times* should report the formation of a 'Temiar Squadron of veteran sharp shooting aborigines'. Noone fought hard to get his 'big battalion' idea accepted. Reports showed that Orang Asli units were effective jungle warriors. Reports of their valour and skill had a powerful impact on government thinking. Even so, it was on the eve of independence in September 1956 that Noone finally succeeded and the platoon-size 'Temiar Offensive Unit', the 'Senoi Pra'aq', was formally established. The British kitted out three sections of thirty aborigine warriors in standard jungle green. Their official badge showed crossed blowpipes with a buffalo head against a green background. The 'Senoi Pra'aq' was issued, however, with modern weapons.

To begin with there was considerable reluctance to make much use of the Senoi Pra'aq. The myth of Orang Asli timidity, like that of the lazy Malay native, was hard to shake off. It was not until March 1958 – two years before the Emergency was officially declared over – that the Senoi Pra'aq were unleashed on the battered relic regiments of the MNLA. In his autobiography, Richard Noone eulogises the lethal talents of the Senoi Pra'aq: they could move through the jungle at speeds that 'astonished even the SAS'; 'we went on from success to success,' he boasted, 'our record of terrorist eliminated was higher than any other security-force unit …'.

By the time Noone recruited the Senoi Pra'aq, the security forces had pushed the MNLA out of the southern peninsula states Selangor, Negeri Sembilan and southern Perak into the Temiar heartlands in the north. Here they found temporary refuge in one of the world's densest and most inaccessible jungle terrains – a hostile world of twisting, unmapped river valleys and steep, thickly forested peaks. In the early part of the decade, the last battles between the Chinese nationalist KMT and the communist MNLA had been fought in this lost world – a savage, take no prisoners war that few noticed was happening. This was where the Senoi Pra'aq would be deployed in the last years of the Emergency. They would be launched into a region officially called the 'Bamboo Operations Area' that extended down both sides of the Main Range. Under the auspices of the SAS, training of Semai and Temiar recruits lasted about three months. Most proved themselves adept jungle soldiers – 'tough nuts' in British army parlance. Few showed any compunction about killing outside their own clan areas. They fought very effectively as hunter-killer teams right across the 'Bamboo Operations Area' – and the evidence of their 'kill rates' suggests that Noone had been right about their potential as ruthless warriors. It was the Senoi Pra'aq that liquidated the last MNLA units.

Although SAS accounts ennoble these expert jungle fighters, Senoi Pra'aq veterans are more straightforward. Hunting communists was 'fun' – and lucrative. They especially enjoyed 'hunts' that took place over several days and gave them the opportunity to make use of traditional tools like parangs and blowpipes. Many Senoi Pra'aq fighters put their faith in the animist magical powers conferred by incantations (*Jampi*) and necklace charms (*Tanka*). Some Senoi Pra'aq fighters became famous because bullets appeared to pass through without harm. These legends may have a simple explanation: by the end of the 1950s, the MNLA supplies of ammunition had deteriorated to such a degree that it was unreliable and underpowered. Bullets often needed to be baked overnight in hot sand. This meant that the guerrillas would open fire with rounds that were spent by the time they reached their target. But invulnerability to enemy fire was all grist to the mill of Malaya's 'killer elite'.

4

A WAR WITHOUT END?

Sham Showdown at Baling

Shortly before 10 a.m. on 28 December 1956, a meeting of curious poignancy took place on the jungle fringe at Gunong Paku not far from the small town of Baling in northern Malaya. Chin Peng, the Secretary General of the Malayan Communist Party and military commander of the MNLA was about to take part in peace negotiations with the new Chief Minister of the Federation, Tunku Abdul Rahman. As he emerged from the jungle fringes, Chin Peng was astonished to see his old friend from Force 136 days, John Davis. 'To me he looked unchanged,' Chin Peng recalled, 'seemingly not a day older.' Davis held out a hand and said in Cantonese 'Long time, no see.' Chin Peng was 'momentarily taken aback'. There was no time for affable reminiscence. Davis, now working as a district officer in Penang, was there as 'conducting officer' charged with ensuring the safety of the MNLA party. From the rendezvous, Davis escorted Chin Peng and the three-man communist delegation to the English School in Baling. Here they would be billeted in a small brick bungalow, with their own cook. Their hosts had thoughtfully provided supplies of toothpaste and soap. Barbed wire surrounded the bungalow. Hundreds of British troops were stationed around the school building and an army of journalists and cameramen swarmed nearby to see with their own eyes and lenses the man the *Daily Mail* referred to as 'a tiger emerging from his lair'. A breathless voice-over on one newsreel proclaims: News Flash: 'All necks strained for the No 1 terrorist. There he is, that's him, Chin Peng directly responsible for a brutal seven year campaign of murder and terrorism against the ordinary people of Malaya.'

At 2.20 p.m. sharp, Davis led Chin Peng and the MNLA delegation from their billet to the classroom where talks would begin. A security zone had been cleared around the school and army marksmen had been deployed with orders to shoot dead any intruders. In photographs, Chin Peng looks surprisingly at ease. Flanked by Rashid Maidin and MNLA propaganda chief Chen Tien, he took his place at a long table covered with a white cloth. On the other side of the table sat Tunku Abdul Rahman, the Chief Minister of Singapore David Marshall and the

MCA leader, Tan Cheng Lock. At a signal, the press corps stampede unleashed a cacophony of clicking, whirring and flashing. All journalists had been forbidden to talk to the MNLA delegation.

Negotiations that take place between warring parties when neither has yet 'won' customarily but not invariably involve a hidden balance of potential concessions and gains, even if one side is demonstrably in a weaker position. However unequal, there is give and take. Neither party can risk losing face by leaving empty-handed. Even in the aftermath of defeat, the lesson of history is that magnanimity is preferable to the ruthless enactment of retribution: the lesson of Versailles. The Baling talks that took place in Malaya on the eve of independence had a very different dynamic. The negotiations were a sham, a work of political theatre. The real agenda was not ending the Emergency as Chin Peng naively believed but forging a new government fit for independence. A few days after the talks ended, Tunku Abdul Rahman flew to London and secured agreement with the British that Malaya would at last become independent the following year on 31 August. This was a triumph for the Tunku. But his diplomatic feat was the gift of Baling: the last stepping stone to *merdeka*.

The Baling talks took place in the shadow of the Suez Crisis. In October 1956, the British Prime Minister Sir Anthony Eden had hatched a secret plot with the Israeli and French governments to seize back the Suez Canal from Egyptian President Colonel Gamal Abdel Nasser. The debacle that ensued when Israeli, British and French troops invaded the Canal Zone brought to an end Britain's role as a world power and entrenched the United States as a global hegemon. Since 1945, there had been tectonic shifts in the global relations of the great powers. By 1948, the Soviet Union dominated Eastern Europe and was pressing on the northern ramparts of the fading British Empire. The conquest of Germany and Japan delivered immense power to the Americans across the Western hemisphere and in East Asia. The Soviet Union and the United States had thus become globally competitive powers. British power had not completely evaporated. What we now call decolonisation was in reality a period of retrenchment. Empire was redefined not abolished. This reflected American pragmatism about power sharing and would have most impact in what was still known as the 'British Southern World': that vast swathe of territory that stretched from the Middle East and South and East Africa, across the Indian Ocean, through Malaya and Singapore to Australia and New Zealand. The security of this sprawling territorial conglomeration depended on a chain of military bases in Cape Town, Suez, Iraq and to the east in Singapore. The Indian Ocean had once been called a 'British Lake'. Even after 1945, this was still an apt description. India and Ceylon (Sri Lanka) won independence very soon after the war ended. But the Colonial Office in London hoped that British power in the wider region could be maintained for some time to come along with all the old dividends of empire. So far, the new global powers had left the 'British Southern World' to its own devices. But only the most deluded imperialist imagined that this state of affairs could be sustained indefinitely. The spark of nationalist revolt had fallen on combustible tropical tinder right across Southeast Asia from French Indochina through British Burma to Dutch Indonesia and British Malaya. Malaya was the dollar-earning machine of the 'new' empire: revenues from rubber and tin shored up Britain's wounded finances and ameliorated its dependence on American largesse. It was mainly thanks to these Malayan earnings that the sterling area was restored to dollar solvency by the beginning of 1951. The Emergency cost the Exchequer and the Federation government dear. So there could be no question of pulling out of Malaya. Likewise, Singapore was essential to regional security – especially as the winds of revolt blew south from communist China into French Indochina and beyond. In 1956, the Suez disaster profoundly disrupted this delicate equilibrium. The winds of change would reach hurricane force.

In Malaya, the British had clamped down on both the communists and Malay radicals. The emerging political landscape was dominated by chauvinist Malays in UMNO. The party leader, Tunku Abdul Rahman, had forged an expedient alliance with Chinese and Indian parties to placate British anxieties about communalism. The only significant opposition to the power of UMNO came from Islamic parties and extremists like the Peninsula Malay Union (PMU) which denounced any attempt to ally with Chinese or Indian parties. The PMU gained little momentum in this period though an early admirer was a journalist and doctor who called himself 'C.H.E. Det': the nom de plume of Dr Mahathir Bin Mohamed. Tun Dr Mahathir would become the fourth and longest-serving Malaysian prime minister at the end of the century.[48] Dr Mahathir warned PMU leader Hashim Ghani 'should be under no illusion as to the chances of his countrymen in competition with the superior organisation, financial position and education of the non-Malays'. Ultranationalism is always seeded by fear. When Mahathir became Malaysian prime minister, he would direct his venom not only at the Chinese but an imaginary global conspiracy of Jews.

The emergence of this vibrant new political space in Malayan public culture changed the way the British exercised power. The rise of Malayan political parties heralded the end of the traditional colonial embrace. Political leaders replaced the rulers. They could not be 'persuaded' to toe the line over a cup of tea or quietly pensioned off. Colonial rule had to evolve to stay in charge. Post-war British prime ministers, Attlee then that old reactionary Winston Churchill, reiterated their promise of *eventual* self-government. In 1948, when the Emergency began, independence was widely assumed to be at least a quarter of a century in the future. In 1950, the Commissioner General Malcolm MacDonald was talking of ten to fifteen years. General Templer appears to have looked forward to self-government some time in the early 1960s. But by the time Templer left Malaya, the pace of constitutional change had switched into high gear. There were many forces driving the rush to *merdeka*. The success of UMNO had made Malays impatient. From the British point of view it was essential to keep the Malays 'on side' because they formed the vast bulk of the local security forces. On the Chinese side, the Emergency had isolated the communists and brought forward a viable new elite that was prepared to concede the trappings of power to Malays. On a broader scale, the 'British Southern World' looked a great deal more fragile than it had in 1948. The strategic interests of India, Pakistan, Burma and Ceylon which had become independent soon after the war looked increasingly volatile. Communist China had waged war in Korea; Indonesia looked distinctly unstable; the French had been ousted from Indochina. There was no question that Malaya had to be stabilised. MacDonald advised that: 'If we were to resist the pace of change, we should lose the present support of Asian leaders [...] we must be in harmony with Asian leaders so that there is no discernible difference in views on which world opinion can take sides against us.' British Foreign Secretary Ernest Bevin was blunt: 'Our support of nationalism in South and South East Asia provides the best possible counter to communist subversion and penetration.'

This is not to suggest that the British serenely granted Malaya independence. However affable the Tunku may have appeared, he drove a hard bargain. He forced the British to compromise their demand for a multiracial party: the Alliance was always a marriage of convenience. The communal parties would never truly merge. It was Alliance pressure, cleverly applied, that overrode that British condition for independence. This meant that *merdeka* would leave many unresolved matters in its wake. The tricky position of the Chinese MCA was astutely analysed by Sir David Watherston in a memorandum to MacGillivray:

> The MCA finds itself in acutely difficult position[sic]. On the one [sic] it realises that it owes its position in the Alliance to Malay votes and that the adoption of 'jus soli' [citizenship according to place of birth] now as a plank – the most important plank – in its political platform could only lead to an open breach with the Alliance. On the other hand, it sees that the strength of the demand for 'jus soli' from the influential Chinese business class (which constitutes the main support of the MCA) is such that this class will abandon the support of the MCA unless it takes a stand on this question. If this support was lost, the MCA might well disintegrate as it has never had any real roots among the rank and file of the Chinese population.' (18 April, 1956)

The Alliance had merely papered over communal strife.

Then there was the pressing matter of Singapore. After 1945, the British reclaimed Stamford Raffles' great port city and restored its prestige and power as a naval and military base and commercial hub. Singapore was divided from British Malaya by the narrow Straits of Johor but the British forged a very different strategy on the other side of the causeway. Singapore would remain Britain's iron gate in Asia, shielding its commercial interests in the region and providing a bulwark against the spread of communism. As one of the Straits Settlements, Singapore had eclipsed Malacca and Penang to become the commercial furnace of Southeast Asia, luring into its swarming shipyards, shop houses, factories, offices, and brothels a rich diversity of Asian peoples: Arabs, Tamils, Malays, Javanese, Sumatrans, Jews, Filipinos, Japanese. But the city's commercial and cultural life was dominated by the overseas Chinese. Singapore was in essence a Chinese city and British power depended on Chinese co-operation. After the war, Singapore's economy lay in ruins. There was widespread labour unrest and a vibrant communist movement. As in Malaya, the British sought out a compliant elite to retain power and quash troublesome radicals. Their natural ally was the Chinese business class that shared the same fear of communism and a labour movement that was, of course, led by Chinese leftists. In 1948, the British introduced a new constitution that gave Singapore, for the first time, a legislative council with six elected members, increased to nine in 1951. This was a sham token democracy: a narrowly defined franchise, the insistence of English as the official language and suppression of all left-wing organisations ensured that politics was reserved for a jealously protected elite represented by the Progressive Party (PP) that was founded in August 1947 by English-speaking, London-educated lawyers Tan Chye Cheng, John Laycock and Nazir Ahmad Mallal. Like Dato Onn in Malaya, the PP leaders embraced the 'slow road' to self-government. The PP backed British efforts to clamp down on labour unrest and accepted the extension to Singapore of the 'Emergency Regulations' in 1948. At the beginning of the 1950s, the British were ambushed by a new generation of Singaporean nationalists – and a brash young national leadership that would soon dominate the political life of the colony. Lee Kuan Yew, also educated in London, had once backed the PP and worked as John Laycock's election agent. But Lee and other impatient Singaporeans like David Saul Marshall wanted a swifter end to colonial rule. Lee was in some ways a thoroughly Anglicised subject of the British Empire but his social intimacy with representatives of the imperial power had quashed any illusions he might have entertained about its permanence and exposed the coarseness of England's 'beer swilling bourgeoisie'. The flamboyant Marshall was born into a Jewish family with roots in Iraq. During the war, he had survived forced labour in iron mines on Hokkaido. A fiery orator, Marshall established the centre-left Labour Front coalition, while the highly competitive Lee countered with the People's Action Party (PAP) which was reputedly penetrated by the MCP. In the troubled aftermath of the 'Maria Hertogh' affair and an eruption of social unrest, Britain sought to reinforce the Progressive Party. The 'Rendel Constitution' inaugurated the formation of a mainly elected assembly and extended the franchise. To the dismay of the British, the socialist Labour Front was the surprise winner in elections and Marshall emerged as Singapore's chief minister. Goaded by Lee, Marshall threatened to resign if the British refused to offer self-government immediately. The sticking point for the British was their determination, backed by the United States, to hold on to Singapore as a military and naval base. Marshall was a volatile individual who was innately hostile to communism. This would make him a very useful negotiator at Baling at the end of 1955.

What of the communists? By 1955, four years after the reorientation of 1951–52, the MNLA was a severely weakened insurgent force. Chin Peng and the Central Committee had retreated to the Betong Salient on the Thai border where the communists were sustained by a large Chinese minority that had not been resettled in villages. In the autumn of 1953, General Templer had initiated a bold experiment in Malacca where Special Branch intelligence showed that the communists had been almost completely eradicated in specific districts. These were declared 'white areas' and most Emergency Regulations, except registration, were lifted to reward local people. Rice rations increased and shops could stay open day and night. Curfews were abolished; tappers were permitted to take midday meals to work; and people and goods moved freely for the first time in nearly a decade. Templer warned that these onerous restrictions would be immediately reimposed if there was any resumption of subversive activity. He calculated – and was proved right – that the benefits of living in a 'white area' without curfews and other restrictions would make it very difficult for the Min Yuen to reactivate their organisation – and the MNLA to mount attacks. Templer's strategy was controversial. Whenever a new 'white area' was proposed, the Special Branch and other agencies issued dire warnings about how easy it would be for a handful of hard-core terrorist supporters to revive the communist networks. In the long run, Templer's daring paid off. Not a single 'white area' ever had to revert to 'black' (though there were still 'black areas' in Kelantan as late as 1965).

After 1953, an archipelago of 'white areas' was gradually extended across the peninsula much to the dismay of the Central Committee. During the two years of Templer's authoritarian rule, fully two-thirds of the MNLA fighting units were eliminated. Between 1951 and 1957, the security forces killed 9,000 guerrillas, far outnumbering new recruits, and overall strength fell from roughly 8,000 to 2,000. In 1953, the MNLA killed less than one-fifth of the number of security forces and civilians that they had in 1951. The communist movement was internally battered by betrayal, surrender and for those that fought, on famine. The MCP was not defeated. From the point of view of the government, the communists were still a threat. Chin Peng himself saw the move to the Thai border as analogous to Mao Zedong's 'Long March' which had allowed the Chinese communists to reorganise and regroup out of reach of their Kuomintang enemies and the Japanese. Arguably the 'Betong Salient' was the single 'base area' (in the Maoist sense) established by the MNLA.

The cost of retreat was isolation. From Chin Peng's perspective, the political initiative was slipping away into the hands of the Alliance Party. So it was that in May 1955, Chin Peng hatched a plan to reach out to the Alliance. He invented a high-ranking communist official with the Mandarin name Wu Xing, which would transpose as 'Ng Heng' in Cantonese. This subterfuge was a face-saving 'get out' if the Alliance rejected the proposal outright if the peace offer was denounced by rival communist factions as 'ideologically unsound'. Party spokesman 'Wu Xing' sent a signed letter responding to the Tunku's amnesty offer and proposing talks. The Alliance offer had stipulated that amnesty would be granted only if the communists surrendered first. Wu Xing unsurprisingly rejected this scenario – and insisted that the terms of any amnesty had to be negotiated. Chin Peng's account of the run-up to the Baling talks in *My Side of History* reveals inadvertently that the MCP negotiating stance relied on bluff: 'Wu Xing' boasted that: 'In spite of the thousands of methods adopted by the British government to liquidate us, it has failed to do so. Neither has it defeated us in war, because we are supported by masses of people [sic] and hence we will never be defeated.' This was equivalent to waving a plastic toy gun.[49]

'Wu Xing's' letter was sent not to the high commissioner but to the United Planters' Association of Malaya (UPAM) and copied to the MCA leaders Tan Cheng Lock and H.S. Lee and the new Chief Minister of Singapore David Marshall. The UPAM passed on the letter to the Chief Secretary of the Federation Sir David Watherston who immediately sought the advice of C.C. Too who had resigned from the Malayan information services when it was reorganised by Alec Peterson. The 'Wu Xing'/'Ng Heng' letter had taken the British by surprise. It was also potentially embarrassing: they did not want to appear to dismiss the chance of a deal.

Too warned the new information head, O.W. Wolters, that the MCP Central Committee would almost certainly keep up the pressure, by sending a second open letter proposing peace. Wolters was sceptical – but three days after the amnesty announcement, Chin Peng wrote directly to the Tunku as Too had predicted. The British had to counter the MCP move. As Watherston explained in detail to Colonial Secretary Lennox-Boyd, the MCP politburo understood that the armed struggle had failed, and recognised that the Alliance could steal its political thunder. The communists could, in short, miss the political boat. Watherston emphasised that: '*the MCP have approached us as an armed force which is conscious of failure*'. Since the MCP had already rejected the mealy mouthed amnesty terms offered by the Alliance, Watherston anticipated that the communists would demand recognition as a legal political party and insist on immunity from punishment for its members and followers. This option was anathema and was thoroughly alarming. It would turn the Malayan clock back to 1948 before the Emergency was declared. The worst-case scenario was that the 'treasonable' MCP inveigle itself back into the Malayan political mainstream as a legitimate party while maintaining a clandestine terrorist organisation that would work towards the defeat of the 'government of the day'. On the other hand, 'outright rejection' would leave the Federation open to charges of unnecessarily prolonging the war. At the end of his long report, Watherston concluded that the only option was to 'issue a statement [...] rejecting the offer, referring to the present surrender policy ...'. It was vital to get over the message that it was the Federation that was offering peace terms – namely that the MCP should surrender – not the MCP. In London, Lennox-Boyd reiterated Watherston's point to Foreign Secretary Anthony Eden: 'The High Commissioner and I have been viewing with apprehension the dangerous possibility of public demand in Malaya for a negotiated peace. If any such negotiations were undertaken they could not but rebound to the advantage of the Communist terrorists ...'. Any concession would open the door to the MCP to return to society 'like maggots into a pile of bread'.[50]

The task now was to get the Alliance leadership onside. And this would prove to be tricky indeed. The Tunku was no longer prepared to meekly follow the high commissioner's orders. 'Events, dear boy events' opined Harold MacMillan famously when asked why he had chosen a less than desirable course of action. The Alliance had by now shown it was a vote winner and the Tunku was now chief minister. The Alliance had satisfied one of the British conditions for independence, i.e. a non-communal party (or so it seemed) – now the only obstacle remaining was the Emergency. Might the MCP offer be used to end the conflict condition and open the door at last to *merdeka*? For High Commissioner MacGillivray in Kuala Lumpur and Lennox-Boyd in London the looming talks became a matter of great anxiety. In public statements, the MCP was noisily presenting itself as an equal negotiating party. Unlike the Alliance, the MCP was, at least superficially, a genuinely multiracial party. The MCP propaganda did not go unnoticed. The majority of the Chinese papers like the *Nanyang Siang Pau*, which had the biggest circulation, openly backed negotiations (not just 'talks') – just as Watherston had feared.

British anxiety about the imminent talks focused on the new chief minister. And the crafty Tunku played their fears to the hilt. The more the British fretted that he might compromise with the communists, the stronger his hand would be negotiating the terms of – and crucially the timing of – independence. The Tunku himself feared that if he did not conduct the negotiations, or talks, as his 'own man' he would be pilloried as a colonial stooge or 'running dog'. British reports frequently alluded to the Tunku's 'unreliability'. He was, Lennox-Boyd concluded, a 'very vain man' pursuing his own cryptic agenda. The new Commissioner General Southeast Asia Sir Robert Scott, who had replaced MacDonald, feared that 'it is unlikely that Rahman will break with the Communists at the talks [...] if the meeting does not end the Emergency the Communists no doubt plan to put the blame on HMG and not on Rahman, a plan to which he would no doubt lend himself ...'. The Prince of Kedah now seemed to regard himself as Malaya's Gandhi.

MacGillivray sensed a closing trap. There was now a very great risk that it would appear that the British did not want to end the Emergency but to keep it alive in order to deny independence to Malaya. This would provoke a renewed anti-British assault by UMNO – the very people whose support the British needed to steer Malaya into the future.

British anxieties deepened after a dress rehearsal where C.C. Too took the part of Chin Peng and Major General Linday 'played' Tunku Abdul Rahman. Too/ Chin Peng offered the following deal: we will lay down our arms if you allow us to walk out of the jungle as free men and recognise the MCP as a legitimate party. Linday/Tunku could not respond to this 'sensibly'; he was in a 'cold sweat'. This alarming pseudo-drama was the reason MacGillivray proposed 'stiffening' the Tunku by inviting his counterpart the Singapore Chief Minister David Marshall to attend the talks. The point was, as Commissioner General Scott pointed out to Eden on 23 October, that: 'Marshall […] has to accept the fact of an overwhelming Chinese majority in Singapore. His anxiety is Communist subversion, and his aim in a non-Communist City State, where all communities can live and trade in harmony, a modern venice [sic] on a British Socialist pattern.' Lord Reading came to same conclusion: '[Marshall] sees himself […] engulfed by a rising tide of mixed Chinese Communism and Chinese racialism [sic], against which he feels he has no defences. He kept on repeating to me … "I am a very worried man".' These proved to be shrewd assessments of Marshall's likely position when confronted by the MCP leaders at Baling. He was, as Chin Peng ruefully recalls, a very aggressive negotiator. If this was not enough, the British shrewdly implied to the Tunku that the issue of the ending of the Emergency might no longer be considered a deal breaker. This was not far short of handing him a negotiating Exocet missile.

The British need not have worried. The Tunku and Marshall both made short shrift of Chin Peng and his negotiating partners. At the end of the first day, *The Straits Times* reported that Chin Peng looked 'thoroughly dejected […] bent almost in despair'. He realised by then that no further progress could be made to secure MCP recognition: that proposal was dead in the water. He believed that he had one card left to play. The following morning, the second day of the talks, Chin Peng made the opening move: though popularly elected, the present governments of Malaya and Singapore were not yet properly independent. To Chin Peng's amazement, Marshall agreed. He then 'played his card':

> *Chin Peng*: If these popularly elected governments of the Federation and Singapore have self determination in matters concerning internal security and national defence then all problems could be solved easily […] then we can stop the war immediately.
>
> *The Tunku*: Is that a promise? When I come back from England that is the thing I am bring with me.
>
> *Chin Peng*: That being the case, we can straightaway stop our hostilities and also disband our armed units.

The Tunku had at this moment won a vital concession from Chin Peng. He would use it with dazzling effect when he faced the British at a much grander venue in London a few days later.

As Karl Hack points out, the outcome of the Baling talks followed from a fundamental imbalance of power at the negotiating table. The MCP genuinely wanted peace and, as we have seen, were prepared to make significant concessions *if* they could emerge from the process with dignity and the right to participate in the political life of Malaya – even in a compromised way. But, as the British documentary record reveals, Chin Peng's opponents on the other side of the table knew that the MCP had been *forced* to negotiate because their armed struggle had run out of steam. The MNLA posed, to borrow Hack's phrase, 'a manageable and diminishing threat'. This information encouraged the Tunku and his Singapore counterpart David Marshall to refuse to make any significant concessions. They grandstanded. For the future leaders of an independent Malaya and Singapore, to agree to recognise the MCP as a legitimate party and permit MNLA guerrillas to walk back into civilian life would be tantamount to state suicide. As the Tunku disingenuously recollected in an interview:

> … It is the words that came from his mouth, which I can never forget to the end of my day. He said, 'As between you and I, you are anti-Communist, I am a Communist, there can never be co-existence, so there is no point in my telling you that I will lay down my arms, there can never be proper understanding, I will always carry on with my communist activities.'

That might be called the 'fairy tale of Baling'. Chin Peng had, honourably, offered precisely that – co-existence. He could not have known of the political skulduggery that had taken place between the British and the Alliance to ensure the right outcome at Baling. Since the Tunku knew that he was no longer obligated to 'end the Emergency at Baling', he was free to exploit Chin Peng's demand that he return from the London talks with agreement on the matters of internal security and national defence. Instead of playing a card, he had handed an ace to his cunning opponent. From the British point of view the outcome was almost entirely satisfying. The Tunku had 'stood up to the communists'. He and Marshall had played their parts well. They had, as promised, sought peace but given nothing.

Hollow Victory

Well before the end of the decade, Emergency war had become a mopping-up operation. Chin Peng admits in his memoir: 'The battlefield outlook for our forces by this time was indeed gloomy.' From a peak level of 8,000 armed guerrillas in 1951, the war had eroded the MNLA to a rump of some 3,000 men by 1955. 'Contacts' dropped from about 1,000 in 1954 to 560 in 1955. The average soldier in Malaya could patrol on average for a thousand hours before he encountered a 'CT' – and usually after a patrol of four hours. The refinement of intelligence gathering by the Special Branch meant that MNLA leaders could be more effectively weeded out. The leader of the platoon that had assassinated the high commissioner in 1951, Siew Mah was shot dead by his own bodyguards. The reward they received was astronomical. These targeted assassinations had a catastrophic impact on morale. The worst enemy of the communist guerrillas was more mundane. It was hunger – an experience still seared in the memories of MNLA veterans:

> *Ah Hai:* We suffered badly. There was no food and we were hungry. A lot of lives were lost due to starvation.
> *Mamat:* We lost people in battle, but that's expected – but we were dying of hunger. We could not walk, we could not move. I was eating sticks: I put into the pot and boiled it with grass and eat it. That was the most bitter experience, that was the truth.

Shortage of food sapped the strength of the MNLA platoons.

> *Wong Kin:* During that time we had to reduce the number of people to the team in order to survive. Big troops were affected because we had to be separated and this weakened our combat strategies.

So it was that the First Malayan Emergency officially ended on 31 July 1960 with much pomp and circumstance on the old Padang in Kuala Lumpur. The occasion perfectly conveyed the ambivalence of *merdeka*. Malaya was now an independent member of the British Commonwealth. The 1st Battalion of the Malay Regiment outfitted in their dress uniform of a green songkok, white tunic and trousers and green and brown sarong marched past the exposed Tudor-style beams of the old Selangor Club and the Orientalist fantasy of the Selangor Secretariat. In the wake of the seven Malay Regiment battalions marched the Royal Hussars, the Brigade of Gurkhas, the Royal Malayan Police, the Senoi Pra'aq aboriginal trackers, Fijians, New Zealanders, Australians, Kenyans and Rhodesians. Above their heads, engines throbbing in the broiling air, hovered Bristol Sycamore helicopters that in the last years of the war had ferried back and forth across Malaya's jungles some of the 40,000 soldiers, 67,000 full and part-time police, and 300,000 Home Guards who together had defeated a communist insurgency that had erupted in a narrow peninsula, home to a mere 6 million people. Buzzing little Pioneer STOL aircraft (manufactured in Scotland) that had dropped millions of leaflets across the Malayan jungles to sap the morale of communist guerrillas led a fly-past of sleek jet fighters that glinted as they banked in the hot tropical sun. Malaya marked its victory against the MNLA by commemorating an empire that had not yet released its grip on the nation's riches. The martial parades and blaring military bands disguised an inconvenient fact. The Malayan communists had not been defeated and the communal hatreds that the British had fomented for more than a century simmered still behind the pomp and pageantry in the Padang. In December 1960, Chin Peng and fellow Central Committee member Chen Tien abandoned the Sadao camp and began an epic journey that would eventually bring them to Beijing.

The Long Shadow of the Emergency

This is not the place to recount the history of independent Malaya since 1957. That history has been blighted by violence and turmoil: a war with Indonesia following the enlargement of Malaya with the addition of the British colonies of Sabah and Sarawak, a bitter struggle with Singapore, war with Indonesia and bloody race riots in the capital Kuala Lumpur. The May 13 riots in 1969 led to a period of outright dictatorship. Driving this was the inheritance of colonialism: the arbitrary borders cut between people and ethnicities. The British and their nationalist Malay allies had fashioned a hybrid kind of independence. In 1948, the British had clamped down not only on the communists but Malay radicals. Though a succession of high commissioners flirted with Dato Onn bin Jaafar and his various parties, it was UMNO and its aristocratic leader Tunku Abdul Rahman who came to dominate the nationalist movement. At the Baling talks, the Tunku cemented his bond with the colonial power by standing up to Chin Peng but also forced the pace of constitutional change. Even in 1952, the new British 'supremo' Sir Gerald Templer had imagined Malaya becoming independent some time in the 1960s. The British conceded eventual independence but right up to the last moment looked for ways fair and foul to slow down progress. The reasons have never been disputed. Britain depended on American dollars earned with Malayan exports and feared that independence might unleash the communal violence that had erupted in India and Palestine. The Tunku's cleverly fought campaign to accelerate Malaya's course along the road to freedom had many consequences. It meant that he became prime minister of a new Southeast Asian nation in the dog days of a communist insurrection. He became both the 'Father of the Nation' and a war leader. To win power under the aegis of British colonial rule, the Tunku had engineered strategic pacts with the non-Malay elites – the Chinese MCA and the Malayan Indian Congress, an alliance that papered over communal divisions. The Alliance was a strategic reconciliation that had very little impact on Malaya's racial divisions. So Malaya was launched on the path of nation building in the shadow of the Emergency. This apparent disadvantage suited the Tunku's authoritarian and chauvinist caste of mind, albeit well disguised by his charm and a kind of bumbling insouciance. The draconian Emergency laws and regulations that had steadily accumulated since June 1948 would not be repealed. Using these laws, the Malayan government restricted freedom of speech, arrested anyone suspected of communist sympathies and detained them indefinitely without trial in the interests of 'national security' and 'racial harmony'. The habit of denying freedom is very hard to break. The new Malayan constitution enshrined the rights and privileges of Malays – as the British had always promised. The Alliance was never a forum of equals, nor was it intended to be one. The 'Reid Commission' that met 118 times in 1956 resisted MCA lobbying that it incorporate the citizenship principle of 'jus soli' for all those born in the country before, on or after Malaya's independence – but this was rejected in favour of the UMNO proposal that limited citizenship to those born on or after August 1957. The British accepted the UMNO package lock, stock and barrel: 'special position of Malays', 'Malay as the national language', 'Islam as the official religion', 'Malay land reservations', and 'reservation for Malays of a certain proportion of jobs in the civil service'. In a series of protracted negotiations with the Malay rulers, the British soothed their concerns about the democracy by inventing a new position of Yang di-Pertuan Agong (He who is made Lord): a 'supreme ruler' elected by the Council of Rulers to serve five-year terms. Article 83 of the Constitution states that:

> It shall be the responsibility of the Yang di-Pertuan Agong to safeguard the special position of the Malays and natives of any of the States of Sabah and Sarawak and the legitimate interests of other communities in accordance with the provisions of this Article.

Concealed within the debates that preceded independence was the officially unstated view that the MCP was a Chinese movement, and that Malays were for the most part 'naturally' opposed to communism. The strategic role of Malaya post-independence would be, at least in theory, to buttress British and American efforts to staunch the spread of communism in Southeast Asia. The development of the Malayan economy after 1957 would depend on Chinese enterprise, and still does. What Lee Kuan Yew called the 'obscurantist doctrine' of Malay rights still marginalises Chinese and Indian Malayans and inspires corruption and deceit. The Tunku's party has in the shape of the 'Barisan National' clung to power to this day. Elections in May 2013 seemed to promise change – but whether through electioneering trickery or outright fraud, the opposition parties fell at the last post.

The Emergency did not end in 1960. For visitors to Malaysia today this may come as a surprise. Most of us encounter a prosperous modern nation bristling with vast fortress-like shopping malls that appears to be at peace with itself. I first spent time in Kuala Lumpur working on a documentary about the coronation of the new Yang di-Pertuan Agong in 2007. That year it was the 'buggin's turn' of the young Sultan Mizan of Terengganu who as every one of his predecessors promised to promote racial harmony. As I began the long tortuous process of getting access to the royal family, I began to get glimpses, albeit fragmentary ones, behind the elaborate façade of Malaysian normality. I heard a lot about race – and sensed that the 'Malaysian races' still looked out at each other suspiciously from behind an impenetrable barrier. Kuala Lumpur was a melting pot that had never melted. I found out early on that the Malaysian monarchy was an ersatz creation of the British colonial government that was designed to protect the political and constitutional rights of a single race and faith in perpetuity. Although the monarchy was a modern institution, its elaborate rituals enshrined a rigid set of deferential codes of behaviour and thought that I soon realised mirrored an authoritarian state. Recently the Malaysian government invested millions in a vast new royal palace in Kuala Lumpur. I was struck by the banality and timidity of the mainstream press: friends urged me to read the blogs like 'Malaysiakini'. To be sure, the bloggers had the measure of their society. I learned about the UMNO conference held in 1987 when Tun Razak's son, the UMNO youth leader Najib Razak, unsheathed a kris dagger and threatened to 'bathe it in Chinese blood'. This blood-curdling display was not a one-off. Kris's are ritually brandished at UMNO conferences to assert the traditional rights of Malays and the practice reached a climax at the 2006 Annual General Assembly when a number of delegates had seemed to experience difficulty keeping their weapons in their sheaths. Malays evidently felt threatened – but by what and whom?

These fears are surprising. The Malaysian state still enshrines Malay hegemony. Amnesty International, as well as a group of courageous Malaysian civil rights lawyers, point out that, since 1960, a succession of amendments to the constitution have substantially altered the checks and balances built in by the Reid Commission in 1957 to favour the executive 'to the severe detriment of the citizen'. The Malaysian executive has relied excessively on 'Emergency powers' – a trick learned of course from the British colonial government. It is a startling fact that during forty-three years of independence, there has been just one short spell of four years between 15 August 1960 and 2 September 1964 when the country has not been subject to an Emergency: the first Emergency, which ended after the twelve-year communist insurgency on 31 July 1960, was followed by the Second Emergency, declared on 3 September 1964 for the whole of Malaya during the 'Konfrontasi' war with Indonesia. The Third Emergency, declared on 14 September 1960, was limited to the State of Sarawak, following the dismissal of the chief minister, Stephen Kalong Ningkan. The 13 May 'race riots' provoked the Fourth Emergency encompassing all Malaysia on 15 May 1969. Finally, on 8 November 1977, the Fifth Emergency was declared in the northern state of Kelantan to deal with a political crisis. In 2000, a panel of Commonwealth judges and lawyers warned that:

The continuation of Emergency after the need for it has passed can have an insidiously brutalising effect upon the administration of justice in any country. We suggest that the Malaysian malaise may be due in no small measure to the gradual acceptance of a state of emergency as the norm of Government.

Here in a nutshell is the inheritance of the British wars in Malaya: 'the gradual acceptance of a state of emergency as the norm of Government'. This political norm has had a dangerous impact on the rule of law. Since 1957, the Malaysian government has passed some 900 odd acts of parliament. Of these, the Commonwealth panel listed fourteen that 'abrogate constitutionally protected fundamental rights'.

Government by Emergency is reinforced by a battery of statutes that limit freedom of speech: the Sedition Act, the Official Secrets Act and the Printing Presses and Publications Act. These derive, of course, from a ridiculous proscription on the public discussion of 'sensitive issues'. Any newspaper that dares to step out of line will be punished by having its licence to publish summarily revoked. The consequence, as I discovered while making a documentary in Malaysia in 2007, was that media and cultural discourse in Malaysia is poisoned by censorship and self-censorship. Any kind of oppositional thinking is denied to the media: publications by opposition parties are restricted to sale to party members only. Foreign newspapers and journals are periodically banned or delayed. Television stations like RTM and TV3 simply ignore opposition parties. There are draconian restrictions on assembly and debate in universities and colleges. In 2011, the ice seemed to be breaking. Many dared to 'assemble' and protest against the current government on the streets of Kuala Lumpur. Such is the power of the executive, with its array of draconian statutes and laws, that few dare to hope that Malaysia will change fundamentally any time soon.

The Malaysian state uses its powers to reinforce the rights and privileges of a race. Although Indonesia belongs in the same Malay cultural world as Malaysia, its history has followed a very different path. Despite the vast territorial expanse of the Indonesian Archipelago, Dutch rule led to the emergence of a precocious and inclusive nationalism. Deeply divided though the peoples of the Dutch East Indies were as Muslims, secular nationalists and communists, all of these constituencies recruited supporters as widely as possible: ethnicity made minimal difference to ideological allegiance. Indonesian nationalists did not by and large regard other ethnicities as the enemy as Malays did and do – but strove to demolish the Dutch colonial regime and its collaborationist native rulers. It was only after the military coup in 1965 and the rise to power of the Javanese-dominated Suharto regime that race began to shape Indonesian politics. Suharto's murder squads targeted ethnic Chinese as well as communists, and the barbarous war against the Fretilin independence movement in East Timor was in essence an ethnic conflict. With the fall of Suharto, and the emergence of Indonesia as one of the fastest growing Asian economies in the twenty-first century, ethnicity has once again receded.

The case of Malaysia was very different. Ethnicity or race dominates political life. The British colonial power imported hundreds of thousands of Chinese and Indians to work in tin mines and rubber plantations – a human inflow that threatened the peoples of the peninsula and Singapore who regarded themselves as indigenous. Malay nationalism which emerged two generations after Indonesian nationalism was preoccupied less with the colonial class than the Chinese. After the Second World War, the Malayan communists and a few leftist Malay radicals alone opposed the British. The MCP did not regard itself as an ethnic party: though it was dominated by ethnic Chinese, the party made sustained efforts to recruit Malays and formed bonds with the truly indigenous Orang Asli. The British invested heavily in a propaganda war that branded all insurrectionaries as an ethnic other. By resettling more than half a million rural Chinese in 'new settlements' the British 'reconditioned' non-Malays to accept independence in ethnic terms. By backing the conservative Chinese elite through the MCA, the British and the emerging Malay political elite, the British made sure that the Chinese business elite would back the ethnic status quo. The economic power and influence of the Chinese in Malaysia has for much of recent history protected their community from Malay assault. The habitual use of 'Emergency' powers and an accretion of anti-democratic legislation check the exercise of true democracy. Our ancestors built 'British Malaya' and significantly shaped its authoritarian successor state. We should acknowledge the sins of the fathers. But it is up to the people of Malaysia to embrace a truly civil society – and end the 'habit of Emergency' for ever.

ACKNOWLEDGEMENTS AND SOURCES

A Guide to Further Reading

I first visited Malaysia at the end of the last century when I climbed Mount Kinabalu in Sabah on the island of Borneo to make a documentary film for Channel 4 television about Low's Gully, *The Abyss*. I returned in 2007 to make a documentary for National Geographic (Asia) about the coronation of the new Yang di-Pertuan Agong that would be broadcast as *Becoming a King*. I wanted to understand this fascinating and in many ways deceptive Southeast Asian nation that our colonial forebears did so much to shape. This book should be regarded as an extended essay rather than a textbook or academic historical study. For that reason I have not encumbered the text with a blizzard of reference numbers and have made minimal use of footnotes. I thank Peter Robinson for encouraging and refining the project at an early stage. I must acknowledge a number of books that profoundly influenced and informed my account of Southeast Asian history and the Malayan Emergency. Benedict Anderson's classic study of nationalism *Imagined Communities* (first published in 1983) opened up the vista of political thinking in Southeast Asia. Anderson's brilliant essays on Southeast Asian history and culture in *The Spectre of Comparisons: Nationalism, Southeast Asia and the World* (1998) and *Under Three Flags* (2005) offer dazzling insights into the nature of Asian political thought. Anyone writing about the Japanese occupation of Southeast Asia and its aftermaths must acknowledge a huge debt to *Forgotten Armies* (2004) and *Forgotten Wars* (2007) by Christopher Bayly and Tim Harper. Harper's earlier academic study *The End of Empire and the Making of Malaya* (1999) is rich with ideas. Anthony Stockwell's edited collections of *British Documents on the End of Empire: Malaya* (3 volumes, 1995) and *Malaysia: British Documents on End of Empire* series (2004) proved invaluable. Cheah Boon Kheng's *Red Star over Malaya: Resistance and Social Conflict, During and After the Japanese Occupation of Malaya* (1983), *The Masked Comrades: A Study of the Communist United Front in Malaya, 1945–48* (1983) and *Malaysia: The Making of a Nation* (2002) are classic accounts by an important Malaysian historian. A groundbreaking study of the Emergency period is Kumar Ramakrishna's *Emergency Propaganda: the Winning of Malayan*

Hearts and Minds (2002). Dr Ramakrishna's penetrating and subtle unpicking of how the British waged a war of ideas is an essential study. Ronald Spector's *In the Ruins of Empire: The Japanese Surrender and the Battle for Postwar Asia* (2007) provides a gripping account of the volcanic struggles that erupted across Southeast Asia in 1945. The work of Karl Hack, listed in the bibliography, had a profound influence on the development of the historical narrative in this book. Dr Hack's generous email correspondence, as well as snatched conversations at the National Archives in Kew and at the Royal Courts of Justice in May 2011, clarified many issues and opened intriguing new research pathways. I am grateful to Dr Andrew Mumford for sending me the manuscript of his important study *The Counter-Insurgency Myth: The British Experience of Irregular Warfare*. Mark Ravinder Frost was generous with his time and comments. I have tried to build on the pioneering research of Ian Ward and Norma Miraflor exposing the bloody events that took place at Batang Kali in December 1948, and published in *Slaughter and Deception at Batang Kali*. I am grateful to John Halford of the legal firm Bindmans and Quek Ngee Meng for responding to my many questions before and after the 2012 'Batang Kali trial' in London.

I thank Dr Yin Shao Loong, a brilliant young social historian and environmentalist and the esteemed Professor Farish Noor for endeavouring at least to put me right on the many aspects of Asian culture and history. I had many enlightening conversations with Gus and Enyd Fletcher. Tim Hatton corresponded with me about his visit to Batang Kali in December 1948.

I would like to thank Christopher Humphrey and Michele Schofield at AETN All Asia Networks, Singapore for permission to use extracts from interviews conducted for two History Channel (Asia) documentaries about the Emergency and the Japanese occupation of Malaya produced by Novista TV in Kuala Lumpur. I am especially grateful to Lara Ariffin, Harun Rahman and Tan Sri Kamarul Ariffin for such stimulating conversations and unstinting generosity over the last few years. It goes without saying that none of the authors or individuals mentioned here or in the bibliography bears any responsibility for factual mistakes in the text or advocates any of the views and opinions expressed herein. I am enormously grateful to David Robson for reading the manuscript and eliminating many infelicities of style and expression.

At the History Press I would like to thank Mark Beynon for his unstinting support, Lindsey Davis, Lauren Newby and our meticulous copy editor Richard Sheehan, who eliminated a number of howlers.

Readers are referred to my blog for more information and a selection of maps: http://malayanwars.blogspot.de

SELECT BIBLIOGRAPHY

Abdullah, CD, *The Memoirs of Abdullah CD*, Strategic Information and Research Development Centre, Petaling Jaya, 2009.

Aldrich, RJ, *Intelligence and the War against Japan: Britain, America and the Politics of Secret Service*, Cambridge University Press, Cambridge, 2000.

Allen, L, *The End of the War in Asia*, Hart-Davis, MacGibbon, London, 1976.

Anderson, B, *Java in a Time of Revolution: Occupation and Resistance, 1944–1946*, Cornell University Press, Ithaca and London, 1972.

Ascherson, N, *Games with Shadows*, Radius, London, 1989.

Aydin, C, *The Politics of Anti-Westernism in Asia: Visions of World Order in Pan-Islamic and Pan-Asian Thought*, Columbia University Press, New York, 2007.

Barber, N, *The War of the Running Dogs: The Malayan Emergency, 1948–1960*, Bantam Books, 1987.

Bayly, C & Harper, T, *Forgotten Wars: The End of Britain's Asian Empire*, Allen Lane/Penguin, London, 2007.

—— , —— , *Forgotten Armies: The Fall of British Asia*, Allen Lane/Penguin, London, 2004

Boot, M, *The Savage Wars of Peace: Small Wars and the Rise of American Power*, Basic Books, New York, 2002.

Borschberg, P, *The Singapore and Melaka Straits: Violence, Security and Diplomacy in the 17th Century*, NUS Press, Singapore, 2010.

Bose, R, *The End of the War: Singapore's Liberation and the Aftermath of the Second World War*, Marshall Cavendish, Singapore, 2005.

—— , *Secrets of the Battlebox: The History and Role of Britain's Command HQ during the Malayan Campaign*, Marshall Cavendish, Singapore, 2005.

Brendon, P, *The Decline and Fall of the British Empire 1781–1997*, Jonathan Cape, London, 2007.

Carey, I, *Orang Asli: The Aboriginal Tribes of Peninsula Malaya*, Oxford University Press, Kuala Lumpur, 1976.

Carter, M, *Voices from Indenture: Experiences of Indian Migrants in the British Empire*, Leicester Unviersity Press, Leicester, 1996.

Cesarani, D, *Major Farran's Hat: Murder, Scandal and Britain's War against Jewish Terrorism, 1945–1948*, William Heinemann, London, 2009.

Chandra, E, 'We the (Chinese) People: Revisiting the 1945 Constitutional Debate on Citizenship', *Indonesia*, Number 94, 2012.

Boon Kheng, C, *Red Star over Malaya: Resistance and Social Conflict During and After the Japanese Occupation of Malaya, 1941–1946*, EDS, London, Singapore, 2003.

——, *The Masked Comrades: A Study of the Communist United Front in Malaya, 1945–48*, Times Books International, 1979.

Chin, Kee Onn, *Silent Army*, Longmans Green and Co., London, 1952.

——, *Malaya Upside Down*, Federal Publications, Singapore, 1976.

——, *The Grand Illusion*, Aspatra Quest, Kuala Lumpur, 1984.

Chynoweth, J, *Hunting Terrorists in the Jungle*, Tempus, Stroud, 2005.

Cloake, J, *Templer: Tiger of Malaya: The Life of Field Marshall Sir Gerald Templer*, Harrap, London, 1985.

Clutterbuck, RL, *The Long, Long War: The Emergency in Malaya, 1948–1960*, Cassell, London, 1967.

——, *Riot and Revolution in Singapore and Malaya, 1945–1963*, Faber & Faber, London, 1973.

Coates, J, *Suppressing Insurgency: An Analysis of the Malayan Emergency, 1948–1954*, Westview Pr, 1992.

Comber, L, *Malaya's Secret Police, 1945–60: the Role of the Special Branch in the Malayan Emergency*, Monash Asia Institute, Clayton, 2008.

——, *Through the Bamboo Window : Chinese Life and Culture in 1950s Singapore & Malaya*, Talisman: Singapore Heritage Society, Singapore, 2009.

Cruikshank, C, *SOE in the Far East*, Oxford University Press, London, New York, 1983.

Dahm, B, *Sukarno and the Struggle for Independence*, Cornell University Press, Ithaca and London, 1969.

Ken, D, in Goscha, CE and Ostermann, CF, *Connecting Histories: Decolonization and the Cold War in Southeast Asia 1945–1962*, Woodrow Wilson Centre Press, Washington DC, 2009.

Darwin, J, *The End of the British Empire: The Historical Debate*, Basil Blackwell, London, 1991.

——, *The Empire Project: The Rise and Fall of the British World-System, 1830–1970*, Cambridge University Press, Cambridge, 2009.

——, *Britain and Decolonisation: The Retreat from Empire in the Post-War World*, MacMillan Education, Basingstoke, 1998.

Dhu Renick, R, 'The Emergency Regulations of Malaya: Causes and Effect', *Journal of Southeast Asian History* vol. 6, no. 2, 1965, pp. 1–39.

Easter, D, *Britain and the Confrontation with Indonesia 1960–66*, Tauris, London, 2004.

Elson, RE, *Suharto: A Political Biography*, Cambridge University Press, Cambridge, 2001.

Emerson, R, *Malaysia: A Study in Direct and Indirect Rule*, University of Malaya Press, Kuala Lumpur, 1964.

Follows, R, *The Jungle Beat: Fighting Terrorists in Malaya*, 2nd ed., Travellers Eye, Bridgnorth, 1999.

Frederick, W, *Visions and Heat: The Making of the Indonesian Revolution*, Ohio University Press, Athens, Ohio, 1989.

French, D, *Army, Empire and Cold War: The British Army and Military Policy 1945–1971*, Oxford University Press, Oxford, 2012.

——, *The British Way in Counter-Insurgency, 1945–1967*, Oxford University Press, Oxford, 2011

Frost, MR & Yu-Mei Balasingamchow, *Singapore: A Biography*, Hong Kong University Press, Hong Kong, 2009.

Grob-Fitzgibbon, B, *Imperial Endgame: Britain's Dirty Wars and the End of Empire*, Palgrave Macmillan, London, 2011.

Hack, K, 'Iron Claws on Malaya: The Historiography of the Malayan Emergency', *Journal of Southeast Asian Studies* vol. 30, no. 01, 1999, pp. 99–125.

——, *Defence and Decolonisation in Southeast Asia: Britain, Malaya and Singapore, 1941–1968*, Curzon, Richmond, Surrey, 2001.

Hack, K & Blackburn, K, *Did Singapore have to Fall? Churchill and the Impregnable Fortress*, Routledge Curzon, London, 2004.

Hall, D, *A History of South-East Asia*, Macmillan, London, 1981.

Hamby, J, 'Civil-Military Operations: Joint Doctrine and the Malayan Emergency', *Joint Force Quarterly* No. 32, 2002.

Hamilton, DW, *Jungle Campaign: A King's Own Yorkshire Light Infantryman*, Praeger, Westport, Conn., London, 1998.

Harper, TN, *The End of Empire and the Making of Malaya*, Cambridge University Press, Cambridge, 2001.

Harrison, T, *World Within: A Borneo Story*, The Cresset Press, London, 1959.

Hasegawa, T, *Racing the Enemy: Stalin, Truman, and the Surrender of Japan*, Belknap Press/Harvard University Press, Cambridge, Massachusetts, 2005.

Hembry, B, *Malayan Spymaster: Memoirs of a Rubber Planter, Bandit Fighter and Spy*, Monsoon, Singapore, 2011.

Heng, P, *Chinese Politics in Malaysia: A History of the Malaysian Chinese Association*, Oxford University Press, Oxford, New York, Singapore, 1988.

Heren, L, *Growing up on the Times*, Hamish Hamilton, London, 1978.

Hering, R, *Soekarno: Founding Father of Indonesia*, KITLV Press, Leiden, 2002.

Hoe, A & Morris, E, *Re-enter the SAS: The Special Air Service and the Malayan Emergency*, Leo Cooper, London, 1994.

Holman, D, *Noone of the Ulu*, Oxford University Press, Singapore, Oxford, 1958.

——, *The Green Torture: The Ordeal of Robert Chrystal*, Robert Hale, London, 1962.

Hyam, R, *Britain's Declining Empire: The Road to Decolonisation 1918–1968*, Cambridge University Press, Cambridge, 2006.

Jackson, R, *The Malayan Emergency: The Commonwealth's Wars 1948–1966*, Routledge, London, 1991.

Jones, A, 'The Orang Asli: An Outline of Their Progress in Modern Malaya', *Journal of Southeast Asian History* vol. 9, no. 02, 1968, pp. 286–305.

Jumper, R, *Death Waits in the Dark: The Senoi Praaq, Malaysia's Killer Elite*, Greenwood Press, Westport, Ca., 2001.

Khoo, Kay Kim, *The Western Malay States 1850–1873: The Effects of Commercial Development on Malay Politics*, Oxford University Press, Kuala Lumpur, London, 1972.

Kua Kia Soong, *Patriots and Pretenders: The Malayan Peoples' Independence Struggle*, Suaram, Kuala Lumpur, 2011.

——, *May 13: Declassified Documents on the Malaysian Riots of 1969*, Suaram, Kuala Lumpur, 2007.

Leary, JD, *The Importance of the Orang Asli in the Malayan Emergency, 1948–1960*, Centre of Southeast Asian Studies, Monash University, Clayton, Australia, 1989.

——, *Violence and the Dream People: The Orang Asli in the Malayan Emergency, 1948–1960*, University Center for International Studies, Athens, Ohio, 1995.

Lee, GB, *The Syonan Years: Singapore Under Japanese Rule, 1942–1945*, National Archives of Singapore, Singapore, 2005.

Legge, JD, *Sukarno: A Political Biography*, Praeger Publishers, New York, 1972.

Lim, T, *Multiethnic Malaysia: Past, Present and Future*, Strategic Information and Research Development Centre (SIRD), Petaling Jaya, 2009.

Loh, Francis Kok-Wah, *Beyond the Tin Mines: Coolies, Squatters and New Villagers in the Kinta Valley, Malaysia c.1880–1980*, Oxford University Press, Singapore, 1988.

Lowe, P, *Contending with Nationalism and Communism: British Policy Towards Southeast Asia, 1945–65*, Palgrave MacMillan, London, 2009.

Macintyre, WD, *The Imperial Frontier in the Tropics 1865–75*, Macmillan, St Martin's Press, London, 1967.

Mackay, D, *The Malayan Emergency, 1948–60: The Domino that Stood*, Brassey's, London, 1997.

Mackie, JAC, *Konfrontasi: The Indonesia–Malaysia Dispute 1963–1966*, Oxford University Press, Kuala Lumpur, London, 1974.

Maidin, R, *The Memoirs of Rashid Maidin: From Armed Struggle to Peace*, Strategic Information Research Development, Petaling Jaya, Selangor, Malaysia, 2009.

Miller, H, *The Communist Menace in Malaya*, Praeger, New York, 1954.

——, *Jungle War in Malaya: The Campaign Against Communism, 1948–1960*, Barker, London, 1972.

Milner, AC, *The Invention of Politics in Colonial Malaya: Contesting Nationalism and the Expansion of the Public Sphere*, Cambridge University Press, Cambridge, 1994.

——, *Kerajaan: Malay Political Culture on the Eve of Political Rule*, University of Arizona Press, Tucson, Arizon, 1982.

——, *The Malays*, Wiley-Blackwell, Chichester, West Sussex, 2008.

Mishra, P, *From the Ruins of Empire: The Revolt against the West and the Remaking of Asia*, Allen Lane, London, 2012.

Ghows, M, *The Malayan Emergency Revisited 1948–1960: A Pictorial History*, AMR Holding Sdn Bhd: Yayasan Pelajaran Islam, Kuala Lumpur, 2006.

Mrazek, R, *Sjahrir: Politics and Exile in Indonesia*, Cornell Southeast Asia Progam, Ithaca, New York, 1994.

Mumford, A, *The Counter-Insurgency Myth: The British Experience of Irregular Warfare*, Routledge, London, 2011.

Nagl, J, *Learning to Eat Soup with a Knife: Counterinsurgency Lessons from Malaya and Vietnam*, University of Chicago Press, Chicago, London, 2005.

Nemenzo, F, *Revolution and Counter-Revolution: British Colonial Policy in Burma and Malaya 1945–51*, University of Manchester, 1965.

Nonini, DM, *British Colonial Rule and the Resistance of the Malay Peasantry, 1900–1957*, Yale University Southeast Asia Studies, New Haven, Connecticut, 1992.

Noone, R, *Rape of the Dream People*, Hutchinson, London, 1972.

Noor, F, *The Other Malaysia: Writings on Malaysia's Subaltern History*, Silverfish Books, Kuala Lumpur, 2002.

O'Ballance, E, *Malaya: The Communist Insurgent War, 1948–1960*, Faber, London, 1966.

Peng Chin, 'My Side of History: Recollections of the Guerrilla Leader Who Waged a 12 Year Anti-Colonial War against British and Commonwealth Forces in the Jungles of Malaya', Media Masters, Singapore, 2003

——,*Dialogues with Chin Peng: Dialogues and Papers Originating from a Workshop with Chin Peng Held at The Centre for the Study of the Chinese Southern Diaspora, Australian National University, Canberra, 22–23 February 1999*, ed. by CC Chin, K Hack, 2005.

Pham, PL, *Ending 'East of Suez': The British Decision to Withdraw from Malaysia and Singapore, 1964–1968*, Oxford University Press, Oxford, 2010.

Postgate, MR, *Operation Firedog: Air Support in the Malayan Emergency 1948–1960*, HMSO, London, 1992.

Priestland, D, *The Red Flag: Communism and the Making of the Modern World*, Allen Lane, London, 2009.

Pugsley, C, *From Emergency to Confrontation: The New Zealand Armed Forces in Malaya and Borneo, 1949–1966*, Oxford University Press, Oxford, South Melbourne, Vic., 2003.

Purcell, V, *Malaya: Communist or Free?*, Published under the auspices of the Institute of Pacific Relations, Stanford University Press, 1954.

——, *The Memoirs of a Malayan Official*, Cassell, London, 1965.

——, *The Chinese in Malaya*, Oxford University Press, Kuala Lumpur, Hong Kong, London, 1967.

Pye, LW, *Guerrilla Communism in Malaya: Its Social and Political Meaning*, Princeton University Press, Princeton, NJ, 1956.

Raj, JJ, Dato, *The War Years and After: A Personal Account of Historical Relevance*, Pelanduk Publications, Petaling Jaya, Selangor Darul Ehsan, Malaysia, 1995.

Ramakrishna, K, *Emergency Propaganda: The Winning of Malayan Hearts and Minds, 1948–1958*, Curzon, Richmond, 2002.

Reid, A, *Imperial Alchemy: Nationalism and Identity in Southeast Asia*, Cambridge University Press, Cambridge, 2010.

Ricklefs, MC, Bruce Lockhart, Albert Lau, Portia Reyes, Maitrii Aung-Thwin, *A New History of Southeast Asia*, Palgrave Macmillan, 2010.

Sandhu, KS, 'Emergency Resettlement in Malaya', *Journal of Tropical Geography* vol. 18, 1964, pp. 157–183.

Sarkesian, SC, *Unconventional Conflicts in a New Security Era: Lessons from Malaya and Vietnam*, Greenwood Press, 1993.

Scurr, J, *The Malayan Campaign 1948–60*, Osprey, London, 1982.

Shennan, M, *Out in the Midday Sun: The British in Malaya 1880–1960*, John Murray, London, 2000.

Short, A, & FN Trager, 'The Communist Insurrection in Malaya, 1948–1960', *History: Reviews of New Books* vol. 4, no. 2, 1975, pp. 34–35.

Smith, C, *Singapore Burning: Heroism and Surrender in World War II*, Viking (Penguin), London, 2005.

Smith, E, *Malaya and Borneo*, Ian Allan, London, 1985.

Sopiee, M, *From Malayan Union to Singapore Separation: Political Unification in the Malaysia Region 1945–65*, Penerbit Universiti Malaya, Kuala Lumpur, 1974.

Spencer Chapman, F, *The Jungle is Neutral*, W.W. Norton and Company, New York, 1949.

Stenson, MR, *Repression and Revolt: The Origins of the 1948 Communist Insurrection in Malaya and Singapore*, Center for International Studies, Athens, Ohio, 1969.

Stewart, B, *Smashing Terrorism in the Malayan Emergency: The Vital Contribution of the Police*, 2nd edn., Pelanduk, Subang Jaya, Malaysia, 2004.

Stockwell, AJ, 'The Malayan Union Experiment 1942–1948', *British Documents on the End of Empire, Series B* vol. 3, HMSO, London, 1995,

——, 'The Communist Insurrection 1948–1953', *British Documents on the End of Empire, Series B* vol. 3, 1995,

——, 'The Alliance Road to Independence 1953–1957', *British Documents on the End of Empire, Series B* vol. 3, 1995,

Strauch, J, *Chinese Village Politics in the Malaysian State*, Harvard University Press, Cambridge, Massachusetts and London, 1981.

Stubbs, R, *Hearts and Minds in Guerrilla Warfare: The Malayan Emergency, 1948–1960* Oxford University Press, 1989.

Sukarno, *An Autobiography*, Gunung Agung, Hong Kong, 1965.

Swettenham, F, *British Malaya: An Account of the Origin and Progress of British Influence in Malaya*, George Allen & Unwin, London, 1948.

Tarling, N, *Southeast Asia and the Great Powers*, Routledge, London, 2010.

Tilman, R, 'The Non-Lessons of the Malayan Emergency', *Asian Survey* 1966, pp. 407–419.

Toye, R, *Churchill's Empire: The World that Made Him and the World he Made*, MacMillan, London, 2010.

Tsuji, M, *Japan's Greatest Victory, Britain's Worst Defeat from the Japanese Perspective: The Capture of Singapore 1942*, Spellmount, Stroud, 1997.

Van den Bijl, N, *Confrontation: The War with Indonesia 1962–1966*, Pen & Sword Military, Barnsley, 2007.

Van der Post, L, *The Admiral's Baby*, John Murray, London, 1996.

Walton, C, *Empire of Secrets: British Intelligence, the Cold War and the Twilight of Empire*, Harper Press, London, 2013.

Wang G & Ong W, 'Voice of the Malayan Revolution: The CPM War against Singapore and Malaysia, 1969–1981', S. Rajaratnam School of International Studies, Singapore, 2009.

Ward, I, Miraflor, N, Peng, C & Kathigasu, S, *Faces of Courage*, Media Masters, Singapore, 2006.

——, ——, *Slaughter and Deception at Batang Kali*, Media Masters, Singapore, 2009.

White, NJ, *British Business in Post Colonial Malaysia, 1957–70*, Routledge/Curzon, London, 2004.

Williams, AT, *A Very British Killing: The Death of Baha Mousa*, London, 2012

Yu, E, *Tunku Abdul Rahman Putra Al-Haj: His Life Journey Leading to the Declaration of Independence (1903–1957)*, MPH, Petaling Jaya, 2009.

NOTES

1. http://bindmans.com/documents/Batang_Kali_Skeleton.pdf
2. http://www.leighday.co.uk/Illness-and-injury/International-and-group-claims/Kenya
3. See *The Oxford Book of Fascism*, ed. Bosworth, R. pp. 526ff.
4. In 1939, Siam had been renamed Thailand by the dictator Field Marshal Luang Phibunsongkhram also known as Pibul Songgram. On 25 January 1942, Phibunsongkhram declared war on the United States and Great Britain as an ally of Japan – and the British refused to recognise the name change and continued to refer to Siam. Siam became Thailand for good in 1948.
5. The Japanese–Thai government included secret protocols guaranteeing the return of 'lost' Thai territories such as the northern Malay states and parts of Burma. This quid pro quo would have significant consequences during the Japanese occupation.
6. See Wade, G., ed., *Southeast Asia in the Fifteenth Century: The China Factor* (Singapore, 2010).
7. Quoted in Milner (2008), p. 41, who provides an especially illuminating account of the coming of Islam.
8. Extracts quoted in Frost, M.R. (2009).
9. This account is based on John Tully's definitive *The Devil's Milk: A Social History of Rubber*, (2011).
10. Though not in 'the Territories in the Possession of the East India Company [...] the Island of Ceylon [...] and the Island of Saint Helena' until 1843.
11. Data from Tully, (2011).
12. Quoted in Carter (1996).
13. '*Mi patria idolatrada, dolor de mis dolores,*
    Querida Filipinas, oye el postrer adios.
    Ahí te dejo todo, mis padres, mis amores.
    Voy donde no hay esclavos, verdugos ni opresores,
    Donde la fe no mata, donde el que reina es Dios.'
14. Milner, (1994), p. 119
15. See Priestland (2009) for an illuminating account of Asian communism, pp. 234ff.

16. A detailed account of this little-known episode is *To' Janggut: Legends, Histories, and Perceptions of the 1915 Rebellion in Kelantan* (2006) by Cheah Boon Kheng. See also 'The Kelantan Uprising: Some Thoughts on the Concept of Resistance in British Malayan History', J. de V. Allen, *Journal of Southeast Asian History*, vol. 9, no. 2 (Sep., 1968), pp. 241–257.

17. The most detailed recent account of the career of Lai Tek is Leon Comber's 2010 'Traitor of all Traitors–Secret Agent *Extraordinaire*: Lai Teck, Secretary-General, Communist Party of Malaya (1939–1947)', published in JMBRAS, vol. 83, part 2 (2010), pp. 1–25. *The Masked Comrades: A Study of the Communist United Front in Malaya, 1945–48* (1979) and *Red Star over Malaya: Resistance and Social Conflict During and After the Japanese Occupation of Malaya, 1941–1946*, both by Cheah Boon Kheng, discuss the case of Lai Tek in detail. Not a single relevant Special Branch file appears to have survived.

18. French Indochina comprised:
- Cochinchina, 1859–1954
- Cambodia, 1863–1954
- Annam-Tonkin, 1883–1954
- Laos, 1893–1954
- Kouang-Tcheou-Wan, 1898–1946. This was located in southern China but incorporated into the Government General of Indochina.

19. *The Voice of the Night: Complete Poetry and Prose of Chairil Anwar* translated by Burton Raffel, Ohio University Center for International Studies, 1993.

20. http://www.lonesentry.com/articles/kempei/index.html

21. Novista Archive, interviews conducted in Malaysia in 2011.

22. There is no up-to-date account of the life and work of H.D. 'Pat' Noone. I have had to rely on two books by Dennis Holman, *Noone of the Ulu* (1958) and *The Green Torture* (1962), and Richard Noone's *Rape of the Dream People* (1972). This fascinating story deserves updating. I am grateful to Geoffrey Benjamin for sharing information about the Temiars and the work of Pat Noone.

23. This is quoted by Holman in *The Green Torture*, p. 59. The account of Noone's speech to the MPAJA is, we must assume, based on Chrystal's somewhat jaundiced memory.

24. Novista Archive.

25. Lim Bo Seng's MI6 file was released by the UK National Archives sixty years after the war in 2005: HS 9/1341/6.

26. UK National Archives, WO 172/1763.

27. Novista archive, J.J. Raj interview.

28. This is one of the many fascinating personal accounts that have been recorded and collected by the National Archives of Singapore's Syonan Oral History Project. The recordings are also available at the Liddell Hart Centre for Military Archives, King's College, London.

29. The full text of Krull's *Diary of Saigon* is available online: http://www.virtual.vietnam.ttu.edu/

30. The main documentary source for this chapter is *British Documents in the End of Empire, Series B Volume 3: Malaya, Part 1: The Malayan Union Experiment 1942–1948*, ed. Stockwell, A.

31. UK NA, WO 203/4403.

32. Huang Yeh Lu *aka* Wee Mon-cheng later became the Singapore ambassador to Japan and Korea.

33. Service, R., *Comrades! A History of World Communism*, (Harvard, 2007), pp.241ff.

34. According to Larisa Efimova: 'The delegates included 18 representatives of youth organisations in India, nine from Pakistan, seven from Burma, one from Malaya, five from Indonesia, six from Vietnam, one from Ceylon, two from the Philippines and seven from China. There were a total of 56 delegates with formal votes. The Conference also included 15 observers from North Korea, Mongolia and the Soviet Asian republics; 22 representatives from Canada, Britain, France and some other countries, including three persons from the USSR, were invited as guests.' (*Journal of Southeast Asian Studies*, 40(3), pp 449–469 October 2009.)

35. Novista archive, interview with Hassan Saleh, 2010.

36. Quoted in French (2011), pp. 74ff.

37. http://www.globalsecurity.org/military/library/report/1991/BHD.htm

38. This is, strictly speaking, an anachronism since the MCP formed the MNLA at the beginning of 1949. I believe it is forgiveable.

39. My source here is Short (1975) and documents cited pp. 162ff.

40. 'The Claimants challenge decisions of the Defendants (or "the Secretaries of State") of 29 November 2010 and 4 November 2011 (a) not to pay "reparations" or financial compensation in respect of killings at Batang Kali, Selangor, Malaya on 11–12 December 1948 ("the killings") and (b) not to establish a public inquiry under the Inquiries Act 2005 ("the 2005 Act") or any other inquiry or investigation into the killings.' No claim has been made for compensation of any kind.

41. My application in 2012 under the Freedom of Information Act to acquire the sworn statements made to the police by the Scots Guards and made available to the applicants' lawyers was, however, turned down.

42. Novista Archive, Tim Hatton interview.

43. These figures are provided by Francis Loh Kok Wah in *Beyond the Tin Mines*. See bibliography for more details.

44. I rely here on Jeremy Lewis, *Shades of Greene: One Generation of an English Family*, (London, 2010).

45. I am grateful to Dr Kumar Ramakrishna for sending me his essay 'The Making of a Malayan Propagandist: the Communists, the British and C.C. Too', JMBRAS, 73(1): 67–90. 2002, and to Anthony Too for spending time discussing his uncle's life and work.

46. According to the OED, a catalyst is a substance that increases the rate of a chemical reaction without itself undergoing any permanent chemical change.

47. http://www.psywar.org/glossary.php

48. Dr Mahathir's current blog is: http://chedet.cc

49. The complete text can be read in Stockwell, *The Alliance Route to Independence 1953–1957*, (1995), pp. 126-128

50. *The Manchester Guardian*, a liberal paper, agreed: 'as the Communists have no intention of giving up their struggle for domination of the country, it would move the battle from the field of open military warfare to the far more threatening and dangerous fields of subversion and infiltration'.

INDEX